08/92

D0045913

Discarded by
Santa Maria Library

818.5209 S534
Shnayerson,Michael
    Irwin Shaw, A Biography
c1989

92
93

IRWIN SHAW

IRWIN SHAW

A BIOGRAPHY

Michael Shnayerson

G. P. PUTNAM'S SONS   NEW YORK

The author gratefully acknowledges permission from the following sources to quote from material in their control:

Arbor House, a division of William Morrow & Co., Inc., for excerpts from *After the Lost Generation* by John W. Aldridge. Copyright © 1951, 1958 by John Aldridge.

Henry Holt and Company, Inc., for excerpts from *Another Way of Life* by John Bainbridge. Copyright © 1958 by John Bainbridge.

Alfred A. Knopf, Inc., for excerpts from *The Fervent Years: The Story of Group Theatre and the Thirties* by Harold Clurman. Copyright © 1945, renewed 1973 by Harold Clurman.

McGraw-Hill Publishing Company for excerpts from *America Inside Out* by David Schoenbrun. Copyright © 1984 by David Schoenbrun.

The Paris Review for excerpts from *Writers at Work: The Paris Review Interviews, Fifth Series,* ed. George Plimpton. Copyright © 1981 by *The Paris Review.*

The Putnam Publishing Group for excerpts from *Seems Like Yesterday* by Ann Buchwald. Copyright © 1980 by Ann Buchwald.

Random House, Inc., for excerpts from *At Random* by Bennett Cerf. Copyright © 1977 by Random House, Inc. And for excerpts from *Stranger at the Party* by Helen Lawrenson. Copyright © 1975 by Helen Lawrenson.

Random House Papers, Rare Book and Manuscript Collection, Columbia University, for excerpts from Irwin Shaw letters.

Saturday Review from "If You Write About The War" by Irwin Shaw. Copyright © 1945 by *Saturday Review.*

Time Inc. for excerpts from "Irwin Strikes Back." Copyright © 1963 by Time Inc.

G. P. Putnam's Sons
Publishers Since 1838
200 Madison Avenue
New York, NY 10016

Copyright © 1989 by Michael Shnayerson
All rights reserved. This book, or parts thereof, may not be reproduced in any form without permission.
Published simultaneously in Canada

Library of Congress Cataloging-in-Publication Data

Shnayerson, Michael.
  Irwin Shaw: a biography / by Michael Shnayerson.
     p.   cm.
  Includes bibliographies.
    1. Shaw, Irwin, 1913–1984—Biography.   2. Authors, American—
20th century—Biography.   I. Title.
  ISBN 0-399-13443-3
  PS3537.H384Z86   1989   89–31019 CIP
  818'.5209—dc19
  [B]

Printed in the United States of America
1   2   3   4   5   6   7   8   9   10

CONTENTS

PART IV. **FULL CIRCLE**

ACKNOWLEDGMENTS

Of the many friends and colleagues of Shaw whom I interviewed, a few deserve special thanks. Peter Viertel, arguably Shaw's best friend of more than forty years, spent three days in Marbella, Spain, patiently answering my questions, and provided more help and encouragement thereafter. Robert Parrish, arguably Shaw's other best friend of nearly as many years, consented to similar sessions in Sag Harbor, Long Island. Willie Morris, a close friend of later vintage, extended true southern hospitality during my visit to his home in Oxford, Mississippi, interspersing his generous reminiscences with scenic tours of the area and rib-eye steak dinners at local haunts. Ross Claiborne, Shaw's editor at Delacorte, provided not only valuable insights but also copies of Shaw's book contracts and sales figures. Thanks above all to Bodie W. Nielsen, Irwin Shaw's companion of roughly eight years during the late 1960s and early 1970s, who first gave me the idea of writing this biography, and was gracious enough to share with me her daily journals of those years as well as her many letters from Shaw, and to draw up crucial lists of potential sources.

My thanks, in addition, for the interviews or information granted to me by the following: the late Charles Addams, Mary Jane Bacon, Lawrence Beckerman, Gene Berlin, Jeanne Bernkopf, Walter Bernstein, Simon Michael Bessie, Julian Blaustein, Bruce Bliven, Jr., Alexander Boskoff, Himan Brown, Ben Bradlee, Marie Brenner, Art Buchwald, Cornell Capa, Robert Caro, Mary Cheever, Lisa Cohen, Louis and Tina Cohen, Larry Collins, Richard Collins, Eden Collinsworth, Ruth Strong Conte, Norman Corwin, Hume Cronyn, Tom Curtiss, Ruda Dauphin, Leon Davidoff, Don Dixon, Kirk Douglas, Philip Drell, David Driscoll, Jack Egle, Albert Ehrlich, Arnold Ehrlich, Jon Epstein, Diana Erwitt, Jimmy Farber, Donald I. Fine, Elizabeth Fondaras, Joe Fox, Bernard Frizell, Blair Fuller, Betsy Gehman, Mike Gelfat, Martha Gellhorn, Brendan Gill, Alfred Giordano, Saul Goldberg, David Golding, Morton Gottlieb, Jacques Graubart, Cecile Gray, Mickey Green, Winston Groom, Elinor Gruber, Tom Guinzburg, Anthony Haden-Guest, Leila Hadley, Enid Hardwicke, Joseph Heller, Addie Herder, Artie Holstein, Leonora Hornblow, Robert Hughes, Marion Javits, Tillie Jessel, Gloria Jones, Kaylie Jones, E. J. Kahn, Jr., Harold Kaplan, Elliott Kastner, Elaine Kaufman, Joe Kaufman, Slim Keith, Rich-

7

ard Hoar Kent, Robert Kotlowitz, Leon Labes, Arthur Laurents, Karen Lerner, Doris Lilly, Alfred Allan Lewis, Norman Mailer, Karl Malden, Fred Malina, John Phillips Marquand, Jr., Ken Marthey, Josh Mason, Carol Saroyan Matthau, Peter and Maria Matthiessen, William Maxwell, Kevin McCarthy, John McCormack, Edith Messitte, Jeffrey Meyers, Drew Middleton, Herbert Mitgang, Ivan Moffat, Kate Mosolino, Arnold Moss, Edward Newhouse, Jack and Marian Newmann, Liam O'Brien, Kathie Parrish, Gregory Peck, Frank Perry, George Plimpton, Val Ponicsan, Maurice Rapf, Pinckney Ridgell, Norman Rosten, James Salter, Nora Sayre, Arthur Schlesinger, Jr., Francine Schoeller, the late David Schoenbrun, Budd Schulberg, Bella Shaw, William Shawn, Andrea Simon, Sidney Simon, Patsy Matthiessen Southgate, Irving Stanislaw, George Stevens, Jr., William and Rose Styron, Gay and Nan Talese, Manon Tingue, Lillian Tucker, Paul Turgeon, Phyllis Cerf Wagner, William Walton, Sam Wanamaker, George Weidenfeld, Jerome Weidman, Herbert Weisanger, Lael Tucker Wertenbaker, Sylvia Wexler, Richard Whelan, William Wilson, Clay Winters, Ben and Irma Wolstein, Clement Biddle Wood, Maurice Valency, Gabby van Zuylen, Gore Vidal, Frank Zachary.

I am indebted to my agent, Sterling Lord, who first believed in this book, and to Neil Nyren of Putnam's, who showed a veteran editor's patience and good cheer as the year and a half allotted to the writing of it grew to three. I am grateful to Tina Brown of *Vanity Fair* for allowing me several months of paid "down time" as a contributing editor, and for having the confidence that I could make up that time. Thanks also to Harold Evans of *Condé Nast Traveler* for allowing a two-day-a-weeker to remain in his editorial ranks. And thanks to my father, Robert Shnayerson, for many wise editorial suggestions on the manuscript.

Much of this book is anchored by the voluminous, twenty-eight-year correspondence between Shaw and his editors at Random House. I am grateful to Phyllis Cerf Wagner for donating that correspondence to Columbia University's Butler Library, and for the cooperation of the library's special collections staff in allowing me to view it. Thanks also to the special collections staff of Boston University's Mugar Memorial Library for the opportunity to pore over dozens of original manuscripts donated by Shaw, and to the staff of the Harry Ransom Humanities Research Center of the University of Texas at Austin for allowing me to view James Jones's papers. For historical information on the U.S. tax code, thanks to Louis Mezzo and Scott Layne of Grant Thornton Accountants and Management Consultants in New York.

Above all, I am indebted to my wife, Cynthia Stuart. Not only did she muster all the support and enthusiasm that writers seem to presume of their spouses; she made it her business to learn as much along the way about Shaw as I was learning. For the better part of these three years, she also worked countless hours uncovering old newspaper clippings in dusty libraries, sifting through microfilmed city records and pursuing genealogical nuggets with zeal and imagination. This book would have been considerably less substantial without her help. For that, I can express only awed thanks, and the promise that her second year of marriage will be different from the first.

For Cynthia Stuart

PROLOGUE

His laugh was what you would have heard first, if you had opened the carved-wood door of the Chesa Grischuna on this particular evening in the winter of 1983.

The Chesa, in the mountaintop town of Klosters, was much like other inns that dot the Swiss Alps, except it was better. From outside it looked like a square piece of white-iced cinnamon cake, but with each layer a bit akilter on the one below it. Inside, the hand of a relentless innkeeper was apparent: every detail fussed over, from the flagstones in the reception lobby to the low, grottolike whitewashed ceilings, the whole a picture of tight, understated Swiss elegance. If you had just come for dinner, you went through the low arched doorway to the right and wended your way past the bar's hand-carved glossy wood tables and hanging lanterns, to the linen-covered dining booths and tables of the main dining room.

Almost every night here, Irwin Shaw's big laugh reverberated against the wood-paneled walls, filling the place and giving it life. Everyone knew him—the waiters and maître d's, the townspeople, the rich Europeans and rich Americans who came to Klosters, by and large, *because* of Shaw. Anyone could hobnob with the world-famous writer and be swept up by that extraordinary warmth. That was how welcoming he was—how life-enhancing, as everyone came to put it. Even those too shy to introduce themselves could sit at neighboring tables and eavesdrop as Shaw's rolling humor washed over them.

This evening, the circle was made up of family and old friends—the columns of the temple of Irwin Shaw's life.

One was Marian, Shaw's wife. Dark-haired, petite and graceful, she had been a Hollywood starlet when Shaw first met her; more than forty years later, after a shocking and bitter divorce, followed by an even more surprising remarriage to him more than a decade later, she was still a striking woman: proper, demure, but with an occasional snap of tart humor that revealed a keen eye.

Another was Adam, the Shaws' only child. Now in his early thirties, Adam was in many ways his father's perfect son. He bore a strong resemblance to his father at that age—same tightly curled black hair and square features in a broad, ruddy face; same big grin and strapping athletic build—

only he was taller, and without his father's beaklike nose. Like his father too, Adam emanated an open American charm, mingled in his case with a European sophistication enriched by having spent his childhood winters in Switzerland and by attendance at the exclusive Le Rosey school. To women he was simply dazzling. But Adam had been pampered, and it showed. His parents' divorce, with its enduring acrimony and then its strange happy ending, had wounded him, and that showed too. Most troubling, Adam was a son in his father's shadow. He wanted desperately to be a novelist himself and had abandoned a promising journalistic career to make good on that dream. Two unpublished novels later, he was living off his father's money and playing polo in Spain.

Also at the table was Irving (Swifty) Lazar, the bantam-sized literary agent whose bald head and huge black-rimmed eyeglasses had become as much a trademark over the years as his legendary reputation for convincing publishers to pay large sums of money for books that he himself may or may not have read. Lazar had represented Shaw since the early 1950s, lining up not only book contracts but movie deals. Because Shaw was laughably helpless at handling his own money, Lazar had come to do that too, in an almost paternal fashion. There could have been no odder couple, and yet the two had become close friends. They had a banter: Shaw would rail at Swifty for being a venal character; Swifty would counter by saying Shaw ought to be grateful he *was,* because without his aggressive agentry, where would Shaw be? As usual, Swifty was in Klosters with his much taller wife, Mary, whose severely cut, straight black hair made her look like a stern Cleopatra, but who harbored a wry sense of humor—a holdover, perhaps, from her own days as an actress.

Rounding out the table was one of the handsomest couples on either continent: writer Peter Viertel and actress Deborah Kerr. Now in his early sixties, Viertel was still as striking as ever—a literary Sean Connery—and imbued with the easy masculinity of the former OSS man he was. Among his buddies had been Ernest Hemingway, John Huston and bullfighter Luis Dominguin. Among his lovers had been many of the world's most beautiful women. He had married Deborah Kerr more than two decades before— after she had left another husband—and with her he now divided his year between Switzerland and Spain. Novelist and screenwriter, champion skier and lover of the good life, Viertel was also Shaw's closest and oldest friend.

Shaw, at the head of the table as always, looked noticeably weaker than he had the year before. He walked with a cane now—a sad comedown from his skiing days—and his paunch had grown. The ruddiness in his cheeks was more the result of heavy daily drinking than of the bracing Swiss air. He still woke every morning as early as six to tap out several pages of his next novel, a discipline that never ceased to astonish his friends, but by noon he would retire to the back terrace of the Chesa and start in on the crisp local white wine, Dezaley, corralling anyone he could to sit and drink with him. There was a new, brooding side to him as well, a darkness that closer friends sensed under the surface.

The dinner started uneventfully enough. There was venison and trout—the Chesa's specialties—and inevitably the cold bottles of Dezaley. Lazar, just in from New York, was in an especially festive mood. "Just sold the American rights to the Joan Collins book," he announced. "Guess how much I got for her?"

There were halfhearted guesses; Shaw just waved him away.

"Two million!"

There was a silence. Lazar waited for Shaw's laughter to fill it, but the laughter didn't come. Down the table, Shaw's face grew suddenly redder.

"You know, Irving," he said in a voice shaking with rage, "I feel it is *demeaning* to be represented by you. *Do you understand? Demeaning!*"

For a second, Lazar was too shocked to speak. There was nothing bantering about that tone. There was nothing humorous about it at all.

"How dare you speak to me that way after all I've done for *you!*" Lazar managed.

There were two or three more furious exchanges: Shaw excoriating Lazar for taking on the likes of Joan Collins as a client, Lazar coming right back like a tough streetfighter. It didn't make sense, really. Lazar had chased after big deals all his life; Shaw knew it as well as anyone. Why was he so suddenly enraged?

But now there was a difference. As much as Shaw was yelling at Lazar, he was yelling at himself. It was he who, at the height of his literary success, had chosen to accept the lucrative screenplay assignments Lazar had dangled in front of him. He was the one who had written the novels more hastily, for higher advances, as time went on, trading critical acclaim for commercial success. Shaw had done this to himself. And now he was old and sick, and there was so little time left.

He pushed his chair back, stood up unsteadily, and reached for his cane. "I'm sorry," he said shortly. "I'm going home.'

Adam, ashen-faced, rose to help his father. As the others looked on in silence, the two of them made their way slowly through the dining room, past the tables of startled eavesdroppers, out into the cold, clear, snowy night.

One year later, at seventy-one, Irwin Shaw was dead of prostate cancer and its complications, in a hospital room in Davos, the next town down the valley from Klosters. His obituary appeared on the front page of *The New York Times*, and if readers had time that May morning in 1984, they noted that the Brooklyn-born Shaw, known to an entire younger generation as the author of the bestselling *Rich Man, Poor Man* and other commercial fiction, had had his first success as a left-wing playwright in the 1930s, gone on to write a string of lyrical, much-admired short stories for *The New Yorker,* produced a World War II novel heralded upon its publication as a masterwork, and been considered one of the finest writers of his day.

At the time of his death, every one of Shaw's dozen novels was in print. Fourteen million hard- and softcover copies. Twenty-five languages, including, as Shaw had enjoyed pointing out to interviewers, Icelandic and Macedonian. Half of those novels were early works, written in the late forties, fifties and early sixties, but a bookstore browser wouldn't have guessed that from the covers—all of which bore the same script design that had first graced *Rich Man, Poor Man,* the spectacular bestseller that had pulled the old books back into print.

The irony was that television had been responsible for revitalizing Shaw's long literary career to this extent: *Rich Man, Poor Man* had been a respectable bestseller when first published in 1970, but the trendsetting miniseries six years later had fueled the book's second, more dramatic ascent. Overnight, television had beamed Shaw's name to millions who had heard it dimly before, if at all. Shaw had had nothing to do with the miniseries—which merely confirmed his conviction that life was ruled by accidents—but he could hardly argue with the fresh wave of fame, and the money, and the new readers that its success conferred upon him. He could and did argue with the critics who, because of that television fame, dismissed him as a strictly commercial writer.

Mostly, he argued in vain. Even to older readers who remembered and admired the early work, Shaw was the one whose career had taken a disconcertingly commercial zig and never really zagged back. As for the legions of new, young readers, they seemed to assign Shaw, logically enough, a hazy place among the crowd-pleasing talespinners, somewhere off by Herman Wouk, James Michener, Leon Uris. Such was the cost of literary rediscovery in the television age.

The truth was that if Shaw had died in 1950, his place as one of America's finest writers of the thirties and forties would have been far more secure. As a playwright he would have been mentioned in the same breath as Clifford Odets and William Saroyan. As a writer of short stories he would have been ranked unquestionably with John Cheever, John O'Hara and J. D. Salinger. Along with James Jones and Norman Mailer, and perhaps James Gould Cozzens, he would have remained one of the three or four American writers whose novels defined an entire generation's response to World War II. Instead, Shaw's commercial successes came to cloud his achievement.

If Shaw's career was marked by incongruities, so was his character. Heavily muscled and athletic, a man who delighted in his college football prowess, he was also a sensitive observer of nuance and detail, and an elegant, musical stylist whose stories glow with masterful touches. All his life he retained the thick Brooklyn accent that led S. J. Perelman to compare him snidely to a butcher from the Grand Concourse. Yet Shaw was a truly brilliant man: articulate, funny, wonderfully well-read. In temperament, he struck most observers as miraculously uncomplicated, a big, warm, restless bear of a man who always seemed delighted with the people he'd just met, the food he was eating, the places he was seeing. Yet, as he once described himself, Shaw was also a hidden man.

The clues lay within his fiction. The face Shaw presented to the world was invariably a happy one; yet the protagonists of his stories and novels were always cut off and alone, brooding and bitter. In real life, Shaw seemed to adore women, and for several decades earned a reputation on two continents as a ladies' man. Yet his stories and novels are filled with predatory, manipulative female characters, fierce antagonists of life's long romantic wars. To those who knew him, Shaw radiated confidence about his talents, always tackling the next story or novel with seeming assurance that he could see it to a successful end. Yet his fiction is marked by a sense of certain, if unpredictable, calamity and undoing—the fate of even the most blameless and circumspect of men in an immoral and violent world.

By far the most baffling incongruity of Shaw's life was that between the pride he placed in his justly deserved literary reputation and his seeming willingness to squander it. It was impossible to know Shaw and not be keenly aware of his sensitivity on the subject. Was it a poor boy's love of the good life that made him so receptive to the big-money deals? *"Irwin was like a cat,"* one close friend liked to say. *"He loved luxury."* Was it a hunger for the fame that movies and bestsellers brought? *"Irwin courted fame,"* suggested Gay Talese. *"He liked rewards, he liked immediate gratification; he found fame in the way he wrote and what he wrote about."* Was it, as Shaw himself suggested, that screenplays were a welcome opportunity for human contact and collaboration after long, lonely bouts at the typewriter? Or was there some deeper reason?

What seemed indisputable was Shaw's firm conviction that he could simply do it all. Like a tennis player trying to carry on a match with himself by racing back and forth across the net, Shaw in his prime would bound out to Hollywood to knock off a screenplay for money, bound back to New York to stage a dramatic play for art, write brilliant short stories with one hand and epic American novels with the other. If finally he failed to maintain the balance, still he did it *longer,* and with more panache, than any other American writer of his time except Hemingway, with whom Shaw was most often compared. Somehow, among other works, he managed to write one historic play, dozens of classic American short stories and several early fine novels, all while transforming his Brooklyn fantasies of a glamorous life into glamorous reality. Somehow, too, as his reputation burgeoned and his lifestyle grew more glittering, he maintained the generosity of spirit that was his hallmark, a balance of delicacy and grace. Celebratory, empathetic, with envy and malice toward none, he was, as one hostess of the time put it, the only well-known writer to whom you could talk without feeling intimidated. Those who spoke to him only once remembered him fondly for the rest of their lives; among those who knew him well he was, without exception, a man beloved.

Across the sweep of seven decades and three continents, Shaw's life was a rare journey, from Depression-era Brooklyn to Broadway and Hollywood to postwar Paris to an elegant Swiss mountaintop town, from precocious beginnings as the promise of his generation to a bittersweet end among the wealthiest, but most underrated, writers of his time. As forcefully as any Shaw novel, it is in retrospect an ethical allegory, a deep and implacable struggle between art and money in mid-twentieth-century America.

PART I

BROOKLYN
BEGINNINGS

CHAPTER ONE

In the fall of 1920, when Irwin Shaw was seven years old, his family moved to the great green promise of Brooklyn.

In its farthest reaches, Brooklyn was still open country. Its flat-lands—of scrub brush and marsh—dipped southward toward Brighton Beach and Manhattan Beach, Coney Island and Sheepshead Bay. For the scores of Jewish immigrants who had poured through Ellis Island in the last three decades, Brooklyn seemed a merciful alternative to the crowded tenements of the Bronx and Manhattan's Lower East Side. A man could move his family to the ocean! Not only that: in a time of smoldering anti-Semitism across the land, when Henry Ford spoke darkly of "the international Jew," a man could be with his own people, his children nurtured and protected, in what amounted to nothing less than a home-land. And what brought it all suddenly within reach was the brand-new elevated line.

To some extent, the seashore had been settled already. Since the 1880s, it had served as the Hamptons of its day for New York's most affluent families. On Sheepshead Bay, a so-called Millionaires' Row of large, wood-frame summer houses had sprung up. Nearby, the world's finest horse-racing track had been established with Vanderbilt money, and by the turn of the century elegant gentlemen and ladies were driving out daily to place their bets. At the same time, new trolley car lines brought working-class families out for the weekend to the beaches, where they stayed in enormous wooden hotels, and to Coney Island—no longer an island proper, thanks to the landfill road that now linked it to the mainland. Here famous bandleaders played on summer nights, and fireworks delighted the crowds.

By the time the subway settlers arrived, however, that era had ended and another had begun. The millionaires—many of them brewers or liquor merchants affected for better or worse by Prohibition—had moved east-ward into Long Island. The racetrack had closed amid bookmaking scan-dals. Now, with the city's proposal to build an elevated Brighton Beach line, the beaches would be a five-cent ride away from the city—commuting distance for a new generation. Feverishly, real estate speculators began buying block-sized lots for row upon row of two-family, semi-detached

21

houses. In September 1920, their gamble paid off. The Brighton line went through.

For William Shamforoff, thirty-six, a Russian-Jewish immigrant from the Ukraine town of Nezhin, near Kiev, the move to Brooklyn with his wife and two young sons would seem enough of a fresh start to inspire a change of family surname. Shamforoff had been born into an unusually literate family—his father, Israel, had originally been a scribe, and one grandfather a Hebrew teacher. Nezhin was a cultural oasis of the Chernigov region, with a college that boasted Nikolai Gogol among its graduates. Its location on the Oster River, and its railroad junction, made the city an important crossroads of trade, where merchants from Turkey, Crimea, Moscow and Siberia would come to do business, as well as an agricultural center that prided itself on its local pickles. Times were hard, though: Israel's wife, Bessie, lost eight of the fourteen children she conceived. In 1892, after several bad harvests, Israel Shamforoff made the decision to journey alone to America, with an immigrant's dream of getting established in the new country, then sending for his family. Late in the year, he traveled overland to the North German coast, then boarded the *Thalia,* an immigrant ship, for the crowded ten-day trip to New York.

Two years later, Bessie Shamforoff and five of her six children made the passage to join Israel on Manhattan's Lower East Side. What Israel was doing to support himself is left unclear by the 1900 New York census, which defined him merely as an "agent," though within a few years he would work as both a real estate broker and a liquor salesman. (In December 1904, he would also—at last—be granted American citizenship.) The census did note that Israel had learned to read, write and speak English; Bessie, despite six years in America, remained untutored in the language. Of Bessie's two sons William and David—sixteen and ten, respectively— the elder was noted as working a newspaper delivery route, apparently full-time, while the younger was reported to be in school, a luxury that would presumably last until the earliest age he too could help support the family. The family's address was noted simply as Cannon—a short, squalid street not far from the Manhattan Bridge.

William, the elder, would remain short and stocky into manhood, a gentle and dreamy character with an immigrant's fierce patriotism. As with others of his generation, his highest ambition already was to Americanize himself in every way possible, and thus it seemed fitting that, at age twenty-seven, he should marry Rose Tompkins, daughter of an intellectual, politically minded Lithuanian Jewish family who possessed the inestimable pedigree of having been born in America. By then William had spent a year or two in Brooklyn, where his address was listed as Sea Breeze Avenue, in Brighton Beach, and had become established in the millinery business. Upon marrying, the couple moved to the South Bronx, to a small house at 811 Ritter Place, a one-block-long street in the then lower-middle-class but respectable Boulevard section. Their first child, Irwin Gilbert, was born February 27, 1913; a second son, David, was born August 27, 1916. Both children were given the family name of Shamforoff.

As a successful writer, Shaw would later joke about his happy childhood, so happy that had it not been for the Great Depression, he might not have had anything to write about. William and Rose Shamforoff were loving and happy parents throughout those early years, relatively untroubled by their humble status because of the warm network of relatives and friends that surrounded them. Both parents were also avid readers, and Will in particular invested in both children an earnest love of literature. Not untypically, Rose was much the stronger of the two, an ever vigilant housewife, stern decision-maker and hub of a family centered on the home. Quick-minded and artistically talented—she played piano well enough to give lessons, and imparted enough musicality to her husband and children for the family eventually to play as a group, with Irwin on cornet—she had had no real opportunity to pursue her own ambitions, and thus channeled them determinedly into her two young sons. Throughout his life, Shaw would feel a deep gratitude for the drive his mother instilled in him— dutifully writing her a letter every Sunday until the end of his life—mixed with more than a little resentment at the pervasive role she played in his childhood.

Mixed feelings also attended the subject of religion in the Shamforoff household. Will and Rose would hardly have denied their religion. They espoused Jewish family values; the social world they inhabited was almost entirely Jewish. Yet they were determined to become assimilated Americans in every sense and made a conscious choice not to speak Yiddish in the house. The further choice to amend the family name to Shaw seems to have been made jointly by William and his two brothers, David and Daniel, three years after their arrival in Brooklyn. Young Irwin, however, resented the decision enough to retain the name Shamforoff through high school. He also insisted on being bar mitzvahed, though because he knew not a word of Hebrew—let alone Yiddish—the occasion became little more than a birthday party.

As an adult, with no further religious training and no synagogue affiliation, Shaw would still feel the need to come to terms with his Jewishness as a man and as a writer. He would call himself a nonpracticing Jew but also an atheist. He would show no interest in writing so-called Jewish fiction, and indeed, no one would think to class him with its practitioners. Yet a deep concern with anti-Semitism would surface in several of his finest short stories and strongly influence *The Young Lions,* his novel of World War II. Most important, he would feel the sting of anti-Semitism himself, in ways that directed his life and work more than many of his friends would know.

Within two years of Irwin's birth, the family moved from Ritter Place, to a house closer to Long Island Sound, at 960 East 163rd Street. William tried to improve his lot as a salesman for a credit company, while Irwin went to first grade at an airy new public school in the Bronx named for the poet Joseph Rodman Drake, to whose nearby grave the schoolchildren would make solemn pilgrimages. On fair-weather Sundays, the family would journey by trolley through the farmland settlements of Brooklyn to Coney Island to visit various relatives. World War I was on at the time, and Irwin's first awareness of it was in Sunday beach-combing expeditions. "The beach was stained by oil, congealed into tar, and littered with thousands of small, three-inch long capsules of yellow powder, from ships that had been torpedoed off Sandy Hook," he wrote years later. "We took it for granted that the capsules contained gunpowder and we felt daring and solemn as we made small hoards of our loot, later to be left to the new work of the incoming tide. Until then, the war had been an abstract thing."

Sunday trips were one thing; living on Coney Island was quite another. When his parents made the decision, that fall of 1920, to move to what Barnum-like developer Joseph P. Day trumpeted as Brooklyn's "New Flatlands," Irwin felt an exile. For all the gregariousness he would later acquire, Irwin was a sensitive and introspective child, and this first uprooting left its mark. Almost certainly, it instilled in him the sense of apartness, of being an observer, that would start him writing stories by the age of twelve. "Stranded by one of the first waves of subway-borne settlers in a brick building on which the carpenters and painters were hurriedly putting the finishing touches, I stared morbidly out under the elevated pillars to the wintry sea a quarter-mile away," Shaw later wrote. "I could see acres of windswept salt grass, the dark hulks of the old hotel and theatre, the bungalow colony of crowded little frame shacks, with the usual signs of 'Dew Come In' and 'Kill Care Inn' in flaking paint on their flimsy porches, all soon to be replaced by something worse. Conscious of a dark turn in my destiny, I vowed to leave the borough as soon as I could."

Brighton Beach, the neighborhood in which the Shamforoffs began their new life, was filling up mostly with Scandinavian and German families. The modest apartment they chose to rent was in one of the two-family, semi-detached houses that were being constructed in block-long rows, usually before the streets they fronted were paved or lighted. One family would buy a semi-detached house from the developer, live on the ground floor, and rent out the top floor. So would go the unit's adjoining house. Through the thin walls, all four families could hear each other with painful clarity day and night—and an impressionable boy would have fine opportunities to soak up the mysteries of human relations. Because the landlord family in each house controlled the furnace, upstairs voices were almost always raised—and pipes angrily banged—on cold winter days. The Shamforoffs, as it happened, lived upstairs.

The Coney Island public school to which Irwin was now sent presented yet another indignity. A dreary brick building with narrow windows and gas fixtures only recently converted to electricity, it was further distinguished by its rickety outside wooden stairs—stairs its students had to negotiate to get from class to class even in driving rain or snow. At the end of Irwin's first year in Brooklyn came a sweet consolation and show of justice: the building was condemned, the children led out of it in single file to cheer at its demise.

Brooklyn wasn't all bad. The seascape that had seemed so bleak in midwinter became colorful and busy by spring. From Steeplechase Pier, an excursion steamer left every two hours to take in the beachfront. The bigger Iron Steamboat churned from Manhattan's battery and back, bringing crowds of noisy day-trippers. Close by were the docks of Sheepshead Bay, alive with bobbing pleasure boats and yachts. Here fishermen would display their catch of the day, and an enterprising boy could still go digging for clams and mussels. By the end of the decade, gas and oil from the motorboats would end that pursuit, and the fishermen's too.

Not surprisingly, boats figure in several of Shaw's earliest short story attempts. One unpublished sketch called "Champagne" has the sailors of a sinking ship breaking out the captain's best vintage and drinking it, wonderingly, for the first and last time. Another, "Important," is also set on a sinking ship (in the summer of 1934, the Morro Castle, a passenger ship, went down in flames off the New Jersey coast, taking 137 lives and convulsing the papers for weeks). A heroic young man of twenty-nine encounters a beautiful young lady up on deck as waves pound the ship. He asks her what she'll be sorriest she never experienced, now that her life is ending so prematurely. Making love, responds the lady sadly, for she is, as it happens, a virgin. Solemnly, the young man volunteers his services, and the two adjourn to his stateroom. But when the lady begins to undress, the young man stops her; love is too precious to squander in this way. The lady agrees, and begins dressing as the ship goes down.

Though youthfully naive, both sketches offer insight into the mind of a young writer who within a few years would be turning out stories that awed the editors of The New Yorker. Present were a Depression-era empathy with the downtrodden, an innocence that would never quite leave him—even in the later novels of tired roués—and a boyish penchant for spinning fantasies in which he played the swashbuckling hero, fantasies that he seemed to be able to put down on paper with polish and ease.

For a pensive Brooklyn boy, it was a rich and sweet experience to take the walk along an abandoned spur of the Long Island Railroad—built in the 1880s to bring New Yorkers to the horse-racing track and ocean beaches—to the local public library, a two-storefront affair on Sheepshead Bay Road, a good half-hour from home. "A brooding, desert silence hung over the tracks," Shaw wrote later. "And the rich smells of the sea and the rank growth mingled in the heavy afternoon sunlight, and it was easy to imagine, for a boy with a book under his arm, the ghosts of luxurious ancient trains clicking by, filled with strangely dressed ladies and gentlemen, on their way to older amusements at the shore."

One of Irwin's first discoveries in the library was an eight-volume fictionalized history of the Civil War by A. E. Altsheller. There were two heroes, cousins, one a Union soldier and the other a Confederate, and of course each was equally brave and equally convinced his cause was right. Irwin devoured the series, enthralled by its broad canvas, devastated when favorite characters died in battle. He would read other, better-known books of panoramic scale—*War and Peace,* for one—but here was a first example of the genre he would fix on with both *The Young Lions* and *Rich Man, Poor Man.* For a budding young writer, the Altsheller series offered another lesson too: impartiality. Just as Altsheller's Civil War heroes were allowed to hold conflicting views of equal credibility on slavery and seccession, so would Shaw's own broad-canvas characters embody opposing views of World War II, the Cold War and the years beyond. There would be critics who pointed to this as one of Shaw's greatest strengths—the ability to see both sides and present a balanced portrait. There would be others who saw it as his greatest weakness: painting cardboard characters who simply represented differing views and had none of the subtleties and contradictions of real people.

The local librarian, a prim lady whose neat desk was always adorned with a bowl of narcissus, allowed only one book to be borrowed at a time, so Irwin had to make his library walk several times a week. From Altsheller he went on to Mark Twain and Alexandre Dumas—for years, he considered *The Three Musketeers* the best book ever written—and Rudyard Kipling's stories and poetry. Then too, there was the Tom Swift series, the Ralph Henry Barbour sport series, Zane Grey, Owen Wister's *The Virginian* and Owen Johnson's *Stover at Yale.* Here were boyhood dramas of the most traditional sort, in which causes had effects and heroes vanquished villains amid the color and sweep of real storytelling. Small wonder that Shaw, who liked to say he was telling elaborate stories at age five to his parents, should choose, when he started writing them down, to begin at the beginning and follow a straight narrative line to the end.

Clearly brighter than most of his classmates, Irwin was skipped a grade, then sent at the age of ten to an advanced junior high school program at P.S. 136, where he could skip another grade by doing two years' work in one. The Admiral Charles Dewey School lay miles away in Sunset Park, however. Reluctantly, Irwin joined the daily migration of Brooklyn subwaygoers, paying his five-cent fare for the hour's journey to a strange neighborhood of cobbled streets near the docks and railroad yards of Bush Terminal. He found the schoolwork easy enough but proved too light for any team sports, much to his chagrin. As a last resort, he took to reporting basketball games for the school newspaper—and thus did Irwin Shaw's first published words appear. The greater satisfaction was in traveling with the team to play other schools in the farthest outposts of Brooklyn. Neighborhood pride stirred strong passions at these contests, and as Irwin soon learned, it was far safer to lose than win an away game: the defeated home squad would gather like a lynch mob outside the school doors to pound the departing victors with rotten vegetables or more dangerous projectiles.

Closer to home, Irwin joined the Montauk Athletic Club, a band of like-minded neighborhood boys who played baseball in the local school playground. Friday nights in winter, the team would meet solemnly to hear minutes of the club's last meeting and ante up ten-cent donations for the purchase of equipment for the upcoming season. One Saturday each spring, the players would take the subway to downtown Manhattan, to a sporting goods store on Nassau Street, and choose bats and balls and order red sweatshirts emblazoned with the word "Montauk" in flowing script. Duly suited up, the team would solicit challengers through the classifieds in the *Brooklyn Eagle:* "Fast Club, 13–15 class, uniformed, traveling, looking for games. Call Brighton 3022, any evening after six."

It meant a lot to a shy ten-year-old boy to become a part of that team and to realize he played pretty well. It gave him a confidence he hadn't yet known, and it made a permanent mark. Throughout the rest of his life, Shaw would take as much pride in his athletic prowess as in his writing, and his sense of identity would come to rest almost equally on both. One of his very best stories, "The Eighty-Yard Run," would offer a beautifully sensitive portrait of an aging football player; in real life, Shaw would follow professional teams and trade barroom pronouncements with all the swagger and passion of one of his working-class short story characters. To more thin-blooded literary types, the wonder would be how such a keenly sensitive mind could reside beneath the burly football fan with the Brooklyn accent.

It was at the Montauk that Irwin met Jimmy Farber, a boy two years his senior who became his best friend. Despite the age difference, Irwin stood two or three inches taller than Jimmy and looked older, and with his newfound confidence he tended to be the decision maker of the two. That fall Irwin enrolled at James Madison High School—a mercifully shorter ride from home—and he and Jimmy traveled back and forth together. Winter weekends they would head over to Coney Island to play ice hockey on the flooded and frozen-over parking lots. Summers they lived at Brighton Beach. They could make a day out of just going to Nathan's, where a hot dog cost five cents and a roast beef sandwich cost a dime. They would wander along the brand-new boardwalk, or head over to the handball courts nearby. The winner of a game kept the court to take on the next challenger; Irwin eventually became one of the best players around, holding a court for hours. His hands grew hard as marble, he liked to recall years later at dinner parties—so much so that he ended up playing without gloves.

Irwin at twelve may not have quite known he wanted to be a writer, Farber recalls, but that began to change when he went off with his brother to a summer camp, called Iroquois, in the Adirondacks and started reporting his exploits in letters to Jimmy. "He was a junior at his camp," Farber recalls. "I was a senior at mine, and you know at that age those things mean a lot. Anyway, he wrote about how he got on the senior baseball team— something to do with a wild catch he made. It was just a great letter; I read it aloud to my campmates." Nearly four decades later, Shaw would have the narrator of *Voices of a Summer Day* recall a similar diving catch made at camp "that brought him the election of the Best Athlete of the Week."

Irwin also learned to ride at camp. In Brooklyn he'd often gone to the Police Department stable on Ocean Parkway, where fresh horses were broken in for use throughout the city, and thrilled at the pairs of mounted policemen passing by. Now when he came back from camp, he and Jimmy started riding almost every weekend—$1.50 an hour. "We'd ride along Ocean Parkway, go down to Prospect Park," Farber recalls. "It wasn't quite what it sounds; there was a mall on either side of the parkway, and one side was a riding path from the beach to the park. The horses were the sort who knew when the hour was up, and would start lumbering back no matter what you did." Another boy named Fred Malina began riding with them, and despite the fact that Fred went to another high school the three become a triumvirate, meeting after school and rarely socializing with anyone else.

As they grew more independent of their families, they began venturing into Manhattan. They'd go to Gray's Drugstore in the 42nd Street subway arcade and buy cut-rate second-balcony tickets for fifty cents to whatever play they could, minutes before show time. Afterward they'd go out for a "drink," which meant a double malted for twenty cents at Walgreen's on 44th Street. With an extra twenty cents for the subway (a dime either way now, up from five cents), an evening at the theater cost all of ninety cents. The boys saw more than a dozen plays this way before any of them realized a production might actually be less than perfect.

These escapades were far more rewarding than the daily reality of James Madison High, a new and overcrowded school to which Irwin felt little connection at first. Not infrequently he would arrive late in the morning, see that classes were in session, and head off to the downtown Loew's Metropolitan theater, a gathering place for truants from all over Brooklyn, or go rowing on the lake at Prospect Park. In French and geometry classes, he would sit in the back drawing artful caricatures of his teachers, which led to his mother's being called in for tense consultations. One teacher accused him of being "one of those young gentlemen who loll around outside the gate after school hours, smoking cigarettes and waiting

for girls." Irwin, whose crimes were rather more benign, was secretly delighted.

Eventually Irwin made the football team at Madison, but not by much.
At least two years younger than any of his classmates, he weighed in at 155
even as a senior and sat on the bench most of his varsity season. As in
junior high, he had more luck as a writer. For the school paper he wrote
a series of ruminative essays; he also joined a "writers' club" of peers who
gathered after school to trade blistering judgments on each other's short
stories. Irwin's were fantasies for the most part, in which he played some
noble role. A few years later, Fred Malina called Irwin to ask if he might
use a few of them to satisfy a senior short story–writing course requirement
at New York University. Irwin invited him over, led him upstairs and threw
open a chest: inside were more than a hundred stories. " 'Take any six you
want,' " Malina remembers Irwin saying. "So I did—and got a C for the
course."

It was just as Irwin began fancying himself a writer, at age fourteen,
that the bottom fell out of the Brooklyn land boom and that almost
overnight the Shamforoffs slid into bad times.

For William Shamforoff and his two brothers, Brooklyn's continuing
land boom had stirred irrepressible visions of grandeur. Every day, it
seemed, developers would carve another hunk of scrub-brush flatlands into
block-sized lots and pocket windfall profits. How could they lose? Accordingly, the Shamforoff brothers had gone into business together in 1923 as
the storefront real estate brokerage of Shaw & Sons on Coney Island
Avenue. (The inclusion of their father in the company name was more
honorary than actual.)

By 1926, all over the country, land speculation had reached a feverish
pitch. Florida had led the way, its newly minted legions of real estate agents
touting the paradisiacal pleasures of a state made suddenly accessible by the
automobile. Developers bought up huge tracts of land, christened them
with shimmering names, and sold off lots to buyers who resold them later
the same day and doubled their money—all assuming that the "fashionable
set" would populate every development and that Florida would soon
become another California. In New York, as in other cities, the boom had
created suburbs—or visions of them, at least, more than one embroidered
with a Venetian theme of interlocking canals and lagoons. Brooklyn's
developers, having spent the early twenties putting up row houses on the
site of the old racetrack, now looked east of the Sheepshead Bay area. At
the mouth of the inlet, almost touching the beachfront on either side, lay
Plumb Island, where 150 plucky residents ferried their supplies from the
mainland and lived through the winter without heat or electricity. It was
the city's plan, first proposed in the 1910s, to fill in the marshland, link
Plumb Island to the shore, and create Marine Park, where pleasure-boaters
could dock and children could play on the landscaped greenswards. Specu-

lators in Sheepshead Bay had gambled that the Brighton Beach line would
go through—and so it had, boosting the value of their lots astronomically.
It seemed a similarly shrewd bet to buy up block-sized lots around Marine
Park, build entire squares of contiguous brick houses, and sell them off at
a healthy profit when the park was completed and another subway spur
materialized to service the area.

Fired by that hope, Shaw & Sons bought a lot on newly mapped
Brown Street off Avenue U, just a few blocks from one corner of the
soon-to-be-glorious Marine Park, and had plans drawn for a square block
of elegant houses. The partners shifted their base of operations to a cottage
by the site, and hung on one wall a framed editorial by Arthur Brisbane
touting real estate as the best investment a man could make; unlike stocks,
declared Brisbane, real estate could never decline in value. So enthusiastic
were the brothers Shaw that none grew apprehensive on the occasional
days when water bubbled up through their marshy land at high tide, or
took it amiss the time that Will Shaw, inspecting another property nearby
for possible purchase, sank up to his waist in a mudflat and required
immediate assistance to avoid an untimely demise. The market, after all,
couldn't fail.

In truth, the tremors of a national real estate collapse had been
apparent since late 1926, when two hurricanes swept across Florida with
devastating force, uprooting half-completed developments and making
very clear to the millions of new homeowners, many of whom had bought
their lots through the mail from other parts of the country and had not
yet set eyes on them, that there was trouble in paradise. As it became more
and more obvious that the polo-playing rich were not arriving to buy lots
at inflated prices—that, indeed, no one now was buying at all—prices
plummeted.

The tremors traveled slowly, so much so that in 1928 Brooklyn was
still among the first of the northern markets to collapse. Then suddenly
Marine Park looked like a wasteland again. (Only the persistent machina-
tions of Robert Moses would transform it into a park more than a decade
later.) With no buyers for the houses they had yet to erect, the Shaws were
forced to retrench. Smaller row houses, with peaked roofs and a woeful
semblance of English Tudor design, replaced the homes in the prospectus.
Next, Will and his two brothers moved their families into three of them.
Even as mere homebuyers they were unable to pay their mortgages, but
with no one else stepping forward to buy the apartments at list value, the
bank with which they had leveraged the lot development grudgingly agreed
not to foreclose; this way, at least, the brothers might one day be good for
the money. As for the other apartments, those were sold at cut-rate prices,
and the long siege against creditors began.

For Irwin at fourteen, his father's business failure became the first
great formative influence in his life. A comfortably middle-class family one

month, the Shaws were impoverished the next. The phone was turned off, as was the electricity, for months at a time. The shades were drawn to deter creditors who might come by in person. Both Irwin and his brother David began doing odd jobs after school, selling newspapers or delivering groceries; their mother helped by making ladies' hats and opening a small shop in the neighborhood. As Shaw & Sons continued a long and painful decline—not until 1932 would its listing be deleted from the local directory—Will Shaw took to selling housewares door to door. "When he had sold more than five dollars' worth of the household gadgets during the day," Shaw wrote in *Voices of a Summer Day* of Israel Federov, "Israel sat hopefully, his head up. His head was not up tonight."

What Irwin was witnessing was nothing less than the breaking of his father's spirit. Money, or the lack of it, had done this; for the rest of his life, Shaw would hold strong, contradictory feelings about money that infused his sensibility as a writer. He would take pride in his ability to earn considerable money as a writer—enough to support his parents through the Depression, enough eventually to live in great style—and on some level would judge himself as a writer by how much money he made. Yet he would hunger for literary respectability and feel terribly wounded when critics accused him of becoming a commercial writer. He would scare himself with the specter of running out of money, especially as his lifestyle became more and more ornate, yet he would fail utterly to keep track of the money he made, pay bills two and three times, and spend recklessly on nightlife. Most important, the characters in his fiction would be forever haunted by money—by the desire to make it for the status and security it conferred, or by the tragedy of having failed to make it.

One undeniable benefit accrued to Irwin as a result of his father's misfortune: the office typewriter. A heavy steel machine with oversized type, it served Shaw through many of the early *New Yorker* stories that made him famous, including "The Girls in Their Summer Dresses," the original of which, typed on the yellow foolscap Shaw used because it was the cheapest paper available, lies now with dozens of others in the special collections department of Boston University's Mugar Memorial Library. To a boy just beginning to write stories, that typewriter was more than a convenience. It *made* him a writer; and it offered an outlet for the painful emotions the new bad times had stirred.

The young writer testing himself on his hand-me-down typewriter began to soak up the Brooklyn speech patterns he heard around him—and nowhere were they more colorful than at Ebbets Field, where the Brooklyn Dodgers did their best to confound the odds. Plunking down his fifty-five cents for a ticket, Irwin would attend almost all the double-headers, nursing a canteen of iced tea in the unshaded bleachers. On every side would be the ranks of Brooklyn's nightworkers—taxi drivers, milkmen, newspaper-delivery truck drivers—together with the truant and the unemployed. It was here, Shaw liked to say, that he acquired his thick Brooklyn accent, an accent worsened by a slight lisp that he kept for the rest of his life and that made him seem, even at the most glittering social events on two continents, to be talking with a mouth full of hot mashed potatoes. He did not, however, learn to love the hot sun. Along with his heavy build seemed to go a propensity for heavy sweating; on winter days, Shaw would often feel stifled enough to throw open a window, and when he became successful enough to choose where he lived, it would not be by chance that he settled in Switzerland, where even midsummer days were dry and cool.

If baseball provided one literary inspiration, girls provided another even more immediate. Irwin's age and weight might still hold him back from first-string football, but his physique and ruddy square features had begun to exert a palpable attraction. He made one initial misstep: dared by friends on the Coney Island boardwalk one summer day, thirteen-year-old Irwin went up behind a girl perhaps two years older and mustered a greeting. The girl turned, curious, to face him. Then her smile vanished. "Why don't you go home to your mother?" she jeered. Shaken, Irwin vowed never again to approach a girl unasked. The snub was as singular as it was memorable, however. Fred Malina remembers that by age fifteen Irwin was always the one in search of parties. At one point Irwin took up with an older woman of twenty, and Malina and Farber would tag along after him as he visited her on her babysitting jobs. "He was good with girls," Farber recalls. "Even then, he was cheerful and witty. I was two years older, but I was shorter too, so he'd find a girl for me, and we'd double date. One night when I was eighteen, we went to the rec-center evening at a local public school. No one under eighteen was allowed in, but I was the one questioned by the guy at the door, not Irwin. So Irwin talked him into letting *me* in."

Shaw's social life inevitably suffered from the jobs after school and during the summers that were required to help his hard-hit family. He served summonses for a lawyer his father knew. He delivered suits for a custom tailor in Manhattan. He tutored a child who had trouble learning to read. Saturdays he worked off and on at Klein's department store, picking up the raincoats that frenzied women shoppers had discarded and putting them back on the racks for two dollars a day.

With the family's business failure, Will and Rose Shaw appear to have succumbed even more than before to the self-abasement they felt as Jews of immigrant stock in America; and Irwin, clinging to his Russian surname, reacted angrily to that. In one touching scene in *Voices of a Summer Day*, the Shaw-like Benjamin Federov is embarrassed when his father, normally a mild-mannered man, turns apoplectic at learning that his brother-in-law has gone up to Boston to protest the executions of Sacco and Vanzetti. The whole family, rants the father, will be judged for this unpatriotic deed, and Jews everywhere will be branded once again as anarchists who should be deported. Meanwhile, the mother in *Voices* tries to discourage her son from playing football because it's one of the "goyim nochas," the violent "gentile pleasures" that Jews should be sophisticated enough to avoid. The very idea, writes Shaw, "infuriated [Benjamin] because of its echo of the ghetto and what he considered the sickly assumption, incomprehensibly borrowed from their enemies, that Jews were too clever to expose themselves to danger."

His parents' shame in turn shamed Irwin. Ironically, it made him all the more eager to prove himself among WASPs even as he decried Jewish self-denial. Not by coincidence had he dreamed, before the land bust, of going off to Princeton, perhaps the most socially insular college in the United States at this time. To some extent, his love of football—and later, of drinking—would also seem born of the desire to leave his ethnic roots behind. Now, of course, Princeton was out of the question. In the winter of early 1929, some nine months before the real onset of the Great Depression, Irwin enrolled at new, tuition-free Brooklyn College, established in the borough's downtown commercial district. It meant a longer subway ride, a dreary campus life, but also the first real glimmerings of literary success. As if in anticipation, Irwin Shamforoff, fifteen-year-old freshman, enrolled under the more literarily promising name of Irwin Shaw.

CHAPTER TWO

A stranger asking directions to Brooklyn College in February 1929 would have found himself wandering the borough's downtown streets in mystification. He would find no welcoming campus green. He would find no campus at all, just the office buildings through whose doors dark-suited lawyers hurried to and from the nearby Brooklyn courts. Only by standing on a street corner would he at last see a five-minute migration of students from one building to another, stepping briskly across the busy commercial streets to avoid the oncoming trolleys, en route from one class to the next.

To confuse matters further, Brooklyn College didn't even exist in the school year of 1928–1929. In response to the growing tide of Brooklyn students forced to make the long commute to Manhattan, the city had rented classroom space in five office buildings to create a Brooklyn extension of the all-boys City College of New York, as well as one for all-girls Hunter College. The two schools operated independently of each other, the boys attending classes in certain buildings, the girls attending classes in others. Only in 1930 did the city establish Brooklyn College as an official—and coeducational—institution.

In those hard-pressed times, there was a good reason for the swelling student tide at the Brooklyn extension colleges: no tuition fees. Any public high school student with qualifying grades could enroll and keep living at home, his only expenses textbooks and subway fare. For a boy whose father was out of work or soon to be, the public institutions presented the one opportunity in a suddenly dismal world to gain a college degree, to get a foothold on success and escape the immigrant class. "The diploma we sought," Shaw wrote years later, "was first and foremost a weapon with which to extricate ourselves from the dreadful prison of want which was destroying our parents in front of our eyes."

Most of the roughly 1,000 incoming freshmen were Jewish. Overall, they were an extraordinary group, fiercely motivated and highly intelligent. The Latin class was likely to hold at least one student who had read Tacitus and wanted to debate the teacher about him; students in a basic philosophy class were likely to be as familiar with Kant and Hegel as with Coolidge and Hoover. Given the attitudes of the times, many of the graduating women would simply get married, but nearly all the men would go on to be successful professionals; and while Shaw would emerge as the most famous name in his class, he would be followed not far behind by humorist Sam Levenson, poet and novelist Norman Rosten and historian Oscar Handlin.

Even so, Shaw was not thrilled to be there. He hated the prospect of a longer commute again: boarding a bus or walking a mile to the Avenue U station of the Brighton Beach line, then wedging in among the tightly packed bodies at rush hour for a trip that sometimes took upward of an hour. He resented the stark contrast the downtown buildings presented to his dreams of an ivied campus: not only did they lack ivy, but between two of them sprouted the Star Burlesque Theatre, which advertised such strippers as the notorious Ann Corio, who could make her tasseled pasties spin one clockwise and one counterclockwise simultaneously, and where indolent students and faculty alike would duck in for twenty-five cents' admission during midday lulls in the academic schedule.

Depressed and resentful, Shaw stumbled through his classes with no more than a halfhearted effort. At the end of his first freshman term, to his shock, he was asked to leave. The specific cause of his undoing was calculus, taught by an unforgiving professor named Walter Prenowitz, who gave Shaw a flunking grade and, by the competitive standards of the city college system, a one-way ticket out. For Shaw the student, that failure ushered in a year of panic, despair and degradation. For Shaw the now aspiring writer, it was, in its own way, a marvelous gift.

Hounded by his mother's guilt-provoking reproaches and his father's sorrowful eyes, Shaw went in search of a job that summer as the Great Crash loomed. He had no luck whatsoever with the employment agencies; finally he took a job as a shipping clerk in a furniture warehouse for $16 a week, and began a long, dreary chapter of riding a trolley to the end of the Flatbush Avenue line, with a second journey by train into the borough's darkest depths. The day began with sweeping the warehouse. Then opening crates. Then packing orders into cardboard cartons. Then loading the packed cartons onto a handcart and wheeling the cart to the post office, there to wait an hour in line with all the other warehouse clerks. "It was at this period," he wrote later, "that I determined to be a writer or die in the attempt."

This was a job too mundane even to provide material for a story. But from the drivers who delivered the installment-plan furniture—and reclaimed it if customers failed to meet their payments—Shaw heard enough to write a fine day-in-the-life sketch called "Pull Truck," which he never published but which has all the social realism and sharp imagery of his best *New Yorker* stories. In the story, the young narrator rides shotgun on a pull truck with an older, seasoned partner named Moore. First stop is at a tenement walk-up apartment to reclaim a radio from an old woman who pleads with them, then bitterly kicks and spits at the partners as they take the radio away. Next stop is an elegant Bronx house to pull a piano; a little girl standing by declares she doesn't want it anyway, while her mother just sighs. Two more stops after lunch, and then a final one in a tree-shaded Brooklyn neighborhood with respectable houses and neatly trimmed lawns. Neighbors lean forward on their porch chairs as the partners knock on a door. Out goes the sofa, onto the street. In a voice loud enough to be heard by the neighbors, the woman of the house demands the partners "exchange" the sofa as quickly as possible. Moore, scornful of the woman's pretentions, and wanting to impress a pretty girl just passing, replies even more loudly that the furniture will be in the warehouse until the woman decides to pay it off.

Here was a story—written by Shaw at seventeen, to go by his hand-written note to that effect on the original manuscript—in which all the major notes of his mature work were sounded: a palpable sense of the Depression in New York, made real in a few quick strokes; a storyteller's instinct for pace and dialogue; a bitter awareness of the power of money, and a sweet sympathy for its victims. Above all, there was a writer's decision to try to chronicle his time by transmuting his own painful experiences. In this story, unlike most that Shaw would go on to write, the narrator speaks in the first person; even so, his reactions, until the end, are held back, giving the encounters with each hapless customer greater impact.

The copy of "Pull Truck" that lies in Boston University's Mugar Memorial Library has an ending both anticlimactic and perhaps realistic: though infuriated by Moore, the young narrator goes off at the end of his workday, starved, to have a big steak-and-potatoes dinner, only to find he still has no appetite. This, Shaw explains in a handwritten note appended to the manuscript, was a revised ending. In the original story, Shaw explains, the young narrator punched Moore in the mouth, broke three of his teeth, and went off seething with righteous indignation to buy a cup of coffee with his last nickel. That was noble, Shaw writes as a man in his sixties, but life seems less noble now. Indeed, he adds, if he were writing the ending a third time, he would have his young narrator return blithely to the office with Moore, collect his day's pay, order a huge dinner, gulp it down without hesitation, and go off to the movies.

There were other payoffs to Shaw's season of misery and disgrace. In earnest now, he began studying his craft. He read Balzac and Chekhov and Tolstoy; more than one critic would come to feel that Shaw's panoramic novels—*The Young Lions* and *Rich Man, Poor Man* in particular—harked oddly back to Balzac in their effort to capture the fabric of a whole society, and Shaw himself would often compare *The Young Lions* to *War and Peace* (not, it must be said, with too many concessions). He read the Romantic poets—Keats, Byron, Shelley—and a few of the lyric poets, such as Herrick.

He read the Bible ("How many times," he would muse to one interviewer, "have I reread the King James version of the Old Testament?"). And he read—and reread—*The Odyssey* and *The Iliad.* Critics would often knock Shaw's later novels as superficial, but no one ever discussed literature with Shaw and went away feeling the man was ill-read.

Of course, Shaw read more recent masters as well. Like many another sixteen-year-old, he plowed through Thomas Wolfe, William Faulkner and Aldous Huxley. He read James Branch Cabell, whose elegance of style in such novels as *The Silver Stallion* and *Something About Eve* had briefly brought him high critical acclaim. ("His was a fake elegance. Fancy—I quickly turned against it," Shaw said to one interviewer later.) He adored F. Scott Fitzgerald, whose glittering world exerted a powerful attraction. (In particular he loved *Tender Is the Night,* which appeared in 1934, and was astounded by the scathing reviews that greeted it; later in life, when his own novels received similar treatment, he would often cite the reception of the Fitzgerald book as a classic case of how wrongheaded the critics could be.) The writer he read most closely, however—the writer everyone of Irwin Shaw's generation by now was reading most closely—was Ernest Hemingway.

By 1930, Hemingway had become a major literary success. He had had his Paris years; he had published *The Sun Also Rises* and *A Farewell to Arms.* Nearly fifteen years older than Shaw, he represented another generation altogether, and defined not only the nihilistic spirit of his age but a stunning new literary glamour—proof that writers could be physically vigorous, that their lives could be as much chronicled in the press as those of movie stars, that they could drink and carry on and still write brilliantly. That Shaw would come to play a small but pivotal role in Hemingway's life—and face off with the great writer in more than one dramatic and angry encounter—would have astounded the young man just now putting down his first tentative stories.

Eventually in his best work, Shaw would succeed in incorporating Hemingway's spare language and flat rhythms within his own more musical style. His writing would never be the bold experiment that Hemingway's was, but it would attain a clarity and elegance that struck more than one critic as equal to the older master's. Ironically, the greater debt Shaw would end up owing Hemingway—and to far more damaging effect—would be not in his writing at all but in the way he lived his life.

Duly chastened by his bout of hard labor, Shaw began attending evening classes at Brooklyn's City College with an eye toward returning full-time in the fall of 1930. It made for a long, long day, especially when he had to face the dreary subway ride home after sitting through a class in Chaucer or European history. On his few free evenings, he began dropping in at the Civic Repertory Theatre on West 14th Street in Manhattan. It was near one of his jobs—as a shipping clerk in a cosmetics factory—and, thanks to its founder Eva Le Gallienne, it offered a unique opportunity to see classic dramas for no more than fifty cents a ticket. The Broadway plays Shaw had attended with friends had been chosen solely on the basis of cut-rate availability; not many were terribly good. Now, within the Civic Rep's huge, drafty space and jarring green-painted walls, sitting on one of the wooden gallery benches and straining for a view of the makeshift proscenium, Shaw began to see productions of Ibsen and Chekhov, Tolstoy and Gorky. The excitement of theater as a form of social protest had not quite materialized. The Group Theatre would stage its first play in the fall of 1931, and Clifford Odets would not burst onto the scene until 1935 with *Waiting for Lefty.* Still, there was electricity in the air, and Shaw felt it. He wanted to be a playwright too.

To his great relief, Shaw passed the entrance exams to become a freshman again at the school now officially known as Brooklyn College. He might still have been turned down—a return like this was highly unusual—but for the support of a football coach named Lew Oshins.

Oshins, a coach of the "no-pain, no-gain" school who prided himself on having once played the better part of a game with a broken leg, needed all the decent players he could find. With the formation of Brooklyn College, a football team had seemed a fine idea, and Oshins had been hired to create one. Hardly any of the intensely academic students at Brooklyn College had ever played the game, however, and recruiting would have been frowned upon.

To a coach in this predicament, Irwin Shaw looked like a prospect: maybe not a star, but the kid did know how to play the game. He'd put on weight since high school and now tipped the scales at 170 (he stood a little under five-foot-ten); and he'd kept up with regular Sunday scrimmages on a makeshift field at Avenue K and 15th Street. Gratefully, Oshins added him to his meager lineup, and thus began one of the happiest chapters in Shaw's life, one that he would recount, with growing exaggerations over the years, to dinner partners who had never watched a football game, much less heard of Brooklyn College. It would assume an almost epic importance as Shaw told it, to the point that these same dinner partners, interviewed later, would never fail to mention Shaw's early greatness on the gridiron. In fact, as one of the original players rather bluntly put it, Shaw was "a second-rate player on a mediocre team." And yet the team was not without a certain screwball charm.

For one thing, it had no field. The twenty-five gawky young men enlisted by Oshins practiced dutifully every day for their first season in the basement of one of the college buildings on Willoughby Street. The ceiling was only eight feet high, so no passes could be thrown. The room was so small that players could practice only one limited play at a time; spread formations, punts and kickoffs had to be explained in theory. Then there were the pillars—heavy supporting columns that the players had to dodge as they ran. Shaw had a sense of impending disaster as he listened to the players talk philosophy in the locker room and fumble with the minimal shoulder pads and leather helmets that had no faceguards. Sure enough, when the Brooklyn Warriors bused over to New Jersey to meet Trenton State Teachers in their first intercollegiate challenge, the final score was 38–0 in favor of Trenton.

The physical battering the Warriors received put them at risk with another contingent: their mothers. One lineman began having to drop his uniform out his bedroom window on Saturday mornings, then when he left the house claim that he was off to the museum—a lame excuse when he came back with bruises or a black eye. Another player signed in at games with his name spelled backward. More than one Jewish player was forbidden to play on the Sabbath. As for Shaw, "When I came into the sleeping house late on Saturday nights, after coming home from distant games, I would steal burglar-like up to my room with my wounds, but I would always be awakened some time in the middle hours by the touch of my mother's fingers on my lips, as she felt to see if my teeth, which she for some reason considered my chief charm, were still there."

In later years Shaw liked to say he played quarterback, but the position was defined somewhat differently then. These were the days when the same eleven players played both defense and offense in two punishing thirty-minute halves. On defense, Shaw would play wingback. On offense, he would serve as one of four players in a diamond-shaped formation behind the front line. At the top of the diamond, nearest the front line and the hiking center, was a player generally called the quarterback. At the two outer points of the diamonds were halfbacks, of whom Shaw would be one. At the rear point was a fullback. When a play was called, the ball might be hiked to any of these four players.

Almost immediately, the four Brooklyn College backs became known for their prominent noses as the Four Hawksmen, after the Four Horsemen of Notre Dame. In part because his was the first to break—and in part to distinguish him from fullback Jerry Shaw, a teammate generally conceded to be the best player in the history of the college—Shaw was christened "Nose," a moniker he managed to live up to by breaking his nose two more times in his Brooklyn College career, the last time so badly he was blinded for four days. (It is surely not coincidence that a fair number of noses get punched or broken in Shaw's fiction: at the start of *Two Weeks in Another Town,* grizzled ex-actor Jack Andrus walks into a Rome hotel only to have his nose punched by an irrational passerby; in *Beggarman, Thief,* prim Rudy Jordache gains character by having his nose disfigured by muggers.)

Every game the Warriors played that first season was an away game, not only because they had no field but because the visiting team's expenses would be paid by the home team. By scrimping on meals—sandwiches on the bus—and not letting his team stay overnight except on the longest trips, Oshins could supplement his nearly nonexistent budget enough to buy uniforms for his players. A football Saturday would thus begin at dawn with the bus ride to some outpost like Doylestown, Pennsylvania, to play the National Farm School, or up north to take on Rhode Island State (the players occupying themselves on the ride by reading poetry), and end at midnight with the weary Warriors back home—beaten again.

Sorry as the team's record remained, Shaw became a respected enough player after his first two seasons that in October 1932, the school paper noted: "BROOKLYN COLLEGE LOSES IRWIN SHAW." The story explained that "Irwin Shaw, veteran quarterback of the Brooklyn College varsity football team, has resigned from the squad in order to devote more time to his studies." In fact, Shaw had merely found he couldn't come up with such minor expenses as the subway fare to distant practice fields the team now used. His retirement lasted only a game or two, until Coach Oshins relented and began secretly subsidizing Shaw's transportation fare.

Eventually the team got its own field on a vacant property called the Wood-Harmon lot, on which the future campus of Brooklyn College would be built. Still, the players had to line up every day at the start of practice along the outside of the field and walk slowly across it, picking up pieces of glass. And the team's budget grew no fatter. One game was refereed by the opposing coach's brother-in-law, who chose not to notice that one of the opposing team's members was playing with an iron bar strapped from his wrist to his elbow. The Warriors wanted to leave at halftime, but Oshins said no—they had to keep playing or they wouldn't get their expenses, which they needed in order to pay the bus driver to get them home. The team did win a few games in its first four years, the same plucky players staggering through all four seasons, but it never did compile a winning season, and for many members the fondest memories were of every season's longest road trip, to play Canisius College in Buffalo. Canisius always beat them worse than did any other team, but the Warriors got to stay overnight at a country inn called the Elms and dine on hot mince pies.

For all the broken noses and battering defeats Shaw suffered on the football field, he was having a wonderful time. Not only did he love the game, he loved the respect he began to feel from his classmates, and the mentions in the school newspaper, and the cheers of the hometown crowd when at last there *was* a hometown crowd on a hometown field. Here in its own small way was a first taste of fame; and to a poor boy nurturing rich dreams, it was heady stuff.

Little by little, Shaw became a campus character, such as the campus allowed. He joined a fledgling fraternity, Sigma Tau Sigma, and took it rather seriously, though the frat had no house to speak of, and its members self-deprecatingly called themselves the Ducky Wucky Boys. The use of his father's gray Nash on Saturday nights brought much greater clout. As many as four couples would squeeze into it to go to parties and school dances. Later, when the girls had been dropped off at home, the boys would drive out to Sheepshead Bay for bowls of steaming thick clam chowder and platters of hot biscuits at Lundy's, the seaside restaurant that stayed open all night. Grouped near the big potbellied stove in one corner, listening to the waves slap against the pilings under the restaurant itself, the boys would compare their dates of the evening and speculate on their chances— unlikely at best—of going all the way. With Prohibition on, these were liquor-free evenings. Had Repeal already arrived, Shaw and his cronies would likely not have imbibed anyway; they could barely afford the thirty- five cents for a bowl of chowder, let alone a drink. Besides, among these Depression-era adolescents—most of them Jewish, and most quite properly behaved, give or take a yell out the car window—liquor was a foreign substance, associated with the irresponsible twenties that now seemed so distant and wrong. Shaw felt no differently; and with no real talk of liquor at home, and certainly no trace of alcoholism in his immediate family, his own later excesses, so considerable and eventually corrosive, would strike his former school friends as baffling.

Brash with his social and athletic successes, and proud of a physique that grew more granitelike every year, Shaw set his sights on a girl he'd first noticed in one of his classes. Small, with a full figure and dark hair up in a bun, she was more handsome than beautiful. Still, she seemed to stand out. She had an ability to make the boys she was with feel important, and she was something of a flirt, though chastely so; among the several boys she'd already dated was Sam Aaron, who would one day own New York's toniest liquor store, Sherry-Lehmann (and sell wine to Irwin Shaw). When Shaw met her, more than half a dozen boys were already half in love with her, beginning with the captain of the football team, who worked in the dean's office with her. The girl's name was Elaine Cooper; readers of *The Young Lions* would come to know her as Hope Plowman.

Challenged by her other beaux, Shaw played his strong suit: he wrote Elaine a letter every day and passed it to her in class. Some 380 letters later—so Shaw recalled years later—she gave in. Irwin and Elaine began to double-date with a classmate named Leon Labes and his girlfriend, Peggy (like many of his Brooklyn College peers, Labes would go on to marry his sweetheart). They would go to the Brooklyn Paramount and hear Rudy Vallee, then to the Fulton Royale for a late cheap dinner. Recalls Labes: "How many lunches Irwin and I had to go without to afford these dates may seem unimportant now, but that was literally what we had to do." Elaine lived on Marcy Avenue in the then middle-class neighborhood of Bedford-Stuyvesant. This was a long subway ride from Shaw's house in Marine Park, but by such distances was ardor gauged; the longer the ride, the more serious the relationship. In one of the strongest scenes of *The*

Young Lions, the young Noah Ackerman takes Hope Plowman all the way home from a party on Riverside Drive to Hope's house in Bedford-Stuyvesant, reveling, at the end of the night, in the sweet pain of such devotion.

There was a problem, however: Elaine was a Christian Scientist. Her father was even a healer. "She never imposed her beliefs on others," Labes says, "but she went to meetings, and it did interfere with her relationship with Irwin. Irwin wanted to marry Elaine, and he proposed to her, not as an immediate thing, but as something they'd work toward. She told him she loved him but that the only way she could marry him was if he could become a Christian Scientist. And Irwin couldn't do it. He thought about it and thought about it, and had it out with her one day. She told him flatly she couldn't. And later he said to me, 'Leon, I cried all day and all night, I didn't stop crying for twenty-four hours, it's the only time in my life I remember crying.'"

Shaw was writing more than letters at this point. In January 1932, a college literary magazine called *The Odyssey* appeared with two Shaw contributions. One was a wry fairy tale, "The Poet and the Queen," in which a cavalier poet refuses to write verses for the queen and has his head lopped off for his trouble. As a sophomore, Shaw was entitled to a few sophomoric efforts, and this was one, but the tale does bear a noteworthy caveat below the title: "With due and reverent apology to James Branch Cabell."

The other story was more interesting. "Idyll" unfolds as an unspoken exchange of thoughts between a boy and girl in the process of losing their virginity. "I do not especially love you," the boy begins. "But I want you terrifically." Responds the girl: "I like you. You are not so bold as you might be. I imagine I would enjoy you immensely. It is a pity that young men whom one likes are, as a rule, inexplicably hesitant." Eventually the hesitations are overcome. "I am a bungler," the boy thinks as he enters her, "and I do not know how to approach my ecstasy, but I am shaken and I shall not be after as I was before." Responds the girl: "You are hard . . . and I am sure, powerful, and I am not very sane because I am aware that you are hurting me most dreadfully, and I do not care at all."

The story caused an immediate scandal. President William A. Boylan, who owed his position entirely to the serendipity of having been a grammar teacher to Mayor Jimmy Walker some years before, ordered all copies of the issue confiscated and summoned Shaw to his office. Fuming, he proceeded to read the story aloud to its author. Recounted Shaw years later: "This obviously was designed to impress upon me the depravity of my act and be punishment enough in itself to preclude further disciplinary action. I must confess . . . that I enjoyed his performance and thought the story in its oral form most promising."

Shaw also began writing an almost weekly column called "P'Shaw" for the college newspaper, *The Brooklyn College Pioneer.* The column showed unusual professionalism in style, though its mordant wit and world-weary voice occasionally tipped into arrogance. One typical entry addressed the incoming freshman class with these words: "The school has neither halls of marble, nor tradition, nor prestige, athletic or scholastic, to offer you. . . . Our buildings are twined with delicatessen signs instead of ivy, our traditions are wry, sad things." The seasoned author went on to exhort his new colleagues to join the football team or the student council not for college glory—a meaningless notion at Brooklyn College—but for their own amusement. "Why, we even write this column because we enjoy it," Shaw concluded with a "Talk of the Town" touch.

The column was less notable for what it said than for what it failed to say. As Shaw ruminated cheerily on school spirit, the world around him sank into the blackest days of the Depression: only two weeks later, Roosevelt would be inaugurated amid the final collapse and closing of the banks. On the Brooklyn College campus, as elsewhere in the country, economic despair had spawned angry student groups—the Young Communist League on the one hand, the Young People's Socialist League on the other—and in addition to national issues, fierce debate was stirred by the city's decision to impose tuition fees. Meanwhile, in Europe, Hitler's Brown Shirts were becoming more visible daily. In Brooklyn, many students joined the League Against the War and marched in mass peace demonstrations.

That Shaw never touched on even local political issues in his column seems curious, given that just three years later he would make his first literary mark with the fiery antiwar play *Bury the Dead.* In part, his reticence reflected the realities of a city college newspaper supported by taxpayers' money. In part, it suggested that Shaw simply had no political interests at this time, that his real concerns were the all-American ones of football, girls and Saturday night. "Irwin was considered a great athlete," recalls fellow Brooklyn College alumnus Bernard Frizell, who remained a friend through the years. "But the intellectuals pretty much looked down on him."

For all the sophistication Shaw thought he showed in his columns, infinitely more was being brought to bear on the stories he continued to write on the big office typewriter at home. It was as if here, away from his peers, he could put aside the increasingly public self that enjoyed pontificating in print. There was ego in writing stories, to be sure—the writer at twenty knew he was good and getting better—but this was ego sublimated to the story itself.

One result was that for the most part Shaw no longer wrote in the first person. In one lovely, unpublished story from this period called "Romance Comes to Miss Brewster," he captures beautifully the vulnerability of a lonely spinster on a transatlantic cruise ship without once showing his youthful hand. On the cruise, the spinster is beguiled by a handsome gentleman, only to have her hopes crushed when he reveals himself to be a smuggler who just wants her to sneak a large diamond through customs for him. The twist is that she does, then keeps the diamond, riding off in a taxi with it clutched to her chest as a talisman, in its own way, of romance. By remaining oblique and understated, Shaw lets the reader discover for himself the spinster's pathos.

Years later, Shaw would confide to one interviewer that he was a "hidden man" who took "refuge in the third person." This was true even in the way he lived his life as a student at Brooklyn College. There was a public Shaw who played football and wrote his newspaper column, and there was a private Shaw, just now beginning to tap the wellspring of a deep storytelling talent. "Irwin was a very definite guy even then," one of his football teammates recalls. "He just knew where he was going." The private Shaw, the hidden man who went home to write stories, would put it this way: "Except for a girl or two who came into my life when the college was made co-educational, I knew nobody well."

The struggle between the public Shaw, who loved attention, courted fame, and was easily flattered, and the private Shaw, the artist who knew how to pursue his art, would be the crux of the life he chose to lead.

One day in his junior year Shaw, who by now was an English major, asked a favor of a classmate enrolled in a speech class. The professor who taught the speech class, David Driscoll, was a somewhat romantic figure to his culture-starved students. He had visited Paris; he had read James Joyce; he had even smuggled back from Paris a contraband copy of *Ulysses* in a plain brown wrapper. Driscoll was also the faculty advisor of the college dramatic society, and he produced classic plays on a makeshift stage with two spotlights, in a classroom on the second floor of the Lawrence Street college building. That was what Shaw wanted to talk to him about.

On a Wednesday afternoon—during the one midday lull in the academic week—Shaw, at Driscoll's invitation, knocked on his classroom door and asked in a hesitant voice if Driscoll would look at a play he had written. It had been typed on the oversized typewriter; on yellow second sheets. The title was *A Brawl in a Tavern*. Driscoll read one page, then another. He looked up. "You write this?" he said. "Yeah," said Shaw, suddenly shaken. "What's the matter, it's no good?" Driscoll said, "Jesus, it's terrific."

Shaw was ecstatic. This was, after all, the first time he'd shown a serious literary effort to an older critic. Ironically, the play wasn't nearly as good as the stories he had already written, but it did have a certain professionalism. Written as a sketch on the death of Christopher Marlowe, it shows that Shaw was reading—and imitating rather well—his Elizabethan drama. Less happily, *Brawl* reveals two characteristics that would show up again and again in Shaw's work and life: drinking to excess, and artistic self-pity. The Marlowe character guzzles red wine in a tavern and calls for paper: "The wine always makes the ink run free and fine from the point of my pen." He gets drunker and drunker, with much moaning about his art, until he rashly challenges a soldier to a duel and is "pinked." Shaw himself was not yet drinking at all, but the bottle clearly held an allure.

That year Driscoll produced seven or eight of Shaw's plays, including *Brawl,* and became a seminal influence, offering constant encouragement. He never did have the young playwright in a course, but one of his colleagues, speech teacher Arnold Moss, spent painful hours trying to correct Shaw's lisp by putting matchsticks in his mouth and telling him where to lift his tongue. Shaw had trouble with his *g*'s and *s*'s; because of the training, he would spend the rest of his life pronouncing them with inordinate care, getting his tongue in the right position, and often sounding affected as a result.

One other professor made a strong impression. David McKelvey White, son of an ex-governor of Ohio, taught an English course, "Versifaction," that Shaw took in his junior year. White recognized natural talent when he saw it, and took Shaw under his wing. "There's one thing I worry about for you," White told him. "You're going to be successful too early." Shaw, who at the time had not enough money to buy *The New York Times* for three cents every morning, was thrilled at the prospect. White also took him to his first classical music concert. It was at Carnegie Hall, and the music was Brahms; the young football player was hooked. About the time Shaw graduated in 1934, the so-called Rapp-Coudert Committee, a New York State precursor of the House Un-American Activities Committee, began looking into allegations of Communist infiltration of university faculties. One professor at Brooklyn College took it upon himself to name names, and White was on his list. White was fired; soon after, he went to Spain to serve as a machine-gunner in the Abraham Lincoln Brigade and was killed. For Shaw, it provided a bitter first lesson in the costs of Communist witch-hunting, and a strong motivation for giving generous sums to the Spanish Loyalists when White's prophecy came true.

Throughout his college years, Shaw kept working at odd jobs to support himself and help his family. Now, at least, the jobs tended not to be mindless hard labor. In addition to tutoring slow readers, he blithely wrote English papers for more affluent New York University students he met through his old friend Jimmy Farber. The ethics of this bothered him not at all; some of the students, though, were bothered by the vocabulary their ghostwriter used. One word that really stumped them, Farber recalls, was "cryptic." When Farber got to dental school, Shaw also ghosted short profiles of scientists for him for the school paper. The story fee was five dollars; Farber and Shaw split it. Thanks now to Roosevelt's national work plans, Shaw also earned fifty cents an hour at the college library for replacing books on the shelves. When school was out, he earned roughly $75 a summer as a camp counselor, once up in New Hampshire, once in Vermont.

To the classmates who knew he ghosted term papers for profit and who read his weekly columns, the public Shaw seemed more and more the professional cynic. Anyone, of course, had good reason to feel sour at the prospect of graduating into a world paralyzed by the Depression for nearly five years, a world in which even Roosevelt's initial flurry of radical initiatives had begun to sink into what seemed a bottomless swamp of bad times, but Shaw seemed more embittered than most. What particularly irked some of his classmates, however, was his increasingly brazen self-confidence as a writer. It was an irritating combination of traits, this deep gloom about the world at large and hubris about himself; and even later, when his star began to rise, critics would sometimes sniff that contradiction in his work and lambaste him for it. Yet Shaw's better side—his great natural charm and effervescent humor—was fully evident in college too, as it would be throughout the rest of his life. To his classmates, Shaw was both a likable and an exasperating character, full of talent and brio—and a bit too full of himself. Only later, when his success came to warrant it, would his self-image seem appropriate, as if he had grown large enough to fill it.

Shaw the cynic took a stand of sorts in a farewell "P'Shaw" column that summed up his mostly unhappy impressions of four years within his alma mater's unhallowed halls and concluded with the words, "God, gentlemen, how you have bored me." Once again, President Boylan called the offender of college mores into his office. Stern words were invoked about the ingratitude of students receiving a college education at the taxpayers' expense; dark threats were levied about the unlikelihood of said students to be allowed to graduate as planned.

In the *Broeklundian* yearbook, for which Shaw served in his senior year as features editor, more acid words were served up. In a graduating class of more than 500, Shaw was one of a dozen or so students deemed noteworthy enough to be lampooned in brief sketches—but his had a certain bite to it. "He is . . . writing the Great American Play, which fails to distinguish him from the other 412 in the class, not counting the Math majors. Speaks frankly of other people's sensitive spots, and is merciless in his quest for shortcomings." Though the sketch seemed to capture Shaw as many students saw him, it was also true that the editor who wrote it had been irritated when Shaw, asked to write two humorous essays to precede each of the four class sections—one limning the freshman boy, for example, the other the freshman girl—had submitted essays far too long for the space allotted and had then grown huffy at the prospect of having his prose whittled down.

In fact, the essays, unsigned, are lovely pieces. Private references to Shaw's own experiences at Brooklyn College are woven throughout, but most evidently in the two "Senior" essays. "Fate has caught up with him," begins the one on the senior boy. "Life has arrived and is clamoring at the gates. He is too worried about his future to pay any attention to his work and slouches in silence cursing lectures. . . . All during his final semester he is busy hunting a job." The senior girl, who seems modeled on Elaine Cooper, is not even thinking, in these preliberation times, about finding a job; her heart is set on the man who may prove her provider. "Naturally, as her mother reminds her with some bitterness, with all the world to choose from, she would select a young man who hasn't two coins in his pocket to rub together—and worse still, doesn't seem to mind it in the least."

On Valentine's Day, 1934, Shaw graduated from Brooklyn College despite President Boylan's threats. His academic record was commendable enough to earn him a silver key—only a dozen or so students won either gold or silver keys—but perhaps because of his intransigence, he won none of the commencement awards. He did, however, witness a scene that must have filled him with a delicious sense of retribution. The guest speaker at the commencement ceremony was newly elected Mayor Fiorella La Guardia, who had taken his oath of office just days before. La Guardia arrived with a police escort of five and took his seat on the stage along with the day's other dignitaries. First to address the hundreds of seniors gathered in the cavernous, dingy auditorium of the Girls Commercial School—Brooklyn College having no auditorium of its own—was President Boylan. No sooner had he begun his remarks than it became painfully clear that La Guardia was talking to one of the other dignitaries onstage. To the shock of all assembled, Boylan broke off his remarks to announce, "I am disturbed by voices—I cannot continue." Then he wheeled about to face the mayor and launched into a harangue about the college's continuing difficulties in securing a campus of its own, and how this campaign had been thwarted by the city at every turn. Boylan concluded with an impassioned appeal to the new mayor's "*corda*" (*cuore*)—his heart. Upon which the Little Flower jumped up, strode to the podium, and responded, "It is not '*la corda*' but *la tasca* that is failing," and pulled out the linings of his empty pants pockets. "Were it not for the dishonesty of those who preceded me," La Guardia declared in a ringing denunciation of Boylan's patron, ex-mayor Jimmy Walker, "I should be able to give you a new building!"

La Guardia's prepared remarks were more sobering. "This generation turns over a sorry world to the new generation," he told the packed auditorium. "I ask the parents here not to expect too much of these children."

The outlook was indeed bleak for the Brooklyn College graduates of 1934. At about this time, the new *Fortune* magazine observed: "The present-day college generation is fatalistic. . . . The investigator is struck by the dominant and pervasive color of a generation that will not stick its neck out. It keeps its shirt on, its pants buttoned, its chin up, and its mouth shut. If we take the mean average to be the truth, it is a cautious, subdued, unadventurous generation, unwilling to storm heaven, afraid to make a fool of itself, unable to dramatize its predicament. . . . Security is the summum bonum of the present college generation."

Such pronouncements were easy for one of Henry Luce's well-paid staffers to make. For Shaw's generation, caution was the only sane response a young man could make to the Depression's continuing chill. Many of Shaw's classmates spoke that year of taking civil service exams, becoming post office workers, municipal workers or, ideally, public school teachers. This path beckoned to the Jewish students especially, just as the Brooklyn Irish traditionally became firemen and policemen. There was dignity in civil service, some use of the mind—and security. For Jewish students, the other path was into the small family business, usually in the garment industry; on the whole, immigrant Jews had tended to go into business for themselves or with a partner, rather than try to work for large, gentile-owned companies that were likely to discriminate against them. Even before graduating, Irwin Shaw tried both paths.

At his father's insistence, Shaw reluctantly spent a day visiting the small garment-center factory in Manhattan where Will Shaw had finally landed a low-paying job producing hat trimmings. Already his father had pleaded with Irwin not to keep on with this silliness about writing that would never earn a dime, to get serious about life and join the business in which his father had friends and connections. This time, as before, Will Shaw's importuning fell on deaf ears.

With only slightly more interest, Shaw applied for an English teacher's license in the public school system. He breezed through the written exam—then failed the oral, thanks to his still-strong Brooklyn accent and the way in which he mangled his g's. Not long after, he wrote to his own alma mater in the hope of teaching there; his letter went unanswered.

At this point Shaw decided to pursue a newspaperman's job. He might have stood a chance, even in bad times, if the daily New York World had not just laid off scores of seasoned reporters who were now themselves making the rounds of the other newspapers. All Shaw's search produced was a grimly amusing tale of rejection that he wrote up first for The Brooklyn College Pioneer as a special postgraduate "P'Shaw" column, then turned into an unpublished short story called, cleverly enough, "Men of the Old World." "He nursed the idea that he could write," Shaw began his third-person column. "Since newspaper work seemed to be the most immediately possible outlet for his talents . . . he started on the rounds of the newspaper offices with high hope, a new hat violently creased in the prevailing style among reporters, and a choice batch of clipped columns from his files."

In the story, a secretary at the *Herald Tribune* announces the paper would pay such a neophyte only $15 dollars a week even if it did offer him a job; the applicant hurries away. An editor at the *Evening Post* hears "Brooklyn College" and laughs at the thought of its football team. In growing desperation, the applicant sends letters to every publication he can imagine. Quickly, the responses come back, nearly all making mention of the "men from the old *World*" who are also looking for work. Throwing in the towel, the applicant trudges over to Macy's, only to learn the store's employment office is closed indefinitely. With no other recourse, he joins a crowd of picketers in Union Square carrying placards that read "Down With the System." One of the protesters, it turns out, is one of the many "men from the old *World*." The young applicant punches him in the nose.

With no money or career prospects, Shaw, like most of his fellow graduates, continued living at home. One night he called David Driscoll, the dramatic-society advisor who had become a mentor of sorts. Driscoll lived in Manhattan, on Eighth Avenue at 12th Street. Shaw asked if he could stop by, and when he did, he admitted he was flat broke. Could Driscoll think of anything better than the one job offer he'd gotten, working in a radio store?

Driscoll responded as Shaw had hoped he would. Not long before, the drama teacher had been enlisted to write radio scripts for a bright young former Brooklyn College student named Himan Brown, who had had the moxie and luck to become a radio producer. Maybe Brown could use another writer.

A gentle and generous man, Driscoll loaned Shaw $100 that night to tide him over and promised to give Brown a call. For Shaw, it would be a call that changed his life.

CHAPTER THREE

By the time a twenty-one-year-old Irwin Shaw looked to it as a last-resort source of employment, radio had come a long way. The flimsy "cat's whisker" wireless hookups with earphones of the early 1920s had been replaced by handsome mahogany consoles that picked up radio signals thousands of miles away. National programs had sprung up, and national companies to produce them: NBC in 1926, CBS a year later. Soft music and recipes were standard fare at first, but in 1929 two ex-vaudevillians came up with *Amos 'n' Andy,* and most of America tuned in—so attentively, it was often said, that city water usage went down to zero because no one left the radio to go to the bathroom.

By the early thirties, radio had varied its offerings. Personalities were one answer: comedians Eddie Cantor, George Burns and Gracie Allen, Jack Benny, Groucho Marx and others climbed eagerly aboard from vaudeville's sinking ship. Sports figures such as Babe Ruth, Jimmy Foxx and Max Baer came to host their own programs. Fictional heroes appeared, too—Sherlock Holmes, Tarzan of the Apes—and even such established comic-strip characters as Lamont Cranston (The Shadow), Britt Reid (The Green Hornet) and Mr. Keen, Tracer of Lost Persons. The Depression, of course, helped enormously, as an ever larger pool of the unemployed found themselves not only free to follow serial shows but desperate for even brief escapes from dreary circumstances.

In the bleak year of 1934, nearly every family in America was tuning in daily. Radio was the country's great unifying force and solace; and if many shows aimed at the lowest common denominator, positioned as they were by the advertising agencies that underwrote their cost, still there was enormous competition for the writers' jobs that each new show created. Shaw, promising as he might be, would never have landed one—nor would David Driscoll—without the luck of knowing the remarkable Himan Brown.

Brown, whose father worked as a dress contractor, was about Shaw's age. In high school he had gotten involved in plays at the local community center, where a young social worker named Moss Hart was in charge of drama. Hart liked Brown's Jewish-dialect act, and before long had him on the Borscht Belt during summer vacations, doing standup comedy along with other such neighborhood boys as Danny Kaye. All the while, radio's popularity was growing. When Brown heard that a new station, the National Broadcasting Company, was auditioning actors, he read from a popular comic strip of the time, *Nize Baby,* whose characters spoke in the same Jewish dialect he'd honed in his standup routine, and was promptly hired to do *Nize Baby* on Saturday mornings.

After his second week on the air, Brown got a call from a woman named Gertrude Berg who had an idea for a series titled *The Rise of the Goldbergs.* Berg's family owned a hotel in the Catskills; she knew comedy writers willing to help. She signed up Brown to play the father on the show; she played the mother; and the teenaged Brown, already a glib salesman, pitched the package to advertisers. The show became a great success, and Brown, who had been promised half the profits, was soon pushed off of it. He went to Brooklyn College but soon talked his way into producing a new show, *Marie, the Little French Princess,* about a sweet blue-blooded girl who leaves her gilded world for a happier, more fulfilling life as a commoner in America. For a writer he had to look no further than his teacher David Driscoll—and when Driscoll suggested that Irwin Shaw would make a fine writer for Brown's next project, Brown was only too happy to take his advice.

"There was an advertiser at that time called Tasty Yeast," Brown recalls, "a candy bar where you got all this yeast and so on—good for you. I went to see the agency that handled Tasty Yeast; the package I was peddling was *Dick Tracy,* to which I'd gotten the rights." Despite the recent success of *Little Orphan Annie* on the air, the agency was cautious. It agreed to a test of three shows weekly for thirteen weeks in Boston. The agency would supply the actors, as agencies were already wont to do, but assumed that Brown had a staff of writers at the ready. Brown assured the agency he did, then gave Shaw a call. "Irwin said, 'Sure, let's take a whack at it,' " Brown remembers. "So we plotted some scripts together and he wrote them. Mostly we did this at my house, because my family had a second-floor open porch on Carroll Street and Troy Avenue—where all the Hasidim live now."

Shaw wrote the thirteen weeks' worth of scripts, but then a snag developed. Tasty Yeast, it seemed, was not as bursting with nutrients as its makers had led the public to believe, and federal agencies were suddenly taking an interest. Ever nimble, Brown sold the show instead to Quaker Oats as a five-day-a-week series, and Shaw began working in earnest.

The shows were each fifteen minutes long, of which two and a half minutes would be allotted to Quaker Oats commercials. For each thirteen-week series, Shaw and Brown would lay out a general plot line using continuing characters—Pat, Tess Trueheart, Dick Tracy—then refine it every week as they went along. "There might be something with villains and city politics and bribery—a large robbery pulled off or a murder committed and so on," Brown recalls. "We did a lot of mystery things, a lot of creaking around.

"On any given show, Irwin would give me a projected story line, and I would say, 'Don't you think that while we're there we could throw in another red-herring character? That sort of thing. But at the same time, I couldn't use too many actors. For one thing, we were on a very tight budget. And in eleven or twelve minutes you couldn't have that many people running around."

Then too, the shows were *live*. So every character and plot twist had to be timed to the second to avoid having the show run over. "When the clock was on the last minute—fourteen-thirty of a fifteen-minute show— you had to be off, that was it," says Brown. Sound effects had to be timed too. If Shaw wrote, "Telephone rings," there had to be a phone that actually rang, the actor had to pick it up and put it to his ear, and that would consume several seconds.

Even so, it was impossible to tell exactly how long a written script would play. One actor might take too long with his lines; another might speak too fast. When Shaw had written the script as tightly as he could, Brown would take it to the NBC studio on the eighth floor of Rockefeller Center and begin working with the actors. "Shaw wasn't part of that," Brown explains. "I did all my own editing. I would cut sentences or words, change a climax or a scene, because it played differently from how it looked on paper. Then when we rehearsed I would clock it, and clock it, and clock it again."

Radio listeners had shown with *Nize Baby* and *Little Orphan Annie* that they loved hearing comics on the air. Soon *Dick Tracy* was a reasonable success as well, and Brown began combing the comics for another sure bet. He settled on *The Gumps*. Andy and Min Gump were a cranky couple, the Archie and Edith Bunker of their day, and Chester Gump was their independent-minded child. Brown bought the rights, then convinced the Korn Products refining company to buy the show. Again he turned to Shaw as a writer. "I said, 'Irwin, how are you at comedy?' And he was sensational. It was the same family three times a week, with an uncle, some relatives. He did some of the most beautiful vignettes." On that show, Brown cast Agnes Moorehead, who'd never been on radio, to play Min Gump; he chose Wilmer Walter, an important actor of the day, to play Andy Gump.

Shaw wrote both shows for more than two years. At $20 to $25 an episode, the pay was poor compared to what the actors and Brown as producer received. But Shaw was so facile he could turn out five scripts in three days, have the rest of the week off to write short stories, and still earn at least $100—extraordinary money for a twenty-one-year-old boy in the midst of the Depression. (A three-course restaurant meal could still be had in the 1930s for a dollar; a new suit might cost $20, a new Ford not quite $600.) Soon enough, he hired a secretary to help. "I managed to write the equivalent of a three-act play every Monday and Tuesday for the airwaves by lying on a couch and dictating to a secretary," Shaw later recalled. In radio terms: five twelve-and-a-half-minute episodes. "Then I took Wednesday off to rest and worked on my short stories and plays the rest of the week." Even so, Brown recalls that Shaw was always in need of money, always asking him for advances on scripts.

The money wasn't going to clothes and dates. Overnight Shaw had become his family's provider. Suddenly it was he who would deal with the creditors, pay off the monthly bills, and hear out his mother's pleas for a new dress or pair of shoes. At about the time Shaw had graduated from Brooklyn College, the bank had lost patience with his parents for failure to make mortgage payments and evicted the family from 2036 Brown Street. It was Shaw who rented an apartment for them—and himself—in Flatbush, at 1149 East 17th Street, across from the Wingate Athletic Field, so that Shaw could more conveniently play football on the weekends. Will Shaw was only fitfully employed in the garment district; Irwin eventually set his father up in business with a neighborhood friend, Samuel Wechsler. For a year or so in 1935–1936, Shaw and Wechsler tried to manufacture artificial flowers—boutonnieres—and hat trimmings, out of a work space on Seventh Avenue and 34th Street in Manhattan. Wechsler's daughter recalls, "Irwin's father and mine were the most adorable two men. But precisely because of that, they were not suited for business." Quietly, the business collapsed.

Being the provider affected Shaw in very definite ways. Here, first of all, was tangible proof that he could make a good living as a writer. Never again would Shaw see himself as anything *but* a writer; nor would he hold any other sort of job. That his first writing success should bring such money—at a time when his family so desperately needed it—would also set a standard for him that he would never quite be able to push aside: that a writer was judged by the money he made, and the more he made, the better a writer he must be. The flip side of that standard was the fear that no matter how good the money was today, it might well vanish tomorrow, and Shaw now knew exactly how painful life without money could be.

At the same time, Shaw rose to the challenge of being the provider with a remarkable generosity of spirit that never left him. The money he worried about earning he gave away unstintingly, first to his parents and brother, later to his own family, and always to friends in need. Despite his not infrequent grumblings about the burden it imposed on him, he found that secretly he rather *liked* being the provider. It put him at the head of a table; it put him in charge; and as his writer's ego grew, that appealed to him more and more. To a girl named Ruthie Strong, in whom he'd taken an interest, he confided a dream he'd had: "I was riding a bicycle uphill," he told her, "and on my back I was wearing a basket. And in the basket were my parents, my brother—and you."

Unquestionably, the responsibility aged him. The boy of twenty who twitted his professors in print was, at twenty-two, a seasoned, even weary professional writer. Some years later, Shaw set down on paper exactly how he felt about this stage in his life, in a story that remains one of his very best: "Main Currents of American Thought."

Published in *The New Yorker*, "Main Currents" is an all-but-autobiographical sketch of a beleaguered radio writer named Andrew. One of the series he dictates to his secretary is a *Dick Tracy*–like drama called *Dusty Blades*; the other is *Ronnie Cook and His Friends*. The man at the bank tells Andrew he's overdrawn. His mother pleads in her "asking-for-money" voice for fifty dollars for a party dress for Andrew's younger sister, Dorothy—not the last time Shaw would transform the gender of his gentle younger brother, David. As Andrew adds up the other family bills he has to pay, his smooth-voiced agent, Herman, calls to complain that the *Blades* scripts are "slow as gum." (When the story appeared in *The New Yorker*, Himan Brown was hurt enough by the characterization to avoid ever talking to Shaw again; by then, however, Shaw had stopped writing for him.) Andrew's heart lies not with radio writing, but with the play that sits unfinished on his desk, and with the books he buys but has no time to read, like Parrington's *Main Currents of American Thought*, whose title becomes an ironic reference to radio drama and a symbol of the intellectualism to which he aspires.

In a few short pages, Shaw captures a sense not only of his own life but of the times in which he lives. (Among Andrew's obligations is a donation of $100 to the Spanish Loyalists. Barcelona has just fallen; the story appeared in August 1939.) He does this with a storyteller's natural gift, weaving Andrew's brooding thoughts about how to direct his characters in the next week's radio scripts with the real-life demands put upon him by his family. If his portrait of Andrew is tainted with a bit of self-pity, and if the references to *Hamlet* and *Moby-Dick* are pretentious, dropped as they are without narrative reason, still the story is a beautifully realized masterwork.

Following the convention of the day, Shaw ended most of his early stories with a twist, and "Main Currents of American Thought" is no exception. So world-weary is Andrew that he must, the reader presumes, be a middle-aged man at least. The story's last paragraph thus comes as a shock. Andrew takes a precious few minutes from his labors to join a pick-up game of baseball. "The sun and the breeze felt good on the baseball field," Shaw writes, "and he forgot for an hour, but he moved slowly. His arm hurt at the shoulder when he threw, and the boy playing second base called him Mister, which he wouldn't have done even last year, when Andrew was twenty-four."

Shaw would often say later that he never reworked the first drafts of his early stories—rarely, for that matter, reworked anything he wrote—and that many came to him in a single day or less. In fact, the original manuscript of the story reveals another, less felicitous last sentence crossed out, with the famous one scrawled below. "The sun and the breeze felt good on the baseball field," goes the original ending, "and he forgot for an hour, but he moved slowly after ground balls and felt himself missing plays that he could have made easily when he was twenty-two, three years ago."

Shaw would draw on his radio-writing days for another, longer work—his second novel, *The Troubled Air*. But in a broader sense, radio shaped him as a writer. Radio serials moved along by cause and effect, underscored by a strong sense of justice for the public good. Shaw brought exactly these concerns to his fiction and drama. Eventually he would react against them, deciding with a certain bitterness that life was a series of arbitrary events, and subject his characters to random accidents. Even so, many of his best stories show a strong concern with morality, his characters trying, though they often fail, to measure up to a moral standard as homegrown as that of old radio heroes.

Dialogue was radio's other great lesson for Shaw. Radio scripts, of course, had no descriptive passages at all, only dialogue and sound effects. "The training was invaluable," Shaw later admitted, "because in a radio serial people have to talk in their own voices and have to be recognized as certain characters immediately at all times, which is a hard discipline." Realistic dialogue, capturing its time as deftly as the occasional descriptive detail or passing reference to world news, would lie at the heart of many of Shaw's early short stories. One would have to wonder if radio's lessons had not been learned too well: the tendency to move characters too neatly, and to tie up loose ends too tightly, would strike many critics as drawbacks in Shaw's novels. For now, radio's only unfortunate legacy was a case of acute insomnia that would dog Shaw until the age of twenty-nine—when he entered the Army and the whole issue became moot.

At this time, both for extra money and for a perverse sort of fun, Shaw spent his Saturdays playing what euphemistically passed for semipro football in Brooklyn. One of the football coaches at Madison High, Mike Torgan, fielded a private team he called Mike Torgan's Tigers. Shaw, along with a few of his erstwhile Brooklyn College teammates, would line up against other private teams at high school and college stadiums, earning a percentage of the gate receipts, which usually amounted to three or four dollars per player. In an early story, " 'March, March on Down the Field,' " Shaw offers a gritty and amusing glimpse of those games. Scheepers' Red

Devils suit up in a freezing locker room, with much loud griping about the cold, only to learn from Coach Scheepers that so few people have turned out to watch the game that the players will have to settle for half their expected pay. Worse yet, the team's leather helmets have somehow failed to arrive. Too destitute to refuse to play even in these conditions, the players file out of the locker room bareheaded, to march, march on down the field.

Inevitably, Shaw wrote about his family too. An unpublished play from this time, *The Golden Years*, depicts a Brooklyn Jewish family in June 1929. As the play opens, the family's favorite son is about to deliver a high school valedictory speech about the great golden years that lie ahead. The stage is crowded with an O'Neill-like assemblage of relatives; the boy's father is one of four brothers, variously ambitious or dissipated, all overshadowed by a rocking-chair patriarch who makes cynical pronouncements from the corner. By the end of the first act, the boy's father, a good-hearted union man, has been shot by the local racketeer. When the surviving brothers seek revenge, they encounter a smooth, democratic boss who plays peacemaker; the boss knows everyone's secret and how to force compromises on both sides while extracting payoffs from either camp in the process. By the time the last curtain goes down, the play's valedictorian has lost his last vestiges of youthful idealism.

The Golden Years asked the same question that would animate nearly all of Shaw's writing, both in drama and fiction: How should decent people react to the corruption and violence that inevitably seep into their lives from the outside world? While its concluding speeches grew somewhat melodramatic, overall the play packed as strong a punch as the more happily destined *Gentle People* of a few years later. But when Shaw dusted it off after *The Gentle People*'s success and showed it to Harold Clurman, the Group Theatre's director found it unexciting, and the play was never produced.

Shaw genuinely *liked* writing, which couldn't be said of every writer. He liked moving his characters around, and he enormously liked feeling he did it better than anyone else he knew. He was no closet artist, however, content to write for himself. He wanted desperately to get published and escape the treadmill of radio-serial writing. Beginning in 1934, he sent out dozens of stories to Street and Smith's magazines, to *Judge, Collier's, The Saturday Evening Post* and others.

It was a huge and inviting market that had begun to swell after World War I, thanks in part to breakthroughs in printing that allowed for cheap production of mass-circulation magazines. Magazine stories were a prime source of entertainment for millions, and would remain so until the advent of television. As a result, scores of magazines published short fiction—as many as 300 stories a week throughout the country—and a young writer stood a better chance than ever before of seeing one of his efforts in print.

For young writers of especially literary leanings, one of the most exciting periodicals was the new *Story* magazine, started by an American couple in Vienna in 1931 but soon brought to New York under the aegis of Bennett Cerf. In its earliest issues, *Story* published James T. Farrell and Erskine Caldwell, both unknowns at the time. In its February 1934 issue it published a story called "The Daring Young Man on the Flying Trapeze" by another new name, William Saroyan, who became an overnight success much as Shaw would two years later. Another impecunious young writer, John Cheever, published the story "Homage to Shakespeare" in the magazine in early 1935 without eliciting much reaction at all.

Shaw couldn't even get published, but in the summer of 1935 his luck began to change. David Driscoll and his wife, Rose, decided to rent a beach house in Cape Cod with another couple, Brooklyn College professor Maurice Valency and his prospective wife, and Shaw was invited to join them. Because Jews were still frowned on in the area—many listings included the code phrase "churches nearby" to indicate the sort of summer tenants sought—Driscoll and Valency conducted the search. The house they settled on was in West Falmouth, a large Cape Codder, wood-shingled, gray, with a barn and a tennis court, looking across the coast road to the ocean beyond. Arnold Moss, the Brooklyn College speech professor, took a house with his wife a quarter-mile down the road into town. Together with the Driscoll contingent they formed a literary circle of sorts, each of the men writing for radio but harboring far grander hopes.

In the mornings, the typewriters clattered away. Driscoll, with considerable resentment, kept turning out *Marie, the Little French Princess* for Himan Brown—the money was simply too good—but also collaborated on a play with Valency. Valency, an English professor who would go on to adapt *The Madwoman of Chaillot* and other Giraudoux plays, saw himself as a creative writer too. Like Driscoll, he was some ten years older than Shaw, whom he considered a somewhat bumptious character, all jock and no intellect. Shaw was forever turning to Valency to ask for help in changing the ribbon on his typewriter. Valency had a little sailboat that summer, and one day he took Shaw out on it. To Valency's amusement, the big kid turned absolutely green when a sudden wind blew up—he'd never been out on a small boat before.

Shaw was both flattered and a bit awed to be included in this older set; he still addressed his Brooklyn College mentor as "Mr. Driscoll" and would do so for many years after. As a writer, however, he was no less professional than his elders. Like Driscoll, he still wrote for Himan Brown, producing a radio script every weekday morning. Afternoons were for the beach and tennis; Shaw found a few locals to round out an aggressive game of doubles at a nearby rental court and, except for a shaky serve, played rather well. Then, in the last week at Falmouth, he too decided to write a play.

It was hardly coincidence that plays were what the Brooklyn literary set burned to write that summer. For at least three years now, the effects of the Depression had been dramatized in growing numbers of graphic plays called agit-prop (agitation-propaganda) productions. Performed by amateur groups in lofts and small theaters, agit-props reflected the deepening bitterness of hard-hit workers—as well as of the artists who dramatized their plight—and the tilt toward radical solutions, including Communism, to right the wrongs of capitalism. A turning point had come in January 1935 with *Waiting for Lefty,* Clifford Odets's graphic one-act depiction of a taxi strike, produced first by the New Theatre League at its annual new play benefit. So grittily realistic were the characters and dialogue that for the first several minutes of the production, an unprepared audience at the old Civic Rep on 14th Street had not known that what they were seeing was not indeed an angry union meeting. By the time the play ended with the cast shouting, *"Strike! Strike! Strike!"* the inchoate social theater of the early thirties had found its voice. Within months the Group Theatre came out with three more Odets plays, *Till the Day I Die, Awake and Sing* and *Paradise Lost,* all white-hot with the twenty-nine-year-old playwright's impassioned portrayals of laborers and Jewish-American immigrants. Alfred Kazin, in *Starting Out in the Thirties,* captured what Shaw and Driscoll and Valency felt. "How I admired Odets! How grateful I was to Odets! Even his agit-prop play *Waiting for Lefty* bounded and sang, was crazily right in its close-ups. . . . It abruptly sent out such waves of feeling that I found myself breathing to Odets's rhythms. . . . Sitting in the Belasco, watching my mother and father and uncles and aunts occupying the stage in *Awake and Sing* by as much right as if they were Hamlet and Lear, I understood at last. It was all one, as I had always known. Art and truth and hope could yet come together—if a real writer was their meeting place."

Shaw felt all that. But there were no impassioned after-dinner discussions about what was happening to the theater down in New York, at least not that Shaw participated in. And when August came, and he started a play, he kept it to himself. Even then, he made a practice of not discussing what he was writing. He would maintain that privacy for the rest of his life, rarely showing his work to anyone, even lovers or editors, until he felt it was done. "He didn't wear his heart on his sleeve," Driscoll says. "I soon learned with Irwin that you didn't say, 'What are you writing?' or 'How's it going?' He just never wanted to talk about it."

The August play was a one-act allegory about six dead soldiers who refuse to be buried and instead stand up to be heard. (As a private tribute to his mentor, Shaw named one of his soldiers Driscoll. It would not be the last time his characters' names bore some personal resonance.) In fact, it was Shaw's sixth serious attempt at a play. He came up with a first draft in roughly ten days. Its title: *Bury the Dead*.

When *Bury the Dead* exploded on the Broadway stage the next spring, more than one critic pointed out that Shaw's premise was not an original one. In 1931 The Theatre Guild had staged a strikingly similar drama, *Miracle at Verdun*, by German pacifist Hans Chlumberg, at the Martin Beck Theatre in New York. *Miracle at Verdun* opens in one of Verdun's wartime cemeteries, as a tour group arrives to inspect a unique mass grave in which German and French soldiers were buried together. A mysterious stranger stays behind to invoke the dead, and miraculously they respond, shaking off the earth that covers them. Before long they are tramping through the countryside, headed back to their hometowns, only to be received in terror—and then anger. What are the widows to do, who remarried after the war? And who will provide for the resurrected, if all 13 million war dead return? With dark humor, Chlumberg shows the leaders of the free world gathering when they hear the news, their past tributes to the war dead revealed as hypocrisy now that the dead have reappeared. After much debate, the leaders persuade the dead to return to their graves, and the world goes right on building for the next war.

Bury the Dead does open at a gravesite; the dead do come to life; and they do confront the living. One of its vignettes even brings a widow together with her dead husband. But these are borrowings of no more consequence than Shakespeare's. Shaw's play is different in tone: blunt and direct, compared to Chlumberg's ironic detachment. Its scope is smaller than that of *Miracle* too. Not only is it a single act compared to Chlumberg's three, but it remains with the resurrected dead at their gravesite rather than switch to halls of state; and because Shaw offers only a handful of walking corpses and not a crowd, each can tell his own story and establish more contact with the audience. Most important, by taking its premise to a reductio ad absurdum, *Miracle* can conclude only by having the dead agree to return to their graves; the prospect of 13 million resurrected war dead allows no other ending but apocalypse, and so the play's message, strong as it is, remains in the mind, not the heart. *Bury the Dead* is pure agit-prop, a powerful punch in the gut meant to stir its audience to action. Its dead soldiers tell simple, moving stories of how they died and what they miss about life. They hear out the living who want to see them buried—gravediggers, wives, angry generals—but remain unpersuaded. In the violent last episode, hysterical generals begin firing futilely with machine guns at the advancing corpses as one sympathetic observer shouts, to the audience as much as to anyone else, "Tell 'em all to stand up! Tell 'em! Tell 'em!"

The play that Shaw had just written was far closer to *Waiting for Lefty* than anything else. In its realistic dialogue, its structure of vignettes and its final call to action, *Bury* accepted the Odets play as a model of the agit-prop form. What lifted it from mere imitation was the force of its language, and the trait that would be Shaw's signature as a writer for years to come: its electrifying appropriateness to the sensibility of its time.

The New York to which Shaw returned with his play under his arm in September was a city galvanized by the arts. Just that month, Harry Hopkins won passage of his $5 billion Works Progress Administration, of which a small but significant fraction went to start dozens of Federal Arts projects. Among them would be the Federal Theatre, which by the spring of 1936 would produce its first highly successful, socially minded plays. For an unknown like Shaw, however, the hubbub was as frustrating as it was inspiring: with so many experienced actors, playwrights and directors out of work, the Federal Theatre's directors announced in October that only those with previous credits would be eligible for FT plays.

There was one other hope. Central to the social-theater movement was the New Theatre League, a loose affiliation of politically minded amateur production groups. In the League's monthly *New Theatre* magazine, Odets, Archibald MacLeish, the Group Theatre's Harold Clurman and others wrote impassioned essays on the need to forge a theater that must be, as Odets put it, "hot and spiteful, and . . . must probe the future with reference to the past and present." These were the luminaries of the movement who also sat as judges on periodic playwriting contests for new work, the last of which had showcased Odets's *Waiting for Lefty.* First prize was $50 and, much more important, the opportunity to have one's play produced on a Sunday night or two at the Civic Repertory Theatre on West 14th Street.

Confident as he often felt now about his writing, Shaw at twenty-two was abashed at the prospect of submitting his play to the New Theatre contest that fall. Indeed, without the urging of his Brooklyn friend Jerry Moross, he wouldn't have done it at all. Moross was a young composer who had grown up on Avenue K and gone off to New York University at the precocious age of fourteen. Just that year, he had had his first Broadway success with the revue *Parade.* Moross was strongly allied with the New Theatre League, and knew personally the playwrights George Sklar and Albert Maltz. Tentatively, Shaw asked him to take a look at *Bury the Dead.*

Moross was staggered by the play. He was also chagrined: by the time Shaw asked him to read it, the contest deadline had passed. Convinced the play merited serious attention, Moross submitted it anyway. The judges stuck to their deadline, and soon after announced that the winner of the contest was Albert Maltz, for his play *Private Hicks.* But they were as taken with *Bury the Dead* as Moross was. *New Theatre* editor Herbert Kline decided to print the play in its entirety. More exciting yet, one of the League's repertory groups, the Let Freedom Ring Acting Company, chose to stage two performances of the play, on Saturday, March 14, and Sunday, March 15, 1936, at the 46th Street Theatre.

Emboldened by *New Theatre*'s interest in his play, Shaw made the big move from Brooklyn to Manhattan. It was a move he had always wanted to make, a vision that had grown more and more compelling in his Brooklyn College years. "Like spies for an invading army," he wrote of himself and his college mates, "we had stolen in and out of its streets, marking its wealth, the temper of its inhabitants, its deceptively nonchalant defenses, its theatres and museums, the beauty of its women. With its domes and spires constantly in our sight, to spur us on with the tantalizing accessibility of the prize, we laid our plans for conquest."

Shaw rented a two-room furnished apartment on West 12th Street for $55 a month, subsidized by his continuing scriptwork for Himan Brown. Greenwich Village had lost some of its bohemian charm from a decade before, when the likes of Eugene O'Neill and John Reed vied for the love of Louise Bryant and drank in dark Sixth Avenue bars. Still, there was much excited talk of art and politics in places like the Jumble Shop, off MacDougal Alley, or Stewart's Cafeteria on Sheridan Square, where Odets had often come with Harold Clurman. "At midnight it had the festive air of Madison Square Garden on the occasion of a big fight," Clurman wrote of Stewart's. "Here the poor and jolly have-beens, ne'er-do-wells, names-to-be, the intellectual, the bohemian, the lazy, neurotic, confused and unfortunate, the radicals, mystics, thugs, drags, and sweet young people without a base, collected noisily to make a very stirring music of their discord and hope."

Five weeks before the scheduled performances of *Bury the Dead*, the Let Freedom Ring company (the name came from the title of an unsuccessfully produced play about slavery by Albert Bein) held an initial reading in the Village, which Shaw attended. With his football player's build and heavy Brooklyn accent, the playwright posed a disconcerting contrast to his work—so much so that after he had left, the director, Worthington Miner, turned to his actors and said, "I not only don't believe that that boy wrote that play, I don't believe he can read it."

In fact, Shaw went on to act a minor role in the production, mostly to help cut costs. Not only was the budget meager, there was also the fear that Actors' Equity might forbid production of what was technically an unsanctioned play. "There are one or two extra-large bogeymen who are especially imported when a one-act play is going the rounds," Shaw later wrote. "There was the spectre of Equity hanging over a group rehearsing collectively for five weeks, wonderfully underpaid. And there was the large and lively ghost of poverty rattling dismally in the corners of the little halls and the variegated theaters which we begged and borrowed to rehearse in at odd hours." Shaw wrote a curtain-raiser himself, *Roll Call*, about three soldiers on cots in an army tent, waiting to return home from the war, but the play was not used. (The play's setting suggests that of one of Shaw's best stories, "Act of Faith," written some ten years later.) Instead, the troupe went with *Over Here,* a popular war play of 1918 written by Walter Hare. Despite all the difficulties, the two plays did go on as scheduled, to benefit the New Theatre League and the American League Against War and Fascism.

Reaction to the first performance of *Bury* was extraordinary. Word of mouth brought a standing-room-only crowd the second night. On Monday, Herbert Drake in the *New York Herald Tribune* declared it "an impressive play" and Shaw "a playwright to be reckoned with." Added Drake of the play: "It is so strong, so powerful and so compelling a drama that a more important place should be given it." By the next week, Robert Garland of the New York *World-Telegram* reported that "not since Clifford Odets' *Waiting for Lefty* showed up somewhere on the outskirts and worked its way north to success on Broadway has a one-act play aroused such comment and concern as Irwin Shaw's *Bury the Dead,* now being displayed at odd moments and in divers places." Garland went on to urge theatergoers to seek it out, declaring, "This one-acter of Mr. Shaw's is . . . one of the notable theatrical events of the season. I don't say you'll enjoy it. But you'll not forget it for many a war-conscious day."

One of the first to show interest in taking the play uptown was Harold Clurman. There was a problem, however. "The Group offered to produce this promising first play," he later wrote. "But Shaw, very young and impatient, wanted an immediate production, and we had just contracted a strange liaison with Milton Shubert to do a production with him." Clurman noted rather primly that Shaw subsequently had trouble finding backing for the play—and this was true. Producer Alex Yokel announced in early April he would bring *Bury the Dead* within a week to the Fulton Theatre for a regular Broadway run, but more than half of the $1,100 needed to stage the production was still being sought.

Meanwhile, two other rich opportunities had come Shaw's way. One was a call from a talent scout at RKO studios in California. The scout had heard some of Shaw's radio scripts and read *Bury the Dead* before its production. How would Shaw like to fly out to Hollywood to work as a screenwriter at $360 a week on a movie about football called *The Big Game,* with a doubling of his salary in six months if all went well? On March 14, the very night *Bury* debuted as a reading, Shaw signed his first Hollywood contract. With it, he joined the literary migration from New York to Hollywood that had begun in the late twenties when, as Budd Schulberg put it, studio heads began sending an SOS to eastern writers to fill the new demand for talkies. Within the last several years, virtually every writer with a book to his credit had heeded the call: Maxwell Anderson, Robert Benchley, Dorothy Parker, Dashiell Hammett, James Cain, John Dos

Passos. And of course, William Faulkner and F. Scott Fitzgerald. The rush was such that any caviling by purists about the corruptive influence of Hollywood struck most young writers as sour grapes. And if most of the newly hired talent came running back to New York in weeks or months, muttering about the studio heads' heathen tastes, the next recruits could always hope to prove the exceptions and write the rare film whose quality somehow survived the studio system unscathed. Besides, this was still the Depression; who could turn down that kind of dough?

The other call was from a young New York publisher named Bennett Cerf, who wanted to include *Bury the Dead* in his new hardcover line of contemporary plays.

Just two years before, Cerf's still new Random House had published James Joyce's *Ulysses* after an epic court battle in which the government's censorship of the book was overturned. Hero of that victory and now one of New York's most important publishers, Cerf shared an office at 20 East 57th Street with his partner Donald Klopfer—their two desks faced each other—and it was into this office that Shaw was ushered one day in early March 1936. "We were surprised to find that he was a great big bruiser of a fellow who was built like a longshoreman," Cerf later recounted. "He had a lusty, hearty laugh that made you laugh with him. We liked him on sight.

"We knew that in spite of its critical acclaim, *Bury the Dead* was not making a fortune for its author, and so, after a moment's consultation, Donald and I decided to offer him a job at Random House. I approached the subject gingerly because I didn't want to embarrass Shaw by asking what he was living on, so I asked him what he did. He said he wrote for radio, and my very next question elicited the fact that he was earning five or six hundred dollars a week. When we heard this, Donald and I burst out laughing. Here we were offering him a job and he was making more than the two of us put together. He was indeed already a very successful young man. It turned out that he looked so dirty because he had been playing touch football in Central Park."

By early April, Shaw was in Hollywood, living with an aunt and writing in an apartment his relatives found for him. At the RKO lot, where he often took lunch in the commissary, he struck fellow writer Julian Blaustein as seeming about as green as they came. So accustomed was Shaw to living at home that he kept sending his shirts weekly back to Brooklyn in a large cardboard box for his mother to clean and iron. By continuing to write *The Gumps* on the side, he stockpiled enough money to contribute the $500 still needed for *Bury*'s Broadway production—at that time a lavish budget, demanded by the large cast of thirty-five and an unusual number of lights.

For the April 18 opening at the Ethel Barrymore Theatre (the venue having been changed because of the financial difficulties encountered in producing the play), Shaw flew back to New York—a two-day trip with an overnight layover. Despite the glowing advance notices, he had to paper the house with family and friends, including David Driscoll and half the Brooklyn College football team. The play had a new curtain-raiser, a newsreel-like antiwar montage called *Prelude* by J. Edward Shugrue and John O'Shaughnessy (an Armistice Day production would feature a similar one-acter called *Headlines* by the then unknown Tennessee Williams). As staged by Worthington Miner—and performed by the original cast, now rechristened the Actors Repertory Company—*Bury* had been refined into a fast-paced whirl of episodic scenes, with dramatic spotlighting of the dark stage, ghostly offstage voices and the orchestra pit as the grave. The Saturday-night audience watched the curtain go down in stunned silence, then broke into loud cheers, with cries of "Author! Author!" which eventually brought the embarrassed but happy playwright to the stage. Shaw dutifully returned to Brooklyn with his family to spend the night at home, before flying back to Los Angeles to work.

If he had hurried away half out of fear for what the reviewers might say, he needn't have worried. Brooks Atkinson of *The New York Times* declared the next day that "Mr. Shaw's grimly imaginative rebellion against warfare is a shattering bit of theatre magic that burrows under the skin of argument into the raw flesh of sensation. He is a young man, a latter-day graduate of Brooklyn College, and his knowledge of the battlefields must have come at second hand. But his moral indignation is his own, and his dramatic virtuosity is extraordinary. What *Waiting for Lefty* was to Clifford Odets, *Bury the Dead* is to Irwin Shaw." Atkinson went on to acknowledge the play's similarity to *Miracle at Verdun,* but declared Shaw's approach was different enough that the walking-corpse concept became his own.

The other dailies were equally fervent in their praise. John Mason Brown of the *New York Post* wrote, "Seen even at a dress rehearsal, when it was acted before a few scattered people, its effect was so hushing, so heart-breaking and galvanizing that it is not difficult to guess how stupendous its impact will be upon the crowded houses it so richly deserves." Added Gilbert Gabriel of the New York *American:* "Mr. Shaw stands in imminent danger of growing into one of the most powerful dramatists of this land and time. It is a long time since I have seen a large audience so moved, so hotly convulsed, so deeply shaken."

Even in a passionate era, these were extraordinary reviews, written by men who had seen what they felt was history-making theater and been genuinely startled by it. Suddenly, *Bury the Dead* was the talk of the town, the new play to see, even as other plays, among them S. N. Behrman's *End of Summer* and Robert Sherwood's *Idiot's Delight,* were making theater history of their own and adding up to a memorable season of antiwar and socially minded drama. The young playwright was written up everywhere, the columnists delighting in the colorful facts of his football career (exaggerated immediately to serious semipro status) and his radio-serial writing. Only in some of the weeklies did a backlash of critical opinion appear—as if *Bury*'s particular power had worn off a bit with a few days' perspective.

Joseph Wood Krutch, writing in *The Nation*, regretted that Shaw failed to sustain the great drama of his premise. "A symbol as complete and adequate as the one he invented is not improved by being progressively diluted," Krutch wrote. *The New Yorker*'s Wolcott Gibbs was more damning. Acknowledging the decency of the play's premise, he still found *Bury*, strictly speaking, to be a second-rate drama. "Mr. Shaw says that the young men must not die, and he says furthermore that the young men must refuse to die. Obviously nobody in his senses could quarrel with such a thesis as this, even if it had been written by that other earnest pacifist, Dr. John Haynes Holmes, and acted out by the Singer Midgets. Unfortunately, however, it is the function of this department to discuss what goes on in the theatre in terms of dramatic merit rather than sociology, and I am obliged to say that for me *Bury the Dead* was just a little discouraging." Gibbs found Shaw as a writer to have a "florid touch," and as a dramatist to have created "a setup for an easy catch in the throat." Shaw did show great hope, however. "Perhaps," Gibbs concluded in what would seem a prophetic piece of advice, "he ought to remember only that fantasy . . . has a tendency to blur the issue rather than clear it up."

But *Bury the Dead* was more than a play now. Overnight, it had been taken up as a social weapon. In April, *New Theatre* magazine reprinted the play in full, prefaced by a trumpet blast from editor Herbert Kline: "This play should not only harrow those who witness it; it should affect their lives. That is frankly its purpose. If it can draw new masses of people into the militant struggle being waged against the forces of militarism by such organizations as the American League Against War and Fascism and the American Student Union, it will have fulfilled the prime aim of its young author." Out in California, Donald Ogden Stewart had spoken on March 29 in the same terms to 1,200 members of the film community, who first heard a reading of *Bury the Dead* by Fredric March, his wife, Florence Eldridge, and director John Cromwell. "Thank God that that play has been written," Stewart declared to the crowd. "Thank God for Irwin Shaw."

Had Shaw been in the audience that night—he was still in New York, about to head west—he would have felt both flattered and a bit overwhelmed by the fierce sentiments swirling around him. He was arriving in Hollywood just as the writers' war with the studios was coming to a head, and *Bury the Dead* had been snatched up as a banner not only of the antiwar movement but also of left-leaning writers and directors allied in the fight to form a union. As one after another well-known talent stood up to endorse the play, greetings were extended to the playwright himself. "I want to welcome him to Hollywood," said Arthur Kober, a *New Yorker* writer turned screenwriter. "He is here to work as a screenwriter for RKO and as you all know, the screenwriter is an important, oh so important individual in this town."

Dudley Nichols, one of Hollywood's highest-paid screenwriters, who had just turned down an Academy Award for his script of *The Informer* to assert his kinship with the Writers Guild, also welcomed Shaw and added, "It's exciting to know so many people can feel these things and feel solidarity in them."

Clifford Odets, Shaw's role model, spoke too that evening. "What we are doing when we all come here, when our writers write plays like this one, when our actors and directors are interested enough to read them, is making ourselves an outpost of civilization. And what I think we all will agree upon is that more and more our kind of people must push forward until that outpost of civilization covers the whole damn world."

So stirring was *Bury the Dead* to this crowd that all factions that night claimed the young playwright as one of their own. To the Communists—of whom Odets still counted himself one—Shaw was clearly a blood brother. To the more moderate leftists, his play was admirably nondoctrinaire. And to those whose main concern was closer to home, in forming a union for collective bargaining power, this Irwin Shaw, with his overnight fame, would surely lend another important name to the rolls of the Writers Guild.

Everyone wanted to sign up Irwin Shaw. There was just one hitch. No one had asked him if he wanted to join.

CHAPTER FOUR

Less than two weeks after Shaw's return to Hollywood from the triumphant Broadway opening of *Bury the Dead,* the writers' war exploded.

Fierce feelings had been building on either side ever since the 1933 passage of President Roosevelt's National Industrial Recovery Act, with its controversial Section 7A granting workers the right to organize unions and bargain collectively. In these darkest days of the Depression, Hollywood writers and directors were among the most highly paid workers in America; still, they could be fired at will, replaced by fresh talent at a fraction of their salaries, and in various other ways made to feel their utter helplessness at the hands of all-powerful producers. In the spring of 1933, when the movie industry suffered its first real dip and producers imposed drastic pay cuts across the board, angry writers had banded together to form the Screen Writers Guild.

Over the next three years, the Guild had struggled largely in vain. Most top writers—those making between $1,000 and $5,000 a week—remained loyal to the producers who paid them; and lower-salaried writers could always be replaced by eager new arrivals. The only answer, clearly, was to join up with the New York–based Authors League of America and the Dramatists Guild, and thus to represent some ninety percent of the country's working writers. As 1936 unfolded, the rival guilds put aside their differences, worked out an amalgamation plan, and scheduled a vote on the issue for May 2, 1936.

Grimly, the producers fought back.

In the weeks before the vote, four well-paid writers—instantly dubbed the Four Horsemen—made the rounds as studio loyalists to convince their colleagues that amalgamation was a closed-shop proposal stirred up by Communists. Screenwriting was a "soft racket" that paid extraordinarily well, as one put it; why rock the boat? Then, on May 1, the producers held a three-hour meeting chaired by Irving Thalberg. It was decided that each studio head would address his writers directly. The day of the vote, Pandro Berman of RKO spoke to a gathering that included one of his newest writers, Irwin Shaw, urging a vote against amalgamation.

That night, a remarkable truce was struck—or so it seemed. Instead of voting against amalgamation, the studio loyalists declared they could see their way to a vote for the *principle* of amalgamation, if allowed two weeks' breathing time before a separate vote for the *act* of it. Embracing their new comrades-in-arms, the Guild faithful went along with this compromise and put several studio loyalists on their reformed board.

Days later, these same loyalists announced their resignation and the formation of a *new* group called the Screen Playwrights. Other writers jumped ship to join them, and soon enough it became clear that the producers were behind it all, offering large contracts to lightweight writers in return for joining SP, and thus completely deflating SWG's momentum. By summer, the Guild had lost nearly all its members, and it was left to the original few to start the long, painful process of building it back up.

This was the sad drama that Budd Schulberg would capture so bitterly and well in his 1941 classic novel, *What Makes Sammy Run?* And these were the lines of battle that seemed to demand clear fealty to one side or the other. Only a young new arrival might avoid taking a stand, simply failing to join the Guild in time to cast his vote on the fateful day. Shaw, as it happened, waited until January 1937 to join the Guild.

In fairness, Shaw was in a difficult position. He sympathized with the Guild writers who assumed he was one of them, but like any other twenty-three-year-old just offered a chance at Hollywood's brass ring, he felt more concerned with getting established than fighting the good fight. He also felt that while *Bury the Dead* was hortatory, it was still ultimately a play, not a political platform—and that he was a writer, not an organizer. "I am not a pacifist, and *Bury the Dead* is not a pacifist's play," he declared in an emotional piece about his overnight success that appeared in *The New York Times* the day after the May 2 Guild vote. It was a distinction that more than one critic in later years would refuse to accept, concluding, as a result, that Shaw had ducked his political responsibility and sold out. But neither now nor later would Shaw pretend to be anything but a writer concerned with the state of the world. It would be the critics who presumed more, and who were thus disappointed.

What Shaw cared about was knocking out scenes for *The Big Game*, his football picture, in the apartment his relatives had found for him at 325 North Oakhurst Drive in Beverly Hills. He also cared about a girl he'd just met, an actress who, as it happened, had performed in the March 29 reading of *Bury the Dead* for a planned Los Angeles Contemporary Theatre production. Her name was Marian Edwards, and she was a dark-haired beauty, all of nineteen, who had subsequently auditioned for a part in the actual production. Among those judging the audition had been the young playwright himself, who regretfully found her unsuited for the part. That, however, had not prevented him from being strongly attracted to her.

Marian—the prettiest girl in all of Hollywood, as Shaw described her in letters to his New York friends that spring—had grown up in the business. Her father, a Hungarian immigrant who went by the name of

Snitz Edwards, had started in vaudeville as a comic; in 1920, at nearly sixty, he established himself as a highly successful character actor, going on to appear in more than fifty silent films. Diminutive and rather sinister-looking, he usually played villains: in Lon Chaney's *The Phantom of the Opera* he played Florine Papillon; he was Douglas Fairbanks's evil associate in *The Thief of Bagdad*; he appeared also in such Buster Keaton movies as *Battling Butler*, *College*, and *Seven Chances*. His last appearance was as a gangster in Jimmy Cagney's *Public Enemy* in 1931. (As the member of a rival gang, Snitz betrays his boss's whereabouts by making a furtive call to the feds from a phone booth; so short is he that he can barely reach high enough to dial.) By then, of course, the silent-film age was over, and like many of its stalwarts, Edwards was uncomfortable with talkies. He also suffered increasingly from arthritis; in May 1937, barely a year after Shaw met Marian, he died.

Eleanor Edwards, Marian's mother, had also worked as a screen actress in the twenties, though only in a smattering of films, and always in minor parts. Some twenty-five years younger than her husband, born in New York of English-Irish lineage, she bore him three daughters—Marian, Evelyn and Cricket—of whom Marian was the youngest. At a time when Los Angeles retained some semblance of its origins as a Spanish town in the San Fernando Valley, the Edwardses lived comfortably in a wooden house on Third Street near Vermont Avenue, and the girls went to local public schools, eventually to Beverly Hills High. Snitz Edwards, though, never made more than a decent living from his movie roles, and when he stopped working in the middle of the Depression, his teenaged daughters found themselves forced to help support the family.

For Marian, the prettiest of the three—petite, with doll-like features—that meant trying to get work as a chorus girl in movie musicals, with the hope of eventually becoming an actress. She took ballet lessons while still in high school, then joined a stock company of actors and dancers at MGM who performed in the "two-reelers," or shorts, that were regularly shown with feature films at that time. There were travelogue two-reelers, straight newsreels, comedy shorts and song-and-dance numbers; Marian did several of the song-and-dance numbers. Generally she'd get a call at six in the morning and go off to a day job that, in a still unregulated business, often wouldn't end until two or three in the morning. By that time, her dancing shoes would be soaked in blood.

Through much of high school and beyond, Marian's serious beau was an aspiring young screenwriter named Richard Collins, who would figure significantly years later in the HUAC hearings. "I must have been fifteen when I met her, and she was two or three years younger, and by the time I graduated from high school we were dating," Collins recalls. "I went to Stanford for a year, but we stayed in touch, and there was talk of getting married. She was, unquestionably, one of the two great interests in my life.

But then I went to New York to try and advance my career as a junior writer—I was really trying to make a living at that—and that's when Marian, who was still in California, met Irwin."

Marian had two close girlfriends who were also dancers, Louise Sidell and Virginia Ray, better known as Jigee. Both were lithe, bright, funny and beautiful, but Jigee had a quality about her, a flirtatious charm, that was quite extraordinary. By the time a dinner party was over, it was later said, Jigee would have established a secret with every man at the table. It was Jigee who threw Marian and Irwin together and then continued to play an important role in both their lives.

By then Jigee had begun to date Budd Schulberg, the shy son of Hollywood producer B. P. Schulberg. She had met him through Schulberg's closest friend, Maurice Rapf, himself a Hollywood producer's son, who had fallen in love with Jigee when she appeared in a school picture he had helped originate as a studio apprentice during a college summer. "Jigee had very long dark hair, and very rosy cheeks," Rapf recalls. "She wasn't pretty in the true sense of the word. She was small and had big hips, but nobody ever paid attention to that. The fact was, she could string along a guy better than anyone I ever knew. She had a way of providing intimacy without sex—not that she didn't ever play around. But an awful lot of guys felt very close to her without ever making the grade."

Schulberg fell hard for Jigee when he returned to Hollywood after graduating from Dartmouth in 1936, and managed to ease her away from Rapf, who ended up marrying Jigee's friend Louise Sidell. Into this circle arrived Shaw, who had met Schulberg briefly in New York through Herbert Kline of *New Theatre*. By one account, Shaw asked Jigee out for dinner; at the last minute Jigee had to cancel and sent Marian in her place. From this near–blind date—each presumably recognizing the other from Marian's unsuccessful audition for *Bury the Dead*—began the relationship.

The turning point may have come soon after, at a dinner party at Schulberg's house. Marian came to the party with her longtime boyfriend, Richard Collins. "There were maybe eight of us at the table," Schulberg recalls. "And Jigee and I said to each other after that, when everybody had gone, that Dick had lost Marian that night. You could feel the pull. Irwin was enormously magnetic. He was successful, he was physically appealing, strong-looking, fun-loving, had a great laugh, attractive to women but very much a man's man too." As for Marian, she struck Schulberg as remarkably like Jigee. "They were both sort of dazzling, Jigee and Marian, they sort of supplemented each other, and they made us feel extremely intelligent because they agreed with us. It's almost hard to separate them in my mind—little Wonder Women eighteen or nineteen years old." Despite her modest background, Marian had a definite sense of elegance about her that struck Shaw as upper-class. And the young Shaw, as his friend Ruth Strong

observed, envied the upper class their ease, and entrée, and style. "He
envied people who spoke well, who were easy in their manner and speech,"
she recalls. "He didn't make a secret of it. He openly admired it." Marian's
shoes might still be bloody from dancing as a chorus girl; but she was an
actress, and from the start she instinctively knew which role to play.

Romance and radicalism were wonderfully entwined in Hollywood at
this time, and in varying degrees, Shaw's circle reveled in both. It was said
that the town's most beautiful girls were members of the Communist Party,
and that that was why more than a few male members joined; certainly
Jigee's presence at a Communist meeting imbued the dreariest political
diatribe with excitement. Everywhere there was gathering and drinking
and political talk. One typical evening, Schulberg recalls, he and Shaw and
Clifford Odets got gloriously drunk together in Odets's kitchen, and spent
most of the night earnestly discussing the specter of war and how to dispel
it. Odets was drawing away from Communism by now, but Schulberg had
joined one of the several Marxist study groups springing up in Hollywood,
and along with Maurice Rapf he would join the local Communist Party
when it coalesced the next year. Shaw never did evince any interest in
joining the study groups or the party, Schulberg recalls. Nor did anyone,
after the hoopla of his arrival, think to recruit him. "I don't know what
it was about Irwin that protected him from going all the way," Schulberg
says. "He seemed to maintain a quizzical attitude toward the party itself
while being sympathetic toward the general movement."

The fact was that Shaw preferred to keep his political rhetoric generic.
In his "Notes on *Bury the Dead*" for *The New York Times*, which also
appeared at this time as flap copy on Random House's fast-selling hardcover edition of the play, he wrote: "I feel that life is too fragile and fine
a thing to be treated as butcher's meat in the markets where nations buy
and sell land and honor in their discreditable transactions." Though a
patriot, Shaw wrote, he would consider the country to have committed a
"criminal plot against my life" if it waged war at this time. For what, he
asked melodramatically, did countries fight each other? "A piece of land,
a few gallons of oil, free passage of tramp steamers carrying guncotton from
one port to another, a diplomat's reputation . . . What madman dares bid
me get up from my typewriter to trudge, gun in hand, into shell and shot
for these academic abstractions?"

In early July, Bennett Cerf, just back from a trip abroad, wrote Shaw
to say that everyone was talking about *Bury the Dead*, and to ask eagerly
what he might hope to publish next. Shaw by now had finished *The Big
Game* and was working with two or three other studio writers to come up
with a treatment for *The Saint in New York*, a first adaptation of the popular

detective series that would spawn several sequels starring George Sanders (*The Saint in Palm Springs*, and others). Flushed with his new image of literary success, he suggested that Cerf might want to publish a final script of *Saint*, but also referred to a play he was working on, *Salute*, a satire on false patriotism whose unlikely premise was the visit to a public high school by a high military officer who reacts with shock when a feisty girl refuses to salute the flag in assembly. If Cerf could publish *Boy Meets Girl*, Shaw declared—referring to the previous season's most popular Broadway comedy—then he could certainly publish *Salute*. More winningly, he added that he had bought more copies of *Bury* than anyone else and was giddy about the play's success.

The same day Shaw wrote to Cerf—July 19—General Francisco Franco was reported to have declared a military revolt against the elected government of Spain, beginning the civil war that would end as such a tragedy for democracy, and set the stage for World War II. In Hollywood the revolt provoked a new cause. To some extent it also provided an outlet for writers who felt both stymied by the Guild debacle and guilty for leading an easy life while the outside world simmered. "Some sour commentators jeered that the Hollywood writers who had been worsted by the rigors of the creative life in the East now used their social preoccupations as a sop to their ailing consciences," wrote Harold Clurman. "Another theory among the cynics was that a vicarious participation in the Spanish fracas helped many a benighted Hollywood scribbler add stature to himself that he could not acquire through his work."

There was, Clurman conceded, some truth in this, but perhaps it was truer to observe that the spiritual hollowness of the screenwriter's life created a greater than normal desire to do some worldly good. Unquestionably, in a lonely town where writers had little contact with each other unless hired to rewrite each other's work at the studio, the war became a social link. Every party that summer became a fund-raiser for the Loyalists, every gathering galvanized by a speech.

In fairness, Shaw's reaction to the political issues of the day was less solipsistic than it might seem. From 1936 until 1942, when he went off to war, Shaw contributed money and lent his name to half a dozen causes in Hollywood and New York that were either liberal or left-wing, depending on who characterized them. His principal involvement was as a member of the League of American Writers, the Hollywood group formed by Donald Ogden Stewart, John Howard Lawson, Albert Maltz and others in 1935 to mobilize writers against the threat of fascism in Europe, and to remind them of their power and responsibility to write films with simple, clear, antifascist messages. Shaw eventually signed a fair number of political protests, many sponsored by LAW. In May 1938 he signed a LAW protest against Franco in Spain, and another against the Moscow purge trials. In

November 1938 he signed the call for a humanitarian Western Writers Congress; in April 1939 he signed the call for an increase in the Federal Arts Project; in February 1940 he signed a protest against attacks on the Abraham Lincoln Brigade; the next month he participated in the fourth annual conference of the American Committee for the Protection of the Foreign-Born at the Hotel Annapolis, in Washington, D.C.; in May 1940 he joined the Committee to Free J. B. McNamera, a radical accused of bombing the offices of the *Los Angeles Times*; on November 15, 1940, he served as a sponsor for a mass meeting of the American Committee for Friendship with the Soviet Union; on December 8, 1940, he spoke at a Brooklyn Academy of Music fund-raiser against the Rapp-Coudert Committee; in April 1941 he joined the Citizens' Committee for Harry Bridges, a man accused of being a dangerous alien.

That Shaw's limited role in these obscure organizations has not slipped into oblivion must be attributed entirely to the Federal Bureau of Investigation—an unwitting participant in literary history, to say the least. All it had taken was a play like *Bury the Dead* to put Shaw on the FBI's long list of writers to be watched. From now until after the war, every petition he signed, every committee he joined would be noted in Shaw's classified file, with the stern—and incorrect—observation that all those groups were Communist fronts.

Occasionally over the next years, Shaw also helped the left by teaching writing courses for free. From 1934 to 1936 he taught occasionally at the New Theatre School in New York. In 1940 he helped LAW start a school for writers in Hollywood. The aim was twofold: to give novices a chance to study with successful professionals, and to impart a vaguely Marxist view of American literature. The school, in effect, was a Marxist study group without the involvement of the Communist Party. By then Shaw had also joined the Hollywood Anti-Nazi League; and this too was looked upon disapprovingly in the strange political climate of the times. Hitler might be a dictator, but Hollywood writers shouldn't get involved in foreign policy, went the thinking of the day; besides, the studios still distributed films to Germany and Italy. As far as the FBI was concerned, the Anti-Nazi League was simply another Communist front, so the point was moot: this involvement too was noted in Shaw's file.

Shaw was not a joiner, as Schulberg had pointed out. He would not even really be a "fellow traveler," though the term for Communist sympathizer was a malleable one; generally, he didn't care for meetings and structure. He was, quite simply, a concerned liberal in a volatile age, taking commonsense stands against fascism and anti-Semitism, signing the occasional protest, chipping in the occasional contribution. In the eyes of the FBI, however, that would make Shaw not only a premature antifascist—to use the era's most absurd moniker—but an out-and-out Communist.

For now that file would merely rest in a drawer in an office at the FBI. Later, during the war, it would be used to hurt him.

By the end of summer 1936, Shaw was happy to leave the Hollywood circuit. His RKO stint had embittered him to the studio system—in later years, he would claim he had demanded that his name be removed from the credits of *The Big Game,* though it appeared in reviews that fall—and he was eager to see *Salute* reach the stage. Anticipating his return, he sublet for a brief period his old friend Jimmy Farber's apartment on 34th Street between Park and Madison avenues, the top floor of a walk-up. Marian went back east ahead of him, in the hope of landing a part in the Broadway cast of *You Can't Take It With You;* she had met Moss Hart in Hollywood, possibly through Shaw, and that had led to an audition in New York. She failed to get the Broadway role but did perform in a short road-show production that played one week in Jamaica, Queens, and one in Brighton Beach, Brooklyn. Farber had a girlfriend of his own, and when Shaw returned, the two couples would go out together. Farber did feel that his old friend had changed, as did Jerry Moross, the composer who had provided such a vital link in Shaw's nascent career. "It's fair to say that Irwin became arrogant," says Farber.

Certainly, Shaw was brimming with energy. In September and early October, he finished the first draft of *Salute,* wrote a one-act play called *Roll Call* to precede *Bury the Dead,* began work on two other plays (*Quiet City* and *Siege*), sketched out a novel idea, *and* wrote a quick scenario for RKO. Through most of this time, the new hope of Hollywood and Broadway lived at home, in Brooklyn, with his parents.

If he was also arrogant, the young playwright must have been taken down a peg by the reviews that greeted *The Big Game* in October. Part football movie, part thriller, it chronicled an attempt by gamblers to kidnap a star quarterback the day before his big game. Wrote Bosley Crowther in *The New York Times:* "Perhaps the most puzzling dramaturgic phenomenon of recent date is Irwin Shaw, the Brooklyn youth who wrote a startling one-act play called *Bury the Dead* last season, on the strength of which he was hoisted on numerous shoulders and borne in triumph to Hollywood, only to turn out a picture called *The Big Game.* . . . Mr. Shaw could hardly have been expected to figure, in his maiden screen effort, as a second George Bernard, and R.K.O. deserves at least half the blame for so flagrant a misuse of talent." Still, implied Crowther, he did deserve the other half for taking it on. Other reviewers agreed, and *The Big Game* soon sank without a trace.

Here, in Shaw's first year of success, were the roots of a conflict that would entangle his entire career: the drive to write great works, and the desire to earn the big nickel that Hollywood, and later commercial book publishing, could provide. As a twenty-three-year-old who still lived with his parents, Shaw could hardly be blamed for wanting to earn his way to financial independence. Then too, how many writers in the 1930s could afford to toil monkishly at novels without *some* other income? Still, as Crowther had observed, Shaw's case seemed especially distressing. It was one thing to go from writing, say, a comedy of manners to a movie script of similar content. It seemed quite another to go from searing social drama to silly entertainment. If nothing else, this overnight success seemed remarkably facile.

Pandro Berman, head of RKO studios, had told his new young screenwriter the way to be happy: scrap his foolish ideals, buy a house and pool in Los Angeles, and get married. But Shaw, stung by his failure with *The Big Game,* resolved to stay in New York and secure his reputation as a playwright of social protest.

There was no shortage of issues to protest. Despite Roosevelt's reelection and the ever growing web of federal work programs, the Depression appeared impossible to budge, and bloody strikes were breaking out one after another. Overseas, Franco's army, abetted by Hitler and Mussolini, seemed increasingly likely to vanquish the Loyalists, and from Germany now emanated the ugly undertone of anti-Semitism and the growing possibility of another world war.

Shaw took on both foreign fronts. That fall, he wrote a one-acter called *Church, Kitchen, Children* about a young Jewish doctor and an Aryan nurse divided by Hitler's new racial laws; the play was given two public readings by the Hollywood Anti-Nazi League for the Defense of American Democracy, and while it ended up orphaned without a formal production, it furthered the parallel between Shaw and Odets, who had followed up *Waiting for Lefty* with his own anti-Nazi one-acter, *Till the Day I Die.*

Shaw addressed the Spanish Civil War with the two-act drama he had first called *Brittle,* then retitled *Siege.* (*Salute* was put quietly on the shelf in this period.) Set on New Year's Day, 1937, the play unfolds the fates of several desperate and starving Loyalists in a besieged fort in Madrid. One of them is quite religious, one cynical and so on through various types. The cynic, Mateo Guiterra, is a luggish sort Shaw likens to an American prizefighter. He doesn't hesitate to leave a wounded comrade on the battlefield to save himself, but he is also the one to whom the beautiful Teresa finds herself drawn (despite a husband in the vicinity). As with many Shaw characters to come, there is, in Guiterra's swagger, a fantasy reflection of the muscular playwright.

By torturing a captive, Guiterra learns of a cache of food hidden in neighboring barracks, across an open stretch controlled by enemy fire. In the earnest debate about what to do, much is said about the nature of the conflict the Loyalists are engaged in and the role of pacifism (represented by the intellectual writer, Teresa's husband, who refuses to fight). When a wounded Loyalist is brought in, the issue of whether to fight or surrender is sharpened. The wounded Loyalist becomes the advocate for dying in combat. Guiterra, ever cynical, suggests appeasement. That, the other Loyalists agree, is unthinkable: they unite, kill Guiterra, grab their grenades, and charge off to certain death as the curtain falls.

For Shaw, who finished the play in March 1937, *Siege* marked a complete change of heart, in little more than a year, from the seemingly unequivocal pacifism of *Bury the Dead*. Alarmed, as any thinking person, by Franco's revolt, Shaw meant the play to serve as an answer to *Bury* (even to the extent of having an identical-sized primary cast of six soldiers). He had believed in the earnest cries of his dead soldiers for an end to war, he seemed to be saying; but in a single year the world had changed. The young playwright had also come to feel uncomfortable with the one-dimensional image of himself projected by *Bury*. There was more to him than that, was the message between the lines of his characters' earnest declarations.

With *Siege* out of the way for the moment, Shaw took time to earn a quick piece of RKO cash, writing the scenario for Patrick Quentin's *Puzzle for Fools*. The story line must have appealed to him: a former "great white hope of the American Theatre" checks into a sanatorium with the announcement that he's been drunk for three years. For love more than money, Shaw also wrote a radio drama on request called *Supply and Demand*, to be broadcast on CBS's important new Columbia Workshop program, for which Archibald MacLeish had provided a first installment. Shaw's play, broadcast in May, opens on the New York waterfront on Thanksgiving Day, as truckloads of turkeys are being dumped into the river because of a market surplus. Two hungry observers come upon the scene and philosophize about it, their remarks provoking flashbacks that illustrate other examples of "supply and demand." Norman Corwin, whose dozens of radio plays and books about radio made him a leading figure of the form, observes that Shaw's appearance on the program conferred considerable status: "The Columbia Workshop really became the ranking prestigious program on radio. There was nothing like it. To have your script done by the workshop was the highest honor radio could bestow."

Shaw by now had ceased writing serials for Himan Brown, and *Supply and Demand* provided a triumphant finale to his radio days. The show was directed by *Bury the Dead*'s Worthington Miner and produced by the Workshop's guiding presence, Irving Reis, who would turn up in Shaw's Army unit in London during the war. It was, in all respects, the dignified second step for a playwright whose future, despite Hollywood detours, was deemed incandescently bright.

If Shaw had been asked in 1937 what sort of writer he was, his immediate reply would have been that he was a playwright and, for money, a scenarist; this pattern continued over the summer, when RKO loaned him to Walter Wanger to write an original screenplay for *Arabian Nights*. All the while, though, Shaw had kept writing short stories. He hadn't sent any out in some time, but this hardly suggested some private passion; Shaw was a pragmatist about all his literary efforts, and fully intended to publish everything he wrote. Finally, in November 1936, *Stage Theatre Guild Quarterly* had published Shaw's first story: "Flash in the Pan," a sketch about a nervous young playwright attending the opening night of his second play.

Although overlooked by critics and never included in any of Shaw's collections, "Flash in the Pan" is a vintage piece suggestive of his most famous story, "The Girls in Their Summer Dresses." Similarly, it captures the intimacy of a married couple who are, essentially, Irwin and Marian. By 8:00 P.M., as the story opens, the reputed "proletarian" playwright has downed four drinks and worked himself into a thoroughly black mood about how his play will be received by the critics. They loved his first one, but now the playwright is sure he'll be labeled a flash in the pan. Grudgingly, he accompanies his wife out onto Fifth Avenue while keeping up a steady stream of self-pitying remarks which she coolly deflects. The biggest problem, he says as they ride uptown in a taxi, is that he can't write second acts: nothing happens in this one, why didn't he see that before? The playwright slinks into the theater with the first act already up and twists in agony as the actors mangle their lines, refusing to be heartened by the audience's receptive laughter. As the curtain goes down, he tries to pull his wife to the door, but she stands up and loudly cries, "Author! Author!"—as sure a show of wifely devotion as any man could want. Unmollified, he walks the streets with her, waiting for the next morning's newspapers to hit the stands. At 3:30 A.M., the papers arrive at a newsstand on 50th Street and Sixth Avenue. The playwright's wife collects the *News*, the *Mirror*, the *American*, the *Times* and the *Tribune*, and walks over to a corner street lamp to start reading. As one positive review follows another, her husband asks her gravely if any of the critics have called him a flash in the pan. "None," his wife rejoins. Late the next morning, as they lie in bed, poring now over the afternoon editions, the playwright does find one critical barb in a review in the New York *Sun*. Only in the second act, reports the *Sun*, does the playwright's touch falter. Devastated, the playwright swears, then falls back against his pillow to wallow in black thoughts. Beautifully written, gracefully shaped, with self-deprecating humor and a deft sign-off, "Flash in the Pan" is a story that deserves literary rediscovery. It also stands as the first of many instances in which Shaw's fiction cannily predicted occurrences in his personal life.

A greater short story success came with Shaw's first appearance in the pages of *The New Yorker*, in October 1937. For a story titled "No Jury Would Convict," the author received a check for $75—and entry into the most significant literary relationship of his life.

As with several of Shaw's earliest stories, "No Jury Would Convict" is not so much a narrative as a brilliant exercise in capturing the earthy talk of rough-hewn New Yorkers. The setting is one Shaw knew well: the bleachers at Ebbets Field as the feckless Brooklyn Dodgers take on the Jersey Giants. Among the Dodgers fans is one who actually lives in Jersey City but roots for Brooklyn anyway, making the long trip game after game, season after season, despite the Dodgers' dismal record. This time is no different: the Dodgers blow a late-game rally, and the Jersey City fan, briefly buoyed by hope, sinks back into despondency, muttering that someone should shoot the Dodgers' coach ("No jury would convict"). Shaw's ear for dialogue gives the story its power; the characters almost leap off the page. Beneath the banter lies the poignancy, unstated until the very last line, of men whose strongest feelings of love and loyalty and despair are stirred by the figures on the field, and whose love, for the Dodgers at least, is made all the deeper by the sweet pain of loss. Bitterly, the disappointed fan declares he'll root for a winning team next time. "And he went back to Jersey City," writes Shaw, "leaving his heart in Brooklyn."

By relying on dialogue, Shaw was playing to his proven strengths as a radio writer and dramatist. By setting his characters in Brooklyn, he was wisely writing what he knew. In neither respect did his story break entirely new ground. By the early thirties, Damon Runyon's sketches of Broadway lowlifes had become a fixture of *Cosmopolitan* and other magazines, showing just how important colorful dialogue could be. In *The New Yorker*, Thomas Wolfe's "Only the Dead Know Brooklyn" in 1935 had been a tour de force of straight Brooklynese. But Wolfe's story had made hilarious fun of that dialect. Shaw's story showed an unabashed empathy for his characters—and that, in the pages of the still effete *New Yorker* at least, *was* new. It would be a year, however, before the editors of *The New Yorker* took his next story and began to think of Shaw as a regular contributor.

Meanwhile, in November, having moved from his family's Brooklyn apartment to rent a place of his own again at 25 West 10th Street in Greenwich Village, Shaw broke into the country's other most important periodical for fiction with a story called "Second Mortgage."

At this time *The New Republic* was, as Alfred Kazin described it, "not merely a publication but a cause and the center of many causes." As for Malcolm Cowley, the magazine's literary editor, his influence was absolute and unquestioned. For Shaw, Cowley's endorsement carried at least as much weight as that of the editors of *The New Yorker*; years later, when asked where his first published story had appeared, he would make the doubtless honest mistake of answering that it had appeared not in *Stage Theatre Guild Quarterly*, not even in *The New Yorker*, but in *The New Republic*.

"Second Mortgage" was a stronger story than Shaw's *New Yorker* debut, torn right from his family's grim home life in the Depression, its realistic dialogue fleshed out with coolly controlled description. Shaw told

it in the first person—one of the few times he would do so in his fiction—
and portrayed parents who were clearly his own, hovering behind closed
curtains to avoid bill collectors. The story takes place on a Sunday, so that
when the doorbell unexpectedly rings, the narrator-son decides to answer
it. In comes an anxious Mrs. Shapiro, who, it turns out, was swindled into
investing her money in a trust fund that granted second mortgages. Now
the mortgage holders have failed to make their payments, and the trust
company has gone bankrupt, and all that the heartsick Mrs. Shapiro can
do is go door to door to the families who held those mortgages, hoping
to coax any amount of money from them. When Mrs. Shapiro finishes her
sad story, her listeners sympathize—but have nothing to give her. Helpless,
they promise to scrape up some cash by next Sunday, and on that thin
thread of hope, Mrs. Shapiro leaves. The next Sunday, when the doorbell
rings, the family sits silent, unmoving, behind the closed curtains.

Despite the first-person narration, Shaw remains as still and expres-
sionless throughout as his parents do—the invisible observer—and thus
imbues the simple story with its understated power.

Siege, self-conscious by contrast, was traveling a rocky road to production. In early September 1937, a producer named Irving Cooper announced he had signed up the play. "So speedily are production plans
advancing," *The New York Times* reported, "that Mr. Cooper speaks of
rehearsals in two weeks, with a cast of ten men and two women. He and
Mr. Shaw left yesterday to discuss the whole thing in the quiet of the
countryside, Mr. Cooper pausing to describe his new purchase as both
'realistic' and 'a romantic play about death.' " Somehow, Cooper quickly
lost his confidence and backed out of his producer's role. Shaw then
pleaded with Harold Clurman to put on the play, but Clurman found it
"weak and unclear," and cautioned Shaw against his "facility." Finally,
Shaw persuaded Norman Bel Geddes, the well-known scenic designer, to
back a production at the Longacre Theatre and also to create the sets.

By opening night, Shaw had suffered a sharp loss of faith. Anguished,
he prowled the neighboring streets around the Longacre as theatergoers
began to arrive, and by chance ran into Clurman. Trembling, Shaw asked
if Clurman was headed to the Longacre too. When Clurman said he was,
Shaw grabbed him by the lapels and pleaded, "Please don't see my play!
It's going to be terrible!"

"Do you mean it?" Clurman asked.

When Shaw made clear he did, Clurman wrote him a check on the
spot for $500. "This is an advance on your next play," the producer
declared. "Go home and start writing it."

Unfortunately, Shaw's fears were well founded. *The New York Times'*
Brooks Atkinson ridiculed Bel Geddes's too-handsome prison set, with its
dungeon door rolling open and shut on roller skates, and wrote: "*Siege*

consists in swinging the scenery back and forth while guns rat ta tat tat, actors stroll back and forth and besiege the audience with a gas attack of dialogue. . . . The talk has no form, no style, and no point of view." Having prized Shaw the year before as a fresh new talent, Atkinson now declared, "he is hardly experienced at all," and defined him as "the author of a one-act anti-war play which contained one good dramatic idea." Other critics concurred, if not so harshly, and *Siege* closed in six nights.

Shaw had been last year's Clifford Odets. Now he was learning what it was like to be last year's Irwin Shaw. Odets, wrestling with his own demons in Hollywood, had put it searingly well: "The young writer comes out of obscurity with a play or two. Suppose he won't accept the generous movie offers. Why, that means he's holding out for more. Suppose he accepts—an ingrate, rat, renegade. If he won't wear evening clothes, that's only because he's trying to be different. But when he wears them, you may be sure he's turned capitalist overnight.

"If he's written two plays about the same kind of people, everyone knows that that's all he can write about. But when he writes about a different class, he is told to go back where he came from and stick to his cast (or caste).

"He gets party invitations and when he won't accept, he's too serious. But when you see him at a party or a bar, you knew all the time he was a playboy.

"Suppose he rapidly follows one play with another, why he's writing 'quickies'! But if they come further apart, it is a sure sign he's already written out.

"If the reviewers praise him Tuesday, it's only because they're gentle quixotic fellows. But watch them tear him apart on Wednesday! . . . The young writer is now ready for a world cruise!"

In truth, Shaw's triumph with *Bury the Dead* was too recent and impressive to be undone by a weak second play. New York's prominent partygivers were just getting to know him; the city's most attractive eligible women were just learning what a catch he might be.

The most brazen and beguiling of those was Helen Brown Norden, better known by her later married name, Helen Lawrenson. Norden's colonial stock and quiet childhood in a small town in upstate New York did nothing to explain the tart wit and sassy spirit she had acquired by the time she came to New York in the early thirties after graduating from Vassar; perhaps they compensated for the awkwardness she felt as a tall and often ostracized teenager. At any rate, she began her journalistic career as a writer of wry captions at *Vanity Fair*, and soon established a close, volatile friendship with another of the magazine's editors, Clare Boothe Brokaw, as well as a fond sexual liaison with the magazine's owner, Condé Nast. By 1937, when she met Shaw, Norden had left *Vanity Fair* to pursue her own writing; Clare Brokaw had left to marry Henry Luce. Free-spirited, Norden never took her affair with Shaw terribly seriously. But she was energetic about it. "Nice woman," Shaw confided years later to Joseph Heller. "But all she ever wanted to do was go to bed." It was during that period, in late 1937, that Norden introduced Shaw to Clare Luce.

"Clare asked me to bring him to meet her," Norden later wrote of the woman whom she had come to see as extraordinarily shrewd in her social manipulations. "When we arrived, she was waiting for us at a table in the Waldorf Grill, reading a copy of his one-act antiwar play, *Bury the Dead.* I never saw her dressed so simply: a tailored dark dress, no jewelry except a wedding ring. Her manner was friendly, but also respectful. She asked him to autograph the book; she asked him the right questions about his work and ideas and aims. Only once did she make a wrong move. After we left her, Irwin said, 'She's quite a girl. But she's no friend of yours. When you went to the can, she said, "Brownie's an old man's darling." He knew about [Bernard] Baruch, so I just laughed and said, 'Well, he's more her old man than mine.' "

Despite this, and despite the fact that *Time*'s unsigned notice of *Bury the Dead* had been snide, with its reference to Shaw as a former "third-rate semi-professional football player," Shaw was intrigued by the invitation that came in January 1938 for him and Norden to join the Luces for a weekend at Mepkin, their 7,000-acre plantation at Moncks Corner, South Carolina.

The first thing Shaw noticed, when he and Lawrenson arrived, was that Clare seemed to dominate her powerful husband. Forthright, even reckless at that time in her life, Clare demonstrated to Shaw the way to wring a bird's neck and encouraged him to try. Recounts Wilfrid Sheed in his biography of Clare Luce: "On the same principle, she got him to ride a somewhat mettlesome horse (which he did with ease, having ridden in Prospect Park as a kid). It went without saying that Clare was also a good shot. By what seemed like dint of will, she was good at just about everything. . . . As an old football player, Shaw found this tomboy stuff exhilarating, not depressing as some might."

Shaw elaborated on the visit years later in a bitter diatribe about *Time* and the Luces published in a short-lived magazine called *fact.* Henry Luce, he recalled, was reviled by his household staff. "They thought he was absurd and their relations with him were based on covert contempt. . . . He was timid on a horse and clumsy with a shotgun, in contrast with his wife, who probably would not be timid in the ring with Sonny Liston." Shaw was advised to keep his horse at a walk so as not to embarrass his sensitive host, but went recklessly galloping all over the estate. "Besides this ungracious exuberance," he admitted, "I outraged the principles of hospitality . . . by going on ahead one day and making [my] gelding prance up to the top of a little knoll, where I sat stiffly, like a general reviewing troops, my arm outstretched in the Fascist salute as Mr. Luce and entourage came upon the scene on their sedate nags. This would be a bad joke at any time but it was especially foolish at that period, when Luce, avid for power, was trying various political garments on for size and was not averse to a little preliminary flirting with the Far Right."

The weekend was important for two very different reasons. It provided one of Shaw's first glimpses of real wealth, which he thoroughly enjoyed; this hobnobbing with high society was *fun*. At the same time he felt, rightly or wrongly, that he had offended *Time*'s founder. In years to come, when *Time* lambasted one after another of his plays and novels, perhaps dampening their commercial success, Shaw would look back to his weekend with the Luces and declare that that was when the fix went in.

Black as the world seemed after *Siege*, Shaw had just established the two alliances—to Harold Clurman's Group Theatre, and to *The New Yorker*—that would resurrect his floundering career. With the possible exception of Orson Welles, whose Mercury Theatre had burst onto Broadway that fall for a short-lived but brilliant two-season run, Clurman now could lay claim to being the uncrowned king of theater in New York. The Group Theatre he had founded in the early thirties with Lee Strasberg and Cheryl Crawford as a drama workshop of new ideas—of Method acting, and of plays treated as "artistic wholes" in direct relation to a troubled society—had hit its stride in 1935 with Odets's four agit-prop dramas, then achieved commercial success two years later with Odets's *Golden Boy*. In a sense, that success had already begun to destroy the Group. Odets had gone off with much guilt and confusion to Hollywood and embarked on a stormy romance with actress Luise Rainer. Back in New York, fierce bickering among the theater's founders had resulted in Strasberg's and Crawford's departures, with Clurman declaring himself in charge. For the moment, though, it was still terribly exciting to have one's next play produced by the Group, and for Shaw, the check Clurman had written so dramatically on the street seemed nothing less than a return ticket from ignominy.

Clurman, for his part, held Shaw in as high esteem as he did Odets, and would nurse great expectations for each of the next several Shaw plays after other principals in the Group had grown disillusioned. Some ten years older than Shaw, he felt an almost fatherly affection for the young playwright who radiated such athletic vigor.

In March 1938, Clurman took Shaw and Molly Thacher, wife of Elia Kazan and the Group's official playreader, on a boat trip to Cuba. Their mission was twofold: to confer about the draft of a new play Shaw had just submitted, and to soak up atmosphere and color for an as yet unfinished play about Cuba that Odets had tried to write the previous year. For Shaw, who would become such a European traveler, the trip was his first outside the United States. One of his more vivid experiences during the ten-day interlude was seeing his first and last pornographic movie; a nice Brooklyn boy for all his growing sophistication, Shaw was shocked by the "twenty-minute, badly-lit monstrosity." Of more consequence, he hit upon another play idea during the trip, based on the memory of two old men fishing off Coney Island's Steeplechase Pier. That idea would emerge, in less than a year, as his most commercially successful drama, *The Gentle People*.

By late spring there was more cheering news. Prestigious *One-Act Play Magazine* asked Shaw to turn "Second Mortgage" into a drama and published it in May. Another contributor, William Saroyan, submitted a play version of a story called "My Heart's in the Highlands"; soon the Group's decision to stage *Highlands* would bring Saroyan and Shaw together. For Memorial Day, the Columbia Workshop performed an abridged version of *Bury the Dead*. The play, which had run a respectable sixty-five performances off-Broadway, had gone on to be produced in regional theaters all over the country and even in Europe, often on a twin bill with *Waiting for Lefty*. Shaw's play was more than a drama now; it was an international symbol of the peace movement.

Galvanized, Shaw vowed to finish both *Quiet City*, his new play, and *The Gentle People* by summer's end, in time for the Group's next season. He took a house with Marian in Woods Hole, Massachusetts, at the corner of Agassiz and Gansett roads. By late June he was able to report in a letter to Cerf that *The Gentle People* was half done, and that both plays would be knocked off by August. As Harold Clurman sailed back from a summer in Europe, Shaw sent him a wire on board requesting an immediate reading of *The Gentle People*, which for the moment had supplanted *Quiet City* as his main interest.

The play Shaw showed him was subtitled *A Brooklyn Fable*, a qualifier the playwright insisted on keeping in the program notes when the play was produced. Its two central characters, Jonah and Philip, are Brooklyn fishermen who have little to live for but their nightly excursions off Steeplechase Pier and the dream of saving enough money to buy a sea-fishing boat they can take down to Cuba. (In its waterfront setting, and in the pipe dreams to which its characters cling to get through the drabness of their ordinary lives, *The Gentle People* recalls Eugene O'Neill's sea plays.) Jonah, a Jew, suffers under a henpecking wife. Philip, a Greek, is being aggressively courted by the fat woman who owns the restaurant in which he works as a cook; if he refuses to marry her, he'll lose his job. One evening, a young racketeer named Harold Goff strolls out on the pier to demand five dollars a week as "protection" for their rowboat. The fishermen are furious but helpless, and finally acquiesce. Then Goff begins going out with Jonah's impressionable daughter. In passing, the daughter tells Goff that Jonah and

Philip have already saved $190 toward their dream boat. Goff goes directly to the two men to demand the entire sum. Only now, with their dream imperiled, do the two reluctantly decide to kill Goff. The surprise is that all works according to plan: Goff is felled by a piece of pipe and pushed into the bay, and though the two fishermen are foolish enough to keep his fancy wallet, they outwit a suspicious policeman by dangling it overboard on a hook while he searches their boat. Justice, of the eye-for-an-eye variety, is served; good wins out over evil; the fable ends.

Clurman's reaction was mixed. He liked the play but was worried because "it was both delicate and melodramatic, saying a little more than its simple fable indicated, yet not enough for the elaborate structure the production demanded. It was full of plot, yet somehow more narrative than dramatic, heavier than it was meant to be, lighter than the author's and the Group's reputations promised. After several days of hesitation I announced to Shaw: 'It pains me to tell you I've decided to do your play.' " But instead of having *The Gentle People* lead off the fall season as planned, Clurman postponed its production to January.

Somewhat greater enthusiasm greeted Shaw's next submissions to *The New Yorker.* His second published story, "Borough of Cemeteries," appeared in August 1938. Like his first, it drew on Brooklyn characters and talk: two taxi drivers get into a drunken argument in Lammanawitz's Bar and Grill and end up driving their taxis into each other like bumper cars, destroying their livelihoods but salvaging honor. November saw publication of a third Brooklyn story, " 'March, March on Down the Field,' " the wry glimpse of Shaw's days as a Saturday semipro football player; December brought "Little Bernhardt," a trifle about a boy jealous of his actress sister, whom his father proudly dubs a little Bernhardt. This last revealed a weakness that would mar more than a few of Shaw's stories to come: a sympathy and affection for certain characters, particularly children, that could tip into bathos.

The New Yorker was taking notice of its newest contributor, and to the astonishment of its editors, he seemed to have dozens more stories in hand. In November he submitted to Random House a choice of eighteen for what would be his first collection. Among them were three that would appear in *The New Yorker* within the next watershed year: "I Stand by Dempsey," "Lemkau, Pogran and Blaufox" and, most important, "Sailor off the Bremen."

Meanwhile, with less than three weeks until its January opening night, *The Gentle People* went into rehearsal.

It was not a gentle time. The Group actors disliked the play's apparent endorsement of violence against tormentors. Many also thought that by indulging its flashes of winsome humor they would be presenting a too-frivolous production at a time when the world, more than ever, needed changing. By having one of his fishermen be Jewish and the other Greek, Shaw had intended to make the point that America was a last refuge of the free in an increasingly fascist world, and a melting pot that needed protecting, but Group members still felt the play was lightweight, one that hinted at political statements but avoided declaring them by cloaking the play as a fairy tale.

More than one woman in the Group also found Shaw's female characters objectionable: shrewish, selfish, or both. His women in *Bury the Dead*, as columnist Dorothy Bromley had already observed, had shown themselves to be self-centered, or at the very least prim, in counseling their dead husbands and sons not to fight fate, to do the proper thing and be buried. "I'm inclined to think," wrote Bromley, "that love can be, if only rarely, a deeper thing than this young dramatist of twenty-three has suspected." The one female character in *Siege*, like the feckless daughter in *Gentle People*, had pushed aside the good but gentle man who loved her and gone right for the soulless braggart. As for the principal two female characters of *Gentle People*, they came across as nothing less than castrating monsters. In part Shaw was simply subscribing to a much-accepted attitude of the times. As shrewish or selfish women came to populate one after another of his fictional works, however, the complaint would assume an added, and rather disconcerting, weight.

Rehearsals continued, and more tension arose with Clurman's choice of Franchot Tone to play the gangster Harold Goff. Tone had been one of the Group's founding members in 1931, but had heeded the call to Hollywood and become a movie star. Like Odets, he continued to profess the greatest admiration for the Group and felt much of the same guilt at abandoning the cause. Now he volunteered not only to play the unflattering role of Goff but also to be the production's chief financial backer. Other cast members had mixed feelings toward him, and Clurman, who had elected to direct the play himself, hardly helped matters by choosing not to invite Tone to production meetings on the theory that he was just a cast member. "It was not my intention to snub him in any way," wrote Clurman, "but Irwin Shaw pointed out that, whatever my intention, my behavior was tactless." Clurman added that Tone bore the slight with good grace—but this was perhaps because he was more concerned by the warnings of friends that, as a leading man in the movies, he had made a serious career mistake in accepting the role of a gangster on stage. By the end of the season, he would sever relations with the Group.

The rest of the cast offered clear indication of the Group's extraordinary, if tottering, eminence at this point: Sam Jaffe, Karl Malden, Sylvia Sidney, Elia Kazan, Lee J. Cobb and Martin Ritt were among the players, while Boris Aronson created the five elaborate sets (including a boat off the pier). Such a concatenation of talents stirred more than the usual excite-

ment on the opening night of January 5, 1939. Limousines lined the curb
outside the Belasco Theatre. Droves of fur-coated ticketholders hurried in.
"The audience liked everything," noted Burns Mantle the next morning
in the *Daily News,* particularly a comic-relief scene in a Turkish bath
dominated by Lee J. Cobb, which long outlived the rest of the play in many
theatergoers' minds. George Jean Nathan, writing in *Newsweek,* found the
play "a peculiarly evocative and hintful parable of humble and beset humanity," while Brooks Atkinson of the *Times* called it "an amiable yarn
populated generally with likeable people and expressed in genial dialog."
Sydney Whipple of the *World-Telegram,* however, declared that the play
"fails to be convincing," even "under its sugar-coated classification as
'fable.'" As for *Time,* its anonymous reviewer pronounced *Gentle People*
an "absurd play . . . a piece of hanky-panky, awkward, grotesque, unreal."

Whatever the merits of the production, the more interesting debate
about *Gentle People* concerned the play's politics—whether it had any, and
if so, whether they were properly conveyed. Clurman admitted he may not
have struck the right tone in his direction—"the appearance of realism
with a simplicity that was not quite that"—to communicate a fable that
was at the same time a message about fascism and how decent people, if
pressed, would rise up against it. "Perhaps a more frankly fanciful treatment might have served the play better," he added, though he had firmly
rejected Shaw's suggestion to unfurl across the backdrop a banner that
read "Once Upon a Time . . ." Most Group members simply felt Clurman
had botched the job—and so did Shaw, who anguished as he read reviews
that scoffed at the political undertones as being ill-formed or naive. Finally,
in what would become a Shaw trademark, he launched a defense in print.
John Anderson, a critic for the New York *Journal-American* who had
written favorably of the play, received and published a glowing letter from
Shaw that praised him for understanding the political points he'd tried to
make:
      "The gentle people of the title represent the ordinary man—peaceful,
modest, good in heart, oppressed," Shaw explained. "The gangster is a
symbol I took ready-made from popular speech and thought. . . . The
action of the play is the action of oppression by force. . . . Finally, driven
to the utmost desperation, the gentle people have recourse to the only
measure that promises any relief: the measure of the gangster, force.
. . ." That made for a ponderous theme, Shaw acknowledged, which was
precisely why he had chosen to express it as a winsome fairy tale.
      It was perhaps not the sort of thing another playwright might do. But
Shaw was emerging as a man of as much sensitivity about his work as
confidence, as much possessed of a naphthalike temper for sniping critics
as of a generous spirit and outreaching warmth for almost everybody else.
His reputation was growing, and a persona was developing, one that would

soon seem larger than life to all who met him. In many of the best ways, and in one or two that were somewhat less than that, he was becoming Irwin Shaw in capital letters: famous, lionized, high-living.

The certification of that would come the next month, with a *New Yorker* story called "The Girls in Their Summer Dresses."

CHAPTER FIVE

Irwin Shaw, aged twenty-five, playwright with one hit and one miss, short story writer of seeming promise, veteran of Hollywood's mill, sat restlessly on the twenty-eighth floor of a seedy Eighth Avenue hotel, waiting for *The Gentle People* to go into rehearsals. It was the start of December 1938.

With him was Marian, his on-again, off-again actress girlfriend. He would marry her the next October—but he was not married to her yet, on the morning that he wrote "The Girls in Their Summer Dresses."

Having subsisted entirely on his writing, and without the help of radio serials since *Bury the Dead,* Shaw was both proud and broke. On this particular morning, while Marian lay in bed reading, Shaw tapped out a story about a married couple who stroll up Fifth Avenue on a sunny Sunday. In a sense, nothing happens in the story; the couple exchange idle banter, stop for a drink—end of story. Within those few pages, however, a marriage is revealed. Even on his wife's arm, Michael can't help but take note of beautiful women passing by. He makes little effort to hide his interest, and Frances grimly takes note of his desire. As the women keep passing, Frances's wry tolerance takes on an edge. Her dialogue with Michael is carried on in a Ping-Pong manner that suggests the two have been through this before; also, perhaps, that their marriage is shallow enough that these skirmishes are all they have between them. Finally, Frances gives in to confrontation when they stop at a bar for a late-morning brandy.

"You look at them as if you want them," Frances said, *playing with her brandy glass. "Every one of them."*

"In a way," Michael said, *speaking softly and not to his wife, "in a way that's true. I don't do anything about it, but it's true."*

Near tears, Frances asks what sort of women it is that Michael desires, and why. Resolutely he tells her: women in offices, dressed so neatly . . . actresses, waiting for their big breaks . . . salesgirls in Macy's . . . Presented with the evidence so blatantly, Frances can't help but realize that someday Michael *will* do something about it.

Then comes the story's beautiful, bittersweet twist. Since all hope of an intimate afternoon with her husband has been dashed, Frances goes off in a huff to call the friends she hoped they might avoid.

She got up from the table and walked across the room toward the telephone. Michael watched her walk, thinking, what a pretty girl, what nice legs.

Impersonalized, set back in the crowd, Frances becomes, for a moment in her husband's distracted mind, simply another of the girls in their summer dresses, endlessly alluring, always out of reach.

The beauty of the story is in its subtle soundings of a marriage, in the delicate way its tension builds, and in that last ironic, all-revealing line. Shaw stops short of declaring that Michael is an everyman, and that marriage is an institution doomed to such impasses, though he almost certainly felt so. He does identify strongly with Michael himself; and of course to anyone who ever met him, Shaw simply was Michael, with his big laugh and appetite for life, women and drink, while Marian, delicate and beleaguered, was Frances.

"The Girls in Their Summer Dresses" would trouble many of its female readers through the years. It hardly pleased the woman who first set eyes on it.

"I knew I had something good there," Shaw said years later of the world-famous story he wrote that morning in a single draft. "But I didn't want [Marian] to read it, knowing that the reaction would be violent, to say the least, because it's about a man who tells his wife that he's going to be unfaithful to her. So I turned it facedown, and I said, 'Don't read this yet. It's not ready.' It was the only copy I had. Then I went out and took a walk, had a drink, and came back. She was raging around the room. She said, 'It's a lucky thing you came back just now, because I was going to open the window and throw it out.'"

Shaw found a warmer reception at *The New Yorker*. He had an editor at the magazine now, William Maxwell, who would become as critically respected for his own fiction as for the well-known writers he handled. Maxwell was a tall, patrician man, "so polite," as one colleague put it, "that William Shawn seemed like a roughneck, so polite that you didn't feel put off, but you were held off." Maxwell and Shaw made an odd couple, but that didn't matter: along with his colleagues, Maxwell saw Shaw as a natural, a finished writer who required no guidance. Indeed, Shaw's only problem was that his stories tended to come in long for a magazine that still, in the late thirties, had not published a story longer than twelve typewritten pages. So it was with "The Girls in Their Summer Dresses."

"The original manuscript was twice as long as the version published," acknowledges Maxwell. "I wanted *The New Yorker* to publish it, and they wouldn't have it at its original length; whether before or after submitting the story to [Harold] Ross, I don't remember, I cut it about in half. Everybody, including Irwin, approved of the shortened version, and it was published. When the story came out in a collection of Irwin's stories, he published (to my surprise and satisfaction) the shorter version. The original was repetitive."

The New Yorker paid Shaw $200 and published the story in February 1939, even as The Gentle People was confounding its share of tepid reviews to become a modest commercial success and last a six-month run. The editors whose approval would have seemed a dream to a Brooklyn College student not so long before were bowled over by him. Before the month was out, amid even greater excitement, they published "Sailor off the Bremen," a very different sort of story written in the same week as "Girls," but one that took twice as long to write: two days instead of one.

Like Gentle People, "Sailor" is a morality tale of good people confronted by violence and pushed to revenge. The violence occurs before the story begins, when several Communist Party members stage a surprise protest against Nazism on board a German passenger ship, the Bremen, with a tuxedoed crowd of well-wishers gathered to see the boat off. The German crew members beat the protesters with cold fury, two men holding a protester by the arms while a third delivers the blows. Worst hurt is Ernest, one of the three protesters now nursing their wounds around a kitchen table and recounting their tale to friends. Ernest was unlucky enough to be attacked by a particularly vicious German named Lueger, who effectively blinded him in one eye and knocked out his teeth, laughing as he did his dirty work. Now Ernest's brother Charley vows to beat Lueger himself. He has, as Ernest puts it deploringly, a "football player's philosophy. Somebody knocks you down, you knock him down, everything is fine." Undeterred, Charley and another protester concoct a plan: Charley's sister will flirt with Lueger, get him to take her to dinner, and on the way home walk down a certain block, where Charley will be waiting. As in Gentle People, all goes according to plan. Charley gets his chance and takes it, slamming Lueger again and again, hearing bone and cartilage break every time.

Shaw was still not—and never would be—a party member himself. Clearly, though, Charley is a Shaw-like figure, not only in his football-player size and philosophy but also in his burning desire to exact revenge for a wounded weaker brother. For Shaw, who would always feel protective toward his younger brother, this desire was fierce and deeply rooted, and like an actor drawing on strong personal feelings to color a role, Shaw would return to it again and again: in stories like "Strawberry Ice Cream Soda," in which an older brother sacrifices spare change saved for a date that evening, to buy his younger brother an ice cream soda after he acquits himself honorably in a fistfight with a local tough; in the nostalgic novel Voices of a Summer Day, where the younger brother is similarly battered in a fight; and in the many scenes of siblings that color Rich Man, Poor Man and Beggarman, Thief. When one's own brother is threatened, Shaw seemed to be saying as early as "Sailor," the Old Testament is the only guide one needs.

As it happened, The New Yorker was not the first magazine to which

"Sailor" was submitted. Now that Shaw was a hot property, other magazines were clamoring for stories. *Story* published the gently humorous "God on Friday Night," about a Shaw-like son coming home to confess a marital infidelity to his Brooklyn mother, and to ask her to light prayer candles for him on Friday night. As for "Sailor," Shaw submitted it first to *Esquire,* assuming it was too long and violent for *The New Yorker.* While *Esquire* was still considering it, Shaw stopped off one day at Maxwell's office—"he blew in and out, like a jolly uncle," as Maxwell recalls—to discuss another story. Maxwell asked about the manuscript under his arm. "Oh, that's nothing for you," Shaw told him. Maxwell persuaded Shaw to let him read the story first. Both magazines elected on the same day to publish the story, putting Shaw in an ethical quandary; it was considered improper for a writer to submit a story to two publications. With not that much hesitation, Shaw gave it to *The New Yorker.*

Before the story appeared, Maxwell, a thoroughgoing *New Yorker* editor, went to Greenwich Village and walked the blocks of West 12th Street mentioned in the story as being those down which the unsuspecting Lueger is led to a waiting Charley. The editors knew they had an important story, and they wanted to get it just right.

"Sailor off the Bremen" was an event at *The New Yorker.* It was one of the longest stories the magazine had run, and thus broke the mold that Maxwell had felt limited by only weeks before, when he cut "Girls" down to size; from now on, other fiction writers would feel emboldened to submit longer stories. More important, "Sailor" marked a departure from the tone and perspective of *New Yorker* stories to date.

By and large, the magazine that Harold Ross and his fellow ex-veterans had started in the 1920s as a peacetime sequel to *Stars & Stripes* had retained its original vision in the late thirties as an elegant weekly of social commentary. True, the short, pithy sketches known as "casuals"—in which even social outrages were treated with the wry light touch befitting the magazine's figurehead, Eustace Tilley—were giving way to what Ross called the "grim stuff." There was some social and political reporting now, and tough, occasionally withering profiles (the legendary Henry Luce profile by Wolcott Gibbs had appeared in 1936). But the writers whose fiction graced *The New Yorker* still appeared a pretty precious lot. They wrote about cold-hearted aristocrats and moody Ivy Leaguers (John O'Hara); about affairs those proper folk had with the help (Nancy Hale, John Collier, Walter Bernstein); and about eccentrics and crazies (Robert M. Coates). A few wrote about immigrants and the New York underclass in general (Leonard Q. Ross with his H*Y*M*A*N K*A*P*L*A*N stories; Arthur Kober with his stories about the Gross family in the Bronx), but usually in a faintly patronizing manner. At its best, *New Yorker* fiction gave an honest picture of the upper class, as O'Hara's did, or stirred sympathy for the lower; at its worst it was downright silly and out of touch. Into this brittle assemblage, Shaw's two stories in February 1939 had the bracing effect of a bucket of cold water.

Brendan Gill, who had arrived at *The New Yorker* just three years before, and who was writing stories of his own as well as rewriting "Talk of the Town," says unequivocally: "Irwin was one of the first long story writers—we would gasp at how many inches his stories took up in galleys—and the most ambitious, and he was instrumental in helping change the nature of the *New Yorker* short story. With 'Sailor off the Bremen,' which remains one of our most famous stories, Irwin became the leader; he was almost as revolutionary at that time as Salinger was to be ten years later. We were all thrilled by his stuff; we would all wonder what he'd do next."

By this time there was not any magic circle of *New Yorker* writers and editors into which a newcomer could be inducted with all the ceremony of a college fraternity. The days of the legendary Algonquin Round Table had passed, after the magazine had become such a success that Ross and his knights began getting written up in the columns. In fact, the fiction writers, for the most part, had never been part of that inner circle. They wrote at home and weren't encouraged to mingle. They didn't even see themselves as "*New Yorker* writers"; it would have seemed vaguely demeaning. They were simply *writers* who hoped to sell stories to the magazine among other places. Nevertheless, there were circles—and as staff writer E. J. Kahn, Jr., puts it, "circles within circles"—and Shaw now found he had entrée to most of them.

He began playing tennis regularly with Gill and Robert Coates and a tall, soft-spoken *New Yorker* editor, Gus Lobrano, who would soon take over from Maxwell as Shaw's editor. "We played—very badly—on 40th Street and Park Avenue, on an empty lot on which four courts had been built," Gill recalls. "And then we'd go to a German restaurant called Volk's on Third Avenue—it's where the Mobil building stands today. Eugene Kinkead would play too, sometimes, and so would Dan Lang. I was the worst; Irwin, by contrast, was in great shape, astonishingly vital, with a wonderful laugh. Everybody loved to prompt his laughter. He was always teasing me and remembering coming up to play football for Brooklyn College in New Haven and hearing the cheers go up from the nearby stadium, where Yale was playing Harvard. That sense of being an outsider to the Ivy League was very vivid to him." Shaw was a modest drinker at that time too, Gill recalls. "I remember going with him and the Cheevers to a restaurant on Third, an Italian place called Pietro, on the third floor, just a lot of pasta and red wine. Irwin was a happy wine bibber in those days, and so was John."

The magazine went to bed on Thursday nights, and staffers often gathered for drinks afterward at Blake's, a nearby bar. Shaw would show up there; he would also occasionally head down to the freewheeling jazz parties hosted by staffers Bruce Bliven, Jr., and Jack Kahn in their walk-up apartment on East 4th Street. "We had a piano," Bliven says, "and almost all the instruments in the orchestra, which nobody could play. We just had them. And that enchanted everyone—especially the slide trombone. I considered myself a clarinet player, and Jack would be on the drums, Gus Lobrano would play guitar from time to time, and William Shawn [the up-and-coming editor of factual pieces in the magazine] would play the piano. That's where I first recall meeting Irwin."

Another hangout was the apartment on East 36th Street shared by Jack Kahn's sisters, Joan and Olivia. Their father was a prominent architect who supported his daughters while they dabbled in art. Shaw was awed by that, and even more by the fact that the girls had a maid. "It was funny," Bliven recalls, "because Irwin was the biggest star by a thousand percent in the room; he was a cult figure, really. But he got very, very shy in this atmosphere. He was absolutely enchanted by these people who didn't have to work." Bliven remembers Shaw dating each sister, neither very seriously, and serving as their escort to the opening of several Longchamps restaurants their father had just redesigned. "The daughters thought Longchamps was pretty tacky, and only went to these openings because their father would be there. But Irwin just loved going—he thought having dinner at Longchamps was the epitome of chic."

There were a few who looked somewhat askance at Shaw's big open charm, his guilelessness and his athletic vigor. It was at this time that S. J. Perelman began referring to him as "that butcher from the Grand Concourse"—a nasty jibe about Shaw's ruddy looks and Brooklyn accent more than anything else. There was a code, too, that Shaw seemed to violate in his own good-natured way. *New Yorker* writers were misfits, so went the code. Most were high school or college dropouts; nearly all were destitute (despite the aristocratic tone they affected in their prose). A typical example was Edward Newhouse, a highly respected short story writer of the thirties and forties who had dropped out of high school to ride boxcars around the country because of an editorial in *New Masses* that in effect declared: "Four months in a boxcar will give a kid a better education than four years at Harvard." Says Newhouse, "Irwin wouldn't have done that sort of thing. He was rather more scared of his parents than I was."

At *The New Yorker,* Ross and other editors collaborated in the code. They seemed truly to believe that writers, like priests, should take their vows, live in garrets and wear threadbare tweed jackets, as befitted the dignity of their calling. (This also allowed Ross, a notorious skinflint, to pay more modest story fees to his contributors.) It was a code, too, of blue blood and old money; while the magazine *had* published a scattered few Jewish writers in its first fifteen years, a WASPy, Ivy League ethos prevailed. In such rarefied air, Shaw's own sensibility created a subtle turbulence. Neither a dropout (this was the young man who had fought his way back *into* college) nor destitute, he brought a different code with him: one of pragmatism and gumption, with its accompanying drive (either all-American or Jewish, depending on how one looked at it) for money commensurate with accomplishment. Eventually it would create a rift.

Unlike other *New Yorker* writers, Shaw was starting to travel in wider—and higher—social circles. The New York book publishing and theater worlds had opened up to him; so had Hollywood; and his boyish vigor seemed especially winning to other successful people who had no call to feel challenged by him. Bennett Cerf had him up often to his Connecticut home for tennis. So did Richard Simon, Cerf's Columbia classmate whose own venture into publishing with Max Schuster had also done well. Andrea Simon, Richard's widow and the mother of pop star Carly and opera diva Joanna, remembers Shaw well: "Irwin was tremendously charismatic. Handsome in a way. And one felt that there was never any doubt in Irwin's mind about Irwin, who he was and what he was. There was a certain amount of gentle arrogance that was not offensive. He was very lovable—and kind. He seemed very wholesome for some reason or other; I was told he was very sophisticated. Can you be wholesome and sophisticated at the same time?

"Anyway, he was around a lot. Anyone knowing us casually would have thought he was living with us, down on 11th Street. We also had a big place in Stamford and I can remember Irwin bouncing around on the tennis court—there was so much little boy in Irwin.

"You accepted Irwin being a ladies' man the way you accepted an only child. He had such appeal and charm to women. Rough charm. Nothing smooth about him. You didn't get angry at him for it, although I know a lot of men who did. And yet Irwin seemed to fear nothing.

"That time was a very vital one; everything seemed to have significance somehow, one felt strongly about the things that went on, and it produced so many creative people. And Irwin was a part of it all; if Diego Rivera had painted a mural of that time, Irwin would have been a major figure in it."

Swept along by his triumphs, Shaw went to El Morocco and to "21"—where a flustered Harold Ross wondered how one of his writers could marshal the money and gall to invade one of *his* watering holes. He went uptown to Sardi's; he went downtown to the Village Vanguard, where Betty Comden, Adolph Green, Judy Holliday and the rest of The Revuers were performing their gently satirical sketches to admiring audiences that included S. J. Perelman, Robert Benchley, Ogden Nash, Jack Kahn, Bruce Bliven, Jr., and William Shawn. Sometimes after the show, Shaw would go off with The Revuers to the all-night Washington Diner and help them work up new material.

One of the hottest spots in the Village was Café Society, a basement joint whose walls were adorned with paintings and cartoons by the local talent. There Helen Brown Lawrenson held court, while onstage a number of black musicians entertained the white crowd, among them a young Lena Horne and the boogie-woogie piano team of Ammons and Johnson. Hazel Scott sang at Café Society too, and Zero Mostel headlined the comic talent. Years later, Shaw wrote of being in Café Society on a fateful night in January: "The one moment of absolute gravity recorded in the place occurred on the night of the fall of Barcelona to Franco's troops, when John Wexley, author of the play *The Last Mile,* stood up, weaving drunkenly, his face pale and haunted, and asked for a minute of silence in tribute to the defenders of the lost city. The entertainment was over for the evening and perhaps for a long time to come."

So it was. In March 1939, Hitler broke the Munich pact and seized Czechoslovakia. Before the month was out, Madrid fell to Franco, and the Spanish Civil War was over. "Concurrently with this event," Harold Clurman noted, "came an almost unrecognizable change in the spiritual scene of American life. A certain flatness, a falling off of aspirational force, a kind of treadmill progression subtly characterized the environment from this time till after the outbreak of the war in September."

The end of the Spanish Civil War brought one happy change into Shaw's life: a new friend, Robert Capa.

Capa had just established himself in Spain as perhaps the world's finest war photographer—certainly its most celebrated, and daring, and charming. Now he was back in New York, and it was in a Greenwich Village bar that Shaw first met him. Wrote Shaw years later, "I recognized him immediately: the thick-lashed dark eyes, poetic and streetwise, like the eyes of a Neapolitan urchin, the curled, sardonic mouth with the eternal cigarette plastered to the lower lip." Despite his world renown, Capa, as usual, had gambled his way into debt, and now faced the additional threat of deportation. Despite the willingness of *Life* magazine among others to sponsor him, U.S. immigration authorities refused to grant another visa extension. The night of March 27, Shaw went with Capa to a wild party at which the photographer announced that this was his farewell appearance; within days he would have to leave the country. On impulse, Toni Sorel, a beautiful model who had met him only that evening, offered to marry him. The next morning the two drove off to Maryland, the nearest state where they could be married without a waiting period.

Devastated by Spain's fall, as was his whole generation, Shaw also had new problems of his own. *The New Yorker* was taking more stories, but *Quiet City,* the play he had promised the Group Theatre the previous summer, was going badly in rehearsals. A fantasy about a rich young corporate chieftain who ignores his union problems to go on vacation, it seemed to suffer from a lack of narrative drive, dissolving into an experimental mélange of free-associative vignettes, in which the businessman returns to New York and walks the streets, haunted by suffering voices he's never heard before. In an effort to build enthusiasm for the play among Group members and potential backers, Harold Clurman had tried to persuade Franchot Tone to take the lead role and start rehearsing while The Gentle People was still in production. Tone, already bitter about his role in that play, read Quiet City and refused. Clurman might have abandoned it altogether at this point, but he had promised Shaw a production. With the season nearly over, he decided to view Quiet City as an opportunity to cast several Group members who of late had had little or no time onstage—among them Frances Farmer, whose debut in Odets's Golden Boy two years before had been followed by an embarrassing third-rate movie role. Elia Kazan, who had directed Gentle People so effectively, was told by Clurman to start rehearsing Quiet City at the Belasco amid the still standing Gentle People sets, with minimal funding to be provided by the Group. The play previewed on two successive April Sundays; audiences and cast alike were so unimpressed that Clurman and Kazan made the painful decision to close it down. For Frances Farmer, the failure of Quiet City marked the start of her sad tailspin into undeserved public disgrace as a Hollywood reprobate, leading to amphetamine and alcohol abuse. For Clurman and the Group, the end was much nearer. Only for Aaron Copland would the play be a happy memory: half a century later, his score for it remains a respected and much-performed work.

Despite the debacle, Clurman still thought enough of Shaw as a playwright to enlist him as a judge, along with Molly Thacher, for a Group play contest open to playwrights aged twenty-five or younger. The winner was an unknown named Tennessee Williams, who subtracted three years from his age to be eligible and never put them back; his winning three one-act plays, though lost to time, earned him his longtime agent Audrey Wood.

That spring Clurman also asked Shaw to write a curtain-raiser for My Heart's in the Highlands, the Saroyan play he had decided to produce. Shaw holed up in the country for a week or so and came back with a one-acter entitled The Shy and the Lonely, based on his experience as a summer camp counselor. The play is set in a camp tent, where two teenaged boys urge their shy buddy to make a pass at the ugliest of three camp girls in order to lose his virginity. The effort ends badly, with the virgin boy and ugly girl furious at each other; the shy and the lonely, it seems, cannot even help each other. Winsome but oversweet, the play fell short of Shaw's best work and failed to impress Clurman enough to use it. Shaw, however, referred to it in later years with particular fondness, and was pleased when it was included in a short-play anthology compiled by William Kozlenko. It was, perhaps, a demonstration of that peculiar penchant of writers to favor their least well received work—the runt-of-the-litter syndrome. If the play failed, however, it still changed Shaw's life in one major way, by introducing him to William Saroyan.

They had much in common, Saroyan and Shaw. Both had grown up in relatively poor, second-generation immigrant families (Saroyan's Armenian family had put down roots in Fresno, California). Both had been young men when the Depression hit (Saroyan was five years older than Shaw); and both had leapt from obscurity to overnight literary celebrity. As the thirties social theater exploded, both focused their energies and ambitions on playwrighting, just as both, for money and glamour, took on Hollywood. Both had great triumphs and crashing failures on one coast or the other, and both grew ever larger as public figures. When the decade finally slid into war, they would end up in London as soldiers together.

And then the war would be what pulled them apart.

For now, in what was for each man a pivotal year, they fell upon each other as soulmates. Shaw went to the opening of *My Heart's in the Highlands* and adored it: a perfect production, he felt, with a wonderful cast (including a child actor named Sidney Lumet). Saroyan, he discovered, was not only a writer whose career was in step with his own but also a man of similarly great passions and appetites. He too loved drinking, loved beautiful women, played lousy but earnest poker (Shaw, with a little help from Capa, had learned the game too—another strike, along with his now established taste for red wine, against his Jewish Brooklyn upbringing), and stayed up half the night carousing at Café Society. He felt the same brimming pride in his work that Shaw did, and responded to critical barbs with angry letters that sometimes grew into back-and-forth battles in the press.

Just weeks after the successful opening of *Highlands,* Saroyan turned out *The Time of Your Life,* the play that would become his greatest critical and commercial success. Shaw was busy too. He helped Random House ready his first collection of stories, tentatively titled "Borough over the Bridge." In June *Esquire* published a vintage story, "The Monument," about a proud bartender who refuses his boss's demand to serve cheap, substandard liquor. The next month *The New Yorker* took one of his best and most emblematic stories, "Weep in Years to Come," another deceptively simple sketch of a young couple walking the streets of New York and discussing, this time, the likelihood of war.

By now Shaw had moved confidently beyond his early dialogue stories to fully formed creations that captured, in just a few pages, a sense of the city at a particular moment. New York was more than a backdrop—it was center stage. How a story's characters reacted to the city, to its crowded streets, to its fascinations and hardships, and especially to the dark world events before the war that seeped in through newspapers and radio determined the outcome of the stories and gave them their power. The couple who come out of a movie theater in "Weep in Years to Come" hear a newsboy shouting, "Hitler!" Conversation turns naturally to whether the young man will enlist if war is declared; without hesitation, he says he will. The young woman is taken aback, and asks what good it will do to kill people. Grimly the young man voices the sentiment that more and more Americans were voicing by July 1939: Hitler threatens the free world, and must be stopped. Half a century later, "Weep in Years to Come" retains its narrative force and imparts a delicate, enduring sense of New York in the late thirties.

Much would be made in years to come of Shaw's remarkable *facility* in writing: the speed with which he knocked out stories, the bearish determination that drove him from one to the next. The reputation would not be ill-gotten—and yet behind the smoke a more human-scale writer sweated at his labors, like the real Wizard of Oz behind the curtain. "They think it comes so easy to me," he liked to say. "But I sweat over every word. I'm just glad it doesn't show." For all his outward swagger, Shaw the craftsman was a private worrier, nervous about the next day's output, nervous about the pages that lay fresh before him. By now he had a habit that would stay with him for life, of writing the next day's passage in his head, moving the words around in his mind. Effortless as it seemed, the life of a prolific story writer and bon vivant had its price.

Two more vintage Shaw stories appeared in *The New Yorker* in the summer of 1939. "Return to Kansas City" concerns a boxer who has come to New York to make it big but gives in to the tearful pleading of his wife—another shrewish Shaw woman—to leave their dreary hotel room and return home. "Main Currents of American Thought," the marvelous story based on Shaw's radio-writing days for Himan Brown, followed just three weeks later. By now William Maxwell had left the magazine to pursue a novel, and Shaw had been handed over to Gus Lobrano.

It was, initially, a much better fit. Maxwell, for all his editing skill and respect for Shaw's stories, came across as a formal and somewhat cold man; he was, as one observer put it, "the only one in the group who didn't have a sense of humor." Lobrano, despite a tense demeanor, did. "He was very tall, and very thin," recalls *New Yorker* writer E. J. Kahn, Jr., "and he had a soulful-looking face, and I was always surprised when he told jokes, but he did." Lobrano had roomed with E. B. White at Cornell, then worked unhappily at a travel agency for several years before heeding White's advice to become an editor. After an apprenticeship at *Town & Country,* he had joined *The New Yorker* in 1938; not long after, when E. B. and Katharine White moved to Maine, Lobrano took over the seven-person fiction department.

Perhaps because he wasn't a writer himself, Lobrano hardly ever suggested editing changes, either in Shaw's stories or in those of another of his young writers, John Cheever. There would be factual queries to field from Ross—whether a cocktail mentioned in a story was mixed as described, for example—but otherwise Lobrano had as much respect for his writers' styles as they did. (One change he did sometimes suggest was crossing out the last paragraph of a story when it tried too hard to wrap up loose ends, as did some of Shaw's.) Shaw thought that was fine; he also delighted in going on occasional fishing trips to a family shack Lobrano kept on Cranberry Lake, in the Adirondacks. "I never went there myself," says Mary Cheever, "but John loved it. It was really rough stuff. No plumbing. Nothing there had ever been cleaned." Then there were the badminton games at Lobrano's house in Chappaqua. Writer Edward Newhouse remembers them well: "Irwin and Lobrano and I played together, and it became embarrassing because the loser bought dinner, and Irwin played badminton like a football lineman. After the sixth or eighth time, Gus said, 'This has to stop'—Irwin had had to buy all our dinners. From then on we put the dinners on our expense accounts."

Admired as he was for his stories, Shaw the playwright was having a harder time of it. That summer *The Gentle People* moved on to a harsh reception in London. Up in Woods Hole, where he and Marian took another house, Shaw worked hard but without success to pare down *The Golden Years,* the family play he'd written before *Bury the Dead,* for a fall production by the Group Theatre. Harold Clurman had hoped it would be the Group's salvation, especially when Odets's latest effort collapsed in August. On reading it through, his heart sank; the play, he felt, was hopeless. (As a last resort Clurman had Odets work up an adaptation of Chekhov's *The Three Sisters;* the Group would not survive the season.)

It was in late August that the world skittered into war and that for Shaw's entire generation the most vivid years began. To the Western world's shock and dismay, the Soviet Union signed its nonaggression pact with Germany. In the United States, Communist sympathizers were confounded. They had assumed that Stalin would come out against Hitler and that war would thus be averted. Especially for those who were Jewish and understood the still veiled implications of Hitler's expansionist policies, there was simply no way to justify the pact. Overnight, in California and New York, the Communist movement and all its outlying circles of "fellow travelers" went up in smoke. A week later, Hitler invaded Poland and Great Britain declared war.

That was the same week Random House published Irwin Shaw's first collection of stories. *Sailor off the Bremen and Other Stories,* as it was now titled, was dedicated to Shaw's Brooklyn College mentor David Driscoll, and to Driscoll's wife, Rose. Along with the obvious choices already published in *The New Yorker,* it included a few attempts to broaden Shaw's storytelling borders beyond Brooklyn and Manhattan. Those stories— "The Deputy Sheriff," for example, set in New Mexico, and "Walk Along the Charles River," set in the Midwest—lacked authenticity, but the New York stories added up to real heft, and most critics reported as much. A rare detractor was Alfred Kazin, who grumbled: "I like Mr. Shaw's stories about as much as I like his plays; a good many of the stories, in fact, seem to me thoroughly bad." Kazin went on to brand Shaw "half a writer" whose "stories are a motley of half a hundred influences and impressions, ill-digested patois out of the Brownsville tenements, imitation Irish brogue, creamy sob stories out of *The New Yorker,* and naturalistic violence for the sake of violence, such as James T. Farrell exploited to the full long ago." Kazin concluded that it was "only in the crude but bitterly veracious 'Borough of Cemeteries,' the story of some Brownsville hackies suffering together on a dull afternoon, that Mr. Shaw rises to his promise."

For a short story collection with a print run of 2,000 copies, general critical praise did not translate into money. Having spent much of his year unsuccessfully reworking two plays, Shaw had had to rely on the modest profits from *The Gentle People* and the story fees from *The New Yorker*— averaging $200 per story. For a man who had discovered he liked nightlife, that wasn't enough. That fall, despite his vow not to return to Hollywood, Shaw took an apartment at 1416 Havenhurst and signed on for several weeks of studio scriptwriting, "storing up fat against the long winter," as he put it in a letter to Bennett Cerf. This time out he had a new reason to save: on October 13, in a simple civil ceremony officiated by a justice of the peace in Beverly Hills, Shaw married Marian Edwards.

In that same letter to Cerf, Shaw conceded that *Quiet City* was a failure he would not try to resurrect, and said his next big project might not be a play at all. Instead, he was thinking about tackling something else next spring. Perhaps, mused the former playwright of social protest, he was destined to be . . . a novelist.

PART II

TEMPERED
BY WAR

CHAPTER SIX

The Irwin Shaw who strode into the 1940s was a famous young man, as much larger than life as his own self-image. His very bearing was a picture of success: the full head of tightly curled black hair; the hawklike, almost Roman nose; the big wide shoulders and barrel chest; the football player's rolling, balls-of-the-feet gait. He loved hearty meals, good wine, good scotch. He loved his wife; he loved other women; he loved good fiction and classical music; he cared deeply about political issues. He was also capable of black moods no less real for their relative rarity and evanescence. If his anger was directed at someone else, Shaw could radiate a palpable threat of violence, though he seems to have thrown a serious punch only once in his adult life. Angry at himself, he could sink into uncommunicative silence for hours at a stretch, though friends rarely saw this side.

It seemed only appropriate that a larger-than-life ego accompany the package. In a somewhat ingenuous way, Shaw really felt he was a literary superman. "I'll write fifty more plays," he had told reporters on the opening night of *Bury the Dead*, "and then I'll write a novel." It was as if he were doing so many push-ups, flexing from sentence to sentence, paragraph to paragraph. Yet beneath it all remained the keen sensitivity, the emotional radar that gave him insights into the moods and motives of those around him. Even more apparent was the outsized generosity of spirit that had become Shaw's signature.

He was, in short, a happy man, except in one regard: the theater.

Despite its yielding him one early critical success in *Bury the Dead* and one modest commercial success in *The Gentle People,* the theater had also handed Shaw two decisive defeats. For a literary superman, this was frustrating indeed. Putting aside for now whatever thoughts he had about being a novelist, Shaw dug in with renewed determination to achieve the praise and profits of a major American playwright—a playwright like his friend William Saroyan, who at this time shocked the world by refusing to accept a Pulitzer Prize for *The Time of Your Life.* Shaw planned his year accordingly: three or six months in Hollywood to earn the big money, then back to New York with a new play in hand, to test the fickle critics again. For all the success he would gain as a novelist and retain as a short story writer, Shaw would be haunted for the next twenty-five years by the challenge of achieving a real Broadway triumph. Not once would he succeed.

It was in early 1940 that Shaw, pursuing this course by scriptwriting for Warner Bros. while polishing a play that would reach New York that fall, met a young screenwriter who would become his best friend for more than forty years.

Peter Viertel was just nineteen—compared to Shaw's advanced age of twenty-seven—but had managed to publish a precocious first novel, *The Canyon*, to considerable critical acclaim. A coming-of-age story, the novel chronicled Viertel's southern California life as a son of one of Hollywood's most interesting couples, director Berthold Viertel and his wife, Salka, an actress and screenwriter. It was a life the German-born Viertel had been introduced to as a child when his parents, well established in German theater circles, began to feel threatened as Jews and, speaking no English, emigrated to America in 1928.

Joining the fast-growing community of Jewish émigré artists in Hollywood, the Viertels had fared better than most. Berthold won a director's contract with 20th Century–Fox, then signed with Paramount, where the head of production was B. P. Schulberg, Budd's father. Under the circumstances, young Peter and his brother, Hans, may have felt an early resentment of the Schulberg children, Budd and Sonya, who were also somewhat older than they; certainly in time, Peter and Budd would become rivals of a very bitter sort, with Irwin Shaw caught in the middle.

In 1933, when Berthold's contract with Paramount ended and was not renewed, the frustrated director went back to Berlin to make a film. Salka was left to raise the children on her own; soon after, she and Berthold agreed to an official separation. A woman of keen intellect and indomitable spirit, as liberated as any latter-day feminist, the onetime actress established herself as a cynosure of the émigré artistic community. Her house in Santa Monica, at 165 Mabery Road, became a Sunday salon for the likes of Max Reinhardt, Thomas and Heinrich Mann, Arnold Schönberg and French playwright Marcel Achard. Americans came too: Miriam Hopkins, Johnny Weissmuller, Oscar Levant and others. When a young Greta Garbo came over from Europe, Salka became her closest friend and rumored lover. Soon she was collaborating in the writing of Garbo's American films: *The Painted Veil, Anna Karenina, Ninotchka.*

As a result, Peter grew up more or less on his own. A handsome, athletic teenager, he showed far more interest in tennis than school. He did well enough to get into Dartmouth, but he hated the East and returned after his first freshman term. Back home, he wangled a job as a junior writer, first for Alfred Hitchcock, then for David O. Selznick. In his spare time he wrote *The Canyon*, raced around Hollywood in his Model A Ford convertible, and romanced a succession of beautiful girls.

And kept playing tennis, which was how he met Shaw.

Shaw was playing at the Beverly Hills Club with screenwriter Charles Lederer one day when Viertel arrived as a guest of Billy Wilder.

Shaw had just read *The Canyon* and spoke of it in glowing terms when introductions were made; Viertel had read and admired Shaw's work. More than that, the two were natural soulmates. Both were athletic, virile and sociable. In this politically charged time between the German-Soviet pact and the start of Hitler's surprise campaign against the USSR in June 1941, both were also in agreement that there was no way to rationalize the Soviet choice, and that whatever their former inchoate sympathies as "fellow travelers" with the Communist Party, the time had come to fight the Nazi threat. "Left-wingers like Dalton Trumbo and Budd Schulberg and Jigee went along with the pact," Viertel observes. "I couldn't stomach that. And Irwin certainly couldn't. So that was another bond between us."

At the same time, the two felt a certain unacknowledged rivalry. E. J. Kahn, Jr., a friend of both men, always sensed that deep down each wished he'd been more like the other. Shaw admired Viertel's lean grace and artistic pedigree and, later, Viertel's very active wartime record. Viertel, no less so, admired Shaw's greater literary success and the way he inevitably became the center of any social gathering. Early on, the two boxed a few times. But, says Viertel, "we soon discontinued that. Irwin was very much stronger than I was, but I had a sharp left, and I had had boxing teachers."

There was no way for a nineteen-year-old to compete, of course, with Shaw's Hollywood standing. In a town where junior writers earned $50 a week, Shaw's $500 to $600 put him in the upper ranks. And for the first time he started to live accordingly, buying his suits at high-priced Pesterre's and taking Viertel for steaks at Chasen's. His friends included novelist Horace McCoy (*They Shoot Horses, Don't They?*) and Hollywood's most successful screenwriter of the day, Robert Riskin (*It Happened One Night, Mr. Deeds Goes to Town*). Many, like John McClain (*Turnabout, Lady Be Good*), were newspaper writers who'd made good. Others, like Shaw, had New York theater roots: both Clifford Odets and Harold Clurman were out often, and Viertel met both through Shaw. At the same time, Shaw's own circle expanded to include émigrés he met at Salka's Sunday gatherings.

The work that gave rise to all this socializing was a good deal less exciting. Shaw's principal project at this time was a script titled *The Hard Way*, about a small-town mother with big-city ambitions for her actress daughter. Ida Lupino starred in the movie that eventually made it to the screen, but Shaw left midway through after an argument with director Vincent Sherman. For Viertel, it proved a break of sorts when Shaw steered him to the rewriting job; Viertel and Daniel Fuchs ended up sharing screenwriting credit.

Shaw, whose guilt at playing the Hollywood game always hovered close to the surface, arrived back in New York with relief—and with his new play under his arm. He called it *Retreat to Pleasure* and meant it to be a topical satire. As it opens, an earnest liberal girl named Norah Galligan loses her job as a WPA executive in Ohio because she won't sign an order to take 5,000 people off relief. To her great confusion, three suitors await her upon her return to New York: an unemployed idealist, a wealthy capitalist and a feckless playboy. For no particular reason, she goes to Florida with the capitalist, followed by the smitten playboy and idealist. At the play's end, however, she chooses not to go off with any of them. Infused with a glib, almost madcap tone, *Retreat* was meant to reflect the American mood on the eve of war: self-centered, immature, oblivious to the rumblings of the real world outside.

The calamitous experience with *Quiet City* had soured Shaw on Clurman and the Group Theatre, and so without telling the director, he sold the play in the spring to George S. Kaufman. Unfortunately, Kaufman let his option run out without getting the play into production; and by June, Shaw had no choice but to go back grudgingly to Clurman and let the Group have *Retreat* after all. "For heaven's sake, Harold," he grumbled to Clurman, "let's do a good job this time."

The Shaws took a house in Falmouth for the summer of 1940, and it was here that Clurman came, nursing his disgruntlement at Shaw's "betrayal," to work on *Retreat* as a Group production in the fall. "Shaw had attempted to write a drawing-room comedy with social significance," he felt when he sat down in Falmouth to read the play. "It had some good scenes and pleasant writing, but above all it seemed to me to mirror the soul of the young middle-class intelligentsia and the gloomy, rootless jauntiness of our society generally just after the outbreak of the war in 1939. The play was a little *Heartbreak House,* but unredeemed, despite dexterity, by either a sure hand or a clear spirit. I liked it nevertheless as a kind of document of the day: it evoked an escapist mood that looked toward no eventual release from its underlying disquiet. Shaw was pleased that I could read the play's theme through the froth of its playful verbiage."

Random House editor Saxe Commins, who included William Faulkner among his writers and would come to play an important role in paring down Shaw's novels, was considerably less impressed with the play when Shaw sent him a copy, presumably to be published. "I don't like Irwin Shaw's new play," Commins confided in a memo to Bennett Cerf. "To me it is laboriously casual and careless. Only for moments does it come alive as fantasy. . . . There are pages and pages of goings-on that make little sense. The characters walk on and off as Shaw pulls the strings, not letting his left hand know what his right hand is doing. Apparently the Saroyan success has influenced him. . . . Shaw has picked out the wrong steps to follow, in my opinion. I had hoped he would go forward on his own road in the direction pointed by *Bury the Dead.*"

That put Cerf in an awkward position, aggravated by the fact that

Shaw was annoyed with Random House's handling of his first story collection the previous fall. Shaw felt the collection could have sold better and had taken umbrage when Cerf postponed the fall publication of his second collection because, said Cerf, of the wartime situation. Cerf seems not to have liked *Retreat to Pleasure* any more than Commins did, but felt obliged to promise that Random House would publish it sometime in the fall—all the more reason, he explained diplomatically in a letter to Shaw, to put off the second collection. Shaw wrote back a conciliatory letter admitting he'd been irked enough to talk to other publishers, but only because Random House seemed uninterested in him as a short story writer. *Retreat* was ready, he added. Moreover, with his usual speed he was polishing off another full-length play, *Labor for the Wind*, with yet a third play to be finished by the middle of September! The point of working so quickly, he wrote, was to avoid another mercenary trip to Hollywood in the fall. Shaw fell short of offering an apology for his queries to other publishers, however, and while the heat of the moment passed, the same tension would crop up again and again—Shaw bristling at Random House's seeming cavalierness in what it paid and how it marketed his books—until the final, painful break.

Shaw's choice of Falmouth as a summer retreat was revealing, if only in a symbolic way. Situated at the bottom of Cape Cod's flexed arm, it lay only an hour's drive or so from Provincetown, at the top of the peninsula, yet the two towns were worlds apart. Provincetown, where O'Neill had staged his first sea plays, still drew New York's most intellectual artists and writers. "We were all there, that summer of 1940 in Provincetown," wrote Alfred Kazin. "John Dos Passos still lived at one end of Commercial Street, and Harry Kemp, and Mary Heaton Vorse. . . . People worked till one, when writing broke up for the day and we all rushed to get on the bus to the beach," along whose route one might catch "sight of Edmund Wilson carefully bicycling himself to the Portuguese bakery." The whole *Partisan Review* crowd was there, too, including Mary McCarthy, the "sharply handsome twenty-eight-year-old Vassar graduate" who in her literary attacks seemed to have "come to pass judgment on the damned in Provincetown." Despite his successes, Shaw knew this was not his crowd. His screenwriting set him apart; so did his open manner and overt masculinity. He was as bright, and at his best, as fine a writer, as any of them, but their self-conscious stance as intellectuals was not for him. Later, when the same crowd dismissed him as a writer, those differences would harden into deep resentment.

That summer, as the war in Europe accelerated, *The New Yorker* published two stories that showed Shaw's brooding anger with anti-Semitism. In "Select Clientele," a young Jewish couple, Sam and Esther, go bicycling with their non-Jewish friend Max along back roads near the small New England arts colony where they've come for the summer. At the bottom of a hill four men, surly-looking townies, stand menacingly in their way holding heavy branches. The bicyclists are forced to endure anti-Semitic slurs; as they ride away, rocks are also thrown. Max is the one who insists on revenge and, in an echo of "Sailor off the Bremen," enlists the help of Thomas, the colony's strong handyman. Equipped with pitchforks and bats, Thomas, Max and Sam head out in search of the hoodlums. It turns out that Thomas knows them. Flummoxed, he listens to their feeble excuses and lets them go their way as Max seethes in helpless rage. A vivid snapshot of America's not often acknowledged undercurrent of anti-Semitism at the time—with a bitter nod to Father Coughlin and to the still prevalent custom of advertising summer houses for "select clientele"—the story also demonstrated Shaw's penchant for borrowing real-life anecdotes. In this case, the story came from Daniel Fuchs, Shaw's Hollywood friend from *The Hard Way,* who had undergone much the same experience with his wife during a summer at Yaddo, the arts colony. For all his creative abilities, Shaw felt an almost superstitious need to root his fiction in reality—as if beneath the burly ego was a more tentative writer unwilling to trust his own imagination. It was a need, finally, that would seem a limitation, rendering him too often a sort of fictional journalist, instead of the full-blown artist he aspired to be.

Almost like the second story in a two-part series, "Free Conscience, Void of Offense" uncovered anti-Semitism in the American upper class. The story is set in the autumn of 1938: a college girl and her Ivy League father meet for dinner in a warm, happy restaurant; at the bar up front, well-dressed drinkers are raising toasts to Neville Chamberlain for saving their children from war. The girl tells her father she wants to drop out; he makes the predictable protests. In the background, the revelers at the bar chorus Ivy League fight songs. Then, in a scene that augurs the opening of *The Young Lions,* the drinkers segue to an anti-Semitic chant, amid much backslapping and laughter. To the girl's shock, her father joins in the laughter. He too, she realizes, is a product of the Ivy League world that breeds conformity and prejudice. As with nearly all of Shaw's best stories, the last line is a signature of deadpan irony: that was the year, he writes simply, that Columbia beat Yale 27–14 in the first game of the season. *Plus ça change.*

Despite such continuing success with his stories, Shaw hunkered down with his various plays through the summer and fall. He had more time to himself for writing: Marian landed a part in a Broadway production of *George Washington Slept Here* that opened in October and ran well into the winter. A final draft of *Labor for the Wind* emerged three years later, rechristened *Sons and Soldiers. Retreat to Pleasure,* reworked with Clurman's suggestions, reached the stage much sooner. By the time the critics finished pummeling it, though, Shaw must have wished it hadn't opened at all.

The first problem with the *Retreat* production, as Clurman later reasoned, was that the Group had all but collapsed, undone by internal tensions and the widespread disillusionment with Clurman as a leader. Stubbornly, Clurman decided to direct the play himself and gather a cast from outside the Group if need be. Forced to seek outside financing, he was left with little time to secure the strong male romantic lead he and Shaw agreed was crucial to the production, and even less for rehearsals.

The playboy lead eventually went to a little-known actor named Leif Erickson; John Emery played the reckless idealist, Hume Cronyn the wealthy capitalist, and Edith Atwater the ex–WPA administrator all three men pursue. It was during a preview benefit performance, as Cronyn remembers, that the riot broke out.

"There was a scene in which mother and daughter, played by Helen Ford and Edith Atwater, sit on a balcony at a Florida hotel looking out over the beach. One says to the other: 'There's that nice Mr. Cobble or whatever, he has a very good figure, he swims well too.' They note his progress: 'I believe he's swimming out to the raft.' . . . 'Look who's on the raft—that terrible Myrtle.' . . . 'He's climbing up on the raft; I didn't know he knew Myrtle.' . . . 'He's putting his arm around Myrtle! That's disgusting. Mother, I believe he's Jewish.'

"It was written as satire. But we played it to a benefit house for B'nai B'rith or Hadassah or one of the big Jewish organizations. And all hell broke loose. These were terribly touchy times, and this was taken as literal anti-Semitism. The producer, Lee Shubert, got knocked down at the back of the theater. The curtain had to be lowered; there were people shouting and standing and walking out."

Because his character wasn't involved in the scene, Cronyn was in his dressing room, oblivious to all this, when a white-faced Irwin Shaw and Harold Clurman burst in. "They said, 'Hume, you have to go out and talk to them!' I said, 'Me? Wait a minute. I'm a goy. *You* guys are Jewish. And besides, *you* wrote the play, and *you* directed it.'

" 'Yeah,' they said. 'But they *like* you.' "

The offending scene was quickly scrapped, but as Clurman saw it, the opening night of *Retreat to Pleasure* was a dismal failure. It was "worse than bad: it was weary. It had its pleasant moments, it looked handsome after a department-store fashion, it was not too poorly played, but its origins in dreariness and discouragement were discernible to the naked eye."

In fact, Brooks Atkinson found in it "the drollest writing of the season," and had nothing but praise for the principals. Atkinson conceded, however, that *Retreat* was brilliantly written in subordinate details and "bungled in the major outlines of story," with the play wandering off the mark in a muddled third act. Richard Watts found the core of the play weak and felt restless when the dialogue turned to earnest "discussions of the world's plight." Wolcott Gibbs found the material "discouraging," and declared, with characteristic world-weariness, that "Mr. Shaw's main characters, though handsomely acted, are standard models who have been batting around the theatre for years, talking your ear off." The most interesting pan came from John O'Hara, writing for *Newsweek*. "Here we have again the sad old story of a man writing about something he doesn't know about," O'Hara declared of his fellow *New Yorker* writer in acid-etched prose. "Mr. Shaw can write about the Red Hook district of Brooklyn, about Greenwich Village, and about those hatless young people who are always ascending, descending, or sitting on the steps of the New York Public Library. But I doubt if Mr. Shaw will be remembered as the definitive biographer of the Groton type. After seeing this new play, in which Mr. Shaw has a character who says he went to Groton, I am inclined to doubt that Mr. Shaw ever met anyone who went to Groton. Not that meeting Old Grotties is the way for a promising playwright to be spending his time, but it would seem like a good idea, if you're going to have one on stage for a good fat part of three acts, to sit around and listen to a few Grotties and find out how they talk. At the very least you ought to listen to somebody from St. Mark's."

As far as Clurman was concerned, *Retreat to Pleasure* marked the end of the Group Theatre; a last Clifford Odets play, *Clash by Night*, would be delayed almost a year, open with virtually no Group actors in its cast, and close soon after because of Pearl Harbor. An era had ended. In a decade of galvanizing social theater, the Group had made an unequaled contribution, not only in its best plays and players, but also in the implementation by Clurman and Strasberg of Stanislavsky's Method acting. Shaw's contribution, in the end, had not ranked with that of Odets, as Clurman hoped it would. But *The Gentle People* had been an important Group production. And *Retreat to Pleasure*—well, there was certainly some historical distinction, if a dubious one, in writing the chapter's last page. Most important, though, Shaw had played a real part in one of the most important experiments in American theater. It was a part most readers of Shaw's later novels wouldn't know or even understand, as if one man had lived two, perhaps three successive lives.

Retreat did not mark an end to Shaw's own theatrical career, though he would come to wish it had. But by the time it closed quietly after twenty-three performances—despite a last-ditch rewrite of the ending by its author to make the play less cynical—*Retreat* had changed its creator's life in another, more personal and painful way. Marian, it turned out, had entered into a romance with Hume Cronyn.

The romance was brief but revealing. For Marian, it represented a fitting revenge for the dalliances Shaw had begun to indulge in even during his first year of marriage. Accordingly, Marian was the one who broke the news to her husband, with the expected results. Shaw was righteously indignant—this was not the last time he would demonstrate a double standard of marital ethics—and deeply wounded. A warm friendship with Cronyn was abruptly terminated, his relationship with Marian severely rocked.

All around the Shaws, it seemed, the news of extramarital adventures was fracturing friendships and marriages. The story lines were all entangled, like those of an ongoing soap opera. Only the cast of characters was clear: Budd Schulberg, Jigee Ray, Peter Viertel and of course the Shaws.

In a sense, the story began with Schulberg's decision to hole up in Norwich, Vermont, in early 1940, to write *What Makes Sammy Run?*, based on his embittering experiences in the writers' war of 1936. Schulberg had married Jigee on the last day of 1936 in a ceremony at his father's Los Angeles house. By the spring of 1940, Jigee was bored with Norwich, and with Schulberg's sentimental tie to Dartmouth, his alma mater, a mile or so from Norwich across the New Hampshire state line. She was also, however, pregnant. Another woman might have stayed in Vermont despite her restlessness, but Jigee was not like other women. Resolutely, she chose to head back to California to have her baby there. Schulberg stayed in Vermont with the promise to join her when he'd finished his book.

It was during that summer that Jigee and Peter Viertel first took an interest in each other. Soon after Schulberg returned to Hollywood in the late fall to recoup his finances as a studio writer and attend to the birth of his daughter, Victoria, the affair started up in earnest. "That's sort of a touchy period for me," Schulberg recalls with characteristic understatement. "It was really a period when, you might say, Jigee was leaving me for Peter."

Shaw, as it happened, found out about Jigee and Viertel before Schulberg did, and for a brief time Schulberg felt excluded without knowing why. "I felt a certain tension with Irwin," he acknowledges, "not that he had anything to do with it, but he had sided with Peter. I felt it was a team I was up against—Peter and Irwin and Jigee."

Then came the incident that clarified the battle lines. "We went down to Palm Springs, the four of us," recalls Schulberg. "I felt edgy on the way down. I was still married to Jigee but I felt that all of them were more or less a team. We stayed at a posh tennis weekend hotel. In the talk about driving back, somehow they all ended up together in one car, and I ended up driving back with someone else from Palm Springs to Los Angeles. That was when I first figured out what had happened."

What Makes Sammy Run? appeared in early 1941 to great acclaim, but Schulberg took little pleasure in his achievement. Jigee had taken up openly with the younger Viertel. By spring she had moved out of the big Mexican house the Schulbergs had rented in Stone Canyon and gone off to live with Viertel, taking her baby with her. "And then I remember once going out to the Viertels' house in Malibu, going to see my daughter,"

Schulberg says. "And they were all there: Peter and Jigee and Irwin. I took Vicky off for the afternoon while they sat around. It was horrid.

"I didn't bear any particular ill will toward Irwin," Schulberg maintains. "At the same time, he was more loyal to Peter than to me."

Despite the turmoil, Shaw was writing wonderful stories that elevated these prewar years to a golden period. Four decades later it's difficult to appreciate the excitement he continued to stir in thousands of young men eying the war in Europe with such mixed emotions, and wishing perhaps more than anything that they could simply go on living the happy American life, playing football and falling in love. No other writer seemed to share those bittersweet feelings as intimately as Shaw, or to define them as deftly: tough on the outside, soft within. And if the young men who felt most strongly about Shaw were of a certain type—well-bred, white, urban, politically liberal but only just so—they were hardly the only ones to recognize his talent. The editors of one of the country's two major annual anthologies, *The Best American Short Stories,* not only included "Main Currents of American Thought" in the 1940 collection but dedicated the volume to Shaw. A Shaw story would appear in almost every *Best* collection of the forties, and in two editions of the country's other annual anthology, the O. Henry Awards *Prize Stories.* Most important, *The New Yorker* continued to publish several Shaw stories a year. The magazine also published an anthology of stories from its first fifteen years: 1925–1940. Shaw had three entries, matched only by John O'Hara, Sally Benson and Robert Coates. The leadoff story in the collection: "The Girls in Their Summer Dresses." Shaw was on top of the heap.

It was in January 1941 that Shaw published the story that would rank with "The Girls in Their Summer Dresses" as his best-known and most loved. It did not, however, appear in *The New Yorker.*

As Shaw liked to point out, *The New Yorker*'s editors were a rather unathletic bunch, and the story of a football player reminiscing about an eighty-yard run in a long-ago game—especially a story even longer than "Sailor off the Bremen"—simply failed to excite them. When they turned it down, Shaw sent the story over to *Esquire*'s famous editor, Arnold Gingrich.

"The Eighty-Yard Run," as Shaw titled it, opens with Christian Darling's memory of that run as he walks along the field where he played fifteen years before. It was only a run in a practice game, and Darling never lived up to that promise. Still, it was a magical moment, and all the images flood back: of being a big man on campus; of courting and eventually marrying his sweetheart, Louise; of getting set up in his father-in-law's ink business on the eve of the Great Depression. Bankrupt after that in a fancy Beekman Place apartment, Darling retreats into drink, and then watches as Louise, rising to the challenge, goes to work as an editor at a fashionable magazine and starts to mingle with a smart, liberal crowd that comes to the apartment for cocktails and talks of mural painting and labor unions and Clifford Odets. Louise refrains from any criticism of her husband, remains sympathetic and encouraging, just quietly goes her own way—which renders Christian's decline that much more poignant. Indeed, Louise is that rarity among Shaw women, a strong and memorable character with not a trace of shrew about her. Christian, by contrast, is a dinosaur, on his way to extinction because he cannot adapt to a changing world. Fittingly, he lumbers at last into a job as a college tailor's representative, going campus to campus with the one attribute he has: the look of a "university man." As the story returns to the present, Christian, lost in his thoughts, takes his eighty-yard run once again in the twilight. At the goal line, sweating, he looks up to see a young couple in the stands, gazing down at him perplexed. "I—once I played here," Christian tries to explain. Then he shrugs and walks away.

Shaw would look back on the story as his favorite, and though the analogy that begged to be made between Christian Darling and Shaw himself would be a glib one—Shaw's decline would hardly be so precipitous, nor would he ever stop doing what he loved best—there would be a resonance that could not be denied, and a sympathy that the older Shaw must have felt for his own creation. To one interviewer in the late seventies, he put it in physical terms. "I've noticed as an old athlete myself that as athletes get older they remember most vividly the days when they ran first, when they felt invulnerable, and the whole world seemed to be in their lap, when nothing was in their lap but a fleeting moment of health. And that's what that [story] is about.

"Also it's an allegory. It's a symbol for America, because it begins in the boom times of the 1920s when Americans thought they were sitting on top of the world and nothing would ever stop them, and then the plunge into the Depression, and the drab coming to the realization of what the Depression meant. I used the symbol of the athlete who in the 1920s had this great day. The one great day—in practice, even—and then the long decline into his own private depression which coincided with the Depression of the United States."

Of the many younger writers in New York who looked up to Shaw in January 1941, one of the most admiring was John Cheever, whose own first collection of New Yorker stories would be issued the following year. In March, John and Mary Cheever, newly married, moved to 19 East 8th Street, right across from an apartment to which the Shaws had recently moved, and so the two couples saw more of each other. "Irwin was always sending Marian off to Klein's with ten dollars so he could work in peace," Mary Cheever recalls. In these days the Shaws often seemed headed for a divorce, with frequent battles over Irwin's extramarital affairs. Still, they were charming company, the Cheevers liked them enormously, and throughout his life John Cheever would remain a great admirer of Shaw's stories. He remained mystified by Shaw's other life as a Hollywood writer, however. "Irwin had ways of making money that were completely beyond the ken of Cheevers," Mary Cheever says. "It was just a whole different world that John never understood."

By spring Shaw was back in Hollywood working on a script called *Mr. Twilight* for Warners. As usual, it was a frustrating experience, but this time, in addition to the high weekly pay, there was the pleasure of working with George Stevens, whose sophisticated comedies were making him one of the most respected young directors in the business. On his first Hollywood trip, back in 1936, Shaw had tried to get on a Stevens picture, *Vivacious Lady,* and been turned down. That made the assignment now all the sweeter. Eventually, the studio pulled in veteran screenwriter Sidney Buchman to doctor Shaw's draft, but Shaw shared final credit on the film when it opened the following year as *The Talk of the Town.*

Shaw's work on *The Talk of the Town* coincided with the release of *Out of the Fog,* the well-received film adaptation of *The Gentle People* starring Ida Lupino and also produced by Warners. For the first time, Shaw felt proud of being involved with the movies. Ironically, the extent to which he shaped the story line of *The Talk of the Town* would end up making him one of the targets of Jack Warner's 1947 testimony about Communists in Hollywood. Shaw was not—nor, as the phrase went, had he ever been—a Communist, but *The Talk of the Town* was imbued with a frowsy sort of sociopolitical moral that would later arouse suspicion. Cary Grant, delightfully miscast as anarchist Leopold Dilg, is mistakenly accused of having set fire to a factory and takes refuge in a house about to be rented by a nervous landlady (Jean Arthur) to a prim, humorless Supreme Court nominee (Ronald Colman). Colman arrives and hears about the case but refuses to help defend the still missing escapee, declaring the judicial system will work just fine. Grant comes out of hiding as the cook, and the two have long talks about whether the legal system indeed works with someone like Dilg. Finally, Grant's identity is revealed and the movie heads toward its happy ending, predictable in all respects—except its love angle. As a clever publicity stunt, Stevens and Shaw had Jean Arthur's character teeter between the two male leads so evenly that audiences would be left guessing whom she'd choose until the movie's final frames. Stevens then filmed two endings. The studio distributed half its prints with Grant the successful suitor, half with Colman, and orchestrated a massive campaign to have moviegoers vote for the more deserving man.

Stevens, who had gotten his start as a cameraman for Laurel and Hardy films, was a poker-faced rebel in the movie business, never trying to fight the studios openly but somehow in the end always getting his way to make films that fulfilled his extra-dry comic vision. Shaw adored working with him, so much so that he would pull all the strings he could to join Stevens's wartime photographic unit in London. For now, though, the relationship was largely formal. Separated from Marian, Shaw spent much of his free time with Viertel in the summer of 1941, when he wasn't engaging in romantic dalliances as a mostly unattached husband and man about town. One weekend Shaw and Viertel drove down to La Jolla, taking in the races at Del Mar on the way. "I remember we had an open Plymouth convertible," Viertel says, "and we were driving down the coast road and it was a beautiful day and a guy in a Marine fighter plane strafed us and came right over the top of the car." The two men were on their own that weekend, but the trip seems to have inspired a fine story about two couples driving down to Mexico, "The City Was in Total Darkness," that *The New Yorker* published in August.

Bicoastal decades before a word defined it, Shaw spent time in New York that fall with a circle at least as social as his Hollywood crowd. This was also when he crossed paths, indirectly, with the young J. D. Salinger— through a beautiful debutante named Carol Marcus.

Daughter of a wealthy industrialist, Carol Marcus had grown up in a rambling Park Avenue apartment, gone to Dalton, and spent her after-school hours with her two best girlfriends, Gloria Vanderbilt and Oona O'Neill, the playwright's daughter by Agnes Boulton. None of the three was older than seventeen that fall, but they led an impressive social life. Oona was named the Stork Club's debutante of the year and began going out with the young writer Jerry Salinger, a daring if somewhat unpromising prospect. Gloria took up with a glamorous Hollywood agent, Pat di Cicco, and married him soon after. Carol, an aspiring actress of petite shape and China doll–like beauty, looked younger, and seemed more naive, than her friends. All that changed, however, when she met William Saroyan on an exploratory trip to Hollywood.

"That's how I met Irwin, because Bill knew him," recounts the former debutante, now married to actor Walter Matthau, in the whispery voice that has become a trademark. "And when I came back to New York, Bill followed me. To me, Irwin looked like a prince. He had the most charming gaiety. If you were a girl, you knew you were a girl when Irwin was there. Having lunch with him was one of the most fun things in the world."

Carol's younger sister, Elinor, was thirteen that fall. "There was a circle," she recalls, "and it included Errol Flynn and George Jean Nathan, who was nearly sixty but took me out a couple times. There'd be evenings at Sardi's with all of them, and at the Algonquin several times, or at our apartment. What I remember is that Irwin had a way of never intimidating anyone, of making you feel comfortable immediately."

For now Shaw was having much more fun without his wife in tow, and setting a pattern that would continue even after he reconciled with her: of making trips alone to California and New York and leading a social life so independent of her that acquaintances in later years were often startled to hear he had a wife at all.

Marian for her part felt bitter, not only with her husband for his infidelities (and intolerance of hers), but at Peter Viertel for, in her mind, acting as the catalyst of all the trouble. In October, with the war heating up but the United States not yet involved, Viertel decided to drive up the coast to try to join the Royal Canadian Air Force. Just before he left, he ran into the Shaws, rockily attempting a reconciliation at Romanoff's. "They were sitting at the bar and I went to say good-bye," Viertel recalls. "Marian said, 'I hope you don't come back.'"

As it turned out, Viertel was rejected by the RCAF, thanks to his less than perfect eyesight and the fact that he was German born. By December 7, he was back in Los Angeles playing doubles with Shaw at the Beverly Hills Tennis Club. "Charlie Lederer came out and said, 'You guys, the Japs just bombed Pearl Harbor.' And I remember we said, 'Oh, come on, it's just a joke.' Because Charlie was famous for his practical jokes."

Viertel joined the Marines almost immediately, though he didn't get shipped out until June, and began an active wartime service that would put him in the Pacific and also in the OSS in Germany, passing behind enemy lines. Shaw felt no less strongly about the U.S. decision to enter the war, but he felt obligated to finish the film he was contracted to write, an adventure yarn titled *The Commandos Strike at Dawn* for director John Farrow, about Norwegian partisans resisting a Nazi invasion. He also felt he had to stockpile money for his parents, whom he was largely supporting, and to pay anticipated alimony to Marian. At the same time, he chose not to enlist and finagle some safe desk assignment. Instead, he decided, he would wait until he was drafted, and then see the war the way a writer really should: as a buck private.

That January there was talk of producing Shaw's long-gestating play *Labor for the Wind* for the fledgling Dollar Top Theatre in New York. The Dollar Top, so called because of its intended ceiling on ticket prices, was an effort by Elia Kazan and director Robert Lewis to carry on the work of the now defunct Group Theatre; Victor Wolfson had also contributed a play, and Lewis spoke optimistically of going into rehearsals by the end of the month. Since the Dollar Top's founding the previous summer, however, rising costs had forced its founders to project a top ticket charge of $2.10. Soon after, the theater's plans collapsed, to be transmuted eventually into Lewis and Kazan's successful start of the Actors Studio. For the moment, *Labor for the Wind* would have to wait.

More happily, Shaw's second collection of stories was published neatly on the heels of the appearance of its title story, "Welcome to the City," in *The New Yorker*. Critical response was overwhelmingly favorable, with Shaw treated very much as one of America's best writers. Typical was

H. N. Doughty's review in the *Herald Tribune:* "The warmth of feeling, the heart, the humanity that underlies [Shaw's] stories is genuine and moving. The pathos is not cheap and the humor is not facile." Only in *Time,* with its now established party line on Shaw as a mediocre talent, did the book meet a less than glowing reception: "Irwin Shaw's material is fresh, and he handles it with rich understanding and superb technique—up to a point. Then he lays it on too thick or too pat. Perhaps his professionalism is to blame. Perhaps the author of *Bury the Dead* is more naturally a playwright than a storyteller. Tricks of overemphasis, which get by on stage, look as uneasy in print as theatrical makeup does in a living room."

Shaw rounded out his prewar years in Los Angeles with a script for RKO, *A Yankee Fable,* and spent much of his free time at Salka Viertel's house on Mabery Road. Then he headed back to New York, this time to settle his business affairs and respond to the official request for his presence from Manhattan's Local Draft Board 17.

The golden period was over. Not yet thirty, Shaw had published eighteen stories in *The New Yorker* and several more elsewhere; written one play of historic importance and seen two others to Broadway; and established himself as a top-ranked Hollywood screenwriter. He had also made choices, in what he wrote and in how he lived, that had established him as a literary figure, cutting a swath in glamorous circles on either coast, cultivating expensive habits—and having to earn the money to pay for them. So far the balance of making big money in movies to support the serious writing had held. But somewhere amid the trips from one coast to the other, his marriage had gone awry—was over, as far as he could see. Now the war awaited him, and the only thing certain about it was that nothing would ever be the same again.

CHAPTER SEVEN

On July 10, 1942, the New York *Journal-American* carried this small item: "Irwin Shaw, 29, once so bitter against war that he wrote the one-act play *Bury the Dead*, in which the spirits of slain soldiers rose to speak against the manner of their killing, entered the Army as a draftee." A self-described "free-lance playwright and scenarist," Shaw told his local draft board he had been earning $850 weekly as a Hollywood writer. In passing, the item noted that Shaw was married—but separated from his wife.

Shaw had wanted to see the war from a private's perspective. Now he had his wish.

He entered the war at its darkest juncture. In Europe, Hitler's blitzkriegs had run through Czechoslovakia, Austria and Poland on one side, and Belgium, Holland and France on the other, while Spain and Italy marched meekly to his step. Rommel was in North Africa, pushing east toward Cairo while the pro-Nazi French Vichy forces helped Germany maintain Algiers and its environs. Meanwhile, Hitler's Russian campaign was rolling toward Moscow, seemingly invincible in these warm summer months. A jingoistic America had assumed that its own forces could beat back the German threat easily if it chose to do so, and that Japan was a comical foe. No longer. With the shock of Pearl Harbor followed by a stinging defeat in the Philippines, America's only cause for celebration was its decisive victory in the great sea battle of Midway, thanks to American code-breakers who had learned in advance of the Japanese attack.

It was little more than a month after Midway that Private Irwin Shaw was sent for basic training to Fort Monmouth, New Jersey. Then it was across Manhattan to Queens, where Shaw was assigned to the Signal Corps' picture unit at the converted Paramount studio complex in Astoria.

For all the grousing Shaw would do about the Army, he was one of the very lucky beneficiaries of an intelligent military decision: to have writers and artists put their talents to use by covering the war in print and film for the Signal Corps. In Astoria the talented recruits learned how to write and produce documentaries; then, if the military bureaucracy moved as it should, they went off to wherever the fighting was, typewriters and cameras in hand.

Anyone with a modicum of prewar literary success could qualify for

Astoria, and so it was a colorful bunch that tramped through for short training stints, direct from Romanoff's and the Beverly Hills Tennis Club, "21" and the Algonquin. There were New York writers: William Saroyan, John Cheever and Irving Wallace. There were at least two *New Yorker* cartoonists, Sam Cobean and Charles Addams, the latter qualifying because his first collection had just been published. ("I lived at the barracks out there," recalled Addams years later, "and I remember it wasn't just a matter of making films. We did a lot of drills too, lining up at the crack of dawn and marching through the streets of Astoria. We did KP and all that too. We were all privates. And because those of us who were married were allowed to commute from Manhattan every day, we became known as 'subway commandos.' ") There were Hollywood directors too. Some, like John Huston and Stanley Kramer, were young enough to be recruits. Others—like Anatole Litvak, Ernst Lubitsch, Frank Capra and George Cukor—were beyond draft age but present as volunteers.

Shaw had a bunk in one of the four barracks, but soon into his stay in Astoria he and Marian were reconciled, and the divorce was called off. The turning point may have come on New Year's Eve, at a party hosted by Shaw and another Hollywood writer, Gottfried Reinhardt, in a midtown New York hotel suite. Marian was to arrive from California, and the crowded room buzzed with speculation: Would she show at all? Would she make a late appearance just to needle him? *"Goddammit,"* Shaw was roaring as the hours ticked past. *"Marian's always late."* Then, one observer recalls, Marian walked into the room—and Shaw's face lit up.

No holiday was needed to justify late-night carousing in town. Often now, after the 5:00 P.M. retreat and lowering of the flag, Shaw managed to slip away to Manhattan and come back gloriously drunk. Compared to fighting in the Philippines it was a fool's paradise, but as winter wore on, Shaw began to view Astoria as a terrific waste of time. He already knew how to produce a working script, and the mock documentaries he was asked to work on were depressing fare.

He took some consolation in revising *Labor for the Wind,* the three-act play he'd been tinkering with for at least three years. Its title would change to *Sons and Soldiers* by the time it reached Broadway the next spring, but otherwise the play would remain substantially the same. A multigenerational family story, it was set in 1915 but darted forward to 1942 in a series of nightmares dreamed by the mother figure, Rebecca Tadlock. As the play opens, Rebecca, pregnant with her first child, is told by a doctor that she risks dying in delivery, and so must have an abortion; as it happened, Marian would have several miscarriages before bringing her one child to term. In the future-tense dream scenes that follow, Rebecca sees not just one grown son but two. She pushes the elder to be an artist, but neglects her younger; this situation was also suggested in *Quiet City* and is clearly based on Shaw's own family. She resigns herself to her husband's business failure—from selling swampland in the boom era of the 1920s. When her younger son dies in the Spanish Civil War, she wonders why she suffered through the pain of having him; but when her older son goes off to fight in 1942, she is moved by his somber declaration that the world is worth fighting for, thus at the play's end hardening her resolve to risk having children after all.

In October Shaw sent the play to actress Katharine Cornell, hoping to interest her in the role of Rebecca. Cornell demurred, and the exchange seems to have inspired one of Shaw's few successfully humorous stories, "The House of Pain," about a young playwright who makes the mistake of trying to persuade an aging grande-dame actress to take a matron role rather than a romantic lead.

By early spring Shaw had had better luck. Max Reinhardt, the German director who had come to Hollywood to escape the Nazis and was now a member of Salka Viertel's émigré salon, agreed not only to direct the play but also to serve as one of its producers. Norman Bel Geddes signed on as another producer and, of course, as set designer—a bad omen perhaps, after his overelaborate sets for *Siege*.

Meanwhile, a long-awaited call had come from George Stevens, one of the Hollywood directors past draft age who had volunteered to lead wartime documentary film units. In his quietly insistent way, Stevens had gained permission to film the end of the Africa campaign, and tapped both Shaw and *New Yorker* writer Joel Sayre to help. By April 1943, the three were to fly to Cairo by way of Brazil. They would have to leave a few weeks before the scheduled May opening of *Sons and Soldiers*, however. Still nursing his wounds from the disastrous Group Theatre productions of *Quiet City* and *Retreat to Pleasure*, Shaw insisted on drawing up a contract with the producers that no line of his play be cut or edited in any way. To see that this edict was carried out, he assigned Marian the role of watchdog.

"Marian was at every rehearsal," recalls Gregory Peck, for whom the role of Andrew, the older son, was a Broadway breakthrough and a ticket to Hollywood. "Apparently, Irwin had specified in his contract that there could be no changes, no alterations, no editing of any kind in the script. His wife was there to see to it.

"Several of us felt, and still do, that we might have had a hit if we could have cut twenty minutes from the play. Who knows? Bel Geddes was mainly preoccupied with his sets and the lighting. Max Reinhardt was wonderfully helpful and gentle with the actors, but he was steam-rollered by the blustering Bel Geddes, and frustrated by Irwin's restrictions. He could not cut and shape the script as he had always done in his own theaters in Germany. I hated to see him, in his last production, dominated by lesser talents, and unable to express himself freely."

Karl Malden, who played a young Communist in *Sons and Soldiers*, shared Peck's regrets. By 1943 Malden was actually known as a "Shaw actor," having appeared in both *The Gentle People* and *Quiet City. Sons and Soldiers* was the last play he did before going into the war (his first play after the war would be another of Shaw's). "I think the reason it didn't succeed is that Norman Bel Geddes designed the sets in a way incongruous with the play," says Malden. "The play was supposed to be about a middle-class suburban Jewish family; Bel Geddes did a glamorous Park Avenue set with a grand stairway."

Meanwhile, the Stevens mission had its own share of mishaps. In a letter to his daughter Nora, Joel Sayre described the odd scene that unfolded when he, Shaw and Stevens took leave of their wives in Washington, D.C. Scheduled to fly to Miami en route to Cairo, the "brave task force" discovered that "the Army had failed to provide us transportation. So while our colonels' necks got redder and redder, we proceeded to buy our tickets, including Private Shaw, who hasn't a prayer of ever getting his dough back. However, we landed here (Miami) in fairly good spirits." Sayre, a writer of substantial girth, added that the task force had been put up at the Columbus Hotel. "We've been huddled three in a room (Shaw is fat too, and Stevens is no peeled willow wand either) and now at Larry Shwab's recommendation we've just moved into this beautiful place by the sea. We await transportation by bomber to our next spot on our junket, which we have been told is Natal, Brazil."

This indeed turned out to be the case. Upon arriving in Natal, Shaw sauntered into an officers' club—it's unclear whether he was alone or with his two companions—and was promptly dispatched to the local military jail by a pair of MPs. Only some fast talking on the part of George Stevens extricated him and prevented him from missing his airline connection.

The night *Sons and Soldiers* opened in New York—May 4 at the Morosco Theatre—Shaw was en route at last to Cairo, 7,000 feet in the air over Africa in a heavy transport plane, with the other two members of the "brave task force." He knew neither how his play was being received nor what he would do when he landed.

The first of those questions was answered a week later, when the Cairo Office of War Information queried New York newspapers on Shaw's behalf. Lewis Nichols in *The New York Times* acknowledged the star-studded cast—better known than Peck and Malden at that point were Stella Adler and Geraldine Fitzgerald—as well as Reinhardt and Bel Geddes. But that, he observed, made the play's failure all the more disappointing. "An occasional scene is good, as on the whole is the acting, but . . . *Sons and Soldiers* often appeared talky and scattered, with a good many stock situations and with pretentiousness not always absent." Mused Wolcott Gibbs: "Irwin Shaw is such an accomplished writer of short stories that it is a little hard to understand what happens to him when he sits down to knock out a play. The tight, accurate record of human conversation turns somehow into 'speeches' that are often dangerously close to orations; the humor descends to a frank exploitation of such whimsical characters as vacuum-cleaner salesmen and parody business executives . . . and situations that should arise naturally out of character seem no more than the arbitrary inventions of a desperate though fertile intelligence." *The New Republic's* Stark Young called the play "a muddle and a mess," while *Time,* as usual, added its own special note of acidity. The play, its critic declared, "trots out a lot of flossy china for a terribly bad dinner." After just twenty-two performances, *Sons and Soldiers* closed. Having given Gregory Peck his first important work in the theater, the play, as it turned out, had given Reinhardt his last: within weeks of its closing, the great director died.

The second question was soon answered too. Thanks to the steady advances of General Montgomery's British Eighth Army, the Tunisian campaign was nearly over by the time Shaw arrived in Cairo. Rommel himself had left Africa two months before to plead in vain with Hitler and Mussolini to withdraw the Axis troops. On May 7, British troops from the east and Americans from Algiers completed a pincer attack that won a final German surrender in Tunis, and the war in Africa was finished.

Glumly, George Stevens and Joel Sayre chose to head to the Persian Gulf in search of more action. Shaw stayed on in Cairo long enough to get accredited as a correspondent for the newly started local edition of *Stars & Stripes,* the army's newspaper, and for the magazine *Yank.* Then, with journalistic carte blanche, he took a hot, slow train to Palestine, which was where Walter Bernstein found him.

A fellow *New Yorker* writer who would go on to considerable success as a screenwriter (*The Front*), Bernstein was now working for *Yank.* He had come to Jerusalem to participate in a broadcast for the magazine's one-year anniversary, and soon met up with Shaw. "We were both really fucking off from the Army," Bernstein recalls. "Irwin was writing a play, and I stuck around because I didn't want to go back to Teheran, where I'd just spent six awful weeks. But I had nowhere to stay. So Irwin invited me to come live with him. He had this big room in the home of a refugee lady, Mrs. Feichenfeld. It was just one room, and we both slept in it. We'd get up in the morning and she'd bring us breakfast, and then we'd sit down to write, each of us at separate wooden tables, on which we'd put our typewriters, with our backs to each other. I would sit there awhile, and sharpen pencils, and look at the typewriter, and this noise like a machine gun would start behind me—Irwin's typewriter! After a few minutes he'd turn around and look at me very querulously and say, 'What'sa matter, why aren't you writing?' "

The Palestine trip did little to draw Shaw closer to the organized religion of his forefathers. It did spark deep anger at the plight of European Jews attempting to immigrate to Israel. Hundreds at a time would pay smugglers' prices to cram aboard an old rusted Greek freighter for the illegal trip across the Mediterranean, only to meet a stiff line of truncheon-wielding British soldiers along the Jerusalem docks. Those who hadn't died on the trip would be turned back or taken across Israel to be dumped at the Arab border. Shaw, whose most passionate writing to date had been stirred by injustice, turned out two tough, bitter stories against this backdrop: "Medal from Jerusalem," about a cynical Jewess from Berlin who manages against the odds to immigrate to Israel and tells the Shaw-like protagonist how the rest of her family died in the attempt; and "The Passion of Lance Corporal Hawkins," about a British soldier on the other side, waiting in the military line at the dock for the next ship of Jews to come in.

Shaw did want to see the aftermath of the African war, not just as a journalist but as a writer soaking up material. Back in Cairo before the end of May, he brandished his *Stars & Stripes* credentials to the local U.S. military command, and succeeded in prying loose a weapons carrier truck for personal use. Then he set out alone for Algiers.

It was a surreal scene that lay before him: German tanks and trucks bombed or abandoned in the desertscape, corpses bloating in the hot African sands. Closer to Tunis, Bob Capa was taking vivid photographs of the war's debris. Shaw took his own mental images—pictures that would serve as a backdrop for *The Young Lions*.

Shaw had one other reason to speed toward Algiers. His younger brother, David, had been assigned to an Army squadron that had landed in Africa early on and seen fierce fighting as it pushed Rommel's troops from the west. Shaw hadn't spoken to his brother in almost a year. News of him had come indirectly from home, but there was no assurance that David had survived the campaign's last brutal weeks.

Ever since the Coney Island days, Shaw's love for David had been particularly deep and complex. It was reflected in his work: by now sibling relationships were a touchstone of Shaw's stories and plays, inevitably with a stronger, older brother exhibiting a protective if patronizing affection for his younger brother. (As often, intriguingly, the younger sibling was a sister—so much the weaker and more reliant on her older brother). Pudgy and unathletic, sentenced to a lifetime of living in his brother's shadow, David was also consigned to second place in his mother's eyes, an injustice that made Irwin feel more keenly his brother's keeper. In fact, David had tried to be an artist himself. He had studied painting at New York's Pratt Institute; in the evenings after his workday as a commercial artist, he had written a play about prizefighting, titled *They Should Have Stood in Bed*, with two old Brooklyn friends. The previous year, with a little backstage string-pulling from his older brother, the play had reached the Mansfield Theatre for a brief, unsuccessful run. *Sons and Soldiers* had been dedicated to David as "artist, brother, soldier," and the last of those tributes was perhaps even more pride-provoking than the first: the war, as it does to all boys, had made Shaw's younger brother a man.

All along the 2,000-mile drive, Shaw asked every straggling cluster of weary British and American soldiers for the whereabouts of his brother's squadron. He found it near Algiers. Alighting from his weapons carrier, he walked up to where his brother was standing on a chow line, tapped him on the shoulder and said hello. For long seconds his brother stared at him in utter shock; then the two collapsed in wild laughter.

Shaw was a memorable sight as he pulled into Algiers and checked in at the local *Stars & Stripes* office. Herbert Mitgang, a staff reporter who went on to an illustrious career at *The New York Times,* remembers a striking figure. "Here was Irwin Shaw, whose name we all knew because of *The New Yorker,* and he's got this elegant uniform that made us think he must be some kind of officer or liaison. But it wasn't either British or American, and it had no rank at all. It looked custom-made, and I'm sure it was."

To the delight of the *Stars & Stripes* staff, nearly all of whom were in their early twenties, and thus significantly younger than the famous writer of thirty, Shaw consented to write a few pieces for the paper. Drawing on impressions from his trip, he wrote about a company of American bomber pilots making daily raids on Italy from the Libyan coast in their Liberator planes. The staffers were even more excited when Shaw took them on scenic drives in his big weapons carrier. Half a dozen of them would pile in at once, off into the foothills of the Atlas Mountains, like high school kids cruising Brooklyn streets on a Saturday night. Managing editor David Golding remembers an evening Shaw took him and his buddies to dinner at a black-market restaurant—their first break from army chow in months. "I told him about myself, and he wasn't taking notes at all. Not long after, he told me he'd written up our evening as a story for *The New Yorker,* and they'd sent him a check immediately. So he took us out to dinner again." Less a story than a sketch about a young soldier far from home who misses his girl, "Night in Algiers" appeared in the magazine that September.

Shaw also did some research on a subject he'd started writing a play about back in Jerusalem: the assassination, that previous December, of Admiral Jean-François Darlan. Darlan was the sort of figure destined to play a small but pivotal role in world affairs. A leader of the separatist Vichy government that aligned with Hitler in wartime France, Darlan had had the bad luck to be in Algiers when the Allies launched their surprise invasion of northern Africa in November 1942. He was netted in a general roundup of Vichyites, then persuaded to serve as a mouthpiece for the Allies, who hoped to convert Vichyites by words rather than war. The plan worked, and as reward Darlan was named civil governor of North Africa; the day before Christmas, a fanatic shot him to death in his office. Arriving soon enough after the incident to feel the fallout, Shaw was fascinated by Darlan's role—had Darlan urged his followers to resist the Allies, the Africa campaign would have been bloodier at the very least—and began fleshing out a play in which he would muse on the ironic appropriateness of being saved in confused times by men who were confused themselves. More immediately, he sent off a fine *New Yorker* story, "Hamlets of the World," about a young Vichy lieutenant assigned to take over a command of battle-weary, cynical soldiers just as the Allies land in Algiers; fearing their lieutenant may be foolish enough to resist the Allies rather than surrender, the men simply kill him.

Shaw would have been happy to stay in Algiers a while longer. Herbert Mitgang recalls that he seemed eager to land a writing job on *Stars & Stripes,* and certainly everyone on the staff would have been glad to have him. But when David Golding made an official application on Shaw's behalf through military channels, he was quietly rebuffed; wasn't Shaw too left-wing for a job of that nature?

Whether the FBI had flagged Shaw's service file right from the start is unclear, though it seems likely. What is certain is that on March 22, 1944, a long report on Shaw was forwarded from the FBI's director in Los Angeles, R. B. Hood, directly to J. Edgar Hoover, and that on April 5 of that year, Hoover himself passed the findings on to the assistant chief of staff in the U.S. War Department, to be appended to Shaw's service file for the rest of the war.

These findings, released through the Freedom of Information Act, itemize in numbing detail the political petitions Shaw signed in the late 1930s and early 1940s, the committee boards he lent his name to, the articles he wrote of even the slightest political flavor. Hoover advised that Shaw was "a Communist sympathizer . . . who is said to have been engaged in Communist activities in Los Angeles, California, since 1935." One informer—name inked out—had advised Hoover, who was clearly not up on recent Broadway theater, that *"Bury the Dead* was Shaw's most outstanding revolutionary play and that it followed the anti-war Communist party line of the period 1933–36." The informer added that "this play is said to have been supported by all propaganda agencies of the Communist Party and can still be purchased in Communist bookstores." Hoover declared that Shaw was a "follower of the Communist Party Line and, further, that his efforts are always at the disposal of the Communist Party. In this connection, it has been pointed out that Shaw was mentioned in the *People's World,* generally recognized as the West Coast Communist Party publication, as one of Hollywood's writers who is doing 'good work among the armed forces.' . . . The foregoing," Hoover noted in closing to the assistant chief of staff, "is submitted for your information and whatever action is deemed desirable by you."

Hoover's charges, a ragged clutch of old news reports buttressed by the department's paranoid conclusion that every left-wing social-protest group to which Shaw had lent his name was a Communist front, amounted to nothing less than a military blackball for virtually any position or rank to which Shaw aspired. And if *Stars & Stripes* had been deemed militarily too sensitive for a soldier as pinkish as he, what other posts for a writer were available?

Fortunately there was one: working for George Stevens, who if he was ever apprised of Shaw's record surely must have laughed in derision at the FBI's warnings (and who may even have shown the record to its subject; by the time Shaw settled in London, he was well aware of his FBI standing, and later wove his experience into *The Young Lions*).

Stevens made his way to Algiers in early June to coordinate a documentary film recording the Allies' mop-up operations and the processing of 250,000 German prisoners. General Eisenhower, Shaw learned, was dissatisfied with the film record of the war thus far, and had already tapped Stevens to put together a forty-five-man Special Coverage Unit (SPECOU) in London to film the invasion of Europe—whenever, and wherever, it came. The unit would be linked directly to the Supreme Headquarters, Allied Expeditionary Force (SHAEF), thus allowing the director ample supplies and, in effect, unlimited mobility. If the right bureaucratic wheels could be turned, Shaw was warmly invited to join him.

First Shaw had to drive his weapons carrier back to Cairo. In early July, four days before the Allied invasion of Sicily, he and David spent a last day together on the African coast, drinking rum and pineapple juice, and swimming in the Mediterranean. Then Shaw set out alone. The first evening he made the mistake of getting his weapons carrier stuck in the sand at an Arab coast town, and began to feel somewhat alarmed as the Arabs, like coyotes, drew closer and closer to him. Just before dark, two black American corporals drove up in Army trucks to pitch camp with him and help extricate his vehicle the next morning. The rest of the trip, Shaw gave rides to a variety of characters—two Fighting French parachutists, a battle-hardened British soldier, a studious American sergeant from Spokane, Washington, an Indian corporal, a British liaison sergeant—as much to enlist help in repairing his weapons carrier as to speed them on their way.

Cairo was a hot, unhappy place in the summer of 1943, and Shaw, eager to be off to London with George Stevens, felt a sharp and unaccustomed wave of loneliness. "Walking Wounded," a story *The New Yorker* ran in May of the next year, depicts an American soldier desperate for a furlough from Cairo to see his wife, and bitter at the few British and American women in town. "Ugly, impossible girls no one would ever look at in peacetime, just because there are a hundred men for every woman. . . . Snobbish, overconfident . . . Bitches, all of them." In stories and plays before the war, Shaw had vacillated between a hungry desire for women and the deep suspicion that they were selfish, manipulative creatures. In Cairo the balance gave way. Though it was a fictional character who issued the attack, the writer's own rage was unmistakable—and widely shared. Before the war was over, that very speech, reprinted in *Stars & Stripes*, stirred a huge response of letters from soldiers all over the European theater who felt that Shaw once again had given voice to their own inchoate feelings. The story impressed critics as well, winning Shaw one of the only literary awards of his career: an O. Henry Memorial Award First Prize. (Another story from the Africa period, "Gunners' Passage," about wounded airmen waiting to go home from Accra, would earn Shaw an O. Henry Award Second Prize in 1945.)

Cairo wasn't always so bleak. Walter Bernstein, back from covering the invasion of Sicily, found Shaw living in a very pleasant pension with high French windows and a balcony, writing playful pieces for *Yank* and *Stars & Stripes*. "Irwin got me a room of my own in the place, and we lived this great, sybaritic life. We'd get up in the morning and write. Then we'd go play tennis at noon, when the temperature was incredibly hot, at that British colonial–style sporting club on the little island of Gezira, in the Nile. Irwin was really a free agent at that point; he had no Army responsibilities that I could discern."

One memorable day, Shaw played football too, under the hot Cairo sun. "There appeared a shipment of complete football uniforms," he told an interviewer years later, "and like idiots we put on full pads and had a game. On the sidelines all the British rugby players, who wore nothing when they played, roared with laughter at the tough Yanks fainting all over the field." The only solace from the sun was drinking, but to Shaw's indignation the best bar in town, at Shepheard's British Hotel, was open only to officers. Shaw took the one recourse he had, writing a thinly veiled satire of the situation in *Stars & Stripes*.

August brought a reprieve of sorts: a month back in Astoria, to bone up on filmmaking skills in preparation for joining Stevens in London. Thanks in large part to William Saroyan, it became a memorable time.

Saroyan had lumbered into Astoria that spring like some reprobate student whose arrival disrupts the entire school. He was already a legend, of course. Since turning down a Pulitzer for *The Time of Your Life*, he had had a grandly disastrous encounter with Hollywood, the only constructive result of which was a screen treatment he decided to release that year as a short, winsome novel—*The Human Comedy*. His personal life had been no less dramatic. Determined to help perpetuate his near-extinct Armenian stock, he had demanded that his young beloved, Carol Marcus, prove she could bear heirs before he agreed to marry her. Apparently the demand was met, for a hurried wedding was held in February at the military post in Ohio to which Saroyan had been banished by annoyed superiors who resented his loud declarations of pacificism. Now, with Carol situated across the East River in a penthouse apartment at 2 Sutton Place, Saroyan was proving an utter failure as a soldier.

Shaw arrived just in time to be caught up in Saroyan's great undoing: the making of a training film about how to load a boxcar. "I was their project officer," recalls Julian Blaustein, the Hollywood writer who'd met Shaw on his first trip to Hollywood (and who would go on to be a successful producer). "In fact, our team was me, George Cukor as director, and Bill Saroyan and Irwin as writers. They were all buck privates; together, I think, they made $150 a week. The four of us would sit around in my office working up the film. That's most of what Irwin did in the brief time he was there." Saroyan wrote the film in his own quirky way, with a narrative that began something on the lines of "I am a boxcar. Treat me gently. . . ." Most of the enlisted men thought it was charming when it was finally shown. The officers were less pleased and cracked down hard on Saroyan afterward.

There was a public baseball diamond near the studios, and an ad hoc league had been formed among the men. Shaw played on a team called the Ten Old Men. Julian Blaustein was team captain and played first base; director Stanley Kramer played shortstop; Liam O'Brien, an aspiring playwright, was also on the team. "We didn't like Blaustein much," O'Brien recalls. "We thought he was pompous. And because Irwin and I switched off between second base and shortstop, we'd take turns picking up grounders and throwing him the ball like a fuckin' bullet. 'Hey,' Blaustein would say, 'you don't need to do that!' "

By early September, Shaw was back in Cairo for one last stint on *Yank* and *Stars & Stripes*. He wrote one piece almost every week that autumn; nearly all were set in bars, with soldiers grousing as they downed drink after drink. The pieces exude a tone of joshing camaraderie, which was the prevalent reaction of soldiers to the dreariness and degradation of military life. In addition to his great and growing love of drinking, one thread that appeared in Shaw's military pieces was bitterness toward superior officers. Exciting as his war would be in many respects, it was still a war seen through the eyes of a private, a perspective that would inform *The Young Lions* throughout. Shaw wrote acidly of officers in Cairo and westward toward the battle lines who had stockpiled provisions intended for soldiers at the front. In an unsigned editorial for *Stars & Stripes*, he mocked medal-wearing officers "walking around ablaze with bits of colored silk, looking like a cross between Mrs. Astor's pet horse and General Bismarck." (The prose style was unmistakable.)

In December Shaw returned home for a furlough meant to last through Christmas. Nine days into it, on Christmas Eve, he was mustered out with the official orders he had desperately desired. Thanks to Stevens's help, Shaw was off to London, to a ringside seat at the invasion of Europe.

CHAPTER EIGHT

The London in which Shaw found himself in January 1944 was a city of contradictions. Buildings still lay in rubble from the Battle of Britain nearly three years before, and a renewed "little Blitz" forced nightly blackouts. Yet the restaurants and nightclubs were packed with revelers, and by day the streets were filled with rush-hour traffic. A corner on the war had been turned, and the city was swamped with both British and American soldiers in preparation for the inevitable European invasion. But the weeks dragged by in a glaze of inaction, and American GIs especially grew restless and frustrated, biding time far from home.

There wasn't much Shaw could do yet either, so with George Stevens's permission he attached himself to a British film unit making a three-reel documentary about the planning for D-Day. As the token American on the project, he sat in on high-level meetings with U.S. colonels—a perverse treat for an officer-hating private first class, and certainly one the FBI would have been appalled to know about—and wrote a script. The film was shelved, however, when American authorities decided Shaw had been "hornswoggled" into placing too much emphasis on the British. "Since it was all taking place in the British isles," said Shaw later, "I could hardly pretend it was taking place in North Dakota." After that Shaw spent his time drawing up lists for Stevens of equipment to be requisitioned for the invasion, especially the "eyemo" 35-millimeter portable film cameras that would record the invasion.

Shaw stayed in various rented apartments, thanks to Stevens's willingness to let him avoid the standard military billets to which other soldiers were posted. By the time Saroyan came over in February, Shaw was sharing a three-bedroom Pall Mall apartment with Irving Reis, the director who'd worked on Shaw's radio dramas for CBS, and Saroyan was promptly invited to become a third roommate. Reis was now a captain in the unit, but in this expatriate Hollywood clique, military rank held less sway than one's prewar rank as a writer or director; by that standard, Shaw and Saroyan felt junior to no one in the unit but Stevens.

The whole West End by then was a sort of transplanted American town, and in that tight-knit community Shaw and Saroyan immediately stood out. Word quickly got around that they came to work in a chauffeur-driven limousine; Saroyan was, after all, one of the richer privates in the U.S. Army. At parties, they chatted with generals (Saroyan more amiably so than Shaw). Everything they did flaunted military protocol.

"They were the two worst-dressed soldiers in the entire U.S. Army," recalls Martha Gellhorn, the pioneering wartime journalist still married at the time—though just barely—to Ernest Hemingway. "They had taken real care to be as unmilitary as possible, and they had certainly succeeded." Gellhorn remembers walking with them one day in Green Park. "We passed a desk officer wearing one of those ridiculous rubber bathing caps over his hard hat. He walked past us, then called out, 'Don't you salute officers?' Saroyan and Shaw were both stunned. They just stared. They had no idea whom he might be talking to. Finally they got it, and gave two of the most dreadful salutes you could imagine."

The D'Artagnan to these musketeers, indeed the only other American in London that winter as notorious as they, was Bob Capa. Already ensconced in the supposedly bombproof Dorchester hotel with his girlfriend, Pinky, Capa was nothing less than a connoisseur of revelry in these preinvasion months. His nightly rounds, to which Shaw and Saroyan now became accustomed, usually began at the White Tower, a Greek-owned restaurant Capa had helped establish as a journalists' hangout. The Little French Club on Little St. James's Street was another stopping-off place of choice: a private basement club for the Free French forces, it stayed open later than London's ordinary pubs, and always seemed to have a rare supply of scotch on hand, for which the Hollywood crowd was especially grateful. More often than not, Capa ended up hosting a marathon poker game in his Dorchester apartment, where new players learned that when German planes dropped their bombs nearby, it was bad form to show the slightest hesitation in placing bets.

One of the many younger American soldiers amused and impressed by the musketeers was Barry Bingham, of the Kentucky newspaper family that would be torn by his children's sibling rivalry some forty years later. Bingham, then serving as media director for Admiral Harold R. Stark, U.S. Navy commander of U.S. naval forces in Europe, described Shaw and Saroyan in a letter home to his wife: "They are both G.I.s, you know, and Saroyan looks completely Armenian and incredible in his uniform. You have to look twice to be sure he hasn't got a rug over his arm. He has written 'some plays' in the last few weeks—he doesn't even specify how many—but he can't get anybody to say anything except that they are very fine plays. Nobody seems interested in a production. Shaw is a much more reasonable character. He has written a play—only one—about North Africa, but since it is mildly and obliquely critical of state department policy, he does not think it will get anywhere. Saroyan has read it and says it is the best play to come out of the war so far. I'm afraid that isn't really very high praise, considering *Storm Operation* and the rest. I told Shaw how much I had liked his story in *The New Yorker* about the armed guard officer who performed an appendix operation at sea, and he said his wife had gotten the whole story by picking up a sailor on a train between New York and Hartford. He had given his wife an amber ring out of the profits on the story, he said."

The story, "Faith at Sea," had been published by *The New Yorker* the previous May; the play was the one Shaw had started in Jerusalem, about the muddy politics of North Africa and the assassination of Admiral Darlan.

Shaw had a title for the play now: *The Assassin.* He worried aloud, in social gatherings such as the one Barry Bingham had described, that its political slant would cause it to be censored, and with only one copy of his working draft, he worried even more about losing it. (As a precaution, he began to make carbons of what he wrote, and stored them in a friend's apartment.)

"There were different social sets in the West End," says William Walton, then a correspondent in the London office of *Time,* "and to a great extent those were determined by the women who were there." Pamela Churchill, unofficially separated from Winston's callow son, Randolph, was a prominent figure around town, dating Averell Harriman, whom she would later marry, among others. Helen Kirkpatrick, a Chicago *Daily-News* correspondent, was a tall, Amazonian presence, attractive but slightly square, a favorite of many older journalists. Connie Ernst, who would later marry book editor Simon Michael Bessie, was another central figure, full of fun; like many of the American women on the scene, she worked for OWI, the Office of War Information. And then there was Connie Ernst's roommate, Mary Welsh.

Welsh was another of the *Time* correspondents, a short and shapely woman with a soft voice but lots of spunk. "If you were in a tough spot, she would be there for you," recalls Lael Tucker Wertenbaker, also of *Time,* whose husband, Charles Christian Wertenbaker, had come over to manage *Time*'s invasion team. "She was very courageous, and I think that's one reason she was so attractive to men. And she was very able. Not brilliant, but able. Tough, in a good sense. And trim. She had a lovely torso, and the most marvelous curly hair. You could do anything with that hair." Two men, that year, took a particular interest in Mary Welsh: Irwin Shaw and Ernest Hemingway.

Since Hemingway hadn't yet arrived, Shaw had the head start. Soon enough he was paying regular visits to Welsh's penthouse apartment on Grosvenor Square—penthouses were the cheapest apartments in London and the easiest to find, because of the danger from air raids—and, in that war-torn time, conducting a more serious relationship than many. Even so, the rule was no rules, and so on at least one occasion Welsh found herself balancing Shaw with another paramour. Walton, whose desk abutted hers in the *Time* office, remembers a morning when Welsh came staggering in, muttering about "the most awful night" she'd ever had. It seemed that at nine the previous evening, someone had come across the roof to her cottagelike penthouse apartment and started knocking on her door. "And there I was in bed with Irwin Shaw," moaned Welsh. What was worse, the man at the door turned out to be her other lover, General Robert McClure. The general kept knocking, until finally Welsh had to get up and tell him to go away—without letting him in. "Irwin was terrified, especially because he was so rank-conscious, and McClure was a rather possessive lover. But finally she got him to leave." Adds Walton: "Mary said to me once that Irwin was the best lay in Europe. The two weren't faithful to each other, but they did have an on-again, off-again thing for months, which was considerable in a time and place in which the prevailing attitude was that you really might die tomorrow, so have fun today." (Shaw's sexual prowess seemed to inspire such absolutes: a few years later, a blithely promiscuous woman declared to Carol Saroyan and Oona Chaplin over lunch at "21" that Shaw was the best lay in Hollywood.)

As spring came on, Shaw and Welsh would often join other *Time* employees at the bureau's country retreat, a Tudor-style house in the town of Little Missenden, near High Wycombe. Along with Capa and Saroyan, they would take walks or bicycle rides through the Buckinghamshire countryside, then drink and play poker well into the night. When talk turned to the invasion, as it often did, the revelers had sharply divergent reactions. Capa was making training jumps with a parachute outfit, and fully planning to see D-Day in that fashion. Shaw too was eager to join the first wave, but more sensibly intended to do it by boat. Saroyan remained adamantly antiwar and made no bones about his intention to stay right in London whenever the big day dawned.

By now Lieutenant Colonel Stevens's Special Coverage Unit had become operational. A converted apartment building on Davies Street near Claridge's was used for administrative offices; cutting and editing was done at the Pinewood Studios; and the men were mostly billeted in private homes in the West End, where cots replaced family furniture. Shaw, still in his fancier digs, spent the weekdays on routine assignments, covering military ceremonies, installations and the like. Neither he nor his colleagues ever saw the footage they shot; their completed rolls were shipped directly back to a lab in New York and then either used as briefing information in Washington or spun into newsreels for the theatergoing public. Shaw was one of the unit's four writers whose job it was to write in strong detail what the silent films represented, to give them their context so that the War Department would know what they were about—and to type it all in triplicate.

Saroyan was another of the writers. So was Leicester Hemingway, a blustery and rather pathetic figure spooked by his famous brother. "Leicester wanted to emulate his brother," recalls the unit's fourth writer, Ivan Moffat. "He felt the war would give him the equipment to be a writer, and of course it didn't. He was restless, and ostentatiously wanted to see action. Ultimately, he left the unit for a job in an infantry unit and became a cameraman." Moffat himself was an American-born son of wealthy, artistic parents in London; he had been shepherded into the unit on John Huston's recommendation. Wry and urbane, Moffat, twenty-four, introduced the older Shaw and Saroyan to the private Gargoyle Club on Dean Street, where they spent a convivial evening with Dylan Thomas and Arnold Toynbee. On another occasion he brought them over to meet Cyril Connolly, who studiously ignored the all-American Shaw and then provoked him further by remarking to Moffat, "You're not going over on that silly invasion, are you?"

Despite his unmilitary bearing and disrespect for officers, Shaw felt as patriotically eager for D-Day as any small-town American soldier, and as clear that the war was just. It was an attitude that put him even more at odds with the young playwright of *Bury the Dead* and rendered the FBI's continuing suspicion of him not only unfair but absurd. It also left him impatient with Saroyan, whose strident antimilitary sentiments struck Shaw (and most others) as nothing more than self-pity.

That spring Shaw took a tour of the Allies' coastal installations and in an unpublished account wrote of the tanks and antiaircraft guns that seemed toylike in the peaceful English countryside, and of the British officers manning them who seemed more like householders pushing lawn mowers in their gardens. He saw military exercises conducted with live fire; nearby, white-uniformed cricketeers, unfazed, swung their bats. Underlying the casual chat of the soldiers he interviewed, however, was the same grim determination he himself felt.

On another occasion, Shaw and Stevens saw the preparations from a closer view. As head of a unit that General Eisenhower had personally sanctioned, Stevens was "bigoted"—allowed into high-level military meetings—and to one such meeting he apparently brought Shaw. Dramatically, an officer pulled the curtain from a standing easel to reveal the actual plans for the invasion. Stunned, Shaw and Stevens made a pact not to go out drinking in any public place from then until D-Day, for fear of spilling the beans.

This hardly put an end to Shaw's nightlife, of course. There were still poker parties at Capa's place—he and Pinky had now moved to a penthouse at 26 Lowndes Square—and doubtless a few pact-breaking pub stops along the way. Then, in mid-May, Ernest Hemingway arrived as the *Collier's* reporter for the invasion, whenever and wherever it would take place. Soon after came the fateful lunch at the White Tower, when Shaw found himself introducing Hemingway to Mary Welsh.

Welsh and her roommate, Connie Ernst, had established a sort of Friday lunch salon at the White Tower, on the sensible premise that one of the six or eight men they invited would pick up the tab. On this day, Shaw was lunching with Welsh when Hemingway, looking uncomfortably hot in a woolen RAF uniform, lumbered by en route to his own table. Welsh looked striking that day, in a man's suit she'd had tailored to fit her—the suit in fact belonged to her husband of the time, Noel Monks, who was reporting on the war in the South Pacific for the London *Daily Mail*—and even more so when the heat forced her to remove her jacket, revealing a tight white sweater over her ample bust. "Introduce me to your friend, Shaw," Hemingway said shyly. Shaw complied, and then sat back as the two worked out a lunch date. "Well, it's been nice knowing you," Shaw said as he watched Hemingway walk off.

"You off somewhere?" Welsh asked innocently.

"A monopoly has just been born, you dummy. The Soho answer to DeBeers diamonds."

In truth, Shaw felt somewhat relieved to think Mary Welsh might be taken off his hands so easily. Carefree as she liked to appear, she was growing more serious about him, and Shaw had no interest now in breaking up his marriage; an ocean apart from Marian, he actually felt fonder of her, for all this, than he had since he'd married her. Nor did he yet have any reason to question the admiration he'd felt for Hemingway since his Brooklyn adolescence. There was even a certain masculine pride in discovering that Hemingway was taken with a woman Shaw had known first.

That changed within the week, when Shaw brought Welsh over for drinks to Charles Wertenbaker's suite at the Dorchester. Hemingway held forth with boastful stories and grew increasingly drunk. As Welsh left on her own, he announced that he would come visit her later that evening. He did just that, settling himself on one of the twin beds in Welsh's room and reminiscing about his childhood to Welsh and Connie Ernst. Upon his departure he announced, "I don't know you, Mary. But I want to marry you." From then on, he would view Shaw only with the bitterness of a romantic rival for Welsh's affections. Shaw, for his part, would feel increasing impatience with the famous Hemingway machismo.

As it turned out, both Hemingway and Shaw missed out on D-Day, just a fortnight after that.

For Hemingway, it was a car accident suffered after a wild party thrown for him by Bob Capa on May 24 that put him in the hospital with a concussion and a lacerated scalp; on the morning of June 6, he was still recovering. (Martha Gellhorn scoffed at his condition when she came to visit, which ended their marriage. Mary Welsh came bearing flowers and sympathy, which in a sense started theirs.) For Shaw, it was a heartbreaking mixup in orders. Most of Stevens's unit was to remain in London until the Allies took control of Normandy's shores, but a core group, including

Stevens himself, had obtained permission to make a D-Day crossing on the British cruiser *Belfast*. Shaw was to be part of the group. At the last minute, however, he learned that the British transport orders failed to include him.

The only consolation was that no one in Stevens's group actually accompanied the troops onto the French shores. Nor did another small Signal Corps group on the destroyer *Algonquin* that included Captain Irving Reis. Both groups remained well offshore as transport ships discharged amphibious tankloads of soldiers onto the beaches renamed for the invasion—Utah, Omaha, Gold, Sword—then returned to London. One of the only photographers who did wade ashore was Capa, who braved bullets at Omaha Beach to gain priceless pictures, only to have his film ruined back in Time-Life's London lab by an overly nervous lab assistant. *Life* ran the blurred pictures anyway, but a deeply bitter Capa never quite recovered from the heartbreak of the loss, and ironically titled his autobiography *Slightly Out of Focus*.

In the unreal days that followed, Shaw and other members of the Signal Corps unit remained restlessly in London, listening to broadcasts of the fierce fighting across the Channel, and to firsthand reports from the Stevens and Reis groups. (According to cameraman Ken Marthey, who accompanied him on the initial Channel crossing, a terrified Reis sought the first excuse to return to London via a high-speed press boat bearing film footage of the invasion; then, as Moffat recalls, the captain spent the next days bragging of his courage at the Little French Club. Says Moffat dryly: "There was a lot more boasting than bravery in that unit.") On June 13 the first German V-1 flying bombs reached London. Two or three days later, Moffat recalls, the unit departed London by bus to the campaign's staging area in Southampton. Missing from the group was Saroyan, who had declared his talents were better put to use in London and somehow persuaded military authorities to let him remain there throughout the Normandy campaign in order to write a novel based on his military experiences.

Now there was another wait of several more days, as the men lounged in camouflaged tents discreetly nestled in a pine forest, and traded talk of what they hoped to do after the war. Shaw, for one, busied himself by taking careful notes for the war novel he now fully intended to write. On or about June 21 the unit boarded a converted freighter, along with a battalion of 1,200 engineers, for a slow and grueling five-day trip across the Channel.

The first clue that the voyage would be unpleasant came with the latrine setup. Two outdoor canvas-and-wood latrines were rigged to overhang either side of the ship: the men were to use one or the other, depending on which way the wind blew. During the loading process a jeep smashed into one of them, rendering it unusable; inevitably, the other was the one the wind blew *toward,* resulting in a pervasive stench throughout the trip. Worse, there were only 400 bunks in the airless hold below deck. The 1,200 men thus had to use the beds on a rotating basis, and at any given time there were 800 men above, huddled out in the open. But officers, among whom was numbered George Stevens, ranked private sleeping quarters. During almost every one of Shaw's on-deck shifts it rained. During every one of Stevens's shifts the rain seemed to stop, a phenomenon about which Shaw and the others kidded their superior officer at every chance. Still, as the freighter approached Normandy's beaches, a somber mood prevailed. On deck, Shaw looked out over the gunwale and then turned to Moffat. "A lot of men died on those beaches," he said.

After waiting a final day offshore, the unit disembarked before dawn at Utah Beach, the westernmost of the four D-Day landing sites and in fact one of relatively little resistance and few casualties. It was, however, one of the thinnest points along the Allied line of battle. The men had barely reached their first assigned area, a meadow near the town of Carentan, when three German shells landed in an airfield just across the road from them, no more than sixty yards away. Foxholes were hurriedly dug, each some thirty feet from the next. Shaw looked up from his own labors to see Stevens digging too, and once again was struck by the director's quiet brand of selflessness. It was a rare lieutenant colonel who didn't have his subordinates dig his foxhole for him.

In Stevens's case, there was even more to it than that. The director had a serious asthma condition—another factor, besides his age, that would have kept him out of service if he'd let it. Those first days in Normandy, it rained almost constantly, and the men were forced to remain in their foxholes, huddled under pup tents. Stevens's asthma kept him suffering most of that time, and with the nearby battery of Allied antiaircraft guns that blasted away almost unceasingly, the director got no sleep for days. Still, he maintained the deadpan humor that had infused his prewar films. Receiving a letter one day at mail call, he opened it and read it without expression, then turned to a circle of soldiers that included Shaw. "Everyone, I'd like you to look at this," he said. The letter was a statement of his profits that month from the ongoing success of *The Talk of the Town*. The figure: about $17,000. "And that," he said solemnly to Shaw, "is only for one month." Shaw, who'd spent almost four months writing the script for a one-time fee of $10,000, was stunned.

Stevens appointed Shaw the unit's liaison with the Twelfth Army Group under General Patton. Each evening in those first weeks after digging in, Shaw would take a jeep to headquarters and find out what troop movement or battle point should be covered the next day; often he ran into Capa on these errands, and the two eagerly swapped news. Most of the unit would go off in jeep teams of four—two cameramen, one writer and a driver—with a small trailer hitched on behind to carry supplies. With one exception the cameramen used 35-millimeter eyemos and shot fifty-foot rolls of black-and-white film. The exception was Stevens's team. Back in London, the unit's liberal-minded supply sergeant had "liberated" a cache of 16-millimeter color film that could be used with Stevens's personal 16-millimeter camera. Stevens had actually filmed D-Day in color—the only color film of the invasion that exists—and went on now to capture the entire Normandy campaign and the liberation of Paris in color as well. Because the film was also longer than standard black-and-white, Stevens was able to send back footage that showed more sustained action. Oddly enough, that footage was never made into a film and remains in archives today, a startling yet all-but-forgotten record.

Shaw was in a jeep team with cameramen Richard Hoar Kent and Ken Marthey that began to make tentative forays north into the Cotentin peninsula behind the Allies as they pushed up toward Cherbourg. By June 29 Cherbourg was won, and Shaw's team became one of the first to film the port city's utter destruction. "The whole city was a shambles," recalls William Walton. "The water system had been bombed along with most of the buildings. The night before, I'd slept in a shell hole with Wert [Charles Wertenbaker] and Capa, who spent the whole night playing gin rummy on top of me, and I was so exhausted I slept through the whole thing. Anyway, I remember Irwin walking around on the docks the next day, wearing an ill-fitting winter-issue coat."

A week later Shaw's team recorded a bizarre Fourth of July celebration. Every available artillery gun in the English and American forces all along the front was fired simultaneously at noon; and in the chosen spot near Cherbourg, Generals Montgomery, Bradley, Patton and Eisenhower marked the occasion as a battery of 105s went off behind them. After an invasion of such tactical cleverness, the notion of putting all the Allied generals in one place, within firing distance of the Germans, seemed lunacy to Shaw and other journalists covering the event.

From Cherbourg, Shaw and his jeep team drove east along the D-Day beaches and up to Le Havre to record that city's even greater devastation from Allied bombing attacks. By July 9 they had driven south to record the critical victory at Caen as British and Canadian troops rolled in after long weeks of battle. The rubble was three stories high, and all the towns-people had been evacuated except for the old and the sick, who had been sequestered on the floor of a large church. Shaw and Stevens were among those who removed the helpless people one by one under continuing shell fire—one of the many images of the campaign that would reappear in The Young Lions.

Most days Shaw's team was on its own, and when it was, Shaw was technically in charge. "We moved wherever we saw fit," recalls Ken Marthey. "We had these Eisenhower passes—hell, we could have flown back to the States with that pass if we'd wanted to." They stayed behind battle lines, but faced the still considerable danger of random snipers or skirmishes. Also, says Marthey, "we did have to worry about land mines. We were told not to drive off the road—more mines were planted there than on the roads already traveled—and as a further precaution we put sandbags in the bottom of the jeep. Chances are, a mine would have upturned the jeep anyway." Once at least, Shaw did get shot at. "A bullet went . . . right behind my neck and under the chin of the guy in the jeep beside me," he recounted years later.

Sometimes at the end of a day the men pitched their pup tents in a field and relied on army rations for dinner. They found accommodations in the little French towns they passed through and traded their rations for freshly cooked omelets. Shaw was the negotiator in these happy transactions. Though he'd learned his French in public school and spoke it with his strong Brooklyn accent, he had a fairly good grasp of the language, certainly better than Kent's or Marthey's.

On one occasion, though, Shaw used his French to a less felicitous end. Recalls Marthey: "I do remember that in one town we passed through with Irwin, the townspeople had rounded up women collaborators and shaved their heads. They were about to herd them from the town hall into a police van. Irwin with his very good French talked to the townspeople, and they agreed to transfer them at our convenience—so we could film it. Irwin, I remember, was responsible for setting the van at a greater distance from the building, so that the women ran through a longer gauntlet—spat on and punched and shouted at."

After that Shaw's team drove back west to St.-Lô, as American troops at last overcame fierce German defenses in the third week of July. Along the way they ran into Capa, who hitched a ride in their jeep and told Shaw he never wanted to take pictures again after hearing how the D-Day film had been ruined; before the ride was over, he was snapping away. Another day the team drove into a town no Allies had yet entered and approached a happy throng in the town square. As Shaw stood up in the jeep to declare the town liberated, he looked up at a balcony to see a familiar-looking Frenchman already addressing the crowd. After a moment, he realized it was French actor Claude Dauphin, later to be a close friend.

On July 25 the Allies launched their big push west from St.-Lô into Brittany. For the Special Coverage jeep units, that meant fanning out across the broadening front for an extended period on their own. One of the first towns Shaw's team visited was Granville, on the Normandy coast just north of Mont-St.-Michel. At a hilltop castle, artillery shells dangled outside on wires—booby traps left by the Germans. Shaw's cameramen recorded the efforts of a special Navy squad to demine the castle while on the streets below, thousands of German prisoners went rolling by in trucks to prisoner-of-war stockades. Most memorable, though, was the afternoon Shaw and his team drove up to Mont-St.-Michel.

To four young Americans who'd never seen it, the medieval fortress town perched at the water's edge looked like a castle out of a Walt Disney movie. The Germans who had occupied it as an air-raid station since 1940 had left two days before; some fifty holdouts were camped nearby, or so the Americans were told by the small band of indignant townspeople who greeted them at the gates. Politely, Shaw and his comrades declined to pursue the Germans at that very moment, and instead arranged to stay at a hotel halfway up the town's winding cobblestoned streets. They ate omelets on the hotel's terrace and watched the famous tide come in. That evening German bomber planes roared overhead, using Mont-St.-Michel as a guiding point to drop their loads over Avranches to the right, St.-Malo to the left. Then, as if for the Americans' own macabre entertainment, two German planes burst into flames and fell from the sky, one on the beach within two miles of the town. That night Shaw was awakened by gunfire outside his window. Alarmed at the thought that Germans might be returning, he and Kent took posts by the window and door. Shaw, at the door, heard figures rustling toward him up the stairs. He raised his carbine with his finger on the trigger, and then watched, weak with relief, as three priests swept silently by.

When Shaw and his team reported back to Stevens a few days later, they recounted their adventures so glowingly that the director felt jealous enough to reassign Shaw to a new team and go with Marthey and Kent himself. Perhaps it was Shaw who brought the good luck; now with cameramen Philip Drell and Pinckney Ridgell, and a young driver from Boston named Angelo Tempesta, who before the war had worked as an iceman in summer and a coal man in winter, Shaw ran right into more adventure, this time nearly getting shot by an American MP in St.-Malo.

The city had no sooner been wrested from the Germans than Shaw's team drove in with cameras rolling. Learning that a band of holdouts remained on the tiny offshore island of Cezembre, they rushed over to find an American colonel setting out in a rowboat to negotiate the surrender. Shaw persuaded the colonel to let Ridgell and Drell accompany him to film the event. While Shaw watched through binoculars from the pier, the three cautiously approached the island, white flag held aloft, and managed to put ashore without incident. Leaving the cameras discreetly in the boat for the moment, they walked bravely across open land to the island's garrison to meet the German commander. The commander, it turned out, was in no mood to negotiate. Furious, he gave the three just minutes to get to their boat and hurriedly row back. The team nevertheless gathered footage of St.-Malo, and Shaw elected to pass the completed rolls to another unit member at a prearranged street corner. Unfortunately, the local Army commander had decreed that no one could stop in St.-Malo because of continuing danger from German snipers. Shaw, standing at his street corner, was promptly picked up by MPs and brought to Eighth Division headquarters. A tough sergeant listened as Shaw explained heatedly why he had to get back to the street corner. Then he took out his pistol. "If you try to leave this room," said the sergeant, "I'll shoot you." Placed under house arrest, Shaw succeeded in convincing a corporal clerk to convey his plight to the nearest general. The general signed an order allowing Shaw to remain in St.-Malo long enough to make his rendezvous; then Shaw, wasting no time, got the hell out of town.

Throughout August the westward push continued, as the Germans retreated to Brittany's port cities: Brest, Lorient and St.-Nazaire. With the taking of Caen to the east, however, the more inexorable push was toward Paris. One by one, Stevens's jeep teams turned east and began the head-long journey to reach Paris in time for its inevitable liberation. Shaw's team alternated between General Hodges's First Army and General Patton's Third Army as German resistance melted into full-scale retreat. The question became not whether the Allies would take Paris, but which of its armies—the Americans under Patton or the French under General Leclerc—would earn a higher place in history by being the first to march into the city.

Leclerc won that fight, and with German forces inside Paris routed by the French Resistance, liberation was scheduled for August 25. By the night of the twenty-fourth, Stevens's unit had assembled in the outlying town of Rambouillet, twenty-three miles southwest of Paris, along with dozens of other excited journalists. One was Hemingway, who startled Shaw's cameraman Pinckney Ridgell by parading around his hotel room in the nude as he questioned a respectful circle of French informers. ("I guess he hadn't bothered to dress after a shower.") When Hemingway ran into Shaw, he couldn't resist laying down a challenge. "I have a motorcycle," he said. "Let's look for Germans and draw fire." In light of the fact that the Germans were retreating, Shaw found this a pointless risk and said as much. That night he and his team were taken in for the night by a French plumber, who not only cooked them omelets but brought up his best wine from the cellar.

The order had gone out from General Leclerc that only French journalists were to accompany his tank division into Paris the next morning, but the Americans at Rambouillet conveniently ignored him. Robert Capa talked his way through a phalanx of French soldiers who turned out to have fought for the Loyalists in the same Spanish Civil War battles he had covered. He and Wertenbaker and their jeep driver snaked up through Leclerc's tanks and rode through the Porte d'Orléans right behind the French general at 9:40 A.M., the uncontested first Americans to do so. Not far behind was Shaw's own team, in a jeep covered with flowers from the cheering crowds.

It was a day Shaw would call the high point of his life, one of unparalleled drama and emotion, and also the start of a lifelong love affair with

Paris. As his jeep made its way through a city miraculously undamaged—in the face of certain defeat, the German commander, General Choltitz, had disobeyed Hitler's hysterical order to put up a fierce fight for the city, and instead retreated in order to save it—he shared his comrades' amazement at it all, and at the incongruity of having been in New York scant months before. More than his jeepmates, Shaw also thrilled to the city's literary heritage, to the ghosts of Balzac and Stendhal, and to the more recent echoes of the Lost Generation sipping Pernod at the open cafés along the Seine.

Shaw's team came into Paris with the American Twelfth Regiment as it made its way past Notre-Dame. Its first task was to photograph General de Gaulle's arrival, footage that became part of history. After that the team took off on its own, up the right bank of the Seine toward the sound of artillery fire. At the Louvre, Shaw and cameraman Drell left Ridgell and their driver with the jeep, and set off on foot for the rue de Rivoli. The resistance, they learned, was as much from French Vichy forces as from Germans. Snipers were keeping up a tattoo of fire, and Shaw and Drell were forced to duck into a building that turned out to be the Comédie Française. In the lobby they came upon a makeshift hospital, with the newly wounded being attended, for the most part, by beautiful actresses serving as nurses.

Shaw and Drell returned to the jeep and drove toward another burst of fire, this one from the Chambre des Députés building on the Left Bank, facing the Seine and one of its graceful bridges. From within, a diehard German contingent was firing mortar shells at regular intervals around the place de la Concorde. A resourceful French officer on the other side of the bridge put a German prisoner with a white flag on top of a tank and got in to drive it across. To Shaw's amazement, Drell ran out ahead of the tank to snap pictures of the proceedings—including the later famous images of French women with their skirts billowing in the breeze, hiding behind nearby monuments. When the mortar fire continued, the French officer abandoned the tank and ran the rest of the way toward the Chambre des Députés, accompanied by Drell. Some time later, when the firing from the building had stopped, Shaw ventured over himself to discover that some 400 Germans had surrendered, and that Drell had been the one who first came upon them. They had, in fact, tried to surrender to him, but Drell preferred to have them wait for the French officer to arrive, so he could photograph the occasion.

Later that day Shaw and his cameramen reported in with their film to the Hôtel Scribe, the declared headquarters for all working journalists. Exultant but weary, they registered for two large rooms and took long baths, not minding at all that the only running water was stone cold except for a few designated hours a week, when all the correspondents would rush to shower and shave at once. By cocktail hour, the Scribe's bar was packed with delirious journalists. There Shaw and his jeepmates heard the story of how George Stevens had talked his way into German headquarters with his camera rolling just as the German command was surrendering to General Leclerc. Stevens had filmed the historic moment the same way he did everything else: calmly, coolly, without a hint of emotion.

At Stevens's invitation, Shaw moved the next day into his large suite at the Scribe, to be joined by the late-arriving William Saroyan. The Time Inc. crew—Capa, Wertenbaker, Walton and the rest—fled the hubbub to the more quietly elegant Lancaster, while Hemingway established his own beachhead with Mary Welsh at the Ritz, in large part because the Ritz was the only place in Paris where readily available hot water was to be found. In a fine display of hot-water one-upmanship, however, Shaw got himself invited by another guest at the Ritz, Marlene Dietrich, to take a bath in *her* suite; the two had known each other from Hollywood, and Dietrich was now in Paris entertaining troops for the USO. That evening, Shaw and Dietrich were taken to a lavish dinner by A. J. Liebling on his *New Yorker* expense account, at the end of which Dietrich softly sang songs over coffee and brandy.

Most evenings the various contingents continued to gather at the Scribe, or at the Ritz bar, which was where David Schoenbrun, then a young correspondent for the Overseas News Agency, found them on one of those memorable August nights. "Mike Bessie was waiting for me, Schoenbrun later wrote, "at a table presided over by the broad-shouldered, deep-chested Ernest 'Papa' Hemingway. Despite his dominant personality, Papa was having difficulty controlling the conversation of a dynamic, highly talented group of friends. Robert Capa, *Life* photographer . . . was evaluating critically some of the American generals he had covered in combat. He felt that Bradley was too cautious, Patton too reckless. At his side was his closest friend, ever since the Spanish Civil War, David Seymour, known as Chim, a gentle man, whose large, wide, bald head and smoked glasses made him look like a mad scientist. . . . Next to Chim was Irwin Shaw . . . [and] sitting opposite Irwin was Paddy Chayefsky, another talented writer who would win fame and fortune after the war with films like *Marty* and *Network*. . . . From the Ritz we walked across the Seine to the Left Bank and devoured thick sandwiches at a brasserie on the Boul' Mich'. Then we went to a cellar club for wine and listened to a succession of chansonniers, who sang political and drinking songs. We all joined in on songs we knew and hummed those we didn't. The four-centuries-old stone walls of the cellar echoed with the music and the voices of a hundred men and women. . . . Rarely in life do dreams come true. They did for me that night in liberated Paris."

Like most of his rejoicing companions, Shaw saw the liberation of Paris as a symbolic end to the war, and felt sure the Germans would surrender that autumn. With an almost playful sense of purpose, he and

Stevens and the rest of the Special Coverage Unit established a headquarters in a loft at 47 rue Lauriston, near the Arc de Triomphe, from which they could sally off on short jeep trips to film mop-up operations in the outlying towns. Paris was so much fun that the military authorities were having a hard time pushing units out to the still active front to the east; and they proved no match for the quietly stubborn Stevens, who kept the unit based in Paris well into the next year.

Shaw's longest trip that fall was from Paris to Marseilles, then along the French coast to the Italian border and back north along the Alsatian border. As before, the film he and his cameramen produced was shipped back from Paris to New York for use in newsreels and documentaries, and in many instances remains the only moving-picture record of those historic moments at that penultimate turning point of the war in Europe.

With Stevens's strong recommendation, Shaw was finally given a modest promotion to warrant officer that fall. It made no real difference in his day-to-day duties, but it did provoke a few amusing reactions. Angelo Tempesta, Shaw's driver, took a long look at the black-striped bar on his friend's shirt collar and said, "So what am I supposed to do now, give you a goddamn salute?" In the Scribe bar Hemingway referred to him snidely as "Monsieur le Maréchal," and he informed the waiters at one restaurant that Shaw's rank was the result of his being the illegitimate son of President Coolidge. Recalls veteran correspondent Drew Middleton: "We used to call Irwin 'Marshal' after that; we'd say, 'Marshal, it's your turn to buy the drinks.' He'd get a great kick out of that."

Hemingway's gruffness toward Shaw had taken on a nasty edge, thanks to Mary Welsh. Welsh made no secret of her unabated physical attraction for Shaw. On at least one occasion she even taunted Hemingway by declaring that Shaw had a bigger penis than he did. She seems not to have reported an emotional talk with Shaw at the Ritz bar, in which she flatly asked Shaw to marry her. "I'm already married," Shaw replied, trying to joke it off. Well, she retorted, if Shaw wouldn't marry her, she'd marry Hemingway instead.

That November Shaw went home. The war was still on and he was still in the Army, but he felt the European campaign must be about to end and, as he told Stevens, he wanted to rest up before presumably going off to cover the invasion of Japan. (He was wrong, of course, on both counts: the terrible Battle of the Bulge in Germany would start soon after his departure, and Hiroshima and Nagasaki would put an end to war in the Pacific.) By Thanksgiving he was happily reunited with Marian in the apartment she had moved into early in the war, at 225 East 74th Street. Having borne witness to all the human cruelties of the European campaign, Shaw was delighted to be a subway commando again, and to spend mundane days in Astoria cutting footage the unit had sent back, for documentaries and newsreels about the European campaign. In December he wrote to Philip Drell, who was still in Paris, that he'd grown unashamedly lazy, sleeping late, dining on sirloin steaks, guzzling down good red wine.

There was also time to reflect. In an essayistic piece for *Saturday Review of Literature* in February, "If You Write About the War," Shaw declared he felt sorry for writers who had served in the war, but sorrier for those who hadn't. The war, after all, had become the seminal experience for an entire generation, and writers would be obliged to interpret its impact for years to come. It stood to reason that the best books about the war would be written by those who had seen the bloodshed firsthand; but because of that, Shaw suggested, they would be produced by young writers as yet unknown, writers who may have done no writing at all before they put on their uniforms. A writer of this war would be a boy who "struggled anonymously through the abuse and horror of a rifle company, trying only to survive, like the men around him, through the death and monotony . . . a man who has suffered the full measure of the common experience from Fort Benning to Tokyo, and suffered it not as a notetaker and observer, as any writer inevitably must, but with the same sense of personal, submerged persecution and wry humor as all the men around him." Nor, added Shaw, would he write "like Hemingway or like Remarque, because that was another war, and even though all wars must be considerably alike, there must also be a style for their differences."

These were gracious observations, considering that the very well-known Shaw was already planning his own big war novel. They were also eerily prophetic. Norman Mailer's *The Naked and the Dead* would mark the stunning debut of a twenty-five-year-old writer who had lived through the war. Even truer to Shaw's portrait would be his future close friend, James Jones.

For nearly a year Shaw had been struggling to bring *The Assassin* to the stage. In London, before the invasion, he had submitted it to the military censors, as required, and sweated out their verdict that the play could indeed be produced in England with one absurdly minor change: a passing reference to a Greek whore should be amended to a mention of a whore of Spanish extraction, since England was then allied with Greece. Finally, in March 1945, producer Marcel Varnel brought *The Assassin* to London's Savoy Theatre. Sydney Gruson, then a young *New York Times* correspondent, reported that "where the provinces had been only lukewarm, the first-night audience at the Savoy Theatre gave the play a hearty reception." Also at the opening was American critic W. A. Darlington, who declared this piece of "stage journalism" likely to have a good run, and added that "the Shaw offering has too much human feeling and too much topical interest about it to run any risk of swift failure." The fact that the play had opened was, in truth, more newsworthy than the play itself; it was the first political play to be staged in London in some time, and the first about the war by an American who had been overseas. That it had opened in London before New York was, at the time, no less remarkable. All these considerations served to whet the appetites of American theater for the play's arrival in the fall.

Shaw headed back to Europe in May for one last wartime hurrah before *The Assassin* made its way west to New York. This time he was assigned to work for another Hollywood director, Anatole Litvak, on a film about the retraining of American troops in Europe for the expected invasion of Japan.

The Russian-born Litvak had been an entrenched member of Hollywood's new émigré set before the war, his success already established with films like *Mayerling* with Charles Boyer, and *Flight in Darkness,* made in France in the mid-thirties. Upon arriving in Hollywood he had married actress Miriam Hopkins and made more successful films, *Tovarich* and *Confessions of a Nazi Spy* among them. Like Stevens and Capra, he had put aside his burgeoning career at post–draft age (he was nearing forty when the war broke out) to help make wartime documentaries. He was a difficult man—arrogant, with a Russian stubbornness to match his accent—but he and Shaw would remain combative friends and sometimes colleagues until Litvak's death some thirty years later.

Almost as soon as Shaw and Litvak arrived in Paris, the shooting plan changed. The French had survived their quick bout of gratitude to the American forces and wanted to know why the Americans felt obliged to make use of French railroads to mass troops and supplies for the Japanese invasion. A film, perhaps, would help them see why. To help, Litvak rounded up two other capable hands: Broadway producer, director and writer Josh Logan, and French writer Maurice Druon, whose novels would eventually earn him a place in the Académie Française.

While a shooting itinerary was being drawn up, Shaw had several joyful reunions in Paris. One was with George Stevens, to whom Shaw was able to report that he had turned one of the lieutenant colonel's wartime anecdotes into a short story. "Part in a Play," about a failing French actor who achieves his dreams of stardom by performing as a collaborationist in Nazi Paris, appeared that July in *Collier's.* Another was with Peter Viertel, who had just driven a jeep over from Austria. Viertel, it turned out, had had a far rougher war than Shaw. Having joined the Marines soon after Pearl Harbor, he had been sent to the Pacific and endured an unusually brutal series of front-line assignments. Only later did he learn he'd earned the rough treatment by referring to his officers as fascists in letters to Jigee. The letters, of course, had been read by Navy Intelligence. Viertel had tapped family connections to reach no less than Secretary of the Navy James Forrestal, and had had the black mark expunged from his record. Eventually he had found his way to Europe, working as a Marine officer in tactical intelligence behind enemy lines in France and Germany because of his fluency in both languages. "I found out Irwin was in Paris through Bill Walton," says Viertel. "We met up like two happy idiots."

Capa surfaced too, and that particular reunion had one very specific result. On June 6, Capa and Shaw learned that Ingrid Bergman was coming to Paris that day and would be staying at the Ritz before embarking on a USO tour of Germany. By the time she arrived, there was a note under her door that read:

Subject: Dinner. 6.6.45. Paris. France
To: Miss Ingrid Bergman.
Part 1. This is a community effort. The community consists of Bob Capa and Irwin Shaw.
    2. We were planning on sending you flowers with this note inviting you to dinner this evening—but after consultation we discovered it was possible to pay for the flowers or the dinner, or the dinner or the flowers, not both. We took a vote and dinner won by a close margin.
    3. It was suggested that if you did not care for dinner, flowers might be sent. No decision has been reached on this so far.
    4. Besides flowers we have lots of doubtful qualities.
    5. If we write much more we will have no conversation left, as our supply of charm is limited.
    6. We will call you at 6.15.
    7. We do not sleep.
Signed:
Worried.

Bergman had never heard of either Capa or Shaw, but was charmed into coming to dinner. Unfortunately for Shaw, she was charmed in a somewhat more dramatic way by Capa. The evening marked the start of a torrid romance between the actress and the photographer, with Capa following her to Berlin and back to the States before the affair collapsed nearly two years later. Sometime in that first whirlwind week, a memorably awkward moment occurred at a lunch in St.-Germain-des-Prés. Present were Shaw, Capa, Bergman and three other friends, including Bill Graffis, a wartime buddy of Shaw's. Perhaps because Bergman had so clearly chosen Capa over him, Shaw made remarks that betrayed a certain self-consciousness about being Jewish. That, he suggested, might be one reason why he had achieved only the modest rank of warrant officer, and was wearing the uniform he had on that day. "Listen," Capa retorted, "you are lucky just to have a uniform and to be alive in it." Recalls Graffis: "It was an almost embarrassing snub." Shaw, his vanity wounded by the whole affair, referred to Bergman ever after as "that cow!"

As for the filmmaking mission, it devolved into a glorious junket. From Paris the crew drove east to Germany, passing through Cologne, Bonn and Munich, and ending up in Berchtesgaden, Hitler's Bavarian mountain retreat. "All that while," recalls Pinckney Ridgell, who went along as a cameraman, "we were filming at Litvak's direction—and a brusque direction that was. He was white-haired, short and gruff. But somehow—I guess because he was a well-known director by then—he had beautiful girls, actresses many of them, appear out of nowhere wherever we stopped." The crew finished filming just as President Truman sanctioned the bombing of Japan; with the Japanese surrender on August 15, the entire project was shelved.

Shaw returned to New York in time to help producers Carly Wharton and Martin Gabel start rehearsals for *The Assassin* with a cast that included Frank Sundstrom, Richard Keith and an also just returned Karl Malden, with sets by Boris Aronson. On October 13 he was discharged from the Army; the date also marked his sixth wedding anniversary, six years of a marriage in which more time had been spent apart than together. Four days later *The Assassin* opened on Broadway. For Shaw, it ushered in peacetime with a rude and painful shock.

CHAPTER NINE

Almost as if the war had been only a bad dream, the writers of Shaw's generation put their uniforms away and reveled in the mundane pleasures of peacetime. "One week after I put on the gray suit," Shaw exclaimed, "a nebulous golden haze somehow settled on those years of my life which I turned over to the War Department." Small matter that like many of his peers, Shaw was all but destitute upon his return, that in fact he had only $300 in savings despite his prewar successes. Being alive was happiness enough; and being alive in New York, the city whose halcyon years were arguably the postwar forties, was to have slid from a bad dream into a beautiful one.

Herbert Mitgang, the young *Stars & Stripes* correspondent in Algiers now back to begin his career at *The New York Times*, remembers a huge party thrown by the Shaws late in the summer of 1945, in their ground-floor apartment on East 74th Street. E. J. Kahn, Jr., was there—the *New Yorker* writer, as it happened, lived just upstairs, on the fourth floor, with his wife, Virginia, and the two couples would often have drinks together over the next few years. A. J. Liebling was there too, his friendship with Shaw enriched by shared wartime experiences. Mitgang brought his new wife, and also a character Shaw adored, Milt Estoff. Asked his profession upon entering the war, Estoff had truthfully informed the Army he was a bookmaker—as in bookie—only to be transferred to *Stars & Stripes* in Algiers because some officer had assumed him to be a literary type. Shaw continued to take as much pleasure in characters like Estoff as he did in well-known writers. Even later, hobnobbing with Europe's society rich, he wouldn't lose his capacity for that.

Shaw had at least three goals as a writer as he settled back into New York. He knew he wanted to tackle a big war novel; in addition to the notes he'd taken overseas, he had an ambitious notion to structure a Tolstoyan tale of three soldiers, at least one a German, and somehow to frame the whole by following a bullet through its various stages, from natural iron in the ground to the projectile's flight into a human heart. He also wanted to keep writing stories for *The New Yorker*; he hoped to have a collection published the following year. Meantime, he had a play on his hands.

Martin Gabel, a bantamlike actor with a booming bass voice, had signed onto *The Assassin* as both producer and director. An original member of Orson Welles's Mercury Theatre, and a loyal friend from Shaw's own early stage days, he would go on to a long and dignified theater career and also marry Arlene Francis. As a director, unfortunately, he tended to be earnest and heavyhanded, exactly the wrong approach to Shaw's already earnest plays. Nor did it help that for *The Assassin* Gabel hired almost exclusively radio actors he'd worked with in the past. (Karl Malden was one of the exceptions.) In addition, as with *Sons and Soldiers,* Shaw's own reluctance to have his words revised in any way during rehearsal was seconded by Marian, who once again served, in one observer's words, as a "tiger" over Gabel and the cast.

Still, there was nothing in the play to suggest the walloping it would get from New York critics. As Shaw had cleverly structured it, the Admiral Darlan story pivoted on a foppish young royalist named Sir Robert de Mauny. De Mauny gets drawn into killing the opportunistic Darlan (named Vespery in the play) not only to help bring a French king to power, but also in the naive belief that the Vichyites directing him will somehow spirit him out of prison. The story unfolds seamlessly and well; the dialogue, with the exception of a few tendentious speeches about the noble ideals involved, is brisk and believable. Karl Malden does remember struggling with one long address, central to the play's message, about the importance, in muddled times, of trusting the quality of men's souls rather than the brand of their politics. "Not having Martin Gabel's voice, I tended to deal with long speeches by delivering them so fast they were half over before the audience knew what was going on. Gabel, as the director, wanted rotund tones. Finally I said to Martin, 'Okay, tonight I'm doing it your way.' So at one of the out-of-town tryouts I did, and afterward Irwin came up to me in consternation and said, 'What the hell were you doing out there?' 'Trying to do it like Marty Gabel,' I said. 'Fuck Marty Gabel,' he said. 'Go back to how you did it before.' "

After a rocky tryout in New Haven, *The Assassin* opened at the National Theatre in New York on October 17 to uniformly poisonous reviews. Lewis Nichols in *The New York Times* said flatly: "*The Assassin* is not a good play. It is too often wordy, too often high-sounding without substance, it has too many waits and too little dramatic drive." Howard Barnes called it "more trite than trenchant," and Stark Young complained that "there seems to be no line running through it, and since it follows the death of Admiral Darlan closely enough for you to know the outcome even before the curtain rises, there is no suspense." The most perceptive criticism—and also the most damning—came from Shaw's home court. Wolcott Gibbs in *The New Yorker* suggested that in writing a play that was a hybrid of a melodrama and a political document, Shaw had made a calculated effort to please either side of the aisle. "It is hard not to suspect that he hoped to enjoy the exemptions from criticism provided by both these forms—if, that is, his play struck a good many people as too shapeless and talkative for satisfactory melodrama, it should be remembered that he was dealing with important political ideas, and if, on the other hand, just as many people found these ideas elementary and perhaps debatable, it should be remembered in that case that the creation of popular entertainment puts a heavy handicap on the social thinker."

Shaw had been pilloried before; gone off to sulk; come back renewed. This time he struck back. The Random House edition of *The Assassin* that came out in March 1946 sold only a few thousand copies, but its vitriolic preface stirred seismic reactions in the press and the theater world.

With grim humor, Shaw noted that *The Assassin* had opened in New York four days after his discharge from the Army, and that when he'd read the reviews, he'd had to wonder if he should have been relieved of duty. "The critics, it developed, had done me more harm than the German Army. It is true that the Germans had tried to kill me, but they, at least, had missed." Writing from "the foxhole of his discontent" after the play's short run of thirteen performances, Shaw ruminated on the nightmarish factors that had come to confront a playwright for the American stage. Finding actors, for one: all the good ones had gone out to Hollywood. Dealing with the unions, for another: their arcane rules governing every aspect of a theater production made rehearsals a sure passage into madness. Worst, though, were the critics. "I know that it is considered more sporting to treat the critics with a kind of amused resignation," Shaw wrote. "But I do not feel sporting about the critics . . . and I would no more think of sitting down to dinner with certain of the critics on the New York papers than I would think of breaking bread with the master of Buchenwald." Railing specifically at the *Herald Tribune*'s Howard Barnes and the *Times*' Lewis Nichols, Shaw blasted New York's theater critics as a despicable lot of patronizing and ignorant men intent on writing the caustic, negative reviews that allowed them to indulge in bitchy humor and bad puns at the expense of the hapless playwright. The critics, Shaw wrote, were not just acerbic, they were downright nasty, hastening to kill off any honest play that seemed imperfect, in favor of the "slick, dollar-catching jobs that keep our theatres alight." And who were these powerful arbiters of public taste? Not playwrights themselves; not even people with any past experience in the theater. Better, Shaw concluded, that playwrights write criticism, for they at least would sympathize with their subjects.

Shaw was not the only playwright of the season who felt ambushed. Three weeks before *The Assassin* appeared in print, a much-discussed broadside was launched by Harold Clurman, Elia Kazan and Maxwell Anderson, who reacted to the baleful reviews of Anderson's *Truckline Café* by declaring drama critics to be "the Jukes family of journalism." Shaw's polemic caused an even greater stir. A. J. Liebling, given an early copy, titled his January 1946 *Esquire* column "Five Yards Through Wolcott

Gibbs," and offered support for Shaw, the ex-gridiron star, for getting up from "a mountain of tacklers" and fighting back. Russell Maloney in *The New York Times* more dryly declared the preface to be "one of the theatrical documents of our time. It is all the more effective because it is hysterical, immoderate, and occasionally downright unfair. It proves only one thing, and that only in a symptomatic way: that one of our major playwrights has been clean unhinged by the conditions of the American theatre." The most intriguing reaction, though, came from the editors of *The New Republic.* Declaring Shaw might have a point in suggesting that playwrights serve as critics, they offered him the theater critic's chair at the magazine, duties to start the next September. Gamely, Shaw accepted.

The Assassin 's demise squashed Shaw's hopes of being able to live off the play's profits and focus on his war novel. There was no choice but to heed Hollywood's call; that spring Shaw signed on as screenwriter for *Arch of Triumph,* a film about wartime to be made from the novel by Erich Maria Remarque.

This time Shaw was represented by an agent—the remarkable Leland Hayward. Hayward was an unlikely Hollywood figure, a New York blue-blood whose father had commanded the only all-black regiment in World War I. He had backed into becoming one of the first agents in the film business by taking a job, after Princeton, selling Canadian distribution rights to American films, and by 1945 he had established offices in both New York and California. The bicoastal style applied to his personal life as well. After a tempestuous marriage to a society girl named Lola Gibbs, he started a romance with Katharine Hepburn on the West Coast while taking up with Margaret Sullavan on the East Coast; married Sullavan when she got pregnant (but did not bother to tell Hepburn, who learned of the wedding from hearing Walter Winchell announce it on the radio); and was already drifting into his next marriage, to Slim Hawks, soon to be ex-wife of director Howard Hawks. "Charm was the trick," recalls Slim, now Lady Keith. "He could make you like anything; sell you anything. He wasn't very strong-willed, though; it was very hard for him to fire anybody. He was a gentle, nice man, bounding with energy, and his clients either loved him or wanted to kill him. It was curious to find him in this burly, dog-eat-dog show biz world. But between him and Myron Selznick, who was David's brother, they really invented the theatrical agent."

It was a heady world that Irwin and Marian Shaw entered when they rented their beach house at 18 Malibu Road. Along with Hayward and his contingent—clients who included Ben Hecht and Charles MacArthur—the Shaws began to get invited to parties given by Samuel Goldwyn, David Selznick and Sam Spiegel. There were personal friends too: Peter and Jigee Viertel were building a house on fifteen beautiful acres in Zuma Canyon, just north of Malibu at Trancas Beach, with Robert Parrish, a film cutter

Shaw had met in liberated Paris, and Parrish's wife, Kathie. Initially, Shaw bought a neighboring lot above his friends' spread and christened it with a sign that read "I. Shaw." When he learned how expensive it would be to drill a well from this greater elevation, he sold the property to his wartime colleague Irving Reis. A circle had been established, however: the three couples—Viertels, Parrishes and Shaws—would remain close friends the rest of their lives.

Sunday lunch at the Shaws' beach house soon became a weekly ritual. Marian would make perfect salads and sandwiches. Shaw would make perfect drinks, exulting in his ability not only to mix a gin martini or a whiskey sour with just the right proportions but to fill the necessary number of glasses exactly to the brim. In addition to the Viertels and Parrishes, regulars included George Stevens, Ivan Moffat, Bob Capa and Irving Reis; Chester Erskine, a friend from New York theater days whose status as a triple-threat boy wonder—director, writer and producer—had taken him from Broadway to Hollywood, where he would soon produce Arthur Miller's *All My Sons*; Artie Shaw and Ava Gardner, who lived next door; and other lesser known but no less redoubtable characters such as Mike Burke, an OSS veteran who looked like Cary Grant. Burke had met Shaw in liberated Paris and was in Hollywood to serve as a technical advisor on a film about the war.

Salka Viertel's house in Santa Monica remained the other gathering place for Americans and European expatriates alike. "I walked in the back door one day," recalls Bob Parrish, who was new to the scene, "and there was a guy with short hair cooking at the stove. In the living room, Arthur Rubinstein was tinkling on the piano, Greta Garbo was lying on the sofa, and Christopher Isherwood was lounging in a chair. 'Who's the guy cooking in the kitchen?' I asked no one in particular. 'Bertolt Brecht,' came the reply." In such company, Shaw was a welcome and regular guest.

Shaw's return from the war had augured a second honeymoon of sorts with his wife. By spring, though, the old patterns had reemerged. Marian's acting career had gone quietly adrift; her main involvement in the theater was that of midwifing Shaw's plays, and in all other respects too she led a life ancillary to her husband's. She was a splendid hostess—bright, funny, always organized—and she oversaw the day-to-day household details with unfailing thoroughness, a role Shaw was utterly incapable of playing himself. Without a life of her own, however, she focused all her energies, and anxieties, on her husband. In particular, she nursed a keen jealousy of any woman in whom he seemed to take an interest; an untoward glance or gesture on Shaw's part could tip Marian's intense love into rage.

Shaw, of course, brought much if not most of the jealousy upon himself. The author of "The Girls in Their Summer Dresses" had never made any effort to hide his appetite for other good-looking women, and despite the doubtless sincerity of his marriage vows, prolonged monogamy was simply not his style. "Irwin just wasn't cut out for marriage," says Peter Viertel. "Let's face it—he was a man of the flesh." With Marian in New York before the war, Shaw had shown a blatant enough interest in other women to provoke certain of his wife's girlfriends into banding together as what one observer called "Marian's mafia," loyalists who offered sympathy to Marian and harrumphed about her husband's behavior. Now in Malibu, Shaw resumed the pattern of casual dalliances. Leonora Hornblow, wife of producer Arthur Hornblow, was one frequent companion in this period. Stylish and quick-witted, she possessed two other traits that would often be found in Shaw's women: she was wealthy, and she was coquettish, the sort of woman who walked into a crowded room and managed, without being in any way undignified about it, to send a message of interest to the men around her.

Shaw's sexual exploits were a subject of inevitable gossip, amusement and speculation among his friends. If they stopped to wonder *why* his appetite was so voracious, they usually came to the conclusion that he possessed an out-of-the-ordinary physical sex drive. Shaw himself rather liked this explanation. In his foxhole in Normandy, he had not so jokingly put his helmet over his groin to protect it, as he told one Army buddy, for women everywhere. In *The Young Lions,* he would have his protagonist, Michael, do the same thing, and think back on all the women he'd slept with before the war, an unbroken chain of lovers weekly or more frequently, since the age of sixteen.

Another explanation was the times in which Shaw lived. Any rules of marital propriety had seemed irrelevant during war, and in the years immediately following, the yoke of outward conservativism assumed by most returning soldiers, in politics and in the home, created a secret backlash of reckless behavior, of marital infidelities within a haze of dry martinis. In Shaw's case, however, there was something more.

For Shaw, women could be divided into two categories: those he hadn't yet slept with (and who were thus lovely, pure girls, a pleasure to be with) and those he had. Shaw was no cad: as his affairs drifted to an end, usually because of a convenient departure from one elegant venue to the next, he remained gracious and warm to ex-lovers, and they in turn generally continued to regard him with great fondness—no small tribute. Still, in Shaw's mind women soon seemed to lose the freshness that had made them such delectable prospects in the first place. They began to make *claims,* as Shaw would put it in novel after novel, and in so doing they began an inevitable passage, sometimes gradual, sometimes not, from lover to shrew. The ultimate shrew was a woman whose claim was unshakable, who made increasing demands and drove the beleaguered author to seek comfort in the next, more sympathetic lover. This was the woman who stirred in Shaw's depths the dark bile that colors almost every one of his female characters in print, making them predatory creatures who remain one-dimensional and finally absurd—the weakest aspect of his fictional world.

Whether or not Shaw's feelings about women were rooted in resentment he may have felt toward a suffocating mother is an intriguing but unanswerable question. What does seem undeniable is that Shaw's infidelities had as much to do with provoking his wife as they did with pursuing new sexual conquests—and that Marian's reactions were part of the way the two communicated with each other. Vengeful and jealous as the affairs would make her, the fascination is that she remained, year after year, to do battle with each next marital threat, and thus in an unintended way to flatter her husband by revealing, again and again, how dependent she was on him and how much she loved him. At the same time, the dramas provided Marian with a focus for her anxieties and frustrations—a purpose, even, in a sometimes purposeless life. In the eruptions that followed each discovery, they may also have given her a needed balance of power, at least to affect the moment, a balance otherwise lacking in a marriage to a man whose fame and charisma made him much the more powerful partner. If the pattern was yet indistinct, future incidents would make it painfully clear: both Irwin and Marian thrived on the volatile brew of Irwin's extramarital affairs.

In a surreal way, the war had followed Shaw home. *Arch of Triumph* was set in wartime Paris, and the dutiful screenwriter would drive from Malibu to the newly formed Enterprise Productions (a profit-sharing gambit in which Shaw had a stake) with his latest chunk of dialogue, to see sets of Paris under construction and meet with director Lewis Milestone about the script. The story concerned a brilliant Jewish surgeon who has fled Nazi Germany and lives in Paris without papers, performing "backdoor" operations for incompetent doctors. Ingrid Bergman starred in the role of a beautiful and mysterious widow. Offscreen, taking stills of the ongoing production, was Robert Capa.

Capa had moved into the Garden of Allah hotel, and was restlessly trying to parlay his wartime connections with directors like George Stevens and Anatole Litvak into a Hollywood career. It was already proving a frustrating gambit, but his romance with Bergman, conducted in utmost secrecy because Bergman was still married, continued to thrill him, and some of his happiest moments were the trysts he arranged with her at Shaw's Malibu beach house, when the good-natured Shaw arranged to be elsewhere.

The war in its darker hues had stayed with Shaw too. That April marked the first and only appearance of a veterans' magazine of humor and commentary called *Salute*, put out by former *Yank* and *Stars & Stripes* staffers, including Walter Bernstein, Herbert Mitgang, David Golding and cartoonist Bill Mauldin. The hope was to repeat magazine history: out of such roots after World War I had grown *The New Yorker*. The staff proved unable to publish a second issue, but one was enough to alert FBI file-keepers. Shaw's inclusion on the *Salute* masthead as a contributing editor, together with the humorous piece he contributed about his scorn for military superiors and his relief at being out of uniform, was duly noted in his FBI file. A conservative Michigan congressman was quoted at length in the file from his remarks for the *Congressional Record*; he described *Salute* as a "shrewdly camouflaged publication." The FBI noted that the congressman "specifically referred to an article on page 10 entitled 'What I Think of the Army,' by Irwin Shaw."

Ironically, for all the bitterness Shaw had felt at the occasional pig-headedness of his military superiors in the war, he had come home far more patriotic than when he left, with an abiding faith in the rightness of America's role in the conflict. Had the FBI scriveners wanted some current proof, they might have looked at the front page of *The New York Times Book Review* the first Sunday in June. There they would have found the unusually harsh treatment accorded by Shaw to a wartime novel by his old friend William Saroyan.

The Adventures of Wesley Jackson was the novel Saroyan had skipped D-Day to start writing, the novel that an exasperated U.S. Army had let him continue writing in London. Saroyan had mistakenly assumed the Army would grant him a furlough when he finished; but his superiors were scandalized by the picaresque work, with its bitter indictment of the war and the military, and no furlough ever materialized. Asked to review it, Shaw too was shocked. "Once more Saroyan is full of love for the entire world," he wrote. "He loves the Germans, he loves the Japs, he loves the Bulgarians and Finns and Rumanians. The only people he can find to hate are the Americans. He forgives the Germans Dachau and Belsen without blinking an eye, but he cannot forgive the sergeant who assigned him to KP in New York City. . . . It seems to me that a writer, no matter how far-fetched and fanciful he may be, should have some compulsion to present the truth." Shaw's was the traditional view of storytelling, the view he would maintain unwaveringly throughout his life. When it came to a novel that seemed so plainly autobiographical, set in such a terribly real war, it was hard to disagree with him, but Saroyan, who had felt that any liberties were allowed in the name of Art, was devastated by the review. Though the two men saw each other occasionally in Paris in later years, their friendship was never the same.

Shaw broke another bond the next month, officially signing off as screenwriter on *Arch of Triumph*. Milestone and his producer, David Lewis, had insisted that Shaw's script focus on the romance between Bergman and her costar, Charles Boyer. Shaw had wanted the main drama to be the struggle between the Jewish surgeon and the war itself. In what was reported in *The New York Times* to be an amicable settlement, Shaw had his name removed from the credits and also withdrew as a profit-sharing partner in Enterprise Productions. On July 13, Shaw wrote to Bennett Cerf that he was finished with the movies—for a while at least—and was now throwing himself into his war novel which, he predicted with typical high confidence, would likely be finished by the end of the year.

A welcome reaffirmation of Shaw's literary stature had come in May with the news that he had been selected as one of two dozen artists to receive a grant of $1,000 from the American Academy of Arts and Letters, along with such figures as Malcolm Cowley, Langston Hughes and Marianne Moore. The grant would prove the Academy's sole acknowledgment of Shaw's work, and in retrospect, its timing would seem apt: if only symbolically, it seemed to define Shaw's high-water mark in the literary world, the world whose epicenter was the Academy itself. Shaw would go on to garner far more widespread acclaim with *The Young Lions* just two years later; but among the Academy's literati, the novel, for all its merits, would seem disconcertingly commercial, and Shaw would never again be considered an artist in the strictest sense, much less a prospective candidate for Academy membership. For the moment, the grant seemed to inspire a fine story, "Prize for Promise," about a struggling playwright who wins a $1,000 grant and goes to receive it, along with five other hungry artists, at a richly appointed foundation office, only to be humiliated after a long wait by a well-fed executive who announces that because of the well-known fiscal irresponsibility of artists, the grants will be meted out in weekly stipends.

That summer marked the publication of Shaw's third collection, *Act of Faith and Other Stories.* The title story, which had appeared in *The New Yorker* in February, would be chosen for both the O. Henry Awards and *Best American Short Stories* collections, and would be included in *The New Yorker*'s own anthology of war stories. The honors wouldn't come by chance; "Act of Faith" remains one of Shaw's best stories, arguably the finest of those about the war. In a scene that recalls *The Shy and the Lonely*—Shaw's one-acter about three young men in a summer-camp tent, hungering for girls—three battle-weary American soldiers trade gripes in their tent in Reims. It's July 1945 and the soldiers have a pass to go into Paris, but they haven't been paid in three months and they're broke. After a futile attempt to float a loan from their commanding officer, talk turns to what they might pawn. One of the three, a Jewish soldier named Seeger, has the one souvenir of real value: a German Luger. At first he refuses to surrender it. Then he reads a letter from his father, a letter of despair about the hatred Americans still feel for Jews despite the atrocities of the war. Everywhere one goes, his father writes, there's murderous talk of Jews, and angry mutterings that Jews have profited from the war. Shaken, Seeger puts the letter down and offers the Luger to his buddies, searching their faces for any trace of anti-Semitism. To his relief, he finds only honest camaraderie.

Critics hailed the collection as the work of one of America's best short story writers. Robert Gorham Davis declared: "Irwin Shaw is a moral writer who conceives moral problems simply, feels them deeply, and dramatizes them with an often terrifying historical relevance." A particularly touching tribute came from Budd Schulberg, who put aside any lingering animosity toward Shaw to report he'd read the collection "with a sense of profound satisfaction." Of the title story and its concern with anti-Semitism, wrote Schulberg, "Shaw has stood up to his subject with great courage and refreshing health. The esthetic solution for the story is in the best artistic tradition. It doesn't fudge or preach. It is profoundly apprehensive but unneurotic. It frightens the hell out of you and then it shakes you up and says, Come on, this is America. What are you scared about?" Concluded Schulberg: "This is the way Shaw came out of the war, thinking and writing even better than in the shabby old umbrella and nonintervention days. And now, if the playwright will only permit his Siamese twin, the vastly superior prose writer, to hang on to that typewriter for a while, we are going to have something very solid and exciting and lasting from Mr. Shaw."

Mr. Shaw didn't go along yet with that assessment of his playwriting, but he did hang onto his typewriter now with more sustained intensity than he ever had before. He knew he was brimming with fresh wartime material; he also knew he would never be judged a great American writer without a great American novel. *The Young Lions,* or by its original working title, *The Bloodletters,* was meant from its inception to be nothing less than that. In the end, the novel's greatest strengths—and its perceived weaknesses—would trace to that conceit.

The rest of the summer and fall of 1946, Shaw adhered to a tightly disciplined schedule: up by six every day, he wrote all morning and often into the afternoon. With Viertel and other friends he maintained his usual secrecy about the novel's story line and characters—half superstitious, and as he occasionally admitted, half afraid that some other writer might steal his ideas—but at the day's end he did tend to brag about how many pages he'd knocked off. "It was incredible," recalls Viertel. "Ten pages, twelve pages—as many as twenty-five pages in a single day. We'd all just shake our heads in amazement."

The routine continued when the Shaws moved back to New York in November. By early spring, though, with the novel two-thirds finished, Shaw hit a snag. "I was going along and all of a sudden I stopped in the middle of a paragraph," he told Pete Hamill years later. "And I stopped in the middle of that paragraph for *seven months.* Seven months I looked at the middle of that paragraph. What I finally did was I stopped for six weeks and didn't do anything." Sometime during that seven months Shaw took a break to write his longest story yet for *The New Yorker,* "Widows Meeting," a tale of two sisters who fall in love with the same German before the war: the one who wins him follows him back to Germany and ends up an ardent Nazi, unshaken by Germany's defeat and her husband's death; the one who loses him marries an American boy who gets killed in the war, and must then face her sister, one widow to another. The story touched on the same concerns that would animate *The Young Lions.* How could a human being be drawn into the moral abyss of Nazism? Was there a core of human decency in every person that somehow got tainted in some? Or was there a darker core in the German character that would always give rise to national arrogance and fascism? "Widows Meeting" suggested not that such a core was intrinsically German, but that it did reside in certain people, as a sort of genetic predisposition to evil. And that Nazism brought it out.

The summer of 1947, the Shaws again took a beach house in Malibu. In a July letter to Bennett Cerf, Shaw downplayed his writer's block, reporting he had finished 1,200 pages of *The Young Lions.* The output was extraordinary and seemed to underscore Shaw's private intent to write a novel every bit as broad in scope and sheer length as *War and Peace.* He was, he admitted to Cerf, getting a bit stale, and as a change of pace he took a month off to do something he'd never tried before: cowrite a play.

The play was a historical drama called *The Survivors,* about Civil War soldiers from both sides returning to the same small hometown; the co-writer was Peter Viertel. Given Shaw's healthy ego about his own writing, fireworks might have been expected from the collaboration; but Shaw fully believed that writing, as John Cheever liked to put it, was not a competitive sport, and he approached *The Survivors* with the same good cheer and supportiveness for his coauthor that would astound nearly every writer he met for the rest of his life. "*The Survivors* had started as a movie idea of mine," Viertel recalls. "I had a lot of people bidding on it, and even got an offer of $35,000, but Irwin talked me into doing it as a play with him. We got an advance of $25,000 for it that way, and Irwin made me keep it all.

"We worked out an outline, and then one guy would write one scene and the other guy would write the other scene. And we'd kind of work on it together. We had no problems that way, no problems at all. . . . We said, 'One thing we know for sure: We don't want Martin Gabel to direct it.' But when we finished writing the play, Gabel read it and said, 'I want to direct it,' and we promptly said, 'Okay.' "

The two friends did have one rough moment that summer when a story of Shaw's called "Mixed Doubles" appeared in *The New Yorker.* Beautifully paced, it opens with a casual Sunday tennis match between two suburban couples, seen through the eyes of one of the wives. Proud of her husband's military bearing, his vigor, his prowess on the court, Jane Collins feels other, less happy sentiments as the playing grows more serious and the score tips back and forth. At match point her husband serves once, twice—into the net. And Jane sees once again that this is how he is, that off the court as well as on, he will always, at the crucial moment, double-fault. If the story wasn't an outright portrait of Peter and Jigee Viertel, friends felt, there certainly were some remarkable similarities.

There were other colorful characters around Shaw at this time, but none more so than Irving Lazar, the plucky, pint-sized agent better known as Swifty. Lazar was just starting out in Hollywood, but he had come a considerable distance already. He had grown up in Stamford, Connecticut, the eldest of four sons of a German immigrant father who worked as a butter-and-egg commission merchant and small-time banker. Lazar had had a scrappy upbringing, usually working after school to help make ends meet, then earned his way through Brooklyn Law by attending night classes and working days as a secretary for lawyer-philanthropist Samuel Unter-meyer. One of his first law clients had been Sophie Tucker, or so the legend went, and that had interested Lazar in the business. He had become an agent when some impresario walked into his office bemoaning his need for a Hawaiian musician. Lazar knew one but couldn't remember his name, and so had simply declared that he could get "Johnny Pineapple," upon which he went out to find the musician, told him his new name was Johnny Pineapple, and got him the club job—taking, in the process, his own first commission.

Throughout the 1930s—he was five years older than Shaw—Lazar had worked as an agent for big bands and vaudeville acts for the Music Corporation of America. His big break had come during the war: as a second lieutenant in the Army Air Corps, he had put his agentry tricks to work by cabling both General "Hap" Arnold and playwright Moss Hart that each wanted to meet the other to discuss the production of a patriotic, war-effort movie. Out of that meeting had come *Winged Victory,* the 1944 smash directed by George Cukor, which brought $5 million to the Air Corps relief fund and earned Lazar his captain's wings.

At the war's end, Lazar had set up his own small office as an agent in Los Angeles, principally encouraged by Moss Hart. (One story has it that Hart asked Lazar what he wanted for Christmas. "Cole Porter," Lazar answered; and Porter became a client.) Soon his client list would include George S. Kaufman, S. N. Behrman, Johnny Mercer, Ira Gershwin, Frank Loesser and George Cukor. Already, he was traveling in the right circles, amusing Hollywood's finest with the glibness of his deal-making and his fetish for cleanliness (one of the most repeated jokes about Lazar was that he would madden hotel managements by calling for piles of clean white towels and laying them in paths across the room of his suite).

"He was entertaining and funny and as gutsy as hell," says Viertel. "He used to come out to Zuma Beach on Sundays—he either went to the Gershwins' or came to us. He'd drive out in this big open car, he was a real menace on the road. We had a rubber boat, a Navy life raft, and we used to ride the waves in it. And Swifty always got in it with us, riding those big breakers. Only later did we discover that he couldn't swim."

Lazar did stretch the facts occasionally. Bob Parrish remembers Lazar cornering him at the 1948 Academy Awards after Parrish won an Oscar for his first Hollywood editing job, on *Body and Soul.* "I want to represent you, kid," Lazar told him. "But cutters don't have agents," Parrish replied. "You won't be a cutter forever," Lazar said, "and besides, I rep your closest friend, Irwin Shaw." A week later Parrish and Lazar were among a lunch circle at Shaw's beach house, and Parrish mischievously turned to his host. "Say, Irwin, who represents you?" he asked. Shaw promptly replied that Leland Hayward did. Instead of cringing, Lazar laughed uproariously. "All right," he said, "I don't represent Irwin yet. But I *will*."

At the same time, Lazar *was* amusing, and in the end that exonerated him from all charges among his friends. "There're only two kinds of people in this world," Martin Gabel would declare in his resonant bass voice. "When they walk through the door you either say 'Oh boy' or 'Oh shit.' And my friend Swifty is of the first category.'"

With summer's end, Shaw had to leave this happy circle to return to New York and take up his new duties as a theater critic for *The New Republic.* It was an arrival noted with no small interest by other critics, among them John Chapman, who caustically offered "a scorching warm welcome," and Richard Watts, Jr., who more equably pointed out that Shaw's namesake, George Bernard, had gone from drama criticism to playwriting, so why not the reverse? In his own first column—dated September 29—Shaw acknowledged that friends and colleagues alike had been as shocked by his decision to turn critic as if a town harlot had announced she had seen the light and would shortly be going to the dark continent to convert the natives; hard to say whether the outcry was more for the church or the lady's prospective congregation. But a playwright's perspective, Shaw suggested, was likely to be no more or less biased than a professional critic's. Indeed, a playwright might bring the fresher view, born out of recent experience. Shaw admitted the danger: that he might well have to speak ill of works of playwrights more accomplished than himself. But at least, he suggested, seeing all those plays might make him a better playwright. Anyway, he concluded, "what better opportunity could a man find to lose several old friends and win many new enemies? The blood surges through the veins in an invigorating, fresh flood at the prospect."

Less than a month into his new role—a month of appraising, among other plays, a revival of George Bernard Shaw's *Man and Superman* (the critic Shaw rued that it "made even the most robust of today's playwrights look as though they were suffering from anemia")—Shaw was dealt a painful and undeserved blow. In a harbinger of things to come, the House Un-American Activities Committee convened hearings in Washington on the explosive subject of Communism in Hollywood, and determined that four directors and fourteen writers, Shaw among them, were Communists in deed and intent.

The hearings were chaired by J. Parnell Thomas, a Republican congressman from New Jersey, with a panel that included the junior Republican congressman Richard Nixon of California. They were the first such deliberations to probe the motion picture industry since 1941, when charges had arisen that Hollywood was injecting war propaganda into its films. Three top movie executives had voluntarily agreed to appear before the Committee: Louis B. Mayer of Metro-Goldwyn-Mayer; Sam Wood, a director (*Goodbye Mr. Chips, For Whom the Bell Tolls,*) independent producer and organizer of the Motion Picture Alliance for the Preservation of American Ideals (an anti-Communist watchdog group); and Jack L. Warner, vice-president in charge of production of Warner Bros. The three denied the Committee's strong sentiment that the wartime movies *Mission to Moscow* (Warner Bros.) and *Song of Russia* (MGM) contained Soviet propaganda. (America's wartime alliance with the Soviet Union had already become a dim and disturbing memory.) However, they allowed that certain writers and directors in their midst could be labeled Communists, including Clifford Odets, Dalton Trumbo, John Howard Lawson, Albert Maltz, Robert Rossen and Irwin Shaw (described in the *New York Herald Tribune* as "author of several successful books and plays and an active screenwriter"). Sam Wood, the most ardently anti-Communist of the trio, went so far as to declare of Hollywood's covert Communists, "If you want to drop their rompers, you'll find a hammer and sickle on their rear ends." Shaw in particular was named by Jack Warner as one of six film writers Warner had fired for trying to inject Communist propaganda into their screenplays.

Shaw was outraged. Through his lawyer, Lloyd Paul Stryker, he issued a formal denial of Warner's charges, pointing out that the one script he had written for Warner in 1941—*The Talk of the Town*—had been so well liked that Warner had promptly offered him a three-picture contract at twice the money—an offer Shaw had turned down in order to serve in the Army—and persisted with ever higher offers in the intervening years, including one the previous Friday! He also joined a hastily formed Committee for the First Amendment, a group of 300 independent movie producers, directors, writers and actors, to petition lawmakers to come to their senses. Within a week Shaw made his response more emphatic with an angry opinion piece in *The New York Times*.

"Being a writer these days is a complicated business," he began. "You are liable to wake up one morning and see by the headlines that Jack Warner has proclaimed to a Congressional committee that you are 'un-American' and that he has fired you for trying to inject 'un-American doctrines' into the work you did for his studio." Shaw pointed out that since the hearings no one had called him to respond to the charges, and went on to declare that he was in no way "un-American," that he certainly had never entertained the notion of overthrowing the government of the United States, and that to cap it off, he had been elected to the anti–left wing slate of the council of the Authors League of America. He wryly observed that he no longer even had the courage to read the bitter denunciations of his work in *New Masses,* and that the only operative theory in Hollywood at the time was whether a screenplay would turn a buck. But very well, he concluded: let the impoverished New York theater benefit from the proceedings by having the so-called Communist writers make their way back to its rough-hewn stages—until, that is, the movie producers noted their diminishing coffers and begged to have them back.

Years later, Shaw would see Jack Warner on the avenue Georges V in Paris, strolling along with Darryl Zanuck. "I refused to offer him my hand," Shaw reported with satisfaction. " 'I don't know why you're like that,' [Warner] said plaintively. 'You ought to thank me for knocking you out of the movie business. Look how successful you've become since then, writing books.' "

Shaw, unconvinced, walked on.

It was from the Thomas hearings that the Hollywood Ten were named and officially exiled from the motion picture industry; it was from the hearings that the blacklist began. Shaw was not one of the Ten, and when the Red-baiting fever reached its next peak in the McCarthy era, he would not be called to testify, nor would anyone else's testimony identify him. He would not even be kept from working on films—he would write or cowrite several over the next few years, straight through the McCarthy hearings. Nevertheless, Shaw felt that he *had* been at least graylisted, that his name now gave pause to producers and studio heads, and that he, like many of his colleagues, would be quietly excluded from consideration on many films. As far as Shaw was concerned, his name would remain tarnished until November 1954, when David O. Selznick, eager to produce a live adaptation of "The Girls in Their Summer Dresses" for a television spectacular honoring General Electric, met resistance to the prospect of using Shaw, and promptly squashed it with a phone call or two. It is not hard to believe that Shaw's suspicions were well founded, or to imagine that the FBI, with its active file on him, occasionally did its part to apprise a timid studio head of the true dark nature of Irwin Gilbert Shaw.

For the moment these fears remained abstract. Shaw's immediate concerns were to see *The Survivors* to Broadway, and to finish *The Young Lions* in time to compete with another prospective war novel already stirring talk, Norman Mailer's *The Naked and the Dead.*

Martin Gabel had managed to persuade Viertel and Shaw, despite their vow, to hire him as director of *The Survivors.* No less notable was the casting of Hume Cronyn in one of the lead roles. How could Shaw agree to use the actor who had been involved with his wife before the war? "Ah, well, it didn't bother him really," Viertel says. "Irwin wasn't a grudge holder, and Cronyn was a good actor, so what the hell."

Despite its 1865 setting, the play conveyed clear and heartfelt sentiments about the difficulties of post–World War II diplomacy. The major landholder of a Missouri town returns from the Civil War, having fought on the Union side and been taken prisoner. His old rival, who fought as a Confederate and may have been responsible for his imprisonment, demands access to the landholder's river water for his dying cattle. At first neither man is willing to compromise; gradually a settlement comes within reach, but at the last minute violence erupts and the two rivals end up dead. Says one character, summing it up: "Violence can't be kept on nice, neat tracks. It spreads in all directions and God knows how many innocent people it will touch before it's over—"

Timely in its own way, with plenty of Western drama and gunfire, *The Survivors* intrigued Hollywood producers even in its playwritten form. Paramount came fishing in early November, and a preproduction deal with Universal International nearly materialized. The offers fell through, however, and when the play died a quick death on Broadway, so did its authors' hopes of cashing in big.

The failure of *The Survivors* was as frustrating, and in its way as mysterious, as that of *The Assassin.* The cast could hardly be faulted: in addition to Cronyn, it included E. G. Marshall, Richard Basehart and a young Kevin McCarthy, none of whom drew any critical fire. The sets, once again, were the work of the incomparable Boris Aronson. The writing was well honed, the story an appealing melodrama, and Brooks Atkinson, for one, found the whole production admirable when it opened January 19, 1948, at the Playhouse, without the benefit of out-of-town tryouts. The authors, who had repaired after the show to the Central Park South apartment of Bernard Hart—brother of Moss and coproducer of the play along with Martin Gabel—sat up drinking until they could call *The New York Times* and get a copy reader to read Atkinson's review to them over the phone. "Peter Viertel and Irwin Shaw have written a rattling good play with a meaning," the review began. Atkinson went on to praise in glowing terms the play's clever interweaving of shoot-'em-up excitement and intellectual truth-telling. Performed by "a first-rate company," the play "deserves the wide hearing it is bound to have," he reported. The authors, tensed for disaster, looked at each other in amazement. "There you are,

Irwin," Viertel said jubilantly, "you're lucky again, everything works out for you."

Regrettably, other critics came away far less impressed. Howard Barnes, while noting the play's blend of melodrama and message, declared that "the net effect is definitely depressing. . . . The resolution . . . is about as unsatisfactory as any climax that has been witnessed hereabouts for some time." Wolcott Gibbs simply damned the production with faint praise, calling it "on the whole, a sound and interesting play," but noting that the authors, "to hold their conflict in balance . . . did things that I think hurt the play dramatically." Gibbs's review came as an obituary, however: by the time it appeared, *The Survivors* had closed after just eight performances, killed by its own earnest mood and pitch (a mood further darkened by Martin Gabel's ever earnest direction) and by that dread word "depressing" in print and word-of-mouth.

This time Shaw had the odd opportunity, in his critic's column, of remarking on his own play's quick demise. "Somewhere in the middle of rehearsals," he rued, "after an early run-through, the collaborators made a mournful discovery. They discovered they wished to rewrite the script almost entirely, discarding the realistic three-act form in which the work had been cast, and employing a looser, impressionistic style which would have given considerably more movement and tension to the play." By then, of course, too much was at stake. An opening date was scheduled; neither the actors nor the unions could afford to delay; advertising had to be drawn up and the right word-of-mouth generated. Like a new car on a Detroit production line, the play moved irreversibly and unstoppably to its end point—where, like a car, it had to be sold.

A month later Shaw surrendered his critic's post at *The New Republic* to an old friend and colleague—Harold Clurman. It was time, he declared, to devote all his energies to finishing the book he secretly hoped would be his Great American Novel.

CHAPTER TEN

No one at Random House seemed to like *The Young Men* as a title, wrote Saxe Commins to Shaw on April 14, 1948. How did he feel about *The Warriors?*

Shaw was back in California, taking a brief vacation at the Rancho Yucca Loma, in Victorville. Even at that distance, though, there was no mistaking the excitement in New York about the imminent publication of this first novel. Bennett Cerf had read it and declared he was bowled over—nothing less than a press run of 50,000 copies would do. Shaw had been a professional writer now for more than a decade and hadn't come close to selling 50,000 copies of all his works together. The only problem, besides the title, was that Shaw had turned in an impossibly long manuscript, more than 1,300 pages double-spaced. Not only was it economically unfeasible to print such a doorstop; Commins also felt the narrative could be improved by hefty cutting.

Accordingly, Shaw returned to New York in early May, to sit down with Commins for three weeks of marathon editorial sessions. By the time he flew back to California, he had, with Commins's help, cut more than 100,000 words—as many as 400 manuscript pages—among them the entire leitmotif of the bullet. To Commins's relief, the cuts were accomplished with little or no tension. "No work I have done in many years," he wrote to Shaw, "has been so pleasant, so congenial or so fruitful. I look forward to working with you on many, many more novels. This is your field!"

From another Malibu beach house at 2163 4-A Roosevelt Highway, Shaw dug into a still imposing stack of galleys and came up with a biblical title for his novel from the Book of Nahum 2, 13: "Behold, I am against thee, saith the Lord of hosts, and I will burn thy chariots in the smoke, and the sword shall devour thy young lions: and I will cut off thy prey from the earth, and the voice of thy messengers shall no more be heard." He dedicated *The Young Lions* to Marian, a decision that assumed a special poignance in early June, when she suffered a miscarriage at a cocktail party, the latest of several in their nine years of marriage.

The pared-down novel Shaw now held in his hands was a work of enormous power, a grand slam of a story that was, in fact, three stories interwoven: that of Noah Ackerman, a poor American Jew who joins the wartime army only to encounter harsh anti-Semitism from his fellow soldiers; Michael Whitacre, a successful but cynical American stage manager who ends up in Ackerman's unit; and Christian Diestl, the dedicated Nazi whose destiny finally brings him face to face with both of these Americans. In its geographical sweep and color, *The Young Lions* captures a wider swath of World War II than any other novel of its time. Mailer's *The Naked and the Dead* was set in the Pacific Theater, and James Jones's *From Here to Eternity* in Oahu, Hawaii's Schofield Barracks in the days leading up to Pearl Harbor. *The Young Lions* ranged from New York to Africa to Europe. In style, *The Naked and the Dead* and *From Here to Eternity* achieved a rough-hewn grace that set them apart from Shaw's more liquid prose, and there are critics who have always faulted Shaw for that, finding *The Young Lions* too facile to be a convincing chronicle of war. Four decades later, however, *The Young Lions* remains at least as compellingly readable as its better-remembered companions. It's also the only one of the three that attempts a psychological portrait of the enemy.

Like Mailer and Jones, Shaw managed in *The Young Lions* to transform his personal wartime experiences into universal terms, and to capture the voices around him, of Hollywood writers and Brooklyn trolley riders, of soldiers from the South and soldiers from the plains country, of the French and Italians and British and, in Shaw's case, of the Germans as well. Beneath a story that moved with cinematic speed were the same concerns that had animated much of his work to date. How did violence grow in the human soul, and how could it be contained? And how should decent people—gentle people—react to its random force?

Still, the many autobiographical details of *The Young Lions* glint through the novel like mica. Shaw's story opens on New Year's Eve, 1938, with establishing scenes for each major character. The Austrian ski town where Christian Diestl works as a ski instructor has little to do with Shaw's life (it was likely based on his 1945 trip with Anatole Litvak to Hitler's Bavarian retreat), but the New Year's Eve party in Manhattan that Michael Whitacre attends is a rich slice of Shaw's own prewar literary life in New York, and Whitacre is essentially Shaw in the harshest possible light: successful, glib, superficial, a man who lacks a moral compass and, knowing that, secretly loathes himself even as friends warm to his easy charm. Like Shaw, Whitacre gives money to a man raising funds for the Spanish Loyalists and knows he's done it just to buy off his conscience. Like Shaw, Whitacre drowns his self-loathing in drink and vows to go on the wagon, yet surrenders at the first temptation. Like Shaw too, Whitacre attracts women, and responds to their flirtations, while his actress wife keeps a jealous eye out for his indiscretions, sniffing at his collar when she greets him, for traces of strange perfume. Many of the protagonists in earlier stories had suggested their creator, but never had Shaw etched a self-portrait with such unsparing scorn. It brought his darkest side to light, a show of real artistic courage. It also created a pitfall into which Whitacre finally leads his creator in *The Young Lions*—as do other, similar protagonists in the later novels. In short: self-pity.

At first glance the character of Noah Ackerman, a rootless young Jew who sees the new year in by attending the lonely death of his immigrant father in a shabby California hotel room, seems very little like Irwin Shaw. Ackerman drifts east to New York, is taken under wing by a friendly young intellectual, and falls in love with a girl named Hope Plowman, who makes him escort her all the way home by subway and trolley from a party on upper Riverside Drive to her Brooklyn rooming house. But there are hints in these episodes of a younger Shaw in Noah, hints that accumulate until it becomes clear that Noah is the honest and brave Brooklyn Jewish boy Shaw believes he once was before overnight success corrupted him. (Not by chance is Whitacre a WASP.) Noah's dying father, like Shaw's own, is a Russian immigrant whose business schemes always went awry. The friendly intellectual who takes Noah in suggests Shaw's old Brooklyn College mentor David Driscoll. And the character of Hope Plowman is clearly an homage to Shaw's college sweetheart Elaine Cooper, with her dark hair pulled back in a tight knot as Elaine's was, her small waist but somewhat heavy legs, and her earnest, direct manner. Like Elaine too, Hope has a sternly religious father—New England Protestant rather than Christian Scientist—who must approve his daughter's suitors. The difference is that in fiction Shaw could steer the romance into wedlock: Noah travels up to Vermont to ask Hope's father for his daughter's hand in marriage, and after a few rough moments the father concedes.

The fascination of all that happens to Michael and Noah after these establishing scenes is that each represents a side of Shaw's own character, reacting in different ways to the tempering fire of battle and finally merging in the novel's dramatic finale.

By the time the U.S. enters the war, Michael Whitacre's peacetime life is falling apart. His wife seems involved with an actor (as Marian was involved with Hume Cronyn), and he himself has become enamored of a lissome young woman, enough to allow his marriage to collapse. Like Shaw, he is both beguiled by the next pretty girl and bitterly convinced that women "lie their way into heaven without the flicker of an eyelash." Like Shaw too, he hungers for the war as a welcome test of real courage for his soggy character. The day of Pearl Harbor, he's playing tennis in California, as Shaw was. He thinks of enlisting right away but discards the notion because the producer of the play he's helping cast pleads with him to see it through, and because he needs money for his family. (The playwright of Whitacre's current production is a boorish former leftist who wrote two plays about the working class and now makes tendentious remarks at the Polo Lounge about artists having to remain above the fray of war. Shaw is mocking himself here, but also weaving in a bit of William Saroyan.) At

the same time, he resists the easy opportunity to cadge an officer's rank
through his Hollywood connections and serve out the war in some safe
venue. Instead, he grimly decides to let himself be drafted and fight the war
as a private. Clearly, Shaw wanted the record set permanently straight
about his own delayed entry into the war.

As for Ackerman, he enlists, bids his new wife farewell, and is shipped
to a southern boot camp, where his own painful rite of passage begins when
fellow soldiers revile him as a Jew. Whitacre, assigned to the same unit,
looks on in helpless frustration as Ackerman takes on his tormenters, one
after another, in boxing matches that leave his face disfigured but his pride
intact. Sickened by the anti-Semitism, Whitacre surrenders his ideals and
applies for a transfer to officer training school, only to learn that his record
is blighted by an FBI memo declaring him to be a Red.

Transferred with the help of Hollywood connections to a London unit
that stages entertainment shows for soldiers, Whitacre loses track of Ackerman for a while and revels in the happy, preinvasion life that Shaw himself
led in London with George Stevens's unit. The plucky Louise M'Kimber,
who works for the Office of War Information and blithely takes Private
Whitacre to cocktail parties of five-star generals, is modeled on Mary
Welsh. The poker-playing Hungarian correspondent who turns up in a
basement canteen is drawn from Robert Capa, and the absurdly intense
correspondent from *Collier's* who talks of wanting to write an essay on fear
is based on Ernest Hemingway. Less clear but still identifiable are George
Stevens, as Pavone, the coolly detached head of Whitacre's unit, and
Leicester Hemingway, Ernest's blustery brother, as Keane, the foolish soldier who worries about his bowels and broods on the success of his brother,
a Congressional Medal of Honor winner. (Also in the unit: an Italian
iceman from Boston named Stellevato, based on Shaw's Normandy jeep
driver, Angelo Tempesta.) Shaw's gift is not only in capturing their like-
nesses on the page but in recreating their talk and opinions of the war with
journalistic vividness, and in further limning those times with the random
talk of passersby (even stacking the comments of soldiers in short "inter-
mission" chapters that recall Dos Passos). As in his *New Yorker* stories,
Shaw also intersperses his fictional narrative with news bulletins and headlines. Compelling as his story is, its real purpose is to create a more graphic
reality of the times, and ultimately, of the war.

With the Normandy invasion, Shaw's Americans confront the horrors of war and are tested. (Ackerman goes in on D-Day; Whitacre does
not.) The results, as in life, are surprising. Bullying officers crumple; runts
like Ackerman turn out to be heroes. Whitacre, overweight and overwhelmed, proves less a coward than a helpless child, and only with Ackerman's guidance does he avoid certain death. Ackerman has found the
secret of survival: being in a unit with battle-tempered buddies who won't
betray you. Having found such a unit, he exudes a strange and radiant

serenity, an outlook that in peacetime might be deemed insanity but that in war becomes a kind of hyperclarity.

It's not unlike the outlook that Christian Diestl himself acquires to survive the war.

Diestl's story, though woven episodically through those of Whitacre and Ackerman, stands apart in more than the obvious sense. Shaw borrows from his African experiences to enrich his portrait of the tough Nazi soldier, but many of the details, and much of the flavor, are necessarily imagined or absorbed secondhand. Yet Diestl's emerges as the most vivid of the three stories.

One reason is that neither of the Americans has as complex a character as the German. Whitacre's capacity for self-loathing, intriguing at first, grows tiresome. His scenes become the novel's slowest moving; not coincidentally, he is the only one of the three whose interior thought process we are allowed to see. Ackerman is admirable but also one-dimensional, devoid of any interior conflict. But Diestl is a fascinating enigma. A sensitive lover and political intellectual, he nevertheless grimly accepts Nazism, and the extermination of the Jews, as a means to an end. Well-mannered, scornful at first of fellow soldiers who indulge in black-market dealings, he proves capable in the end of the most barbaric acts. Like Ackerman, Diestl acquires a strange clarity to cope with the war, but whereas Ackerman's is a kind of rough Christianity, Diestl's is the clarity of evil. That Shaw keeps Diestl from becoming a one-dimensional character—even as a war-hardened Nazi, Diestl has feelings—is an exercise of true art. Still, the story's underlying thesis is unmistakable: that Americans, for all their blunders, are essentially good people, and that Germans, complex as they may be, retain a combustible core of national arrogance that awaits only the match of a demagogue like Hitler to explode into aggression again.

Shaw identified with Whitacre; he sentimentalized Ackerman. Diestl he felt coldly removed from, and perhaps as a result, he moves him more briskly through scenes of great action that serve both to harden Diestl's character and to startle the reader in a way the American scenes less often manage to do. (Here, as in stories like "Sailor off the Bremen," Shaw seems to write best when his motivation is rage at injustice.) Consigned to a backwater post in Nazi France under a cruel superior named Hardenburg, Diestl grows cynical about the German army, just as Whitacre does about the American. That cynicism plumbs new depths when he returns to Berlin on a leave and ends up in bed with Hardenburg's wife, a fleshy virago who takes gifts for sexual favors, from both men and women, and becomes a fascinating personification of her city in a soulless time. Transferred finally to Africa, Diestl's unit struggles through the wind-swept sands—killing, in perhaps the novel's single strongest scene, an entire unit of British soldiers at dawn—until trapped by Montgomery's persevering troops. It is then that Hardenburg demonstrates ultimate pragmatism, leaving his men to die on a sand dune and escaping by motorcycle with Diestl on the back. (Hardenburg never does discover that Diestl has slept with his wife.) The odyssey that takes them west toward Algiers is, of course, modeled on Shaw's own drives across that battle-scarred land.

The motorcycle escape ends with a land mine, and Hardenburg, in a somewhat overt touch of symbolism, has his face blown off. Swaddled in bandages in a hospital bed, he rants on about Nazism, imparting the true essence of it; one senses the journalist in Shaw wanting to capture on the page exactly how Nazis rationalized their mission as a lesson to future generations. Diestl, the perfect Nazi, takes the lesson literally, and accepts Hardenburg as his spiritual leader: the devil has gained a devotee.

As Diestl carries on his personal retreat up through France and home to Germany, there are more scenes that suggest Shaw's own war: bombed-out villages in southern France; villages on the Normandy coast in which Nazis struggle to hold power over seething French peasants; Paris in the last weeks of Nazi occupation, with Resistance fighters growing bolder every day. Most shocking are the piles of bodies at Dachau, in a scene described to Shaw by George Stevens, who participated in the camp's liberation. The American lieutenant who allows a memorial service to be held by the camp's surviving Jews, over the objections of non-Jewish prisoners, is modeled on Stevens.

The novel ends in a scene of seeming tragedy. Diestl, resolute to the last, spies Ackerman and Whitacre strolling on a path near Dachau. From a hidden vantage point, he picks off Ackerman with a shot through the throat. Whitacre plunges after Diestl and in man-to-man combat emerges the victor. War has no happy endings and the violence that war unleashes always runs off the track, but Whitacre, Shaw's protagonist, has at last been tested and has found he is not lacking. The novel ends as he shoulders the body of his dead friend and walks back to civilization; symbolically, he has now absorbed Ackerman's character, his strength and courage. The two characters have finally merged.

Which is exactly what Shaw hoped the war had done for him.

That summer, with the novel not due out until October, Shaw let Hollywood seduce him again. With screenwriter Charles Schnee, he worked on the film *Easy Living,* the plot of which must have amused him: an aging football star wants to retire, but first must satisfy the living standards of his overambitious wife. With his brother, David, he wrote a script called *Take One False Step* for Chester Erskine, a light mystery about a college professor who meets up with a blonde from his past on a business trip and gets involved with the police. Both films appeared the next year to critical yawns.

Understandably, Shaw's mind wasn't on the work. From Random House there were still almost daily communiqués as *The Young Lions* went into print. And then there was the matter of that other war book, out and already on the bestseller lists.

The Naked and the Dead had appeared with great fanfare in May, and its young author had already been compared to Dos Passos. Much of the stir had been generated by the book's rough language—the famous "fugs" that appeared all through it. Then too, it brought home in graphic terms the war in the Pacific, which had remained puzzling and remote to many Americans. For Shaw, though, the most startling aspect of The Naked and the Dead was that he and its author bore so much in common.

Like Shaw, Mailer had grown up Jewish in Brooklyn. Like Shaw, he had burst onto the literary scene at a young age. Like Shaw too, he had struggled, with vaulting ambition, to write the big book about the war. When The Young Lions did appear at last, comparisons were inevitable— "Which is better?" was a colorful issue of debate at New York cocktail parties that fall—and no two people brooded more on the matter than the authors themselves.

"Similarities? Well, there were and there weren't," recalls Mailer. "What I mean is, ethnically we couldn't have been closer. We grew up just a few miles apart, same middle-class Jewish background. But he was an athlete, and I always used to resent that. I was jealous! So I always respected him, and I always felt edgy toward him. And that really got into our relationship right in the beginning. It had nothing to do with him, it had to do with me. When I finally met him, I was very tough on him because of this, the fact that he could play ball better than me and was bigger. Remember too, he was also ten years older than I was—that extra half a generation. So I looked on him almost as one would on an older brother."

Both writers, in turn, looked up to Hemingway. It was Hemingway who had set the new standard of the American writer as sportsman and risk taker, Hemingway who defined the new literary machismo. Mailer, however, says he felt less of an emotional tie. "Irwin had really grown up in the Hemingway period. By the time I hit the surface in 1948, Hemingway was already so established, so much at the summit, that you didn't need to think about him that closely." (Two years later, when Hemingway referred to "young writers from Brooklyn who think they're Tolstoy" in Lillian Ross's profile of him in The New Yorker, Mailer wondered whether it was he or Shaw who was the object of the great man's scorn. "At the time it was written I thought he was referring to me. But it may be that Hemingway, who was nothing if not sly about these things, wrote it in such a way that it could hit both of us equally. He always liked to kill the competition, and this way he could kill two birds with one stone. Wow! Elegance!" In fact, Shaw was the likelier target, thanks to Leland Hayward's widely publicized declaration that The Young Lions was the greatest war novel to come along since War and Peace. "And it may be," Hayward added, "that when I reread War and Peace, I may have to change my mind in favor of *The Young Lions.*)" That generational difference, and Hemingway's lessening influence over time, may have helped to distinguish their prose styles. "I always thought Irwin was a much more polished writer than I was," says Mailer. "And I tried to polish much less. It's like boxers and sluggers: the slugger says, 'Well, I can't box as well as he can but I can hit harder.' That's about the way I saw it."

The critical reception to *The Young Lions* was immediate and, overall, thunderously positive. In those first weeks of October many reviewers seemed deeply moved by the book, even awed. "This is the moment Irwin Shaw's friends have been waiting for since 1936," began Richard Match for the *Herald Tribune* book review. Declaring that Shaw had overnight become one of America's most important novelists with *The Young Lions*, Match added, "It is almost as if a DiMaggio had cast aside his center-fielder's glove one afternoon, turned up that night at Madison Square Garden, and knocked out Joe Louis in the first round. Irwin Shaw's new novel is that impressive." Wrote William McFee: "The reviewer is too close to it at present, too moved by its art to say just how great it may be." Marc Brandel agreed only somewhat more calmly. While the book did strike him more as a collection of stories than a unified novel—a criticism others would voice of future Shaw novels—*The Young Lions* still deserved to be "one of the most widely read books of the year. Reading it is a true emotional experience."

All over the country that fall, newspaper critics trumpeted the book. Off Random House's presses rolled one printing after another—five additional printings of 15,000 copies by the turn of the year. *The Young Lions* made its maiden appearance on the *New York Times* bestseller list on October 24, ranking fifth, with *The Naked and the Dead* securely in first place. By November 6, *The Young Lions* had hit the top spot, with *The Naked and the Dead* just below it. For the next several weeks the two traded off, until finally, in late December, they slowly began to fall.

Not every critic joined in the cheering, however. Off to the side, a small but influential New York literary elite regarded Shaw's great success with mixed emotions. To the intellectuals of *The Nation* and *The New Republic,* to critics like Irving Howe and Leslie Fiedler, there was something disturbing about Shaw and *The Young Lions,* an aftertaste of betrayal. Where was the young Jewish leftist whose brilliant first play had been a proletarian howl of protest against war? Where was the writer who had gone on to voice the sorrows of working-class people in his short stories? Who was this stranger who had emerged from his shell, to make money writing movies for Samuel Goldwyn and now more money with a fat commercial novel that took an all-American, down-the-middle stand?

It was a backlash just beginning, but one that Diana Trilling expressed succinctly that fall in *The Nation.* Shaw, she suggested, had been a bellwether: "When liberalism took its boldest stand on a hatred of war, Mr. Shaw raised the bones of the war dead. When liberalism had had its surfeit of quietism, Mr. Shaw issued the call to action. When resistance mobilized, Mr. Shaw was in the forefront of the celebrants of the fighting democratic spirit. When the open enemy of fascism abroad had been conquered, Mr. Shaw was quick to name the lurking enemies of democracy within our walls. As an artist he has been an exemplary citizen—devoted, energetic, too intelligent to be too pious yet too pious to be disturbing, his talents as a writer beautifully tuned to the intellectual pitch of his society." Now, Trilling wrote, the liberal artist is freed "for his original job as explorer of the complexities." Shaw had the opportunity to be that liberal artist, but in view of what Trilling felt were serious flaws in *The Young Lions*—lead characters who failed to breathe; not infrequent patches of bad prose; overall a failure as the study in social determinism the novel was intended to be—it would take another book to see if Shaw could handle the complexities to which his bellwethering had brought him.

If there was wariness in Trilling's tribute, there was barely veiled rage in *Time*'s unsigned pan of the novel. Again, the tone was a harbinger of critical ire to come. "Before the war, Irwin Shaw won easy fame and money by turning out smooth and clever plays and stories—for many tastes, rather too smooth and clever. Now, with his war experience to draw upon, Shaw has thrown all his energy and talent into an ambitious novel. . . . The sad news is that he has failed; his novel is depressing evidence of how hard it is for a writer to slough off youthful habits."

Easy fame and money. Whatever the truth in critics' barbs, these were the irritants that would sharpen them.

Buoyed by his success, Shaw returned to New York in November to go apartment-hunting. For several weeks, he and Marian lived in transition at One Fifth Avenue. By the turn of the year, though, they moved to the Chelsea apartment that would be their last real address in New York, a handsome duplex in an old brownstone at 349 West 22nd Street.

Shaw did continue to work. There were new stories: the most memorable of that period is "Climate of Insomnia," perhaps inspired by the screenplay for *Take One False Step,* about a college professor who spends the weekend brooding over an unreturned phone message from a colleague that may mean blacklist trouble; it appeared in *The New Yorker* the next April. But the success of *The Young Lions* was also ushering in a time of richly earned fun.

In February Shaw let Peter Viertel talk him into going to Ketchum, Idaho, on a first-ever skiing trip. Viertel had arrived earlier and found himself staying at the same motel as Ernest Hemingway. Both men were rugged outdoorsmen, both had seen considerable wartime action, and when introductions were made, the two took an instant and enduring liking to each other. It was a friendship in which Viertel would become something of a respectful younger brother, joining Hemingway for fishing in Cuba and bullfights in Spain, and also serving as screenwriter for *The Old Man and the Sea* and *The Sun Also Rises* (and, as it happened, trying to shrug off Papa's frequent insults about Shaw). By the time the Shaws arrived, however, Hemingway had left, throwing out an ill-fated invitation for the Viertels to join him on a cruise to France the next fall, and a tense situation was avoided.

Bob and Kathie Parrish came along on the skiing trip, and both Parrish and Shaw took to the slopes of nearby Sun Valley with gusto, if not grace. Parrish promptly broke his leg. There were amusing distractions: the Shah of Iran was around, surrounded by bodyguards whenever he went up to take a run. (Introductions were made, and the Shah later came to Klosters.) Darryl Zanuck was there too, accompanied by a personal ski instructor. At the top of a run, just off the ski lift, Zanuck would say to his instructor, "Jeez, it's cold up here, feel my mustache." The instructor, to the great amusement of Shaw or Viertel or Parrish standing by, would have to take off his gloves, lift off his goggles, and *feel* the mustache. Zanuck would become a Klosters regular.

A curious understanding obtained within the group about another sort of fun. As long as Marian was present, the Shaws were treated as a happily married couple—which they often were. But as soon as Marian left, Shaw would do his level best to seduce the nearest attractive woman he saw, and his married friends simply had to laugh along with him. Viertel, for one, privately shared Shaw's out-of-sight, out-of-mind attitude toward marriage, and stories of his own extramarital affairs with many of the world's most beautiful women still circulate among his friends. Others, like Parrish, demurred out of circumspection and a refusal to judge the friend whose jubilant company lit up their lives. Still, it made for some strange times. On that trip, recalls Viertel, "Marian left early and Irwin stayed on and really had a good time, out till four o'clock in the morning with some babe. But what happened was that Marian was on a train headed out of town with Willie Wyler [and Bob Parrish in a leg cast], and the train stopped about sixty miles out of town in a snowstorm." When the conductor radioed back the news, Viertel kidded a woozy Shaw that Marian was due back any minute.

The Shaws had spent the previous New Year's Eve in New York with Simon Michael Bessie, the editor, and the woman he'd since married from wartime London, Connie Ernst. The two couples had been in a ruminative mood, with talk of miscarriages—Connie had had one recently too—and Europe, which Shaw and Bessie yearned to see again, this time under happier circumstances. For the Shaws, a European trip now began to take on the definite shape of a New Year's resolution. By the time he returned from Ketchum, Shaw had lined up the work to make it happen.

First priority was *The New Yorker,* for which Shaw agreed to visit the newly established state of Israel and write a nonfiction piece of reporting on what he found. Despite his disdain for organized religion, he was engaged in an earnest bout of soul-searching about his identity as an American Jew, and was also eager to see how Jerusalem and Tel Aviv had changed since his wartime weeks there. Then too, he would write for the new travel magazine *Holiday,* giving its editors, in effect, his leftovers about Israel. All this would allow him to do some traveling of his own, in particular to explore the south of France with Marian, who had never been to Europe before. It would also give him a chance to work with Robert Capa.

Always drawn to the drama of war, Capa was eager to make a visual record of the new Israeli state, and talked a somewhat dubious Shaw into writing his *Holiday* story as a collaborative project. There might be a book in it too, Capa enthused. Accordingly, in early May, after traveling with Marian by freighter to Genoa and spending a few sunny vacation weeks in Italy, Shaw headed east to meet Capa for an adventure both moving and a bit madcap.

They started in Tel Aviv, visiting President Chaim Weizmann at his research institute, noting the new theaters and symphony orchestra, sitting in on a session of the Knesset. Capa, Shaw discovered, had become such a hero that he himself went all but unnoticed—the fellow, as he put it, who held the photographer's lights. Still, Shaw was able to interview all manner of proud Israelis—farmers, army officers, intellectuals—and gain a vivid, balanced view of Israel's historic transition. When the two went on to Jerusalem, they witnessed the tumultuous one-year anniversary celebrations of statehood. Capa was able to persuade camera-shy Orthodox Jews to pose for him, and to record the preparation of a Bokharan Jewish bride. He was all for plunging right into that part of the old city controlled by the Arab Legion, too, despite the stern warning of Jewish officers guarding the Mandelbaum Gate that the Arabs inside would tear apart the Americans. To Shaw's consternation, Capa was even ready to disguise himself as a Bedouin camel driver to smuggle himself in; fortunately, his zeal was thwarted, and the two ended up relying on an Arab photographer for pictures of the Great Mosque.

Capa then went off on his own, traveling north to Haifa to record the appalling sight of Jewish immigrants from all over Europe arriving in boats with the hope of living in a new homeland, only to be steered to internment camps. Shaw, who had witnessed and written about that tragedy before, had no stomach for seeing it again. After finishing a long "Letter from Tel Aviv" for *The New Yorker,* he traveled back to Rome on May 24 to rendezvous with Marian and take her off on a happy, monthlong whirl of cafés and restaurants in Italy and France.

By July the Shaws had settled in Cap d'Antibes, in a huge, pine-shaded house, the Villa Shady Rock, that fronted the Mediterranean. The house's coastal side was still painted gray-green in camouflage patterns, a reminder of German wartime occupation. In the kitchen was an electric refrigerator, a rare luxury; in the master bedroom was a huge old bathtub with a view of the sea. The house came with two servants, there was a tennis club around the corner, and as Shaw wrote sheepishly to Donald Klopfer, it was not a place in which he expected to get much writing done.

Mornings Shaw would take an early swim, then pick up fresh milk and cream for breakfast from a nearby farm. Then he might take a stroll into Antibes, to gaze covetously at the yachts in the harbor and pick up fresh fruit at the market. The next several hours were reserved for the beach, at Antibes, or at Golfe-Juan, where Picasso could usually be found cavorting with his young child, or at Eden Roc, where the superrich reclined, until the lengthening light stirred thoughts of dinner. Always a hearty eater, Shaw particularly liked seeking out the best bouillabaisse in Cannes, or venturing to Golfe de la Napoule or Monte Carlo or the walled hilltop town of Cagnes. In Antibes itself, there was a sailor's bar across from the best restaurant, and Shaw would stop in toward the end of the evening to engage in the local sport of chest-hair pulling. "The players merely reached inside their shirts, grabbed as much hair as possible, and yanked," Shaw wrote later. "Then they carefully laid the hairs out on a paper napkin to be counted by a referee chosen for his honesty." The loser bought the next round of drinks.

Generous by nature, happy to share the sunny pleasures of this Riviera retreat, Shaw was quick to invite friends to stay, and he had his first taste of playing the grand, gregarious American host in Europe, a role that would come to define him almost as much as his writing. Marian played the supporting role of perfect hostess with consummate good grace, planning meals and overseeing the household staff, whisking away dirty ashtrays and replenishing drinks. Her patience was sorely strained, however, by the houseguests who wouldn't leave: Robert Capa and fellow photographer Gjon Mili.

For all his success and celebrity, Capa had always nursed a brooding, self-destructive bent. Now, in the boredom of peacetime, his life was spinning out of control. As soon as he and Mili arrived that summer—taking advantage of the free room and board at the Shaws' while on extended assignment to photograph Picasso—they took to gambling late into the night at a nearby casino in Cannes, drinking to excess, and bringing back a colorful variety of casual dates, even prostitutes. More than one morning Shaw had to raid Marian's closet for clothes that the photographer's dates could wear to avoid shocking the neighborhood as they left. In one of the most transparently autobiographical scenes he ever wrote, Shaw has his protagonist Jesse Craig in *Evening in Byzantium* reminisce about his 1949 summer in Antibes and the houseguest who went a long way toward wrecking it. Craig's wife, the slim and tan Penelope, goes waterskiing on the bay of La Garoupe, a graceful figure in her one-piece black bathing suit, and Craig recalls many romantic moments, the two of them dancing in nearby cafés, going for noon swims in the Mediterranean (Penelope's cheery announcement of "Swim call" echoes Marian), sipping cocktails on the patio overlooking the sea. But the Craigs' houseguest, an embittered playwright named Brenner, inevitably gets on Penelope's nerves. In real life, Shaw told Capa's biographer Richard Whelan, Marian finally forced him to ask Capa and Mili to leave. In *Evening in Byzantium,* Jesse Craig refuses to do that and goes off to Paris on a business trip, leaving Brenner back at the villa with his wife. Furious, Penelope takes creative revenge: she sleeps with the playwright while her husband is gone. The added shock is that Penelope, just days before, has announced she's pregnant.

Marian Shaw, as it happened, became pregnant that summer too.

When the Shaws returned that fall to West 22nd Street, they were told in no uncertain terms that if Marian hoped to avoid yet another miscarriage, she would have to spend the remaining months of her pregnancy in bed—all day, every day. So grave was the danger that bricks were put under the bed's lower legs so she would be at a safer angle. It was an extraordinary sacrifice, but one Marian was willing to make; after several miscarriages and ten years of marriage, both Shaws were desperate for a child. Irwin's desire was possibly even keener than Marian's. Nonpracticing Jew that he was, he had still inherited the conviction that all Jews, historically beleaguered, must procreate to survive as a people.

Shaw was not, however, the sort of patient and loyal husband who could endure too much bedside vigil. In the morning he would work on stories in another room. Restless by midafternoon, he would saunter down Eighth Avenue, full of brio and ready for a drink. *New Yorker* writer Bruce Bliven, Jr., who lived in the Village, remembers seeing him often on that afternoon stroll, brimming with happy confidence in his own talents and urging Bliven to join him for drinks in the nearest bar.

Sidney Simon, a New York sculptor, remembers Shaw as one of a bachelor group that for a while held parties on a regular basis and maintained a mailing list of interesting single women to invite. George Plimpton and Charles Addams were in the group, Simon recalls, as were Arthur Altschul, Cass Canfield, Jr., and the Capa brothers, Robert and Cornell.

Many of these same names turned up at parties cohosted by Simon in the Sullivan-MacDougal gardens, the private enclave framed by the brownstones on either street in the Village, on a block bordered by Houston Street to the south and Bleecker Street to the north. Record producer John Hammond, who lived in one of those brownstones, invited musicians. Bob Shaplen, the Far Eastern writer for *The New Yorker* at the time, brought in friends from the magazine, and editors Simon Michael Bessie and Hiram Haydn brought other colleagues and writers.

Sundays as a rule, Shaw played with other writers in a pick-up touch-football game in Central Park, inevitably appearing in his Brooklyn College sweatshirt and, less appealingly, his cleats. Merle Miller would play, as would Paddy Chayefsky, Karl Malden and Walter Bernstein. "I remember playing with Irwin in the period that Marian was pregnant," recalls Bernstein. "And we all knew she wasn't allowed to get out of bed. Yet when we came back to the Shaws' house after the game, there would be the ice out, and the liquor, and the canapés, all beautifully arranged. Marian would have gotten up to do all that."

Surprisingly, one of the other regulars in the game was John Cheever. The runt of the group, Cheever often grumbled that the others blocked too roughly. Still, he came out to play. Walter Bernstein remembers blocking out Shaw in one game to allow Cheever to run for a touchdown. "Irwin never forgot that—that I had the nerve to let Cheever score."

In fact, Shaw and Cheever still saw a fair amount of each other. Not only were they fellow *New Yorker* writers who could gripe about the magazine's low pay and cavalier treatment, but Cheever had also gone through Astoria, albeit later in the war. It didn't hurt that both men liked to drink as much as they did, either. The Cheevers often had dinner with the Shaws, and Mary Cheever remembers the banter that Irwin and Marian would engage in as the Cheevers looked on. "Irwin would make fun of her hair, for example. Marian had this wonderful dark hair, and Irwin would say, 'My wife has this marvelous black curly hair, and she dyes it! She puts peroxide on it!' But she was always debunking him too. Because sometimes Irwin was just impossible. He was so full of himself. Like he'd show his muscle and Marian would say, 'Oh, how disgusting!' "

Still, the differences between the two men were more illuminating about each than were the bonds. Simon Michael Bessie, who eventually became Cheever's editor, says Cheever was both fascinated with and baffled by Shaw's garrulousness, his bluster and particularly the ease with which he dealt with producers like Samuel Goldwyn. Adds *New Yorker* writer Edward Newhouse, who knew both men but was far closer to Cheever: "Cheever operated in a fantasy world; he would often embroider his anecdotes. Irwin, on the other hand, lived in the real world; he wrote to order. He also lived in a playwright's world. By the third act, a play had to be winding up, its strings pulling together. He'd learned that from his radio days, and it influenced the way he wrote his stories and novels—in Irwin's world, cause and effect were always at work."

"Put it this way," says Bessie. "What Irwin wouldn't have known about John was quite a lot, whereas I don't think there was much about Irwin that John couldn't easily know."

With luck and great care, Marian did manage this time to avoid a miscarriage, and certainly Shaw must have shared her euphoria at the prospect of delivering a child. But the hours surrounding the birth of Adam Shaw on March 27, 1950, were marred by two of the most disconcerting experiences of Shaw's life.

Marian's labor pains began on a day roughly two months before she was due, and by late afternoon Shaw had delivered her to Doctors Hospital. Then, apparently, he spent the rest of the day trying to get a highly attractive young woman into bed.

Leila Hadley was a well-known, stylish lady about town at the time. She liked to travel and gave parties that drew both a literary and a social crowd. Shaw had gone to a few of them, and taken a strong liking to his hostess. "Then came the day Marian went into labor with Adam," Hadley recalls. "After Irwin took her to Doctors Hospital, he came over to my apartment. He said Marian had told him to come on over, because he was so agitated. But then—he proceeded to make a lunge for me! I mean, he started pursuing me around the apartment, pawing me. I was just stunned, and in tears, because I was still so naive and so in awe of this great writer." The situation had an almost zany edge. "I kept saying, 'What about the *baby*, what about the *baby*??' And he actually called the hospital from my apartment. But I couldn't get him out of there for nearly four hours."

That very evening, Shaw joined friends for dinner at "21." On his way out, he passed Ernest and Mary Hemingway, just arrived in New York by boat from Le Havre, dining with the Harold Rosses. Hemingway had always felt a competitive edginess toward Shaw, but *The Young Lions* had pushed him to fury. Now he lit into Shaw, excoriating him loudly and bitterly, declaring he knew full well that Shaw had based characters in the novel on him, his brother and Mary. It was difficult to tell what he was most insulted by: the mocking portraits of himself and Leicester; the breezy acknowledgment in print that Shaw and Mary Welsh had had an affair (and that Louise M'Kimber had asked Michael Whitacre to marry her); or perhaps worst of all, the sheer effrontery of this Brooklyn Tolstoy to presume he could write about the war at all, when clearly the war was Hemingway's exclusive purview. At any rate, the exchange left Mary and the Rosses shaking. But Shaw, marveled Mary Hemingway, stood his ground unblinkingly, "failing to bleed from every pore."

Shaw had reason of his own to feel furious with the older writer. In November Hemingway had made good on his invitation to the Viertels to join him on the *Île de France* from New York to Paris. At the last minute, Peter had had to stay behind to finish a screenplay, and Jigee had set off alone with Ernest and Mary. Jigee, who had never had a drink in her life, was induced by Hemingway to join him for cocktails as the voyage got under way. She proved to have a genetic propensity for alcohol abuse and within days established an appetite for drink that transformed her, in her early thirties, into a severe alcoholic. Whether she actually had an affair with Hemingway on the trip is unclear—at least one printed account of the trip declares she did, while Viertel says she didn't—but Hemingway certainly took her under his wing, as he often did at this stage of his life with younger women; and when Viertel met up with the trio in Paris, it soon became apparent that his marriage was doomed.

Over the next months, there would be other omens of a souring in what should have been a time of enduring triumph and celebration for Shaw the writer and Shaw the man. Finally it would seem the only answer would be to leave New York, leave Hollywood, to try to recapture the sweetness of the summer in Antibes by moving to Europe, first for another summer, then for a much, much longer time.

CHAPTER ELEVEN

There was an omen in the news the *New York Herald Tribune* reported on April 23, 1950: two American plays, it said, were being produced in Vienna by Communists. Arthur Miller's *Death of a Salesman* and Irwin Shaw's *The Gentle People,* went the story, "are providing the Communists with grist for their propaganda mill. The party press and the official Soviet Army newspaper have been able to use these plays . . . as 'confirmation' of the picture of social conditions in 'capitalist' America."

The climate of anti-Communist fear had cooled since the 1947 hearings, and after the indictment of the Hollywood Ten, the entertainment industry had been left more or less alone. Now the real nightmare was about to begin.

In June the U.S. Supreme Court declined to reconsider the cases of the Hollywood Ten, who had been found guilty of instilling Communist propaganda in films to which they had contributed as writers and directors. The ruling validated Hollywood's pious expulsion of the Ten, and the existence of a Communist threat. In August jail terms of up to twelve months were meted out to each offender.

Also in June, Communist North Korean troops crossed the 38th Parallel, and President Truman took the first steps toward committing the country to war. With American soldiers preparing to put their lives on the line against the Communist threat, the government evinced an abrupt new toughness on possible Communists in its midst, and would soon draw up loyalty oaths for its employees. "Fellow travelers" and other liberals of the gray zone between patriotic Americans and active Communists would no longer be tolerated. One was either a pure anti-Communist—or an unadulterated Red. With the simultaneous publication of a 200-page document called *Red Channels,* that distinction became dramatically clearer.

In the paranoid mood of the time, no one stopped to question the authority of the four fervent conservatives who took it upon themselves to publish the red-bordered, paperbound listing of suspected Communists in the entertainment industry, mostly in radio and the new, potentially far more dangerous medium of television. Nor did the flimsiness of the accusations seem to matter. To a skittish industry, the mere fact that a name was listed seemed proof of that person's guilt. Indeed, the more seemingly proper the figure, the more alarming the accusation. American Communists, as the Red-baiters declared in stentorian tones, usually had two personas: the one the public saw, and a dark, private life of intrigue and conspiracy. Among the *Red Channels* names were those of Dorothy Parker, Judy Holliday, Lillian Hellman and Irwin Shaw.

Liberal journalists hastened to dismiss *Red Channels* as the absurd document that it was, the handiwork of a few frustrated ex–FBI agents who hoped to make a name—and money—for themselves. Within weeks of its publication, however, an incident occurred that confirmed the document's impact and established that a new round of blacklisting had begun. The incident seemed to reenact, in perfect detail, Shaw's nearly finished second novel.

It began with the announcement by NBC that *The Aldrich Family*, a successful radio comedy, would be brought to television, and that its star would be actress Jean Muir. The choice of Muir was a political as well as an artistic one: she had been named in *Red Channels* as having "attended Communist study groups" a decade before, and in ignoring that charge, NBC, intentionally or not, was taking a stand. Theodore Kirkpatrick, the editor of *Red Channels*, realized that NBC might deflate his campaign and end his newfound prominence, yet he and his cronies couldn't attack the network without seeming to overreach themselves. So Kirkpatrick found a willing advocate, a Greenwich, Connecticut, housewife named Hester McCullough who had railed at Ed Sullivan that spring for inviting to his show two performers she felt were Red-tainted. McCullough called network executives; she organized a letter-writing campaign. In remarkably short order, the sponsor of *The Aldrich Family*, General Foods, swung into line and announced that Jean Muir would be dropped from the cast. Shaw's *The Troubled Air*, appearing the next year, would confront the issues raised by that sorry affair.

For the moment Shaw chose to respond to *Red Channels* and the scare in another, more immediate way that shocked many of his friends. "Several weeks ago," he announced in a letter to *The New York Times* that appeared August 20, "I had to perform an unpleasant duty: I had to inform my agents to refuse permission to any groups or persons here or abroad to present my play, *Bury the Dead*."

Shaw was responding, he wrote, to the alarming reports that his plays were being performed as propaganda tracts by Communist groups. "It is to balk these double-tongued gentlemen, with whatever small means are at my disposal, that I have withdrawn my play. I do not wish the forlorn longings and illusions of 1935 to be used as ammunition for the killers of 1950."

Well meant as this gesture seems to have been, it had the misfortune of appearing as a response to Shaw's inclusion in *Red Channels*, an impression hardly mitigated by Theodore Kirkpatrick's announcement soon after that in his weekly newsletter, *Counter Attack,* he would take approving cognizance of Shaw's action. The Shaw letter sent ripples through the press, from *Time*'s leering coverage to the predictable howl of outrage from *The Daily Worker,* which treated Shaw as a scurrilous traitor to the cause. Among his friends, there was widespread consternation that the wrong signal had been sent—consternation that would only grow with the publication of *The Troubled Air.*

It was hard to find fault with a man who objected to the subverting of the message of his plays by Communists. Still, Shaw's loud public outcry, both in 1947 and now, was puzzling. Why, his friends wondered, hadn't he just shrugged off the news about the plays? Yanking *Bury the Dead* would hardly stop the flow of Communist propaganda. Quite the contrary, yanking it provided much more important propaganda for the American Right. There was a sense, in all this, of an ego too easily bruised, of a certain self-centeredness beneath the rhetoric.

On New Year's Eve, 1949, the Shaws had traveled to Quogue, Long Island, to spend the weekend as guests of Ted Patrick, the editor in chief of *Holiday* magazine. Joe Kaufman, a genial partygoer whose family money had enabled him to live a nineteenth-century life of leisure, remembers that party vividly. "Ted was urging Irwin and Marian to come out the next summer, said he'd find the Shaws a house and so forth. I went up to Ted later and said, 'I don't think that's a very good idea, Ted. You know the trouble *I'm* having. How do you think the Shaws will do with that?'"

The trouble was anti-Semitism. At least since the early 1900s, when the big houses had gone up, Quogue had had a reputation as a WASPy enclave, which was almost certainly why John and Belle O'Hara, for example, had made a point of summering there. Kaufman was only one-quarter Jewish. Still, he'd recently been asked to resign from a tennis club to which he belonged when the fact had come to light. Kaufman had told the club's president that he would gladly accept the decision if the president would be so kind as to send him a letter stating that the club did have a policy of discriminating against Jews—which was why Kaufman's "trouble" was continuing. What, he wondered, would happen to the tennis-loving Shaw, whose Jewishness was strikingly apparent?

"Don't worry," Patrick assured him. "I'll take care of it."

To Kaufman, it seemed almost as if Patrick and his fellow townsman O'Hara were laying a trap for Shaw, luring him out to this haven of anti-Semitic Old Money to set him up for a fall because he seemed to betray an overeagerness to be accepted in such circles. Certainly O'Hara was capable of it: studiedly snobbish to a legendary degree, he also felt competitive with other writers, and Shaw, one of his few peers at *The New Yorker* over the last decade, may have stirred his deepest bile. (It didn't help that O'Hara had broken with the magazine the previous year, and that Shaw was still publishing there.) As for Patrick, he was a strange and complex man, an enigma even to his closest colleagues at *Holiday.* "None of us knew Ted, although we got drunk with him every week," muses Frank Zachary, then *Holiday's* art designer. "He was very cold, a man in an iron mask."

Like O'Hara, Patrick adored living well and fraternizing with the rich. With the success of *Holiday,* he spent half the week in Philadelphia, where the magazine's staff was based, then came to New York and ended up in his big Dune Road house in Quogue for the weekends. Like Shaw, he was a prodigious drinker who played a good game of tennis. Like Shaw too, he loved good food and wine, and steered *Holiday* into doing some of the first reviewing of restaurants in the country. Sandy-haired, with a reddish complexion and a somewhat grating voice, he was, says Zachary, "extremely affable when he wanted to be—but stay out of his way when he was drinking." Could he have set Shaw up? If he didn't, says Kaufman, he certainly failed to help when the inevitable occurred.

At Patrick's suggestion, Irwin and Marian took a house on Dune Road opposite Patrick's, directly facing Quogue's little inland bay. For several weeks the summer seemed idyllic. Charles Addams was there; the *New Yorker* cartoonist at that time was married to Barbara Day (who would later marry Joe Kaufman, and after him John Hersey) and would see the Shaws often. "There was a little circle," he recalled years later. "Ted Patrick would have parties, and St. Clair McKelway [of *The New Yorker*] would come down, and of course John and Belle O'Hara would be there." But the O'Haras kept their distance from the Shaws. "One night," said Addams, "I said to Belle, 'Why don't you ever ask the Shaws over? And she said, 'I like *attractive* people.' "

Sometime in August, Shaw learned that he was no longer welcome at the tennis club where he'd been playing almost daily. Why he'd been allowed to play in the first place is unclear. It may have been that Shaw's eminence cowed board members initially, and that his bearish playing style and occasional loud remarks hardened their resolve. "The pretext for asking the Shaws to leave was that they were monopolizing the court," says Kaufman, "but Irwin knew what the reason was."

Kaufman was aghast, and went off to enlist Ted Patrick's support in confronting the board members, because Patrick was such a prominent summer resident. But he refused to get involved. "I said, 'Ted, you're just a coward,' " recalls Kaufman. But that was where the matter was left to stand.

Shaw was deeply wounded by the rejection—more wounded, perhaps, than other men might have been. Having pushed away his parents' ingrained identity as immigrant Jews, he still felt guilt in abandoning those roots, as *The Young Lions* demonstrated. Desirous of assimilating into WASP society, he remained strongly aware of his own Jewishness and made no effort to disguise it. In short, he wanted it all—and in Quogue, he had chosen the sort of place where that simply wouldn't happen.

The following May, just before the Shaws set off for Europe, William Walton, the *Time* correspondent from wartime London, asked Shaw over drinks why he felt obliged to spend his summer abroad. Shaw looked him squarely in the eye. "Because of the anti-Semitism here," he told Walton.

Later, after the move to Europe became permanent, Charles Addams caught up with Shaw one day in Paris and put the same question to him. "I asked him if the tennis club thing had had anything to do with his decision," recalled Addams. "And he said yes, it did."

Back in New York that fall, there was a far happier social life to resume. "In those days," remembers Marion Javits, "there were always two or three hostesses who entertained groups of people." Javits herself, married to the future senator from New York, became known for Sunday-night dinners at Luchow's restaurant on 14th Street—happy, casual gatherings that commingled the art world and East Side society to which the Shaws often came. Then there were Arthur and Joan Stanton. Soon after the war, Arthur Stanton, who was Jewish, had been presented with the American franchise for Volkswagens, the German cars Hitler had helped design, after Henry Ford declined to handle them because he felt they were too small. It was a business move of great shrewdness, if dubious ethics. Shaw, for one, shrugged off the implications and embraced Stanton as one of his closest friends. Years later, his major anthology of stories, *Five Decades*, would be dedicated to Stanton. Over that time, the friendship also resulted in the frequent serendipity for Shaw of a free or at-cost Volkswagen. "The Stantons would have theater people—Joan entertained beautifully," says Javits. Arthur's brother Frank, who served as Arthur's business partner, was also part of the circle, and a good friend of the Shaws. Alfred Crown, an aide-de-camp to Samuel Goldwyn, and his wife were close to the Shaws too, as were Arthur and Leonora Hornblow, Eli Wallach and Anne Jackson, and Edmond de Rothschild, and of course Martin Gabel and Arlene Francis, and Bennett and Phyllis Cerf. "But Arthur and Joan Stanton in particular did have a court, and they were very politically oriented," says Javits. "And in that court, age didn't seem to matter. That was because of the war. If you'd been in the war, you were part of the same generation. I had a husband who was twenty-one years older than I was, but he'd been in the war, and that made him an equal of those people."

The Shaws entertained too, though not grandly. By now the pattern was clear. Marian prided herself on serving as the perfect hostess, and in doing so created the backdrop for Shaw to carry on as the charming host who usually dominated the conversation with his energy and wit. It was an arrangement that pleased Marian because she carried it off well. It pleased Shaw because an orderly home was important to him—a holdover from a childhood in which his mother had managed the same role—and because he was so constitutionally incapable of maintaining that order himself. But the arrangement had a darker side too.

"One evening Irwin ran into my wife, Naomi, on 57th Street," says *New Yorker* writer Bruce Bliven, Jr. "And she called me up—I was home on Washington Square—and she said, 'I've just run into Irwin and he says we simply have to join him for dinner.' Well, I was writing something I wanted to finish, but Irwin was so insistent—and he'd already had a fair amount to drink, he was feeling very, very good—that I said, 'All right, we'll meet.' So I joined them at some bar, I think it was the Russian Tea Room, and we had a couple drinks. And then all of a sudden Irwin said, 'I've got to go home, I was supposed to be home for dinner.' He went on and on about how we had to join him, so finally, reluctantly, we did. We all got into a taxi and went to Irwin's place on West 22nd Street. And it turned out that Marian had had a small formal dinner for six set up! And here came the drunken Blivens and a drunken Irwin. And Marian was just ready to murder us all. And the worst of it was, we knew all the other people there—I remember Martin Gabel and Arlene Francis in particular—and Naomi and I just wanted to die. Marian tried to smooth it over for our sake, she looked adorable, hoping to have this perfect little party, but we'd been set up by Irwin, and he'd just botched the whole thing.

"Naomi and I have thought about that night ever since," Bliven adds, "trying to figure out why Irwin did that. Because he couldn't have failed to notice that Marian was knocking herself out. It was a formal dinner, all arranged. And yet he hadn't called ahead, had just stayed out carousing, and then brought us back to protect him. It was more than thoughtless, really—it was cruel."

As much as any difficult marriage can ever be one person's fault, the Shaws' seemed to be Irwin's. It was Marian who kept wanting the marriage to be right; and it was Irwin who kept smashing her carefully built conceit of domestic bliss, almost always drinking too much in the evenings now, marring her dinner parties, upbraiding her in front of their friends, chasing other women. Some friends ascribed the problems to passion: Irwin and Marian felt so intensely about one another that fights were bound to arise. Some felt Shaw, in his confrontations with Marian, acted the mischievous child, baiting her to stir a reaction. And then there were those—more than there would have been a decade before—who felt the marriage was bankrupt. Carol Matthau, a weekend guest in Quogue in the last days of her marriage to William Saroyan, found Marian overwhelmed by the world in which she found herself. "She was in a world that impressed her but made her mad because she was in over her head," recalls Matthau, who later had a bitter falling-out with Marian. "And so her whole career was devoted to being Mrs. Irwin Shaw, to worrying who he was seeing and whether he was flirting with someone. Irwin hated her, as far as I could see. He loved life, but he hated her. I thought it was the worst marriage I'd ever seen."

Clearly Shaw's drinking had become a corrosive factor in that marriage. But did he drink this much *because* the marriage dissatisfied him? Or was a rocky marriage just one result of a habit that had its roots elsewhere?

It was a conundrum Shaw's friends debated without ever reaching an answer. Neither of Shaw's parents had been more than moderate drinkers; nor had drinking been common among the poor Brooklyn families, especially the Jewish ones, of young Shaw's acquaintance. An athlete might have seemed only less likely to drink, and in any event, Shaw had had little or no money to spend in bars until his mid-twenties. The answer seemed to lie in an odd tangle of circumstance, the top strand of which was youthful success.

The celebrated playwright of *Bury the Dead* had been, after all, a pink-faced twenty-three-year-old. Confident enough of his own abilities to have aimed so high so soon, he had been stunned nonetheless by the magnitude of his success. He'd realized he could hold his own in the café-society crowds to which he now had entrée, but like Michael Whitacre in *The Young Lions,* he'd seemed not to believe his quick mind and wit were more than a front. Beneath the swagger, he would hint in novel after novel, was the real Irwin Shaw—a brooding self-doubter and sell-out. Drinking inflated the private Shaw to the public persona; it stirred the laughter that made everything work. It also eased the private tension of writing every day, and of never really knowing, despite his enormous energy, if his talent would stay true. With appetites so hearty, and a constitution so strong, Shaw also simply *consumed* more than many men did in order to feel the same effects. Now his tolerance appeared to be diminishing, but in the irony of alcoholism his thirst kept growing. As yet Shaw hardly stood out in such a hard-drinking era. But patterns had been set, and if no one else noticed or cared, Marian Shaw did. Angry and worried by turns, she raised a lone voice, and Shaw, of course, resented her for it. So, in an inevitable cycle, did drinking and marital tensions exacerbate each other in the Shaw family.

In September, Shaw became writer in residence for a term at New York University's Washington Square campus. He still lived in Chelsea; the position simply involved teaching a writing class to twenty-five students two nights a week. It was the first time the university had had a writer in residence, however, and for Shaw, who still keenly remembered how far NYU had seemed from Brooklyn College, it was a gratifying honor. At the same time he seemed a bit wary of what the job might entail. Told by an interviewer that writers in residence were expected to be available for home consultations with students on an ad hoc basis, he spluttered, "Lord, I don't want them to pop in here!"

Far more gratifying was the publication in October of Shaw's fourth collection for Random House, *Mixed Company: Collected Short Stories.* Many critics took the opportunity to assess Shaw from the long view as a now proven master of the short story, and offered some of the warmest tributes he would receive for the rest of his career. "Mr. Shaw is probably the most artistic and articulate exponent of the socially-conscious short story writing today," proclaimed William Peden. "I know of no American writer with the possible exception of John O'Hara," wrote John J. Maloney in the *New York Herald Tribune,* "who can, within the limits of the exacting form of the short story, so incisively depict the foibles and the follies of our age as Irwin Shaw." Added John K. Hutchens: "[Shaw] has his peers among American short-story writers now practicing, but just offhand, I can't think of more than two or three."

Yet Shaw, ever sensitive, nursed grievances about both Random House and *The New Yorker.*

A year before, Bennett Cerf had shown what seemed to Shaw a certain niggardliness about publication rights for the paperback book of Shaw's articles on Israel accompanied by Capa's photographs. Despite the excellent sales of *The Young Lions,* Shaw felt that Random House was longer on status than marketing savvy, and he wanted this more commercial venture to be handled by Simon & Schuster. Cerf was reluctant to let the book go. Finally, in the face of Shaw's ire, he reversed his stance on what he dismissively termed a dollar pamphlet, and the book was indeed published in the spring by S&S, as *Report on Israel.* Now, despite its glowing reviews, *Mixed Company* was selling poorly, and Shaw was annoyed again: Random House must not have been putting the needed money into marketing the book. The fact that he was working long days now on *The Troubled Air,* writing five or six pages at a clip, so that Random House would have it in time for its June list, made him feel all the more unappreciated by Cerf.

It was *The New Yorker,* however, that annoyed Shaw far more. Ever since his return from the war, he had felt a certain coolness from the magazine's editors. An anthology of wartime stories had managed to include only one of Shaw's several fine contributions ("Act of Faith"), as opposed to the inclusion of three stories in the 1940 anthology, a not so subtle slight. Nor was it any longer satisfying to Shaw to spend a week on a *New Yorker* story and get paid $400 when he had the opportunity to earn $3,000 to $4,000 a week as a Hollywood screenwriter.

If Shaw felt ill-treated by *The New Yorker*'s editors, they in turn felt ill-treated by him. In the bookish, Manhattan-based world the editors inhabited, Shaw's trips to Hollywood and the extraordinary fees he pulled down for screenwriting work were both confounding and offensive, a profane scramble for manna in the temple of art. Perhaps out of envy as much as anything else, they simply couldn't accept Shaw's assumption that a writer could swing from serious fiction to screenwriting and back without intellectual injury. No one felt that more strongly than Gus Lobrano, Shaw's earnest and mild-mannered editor.

"Lobrano was the managing editor of *The New Yorker* at that time," recalls Edward Newhouse. "His eyes were bad, he was eight or nine years older than the rest of us, and when he'd tried to enlist in the Army during the war, all the armed services had turned him down. One day, coming home on the Hudson train, he saw an advertisement calling for volunteer longshoremen to help load ships for the war effort. Without telling anyone but Ross and his wife and me, Lobrano began to take the train from Chappaqua every Saturday to work as a longshoreman. And he did that throughout the war—that's how quietly moral he was."

It didn't bother Lobrano if a *New Yorker* writer succeeded in selling his stories to the movies, as Edward Newhouse did in 1950 when Sam Goldwyn decided to stitch them together into a patriotic movie called *I Want You*, about World War II veterans dusting off their uniforms to defend democracy in Korea. That was just serendipity—the fat hand of Hollywood dispensing money to a humble writer back in New York. But for a writer to go *out* to Hollywood and work as an indentured servant— that was something else again. That fall, after Newhouse resisted Sam Goldwyn's offer to write the screenplay for *I Want You*, Goldwyn turned to Robert Sherwood, who had written the hugely popular *The Best Years of Our Lives*, to which Goldwyn envisioned *I Want You* as a sequel of sorts. When Sherwood turned him down, Goldwyn turned to Shaw, and Shaw accepted. "The notion of Irwin going out to the Coast to work for Sam Goldwyn made Gus Lobrano acutely uncomfortable," Newhouse recalls. "How could a man do it? It went against Gus's grain."

Once again Shaw was playing his balancing act, going for the big money and gambling he wouldn't lose his literary status. It was an act that was getting harder and harder to sustain, and this time there was another fateful factor. This time Shaw went alone, soon after Christmas, 1950, leaving Marian and his not yet one-year-old son in New York. He must have known this latest screenwriting stint would last several weeks at least. In the end, it lasted more than four months and, in both actual and emotional terms, amounted to a marital separation. The responsibility of family, and Marian's strong desire for an ordered, proper life, had suddenly come to seem intolerable.

If Shaw had also hoped to leave behind him the ugly rumblings caused by *Red Channels* in New York, these were hopes misplaced. Hollywood had caught a new dose of Communist hysteria, and the community was divided between conservative producers and studio heads who wanted to root out suspicious people, and liberals who decried loyalty oaths. In October the archpatriotic Cecil B. DeMille had led an emotional drive to oust director Joseph Mankiewicz from the Screen Directors Guild, only to be rebuffed in a showdown meeting by Mankiewicz's supporters, among them George Stevens, who gave a turning-point speech. Now, though, the House Un-American Activities Committee in Washington was readying a new roll call of Hollywood witnesses to testify at hearings beginning in March, and in the movie community, that stirred new fears.

In January, at Goldwyn's behest, Shaw checked into the Beverly-Carlton Hotel, a comfortable if second-rate place, since demolished, at the junction of Olympic Boulevard and Canon Drive. (Observes Viertel: "The Beverly-Carlton was where writers stayed when the company wasn't picking up the tab.") Across the street was an adjunct building with four residential apartments on the second floor, and it was into one of these that Shaw moved. By an odd coincidence, his old Brooklyn College speech professor and Cape Cod housemate, Arnold Moss, was occupying one of the others. Moss had gone on from his radio days to become a fairly successful movie actor. "Then, in addition to Irwin and me," Moss recalls, "Lillian Ross was staying in one of them. And in the fourth apartment was a young starlet whom we never saw—she never got up, apparently, until five in the afternoon—but in front of whose door flowers arrived all the time." The starlet was Marilyn Monroe.

"Irwin and I would go out all the time," recalls Moss, "and I met a lot of fascinating people like Salka Viertel, who would sit like a queen with every young man in town at her feet. We'd go to parties almost every night; sometimes we wouldn't get home until six in the morning. I'd go back to my room and try to sleep, and by seven o'clock I'd hear his damn typewriter going. The discipline of the man was fantastic." Then there were nights when Shaw found a girl and went off on his own. "He was definitely alley-catting around," says Moss. "But there was almost an innocence about Irwin with women, a childlike quality. Which was often what attracted women to him, I thought."

Shaw managed to maintain a happy rapport with the autocratic Goldwyn until he had to turn in a chunk of script. Abruptly, the relationship chilled. Goldwyn objected to what he called Shaw's bitterness and subtlety in the treatment of Eddie Newhouse's stories, woven together for I Want You. What Goldwyn seemed to want, Shaw snapped back, was some sugar-coated recruitment poster of a picture with no subtlety in it at all. By March 1, though, Shaw was able to write Leland Hayward that he had come up with a way to recast the script that pleased both men, and that he and Goldwyn were now "two lovebirds in a cage."

Cheering too were the packages of galleys for The Troubled Air that arrived from Random House, accompanied by exuberant notes from Bennett Cerf and Saxe Commins. Everyone who had read the book so far, they declared, had come away from it as excited as from The Young Lions, and Cerf confidently predicted it too would shoot to the top of the bestseller lists when it appeared in June.

They were right to be excited. Begun more than two years before, *The Troubled Air* nonetheless managed to capture the heat of the moment, then cool it with a rational eye that took note of, and carefully balanced, all the subtleties of the conflict between Red-baiters and the suspected Reds they targeted.

Like a good detective story, which in a sense it is, *The Troubled Air* unfolds from its initial drama. In this case morality, rather than a murder, is at stake. The lives of the cast members of a successful radio serial are suddenly shaken by the publication of a *Red Channels*–like publication called *Blueprint*. The show's producer, a functionary named O'Neill, tells his director, Clement Archer, that certain of the actors have been named in the tract as Communist sympathizers, and that the show's sponsor has warned they must go. "It's the temper of the time," O'Neill tells a shocked Archer, "and maybe you can't blame them too much." Archer, an honest and uncertain liberal in the mold of Michael Whitacre in *The Young Lions*, bargains with O'Neill for time to question the tainted actors, to see if he can determine for himself whether any are Communists, and still save the jobs of those who aren't.

In his rounds, Archer comes to appreciate the complexity and tragedy of the situation. One actor declares he *is* a Communist and has no intention of covering it—though why should any American lose his job for espousing a different political view? Another admits to the dim memory of attending some rally that turned out to be Communist related; sadly, even that mistake makes her a hard one to save. When Archer announces to O'Neill that he's decided to fire some but not others, the producer bristles, and soon reports the sponsor won't accept the deal. In one of the novel's strongest scenes, Archer commits a breach of protocol to pay a pleading visit himself to the sponsor in Pennsylvania, and encounters an affable, red-faced executive whose eyes turn hard as he rattles off his very convincing rationale for targeting any suspected Communists, even those whose complicity is unproven, in a time of national emergency. (Here, as in the long speech by the Nazi lieutenant Hardenberg in *The Young Lions*, one senses an underlying journalistic intent to put down on paper all the hues of a dangerous political logic, as a record and a lesson.) By the time the sordid business is finally over, the show's composer has committed suicide. Worse yet, Archer's hard-fought victory in saving the actor who is his best friend turns out to be pyrrhic: despite his earlier denials to Archer, Vic Herres is revealed to be a card-carrying Communist after all.

As in *The Young Lions*, glints of Shaw's own life appear throughout the story. The details of the radio show, and the opening scene of its taping, snap with authority from Shaw's radio-writing days in the thirties. Archer's own first job in the business was as a writer on a radio drama about a poor immigrant girl with "vague and secret royal connections in the old country"—a joking reference to *Marie, the Little French Princess*, the show for which David Driscoll wrote. Success came easily to him—easily enough to make him feel guilty—and for Archer, as for his creator, one way of placating his conscience is by loaning money to friends in need. ("To Archer, whose family had always been poor, the quick and generous proferring of money had always been the touchstone of friendship.") Archer's wife, Kitty, is tending a delicate pregnancy, mindful of past miscarriages, and pouts in the bedroom when the distracted Archer fails to pay her enough attention. (Interestingly, at several junctures Kitty *keeps* pouting until Archer spills his latest bad news. But Archer has set her up to look peevish by not sharing the bad news immediately.) Later, O'Neill says he's been quarreling with his wife and invites Archer along to a scheduled lunch with her because he can act "as a buffer state." In a more sympathetic insight, Archer looks at Kitty beside him in a darkened school auditorium as their daughter performs in a play onstage, and wonders if his wife, who once wanted to be an actress herself, is "going over in her head . . . the claims of love, the blunting of ambition, the arrival of children, the slow submersion of herself in [her husband's] career."

Not until early May did Shaw return to his wife and son in New York. By then the HUAC hearings had gone into high gear, and for all the excitement Shaw felt about the imminent publication of *The Troubled Air*, he was also apprehensive about the very real possibility that he might be named by one of the film industry witnesses—many of whom were friends.

The hearings had opened in March with the testimony of two cooperative witnesses, actors Larry Parks and Sterling Hayden. Both named names. Then came actor Howard Da Silva, who resolutely invoked the Fifth Amendment and was promptly punished by producer Irving Allen, who excised his image from an already completed film and reshot the sequences with another actor at a cost of $100,000. More depressing yet, director Edward Dmytryk, one of the original Hollywood Ten, took the witness stand and cooperated completely with the Committee. For Shaw the most startling testimony came in late April: from Marian's old beau Richard Collins and, shortly after, from Budd Schulberg.

Both named names. Indeed, it was Collins's naming of Schulberg that angered Schulberg enough to make a "friendly" appearance himself. Neither named Irwin or Marian Shaw, nor did the Shaws feel they had anything to hide. Already, though, they had seen how the most tenuous affiliations with vaguely Communist groups, from fifteen years past, could be distorted by right-wing crusaders to appear as damning fact. Marian's early association with Richard Collins might still be somehow used against her, and who knew what the inclusion of Irwin's name in *Red Channels* might yet mean? Later, when friends speculated on the real reason the Shaws had moved to Europe, the consensus would usually be that Shaw had moved to evade onerous taxes on his screenwriting income, and there

Irwin Shaw *(second from right, standing),* one of the "Four Hawksmen" of the Brooklyn College Warriors, 1930. (Brooklyn College, Library Special Collections)

A playwright and author at twenty-three. *Bury the Dead* was about to make him famous. (Columbia University)

Shaw with the cast of *Bury the Dead.* "I not only don't believe that that boy wrote that play," the director said. "I don't believe he can read it." (Brooklyn College, Library Special Collections)

Bury the Dead, 1937. "Thank God that that play has been written," said screenwriter Donald Ogden Stewart. "Thank God for Irwin Shaw." (Billy Rose Theatre Collection, The New York Public Library at Lincoln Center)

The Gentle People, 1939, Shaw's most commercially successful play. (Billy Rose Theatre Collection, The New York Public Library at Lincoln Center)

As a member of George Stevens's Special Coverage Unit of filmmakers in Cairo in 1943, Shaw roomed with future screenwriter Walter Bernstein. (Walter Bernstein)

Members of the Special Coverage Unit at their London base in spring 1944. Shaw is first on left, standing; Stevens is sixth from right, standing. (Pinckney Ridgell)

Members of the unit at a staging area in southern England, awaiting invasion orders, early June 1944. Shaw is third from left; in the center is Leicester Hemingway, Ernest's brother. (Pinckney Ridgell)

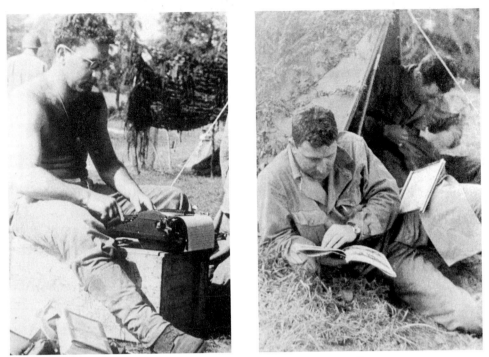

Shaw in Normandy, July 1944. (Philip Drell)

Shaw with Philip Drell in Normandy, July 1944. (Philip Drell)

Impromptu bathing, August 1944. With Shaw is colleague Ken Marthey. (Philip Drell)

With George Stevens, prowling a ruined French town, August 1944. On August 25, Shaw's was one of the first American jeeps in a liberated Paris. (Philip Drell)

Driver Angelo Tempesta, Pinckney Ridgell and Shaw contest a loaf of French bread, May 1945. (Philip Drell)

Ridgell, directors Joshua Logan and Anatole Litvak, and Shaw in the Bavarian Alps near St. Anton, July 1945. (Pinckney Ridgell)

Two Shaw-orchestrated weddings. *Top:* William Styron and Rose Burgunder, Rome, 1953, with some of the "tall young men" in attendance. *(Left to right)* Bernard Burgunder and wife, Anne Wigglesworth, Marian and Irwin Shaw, John Phillips Marquand, Jr., Tom Guinzburg (partly hidden), Rose Burgunder Styron, Peter Matthiessen, William Styron, Claire and Robert White, judge, Frank Wigglesworth. (William Styron) *Bottom:* Gay Talese and Nan Ahearn, Rome, 1959. Newlyweds with Shaw, flanked by witnesses. (Gay Talese)

would be some truth in that. But the poisonous events of April and May 1951 could not have failed to play a part.

Shaw's tax situation *was* troubling—the dilemma of the successful writer. "One day that winter," recalls Edward Newhouse, "Irwin and John Cheever and I had lunch at some elegant East Side bistro. Shaw was in New York for a few days, out from under the thumb of Sam Goldwyn. I remember he was also a new father, and John and I, having gone through early fatherhood already, were full of authoritative advice on how to go about it. Then Irwin began complaining about his financial situation. He pointed out to me and to John that he had to earn a lot of money to pay taxes on the money he had earned *last* year. John and I walked downtown afterward, and John was pretty low. He felt broke, and the idea of Irwin's predicament was not only alien but repellent to him."

The initial plan, in any event, was simply to spend another summer in Antibes, this time in a pretty little white stucco house on a waterfront estate called Clocher de la Garoupe, owned by a rich Englishwoman, Lady Norman, whom the Shaws had befriended two summers before. They would leave in late June, just after the publication of *The Troubled Air*.

Shaw's second novel, every bit as ambitious as the first, appeared to sharply divided reviews that made for quite a sendoff. Milton Rugoff in the *New York Herald Tribune* declared *The Troubled Air* to be "Irwin Shaw at his characteristic best, seizing passionately on a vital social issue and presenting it with a firm grasp not only of the intellectual and moral values but of the many kinds of human beings it involves." But more than one critic expressed skepticism about the surprise ending in which Vic Herres is revealed to be a Communist after all. "It seems incredible," wrote Stephen Stepanchev in *The Nation*, "that Archer should be unaware, after fifteen years of intimate association, that his friend Herres is a Communist. Exercising astonishing self-control, the latter makes no attempt to influence Archer's political thinking or to recruit him for the party's various agencies and drives."

The ending epitomized the problem many of Shaw's peers had with the whole novel: that it aired all sides of the issue and failed to land on any one of them. "This was not a time," recalls Walter Bernstein dryly, "that needed moral ambiguity." This was especially troubling, as Lionel Trilling pointed out, because Shaw had so consciously taken up the mission of advising the uncertain liberal to whom his novel was directed on how to act. "To those people as his audience and by means of these people as his characters he has tried to represent the social and political activities of our time," Trilling wrote, "setting forth in terms of the private life what economic depression, commercial corruption, fascism, xenophobia and war really mean, and to suggest the right responses of feeling and action to these grim commonplaces of danger."

Norman Mailer remembers confronting Shaw at a party at William Styron's house in New York, just after the novel's publication. "I felt it was practically a sin at that time to come out against the Communists. I wasn't pro-Communist, but everybody was attacking it and it was just too easy. I think he was wrestling with the issue in the book, and wasn't clear about what he felt. Anyway, I remember kidding around with him when we met. I was sort of imitating Johnny Weissmuller, and I said, 'Irwin, you— physical courage. Me—moral courage.' And he was very upset about that."

The novel's ending also stirred some of the conservative reaction that Shaw's liberal friends had feared. "Those wonderful people who in the 1930s and half of the 40s wanted to play at conspiracy against their own country . . . have in this year 1951 to face confession, contrition and penance," wrote George Sokolsky in the New York *Journal-American* in an astonishing display of misinterpretation. "And if they imagine otherwise, Irwin Shaw tells them in the last five pages of his novel: for there is no other way. As a matter of fact, the convinced, the active, conspirational Commu- nist . . . means to destroy us and he is proud of it. The banners of truth are indeed flying high if a young American writer could produce this novel."

Above all, critics felt confronted by a political novel that succumbed to the dangers of the form. Wrote Trilling: "Whatever political satisfaction *The Troubled Air* may give, it gives but little pleasure as a work of fiction." Added *The Nation*'s Stepanchev: "That the political novel is difficult to shape has been the discovery of many writers since 1945. There is always the danger of oversimplifying human desire and of losing the thickness of actual experience. . . . So exacting is the form . . . that for successful examples one must still turn to Dostoevsky, Kafka and Malraux."

In the week before they left, the Shaws were treated to a farewell party at "21." The Javitses were among the many friends who attended, and Marion Javits remembers a strange mood amid the laughter and well- wishing. "Their leaving seemed rather sudden," she recalls, "and perhaps it's just coincidence, but I've always associated Irwin's departure for Europe with the first grating sounds of the McCarthy era. There were so few intellectual voices to be heard, and it saddened me that Irwin's was leaving us."

Shaw could not have known, as he and Marian boarded the French Line's *Liberté* that June for the six-day journey to France, that much more than a summer would pass before he returned to live in the United States—that for the next quarter-century he would make his homes in Paris and in the tiny Swiss ski village of Klosters. He felt an excitement, however, not dissimilar to that he had felt in going off to the war. It was the anticipation of a galvanizing, catalytic experience, one that would cleanse him of all that now seemed sour in his life.

It was a move that in the end would diminish him as a writer, cutting him off from the world he knew and captured in his most memorable stories. Shaw would spend the rest of his life trying, with only intermittent success, to disprove the dictum that no writer should leave his literary roots. But in the process he would embark on a buoyant, nonstop celebration of good food, good wine and good friends, becoming almost as famous for that as for his writing—and creating, as more than one friend would put it, a veritable artwork of his life.

PART III

THE GREAT
ADVENTURE

CHAPTER TWELVE

It seemed fitting, in an odd way, that two of the other passengers traveling to France on board the *Liberté* that summer should be Ben Bradlee and Peter Matthiessen.

Both men were a good deal younger than Irwin Shaw—they in their twenties, he in his late thirties—and both stood in considerable awe of the famous writer they discovered in their midst. Presentable as their credentials were, promising as their respective careers, neither man would have presumed to approach Shaw without some excuse. "I was en route to being assistant to the press attaché in Paris," Bradlee recalls. "Shaw and I didn't know each other. Irwin Shaw one had heard of; no one had heard of Bradlee. But my son was about the same age as Adam, and so Irwin and I became friends on the boat." The as yet childless Matthiessen, bound for Paris to write a novel, was more diffident. "My first wife, Patsy, and I were newly married, but we were in steerage, or whatever the lowest class was, whereas Irwin was traveling first class. Below deck, we got to know Adam's nurse, a young Danish girl who said she'd introduce us to the Shaws. But I don't think she did; I don't think we actually met until we were all in Paris." Before long, both men would forge warm and enduring friendships with Shaw. Yet something of this initial relationship would remain, not only for them but for others in Shaw's Paris circle: the bright young journalists and writers, taken up by this larger-than-life literary lion who turned out to be even more the paterfamilias than his new friends might have bargained for.

Shaw had always had the capacity to work hard, then play hard, to the astonishment of other writers whose own sense of brooding guilt never let up. Now, more than ever before, he set a course for pleasure: hard-earned, guilt-free, unrestricted. From the moment he and Marian, Adam and his Danish nanny set foot on the sunswept grounds of Lady Norman's estate, the Shaws commenced a summer whirl of sybaritic fun and social entertaining that made their previous Antibes summer seem a quiet retreat.

"They were leading an F. Scott Fitzgerald life, collecting people," remembers Countess Enid Hardwicke, who came with her then husband, British director Roy Boulting. "The house they had rented was off to one side of the property. It wasn't a guest house, just a white stucco contemporary that Lady Norman and her husband had built. It was very nicely furnished, with a long living room and a fireplace at one end, and a gallery going up. I remember Lady Norman, a grand old weathered lady everyone knew, coming by to say hello." Boulting had come to be considered one of Britain's most progressive movie directors—as had his twin brother, John—and he and Shaw had become close enough friends that each would name the other godfather to his son. They had met during the war, when Boulting directed the documentary *Desert Victory,* on the Africa campaign; 1951, as it happened, was the year the Boultings' classic thriller *Seven Days to Noon* was released.

Most visible among the other visitors, Hardwicke recalls, were Arlene Francis and Martin Gabel. "Arlene used to wake up at about half past noon and start telling marvelous stories, and Martin would be there next to her; it was like Ping-Pong. They'd all start making dry martinis, and there was laughter, laughter, laughter." Moss and Kitty Hart came to visit, staying at the nearby Hotel du Cap. So did Josh and Netta Logan, Alan Moorehead, Constance Cummings, and Leland and Slim Hayward. They came drawn by Shaw's enormous charm. "You just gravitated to him," recalls Slim Hayward Keith. "You knew he was laughing because he himself had said something funny, and you didn't want to miss that."

There was tennis and swimming, but much of the laughter arose over cocktails on the terrace overlooking Cap la Garoupe bay. "I remember sitting on the terrace drinking champagne, and I did a terrible thing which Irwee just loved," remembers Slim Keith (who called Irwin by this diminutive as a matter of course). "Somebody said, 'Is Garbo here?' And you see, Leland had had a romance with Garbo, I used to try to get him to tell me about her. But for some reason at that moment I felt he was my man and no one else had ever touched him as far as I was concerned, and I took this glass of champagne and threw it in his face, and Irwee collapsed with laughter. Everybody else was terrified." She stalked out and somehow found her way back alone to the hotel where they were staying. "I locked myself in my room, and Leland kept knocking on the door and I'd say, 'Go away, I'm not coming out ever.' Finally, when I thought he'd gone away, I opened the door and snuck out barefooted down the hallway and he came after me in shorts and a pair of black socks, and he was the most ludicrous thing I'd ever seen, and I just collapsed—'Too funny,' I said. 'Forget it.' Irwee always talked about that afterward. 'Any girl who could do that,' he said, 'is all right by me.' "

Amid these shenanigans, Marian again played the hostess—a tough role. "She played way down, way under him," says Slim Keith. "He was the star, the number-one guy in the room, and she never tried to usurp that. She put up with a lot too." Enid Hardwicke found her "charming, but rather subdued. She had a very cultivated way of seeming, a French-snobbish way of speaking, that she'd acquired since coming to Europe. Irwin used to be very funny about that—when she wasn't around, of course." To well-bred ladies like Enid Hardwicke, Marian would never succeed in shaking her middle-class American heritage. "She would have loved to have been born French and lived in the Sixteenth Arrondissement, but she hadn't. And the funny thing was, she never got any closer to it. Nothing ever happened to Marian in all those years with Irwin. Nothing ever rubbed off. She remained bourgeois, she just became the ultimate bourgeois."

Back in the States, *The Troubled Air* continued to stir critical ire. By August 3, an exasperated Saxe Commins wrote Shaw that he was confounded. Everyone who'd read the book, from professors to lowly clerks, had loved it, Commins reported, yet the critics seemed unable to get beyond the notion of the novel as a political tract. There was consolation in numbers, however: the book had quickly gone through its initial printing of 35,000 copies, and climbed onto the *New York Times* bestseller list.

Not yet had the critical consensus formed that Shaw was a strictly commercial novelist of naive political thinking and unoriginal style. That indictment, first sounded by *Time*'s anonymous snipers and Diana Trilling, and now by scattered critics of *The Troubled Air*, would not become a predictable chorus until the arrival of Shaw's next novel, *Lucy Crown*. This was the season, however, that a young critic named John Aldridge made his reputation with an attack on Shaw and nearly all his contemporaries in a book-length study titled *After the Lost Generation*. As much as any one work of criticism might be said to hasten a writer's decline, this book hastened Shaw's.

The tragedy of post–World War II writers, Aldridge declared, was that the Lost Generation of World War I writers—particularly Hemingway— had already worked their ground. Hemingway, Dos Passos and Fitzgerald had already run up against the shock of war, violence and death; it had ruined the nineteenth-century illusions with which they'd grown up. They had already made the harsh decision that in such a world, the individual is thrown back on his own values for survival and must sweat out what those values are. They had already dealt with sex too, in a new and shocking way. From all this they had emerged numb, imbued with the profound sense of nothingness that signaled both the loss of faith and the chance to start anew. And they *had* begun anew, in a new place—as "Lost Generation" exiles in Europe—to fashion a different kind of writing that would make sense of their time. It was Hemingway, of course, who had forged the clean, pared-down style that not only became a sort of fictional catharsis, Aldridge observed, but perfectly captured the human reaction to war with its terse, flat tones.

The novelists of a generation later, wrote Aldridge, had the same wartime horrors and losses with which to come to terms, but the terms had already been defined and there was no better way to express them. Worse yet, these new writers hadn't even had the benefit of growing up in a pre–World War I world of relative grace and innocence, and so had nothing to be shocked about. The youngest generation had grown up instead with a legacy of war, with a Depression and food lines and bloody union battles. Their sense of loss was hollow, and so were the novels they'd produced about their war: more technically accomplished, perhaps, but less original.

Shaw was among the writers, Aldridge felt, whose only real contribution to the literature of war was to broaden the canvas. Hemingway had focused on one character's experience, while Shaw, Mailer and others tried to capture whole armies. What Shaw's generation had done was, in effect, to substitute journalism for meaning. In the twenties, journalism had been used by Dos Passos and others to create sensational fiction. But now that the world had lost its capacity to be shocked, journalism was a used-up form, and as the events of the war began to be forgotten, the dramatic impact of journalistic novels faded with them. "The achievement of Mailer and Shaw, as of most of the other war novelists, consisted mainly of an exceedingly workmanlike job of recording in minute detail the progression of event after event, violence after violence, in a war situation which was by itself perfectly suited to their purpose. Wars have a beginning, a middle, and an end and are, therefore, vastly more adaptable to fiction than the normal human situation which, lacking innate form, must be artificially arranged," Aldridge wrote. "A young writer who has produced one war novel has thus actually revealed relatively little about his true or potential stature as a writer. . . . He is able merely to present the war, and his presentation will be effective if it is true to the facts and for as long as the facts retain their freshness."

To some extent, the acuity of Aldridge's attack was softened by the lumping of World War II writers into one hapless bunch, but Shaw came in for harsh words of his own. He had been shaped, Aldridge wrote, as much by *The New Yorker* as by Hemingway, to lamentable effect. What *The New Yorker* demanded of its writers was an all-knowing, world-weary tone, with no emotion more strongly expressed than by a nuance, and Shaw had responded with "neat, bloodless prose." Complained Aldridge of *The Young Lions:* "Everything about the book has an air of prefabrication and contrivance. . . . There is no suggestion here, as there is in the best of Hemingway's stories, of violently controlled passions." Shaw's characters, wrote Aldridge, "are simply sterile, meaningless shadows, talking mannequins, acting out the slick pantomime of life which Shaw has manufactured for them." In the end, "they are lost in a confusion of message and cheap rhetoric."

Happily ensconced in his Riviera kingdom, powerful in his accomplishment, holding his glass like a scepter, as he would say of one of his own characters, nevertheless Shaw must have felt a tremor of uncertainty as to where this volatile new decade would lead him.

In late September the Shaws prepared to travel to Cherbourg for what they assumed would be their return trip to New York on the *Liberté*. Shaw took time to respond to an inquiry as to his whereabouts and activities from the *New York Herald Tribune*: "Writing about yourself without the usual soothing disguise of fiction I find is rather troublesome and usually all I ever want to know about any other writer is whether or not he's alive or dead," Shaw wrote back. "For the information of your readers I am at the moment alive, sitting in the sun on the southern coast of France, recovering from many months of work and hoping that there will be no war. . . . There are some short stories I want to write and I have been playing with the idea of dramatizing *The Troubled Air*. There is also a novel I have been thinking about for a long time, a good part of which is laid in Europe. I am waiting for the morning when my conscience will suddenly tell me that sloth is sin before making the next plunge."

Unclear as his plans were, it seemed easy enough to change them. En route to Cherbourg, the Shaws ran into a couple who announced they would not be using their Paris apartment for the coming season, and that it was therefore available as a sublet for $75 a month. Without hesitation, the Shaws canceled their return-trip tickets and reveled in the chance to live in Paris for a season or two.

The apartment, at 24 rue du Boccador, had more than cheap rent to recommend it. It was in a wonderful old building with a typically Parisian wrought-iron elevator, near the Champs-Élysées in the heart of the Eighth Arrondissement—the so-called American Arrondissement, because of the postliberation journalists who'd never left. Among the Shaws' new neighbors was Theodore White, who with his wife, Nancy, had come to Paris after his famous falling-out with Henry Luce, and was living off his royalties from *Thunder Out of China* while working for a shoestring operation called the Overseas News Agency. Across the hall from the Whites was Raoul Lévy, a young Belgian filmmaker who would go on to discover Brigitte Bardot. Lévy was full of charm and life, and even more so was Theo Bennehaum, a reckless Russian Jewish immigrant engaged at the time in the unglamorous business of making ballpoint pens. Bennehaum was so flamboyant and charismatic that he could make his deals seem the stuff of high comedy in the telling, yet so shrewd about the complications of postwar international finance that he would soon go on to become an advisor to major American corporations. As for the garret, it housed a twenty-six-year-old American reporter and ex-Marine who eked out his living contributing pieces to a food-and-nightlife column for the Paris *Herald Tribune*. The reporter's name was Art Buchwald, and almost every day, it seemed, he, White, Bennehaum, Levy, Shaw and an ever changing cast of supporting characters would gather in one of the Boccador apartments.

Correspondent David Schoenbrun lived a couple of blocks away and remembers the building as a sort of "fantastic theatrical set with three floors on the stage. We would go for cocktails to one apartment, dinner at another. It was a time when Paris had the single greatest collection of American and foreign correspondents gathered in one capital at one time. And Irwin very quickly became the center of that group. He admired us as journalists because we led dramatic lives, and I think he soaked up our experiences, living vicariously through them. Whereas we admired him for a literary talent that all of us would have sold our souls to have."

Close by the apartment were some of Paris's most famous cafés, and it didn't take Shaw long to develop his favorites. One was the Café des Deux Magots, where artists, writers and journalists gathered. Then there was Alexandre's. "You'd say, 'See you tonight at Alexandre's'—that was across the street from Fouquet's," recalls Art Buchwald. "And there would be Irwin, Peter Viertel, John Huston, Bob Capa, Gene Kelly, so many more. We'd all sit there until two or three in the morning." There was also Chez Carrère, a club on the Champs-Élysées, where Shaw might run into anyone from Robert Capa to Sydney Chaplin—the actor's son—to Noel Howard, an assistant film director who had served the Free French forces as a night-fighter pilot in the war.

The days began as blithely as they ended. Shaw had come to Paris intending to write a play or screenplay of *The Troubled Air*, but that plan had been thwarted. The American Legion, of all groups, had put pressure on Hollywood to keep the book from becoming a movie. On the East Coast, plans to bring the story to the stage were blocked by right-wingers who threatened to picket the theater and blacklist anyone involved. All this was discouraging to any thought of work; then too, Paris was distracting. By October 17, Shaw was able to report sheepishly in a letter to Leland Hayward that his sloth, as he liked to put it, had been almost complete since his arrival. Tentatively, he said, he had agreed to do the screenplay for Anatole Litvak's film version of Alfred Hayes's *The Girl on the Via Flaminia* (to be titled *Act of Love*). Other than that, he might write some stories "to keep my franchise up." And, he added, there was a novel he was contemplating vaguely—"when I feel strong enough I'll start to bat it out"—that would eventually become *Lucy Crown*. Based on a true story he'd heard in 1938 and carried around in his notes ever since, *Lucy Crown* would be Shaw's effort to come to terms with the deep complexities of adultery.

One way to spend a morning was on the tennis courts of Parc St.-Cloud. After a vigorous game with Peter Viertel or some other companion, Shaw would repair to the old hotel terrace, on a hilltop overlooking the courts, for drinks and hors d'oeuvres. Bradlee remembers playing tennis often with Shaw and others "in some fucking garage over in the Seventh Arrondissement. Wooden floor; very, very fast game. And Irwin was really the most competitive bastard that ever lived, as far as sports went. Gradually, he would weed out the players he couldn't beat."

With Capa in particular, Shaw would also go out to the races in the afternoon. There the two would run into anyone from Anatole Litvak to Howard Hawks, John Huston or Aly Khan. Often at night, the pack would gather back at the Shaws' apartment for dinners that turned into free-wheeling debates. "There was a group of men," Enid Hardwicke recalls. "Art Stanton, Peter Viertel, Capa, Irwin . . . they'd talk late into the night. They wouldn't even leave the dinner table. Marian would come eventually and bring another plate of cheese, another bottle of wine at one or two in the morning. Irwin would talk to me about those men with such pleasure, such tenderness. He truly enjoyed himself through their lives and their successes. I always thought of him as a true man for that."

As well as hobnobbing with established writers and film people, Shaw took a somewhat paternal interest that fall in a small but growing circle of young blue-blooded American expatriates he came to call the "tall young men"—the circle that would eventually produce *The Paris Review*.

One of the first "tall young men" was Peter Matthiessen, Shaw's unknown shipmate. Matthiessen can't remember quite how they ran into each other, whether they recognized each other from the boat or just found themselves in the same café, but he does remember how that first meeting ended. "Irwin and I went to the Deux Magots—Patsy wasn't with us—and we had quite a few drinks. Finally Irwin realized he was late for supper. 'Listen,' he said, 'I want you to come along and meet my wife.' I knew I shouldn't be doing that. I was late myself, and I had lost track of where I was supposed to be. But we were feeling great. We took a leak between the cars outside, then went to his place. By the time we got to his apartment, Marian was spitting mad—she had a right to be, but she handled it well, she was very polite under the circumstances. I realized I'd been dragged home as a decoy, and I got out of there as fast as I could."

Despite that unprepossessing beginning, the Shaws and the Matthiessens became close friends. That fall and the next, Matthiessen recalls, they had Thanksgiving dinner together. Matthiessen was fascinated by Shaw as a major literary figure, but Shaw, in turn, was intrigued by the younger couple. He enjoyed encouraging Peter as the recent Yale graduate struggled with his first novel, and he could hardly help but notice that Patsy was a truly legendary beauty, blonde, sexy and bright. The Matthiessens' apartment on rue de Perceval was also becoming a hangout of sorts for the young expatriate crowd. "It was an extremely bohemian apartment," recalls Patsy Matthiessen Southgate (since divorced from Peter). "It was an artist's studio, a great big atelier with vines growing over the windows, and a coal stove, and it was freezing cold—just what you wanted if you were twenty-three years old and living in Paris. It was perfect. The irony was that while we were living in abject poverty, to Irwin we were the rich guys—the Yalies, the Harvard graduates, the upper class—and he was the poor guy from Brooklyn. Of course, he was the poor guy living in considerable wealth, everything was top of the line. He enjoyed having us around for that reason."

Tennis and the races were fine amusements in Paris until the weather turned cold. Then, Shaw discovered, the fun was in skiing. That December he joined Peter Viertel for a skiing vacation in the tiny resort town of Klosters, a two-hour drive from Zurich in the Swiss Alps. It was a vacation that would change his life.

Viertel had first seen Klosters some years before on a screenwriting assignment. Since then, he and Jigee had sold their house in Zuma Canyon and taken to dividing their year between Klosters and Paris. "The masses hadn't caught onto skiing yet," Viertel recalls. "It was just a group of pals. We all lived at the hotel. That was before they salted the roads, and at night there were no cars on the main road between Davos and Klosters and we'd take sleds out there and make great runs in the moonlight."

Shaw was entranced by the tiny two-car train that climbed the Alps from the Zurich station and by the picture-postcard views along the way: thatched-roof cottages on the snow-capped hillsides, cows whose far-off, tinkling bells made ethereal music, clean white railway towns. Brooklyn boy that he was, he marveled at the pristine beauty of Klosters's wide streets and its houses with carved-wood façades. One block from the station was the hotel Viertel spoke of. The Chesa Grischuna, with its wooden fretwork and flower-painted white walls, looked incredibly *gemütlich*; and if it seemed somewhat less refined than it would soon become, it was also a good deal cheaper. "I think a double room cost twenty francs a day with a meal, and that would come to perhaps five dollars a day," says Viertel. "Terrific food, pleasant surroundings, great atmosphere. A beautiful life."

In fact, Klosters was a satellite to the sanatorium town of Davos, where tubercular patients had first begun coming in the nineteenth century. The patients' families had stayed in Klosters, establishing a tradition that belied the town's salubrious air and clear mountain views. Having agreed to stay a month, Shaw found he could actually get more work done here on vacation than he could in Paris. "We all did the same thing," says Viertel. "We worked in the morning and then went skiing about twelve or one o'clock. Irwin became enamored of skiing. He really loved it with a passion." The only imperfection in this snowscape scene was that Viertel was about to leave his pregnant wife.

As far as Viertel was concerned, his marriage had collapsed in the wake of Jigee's transatlantic passage with the Hemingways more than two years before. Neither he nor Jigee had stayed faithful to each other since then, and Jigee's escalating problem with alcohol had only exacerbated the tensions (Viertel never did gravitate to drink the way his friends did; in fact, as Shaw's drinking became more severe over the next years, he grew proportionately less good-humored about it.) Desperate, Jigee had gotten pregnant several times in an effort to restore some harmony to the marriage, but Peter had always resented the plan, and in the end Jigee had had several abortions. In the late summer of 1951, Viertel apparently moved out to embark on an affair with a beautiful, effervescent model named Bettina. When Jigee called to say she was under suspicion as a former Communist by the FBI, Viertel went back for a weekend to calm her down. That was when another child was conceived. This time Jigee determined to bring the baby to term. Viertel refused to acquiesce to what he felt was emotional blackmail, and on March 1, with Jigee a little more than seven months pregnant, he officially left her for Bettina.

"I remember going to visit Jigee in the hospital when she had her baby," remembers Patsy Southgate. "It was a terrible thing. And I think that Marian deeply identified with Jigee, and that this became a serious issue between her and Irwin, whether Peter's behavior was justifiable or not. I think Irwin was more philosophical about it, and Marian felt this was really scandalous behavior."

In the winter and spring of 1952, Shaw wrestled with the screenplay for Anatole Litvak's *Act of Love,* slowed down by the director's insistence that the wartime drama be transposed from Rome—as in the novel—to occupied Paris, in order for Litvak to work (and eat and drink) in his favorite city. Litvak, with whom Shaw had made his 1945 swing through Europe, had acquired something of a rakish image after an incident in the late forties at the Trocadéro restaurant in Paris, when an attractive lady was seen under his table, engaging him in oral sex. Playing the male lead in the film was Kirk Douglas, who would become a drinking companion of Shaw's and perform in the film version of Shaw's own novel *Two Weeks in Another Town,* in which he would epitomize the tough, hard-drinking, down-on-his-luck protagonist of all Shaw's later works. *Act of Love* would appear the next year to enthusiastic reviews—one of Shaw's few screenwriting successes—but what made the assignment most notable was that it provided Shaw with his first major bundle of tax-free European movie money.

The big European tax loophole had not been Shaw's main motive for coming to Paris, though critics would later carp that it had. His love of Paris, of French food and wine, and of his romantic hopes of being able to write better in Paris amid the ghosts of the Lost Generation—these were the immediate reasons, abetted by the dark tides back home, of the burgeoning anti-Communist movement, and of anti-Semitism, real or perceived. Unquestionably, though, the loophole became a strong inducement to stay.

For decades, the American government had waffled on the question of taxation for Americans living abroad. Prior to 1925, an American abroad for any length of time had had to pay full U.S. taxes. In that year, the Republican administration of Calvin Coolidge cleanly reversed the policy. Through the Depression years, the Roosevelt government kept redefining the policy to squeeze at least some tax monies from expatriates, deciding, for example, that all U.S. government employees abroad had to pay full U.S. taxes. By the late forties, the code had become so narrowly defined that an American had to live abroad twenty-four consecutive months before qualifying for the exemption, then continue to live abroad at least six months of every year to maintain it. The exemption itself was defined narrowly too. Instead of ducking all U.S. taxes on *any* income, a qualified expatriate was exempt only from taxes on income earned abroad and *paid* to him abroad. Money paid through U.S. channels was subject to normal U.S. taxes, as was dividend income—book royalties, say, or stocks and bonds. In 1951, the year Shaw decided to stay in Europe, the code was narrowed again. Defining what it called the "physical presence" rule, Congress declared that an American had to live abroad seventeen of eighteen months to qualify for the exemption. If he did, however, he would still be exempt from paying U.S. taxes for all monies earned abroad. There were few Americans now who could meet that criterion, but for a fortunate few, among them American actors, movie directors or screenwriters who could be paid through a studio's European offices for a movie made abroad, the game was still on.

It had taken Shaw a while to understand the loophole's implications: he was, by nature, helpless to cope with his finances in any detail. But even for a man reputed to have once asked for a pencil to multiply 1,000 by 5, the bottom line must now have come clear. Book publishing was still a tweedy gentlemen's business, and despite his reputation, Shaw would continue to receive the same modest advance for each novel written in Europe as he had for his first two books: $15,000. (Even by 1960, when he wrote to Cerf to ask for a higher advance for *Two Weeks in Another Town*, he would be told that no other Random House writer was getting any more than he.) Moreover, this payment, expected to support his family over the two or three years it might take to write the next novel, would be issued from New York and was thus subject to U.S. taxes. Movies, though—there was the lucre. Shaw had written his script in Paris, he had been paid through foreign channels, and if he simply remained in Europe to qualify for the seventeen-out-of-eighteen-month "physical presence" clause, he could pocket his entire fee. For Shaw, that fee was fast approaching $100,000.

Flush with his movie pay, Shaw in the summer of 1952 took a large hilltop villa on the Basque coast, in the foothills of the Pyrenees, above the summer resort fishing village of St.-Jean-de-Luz.

Among the Americans who had taken to summering in the area were Charles Wertenbaker, the hard-boiled *Time* bureau chief from wartime London, and his correspondent-turned-novelist wife, Lael. Wertenbaker had retired from *Time* in 1947 and had come at his wife's urging to live year-round as a writer in the neighboring village of Ciboure, six miles down the road and across a small bridge over the Nivelle River. The Shaws' house was in a lush area called Chantaco, abutting the Chantaco golf and tennis club. Joe Kaufman, the gentleman of leisure from Shaw's Quogue summer, who came to St.-Jean-de-Luz as well, remembers the relationship between Wertenbaker and Shaw as being somewhat mismatched. "Wert was a little hostile to Irwin, though they were friends. Irwin sort of grated on Wert's nerves. Wert had one of the coldest minds I've ever known. A realist, unsentimental. And Irwin was just the opposite."

Shaw felt closer to another neighbor that summer, the ruefully funny screenwriter Harry Kurnitz. Like Shaw, Kurnitz had grown up in a New York Jewish immigrant family and retained a gruff New York accent (in his case, from the Lower East Side). Like Shaw, he had parlayed raw writing talent into great commercial success. A top-ranked screenwriter (*Shadow of the Thin Man, Witness for the Prosecution*), he would also become a successful collaborator on musicals (*The Sleeping Prince*). His greatest gift, however, was his personal wit. "For something like twenty years," wrote Kenneth Tynan, "busily commuting between America and Europe, he patiently lived with the knowledge that he had been elected Hollywood's court jester." In both temperament and appearance—watery-eyed, with heavy black spectacles and stooped shoulders—he resembled a more gregarious Woody Allen. After a feud with Lynn Loesser, whose husband, Frank, wrote the music and lyrics for *Guys and Dolls*, Kurnitz declared, "Lynn is the evil of two Loessers." After testing one of Art Stanton's new Volkswagens, the tall—six-foot-three—writer extricated himself with considerable difficulty and announced, "I've been in roomier *women*." Always joking about his chaotic personal life—Kurnitz had been married once, briefly, but remained a bachelor ever after—he turned gruffly to Peter Viertel one day and said, "Give me a money order, I want to write home."

In a jocular way, Shaw and Kurnitz referred to themselves as the Jews: the American Jews, the Jews who had made it on their own in New York and Hollywood (or, as others sometimes put it, the denizens of Upper Bohemia). That was also to distinguish themselves from the "tall young men" who began to drift down from Paris.

The Matthiessens led the way, renting a simple apartment in a rooming house. Like literary serfs visiting the master's house, they would drive up for dinner at the Shaws', up through a long winding driveway to the beautiful Spanish-style villa called Propriété Bailenea. In the late-summer light, there was a wonderful view over the pink roofs of St.-Jean-de-Luz and of the lighthouse of Ciboure against the sea. Inside the main living room was a grand piano, a tapestry-sized portrait of a stern-faced woman on a green horse (Shaw jokingly referred to her as the landlady), and four large, sepia-tinted plaques illustrating the seasons. In the dining room, the guests would be served in formal grandeur by a retinue of Basque servants. Notables might include Kurnitz, Anatole Litvak or even Swifty Lazar, who would stay at a hotel in nearby Biarritz, and other film people. "Nearly all of the Shaws' friends that summer drove Jaguars," Patsy Southgate says. Finally the Matthiessens felt obliged to reciprocate. "Our apartment simply had a kitchen and a bedroom, so we ate in the kitchen. And I remember serving this terribly overdone roast beef that turned a desperate shade of gray. Marian suggested I slice it and serve it cold with chutney, but it was beyond hope." No matter: Shaw was too busily engaged in conversation about the season's most controversial book, *Witness,* by Whittaker Chambers, to notice.

Another of the tall young men who came down that summer was a shy William Styron.

Styron had published his extraordinary first novel, *Lie Down in Darkness,* the previous year in New York, to generally favorable reviews. He had come to Paris in the winter with the venerable aim of sowing his literary oats after a first success and experiencing the expatriate life. "I was writing *The Long March,*" Styron recalls, "and I was living in a little fleabag of a hotel on the rue de la Grande-Chaumière, in Montparnasse, right around from the Dôme, a street just off boulevard Montparnasse. It was clean, but it was really humble, and very, very cheap."

The Matthiessens lived a ten-minute walk away, and Styron had actually come with a letter of introduction to them through Michael and Cass Canfield, Jr., and their half-cousin Blair Fuller, who would himself become another of the *Paris Review* crowd. Before he had time to use it, he got a call from Harold Humes.

Doc Humes, as he was known, had bought the magazine *Kiosk,* which covered restaurants and nightlife and the like, and changed its name to *Paris News Post.* He wanted to run a short story in every issue and so had enlisted Matthiessen as fiction editor. "The first story I got for him was Terry Southern's first story, 'The Sun and the Still-Born Stars,' " recalls Matthiessen. "It was a very good story, one of the best Terry ever wrote. And when I saw that story in this flimsy magazine, I thought, If we're going to do good stories, let's start a real magazine, with fiction by young writers, and interviews with famous writers to carry the fiction. Doc wanted to be the head of it, and I didn't, I just wanted to take care of the fiction and work on my first novel, but it didn't take long to realize that the magazine just wasn't going to work with Doc in charge. Lovable and intelligent though he was, he couldn't work with people. So I got in touch with [George] Plimpton, who was at Cambridge in England. I knew he had run the Harvard magazine and I asked him to come over to Paris and run this one. He said sure—can't imagine why—and it ruined his whole life."

Somehow, Doc Humes got wind of Styron's arrival in Paris, and invited him out for a drink—which was how Styron met Matthiessen. Plimpton, whom Styron happened to have met in London the month before, showed up too. This group, with the help of a few others, would put out *The Paris Review* the next year. It was through these new friends that Styron met Shaw.

"I had had this tremendous fixation on Irwin even in New York," says Styron. "I had a basic admiration for his stories, they made a powerful imprint on me. And of course I'd read *The Young Lions.* I remember once, with that dazzled feeling one has in one's early twenties, I had been in a restaurant in Greenwich Village and someone walked in who resembled Irwin very much. I remember this thrill going up my back, and saying to whomever I was with, 'I think that may be Irwin Shaw!' "

Styron was impressed first by Shaw's "spontaneous goodfellowship and friendliness"—and then by his car. "There weren't many cars in Paris that year, it was so close to World War II still, the French automobile industry hadn't really cranked up, so practically all you saw were prewar automobiles, bicycles and a few Volkswagens, which were sort of declassé. But there was Irwin—in a beautiful big green Ford convertible. It drew attention wherever he went."

The Hollywood money, and the Hollywood people, loomed large in Styron's first impressions of Shaw. "He was the first Hollywood-connected person I'd met. In fact, he was the first Hollywood-connected person *any* of us had met. And it would always give us a bang when Irwin would say, you know, 'Sam Goldwyn's in town.' And indeed, there would be Sam Goldwyn. And there would be John Huston, who was then married to Ricky Soma, a gorgeous beauty. And Gene Kelly, and Harry Kurnitz. And Darryl Zanuck!" One night Zanuck threw a huge birthday party for Sam Goldwyn, Jr., and Styron got his first blissful taste of fine wine. "The party was at a restaurant—I still remember the name, Chez Joseph, on the Right Bank, somewhere near the Étoile. I just had never thought of wine as being much of anything, you know. I had been drinking a little dago red in New York. But this must have been a prewar Château Margaux. And it was a revelation to me, to be in this splendid, small, chic restaurant drinking this magnificent wine, with Irwin and everyone else, and Darryl Zanuck paying for it all. It was my first taste of the haute monde."

Another time that year, Shaw invited his new friends to a preview screening of a Sam Goldwyn movie, *Hans Christian Andersen,* with Danny Kaye. "The movie was terrible, even with Danny Kaye," Styron recalls. "But everyone was so eager to please old Sam Goldwyn, because this was his idea of one of the great movies of all time. I was sitting very close to

Goldwyn, and Irwin was sitting perhaps one seat behind—and Irwin fell asleep! Not only that: he was snoring. And everyone was petrified that the old man would hear Irwin snore. But this was the carefree attitude Irwin had about people like that. We were all much too awestruck by someone like Goldwyn, whereas Irwin took him in his stride."

That summer Styron and Doc Humes drove down through the French countryside in Humes's Volkswagen, stopping off in St.-Tropez and making their way west to St.-Jean-de-Luz. For a week they stayed in a rooming house and joined in the daily festivities that began on the beach about noon or one o'clock, the writers having all spent their mornings ostensibly engaged in literary pursuits. Marian or one of the other women would usually bring food, and everyone would drink Pimm's Cup steadily through the afternoon. After a respite for late-afternoon showers, the drinking would resume at cocktail hour. Dinners would be either at the Château— as the summer crowd had taken to calling Shaw's house—or at one of the local restaurants, where Shaw would inevitably pick up the tab. For the tall young men, it was a magical time. "There was such a generosity in Irwin," says Styron. "He had this enormous basic attractiveness, a marvelous sparkling animation, this kind of buoyant quality."

Between the older writer and his young friends, however, there were undercurrents of a more complex relationship. As much as the younger writers admired Shaw's literary accomplishments, they were suspicious of his commercial success and scornful of his Hollywood dealings. If F. Scott Fitzgerald had been a sellout, as they tended to believe, where did that put Shaw? Simon Michael Bessie remembers sensing that reaction. "Seeing Irwin with them was almost like seeing an old prizefighter with his court. It was my feeling from talking to some of them at the time that Irwin provoked mixed reactions. They thought he was a character, they thought he had standing as a writer. But they thought he was sort of a doddering old fighter; and they were fascinated to see if he had another fight in him."

Shaw only fanned these doubts by taking such obvious pleasure in his newfound wealth. "He was conspicuous as a consumer," says Patsy Matthiessen Southgate, and to the tall young men, there was something decidedly Jewish about that. "If a WASP bought a leather jacket," says Southgate, "he would make a big deal about how it had been on sale, how he'd gotten it for fifty percent off. With Irwin, the story would be 'Feel it' ard 'Guess how much it cost,' and I wouldn't be surprised if he actually jacked up the price. I mean, to us, the idea of Irwin's having been considered a Communist was really unbelievable."

Of course Shaw felt ambivalent about the money, as he always had. The Depression upbringing still drove him to earn all he could, to stave off the risk of ever being poor again. However much he might gripe about Hollywood, on some level he still measured success by the bottom line. His intellect, and his integrity as a writer, told him otherwise. "That was something we were always aware of with Irwin—that he'd sold out," says Patsy Southgate. "Beneath all this laughter and drinking, I felt a lot of sadness; I think he was highly aware of having betrayed a lot that he believed in himself, and a lot that he wanted to be true to. It wasn't that he'd sold out in any way that made you contemptuous of him; it was just that this was all so much more fun, and he was really turned on by that."

The young men were a mirror for Shaw, reflecting an image he didn't want to see, in a way that none of his Hollywood friends did, even Peter Viertel. It provoked sadness, as well as Shaw's incipient competitiveness. For all the camaraderie, recalls Peter Matthiessen, "he was ferociously competitive with his younger friends."

It came out on the tennis court, or on the beach, where Shaw would joke about being the best-built writer of his generation, and it lay just beneath the somewhat patronizing manner with which Shaw occasionally regarded the *Paris Review* crowd: acting the mentor to students who hadn't asked for one. Not long afterward, Peter Matthiessen and Ben Bradlee decided to collaborate on a *New Yorker* piece for the "Annals of Crime" series. "Ben did the research, and I did the writing," says Matthiessen. "When we were through with it we gave it to Irwin, who said he would send it in with a recommendation. He wrote us a note to William Shawn, and we never told him that we didn't use it. We loved him, but we just shook our heads over that note. The tone of it was sort of: 'A couple of young friends of mine have tried their hand at . . .' It was such faint praise and so patronizing that it would have shot the piece smack on the head. And the piece was pretty good. *The New Yorker* took it, it became quite a well-known piece, and we were not the least bit embarrassed by it."

Styron agrees. "I know what Peter means. There was a bit of that. There was a bit of—well, Irwin couldn't have been much beyond his late thirties, yet he was the grand old man. But I think we both felt we could take it or leave it. It wasn't that constant, either. And there was such a generosity in Irwin, I don't think we let it get us too far down."

Then too, Shaw could still make everything a joke.

Sitting one day at lunch back in Paris with Bradlee and Joe Kaufman, Shaw turned contemplative toward the end of the meal. He listened to his companions talk on awhile, and then suddenly he put his glass down and looked at them both. "You know, I've been thinking about it," he said, "and the fact is—there isn't *anything* I can't do better than either of you."

The lion was still young. Still confident. And still powerful.

CHAPTER THIRTEEN

In Europe, that fall of 1952, Shaw was more than a well-known writer. He was a *figure*, in a way that wouldn't have been possible in New York or even in Hollywood. A year after his arrival in Paris as a long-term resident—and with no departure date in sight—he was one of that colorful band of expatriates a traveling American might hope to meet. Tall young men kept turning up to help launch *The Paris Review*. Actors and directors—Gregory Peck, Kirk Douglas, William Wyler and others—kept arriving to make films as word got out about the tax loophole. To one and all, Shaw played genial host, either from the apartment on the rue du Boccador, or at restaurants nearby. When first one and then another of his younger friends got married, Shaw extended his role by planning and paying for their wedding receptions, acts of generosity that Art Buchwald, William Styron and later Gay Talese would never forget. Ironically, as he tended to his friends' marriages, his own continued to teeter. And as he basked in literary celebrity, his writing began to drift.

Art and Ann Buchwald returned from a ten-day honeymoon in late October to find a surprise homecoming party awaiting them, courtesy of the Shaws. "Only Irwin could have foreseen our letdown in coming back to our dingy old rooms," Ann Buchwald later recalled. "The Shaws rounded up all our favorite pals, then added new faces [like] Rose and Bill Styron, George Plimpton and the Peter Matthiessens. The party went on till dawn." The most memorable moment of it, though, had more to do with the Shaws' own marriage. "As the party was getting into full swing, a glamorous—but uninvited—brunette made an impressive entrance on the arm of one of Irwin's pals, who should have known better. The woman was a well-known divorcee, and gossip was that she had been making a serious play for Irwin. They'd been seen together at lunch and at sidewalk cafés that autumn; her name could never have been on Marian's invitation list.

"But no one would have guessed the truth watching Marian's face. Her smile remained warm and welcoming as the woman approached. Only a few of us saw Marian deftly raise her right foot and with split-second timing trip the brunette at the precise moment she rushed past Marian to greet Irwin. Afterward, Marian acted as shocked as anyone to see the elegantly dressed intruder sprawled on the floor, and was the first to help her to her feet, gathering up the scattered contents of her evening bag, smoothing her dress. Then Marian graciously ushered the woman to the door, and as far as anyone ever knew, out of Paris altogether."

There were other incidents, no less dramatic, that grew into legends among the Shaws' many friends. Not long after this, one story went, Marian returned to Paris from Klosters with a broken leg from a skiing accident. She had heard rumors that Irwin was having an affair with a blonde starlet named Lynn Baggett, who had married Sam Spiegel. When she saw the two of them enter the lobby of the Georges V hotel, she hobbled furiously up to Shaw's companion and kicked her hard in the rear with her cast-encased leg. The ingenue went flying onto the rug—then, as she picked herself up, managed to splutter, with a certain amount of logic, "Why don't you kick your *husband* instead?"

Another time, David and Dorothy Schoenbrun watched the Shaws go their separate ways at a cocktail party and marveled once again at how Shaw, despite his obvious affection for his wife, could spend the entire evening flirting with every attractive woman in the room. As the party wound down, Shaw, his face happy and flushed with drink, came to gather Marian to go home. "Well, honey," Shaw asked her, "did you have a good time?" "Yes, dear," she said, "I had a knockout time," and proceeded to take off her shoe and hit him on the head with it.

There were arguments in restaurants; there were arguments at dinner parties. Patsy Southgate recalls Marian "regularly taking off her wedding ring and throwing it across the restaurant, or onto the tracks of an oncoming train, or casting it into the surf. Irwin was always buying her new wedding rings. It was sort of a running joke." Shaw raged at Marian for small crimes: being late was the most recurring charge; spending too much money, at the hairdresser's or the couturier's, was another. More often than not, Marian raged at Shaw for the larger crime of infidelity.

Shaw's emotions had always been volcanic and it was often he who seemed to provoke the fierce arguments, but Marian, for all her outward appearance of cool containment, could summon the rage to respond in kind. As real as these feelings were, though, it wasn't just bad timing that kept them erupting in public. Like George and Martha in *Who's Afraid of Virginia Woolf?*, both Irwin and Marian played off their stunned friends, daring each other to react in front of them, and thereby raising the stakes.

Arguments in public were more hurtful, but they had a way of venting poisonous emotions more cleanly and completely. For Shaw, especially when another woman was involved, they became dramatic demonstrations that Marian still loved him—loved him desperately, if she could be so jealous. "God, it's great," he told one friend. "Can you imagine how much *energy* she expends on it?" Upon seeing his wife kick Lynn Baggett in the lobby of the Georges V, Shaw reportedly looked at her in awe, broke up in admiring laughter, and promptly took her out to an expensive dinner. Benjamin Federov, in *Voices of a Summer Day,* reacts with drunken irritation as his wife comes over at a cocktail party to break up his flirtation with another woman, then watches with secret delight as his wife "accidentally" spills her drink all over the other woman's dress. The result, again, is a romantic reunion dinner.

Certainly the marriage continued to generate sparks of passion. Bob and Kathie Parrish remember a party at the Chesa Grischuna in the early fifties in which Shaw flirted blatantly with every attractive woman in the bar. At the end of the evening, the Parrishes repaired to their room upstairs. "As we were readying for bed," says Kathie, "we heard Irwin come into his room across the wall and say to Marian, 'You're still the prettiest of the bunch.' And you could hear he was utterly sincere."

There was another aspect to the public arguments, one that had begun, perhaps, with Scott and Zelda Fitzgerald, continued with Hemingway, and was becoming only more apparent as the century unfolded. Famous writers *were* figures now, publicized like movie stars in the press and on radio, with the day of the television talk show not so far off, and figures had license: license to drink more, make love to more women, engage in more public arguments. Among normal people all this would make for unforgivable behavior. Among famous writers it was expected and condoned, even relished: by the next day, veterans of a Shaw dinner squabble would be on the phone to each other, recounting this choice new anecdote and taking secret pride in having had a ringside seat.

The danger for Shaw was the danger for any famous American writer of his age: an unrestrained ego, and the subsequent loss of the self-critical faculty, in both one's life and one's art.

Having left his native country for what now appeared to be an extended stay, sooner or later Shaw had to decide what kind of fiction he was going to write—stories that plumbed his past or stories that came to terms with his new life in Europe. "In the French Style," a story for *The New Yorker* that fall, helped supply the answer.

Beddoes, a world-weary traveler, returns to Paris from an assignment in Cairo—he seems to work for the U.S. State Department—to find that his American girlfriend, Christina, seems changed. Her hair is natural, her nail polish is gone, and she insists on drinking hot tea in the café where Beddoes meets her. Soon enough, Beddoes learns she's agreed to marry a nice young doctor visiting from the States. She's tired, as she says, of being passed along the circle, from one expatriate American journalist or State

Department hand to another. In a few quick brushstrokes, the scene is casually complete: a portrait of Americans in Europe, pleasure-seeking, rootless, ultimately sad until they head back home.

The story was based directly on an incident Shaw and Bob Parrish witnessed while drinking at Alexandre's. Over the low divider between the tables, the two overheard Bob Capa telling his latest girlfriend he'd be going off to China the next day. In the way he spoke to her, it was clear that Capa thought not only that his girlfriend should be excited for him, but that she should faithfully await his return. "Well, I won't be waiting," the girl replied in what became the story's last speech. "I met a dentist from Seattle and I'm going back with him. . . ." In real life, Capa took the news stoically, got up to leave, and walked about ten steps. Then, as Shaw and Parrish watched, fascinated, he returned solemnly to pat her on top of the head, as if to put a benediction on the end of their life together, before walking off again.

Shaw's decision was made, and essentially it was an admirable one. By writing about Americans in Europe, rather than about Europeans, Shaw was recognizing both the limitation and the strength of his situation. The limitation was that while he spoke enough French to get by, he would never acquire either the accent or the manner to pass as a European. The very idea of Irwin Shaw as European was absurd: everything about him shouted "American." In all his time in Europe, the majority of his friends would remain American or English. His literary perspective would remain American too. The strength was Shaw's deep understanding of, and sympathy with, the hopes and sorrows of fellow Americans.

Then too, Shaw was hardly unaware of the expatriate literary tradition. If Henry James could write about Americans in Europe, to be followed by the Lost Generation, why not Irwin Shaw?

It made perfect sense. Except that fate had plunked Shaw down in Europe at a somewhat less than momentous time. The turn-of-the-century Americans of Henry James's novels had made a fascinating study because they came as the first generation of newly minted, Industrial Age wealth, clashing colorfully with Europe's Old World money and values. A character like Daisy Miller embodied all that was American at the time: bad manners and taste, but also the brashness to bull her way through. The Americans of Hemingway's Lost Generation were intriguing, as Aldridge had observed, because they had gone into the Great War with Old World illusions and come out of it forced to redefine themselves. Each of these generations was somehow new and fresh. The Americans of Shaw's Europe, on the other hand, were jaded, often rich and spoiled, and ultimately boring. They were abroad on holiday, on business, or perhaps on a prescribed adventure. Most of them arrived fully formed, and they left, for the most part, unchanged. In retrospect the most interesting of them may have been the tall young men, and *they* were over in Europe consciously imitating the Lost Generation.

They made characters who were hard to care about in print.

In Klosters that winter, Shaw turned forty feeling more or less content. Not only could he enjoy the prospect of earning more movie money—he was about to go to Rome to work for Ben Hecht as a screenwriter on an ambitious adaptation of *The Odyssey*—but he was keeping up his franchise, as he liked to put it, as a short story writer: *The New Yorker* had just published "In the French Style" and "The Sunny Banks of the River Lethe," a winsome story about a forgetful encyclopedia researcher. Of his much-brooded-about next novel, however, Shaw had unexpected doubts.

In late March 1953, the Shaws drove down to Rome in the big green Ford convertible, and moved into an elegant hotel apartment on the outskirts of the city in a relatively tall building, the Residence Palace, at 69 via Archimede. They were due to stay until June 15, then head over to St.-Jean-de-Luz for the summer. Besides his screenwriting fee, Shaw had just received Random House's advance of $15,000 for *Lucy Crown*, a commitment he would come to regret. For the first time, Irving Lazar was handling the book business, not just the movie deals, and in the letters to Shaw from Random House's cofounder Donald Klopfer, there was an undercurrent of resentment about that; why, Klopfer might have said if pressed, should that brazen little agent be allowed to interfere with a personal relationship between Shaw and Random House editors that dated back nearly twenty years?

Soon after Shaw's arrival, two of the *Paris Review* crowd passed through and paid a memorable visit. One was Tom Guinzburg, a publishing heir whose father had started Viking Press and who would have to return to the States in June, upon his father's premature death, to take over the business. The other was John Marquand, Jr., who went by the name John Phillips in an effort to get out from under the shadow of his own famous father. It was an effort that had failed: the publisher of his first novel, *The Second Happiest Day*, had insisted on using Marquand's real name for publicity value.

The novel had just appeared, and Shaw was very consoling about the name fiasco. He also chose not to mention that in his youth he'd written an admiring letter to John Marquand, Sr., and never received a reply. "That night," recalls Guinzburg, "we all went out for dinner and had a lot to drink. Later we came back to Irwin's and sat around the fire, and Irwin began to get very sulky, lecturing Marquand and me about the decline of standards in publishing, how difficult it was to write well and maintain standards when everyone wanted escapist literature. He himself was suffering from this, he said, being forced to write this kind of stuff, writing for the audience rather than himself. The novel he'd been working on for a year or more, he said, was a good example of that.

"And with that, Irwin got up from his chair, went into his bedroom, and came back with this huge manuscript. 'I'm sick of it,' he declared, and to our utter shock he heaved the manuscript into the fire."

The young visitors had the distinct impression that the manuscript in question was *Lucy Crown,* and were thus even more surprised, some three years later, to see the novel appear. "We figured out that Irwin, of course, must have had a spare copy," Guinzburg says. It seems highly doubtful that the manuscript was in fact *Lucy Crown,* since Shaw had just written Donald Klopfer on March 26 from Klosters to report with disgruntlement that he'd written only twenty pages of his new novel. Still, whatever the manuscript was—working notes for *Lucy,* perhaps, or another project altogether— Shaw's bitter doubts were clear.

That was the spring William Styron got married to a young American woman named Rose Burgunder, and Shaw orchestrated the entire proceedings.

"Rose and I had met in Rome," explains Styron. "We were living near the American Academy because I'd gotten a grant, and Irwin and Marian were over there in that part of Rome called Parioli, which is the kind of nouveau-riche area. The Residence Palace was a virtually brand-new, sort of fancy high-rise, a kind of mixture of French, English and Italian. It was as elegant as you could get and still live outside the downtown part of Rome where the hotels were.

"We saw a lot of Irwin and Marian down there. We went out to restaurants. We saw a certain number of the movie people. And we took very nice trips outside Rome, to Anzio and Orbetello, and to the beach at Ostia, where we wandered around in the ruins. We'd find good places for lunch and drink good Italian wine, just the four of us."

Rose, the shy daughter of a wealthy Baltimore department store owner, was particularly struck by Marian. "I remember thinking how beautiful she was. And to me in those days she seemed like an older woman who had managed to stay so gorgeous—she was probably only ten years older than I was. I remember thinking, 'That's the way I want to look in ten years.' We'd have tea and chocolate at the Caffè Greco in Rome, and there was always a banter going on—Irwin was particularly amusing. Still, I remember being terribly surprised that they would give us a wedding, since I knew them so slightly."

At Shaw's insistence, the Styrons invited all their Paris friends down for the May 4 ceremony. There were more of them now, because the first issue of *The Paris Review* had just appeared, graced with a prefatory credo from young Styron. George Plimpton came down, as did John Marquand.

Peter Matthiessen and Tom Guinzburg cabled their regrets: Guinzburg was busy, and Patsy Matthiessen was very pregnant. Cabled Shaw in return: "What do you mean, you're not coming to Bill's wedding? Don't you realize a man only gets married two or three times in his entire life?" Amused, Matthiessen and Guinzburg agreed to come after all.

The wedding itself was a civil ceremony held in the Campidoglio, Rome's capitol building. Bride and groom sat on high-backed gold chairs, and a Roman dignitary with colorful sashes and a big hanging medal officiated. The reception was held at the Shaws' apartment, and to the new bride, most of the guests were just famous names. "The one I remember best was Lillian Hellman," recalls Rose Styron. "She was not at the wedding, because we didn't know her, but when we went back to the apartment, she and Bill and I were on the elevator together, just the three of us going up. I remember all this rustling brown silk, with a little brown feathered hat, and a veil over her face—that was her style. Later we sensed that Lillian didn't have a lot of respect for Irwin as a writer. But she always liked him, and Lillian liked very few people."

Upstairs, they found another surprise. "Marian, who spoke no Italian, had gone to get our wedding cake. She tried to indicate to the baker that she wanted a very large, five-tier wedding cake. What they brought was their window display, which had five separate cakes on it with a little bride and groom on top." While the older guests made for the bar, some of the younger ones engaged in a game of romantic hide-and-seek. Writer Hortense Calisher, it seemed, had become smitten with John Marquand, but he failed to share her ardor. Like rowdy fraternity brothers, Tom Guinzburg and his confreres led Calisher in and out of elevators, vowing at every turn to bring her to Marquand, who was hiding in a cloakroom.

Of the bitter Shaw they'd seen only two months before, throwing his manuscript into the fire, there seemed not a trace.

The Shaws returned to St.-Jean-de-Luz in June, dragging a skein of friends from Europe and America like local tuna fishermen dragging their nets. Thanks to Shaw, St.-Jean was the new summer place to be. Ivy Leaguers and Hollywood screenwriters alike wanted to join in the fun, and in St.-Jean, as in Klosters later on, a visit didn't count if it didn't include time spent with Shaw.

One of the new arrivals was George Plimpton, fresh from having edited his first issue of *The Paris Review*. "I'd discovered that putting out a literary quarterly isn't the most demanding thing in the world," Plimpton admits, "and the practice at that time was to go where Irwin was. You knew you'd run into movie people and all sorts of other wonderfully extravagant types, and Irwin was the person who held it all together. He had a house, he was a great host, and really he was a very special person, one of the most vivid people living in Europe. He was like a wonderful uncle—even though we weren't *that* much younger than he."

John Marquand came too, taking a room in one of the boarding-houses with his girlfriend, Sue Coward, whom he'd later marry. One night Marquand, his girlfriend, Plimpton and Shaw went out to a restaurant for dinner. Marquand, reveling in the stories flying back and forth, made the classic writer's move of going off to the bathroom to scribble in a notebook before he forgot them. Just as he was scribbling away, in came Shaw to do the same thing. The two collapsed in laughter, and the incident became a running joke for years.

In fact, Shaw was the one to put his notes to use. That summer Plimpton, Marquand and Sue went off bumming through Europe and encountered the inevitable emotional turbulence in traveling as a three-some. Shaw wanted to hear all about it, and he was especially taken with a story they told one night at dinner, of a small drama that had occurred earlier in the day. From a local pier, the three of them had watched a French couple row a dory farther and farther from shore. Suddenly the boat had overturned, and the couple had begun calling for help. To the onlookers' greater surprise, the man of the couple had begun swimming back to shore, leaving the woman behind. When the man began to show dangerous signs of fatigue, Marquand had gone to the rescue, only to find the distance greater than he'd thought. As he began to feel panicky himself, a tuna boat came along to rescue each swimmer separately, much to Marquand's embarrassment. The adventure became the basis for the Shaw story "Then We Were Three," eventually published by *McCall's* and included in the O. Henry Awards collection for 1957; some years later, it also served as the basis of the movie *Three,* starring Sam Waterston and Charlotte Rampling.

That summer Plimpton and Marquand persuaded Shaw to sit for an interview, one of the first of the writers' interviews that would become such a famous tradition with *The Paris Review.* Shaw was more reluctant at the prospect than he would have been five years, or even two years, before. Frustrated by his attempts to come to grips with his new novel, feeling guilty about the film money he was continuing to take, he had become sensitive about his reputation. He felt particularly on guard with the *Paris Review* crowd, and so did Marian. "I remember Marian as being very defensive of Irwin with us," recalls Marquand. "She was very afraid we were young snots out to knock him down."

The two interviewers found Shaw with a large white bandage on his left hand. He had purchased a new Hillman Minx convertible and had gotten his hand caught in the car's folding-roof mechanism. This did not, however, prevent him from holding a large martini glass in his right hand, or from snapping at the interviewers' first remark, that a long comic story called "The Green Nude" was "pretty funny."

"What do you mean by that? 'Pretty funny'?"

"As a matter of fact, it's very funny," the interviewers hastily amended. "A very funny story."

"Damn right it's funny. Didn't I tell you it was?"

In a casual way, the interview was the most illuminating one ever conducted of Shaw (with the possible exception of the journal's follow-up interview twenty-five years later). What emerged, amid much intriguingly candid talk about *The Young Lions*, writing for radio, and other milestones of his career, was the portrait of an artist part melancholy, part embittered, but also an artist fiercely, even truculently, proud of his achievements. "Do you really enjoy writing, Mr. Shaw?" the interviewers asked.

"I used to enjoy it more," Shaw admitted. "It's tougher now, as one's power dwindles. Also, the variety of choice increases. There used to be only one sentence to write. You wrote it and it was good and you let it stay. As you grow older and more experienced you find that where you had one sentence before, you have thirty possibilities now and you have to stew to find the best."

For all his successes, Shaw was a writer who brooded about failure and had even come to expect it. "Look, failure is inevitable for the writer," he told his interviewers. "Any writer. I don't care who he is, or how great he is, or what he's written. Sooner or later he's going to flop and everybody who admired him will try to write him off as a bum." Later he added: "Failure is more consistent—for everybody—than success. It's like living in a rainy belt—there are some sunny days, but most of the time it's wet outside and you'd better carry your umbrella. Anyway, failure is apt to produce self-pity, and it's been my experience that self-pity can be very productive."

The interviewers asked Shaw about his plays, and he admitted that having produced seven plays, all but one of them commercial flops, he wasn't any longer sure the theater was the right form for him. He was grimly sure, though, of what he felt about the New York theater audience.

"I have a fine play in mind I'll write for them someday," he declared. "The curtain slides up on a stage bare except a machine gun facing the audience. Then after a pause in which the audience is given time to rustle their paper bags and their programs, wheeze and cough and settle in their seats, the actor enters. He's a tall man dressed in evening clothes. He comes downstage to the footlights and, after a little bow, smiles charmingly at the audience, giving them more time to mumble and rustle and cough and whisper and settle in their seats. Then he walks upstage, adjusts the machine gun, and blasts them."

"Oh yes . . ." stammered the interviewers. "Perhaps we ought to move on."

Spontaneous as these sentiments obviously were, Shaw showed no desire to mitigate them, despite the opportunity to do so. "In fact, he edited the interview himself," recalls Tom Guinzburg. "I remember we sent it to him, and he asked himself some more questions and we asked some."

Shaw's contemporaries were very much in evidence too that summer. Art Stanton, the Volkswagen franchiser, came down, as did Sydney Chaplin and songwriter Adolph Green. Bob Capa came in August to recover from a painful slipped spinal disk and stayed in the big house John Huston had rented with his wife, Ricky. By then Huston had departed, so Chaplin and Green also bunked there. "Irwin and John Huston were almost the only ones who rented large houses," recalls Peter Viertel, who came with his model girlfriend, Bettina, to work on a screenplay. "The rest of us just lived in cheap hotels or boardinghouses. But everybody was pals; there wasn't any leader of the group."

In July Shaw and others put aside their political qualms about visiting Franco's Spain, persuaded by Hemingway, who passed through St.-Jean en route to the festival of Pamplona—his first trip across the border since the Spanish Civil War. Viertel met up with him there. Shaw went instead with Charles and Lael Wertenbaker, Plimpton, and Joe and Barbara Kaufman, who had taken a house near the Shaws'. "We stayed quite a ways outside Pamplona, we couldn't get accommodations in town," Joe Kaufman recalls. "But we were there for the full seven days. And Plimpton ran with the bulls."

Kaufman had come to regard Shaw with wryer detachment than did most of the crowd at St.-Jean. "People didn't tend to argue with Irwin," says Kaufman. "But I remember arguing with him one night soon after we arrived in St.-Jean. It turned out Irwin took criticism rather well. Not about his writing, mind you, but about his deportment. In fact, I always felt you had to argue with him to keep up the quality of the friendship."

The Kaufmans and the Wertenbakers went on other bullfighting trips to Spain with the Shaws, often to see Antonio Ordóñez, the rising young star who so impressed Hemingway too. Away from home, Shaw's penchant for playing master of ceremonies could grow irksome, Kaufman found. "We arrived in one Spanish town for lunch, and Irwin said, 'We're all going to have sandwiches and leave within half an hour.' I said, 'I'm going to stay to have four courses, thank you very much.' And he looked at me and said, 'I'm a little domineering, aren't I?' "

Shaw did seem aware of his increasing tendency to make all the social decisions. In *Lucy Crown*, the martinetlike husband Oliver Crown asks himself why he feels the compulsion to make decisions for his wife, his son, even his friends. In part it's the desire to be in control, in part the assumption that he, more than anyone else, sees matters the right way. For Shaw, another element was sheer restlessness. "Irwin could lie in the sun about five minutes," says Kaufman, "and then he'd say, 'Okay, let's go'—on to the next swim, the next round of tennis, the next patio cocktail party."

July saw the publication of Peter Viertel's thinly veiled novel about John Huston, *White Hunter, Black Heart.* Based on his experience writing *The African Queen* and participating in its filming in the Congo, the much-discussed story, about a screenwriter named Peter Verrill, drew a scabrous portrait of the director as a man of reckless machismo, drinking all day and fornicating all night. Huston professed not to have read the book and not to care, and kept right on working with Viertel. Nor, apparently, did he care when Shaw took up with his pretty wife, Ricky, after Huston's departure late in the summer. Upon learning that Ricky's rental was about to expire, Joe and Barbara Kaufman invited her to stay with them, thus enabling Shaw to prolong the affair.

Twenty-five years later, Kaufman found himself reminiscing about that summer with Marian out in Southampton, and made the mistake of telling her about the affair. Ancient history, he thought. "Marian said, 'I wish you hadn't done that.' And I said, 'How can you be jealous after twenty-five years?' But she was. And that became the relationship."

Despite the many distractions, Shaw did manage to turn out two fine stories that summer that appeared in *The New Yorker* the following winter. "Instrument of Salvation" is based on a turning point in the life of Salka Viertel, a kind of private tribute. European Inge Clavered, a former actress now living in America, arrives late to a Fifth Avenue musical party ("she had developed the habit, as a young actress, of entering all rooms after they were full, and the habit had stayed with her") and encounters a German businessman who once tried to sleep with her in prewar Berlin. The businessman had promised to help finance the repertory company that Clavered and her director husband, Bruno, wanted to establish, but after Inge rebuffed him, the money never came through; instead, the growing anti-Semitism in Germany persuaded Bruno to move to California, where he found work as a movie director and had his family join him. Seeing the businessman again after all these years, Inge knows she should still be angry at this man whose decision so affected her life, but the old man's vanity seems harmless, even pathetic. Inge endures a short, polite conversation with him and then watches as he glides off to flirt, absurdly, with a much younger woman. Though the story is as deftly handled as many of Shaw's best, it was unfortunately left out of subsequent anthologies and can be found only in *The New Yorker*'s crumbling pages.

Better known, and much more profitable, was "Tip on a Dead Jockey," written very much in Shaw's new vein of stories about Americans in Europe and based on the experiences of his friend Noel Howard, who as a pilot had smuggled cigarettes to French Africa during the war. Lloyd

Barber, a grizzled American war pilot who's come to Paris in the wake of a wrecked marriage, is approached at the racetrack by a bland-looking little man named Bert Smith who offers a tip on the upcoming race, while clearly harboring some business proposition. "He had little, dapper feet and a bright necktie," Shaw writes of Smith in one of his best character descriptions, "and he had a well-cared-for, international kind of face, with large, pretty dark eyes, fringed by thick black lashes. He had what Barber had come to call an import-export face. . . . It was a face, you felt somehow, that was occasionally of interest to the police." The proposition, it turns out, is for Barber to pilot a flight of Egyptian currency illegally across the Mediterranean into France. Barber considers the offer, and the $25,000 pay, then rejects it when one of Bert Smith's racetrack tips results not only in a loss but in a dead jockey on the track, a very bad omen. Angrily, Smith recruits Barber's fellow ex-pilot Jimmy Richardson. When Richardson vanishes for a month, Barber fears the worst, only to find his old friend decked out in new clothes, his wife sporting a gaudy new ring, at the bar of the Hôtel Bellman. Life's accidents, it seems, defy omens, and often befall the wrong man.

Gritty and suspenseful, "Tip on a Dead Jockey" fully confirmed Shaw's capacity to transfer his canvas to Europe, in the short story form at least. It also stood as a nearly perfect blend of masterly, artistic fiction and richly commercial storytelling. Within a month of its appearance in *The New Yorker* in March 1954, MGM agreed to buy the story. The film that eventually emerged, with a screenplay by Charles Lederer and performances by Robert Taylor and Martin Gabel among others, did reasonably well with critics and audiences. This was the happy blend that Shaw had hoped to accomplish from his earliest days as a writer. It hadn't been easy before, though, and it wouldn't be easy again.

With the summer revelers heading home in September, Shaw decided to stay in St.-Jean-de-Luz through the fall of 1953 to make serious progress at last on *Lucy Crown*. Whether or not he'd actually heaved a first draft into the fire, as Guinzburg and Marquand were led to believe, he seemed now to be starting from scratch. In a letter to Donald Klopfer, he admitted to having done so little work on the novel that he preferred to have Lazar return his advance of $15,000 until the following year; for both emotional and tax reasons, it made better sense that way. Still, he declared boldly, Random House might expect to see a finished draft by the turn of the year, especially since he was considering making the ultimate sacrifice of going on the wagon.

By November 20, Shaw was able to report to Bennett Cerf that he had written 350 pages, an average of about five a day. He wasn't happy with what he'd produced, however, and had even given thought to putting it aside to play with one of two other novel ideas. Still, he would finish the draft, perhaps by January, and see what Random House thought of it. Meanwhile, he added, his nearly four-year-old son Adam was speaking French with a singsong Basque accent that would have thrilled Shaw's old French teacher at James Madison High School.

With Adam old enough for kindergarten, if not first grade, the Shaws had given thought to going home that year, and to enrolling their son in a proper New York school. There was vague talk of returning the next September, Shaw wrote Simon Michael Bessie in November, but he added sheepishly that he and Marian had entertained the same vague thoughts the year before. He neglected to mention that Europe's charms were no longer the only reason to stay. As of 1953, the big tax loophole was changing yet again. For the seventeen-out-of-eighteen-monthers, a $20,000 ceiling on nontaxable foreign income would now be imposed. That was a healthy sum in 1953—easily comparable to $100,000 in 1989—but for the high-rolling Hollywood set, the ceiling still put a crimp in one's lifestyle. There was one exception to the new edict, however. Americans who could prove they were *permanent* foreign residents could still claim one-hundred-percent exemption on their foreign income. And what constituted permanence? Not unexpectedly, the term was somewhat vague. One good indication was full-time European residence beyond a twenty-four-month period. Another was not having an American residence of any kind. Coincidence or not, the Shaws chose that year to surrender their Manhattan apartment. This year too, they rented a chalet of their own in Klosters, rather than stay at the Chesa Grischuna. If they wanted to keep on living in the style to which they'd become accustomed, the new tax ruling made it suddenly clear: they couldn't afford to come home.

The Shaws arrived happily in Klosters on December 1 to move into a large, comfortable chalet, the Haus am Talbach. Once again, Shaw found he could work better in the alpine quiet of Klosters than anywhere else, and soon he had settled into his favorite routine, waking early to write until late morning, and then, after a round of errands in town, heading up the slopes for an afternoon of skiing.

Once again, though, glamorous guests began to arrive, drawn by Shaw's great charm—so many that Klosters began to be jokingly referred to as Hollywood on the Rocks. Leland and Slim Hayward came, as did Anatole Litvak, Darryl Zanuck and Swifty Lazar. Even Salka Viertel came, having just visited Peter in Ireland, where he was working over the Christmas holiday on a new film with Huston. On December 31, she took the tiny Klosters/Davos train up the mountains, to be met by Shaw and a tearful Jigee Viertel, who had been told by Shaw only that "some friends" were arriving. That night, one and all gathered for a festive New Year's Eve at the Chesa Grischuna, overseen by the Chesa's beaming Swiss owners, Hans and Doris Guler.

Robert Capa was among the celebrants that night, but there was a strange air of unquiet about him. He'd had another bad year, as all his friends knew. Not only had he suffered physical pain due to his back injury, he had also been depressed. Pasty-faced and overweight from drinking, convinced that his best years were already behind him, he exemplified the haggard postwar veteran whose angst Shaw had captured so beautifully in "Tip on a Dead Jockey": "We have had our adventures too early. Our love has turned to affection, our hate to distaste, our despair to melancholy, our passion to preference." The only answer seemed to be to find a new war, and sensing that, Shaw extracted a solemn promise from Capa that the photographer not accept any more wartime assignments.

It was a promise Capa wouldn't keep. Over that holiday, he learned of an opportunity to visit Japan for six weeks and take pictures for a new magazine, *Camera Mainichi*. Shaw asked him to bring back a Japanese camera, and Capa gave him an odd look that assumed, in retrospect, a sorrowful portentousness. "The last time I saw him," Shaw recalled years later, "was at the railroad station of Klosters, where he was serenaded by the town band as he climbed aboard the train with a bottle of champagne and someone else's wife."

There was good news from Hollywood that winter. In January Lazar succeeded in selling the film rights to *The Young Lions* for a sum reported to be more than $100,000. The buyers were a New York tax attorney, Jacques Braunstein, and a producer, Robert Lord, who planned an independent production that summer. Shaw would also get a percentage of the film's profits and, for an additional sum, write the screenplay. For 1954 that was very good money indeed. Then, in February, *Act of Love,* Shaw's first screenwriting job abroad, opened in New York to generally favorable reviews, with Shaw praised by Bosley Crowther of *The New York Times* for having "crisply adapted" the Alfred Hayes novel on which the film was based. With the news in March that "Tip on a Dead Jockey" had also been purchased, Shaw was closer to being rich than he'd ever been before.

Thus it was all the more frustrating that *Lucy Crown* refused to take shape.

Not long after he arrived in Klosters, Shaw wrote Saxe Commins an uncharacteristic plea for help. He'd now written 500 pages, he reported, but the novel was in fragments, like separate short stories, that confounded his efforts to put them in order. Marian had read the work and recommended he discard it. Could Commins possibly fly over to Klosters to take a look?

It was a heartfelt request, but still a presumptuous one by the established code of the publishing business, and Commins responded gently that he'd prefer that Shaw come to New York, especially since Commins was still recovering from a heart attack suffered the previous fall. This Shaw did in early February. On the plane he had time to review a long, careful letter of appraisal about the novel from Donald Klopfer, the first really negative response he'd received in nearly two decades as a Random House author.

The problem, in part, was one of literary ego. More than five years of international stature as the author of *The Young Lions,* and more than two years of high living in Europe surrounded by adoring friends, had softened Shaw's self-judgment. Having indulged in long, unbroken stretches of sybaritic fun, he had sat down at the typewriter to bat out a novel in three months, after spending nearly three years on each of his first two novels. So considerable was his talent that it had betrayed him insidiously, by enabling him to produce work that wasn't obviously bad, just facile: a novel whose sentences glided along with smooth syntax, but with less grace, and fewer shining turns, than before.

The other problem was that Shaw was in deep water with his subject. *The Young Lions* and *The Troubled Air* had been based on news events of major importance, events that had touched every reader's life and lent each book a grainy sense of journalistic reality. The personal stories that Shaw had then hung on those backdrops seemed that much more real, and it was Shaw's special gift to be able to make the personal stories, in turn, illuminate the times. But *Lucy Crown* was set against no such backdrop. It was a novel about one family disrupted by a mother's adultery, its setting no larger than the family's front lawn. It had the peculiar quality of a good Shaw short story inflated to outsized proportions. Worse yet for Shaw, it was a story whose central character was a woman.

The *Lucy Crown* that emerged between covers is a simple enough tale made somewhat less so by the use of flashbacks. At its start, Lucy Crown is a widow in her early fifties who finds herself in a Paris bar late one night, looking across the smoky room at a young man who is, to her shock, the son she hasn't seen in many years. The story then flips back to the fateful summer when Lucy ruined her marriage by having a casual affair in the country with the Dartmouth student hired as a companion for her thirteen-year-old son, Tony. The affair is an awakening for Lucy, her first real pleasure after dreary years as a housewife to her circumspect husband, Oliver. But that joy is short-lived. Tony espies his mother making love in a nearby garden house and reports the incident to his father in the city. Oliver grimly drives up to discover that his wife and son now hate each other. One of the two must go. Oddly, Oliver puts the decision to his son, while confessing he'll be brokenhearted if Tony makes Lucy leave. Tony takes the hint, coldly leaving his parents to years of guilt, until his father goes off to the war at an advanced age and gets himself killed. Having arrived back at the present, the novel concludes with an uneasy reunion between Lucy and Tony, and a car trip to visit Oliver's Normandy grave.

Shaw's first draft of *Lucy Crown,* as Klopfer pointed out, had a more jumbled chronology that left the reader thoroughly confused about whose story it was. Lucy was initially presented as a happy mother with an unaccountably surly son. Later Shaw revealed that Lucy had had an affair, but with a very different outcome: a joyful reawakening of herself as a sexual woman after twelve years of marriage, and a subsequent rejection of her son. Oliver agreed to banish his son and keep living with his liberated wife, until Lucy realized in the end that she had misjudged herself. The problem, Klopfer noted, was that the reader would tend to sympathize with the banished son and resent Lucy Crown, when in fact the story should paint Lucy as the sympathetic main character.

The original story revealed a good deal more of Shaw's feelings about women than its final draft. For all his exuberant philandering, Shaw maintained an unyielding double standard. A man could indulge in extramarital affairs because, paradoxically, he couldn't help himself but he could control the situation. But not a woman. Beneath the surface of every proper wife, as the original *Lucy Crown* made clear, lurked a lustful creature whose passions stood ready to wreck her family and herself. There was, in Shaw, the ghost of some old fire-and-brimstone preacher, and in Lucy Crown, a ghost of Hester Prynne. What the novel suggested, oddly enough in such a lover of women, was an underlying fear of what Marian might do someday, and of its consequences for the Shaws as a family.

Shaw returned to Klosters from his editorial conferences in New York with an admirable determination to do whatever was needed to pull the novel into shape, even if that meant rewriting it from scratch. He was particularly grateful to Commins, who had spent long hours with Shaw despite the need to pace himself. Commins, for his part, was left feeling deeply ambivalent about the writer whose work he had first championed at Random House nearly twenty years before. As much as he adored Shaw's stories and *The Young Lions,* in reading *Lucy Crown* he had come to feel that Shaw was failing to live up to his promise. "He is, I believe, a victim of his great facility," Commins concluded sadly. "He does everything too easily and never under the duress of doubt. If it's a story one wants, a paragraph, a phrase or a word, it flows from the top of his mind. This indicates he relies on talent and he has a superabundance of that. It is as if he were improvising all the time, unconsciously, spontaneously, and effortlessly."

In any event, the work would have to wait until after the summer, because Shaw was now obliged to start his screenplay of *The Young Lions*—a project, he confessed, that he already dreaded. Screenplays were hard, dreary labor, he added, not like short stories that could roll around in his imagination until they arranged themselves in the proper order.

By April 27, Shaw was in Paris to meet with the would-be producers of *The Young Lions* and show them his unfinished screenplay. The apartment on the rue du Boccador had been reclaimed by its owners, so Shaw took a room at the Hôtel Bellman on the rue François. That week, with Marian in Klosters, Shaw had a short affair with an actress he'd met on his last trip to New York. It was a sweet, somewhat sad episode that, with startling resonance, echoed an essay Shaw had published in *Holiday* the year before. The essay was titled "Paris! Paris!" and its voice was that of a lover of the City of Light, reciting the pleasures of introducing his city to a beautiful girl who'd never seen it.

"I was a television actress, singing and dancing in New York that year on the Kate Smith show," recalls Betsy Gehman. "The schedule was exhausting, and I'd been planning a trip to Europe that spring to recover. I'd also, as it happened, been reading *The Young Lions.* The other actresses gave me a farewell lunch at which I got pretty well sloshed, and afterward, as I headed down Fifth Avenue to pick up my new luggage at Saks—there was Irwin Shaw, flanked by someone on either side.

"Well, of course, I recognized him from his picture on the book, and I was just sloshed enough to go up to him and tell him how much I liked his book. Whereupon we started talking with great gusto while the other two people stood off at a respectful distance. It was wonderful and, I suppose, a bit sad in a way: he left no girl unturned. Anyway, I told him I was going to Paris and on what boat, and he said I must call him when I arrived. As we parted, I apologized for taking him away from the two people he'd been walking with, and I asked him who they were. 'Oh,' he said, 'they're my mother and father.'

"Halfway across the Atlantic, I got a cable—on board—from Irwin, saying he would be in Paris when I was there and to please look him up. So I did, and we had some marvelous days together. He showed me all around Paris, the way you'd want to be shown Paris, telling me all about the history and the people, how Joyce had gone to Deux Magots, that sort of thing. One of those days Irwin saw a newspaper headline that Roger Bannister had broken the four-minute mile—and he was so ecstatic, you'd think we'd landed a man on the moon.

"We went pub-crawling—the Café Flore, places like that. And out to dinner—to Ludwig Bemelmans's restaurant on the Île St.-Louis. And all throughout he was absolutely attentive and darling. He even put me up in a hotel not far from his own. And no—he didn't try to seduce me, not in the first three or four days at least. Finally, on the last day, he just said, 'Well, do you think we ought to sleep together?' And I didn't really want to. But then I thought, Well, why not. It turned out to be utterly boring— because there wasn't any passion in it, of course. It was sort of like a handshake good-bye."

Shaw was in Antibes, staying at the Hôtel La Bouée on a working holiday, when he got the call from photographer David Seymour, better known as Chim, that Robert Capa had been killed. While in Japan, Capa had accepted the offer from *Life* to go to Indochina and cover France's losing war against the Communists. He had arrived in Hanoi on

May 9—the same day Shaw had left Paris for Antibes on holiday—and on May 25 had set out with a French convoy whose mission was to evacuate a nearby fort in anticipation of a Vietminh advance. Sensing a picture he couldn't get from the journalists' jeep, he had walked up the grassy slope of a dike and stepped on an antipersonnel mine. Along with the myriad other friends Capa had made in his brave and reckless life, Shaw was devastated. In a letter that week to Saxe Commins, Shaw mourned the loss of a charming, courageous man who had been one of his best friends, a loss that seemed to leave "a dreadful hole in our lives." Ironically, only a few years later, Shaw would get a call from Cornell Capa that Chim had been killed in the Israeli-Egyptian war.

Capa's absence seemed only more painful that summer in St.-Jean-de-Luz, where an entire community of friends struggled to come to terms with his untimely death. One consolation was the steady stream of other journalists who now passed through—emissaries, in a sense, from Capa's world. Ben Bradlee, who had gone on from his first Paris posting as press attaché to become a *Newsweek* correspondent, came down on weekends with his buddy Crosby Noyes, whose family was part owner of the old *Washington Star*. "North Africa was starting to be a big foreign correspondent's story," Bradlee recalls. "The way to get down there from Paris was to fly to Biarritz, and from Biarritz to Casablanca or Algiers or Tunis. So what we'd do is catch a Friday-night flight and spend the weekend in St.-Jean-de-Luz. Then on Sundays the plane would come again and we'd fly down to North Africa, work two or three weeks, then take in another weekend at St.-Jean on the way back.

"That," says Bradlee in his best grizzled-editor growl, "was in the tall cotton."

Bradlee stayed with the Shaws a couple of those weekends. He and Shaw would play tennis at Chantaco. Once, and only once, they played golf. "We never played again," says Bradlee. "Because he couldn't do it. He was so muscle-bound he couldn't swing right. Couldn't even back up a car." For Bradlee, it was as much a pleasure to see Marian as Irwin. "She was witty, bright as could be, took no shit from anybody—but very feminine too. She always had a staff down there. And she really made that life work."

Drew Middleton, the *New York Times* correspondent who'd met Shaw in wartime Paris, was another of the regulars that summer. Now the *Times* bureau chief in London, he took a house with his wife in the town for his three-week leave. "One of our big things was that on a Saturday the four of us would get into a car and go down to San Sebastián. We'd have lunch on the way and then see the bullfights. And almost every day we played tennis. In the late afternoon we'd sit on the Shaws' terrace and have drinks while [their] little son Adam ran underfoot. I remember Orson Welles being there that summer, he was a nut about bullfights, always saying

Hemingway didn't really know much about them. He'd gotten very heavy by then—he ate immense amounts, and drank anything in sight, especially sherry—and you knew he was suffering from being out of the limelight. Charlie Wertenbaker was always around too. A magnificent fellow. It was at the Wertenbakers' suggestion that we'd come to St.-Jean-de-Luz. And Chip Bohlen, who had just been named ambassador to the Soviet Union. He'd get into these heated talks with us about the Soviet influence, and Irwin was always very involved in those. The McCarthy era, remember, was still very much with us."

Outwardly, the Shaws remained the gracious, congenial hosts they were. But sexual tensions, aggravated perhaps by an anxiety on Shaw's part at having turned forty, ran beneath the surface like an electrical current. Shaw would activate them by taking an interest in some new attractive woman; Marian would respond with jealous rage; and the woman in question, having been courted by one Shaw, would find herself confronted by the other. The odd part, as more than one woman discovered, was that the Shaws seemed to act in concert.

One female houseguest from this period vividly remembers having Shaw slip into her bedroom uninvited, and try clumsily to seduce her. The woman rebuffed him but noticed the next morning that Marian was acting coolly toward her. To her greater consternation, Shaw returned to her room the second night, renewed the attack, and declared it was "all right" because he'd told Marian everything. In tears, the houseguest rebuffed him again, only to have Marian pull her aside the next morning. "I know you've slept with Irwin," she announced. "All my friends have slept with Irwin—now you have too." When the woman protested, Marian refused to believe her. "You have to be honest," she said. "The only thing that will affect our friendship is if you deny it."

For the guest, the experience ended her friendship with the Shaws and left an enduringly dark portrait of their marriage. At the least, it suggested that behind the famous figure was a man whose appetites, far from abating with age, were beginning to overwhelm him.

CHAPTER FOURTEEN

Perhaps, thought Shaw, a new setting would help with the dreaded rewriting of *Lucy Crown*. It might also distance him from some of the well-intentioned friends who transformed every day in Paris and St.-Jean-de-Luz into a festive gathering. By early November 1954, having revised his screenplay of *The Young Lions*, he and Marian had settled into a new life in London, in an apartment at 22 Mount Street. Still, it was hardly a life of seclusion: thanks to the McCarthy hearings, many Hollywood writers and directors had emigrated to London, Joseph Losey and Carl Foreman among them. Among the Shaws' closest friends were Roy and Enid Boulting, who held an informal salon on Sunday nights at their Chelsea house, when the city was quiet, at which director Fred Zinnemann and actor Peter Sellers were among the regulars. Soon enough, it became apparent to the Boultings that Shaw simply wouldn't be able to abide by London's pub rules. "He was just furious that he couldn't buy a drink between two o'clock and six o'clock in the afternoons," recalls Enid Boulting Hardwicke. "Irwin would say, 'Who are they to tell me when the hell I can get a drink or not? I'm not a child.' They'd rented their apartment for three months, but in about three days Irwin got so mad he packed up and they left."

Actually, Shaw stuck it out until the Christmas holidays. In mid-December, though, he took a sad ferry trip across the Channel to visit Charles Wertenbaker in Ciboure. Only three months before, Wertenbaker had learned he had an incurable cancer. Despite the brave nursing of his wife, Wertenbaker was already so weakened that he preferred not to see many of his close friends, including the Kaufmans, because he felt they wouldn't be strong enough to deal with his condition. Shaw was allowed down with the warning that the trip might be in vain if Wertenbaker was having a bad day.

Fortunately, Wertenbaker felt well enough that day to join Shaw and Lael for a five-hour lunch of laughter and reminiscing on the terrace of a small Basque restaurant, Biriatou. When it came time to leave, Shaw gave his old friend a Spanish-style farewell embrace. Then, as Lael drove him back to the train station, he cried steadily and without shame, "the way soldiers do in war sometimes," Lael later wrote, "over courage, not over death."

It was on February 12, 1955, that another relationship technically came to an end—though this one expired without warning or report.

There was nothing about "Voyage Out, Voyage Home" that would have suggested it would be Irwin Shaw's last short story for *The New Yorker*. Artfully wrought, it was the tale of a twenty-year-old American girl whose father packs her off to Europe in the hope that she'll forget the feckless man to whom she's become engaged. The old treatment works, but not as envisioned: in a Swiss ski resort that resembles Klosters, the girl meets and agrees to marry a dashing young suitor, only to learn that his thinness is consumption. Before she can hope to fatten him up, he suffers a fatal accident on the ski slopes, and the girl is left to return home, feeling much older and wiser than her father will ever know.

A story written against Shaw's new backdrop of Americans in Europe, "Voyage" also underscored a growing conviction on Shaw's part that life turns on accidents, for better but usually for worse. It was an accident on the racetrack that had kept Lloyd Barber from agreeing to pilot a smuggler's flight in "Tip on a Dead Jockey," and sheer accident that his foolish buddy made the trip without being killed. Certainly it was an accident that Lucy Crown's son should happen by the garden house one summer afternoon and look in to see his mother making love to young Jeff Bunner. In Shaw's own life, it was an accident that had taken Robert Capa's life the previous spring, and an accident that Charles Wertenbaker had died of cancer; weren't extramarital affairs accidents too? From now on, accidents would define almost every story and novel Shaw wrote, and characters would be determined by how they reacted to them. It was a cynical vision, and it ran directly counter to the idealism of Shaw's early work, in which good triumphed over evil, often with a punch on the nose, and gentle people carried the day. Now, Shaw seemed to be saying, all the gentle people could do was hope to avoid the bad accidents and be brave if those accidents came. It was a point of view as valid as any other, but it had a built-in liability. Short stories could turn on accidents, but fatalistic novels all too often seemed contrived.

It's doubtful that the editors of *The New Yorker* spent much time worrying over the accidents that cropped up in Shaw's latest stories. They do seem to have worried over certain other factors, and Shaw, for his part, nursed his own grievances. In the end, the rift was one that not only clarified philosophical differences between *The New Yorker* and one of its best-known writers but also defined the complications of being a successful American writer at mid–twentieth century.

For a freelance short story writer, a break from *The New Yorker* did not entail a formal letter of dismissal. Fiction writers for the magazine didn't even have drawing accounts, the serflike arrangement instituted by

Ross for so-called fact writers and artists who received an annual sum as a loan, to be worked off by completing a set amount of work throughout the year. Fiction writers simply began to get their stories rejected, without explanation, until they got the message that they were no longer members of the club. It was a maddening, and more wounding, process. "*The New Yorker* had this terrible psychological hold on everybody," Brendan Gill says. "It was like being a member of a family, and when any of us was rejected it was like being thrown out of the family. It was much more painful than you would expect it to be."

Unexplained as the rejections were, they left their victims, as well as other colleagues, theorizing for years about the "real" reasons behind a break. In a sense, Shaw's case was more complex than most, because it involved not just his writing or compensation for stories but his lifestyle.

In the 1950s, a *New Yorker* writer was still assumed to be a monklike figure, cloistered from the outside world, toiling with painful, consuming dedication to his art. He lived oblivious to money and material comforts, which was a blessing, because he had neither. He remained utterly dependent on his editors for encouragement and financial support, like some hothouse flower in need of watering. He was loyal—and powerless.

"In the old days," recalls Gill, "Harold Ross felt very strongly about loyalty, and by loyalty he meant slavery, that we should all belong to him. One of the reasons he and I were never close was that I had a private income of $3,000 a year, which was enough to make him feel I wasn't a slave to the magazine. Ross always used to say, 'No *New Yorker* writer can afford to drive a car.' Even though he himself drove a Cadillac."

From the very first, Shaw had jostled those dusty presumptions, yet *The New Yorker* had happily published two dozen of his stories over a fifteen-year period. Why should that change now?

One reason was that, thanks to Hollywood, Shaw's high life had grown dramatically higher of late. The sale of *The Young Lions* to the movies, for more than $100,000, had been widely reported. So had that of "Tip on a Dead Jockey," which may have especially annoyed *The New Yorker*'s editors, because they could feel they had made that sale possible by publishing the story, while earning their own very modest salaries. Somehow too, everyone at *The New Yorker* seemed to know that Irwin Shaw earned $4,000 or more for a week of screenwriting work—perhaps because he grumbled to Gus Lobrano and others about the disparity between that fee and the $400 he might hope to earn from a *New Yorker* story that took at least a week to write. "I remember people saying, 'Irwin wants to be the richest writer in the world,'" Gill recalls. "It was a stinging remark based on envy as much as anything else."

In his writing, Shaw happily reported on the circles in which he now moved. For *Holiday* he wrote fluffy essays about swells on either continent. One was titled "Hollywood People," another "Europe Amused." Even the more seriously written "Paris! Paris!" underscored to a desk-bound *New Yorker* editor that Shaw was having the glorious time of an American expatriate with money in the bank, dining in fancy French restaurants, sampling fine wines. For any *New Yorker* editor who managed to miss those *Holiday* pieces, and the continuing squibs in New York columns about Irwin Shaw abroad, there were the stories themselves that Shaw submitted to the magazine about spoiled, rootless Americans in Europe. Intentionally or not, Shaw had become ostentatious.

Surely, though, the magazine's editors mused that year over drinks, there were other reasons for the banishment of Irwin Shaw. The likeliest, they agreed, was the ascendancy of William Shawn. Upon Harold Ross's death in December 1951, the shy and circumspect "editor of fact" had been named his successor. Shawn was already a legend for his reverential dedication to the magazine and all it stood for; he was even less comfortable with a Hollywood high-roller like Shaw than Ross had been. More to the point, the magazine's editor, new to the job, was perhaps less likely than Ross to dispute the fiction department's judgment on any particular writer or story. For its part, the fiction department, though headed by Gus Lobrano and staffed by seven editors, was still strongly influenced by the magazine's matriarch, Katherine White.

"She was a real *femme formidable*," recalls E. J. Kahn, Jr. "She was very influential, not just on her own but as E. B. White's wife, and E. B. White was still our shining star. She could be captain when she wanted to be, and she could be Mrs. E.B. when she wanted to be. And there may well have been a connection between her greater freedom, in Shawn's first years, to make decisions, and Shaw's departure from the magazine." Shaw himself felt that Mrs. White was the one who rejected his work, and that she'd been emboldened to do that because Ross, a strong Shaw supporter for all his grumbling about Hollywood, was no longer alive to protect Shaw's interests.

Bruce Bliven, Jr., for one, rejects that theory: "I know Shaw felt that way, but I can't believe it's true." With at least two or three of the editors in the department discussing each serious story submission, says Bliven, it's unlikely that Mrs. White enacted some personal vendetta. At the same time, he admits, the magazine reputed to be stuffy and unchanging does in fact change dramatically and often, with "little fads" that come in, and then "little purges" that sweep them out. "I think in the fiction department that's been particularly true, that the editors decide they've done too many stories of a particular kind—it isn't very well defined—and that they can't do any more for certain writers. It's very possible that this happened with Shaw."

Certainly another contributing factor was the death, the next year, of Gus Lobrano. Shaw's longtime editor at the magazine had remained a strong supporter, despite his personal misgivings about Shaw's Hollywood assignments. His passing—prematurely, at fifty-four, of what Gill termed a broken heart from not having been named Harold Ross's successor—left Shaw without an advocate. Having already dedicated one collection to Lobrano and William Maxwell together, Shaw dedicated his next, *Tip on a Dead Jockey,* to Lobrano alone, mournfully appending Lobrano's birth and death dates below the name.

The man in the best position to judge Shaw's break from *The New Yorker* was William Shawn. More than three decades later, in the twilight of his long and distinguished tenure as the magazine's editor in chief, Shawn sat in his large corner office, nineteen floors above West 43rd Street, and pondered the question. It was a hot summer day, but there was no air-conditioning on, only three small circular fans ranged around the room, and Shawn, as was his custom, wore a black, 1940s-style suit—buttoned— and heavy, black, shined shoes. Somehow, the suit made him look even smaller than he was: pixielike, with his bald pate and large protruding ears. There was a sense of frailty about him—part guise, part age, perhaps part anxiety at the thought that the magazine's new owner would soon force him to retire.

"Irwin was very much respected and admired, he was one of the promising fiction writers of that time," Shawn began in the slow, searching tones of an exacting man. "Then, in the 1950s, he turned to writing novels and he . . . got into a different kind of life. He was more into the glamour world rather than the quiet *New Yorker* world. He began to be very successful in a worldly sense, and lived well, and got into skiing.

"In a way, Irwin's success may have deflected him from more serious writing," Shawn continued with a slightly pained look. "He always had some sort of division in himself about what he wanted to do and what he wanted to be. But I don't think I can speak on that, because it all depends on what he felt impelled to write, and no other man can say that for him.

"I do know that by the early 1950s, when I became editor, there was a feeling that he was going in a somewhat different direction from the direction we were going in. The word that would have come up in those days was that it was going a little in the direction of slickness and therefore was not for us.

"It was a very gradual thing, and we were always eager to like what he did because of our attachment to him and his work. So it was always very painful to reject something he wrote. I remember conversations with Gus Lobrano about that."

But were there ever any conversations with the writer himself—words of advice, perhaps?

Shawn's pained look gave way to one of surprise. "Why—no. My guess is that nothing was ever said to Irwin."

Why not?

"There's nothing one can say," Shawn replied, gazing off. "It just happens from time to time that a writer . . . changes. . . ."

Shaw's first rejected story—since his early days—was almost certainly the long, lovely tale about Plimpton, Marquand and Sue Coward, "Then We Were Three." In tone and style it was a story of unmistakable *New Yorker* dimensions, yet it appeared in August 1955 in *McCall's*. If Shaw harbored any doubts about his relationship with the magazine, they were dispelled by the appearance of a third anthology of *New Yorker* stories a few years later, this one spanning the fifties. Not one of Shaw's stories was included.

"Irwin never got over his rejection from *The New Yorker*," says Brendan Gill. Unlike most of *The New Yorker*'s writers, Gill traveled in many of the same social circles that Shaw did, and often saw him in subsequent years at gatherings in New York or the Hamptons. "There was scarcely a time in my experience when we were speaking that it didn't come up on some level, his disappointment and enormous bitterness, and this feeling that he had been misunderstood, that we had misunderstood the seriousness of his later writing, of his ambition for himself. He seemed to feel that we felt that he had sold out. I would always say, 'No, it's not like that.' But he never believed me."

Not long after his break with *The New Yorker*, Shaw moved to a new Paris address that left no doubt about it: living well would be his best revenge.

The house at 5 *bis* Villa Madrid lay in the heart of Neuilly-sur-Seine, one of the most beautiful urban neighborhoods in the world. Behind high hedges, stately homes faced each other across wide, tree-lined streets. Nearby were the greenswards of the Bois de Boulogne, a more grandiose Central Park with riding stables and tennis courts. Villa Madrid was a private cul-de-sac within that enclave, complete with gate and toylike guardbooth. Its curving rows of white-granite mansions stood like miniature Park Avenue buildings, solid and austere. Those on the left side of the street backed onto the beautifully groomed Parc de St.-James, with private gardens through their double French doors. The Shaws' house was on the left side of the street, a furnished place—at that time it was impossible to find an unfurnished apartment because under French law a landlord sacrificed his right to remove tenants if the apartment was unfurnished— with a huge sunken living room graced by a fireplace, a large bedroom off to the side, and stairs leading up to another floor with more bedrooms.

Mary Jane Bacon, who began working for Shaw at about this time as a secretary and remained a close associate for several years, remembers vividly the first day she saw the house at Villa Madrid. "Marian came in, she'd just been playing tennis, and she made a great entrance—Marian always made great entrances. As soon as we met, Irwin asked me what I was doing that night, and I said, 'Nothing.' He told me to go back home and change, he was having some people over for cocktails. And when I returned in my little Fiat, everyone who was in the film business in Paris was there: Charles Boyer, Yves Montand, Simone Signoret, many more."

It was the spring of 1955, and Shaw was still finishing *Lucy Crown*, but a good deal of his time was taken up with film assignments. The most frustrating of these was *War and Peace*. Henry Fonda had made it a condition of his decision to act in the film that Shaw write the script; the actor had heard it said that Shaw had considered the novel his favorite since the age of fourteen and had read it every year since. Shaw was indeed so familiar with the story line that he turned out a script in just weeks, which privately alarmed the movie's director, King Vidor. Still, shooting began in Rome, and Shaw, in Klosters, heard nothing further for perhaps two weeks. Then came an anxious call from one of the film's producers. There was trouble; would Shaw mind coming down to help out? At the Rome airport, Shaw learned how bad the trouble was: Fonda had refused to do his next scene. Startled, Shaw asked to see the rushes. As the film ran, he grew more and more annoyed. "Christ," he said, "Fonda's right. I didn't write that. Neither did Tolstoy."

Next he went to King Vidor, a rather sweet and gentle old man. "Where'd those scenes come from?" he asked.

Vidor, a bit abashed, replied, "My wife wrote them."

Shaw was dumbstruck. "Your wife? Is your wife a better writer than I am? Or than Tolstoy is?"

"No," Vidor reportedly replied. "But I like what she writes better. Not only that," he added, "but my wife is a devout Christian Scientist."

"Your wife is a Christian Scientist and you have her writing *War and Peace*?"

In the end, shooting continued with Vidor's doctored script. Fonda reluctantly cooperated. Shaw had his name removed from the film's credits, and drove off in a brand-new consolation Alfa Romeo.

About the same time Shaw learned that his work of the previous year on *The Young Lions* was for naught: the Braunstein-Lord package had collapsed for lack of financing. Over the Christmas holiday season in Klosters, though, he had signed on to write an adaptation of the novel *Fire Down Below*, by Max Catto. One reason was that Shaw's friend Robert Parrish would be directing it. An all-star cast was also being assembled: Rita Hayworth, Robert Mitchum, Jack Lemmon. Then there was the money. With his customary confidence, Shaw felt he could write a first-rate script in no time, and who could refuse another Hollywood offer, especially with a handsome new house to maintain? His restless energy undiminished,

Shaw turned from one movie project to the next as the fifties ground on—without taking the time for quiet reflection and refueling that another writer might have preferred. Like a slugger at bat, he just kept on swinging.

Bacon's job was to help with those assignments, not only by typing but by putting Shaw's scenes into shooting order. "I'd get there in the morning; Irwin would have been up since six-thirty or seven. We'd start our scenes, and he'd dictate dialogue as he paced the room. It was all adaptations of other people's work; after *The Young Lions*, Irwin felt adamant about not writing scripts of his own work."

Almost every night a group would gather for cocktails or dinner at the house. Shaw would start with a sensible guest list but keep inviting whomever he spoke with on the phone or saw in the cafés that day—Alexandre's or Fouquet's—much to the annoyance of Fedora, the wonderful Italian cook who had come with the Shaws from Klosters. Finally the big living room would be filled with a noisy mélange that might include Teddy White, Ben Bradlee, Martin Gabel and Arlene Francis, Shaw's good friend Bill Truehart from the State Department, Harold Kaplan, Peter Viertel with Bettina, playwright Marcel Achard, and perhaps a few tall young men who had stayed on after the establishment of *The Paris Review*, like Blair Fuller, whose attractive wife, Nina de Vogt, became first a friend, and eventually a romantic interest, of Shaw's.

The lovers, Bacon soon discovered, came and went as quickly as scenes in a shooting script. "If Irwin went to a party he just moved all over the place, if you know what I mean. And he never moved quietly. Within a few months of working for him, I heard he'd been doing that forever. There weren't that many important ones; it was just that he'd try to keep one in Rome, one in New York and so forth. Irwin wanted them all. I think he felt it was very generous of him to spread himself around like that, because he was such a great guy. And so of course, Marian lived in jealousy of everyone."

Bacon, who spent enough time with the Shaws over the next few years to be referred to as "the fourth Shaw" by Salka Viertel and others, sensed that Marian wasn't only jealous but also deeply unhappy. "On the surface, it was a great life for her. But under the surface, she and Irwin just didn't get along. They didn't have much to talk about—except people. And Irwin missed the intellectual stimulation.

"On the other hand, if Marian had been intellectual, Irwin would have been very competitive with that. He didn't mind discussing intellectual subjects with me. In fact, if I or someone else did something particularly intelligent he thought that was great, and took all the credit, in a sort of lovable way: it was because of him that we'd done this or that. But he always put Marian down."

The jibes were meant as banter, but they had a cutting effect. "I can't leave Marian," Shaw would say. "She doesn't make any money." Or:

"When I think of Marian, the first thing I see in my mind is her packing her bags. She's always packing her bags to leave." Or: "I've married a woman who only cares about placemats!" Unless the issue was another woman, Marian tended to be cowed by the jibes, or at least not rise to the bait. After all these years, she still felt somewhat in awe of her husband, and increasingly insecure about her own identity apart from his. Often that revealed itself in Marian's strident judgments about plays or movies, the one area where she retained a certain confidence. "She was very bossy and all-knowing in her opinions," Bacon soon found. And usually negative. One night Bacon went with the Shaws to see *Room at the Top,* with Simone Signoret. "Now that's an extraordinary film, right? Yet when we got out, all Marian could do was talk about Simone Signoret's terrible performance. We all just sort of gaped at her."

Now that Adam was old enough to take sides, his father, consciously or not, enlisted him in family disputes. "Irwin and Adam were always ganging up on Marian," says Bacon. "In Adam's eyes, Irwin could do no wrong and Marian no right. He'd see his father putting her down, and he'd do the same thing, which of course made it impossible for Marian to discipline him. Then Irwin would turn around and chastise Adam for not getting along better with his mother. *'If you can't get along with your mother,'* he'd say, *'you'll never get along with your wife.'* "

The parents used Adam; Adam used his parents. It was not a happy family.

By October, following another summer at St.-Jean-de-Luz, Shaw was able to send off his final draft of *Lucy Crown* to Saxe Commins, two years after his brash attempt to knock it out in a quick burst of speed. He still felt more ambivalent about it than anything he'd published to date. All he knew for sure, he wrote to Cerf, was that no one would want to make a movie of it.

He had underestimated Irving Lazar.

"Irwin Shaw's forthcoming novel, *Lucy Crown,* has drawn what is believed to be a record price for pre-publication transfer of screen rights," *The New York Times* reported in mid-January 1956. Producer Harold Hecht and actor Burt Lancaster had agreed to pay $400,000 for the property. Recently formed Hecht-Lancaster Productions would make additional payments depending on the book's sales and a percentage of film profits, so that the ultimate purchase price might reach $750,000. Starring in the role of Oliver Crown, of course, would be Burt Lancaster.

For a man who claimed to do screenwriting strictly as a way of paying his bills, the windfall sale of *Lucy Crown* might have signaled an opportunity to clear the decks of any other film assignments. In February, however, after the now customary holiday in Klosters, Shaw accepted a lucrative offer to go to Monte Carlo for two weeks to assist in the René Clement adaptation of Marguerite Duras's *Sea Wall*, titled *This Angry Age*. He was put up in the Hôtel de Paris, and couldn't resist writing to Bennett Cerf, in a note on the hotel's letterhead, "Now look where I am!" There was, indeed, a charming ingenuousness about Shaw that still shone through, for all the high life he'd experienced these last several years. Mary Jane Bacon, who came to help with the script, recalls heading to the airport with Shaw—Bacon to fly back to Paris; Shaw to fly to Tobago, where *Fire Down Below* was filming. Booked on different airlines, they were supposed to wait for their flights at different café tables, marked by different little airline flags. Shaw kept moving the flags around so he and Bacon could sit together, to the grave annoyance of the authorities. "Look at us, kid," he said with a delighted grin. "Who would ever have thought two people like us would be living such a wonderful life?"

By the time *Lucy Crown* appeared, at the end of March, Shaw was back in Klosters, in a new, bigger house called Chalet Pia. Cerf had ordered a large first printing, hoping to play off the publicity of the movie sale, and to benefit too from an unexpected chunk of money from the film producers for tie-in advertising. As the first reviews appeared, his optimism seemed justified. Charles Rolo in *The New York Times,* noting Shaw's departure from the big canvas of contemporary history, observed that this "venture into fresh territory . . . has produced a continuously absorbing book—sharply drawn, highly charged and painfully moving." Milton Rugoff in the *New York Herald Tribune* declared that Shaw "has told a painful story of human frailty feelingly and well," but made the point that *Lucy* was a study less of adultery as a sin than of the shame that accrued from it.

But *Lucy Crown* left other reviewers disappointed, if not angry. James Kelly in *Saturday Review* found that Shaw's characters "talk smartly and react credibly in the visual tableaux arranged for them. But they do not grow in size or significance. There's an intellectual aridity that locks them forever in coldly dramatic poses, unrescued by affectionate sympathy from their creator." Several critics questioned whether lives could be so irrevocably changed by one unfortunate hour. "Mr. Shaw came to the novel by way of the theater," Lewis Gannett observed, "and his theory of the decisive moment is essentially a theatrical theory. The theater has a scant two and a half hours to complete its drama; the novelist may take longer, and explore at greater length the slow processes which prepare his characters for the moments of fateful decision." Not only was the novel's turning point incredible, some declared; the whole structure was jerry-built. "The major stages of the plot veer drastically away from the probable," wrote J. R. Willingham in *The Nation,* "and one is left with the conviction that despite Shaw's often brilliant parts, there just isn't any structural or thematic justification for *Lucy Crown*."

As usual, *Time*'s anonymous reviewer sounded the most scornful note. "Though *Lucy* makes no visible mark on any literary target, it has already hit the bull's-eye of high finance." The review went on to cite the figures paid to Shaw by Hecht-Lancaster, a fundamentally unfair criterion on which to judge the novel, and one which, perhaps more than any other review in Shaw's career, exposed the envy of Shaw's lifestyle that lurked within many critics of his work. Bernard Frizell, the journalist and fellow graduate of Brooklyn College who was working in those days for *Time*, had a unique view of the situation. "Even though the reviews weren't signed in those days, I happened to know Ted Kalem had written it; Ted was a friend of mine. I saw Irwin at a party soon after that, and he said, 'If I ever catch the sonuvabitch who wrote that review, I'll really kill him.' I didn't tell him it was Ted, but I did go back to Ted and say, 'Hey, why'd you come down so hard on Irwin Shaw?' And Ted, much to my surprise, said, 'Ah, he makes enough money—he can take it.'"

Was it only the money that stirred critics' bile? Or was it now, for some, an issue of class?

In July another review appeared, belatedly, in the pages of *Commentary*. This one was signed by Leslie A. Fiedler, one of America's most important and impassioned new literary critics. Ostensibly a review of *Lucy Crown*, it quickly escalated into a scathing personal attack on Irwin Shaw and all that he stood for, one that in its indictment of Shaw's writing as "half-art" would echo Kazin's remark, over fifteen years earlier, that Shaw was "half a writer."

It was as close to a death knell for Shaw's literary reputation as any single critical piece could be.

Fiedler began by playing off Shaw's remark, in the recent *Paris Review* interview, that he felt "pigeonholed" by critics, who were forever turning writers into types. "As a matter of fact," Fiedler wrote, "it is only what is *typical* about him that makes him interesting enough for critical comment. His books and plays with their breathless pursuit of the very latest liberal-oid cliché-problem, his improbable dialogue (only he himself apparently talks like his own characters), his limp watery prose are scarcely worth more than the sentence it takes to describe them. More precisely, perhaps, they would be worth no more than that sentence, except for the fact that they represent an *ideal* of literary achievement, a style and attitude and choice of subject of which a whole class of readers dream. Irwin Shaw is, in fact, a sociological touchstone."

The bland, upper-middle-class liberals who populated Shaw's novels were projections not only of the author, Fiedler declared, but of his audience: well-meaning sorts who harbored vague "higher yearnings" of social and intellectual concern. Reading an Irwin Shaw novel was all the tonic they needed—just as writing one was tonic for Shaw himself. How interesting, Fiedler opined, that the hack writer–gigolo in the movie *Sunset Boulevard* was seen reading *The Young Lions* in his spare time: "not as an escape, but as an act of piety." But "slickness and sentimentality . . . turned from the service of entertainment and brand names to social awareness and 'human understanding' . . . remain still slickness and sentimentality," Fiedler wrote. "If mere 'decency' of intent could redeem banality, Shaw would be a first-rate writer rather than a symptom."

The savagery of Fiedler's attack seemed mystifying until the critic bared his class colors. The two strongest impulses in all of Shaw's fiction, he noted, were "a desire to get the hell out of Brooklyn and stay out," and a "great, warm, free-floating cloud of sentimentality" and self-pity that translated into an insatiable need for success. Those impulses, Fiedler admitted, were not unfamiliar.

"I, too, began in my own sort of Brooklyn," he wrote, "and I can remember with embarrassing clarity screaming in ecstasy as the soldiers walked portentously across the stage at the end of *Bury the Dead*; it seemed a play written for me and my friends, *our* play. . . . Somewhere in the late thirties, way back in the time of his short stories, we came apart, Shaw and I—crawled, perhaps I should say, into different pigeon holes, where we must wait for the critics to find us." In words that seemed a fulfillment of Diana Trilling's "bellwether" warning eight years before, he added, "The way Shaw has chosen seems to me finally intolerable: to be just right always—not a Communist a month past the time when being a Communist seems (to the most enlightened) a creditable excess; not against war a month past the point when true liberalism demands it; not a millimeter off the precise center between Red-baiting and whitewashing; just eggheaded enough to feel righteous but not too eggheaded to hate critics; able to read the right books in the morning but play a good game of tennis in the afternoon."

In one blaze of red-hot rhetoric, Fiedler had voiced the sentiments of a particular generation. It was a generation of intellectual Jewish liberals old enough to remember the thirties—*Shaw's* generation, or at least the one to which Fiedler felt Shaw had once belonged. It was hard to tell, reading between the lines, whether Fiedler was more incensed because Shaw the young radical had become a centrist liberal, or because Shaw the Jew had betrayed his fellow Jews. Betrayal, though, was certainly the charge.

In an unintended way, that charge said more about Fiedler than it did about Irwin Shaw. Hortatory as *Bury the Dead* may have seemed to its liberal audiences, of what group had its author been a card-carrying member? Certainly not the Communist Party, as Fiedler erroneously assumed. Nor had Shaw signed up in his local Brooklyn chapter of Jewish intellectuals. Fiedler and his loudly cheering friends had pigeonholed Shaw themselves, and then had taken offense when he failed to remain the figure they saw him to be.

What, though, of the writing itself? Of the novel that Shaw had labored over with more difficulty, in the end, than either of his others? Was it really "half-art," as Fiedler alleged?

In truth, it did mark a falling off from Shaw's first two novels, and from the indisputable "whole art" of his best short stories. Certain chapters of Lucy Crown work beautifully: the scene in which Oliver Crown takes Tony out for dinner and gets drunk on the eve of his departure for wartime service, stands on its own as a vintage Shaw short story. However, the intended boldness of Lucy Crown's subject—adultery—masked a sternly bourgeois morality. Suddenly Shaw seemed parochial, even backward-looking. His characters seemed one-dimensional, vessels of one view or another, manipulated through their dark moral drama like puppets moved about a stage. Incapable of the unexpected, they lacked the nuances and incongruities of real people.

The irony was that these limitations had been strengths within the compressed parameter of the short story. A short story demanded that its author be in absolute control. It turned on a single event or emotion, and its characters, with so little time to live, had to be drawn with one-dimensional clarity. They might change by the end of the story, but only from one clear shape to another, and it was up to a reader to supply the depth that a story's characters could only imply. In turning from stories to novels, Shaw had not yet considered that the difference in form meant a difference in art. He had done what had always worked before—just bigger.

In Lucy's wake, for the first time, Shaw experienced the painful silence of friends discreetly failing to comment on his work. Wounded, he took to demanding opinions, and then seething at what he heard. At a dinner in Paris, Leonora Hornblow made the mistake of saying, when asked, that she felt Lucy Crown wasn't up to par for her old friend and that it belonged in the Ladies' Home Journal. For a year after that dinner, the two didn't speak. David Schoenbrun also ran into Shaw in Paris, at the Ritz bar, in the spring of 1956.

"Irwin said suddenly, 'You got the copy of Lucy Crown that I sent you, didn't you?'

"And I said, 'Yeah.'

"He said, 'Well, you didn't acknowledge it.'

"I said, 'Gee, I'm truly sorry, that's the worst thing in the world, as a writer myself I know. I must have been away.'

"So Shaw said, 'Did you read it?'

"I said, 'Of course I read it.'

" 'So what did you think of it?'

" 'I didn't like it,' I said. 'So what's the point in my telling you?' And then I added, 'Irwin, at this stage in your career and our relationship, you're not going to ask someone what they think of your book. You're Irwin Shaw.'

"But he said, 'I do care. And you're my friend.' "

That June, Shaw came back to New York for what should have been a triumphant visit. He had signed on for yet another screenplay assignment, this one a distinguished-seeming adaptation of Eugene O'Neill's *Desire Under the Elms,* for the princely sum of $100,000, and was being put up at the St. Regis Hotel by the producers, who wanted Shaw to meet with them. His arrival also inspired Random House to stage a small literary dinner in his honor in the St. Regis library suite. The invited guests comprised Shaw's inner circle of friends, in publishing at least: the Charles Addamses, the Cheevers, the Kahns, the Gabels, the Simons, the Matthiessens, the Guinzburgs, the Styrons, Mr. Harry Kurnitz, and, as Shaw specified in a letter to Donald Klopfer, "a boy called Plympton [*sic*], of the *Paris Review* (friend of Tom Guinzburg)." It was a festive evening indeed; and yet beneath the gaiety, the guests sensed a new defensiveness in their old friend: about *Lucy Crown,* about the continuing script work, about the whole lavish European lifestyle that seemed to have become as much an impetus in Irwin Shaw's life as his love of writing.

While Shaw was in town on that trip, Peter Matthiessen had a memorable conversation with him over lunch at a midtown hotel. "It was as close as I ever heard him come to admitting he was concerned about his work," Matthiessen recalls. "He said something like, 'I'm writing too many goddamn movies, they're just too slick and they're probably corrupting the serious writing.' I guess he thought I wouldn't agree with him, but I did. I said, 'Why don't you stop, then? You can afford it.'

"He said, 'Well, I have to put Adam through school and college.'

"We'd had a couple martinis by now, and I came out with, 'Irwin, that's bullshit, you've got enough money to put Adam through school a hundred times. Why don't you just drop this movie stuff, go back to your own writing, write what you want?'

"Well—that was not what he wanted to hear. He gave me a terrible look. He was really pissed off; I'd said something too close to the bone. He knew I was right, but I wasn't supposed to say it. I was supposed to be his eager-to-please disciple there. He saw Bill Styron the same way. We liked him a lot, but we just couldn't go along with that idea.

"And I remember that just then, Moss Hart came in and joined us. I didn't know Hart at all, but I was never so glad to see anyone. Because it had suddenly become really awkward with Irwin, and I'd been thinking: How are we going to get through this?"

The writing was suffering. The disciples were deserting. But Irwin Shaw was richer, and more famous, than in his wildest Brooklyn dreams.

CHAPTER FIFTEEN

Never had the irony seemed so clear: by Christmas 1956, Shaw was settled in a new house in Klosters, outwardly leading the life of a rich and happy man, yet the screenwriting done to sustain that life was guilt-provoking hackwork. As for the fiction Shaw turned to between Hollywood assignments, it revealed a new and darker vision, bitter and cynical.

The house this time was Shaw's own, a large and charming chalet built at the then not inconsiderable cost of about $60,000, from his screenwriting fee for *Desire Under the Elms.* Chalet Pia, the house they had rented the previous spring, had been snatched out from under them for the coming winter season by one of the new Hollywood Klosterites, director Howard Hawks. The hell with it, an irritated Shaw had decided; he would be the king of his own castle.

The land parcel he bought lay half a mile or so southeast of the town, enough removed that the Shaw house would be the farthest one out. The distance would allow for more privacy and unimpeded views of the towering, snow-capped Swiss Alps but still be close enough for Shaw to take a daily walk to Klosters's curving streets and clean, chalet-front shops. That fall, while Shaw remained in Paris, Marian supervised the construction—terrorizing the crews into working at record speed, as her husband related with amusement to Bennett Cerf—so that when Shaw arrived for Christmas, he beheld the completed house that would become his most cherished home.

The chalet was a rambling, three-story affair with ten rooms, an overhanging wood roof and wraparound balcony set off by Swiss-style carved-wood balustrades. Shaw named it Chalet Mia, a title that not only meant "My House" but also served as an acronym for "Marian, Irwin, Adam." Soon a rustic farmer's cabin at the foot of the property's sloping front lawn would be refurbished to serve as Shaw's study, with fireplace, simple wood furniture, typewriter and the growing collection of pipes from which Shaw now made a selection every morning as he started to write, tamping down a plug of Dunhill 965 tobacco. The tiny stream that cut through just in front of the cabin would lead Shaw to put in a little arc-shaped log footbridge, no more than two feet across, that he dubbed his "WalkaShaw."

In very real ways, Chalet Mia changed Shaw's life. It made Klosters his base, not just a winter retreat, and in doing so lent an air of greater permanence to his European exile. From now on, even time spent in Paris would be time away from home. Nor would there be any more summers in St.-Jean-de-Luz. Klosters, Shaw would discover that year, seemed almost more marvelous when the winter crowds departed, its crisp dry summer air as pleasant as the Atlantic breezes of the Basque coast. Shaw also continued to feel strongly that he did his best work in Klosters, away from the hubbub and distractions of cities, and that to follow his early-morning hours at the typewriter with an afternoon of skiing was as close to the perfect life as any writer could know. Indeed, most of the nine novels Shaw still had in him would be written here. As the years passed, his own books would share shelf space with thousands of volumes, a prodigious personal library from which Shaw would make constant loans, and in which he took enough pride to make its bequest the first tenet of his will.

To the native Swiss of the town, as well as to the seasonal film crowd from the States, Shaw's decision to buy a house in Klosters had another consequence. It conferred upon him a sort of unofficial status as mayor, or at least as preeminent greeter. To Robert Parrish and others, Shaw was no less than the King of Klosters. He was the one the ever growing holiday crowds came to see; for eager newcomers, the capstone to a perfect skiing vacation in Klosters was an invitation for dinner at Chalet Mia.

Welcoming as Shaw was, the invitation wasn't that hard to come by. Certainly old friends could count on seeing Shaw virtually every day of their stay: Harry Kurnitz and Anatole Litvak, Darryl Zanuck and Sam Spiegel, the Parrishes, the Viertels, the Gabels, Irving Lazar. So could many less well-known regulars, however, who found themselves swept without hesitation into Shaw's glittering circle, and for whom such fraternizing often became the most exciting part of their lives. One early example was a genial New York insurance man named Charlie Tucker, who immediately impressed Shaw because he too had played football in college, then gone on to work in his spare time for twenty years as an official at Ivy League games. Tucker had also served in the war as a lieutenant commander on an aircraft carrier in the Pacific, and as far as Shaw was concerned, anyone who'd gone through the war (let alone with a superior rank) was an instant drinking companion. Shaw would call up Tucker and bellow, with no introduction, *"Hey, Charlie, what's going to happen in that bowl game?"* or *"What do you think of Notre Dame?"* As he did with others, Shaw would also listen with genial fascination to Tucker's stories, and occasionally borrow them for his fiction. His last novel, *Acceptable Losses,* would be based on one such story, and be dedicated to Tucker.

By one in the afternoon, Shaw would have done his writing for the day and gathered all willing hands for a few runs of group skiing. This made for quite a spectacle. "Irwin liked to ski in a pack of as many as a dozen people," recalls Charlie Tucker's widow, Lillian. At the top of the mountain he would push off first and usually lead the group—but not with any particular grace. "Irwin had no form," says Lillian Tucker. "It was like driving a truck." At set points along the trail, he would snowplow to a stop and wait for the others to catch up, concerned with their safety in an earnest, even fatherly way. "Then on his last run of the day," says Lillian Tucker, "he'd stop off at a chalet three quarters of the way down. Everyone would follow him in and he'd say, 'Bring us four bottles of that red wine you brought us yesterday.' And he'd always pick up the tab for that." Dinner would often be at the Chesa Grischuna, where Shaw would introduce newcomers to the cold white Swiss wine Dezaley; or at the Wyneck, farther down the hillside on which Klosters was set, where Hans Guler's niece Ruth served food that was fine enough to provoke endless debates about which kitchen was the better.

Festive as this life was, it couldn't entirely assuage the dark feelings Shaw now felt about his writing. With the encouragement of independent producer Don Hartman and director Delbert Mann, he had labored to make his adaptation of *Desire Under the Elms* as faithful as possible to the original, but for the once young playwright who had been hailed as a bold new voice of the American stage, how noble a task could it be to write camera directions into Eugene O'Neill's dialogue? The screenplay done, Shaw turned back to a story he had started the previous year, one that was fast growing into his next novel, *Two Weeks in Another Town*. He liked what he had so far, Shaw wrote Bennett Cerf, but it was darker than anything he'd written before: an account of a has-been actor who takes a two-week stint in Rome dubbing dialogue for an old, demagogic director whose film is in chaos.

Shaw knew all about those two-week stints. His uncredited work on *War and Peace* for King Vidor had first stirred the idea for the novel, and his two weeks in Monte Carlo the year before had given him more material. Now he went down again, in March, to Rome for another quick fix of movie cash. While he was there, he ran into John Cheever, and the meeting only reinforced Shaw's vision of himself as an embattled man.

From the first, Cheever had been a colleague, breaking into *The New Yorker* in the late 1930s, as Shaw had. Like Shaw, he had written wonderful stories that helped define the magazine's evolution from casuals and once-over-lightlys, and he had published collections at about the same pace. He had also been, and would continue to be, a drinking companion. From the first, though, Cheever had also been Shaw's mirror opposite, not only in character—the reserved manner, the small stature—but in literary sensibility. While Shaw had swept off to Hollywood and Europe, Cheever had remained humbly in New York, a doubt-ridden, near-destitute storyteller living as much in his imagination as in reality. Painfully, he had tried to write a novel, unsure that what he wrote was any good or that he could finish it at all. In 1954 he had submitted a first draft of what he called *The*

Wapshot Chronicle to Random House, to be told by an editor not only that the novel was unpublishable but that Cheever would have to return his $2,500 advance.

Now, at last, the book was being published, thanks to the staunch support of Simon Michael Bessie, Shaw's old friend from wartime London and Paris. After the Random House debacle, Bessie had committed Harper & Row to the still unfinished novel, shrugging off Cheever's warning that nothing might come of the effort, and accepting the demand that no deadline be stipulated or ever mentioned. Not long before Shaw arrived in Rome that March, Bessie sent him galleys of *The Wapshot Chronicle,* and Shaw soberly pronounced the novel "a beautiful job." It was indeed a richly imaginative masterwork, whose tumultuous creation stood in striking contrast to the controlled, first-draft confidence that had shaped nearly everything Shaw had written except for *Lucy Crown.* Though Shaw didn't like to admit it, there was a lesson in that. Soon after, *The Wapshot Chronicle* would win Cheever a National Book Award and election to the National Academy of Arts and Letters, adding to the growing defensiveness Shaw felt about not winning either of those accolades himself.

To celebrate his success, Cheever had taken his family to Rome for a year of adventure and change. He found Shaw staying at the Hotel Excelsior, living high on a movie-studio expense account, with a chauffeur to take the wheel of a big cream-colored car that Cheever always referred to later as a canary-yellow convertible. For the first time, Cheever felt not appalled or depressed by the aura of Hollywood glamour around Shaw— but amused. At some point on this trip, as Cheever fondly related for years afterward, Shaw insisted on using his awkward Italian to instruct his chauffeur to put a pile of newly received mail in the car. "*Sì, signore,*" the chauffeur replied, and promptly went off to dump the letters in the nearest mailbox.

Cheever, the beleaguered writer who had triumphed after all, couldn't help but laugh.

Everything in 1957 seemed to suggest that Shaw's balancing act of art and money had somehow gone awry, that it wasn't possible after all to keep both balls in the air indefinitely, and that now the wrong ball had fallen.

In early July another Shaw short story collection appeared. Shaw had thought to call it *Americans in Europe,* making the framework of his new stories unmistakable, but then Cerf and Klopfer realized that the movie version of "Tip on a Dead Jockey" would open at about the same time. Since the story was to be included in the collection anyway, the promotional value of putting its title on the cover was irresistible.

Perhaps the movie tie-in cheapened the collection in critics' eyes; perhaps the stories did lack a bit of the punch of earlier ones. At any rate the reception, only five years after the much-acclaimed *Mixed Company* collection, was notably chillier. William Peden, writing in *The New York Times,* observed that Shaw's latest characters shared a postwar melancholy, a sense of "having had it," and that the stories too seemed tired. "They don't . . . re-read as well as they read; and they suffer somewhat when read collectively," Peden wrote. "Perhaps Mr. Shaw is no slicker than he used to be, but certainly he is less concerned with ideas than he was some years ago. His frequent superficiality, contrivance and glibness are more apparent than they were when Shaw was centering his stories around fascism, or communism, or war, or racial intolerance and similar 'big' subjects. . . . To this reader, he appears to have become increasingly the victim of his own facility; he seems to have decided to take the cash and let the credit go."

Shaw's movie efforts were hardly more consoling. *Fire Down Below* opened in July to reviews that showed a remarkable consensus. The Caribbean-based love-triangle adventure started white-hot, critics reported, then abruptly cooled when Jack Lemmon, jockeying with Robert Mitchum for Rita Hayworth's affections, got pushed aside by the moviemakers to spend the last half of the picture dealing with a ship collision. "The person who squirts this cold water," declared Bosley Crowther in *The New York Times,* "is scriptwriter Irwin Shaw, who does about as clean a job of dousing a smoldering drama as we have seen lately." Actually, Shaw wasn't to blame at all. In his original script, Lemmon remained on hand through most of the story. According to Parrish, it was producer Irving Allen who chose to alter the movie by drastically recutting it after it was shot.

Of more consequence to Shaw was the adaptation of *The Young Lions,* being filmed at last in Paris and other European locations. After the team of Braunstein and Lord had let the project run aground, producer Al Lichtman had bought the rights for 20th Century–Fox. Lichtman planned a quick, profitable production on a $2 million budget with a short shooting schedule and contract players. Tapped to direct was Edward Dmytryk, one of the original Hollywood Ten who had been sentenced to six months in jail, served a brief time, and then come running to HUAC to name all the names requested of him. To his credit, it was Dmytryk who pushed for a larger budget and top-rated actors, personally enlisting Montgomery Clift to play Noah Ackerman, the beleaguered Jewish soldier; Dean Martin to play Michael Whitacre, the disillusioned WASP; and Marlon Brando to play Nazi Christian Diestl. It was Dmytryk too who made the decision not to use Shaw's script.

Dmytryk found Shaw's script hopeless. It was talky and disorganized—the same problems, he felt, to be found in every Shaw script he'd seen filmed. Worse yet, Shaw had made Michael Whitacre the central character and focused much of the script on Whitacre's problems with his unfaithful wife. Working with scriptwriter Edward Anhalt, Dmytryk restored the narrative balance to all three characters and emphasized the broader issues of the war.

Most important, Dmytryk and Brando decided that the character of Christian Diestl should be made more sympathetic. He should be a decent young man who gradually grows disillusioned with Nazism, rather than the heartless fighting machine he becomes in the novel. Dmytryk and Brando felt that Shaw had written *The Young Lions* in the still heated afterglow of the war, and that as a Jew he had felt an irrational hatred of all Germans. With a decade's cooling perspective, that seemed an untenable view, Dmytryk and Brando agreed; by the same token, one could declare any other nation or people all bad. In fact there were good Germans and bad Germans, and the important point was that all *wars* were bad, that every war, as Dmytryk put it, was a civil strife in which men kill their brothers. That was what the movie version of *The Young Lions* would strive to make clear. It was a "better lesson," Dmytryk declared, than Shaw's point that men, particularly Germans, could be turned by war into animals.

It was a well-meant change, but also a stunning liberty, taken with the very marrow of Shaw's work. As filming began, Shaw made visits to the set and realized immediately what Brando was doing, but he was helpless to do anything about it. One hot summer day, while the film was still in production, David Schoenbrun arranged to interview Brando and Shaw together at Maxim's for CBS, and that was when the fireworks erupted.

Brando, fiercely confident of his own artistic choices, felt even less patient than he might have on another occasion. Some days before, he had gone out to dinner with Dean Martin, and a hot teapot had spilled onto his lap, scalding his genitals and forcing him briefly into a Paris hospital run by nuns (the nuns, Brando reported, were remarkably attentive, gathering in groups beside his bed whenever his dressing needed changing). Shaw, of course, was hardly a less proud or impatient man.

"The cameras were rolling, the sound was running, and I was just interviewing them about the film and the problems that arose," recalled Schoenbrun. "And I had some intuition, I addressed a question to both: Was there any problem in the interpretation of Brando's character?

" 'Yes!' Irwin said.

" 'No!' said Marlon.

"So I said, 'Just a minute now. Marlon, why do you say there's no problem?'

"He said, 'I just read the script and knew what the guy was like and played it straight. I had absolutely no problem. It was a great role.'

"And I turned to Irwin and said, 'Why did you say yes?'

" 'Brando's played him all wrong, that's why,' Irwin said. 'He played him in a sympathetic way because he wants to be sympathetic on screen.'

"Brando said to Irwin, 'What are you talking about, you don't know this character.'

"And Irwin said, 'It's my character, I gave birth to him. I created him!'

" 'Nobody creates a character but an actor,' Brando snapped back. 'I play the role, now he exists. He is my creation.'

"And Irwin said, 'You're a stupid actor, I'm the writer of this story, this is my character, you stupid goddamn—' And he raises his fists, they're big fists, you know. So I grabbed his arms, Irwin was choleric. And finally he calmed down enough to say, 'Well, it serves me right, sitting down and talking to an actor. An actor doesn't have any fucking brains; if he had any brains he couldn't be an actor. An actor is an empty fucking inkpot, you have to pour ink into the goddamn fool to get anything out of him.' "

Later that evening at the Ritz bar, Schoenbrun recounted the story to a mesmerized group that included Hemingway—and Shaw. Hemingway found it wonderfully funny, but Shaw was still too upset to be kidded.

"Now wait a minute," he said to Schoenbrun. "Never mind about your interview. This guy has totally distorted my novel."

"You're a goddamn fool, Shaw," Hemingway shot across at him.

"Why do say that, Ernest?"

"You're a goddamn fool not to know that what you do is sell your book to the movies, go to the bar, and take a drink. You don't think about the movie, you don't look at the movie, you know it's going to be a piece of shit. The idea of selling a book to the movies is to make money."

"Well, that's very much part of the idea. The other part is to make sure that your story is properly transferred to the screen. I'm a writer for movies as well as for books."

"You'd be a better writer if you never wrote scripts."

The two bristled at one another, and for the second time that day, Schoenbrun thought he was about to referee a slugfest.

While the film was being shot, Shaw thought to invite his parents to Paris to get a glimpse of the stars in action. It was an exciting prospect for William and Rose, and of course Irwin would pay for them to come; they could hardly remember a time when they hadn't been supported by their two sons. It was largesse that left them grateful and somewhat daunted, particularly by Irwin, whose fame and accumulating wealth were marvels of the highest magnitude. William Shaw especially felt humbled by it all. The itinerant real estate salesman and hatmaker hadn't worked for years, and yet he and Rose had not only lived in comfort but realized the Brooklyn dream of moving into Manhattan, with a handsome apartment at 760 West End Avenue.

On Thursday, August 22, after a wonderful visit, the Shaws boarded a TWA plane in Paris for a night flight home to New York. Shortly after takeoff, William Shaw suffered a massive heart attack. Within seconds he was dead. Rose Shaw was given the choice of having the plane return to Orly Airport or continue on to Idlewild. Not wanting to inconvenience the other passengers, and seeing no point in turning back, she chose to have the plane fly on. For the duration of the flight, throughout the night, she held her dead husband in her arms. In the morning, having been seen off by one son back in Paris, she was met at Idlewild, alone now, by her other son, David.

Irwin felt devastated by the loss of his father. Mixed in with the sorrow was pity for a man whose life had been so truncated by bad times, who had had to live out his dreams through his son's success rather than his own. Perhaps, too, Shaw felt a wave of pity for himself. A part of his past, the Depression era that had shaped him as a writer, had fallen away.

Like bread dipped in bitter red wine, the novel Shaw had started the year before grew darker through these different misfortunes. He worked on it daily in the fall of 1957 in Paris, driving early in the mornings from the Villa Madrid in his *War and Peace* Alfa Romeo to a new workplace at 18 quai d'Orléans, on the Île St.-Louis. Elizabeth Weicker, a wealthy young American widow the Shaws had met several summers before in St.-Jean-de-Luz, occupied an extraordinary penthouse, an apartment with a wrap-around terrace and 360-degree views of the city, and because she was traveling that fall, she gave Shaw the use of it. (In a true *affaire d'escalier*, Weicker would eventually marry a wealthy Greek businessman, Anastassios Fondaras, after he rented the duplex apartment below her.) Shaw would hammer away at his typewriter for a hard stretch, then stroll out around the balcony, the flying buttresses of Notre-Dame almost close enough to touch, and marshal the energy for another session inside. It was, he told Liz Fondaras years afterward, the most wonderful place he ever worked. As exhilarating as it was, though, it didn't seem to lighten the novel at hand.

By December Shaw was able to report to Bennett Cerf that he'd written 320 pages of *Two Weeks in Another Town*. But when Cerf inquired eagerly in reply if the novel might be finished in time for his next fall list, Shaw evinced a new wariness about setting any deadlines. This time he was going to take as long as needed to write the best book he could. There was, in fact, a huge paradox about *Two Weeks in Another Town*. As cynical as its voice and view were becoming, its author was writing with a growing excitement that this would be the novel that pushed him into the highest literary ranks. This would be the book that won prizes and critical acclaim even as it topped the bestseller lists. This would be the one that proved, once and for all, that Shaw could keep the bright balls of art and commerce up high in the air at the same time.

If one looks back more than a quarter-century later at that all-but-forgotten book, Shaw's excitement isn't hard to understand. *Two Weeks in Another Town* is the most underrated novel in his canon, a richly written, beautifully mature work, more ruminative and resonant than any of his earlier novels or any that would follow. Most impressive, it marked a breakthrough for the short story writer whose first novels had tended to read like short stories strung together. *Two Weeks in Another Town* is the work of a serious novelist, character-driven, smoothly paced, with its own inner world. What keeps it from greatness, finally, is only Shaw's choice of canvas.

Jack Andrus, the middle-aged protagonist of the novel, is a once well-known actor whose career was ruined by a war injury that disfigured his face. Stoically, he has taken up a new life as a State Department bureaucrat in Paris. All that changes with a call from Delaney, the demagogic director who gave Andrus his start. Ego-sodden, Delaney has grown sloppy in his recent films, and his career has dimmed, so much so that the low-budget film he's working on now in Rome may ruin him if it doesn't restore him. Unfortunately, the film's leading man, a has-been, is drinking on the set and slurring his words, and with half the film shot, the only solution Delaney sees is to bring Andrus in to dub the leading man's lines.

Shaw's preoccupation with accidents as the determinants of fate infuses the story that unfolds. As soon as he arrives in Rome, Andrus, whose career was thwarted by an accident, is punched in the nose by a drunken American tourist. No reason; the tourist never reappears; fate has simply asserted itself. One accident leads to another. When Andrus's still bruised nose starts bleeding again the next day, Veronica, the beautiful Italian girl he has just met over lunch at a sidewalk café, helps him up to his hotel room, and they promptly make love. That brings Veronica's madly jealous American boyfriend to Andrus's hotel room later the same day, waving a knife and threatening to kill him. Ironically, the meeting provides the big break for the boyfriend, an aspiring screenwriter and director named Bresach. Andrus sees in him the same passions he himself felt when young, and senses in him a surrogate son (his own first-born having just bitterly written his father off as a sellout). He also realizes, in reading the young man's script, that the passions are fused to talent. When Delaney suffers an accidental fall while horseback riding, Andrus is given control of the film and allows the young director a chance. Bresach galvanizes the set and gets the leading man to stop drinking, and the story seems destined for an into-the-sunset ending until fate intervenes a final time. Delaney, still hospitalized, is persuaded by his jealous wife that Andrus is icing him out from this production and the three-picture deal that bobs just beyond. With the wrath of an Old Testament God, Delaney and his wife banish Andrus, dash the young director's chances, and assure their own destruction. His darkest thoughts reconfirmed, Andrus heads home.

As always in a Shaw novel, characters seem tantalizingly close to figures in real life. Delaney is a composite of several autocratic directors Shaw had known, King Vidor and Anatole Litvak among them. The gaily cynical French journalist who introduces Andrus to Veronica over lunch and refers to himself as the "atrocity editor" because of his extensive wartime experience is reminiscent of Robert Capa; like Capa he goes off on sudden assignment to a war zone and is accidentally killed. As for Andrus's three wives, each seems based on Marian Shaw in a different, revealing way. The closest and most revealing parallel, however, is between Jack Andrus and Shaw himself.

Like most fiction writers, Shaw bristled when friends or critics suggested that his protagonists were modeled on himself. They were characters he had created, amalgams of several real-life people, perhaps, but molded into some new shape. In Shaw's case, that could be said with some justification of the later storybook novels like *Rich Man, Poor Man* or *Beggarman, Thief*. But not at this stage. There were simply too many similarities between Jack Andrus's life and Irwin Shaw's for anyone to read *Two Weeks in Another Town* without gaining the distinct impression that the novel was a portrait of the artist—an artist coming to terms with middle age. Not only were the facts closely parallel—Jack Andrus, for example, is mentioned as having served in the Signal Corps' camera unit in the war—but the bitter judgments, the grim regrets, the clinging sense of hope despite all odds were clearly the author's own sentiments.

Shaw had modeled characters on himself before, but never had he permeated a novel so completely. In that sense he was once again responding with an astounding aptness to the times in which he lived. Like other American writers of the mid–twentieth century—Norman Mailer and James Jones, to name two—Shaw had been lifted to dizzying new heights of fame. The coming of paperbacks and television had helped fuel that, as had the Hemingway-inspired cult of the writer as celebrity; but the new fame had brought with it a newly steep slide. Mailer's second novel, *Barbary Shore*, had been assailed by the critics; so had Jones's *Some Came Running*. Like boxers—Mailer, Jones and Shaw all referred to themselves as such— the American writers of the fifties had reeled from critical punches, even as their egos became inflated by the flattery of those around them. Buffered from the outside world, cut off from new formative experiences, they turned inevitably to writing of the subject they knew best—themselves. They trusted their own guts and ego to pull them through, and so their protagonists, far from being fictional creations, became outsized self-images.

Such a protagonist is Jack Andrus. He's the Irwin Shaw who lurks behind the laughing party man, the real Shaw that friends rarely saw. He's a pragmatist whose youthful passions and dreams have died, who knows accidents will happen and merely hopes to survive them. Experience has taught him to have no illusions about the film business, yet he still guards the wistful hope that good movies can be made and wonders secretly if the best art to come out of the twentieth century will have been created on the screen after all. At the least, he has a "bourgeois sense of commercial honesty" about movie assignments, working hard to earn the big money offered him, that echoes Shaw's own rationales about committing such time and energy to screenwriting.

Andrus's darkest thoughts are directed toward the women in his past. Indeed, as much as anything else, *Two Weeks in Another Town* is a book about women, or rather, the capacity of women to entrap and destroy men. Andrus's first wife, an "awful" actress whom he married when he was too young to know better, turned out shrewish and spiteful when Andrus returned all the way from California to New York to tell her, honorably in advance, that he was in love with his costar and wanted to start an affair. His subsequent marriage to the costar, Carlotta Lee, had its shining hours, but the war cut them short. Stationed in wartime London, Andrus listened to a soldier brag about the Hollywood actress who was sleeping with anyone who called on her, and realized with shock that the actress was Carlotta. (The episode suggests Peter and Jigee Viertel rather than the Shaws.) Recovering in a VA hospital after being wounded, Andrus did his noble best to ignore the stories when Carlotta came to visit, only to have her cringe at the sight of him. Yet when the lawyers took over, it was Carlotta who demanded and won the huge settlement. Andrus's third and current wife, the chic French Hélène, does little to restore his faith in the gender. With her pouting demands on his time, it's no wonder that this latest marriage has its "dead grey patches" and that Andrus hasn't felt the least desire to make love to her in weeks. Even more than the money, Andrus goes to Rome to be free of the "claims, ambushes, demands, entrapments of women."

Of course, he can't escape. Julia, Andrus's first wife, sends shrill letters. Carlotta shows up at his hotel when she learns Delaney has been critically hurt. Hélène makes long-distance checkup calls from Paris at three o'clock in the morning. Small wonder that Andrus regards even the most charming women with suspicion and disdain. Veronica, he decides when he meets her, is the sort of "glossy female brute" who doubtless enjoys breaking men's hearts. Not long after, at a cocktail party reminiscent of but far more nightmarish than the one in *The Young Lions*, Andrus regards the "hunters and huntresses" circling each other. Among them is the star of the film, an Italian woman of rough peasant beauty, cold and decadent, who humors Delaney in order to have her part made larger and who, upon hearing the director has been stricken later on, announces she doesn't like sick men. At the party too is Delaney's wife, Clara, a dried-up crone who snivels from the corner as her husband carries on with the Italian film star. Secretly, she yearns for him to fail, because only in failure and humiliation does he return to her.

All this is painted, against the backdrop of Rome's silent monuments, with the gaudy brilliance of the film it presaged, Fellini's *La Dolce Vita*. Gradually, however, Andrus loses the reader's sympathy. His grumblings about the claims of the women in his life come to seem self-pitying, especially in his chase, as a married man, after the supple Veronica, an affair even he knows is frivolous. His stoicism and detachment mask mere self-centeredness. Indeed, for all his world-weariness, Andrus is a remarkably arrogant fellow who sees himself, privately, as a sort of modern-day Roman hero, with one foot back in classical history. Bresach tells Andrus he has the head and neck of a Roman emperor—a remark often addressed to Shaw. To Andrus, who strolls past the Colosseum at midnight imagining ancient times, the comment makes perfect sense. By the end of the novel, Andrus compares himself to Odysseus, lashed to the mast of the ship, pushing on at last beyond the Sirens.

Worst of all, Andrus is weak. Confronted by the growing complications of the plot, he drinks scotch—lots of it—in solitary, and takes pills to get to sleep, yearning for oblivion. He doesn't deny the charges from his son, and from Bresach, that he's a sellout, but in fact he's not strong enough to accept any blame. Like Shaw, he's a believer in accidents, and his war wound provides the excuse for all that's followed. Andrus never stops to consider that his drinking and womanizing may have affected his marriages. His failures are accidents; those of his wives are betrayals.

At the end of the novel, Andrus goes to Carlotta's hotel room, thinking balefully that it's cheaper than visiting a whore. To his own surprise, the two make love tenderly, forgivingly, and Andrus is cleansed of his bitterness toward her. It is, finally, the only real resolution in the novel; it's the only answer to the accidents and tragedies of life. (Or, as Andrus muses in the plane headed home: "Be delighted!") The catharsis, fortunately, goes a long way toward pulling the novel from the depths of self-pity into which it has descended.

Like any good self-portrait, *Two Weeks in Another Town* is more fascinating for its unintended truths than for its intended ones. At forty-five, after the years of movie scripts and high life in Europe, Shaw knew well that he was deemed a sellout by some, that his status as an artist was declining as his quality of life kept rising. Jack Andrus is a testament to that self-knowledge; and *Two Weeks in Another Town* is ultimately a rumination on the preciousness of youthful talent and passion, and the corrupting power of success on them. Like Andrus, though, Shaw took no blame. Not for the career decisions. Not for the drinking that was tending to blot out the end of every day. And certainly not for the cavalcade of lovers who continued to rock his marriage.

For all the stoic determination Shaw brought to *Two Weeks* in Paris in the fall of 1957, evenings were always taken up with the friends and admirers who bathed in the glow of his gregarious charm. Most of the tall young men had returned to the States, but the American expatriate community had only swelled through the fifties. There were the Hollywood figures playing out their months abroad for the tax break, the journalists and writers, and now too a number of wealthy, social Americans who began to dominate Shaw's circle.

In addition to Liz Weicker, who nursed a keen interest in American writers, there was Clement Biddle Wood, a courtly writer who would become one of Shaw's closest friends and who, after Shaw's death, would be asked by Marian to write an official biography. Wood felt a generation younger than Shaw—a veteran of the Korean War rather than World War II—and when Liz Weicker invited him and his wife to meet the Shaws over a dinner at Maxim's, he felt a certain ambivalence about accepting. "Irwin, you see, had always been a literary hero of mine," Wood recalls. "When I was a teenager I read the stories in The New Yorker; when I was in the Army I read his stuff in Yank; and when I was in college after the war I read The Young Lions. I was dying to meet him. At the same time, I had that feeling you always have about someone you admire, that when you get close you'll find he has feet of clay." To his relief, Wood liked Shaw immediately. "He was very jolly, in his usual uniform by then of sloppy blazer, rumpled flannels, loosely knotted black knit tie. Yet he looked more at home in Maxim's than people far more elegantly dressed."

Wood, like most of the other social Americans, was living in Europe "for the hell of it," ensconced in a large house on the place des Vosges. For some time he'd been holed up at his family's Pennsylvania estate trying to write a novel, and at the age of thirty-two he felt the need to get away. "So I went over to Paris for a year," he says, "and ended up staying there twenty years." That first night, as he did with so many younger writers, Shaw took a genuine interest in Wood's work. "He asked a lot of questions—'What are you working on,' that sort of thing. I was the perfect picture of a blocked writer at the time, and he couldn't understand being blocked at all. Finally he said, 'When you get it into some sort of shape, I'll give it a read if you like.' I was terribly flattered by that. But it was years before I showed him something."

It was Wood, in turn, who introduced Teddy and Gabby Van Zuylen to the Shaws. "We were this young, aristocratic Harvard/Radcliffe couple with money who'd come over to Paris as an experiment and taken a house on the avenue Foch," recalls Gabby Van Zuylen. "But we'd found ourselves locked in with a lot of Rothschilds—Teddy's relatives. Meeting Irwin and Marian opened up a whole new world."

The social Americans felt strongly that Shaw's friendship was a gift, and they were grateful for it—but Shaw was pleased too. Not only were the new friends charming in their own right; they also represented an old-moneyed WASP elite that was as far from Sheepshead Bay as a poor

Jewish boy could get. Shaw was fascinated by their air of privilege, by the talk of schools and summer places and old family names that until recently had seemed the signposts of some distant, unreachable land. He wasn't a social climber; he didn't need to be. Still, he took an almost ingenuous delight in these new friendships as gauges of his own success. Joe Kaufman remembers being driven by the Shaws to a party in Biarritz. "As we approached, Irwin looked at the cars lined up in the driveway and said, 'You know, I never get over going to a party at which there are five Rolls-Royces parked outside.' "

Before heading down for the now established ritual of Christmas in Klosters, Shaw reported to Cerf that he had given in once again to Hollywood's lure and would be doing a screenplay for Darryl Zanuck. (It was a drama, never produced, that took place in various grand hotels in Europe and enabled him, together with Mary Jane Bacon, to do a lot of sybaritic gadding about.) There was a coyness in those words that perfectly captured Shaw's ambivalence about taking on scripts. Outwardly rueful, he harbored pride in being recruited by Zanuck, in knocking off the script as a real professional in the film business, in making the big money. Also, as he confessed to Art Buchwald, there was something to be said for the pleasure of working with others once in a while. "When you write novels you sit alone at your desk for long, long periods of time, and you begin to yearn for the sound of the human voice. And you certainly hear the sound of the human voice around a movie studio.

"In addition to all that," Shaw said, "there is always the hope that you're finally going to come up with a wonderful picture, and you've got to keep your hand in so that you'll be ready when the lucky moment arrives."

In the same spirit, Shaw decided to make a tentative return to the stage, exactly a decade after the failure of *The Survivors.* Rather than write a play, he would translate a French comedy, *Patate,* written by his longtime friend Marcel Achard, and adapt it to the stage in New York. For more than two years, *Patate* had played to full houses in Paris. The title was the nickname of its hapless lead character (the literal translation was "potato"; the connotation was more that of "patsy"), an inventor who discovers that the detestable man from whom he's borrowed money is now sleeping with his daughter. With Irving Lazar handling the negotiations, Shaw and Achard hooked up with producer Gilbert Miller, and an October 1958 date was set.

In March 1958, with Shaw still in Klosters, *Desire Under the Elms* opened in New York to tepid reviews. "Something is curiously missing," wrote Bosley Crowther in *The New York Times,* "something that, by its absence, causes the whole ambitious project to fall flat." This time, at least, Crowther excused Shaw from blame. Somehow the play's translation to the screen had dissipated its sense of brooding menace.

Crowther, and others, thought little better of *The Young Lions* when it opened in early April. Taking skeptical note of Brando's reinterpretation of the novel's Christian Diestl, Crowther wrote of the film: "It is not so much anti-Nazi as it is vaguely and loosely anti-war." Yet Brando, at least, was more interesting than his American counterpart. "[Montgomery] Clift is strangely hollow and lackluster as the sensitive Jew," Crowther wrote. "And [Dean] Martin plays a Broadway showman pulled into the army against his will as if he was lonesome for Jerry Lewis and didn't know exactly what to do."

Shaw himself had mixed feelings as he watched his big first novel on the screen at a preview in Paris. It had much to commend it, he wrote to Cerf, and would probably be a great success, but he felt nearly every idea woven into the story had been neatly cut out by director Dmytryk and screenwriter Anhalt; while he found Clift's performance wonderfully compelling, he couldn't even judge Brando's because it made him so angry. As April unfolded, Shaw's prediction of commercial success for the movie was borne out: the combination of the big popular novel and the three handsome stars in the leading roles brought audiences streaming in. On April 11, Cerf reported to Shaw that the movie had had a marvelous effect on the just published tie-in paperback edition of *The Young Lions*.

A relatively peaceful spring was shattered by the news that Peter Viertel had taken up with actress Deborah Kerr. Kerr's husband and manager, Anthony Bartley, publicly accused Viertel of having begun an affair with Kerr while the two were working together on a film in Vienna. A furious Bartley issued a legal writ against Viertel, demanding custody of the two daughters produced in the course of his twelve-year marriage to Kerr, and the flap became an international incident, marveled over at dinner parties from New York to London to Rome. Viertel, for his part, airily denied the affair as "nonsense and pure malarkey."

If the Viertel-Kerr scandal was cause for gossip in Klosters that summer, another bulletin of personal news brought genuine sorrow. In mid-July Shaw opened a newspaper to read that Saxe Commins had died of a heart attack. More even than Bennett Cerf and Donald Klopfer, Commins had been Shaw's great supporter at Random House, urging his editors in chief to publish *Bury the Dead*, shepherding the short story collections into print, and persuading Shaw to make major cuts and changes in his first three novels. Shaw knew that Commins hadn't been excited by *Lucy Crown* even after its revisions. In his mind's eye, as Shaw worked on the lengthening manuscript of *Two Weeks in Another Town*, Commins was the judge he hoped especially to impress. In a letter to Cerf, Shaw expressed heartfelt grief at Commins's death, and voiced the regret that he hadn't showed Commins the 140,000 words he had so far, to prove that the writer he'd nurtured for more than two decades could still live up to his original promise. Now it was too late.

That fall, Shaw put the novel aside again to make a trip he hoped might redeem the somber year. In Paris producer Jean-Pierre Aumont had decided to adapt *Lucy Crown* for the stage, and on September 22, Shaw flew up for the premiere at the Théâtre de Paris. The next day, he flew directly to New York to catch another premiere: *Patate,* at the Shubert Theatre in New Haven. His arrival, unfortunately, did nothing for his spirits.

Shaw found the New Haven production shrouded in dread. The problem wasn't producer Gilbert Miller, lead actor Tom Ewell, the others in the cast or the staging by Jed Horner. The problem was Shaw's adaptation. Somehow, in his dogged translation, Achard's light farce had grown heavy flat feet. Achard knew enough English to sense the change, as did his wife, Juliette, who began shrilly rebuking Shaw for dragging them into certain calamity. Sensitive about his talents as a playwright, Shaw was quick to argue back. When the local reviews came in sour the next day, the production fell into pitched camps. A Boston tryout the next week brought no better luck, and by the time time *Patate* opened at the Henry Miller Theater in New York on October 28, nearly two frantic weeks of play-doctoring after its scheduled premiere, the only question was not whether it would be savaged but how badly.

The answer was: badly. "In Paris," Brooks Atkinson wrote in *The New York Times,* "Marcel Achard's *Patate* soothes the citizenry. . . . [In New York] it comes closer to drugging the citizenry."

Patate closed quietly after seven performances. As he had a decade before, Shaw flew back to Europe a sadder man, perplexed and defeated once again by the theater that had given him his first success.

CHAPTER SIXTEEN

"What they had," declares Gloria Jones of the extraordinary affection and respect between Shaw and her late husband, "first and foremost, was the war."

Shaw always had had close male friends. It was one of his most admirable traits, revealing a strong generosity of spirit, a willingness to show his emotions that bordered on the sentimental—a wonderful ability, despite the competitiveness that lurked beneath the surface, to forge a real bond of loyalty and love. In this sense, as in so many others, Shaw was a touchstone of his generation: the war had stirred deep and enduring camaraderie among men who might otherwise have been kept apart by their respective families and careers. Among the several significant male kinships of his adult life, however, the one with James Jones stood out.

It was in the early fall of 1958 that James and Gloria Jones found their way to Paris and, despite their inability to speak the language, happily settled in for an open-ended stay. Jones was the writer whose emergence Shaw had predicted with canny accuracy, the young all-American soldier whose raw emotions, fused with natural talent, would produce the definitive big novel of World War II. Illinois-born—he was nine years younger than Shaw—Jones had enlisted in the Army in late 1939 and endured the brutal training and dreary routine of a stateside private in Oahu, Hawaii. He had witnessed the Japanese bombers on Pearl Harbor day, and subsequently seen fierce fighting in Guadalcanal, where he received a head wound from shrapnel and eventually suffered an emotional breakdown. Sent back to the U.S. to recover, Jones met an older woman named Lowney Handy in his hometown of Robinson, and the meeting changed his life. Despite a relative lack of education, Jones felt his first stirrings of interest in literature while in the Army; he now nursed a fierce ambition to be a writer, and it was Handy who provided the essential support and encouragement. So freethinking were Handy and her husband in that provincial midwestern town that Jones was taken in both as a boarder and as Lowney Handy's lover. However, Handy also took a serious interest in cultivating literary talent, and she saw in Jones's rough efforts a natural storyteller's genius. Out of those postwar years under Handy's stern direction came the big novel that made Jones famous in 1951, *From Here to Eternity*.

Like so many of his contemporaries, Jones had had his ups and downs through the fifties. His happiest moments had come with his intense work over the next several years on his second novel, *Some Came Running,* and his arrival in New York, manuscript in hand, in late 1956. There, Budd Schulberg—the omnipresent maker of marriages—had introduced Jones to Gloria Mosolino, a beautiful, curvaceous blonde from John O'Hara's hometown of Pottsville, Pennsylvania. Mosolino had a colorful past—her uncle had been a bootlegger. She had a promising career as an actress, having just finished serving as a stand-in for Marilyn Monroe in *The Seven Year Itch.* Most important, she had a reckless, often bawdy sense of humor and a passionate sexuality that Jones found mesmerizing. Within three months, the two were married in Haiti. Soon after, *Some Came Running* appeared to scornfully negative reviews. In part because of that, in part because Jones had never seen Europe, the newlyweds, with Gloria pregnant, made the decision to have their first child abroad.

This first pregnancy ended in miscarriage before the Joneses arrived in Paris. Still, the adventure of living in Europe swept them up, and Jones's considerable reputation soon resulted in dinner invitations from the tight-knit circle of Paris's literary expatriates. One of these was from Shaw, whom the Joneses met at Alexandre's. Jones had been introduced to Shaw back in the States, but the two men were relative strangers, and Shaw's more elegant lifestyle, plus the fact that he was almost half a generation older than Jones, might have kept the characteristically shy Jones at arm's length if Shaw hadn't made the first move. "The Shaws were much more Right Bank," says Gloria Jones. "And we were much more Left Bank." Settled in a sublet on the Île de la Cité, the Joneses would hang out at Deux Magots and Flore. Only at the invitation of editor Herman Gollob, then a William Morris agent, had they come on this late-summer day to Alexandre's. "But Irwin, who was sitting with Herman, told us to come along to a party he was giving that Saturday night," Gloria recalls. "And it was wonderful—all the movie people in Paris were there."

Soon the Joneses and Shaws were meeting regularly for dinner, usually at expensive restaurants of Shaw's choice, with the older writer picking up the tab, and sharing rich talk of the war, of mutual friends, of the daily struggle to keep turning out pages. One fellow expatriate who often showed up was James Baldwin, who made notable exceptions of Shaw and Jones in his bitter denunciations of what he felt was a deeply racist America. Over the winter that followed, the Joneses met many of Shaw's good friends in Paris. Shaw, in turn, met a more artistic crowd through Jones: abstract painters Paul Jenkins and Alice Baber, and Addie Herder, who made constructions not unlike those of Joseph Cornell; and Cecile Gray, an early New York roommate of Gloria's whose own realistic paintings would come to hang in both Jones's and Shaw's homes.

Shaw's generosity never ceased to amaze these friends, and his willingness to serve as a guide and paterfamilias to newly arrived American expatriates was becoming legendary. In the spring of 1959, in Rome for a quick stint of movie work, Shaw wandered one night into the Hosteria dell'Orso. Upstairs, in the restaurant's nightclub, Cabala, he ran into a young American couple in love in the papal city. The woman's name was Nan Ahearn; the man was writer Gay Talese.

In fact, Talese had briefly met Shaw in Paris in the early fifties. As an Army lieutenant in Frankfurt, he had had the freedom to go where he pleased, and found himself at the famous Hôtel Scribe one night, introduced to Shaw by correspondent Bernard Kalb. Shaw had bought Talese a drink, chatted with him amiably, and the connection had been enough for Talese, who was now working as a reporter in Rome for *The New York Times,* to approach Shaw in the crowded club. When he heard that Ahearn had just started working at Random House, Shaw's face lit up. When he learned that Ahearn had seen and admired the book jacket for the soon-to-be-published *Two Weeks in Another Town,* he was an effusively happy man.

Talese had always been in awe of the older writer. Growing up, he had read the stories, the early novels, and reveled in Shaw's gossamer prose. When he left the *Times* to write the brash *Esquire* profiles that would establish him, along with Tom Wolfe, as one of the top New Journalists, he would struggle to make his dialogue sparkle in the way Shaw's did, and acknowledge that debt in the prefatory notes to his collection *Fame and Obscurity.*

Talese and Ahearn had decided to get married secretly in Rome, while Talese was reporting a story about the via Veneto. Now, to their chagrin, they had discovered how much red tape was involved in the prospect. They shared their feelings with Shaw, and the reaction was immediate. "Don't wait! I'll arrange it! I know someone here!" Shaw declared.

It was no small claim, but Shaw delivered. "It was typical of Irwin," recalls Nan Talese fondly. "He just breathed life into every situation." After staying out too late and drinking too much, the unlikely trio made its way the next day to the Campidoglio, escorted in a fancy car that came courtesy of Shaw. At the simple ceremony Shaw served as Talese's best man and as witness. Afterward, he led the dazed newlyweds to their own surprise celebrity reception, complete with Billy Wilder and Merle Oberon, at a café across the street from the Hotel Excelsior. "For two or three days," recalls Talese, "Irwin made our lives glamorous. And from then on, we were devoted to him."

Having met Shaw at last, Nan Talese returned to New York wondering at Bennett Cerf's wisdom, after Saxe Commins's death, in matching him up with editor Albert Erskine for *Two Weeks in Another Town.* "Albert was much too reserved for Irwin, was sort of intimidated by him," Talese recalls. "They didn't get along." Craggily handsome, a southerner with strict literary tastes and a wintry sense of humor, Erskine in his late twenties had been married to Katherine Anne Porter (she was in her late forties at the time). Robert Penn Warren was his oldest friend, and one of his writers. Faulkner was another; Erskine was considered a Faulkner scholar. "Albert is an absolutely brilliant editor, but very restrained and meticulous, and perhaps a little too cool for Irwin," says fellow Random House editor Joe Fox. "I think Irwin wanted someone who was a little younger in spirit than Albert."

At any rate, there was a notable lack of rapport when Shaw returned to New York in the early fall to go over the galleys of *Two Weeks* with Erskine. Substantial cuts were suggested and made, and Shaw wrote Erskine upon his return to Europe to thank him for his help, but a careful cordiality marked the letters of both men.

It was in Paris that fall that the Shaws were involved in a terrible car accident that almost killed Marian. Driving home late one night from a party, with Shaw at the wheel, the Shaws were blindsided by a taxi. Shaw was basically unhurt, but Marian suffered serious head injuries: a fractured jaw, many teeth knocked out and bad facial cuts that left scars despite plastic surgery. She lay bleeding on the street until a police van arrived to rush her to a hospital for emergency surgery. In *Voices of a Summer Day*, Shaw would recount the incident with sharp vividness and have his Shaw-like protagonist vow that if his wife survived the accident, he would never do anything to hurt her again. By such disasters, in these years, was the Shaws' marriage often jump-started back to life.

When he came to New York now on quick trips, Shaw almost always came alone. He stayed in the Ritz Tower, the well-known residential hotel on Park Avenue. It made everything easier. The Gabels had an apartment at the Ritz, as did Irving Lazar.

By now Lazar was handling not just Shaw's film deals but all his publishing negotiations, and investing Shaw's money for him too. "The investing was very much against my advice," recalls Peter Viertel. "I always said to Irwin that Swifty was not a business manager: 'I don't think he's going to steal from you, but he's working nineteen hours a day on his other business.' But Irwin had a funny thing about money. He didn't want to discuss it. He needed it. He liked making it and he made a lot. But somehow he had kind of a self-destructive air about it. Actually, Lazar did pretty well at the time for him."

The two men, so comically different in physique and character, had established a bantering, love-hate relationship that was in its own way deeply genuine. Elinor Marcus, younger sister of Carol Marcus Saroyan, saw the two a lot that year and the next. Having been married briefly to a French baron and now divorced, she found herself going out with Lazar in a fairly serious way.

"We were a group then: Adolph Green and Betty Comden, Moss and Kitty Hart, George Axelrod, Rex Harrison and his wife, Kay Kendall. And then Julie Andrews and her honey, Tony Walton—Julie had just come over to do *My Fair Lady*. And of course, Irving and Irwin.

"Irwin and Swifty were like the ugly couple, they were always fighting and making up. Irwin was always saying, 'That goddamn Lazar!' Or else, of course, he was saying, 'That goddamn Marian!' I think Irwin really loved Lazar. But what would irritate Irwin so much was that Lazar would tell him what to do, like a mama. And then Irwin would accuse him of not making a good enough deal. We'd all go off to dinner at the Pavillon or to '21' or the Colony." It was a chapter that ended the day Marcus came to the Ritz Tower to announce to Lazar and Shaw that she was marrying a *Newsweek* correspondent named Walter Gruber.

"Irving went white and shouted, '*Who are you marrying?*' Then Irwin got angry at Irving for the way he was reacting. Irving shouted, '*You're messing up your life, you could have anything and you're marrying this jerk.*' And Irwin shouted back at him, '*Well, better than marrying you!*' I left there totally destroyed."

There were others who were less amused by the antic relationship between Lazar and Shaw. Lazar, many of Shaw's friends felt, exerted a corrupting influence, always dangling the next lucrative movie offer, and too often diverting Shaw from the serious if less profitable fiction that his talent obligated him to pursue. In truth, the charge was unfair. Implicit in it was the assumption that Shaw was some helpless child given too many sweets, unable to stop eating them even as they made him sick. It was Shaw, of course, who made the measured decisions to take on one screenplay after another; it was Shaw who, for all his griping, kept Lazar looking for more opportunities.

In December, when Lazar came to Klosters for his now established holiday with Shaw, Viertel and the gang, the usual hysteria surrounded him. Harry Kurnitz, in Klosters to write *A Shot in the Dark*, reported to columnist Leonard Lyons that he had come "to investigate a scandal: the hotel where Lazar . . . stays every year has turned him down because they can't handle his telephone calls. Swifty offered to bring his own switch-board, but they refused. Their best offer was two long-distance phone calls per day, three telegrams and any number of carrier pigeons. To Swifty, of course, that's incommunicado, and so he threatened to pull all his writer clients out of Klosters, which would ruin the town. He says he has an offer from St. Moritz. Klosters retaliated by offering five typewriter ribbons.

"Flash! Swifty just offered Klosters a negotiated peace: Five long-distance phone calls and eight telegrams daily. But they'll have to take down all their pictures of William Tell and put up Irwin Shaw's."

In Paris earlier that month, Gabby Van Zuylen got a call one night from Shaw demanding she be his date. He took her to a restaurant called the Bourgogne, and there were Sam Spiegel and Harry Kurnitz, both with call girls from a well-known brothel. Neither girl spoke throughout the dinner—they just ate—and to Van Zuylen, the sight of them flanking those two such animated but unattractive men made for one of the most hilarious encounters of her life. But the evening had a surprisingly earnest end to it. After dinner Shaw took her for a nightcap at another bar, and what she remembers vividly is how he talked of his about-to-be-published next novel. "He was passionate about it; he talked on and on about it. He was convinced it was going to put him back on top."

Sadly, he was wrong.

The reception accorded *Two Weeks in Another Town* upon its publication in mid-January 1960 was for the most part dismissive. Critics seemed unable to distinguish between the novel in their hands and the reality of Irwin Shaw's life. As far as they were concerned, Shaw was pouring out the sodden woes of being an overpaid screenwriter in *dolce vita* Rome, and what an irksome, self-pitying diatribe was that. Hardly one mentioned the suppleness of the writing, the vividness of the scenes, the rich sweep of the tale that made it a fully conceived novel.

Most damning was Richard Gilman's scornful assessment in *Commonweal*: "We shed our sicknesses in our books, D. H. Lawrence wrote, but there are novelists like Irwin Shaw who seem able only to restate their maladies in each successive work. This sad, sterile, absolutely immobile talent has a medical dossier that reads like this: immaturity; false (or Hollywood-engendered) vitality; melancholia; concern with popularity; arrest at the second or possibly third most superficial level of the Zeitgeist; an ear for talk but not speech; a vision of love that delineates its ape. Nothing can be done for him; there is no cure for pseudo-creativeness."

There were some consolations. Among a smattering of more respectful reviews was that in the *New York Herald Tribune*, whose Herbert Kupferberg found *Two Weeks* "a penetrating story of modern life" that "illuminates brilliantly, almost garishly," its characters, is "swift moving yet with plenty of contemplative insight." London reviewers generally took well to it, and the novel shot faster and further up British bestseller lists than those in the U.S.—not the last time this would happen with a Shaw book. Then too, there was the movie sale. Weeks before publication date, Shaw received word from Lazar that Metro-Goldwyn-Mayer had bought the rights for $150,000 plus a share of the profits (news that Shaw, remembering *Time*'s snub of *Lucy Crown*, tried unsuccessfully to keep from the press; this time it was *Newsweek* that wove the fact into its tepid review).

Commercial success—and critical failure. It was a disparity, now established, that would attend most of the novels that followed. For Shaw, who had shaped *Two Weeks* with all the craft he knew, the reviews were particularly painful. If he had had any doubts of it before, those were swept away: the cabal of New York highbrow critics had their fix in on Shaw. They had him pigeonholed, as he'd grumbled to the interviewers of *The Paris Review*, pegged as the once important storyteller and playwright of the thirties and forties who now came out with "half-art." A middle-aged has-been, with nothing to impart but his own ennui. If they could shoot down *Two Weeks*, ignoring its artistry, its seriousness of intent, there was *nothing* he could write that would earn their endorsement. Not for the first time in American letters, a critically stung author would seem to lean more and more on his commercial success for his sense of self-worth. Readers liked the work; the numbers never lied. It was an understandable and perhaps inevitable defense, but it carried an inherent risk. The more a writer looked to sales for proof of his success, the more he might try to tailor what he wrote to readers' imagined tastes rather than his own.

For the moment, Shaw's strategy was to do nothing—except live well in Klosters that winter of 1959–1960, and in Paris that spring in a new, lovely apartment at 2 *bis* place Lamartine in Neuilly that belonged to Gertrude Vanderbilt Whitney. In Klosters, Darryl Zanuck persuaded him to write a screenplay for Juliette Greco, the starlet Zanuck was desperately in love with (and who was showing less and less interest in him as her career failed to climb under his tutelage). *The Big Gamble*, a dreary drama about an Irishman and his bride seeking their fortune in the Ivory Coast, was a critical and commercial failure the next year. Shaw's only attempt at shoring up his literary reputation was to accept Random House's offer to publish a Modern Library collection of his stories, an honor that also carried with it a depressing sense of finality about his career. Shaw took a quick trip to New York in June to confer with Erskine about which stories to include, and then followed up on a new interest—yachting. For ten days he and Marian bobbed about in the Mediterranean on a rented boat. Despite storms that kept them three days in Portofino, Shaw was enthused about the trip. Ever since his first summer in Antibes, he had vowed to have his own yacht. Soon enough now, he would. As for the rest of the summer, it dissolved into what Shaw acknowledged as the laziest time of his life, a Mediterranean idyll capped by a long, languid stay on a small Greek island owned by shipping magnate André Embiricos.

Back in Klosters, Shaw was happily distracted from his literary broodings by the long-anticipated wedding of Peter Viertel and Deborah Kerr. For all of Viertel's initial denials, the couple had soon become inseparable, and Kerr had gone on to procure a divorce from Anthony Bartley, a painful sacrifice that cost her the custody of her two daughters. Viertel too had had to seek a divorce; despite his open relationship with Bettina in the mid-fifties, he and Jigee had never officially ended their marriage. Kerr and Viertel arranged to be married at the Klosters town hall on July 23. At the last minute, Shaw's bourgeois sensibility kicked up. It wasn't proper for the two to leave together from their house for the ceremony, he declared, and so Kerr came down to Shaw's house to make a separate journey. Afterward, the newlyweds rode through the town in a horse-and-carriage to Chalet

Mia for their wedding reception, where the well-wishers included Yul Brynner and Mel Ferrer.

It was a reckless story with a happy ending, but it did have a tragic afterword. Jigee, the sparkling and flirtatious beauty who in an odd way had come to epitomize the Hollywood Communist movement of the 1930s, slid down the last stretch of a long and pitiful decline. In 1956 she had succumbed to the harsh pressures of HUAC and agreed to testify. Chain-smoking throughout, her spirit broken, she named names in an hour-long session and became, overnight, persona non grata among Hollywood's beleaguered leftists. Worn down, she and her daughter had gone to live with Salka Viertel in New York, where she had slipped further into alcoholism, coupled with heavy drug use. She had also had random, self-destructive affairs—among her later lovers, it was said, was Shaw. In mid-December 1960, in an apartment on Monte Grigo Drive in Pacific Palisades, she apparently went into her bathroom with a lighted cigarette. Whether she had a seizure or simply dropped her cigarette, she set fire to her nylon nightgown. Hospitalized with third-degree burns, she remained conscious for a week, then lapsed into a coma. At the end of January she died, without regaining consciousness, at Cedars of Lebanon Hospital in Los Angeles.

For Shaw, Viertel, and all the other hopeful young liberals of the 1930s in Hollywood, an era seemed to die with her.

Perhaps it was fitting that the year Shaw would come to refer to as his "dark year"—1961—would start with Jigee's immolation and death. Edging toward his fiftieth birthday, Shaw seemed not to know what to write next, and to believe his best years might lie behind him. The letters from Albert Erskine about the upcoming Modern Library collection seemed only to underscore that. Shaw wrote Erskine that he couldn't summon the energy to read the stories once again and make a final selection; Erskine could make the cut. Then came the flap copy with no mention of any of Shaw's four novels, as if they didn't exist. Furious, Shaw dashed off a note to Bennett Cerf to inquire if the omission had been intentional. Cerf's explanation, that he'd wanted the flap copy for a story collection to stress Shaw's credentials as a story writer, seemed ingenuous at best. It was the first of several slights, intended or not, that would bring Shaw's relations with Random House to a head, a process hardly helped by the collection's appearance that year to disappointing sales.

In part to stave off depression, Shaw plunged into a series of distractions. On the ski slopes one day in February with Bob Parrish, he outlined an idea for a movie about Americans in Paris that he hoped to make from his short story "Then We Were Three." This time, he said excitedly, he wanted to circumvent the whole Hollywood process of handing over a script, and all power, to a studio producer. Shaw would write *and* produce the film; Parrish could direct exactly as he wanted to and serve as a coproducer; and with negotiating help from Swifty Lazar, some major movie company might be persuaded to bankroll and distribute the film, surrendering control if Shaw and Parrish agreed to forgo any profits up-front. Parrish was enthusiastic, though not convinced that Shaw would be quite as hands-off about the directing as he vowed. "I knew if I made a picture with Irwin he'd have a lot to say about it," Parrish recalls with amusement. "He had a lot to say about what ski run you took or what you ordered for dinner." Indeed, it was Shaw who made the command decision, some months later, to drop "Then We Were Three" (later made into the full-length film *Three*, with a script by James Salter that Shaw detested) and title the film *In the French Style*, after one of the two stories he now intended to use instead. (That one, about the weary State Department hand who returns to Paris to find his mistress has gotten engaged to a homegrown American boy, had appeared in *The New Yorker* nearly a decade before. The other, "A Year to Learn the Language," about an American girl who ends up staying in Paris long after the end of her academic year abroad, would appear in *Redbook* in the fall. Similar in tone and style, it may well have signaled a final rejection from the editors of *The New Yorker*.) Parrish was delighted with the idea, and over a festive dinner with their wives that night at the Chesa Grischuna, he and Shaw drank to the start of Casanna Productions, named after the ski slope on which they'd agreed to become partners.

As always now in Klosters, there were new and admiring friends, many of them younger writers, to boost Shaw's spirits. One was Larry Collins, the *Newsweek* correspondent who would go on to write major nonfiction works with Dominique Lapierre (*Is Paris Burning?*) and novels (*The Fifth Horseman*). Collins passed through Klosters in the winter of 1961 en route from the Middle East to Paris, where he was to take over as bureau chief, and ran into Shaw at the Chesa. Collins found him "the most extraordinarily open and friendly man. He didn't have a mean, petty bone in his body." Shaw was eager to hear all the news of Beirut, and soon enough Collins found himself headed back to Chalet Mia for a typical Shaw round-table dinner of a dozen notables—Sam Spiegel, Swifty Lazar and the rest. "By the time I left Klosters that winter," Collins remembers, "I was thinking, If I ever write a goddamn book and make some money, I'm going to rent myself a chalet in the mountains just like this."

That year, two other younger writers came to feel the Shaw glow. James Salter, who would go on to write such beautiful novels as *A Sport and a Pastime*, met Shaw in Paris at the Ritz bar and was thrilled. Over the years, as Salter's literary star rose and Shaw's declined, the younger writer would still look up to Shaw with admiration, almost as more of a legendary figure than a flesh-and-blood person. Joseph Heller's first encounter with Shaw was indirect but no less memorable. Simon & Schuster was about to publish *Catch-22*, and Max Schuster's wife sent galleys over to Art Buchwald, an old friend, in Paris. Back came a telegram that astounded Heller—then a complete unknown. "Please convey our congratulations to Joseph Heller whose book *Catch-22* is a masterpiece." The telegram was signed by Buchwald, James Jones and Irwin Shaw, and helped draw critical attention after the novel was published.

In late March, Shaw took on another project that kept him from brooding about a next novel. The dramatic trial of Nazi Adolf Eichmann was about to begin in Jerusalem, and Shaw agreed to cover it for *Holiday* magazine as a handle for understanding how Israel had changed since his visits of a decade before. More immediately, he would file daily reports for Hearst's New York *Journal-American*, fulfilling a long-held, Mittyesque desire to serve a turn as a real news hound. By April 6, when the trial began, Shaw had checked into the King David Hotel with his new fellow journalists and gotten his press credentials. He was still no ordinary reporter, of course. Back in New York, the *Journal-American* devoted several columns to promoting its new star as the writer who in *The Young Lions* had "plumbed the labyrinthine thinking of Nazis like no other fiction writer" and would thus bring "unique insight" to his coverage. But then, this was no ordinary trial. World attention focused on it, with fierce, even hysterical emotions, and as a result, *Time* reported, the case had been "heralded, exploited, rehashed and explored with exhaustive thoroughness."

Shaw acquitted himself honorably, though not without committing the sort of cub reporter's gaffe that earns razzing from a seasoned press corps. Sitting in the courtroom on the trial's first morning, he searched for a metaphor to capture the mood. There was a sense that time had stopped, he felt, and seeing no clocks on the walls, he decided to lead off with an observation to that effect. When he showed his lead to *Newsweek* correspondent Bill Pepper at lunch, Pepper burst into laughter. "But Irwin," he said, "you should have turned around. There was a huge clock right behind you."

At the start of the trial Shaw declared Eichmann a kind of "Twentieth Century Angel of Death," and took a scornful view of the Nazi's defense of himself as a simple soldier obeying orders. By the trial's end, Shaw was taking a novelist's fascination in the complexity of Eichmann's character, marveling at the incongruity of his alleged crimes with his humble manner. Eichmann's voice, Shaw reported, was "gentlemanly, almost soft, with a pleasing timbre to it. . . . There is no distinctive accent, no bite or drive, no hint of the power the owner of the voice once wielded." The Nazi admitted some responsibility for his actions after all, but he went on with surprising believability to describe his horror at the atrocities committed. He was, finally, a "clerk in the grip of a perversion," Shaw declared, a timid "transmitter" of orders that just happened to call for the execution of millions of human beings. Heinous as Eichmann's role was, Shaw wrote somberly, "we were all in some degree transmitters. . . . We did not do enough and because we did not do enough Adolf Eichmann is on trial for his life today."

While Shaw was in Jerusalem, he met an extraordinary man who would become a close friend and appear, in passing, in *Voices of a Summer Day*. In fact, he first met the man's very attractive wife, engaging her in conversation on a coastal beach. When her husband discreetly ambled over to claim her, Shaw good-naturedly got to talking with both of them. Soon enough, he noticed the pale blue numbers on the man's lower arm. Jacques Graubart, a successful diamond merchant in Belgium, had lived through more than one Nazi concentration camp and knew all too well the atrocities being described years later in a Jerusalem courtroom.

The tale Graubart told at Shaw's urging, after a week of drinking and dinners and deepening friendship, was nothing if not Kafkaesque. Imprisoned in a camp near Auschwitz, Graubart had had a strong enough constitution to survive the grueling conditions and the relentless work of repairing railroad cars bombed by the Allies. On January 20, 1945, the camp was evacuated because the Russians were advancing. Prisoners too sick to march were shot; so were those who collapsed during the all-day retreat. A first night was spent at another camp, where the Germans counted the prisoners—1,400. After two weeks of marching in the snow from Poland to Germany—the trip took longer than it might have because the Germans kept to back roads to avoid detection by the Allies—sixty prisoners remained. "Why don't you just liquidate us all?" Graubart asked one of the guards. "So we don't get sent to the Russian front," came the reply.

The camp in which the survivors found themselves—Gross Rosen—made them wish they had died along the way. Everything was mud and corpses. Corpses floated in the mud; prisoners slowly died in the mud. The day after arriving, the survivors received half a loaf of black bread each, which of course they ate. Then they were herded onto train cars with the other prisoners of Gross Rosen—as many as a hundred, standing, in a single car—and told that the bread had been their ration for the seven-day train trip they were now to take. With no room to lie down, and no food, and no bathrooms, prisoners died on their feet. At one point the train stopped, and the survivors were ordered to throw out the corpses; they were sorry to do that, Graubart told Shaw, because the corpses had kept them warm.

The journey ended at Weimar, where in a fine piece of irony, many prisoners were killed by a strafing attack from Allied bombers, whose pilots assumed they were Germans. After more days of travel, the prisoners were marched into another camp, where in their condition they were ordered to work the heavy cables that supplied one of Germany's last remaining underground bomb factories. A work team of twenty went out each day;

only fourteen or fifteen returned. Many of these prisoners were not, in fact, Jewish, and when the Germans announced that non-Jewish prisoners could be shipped to the relatively more comfortable Buchenwald camp, Graubart borrowed a dead friend's jacket and disguised the numbers on his arm. The ruse worked, but when he reached Buchenwald he was ordered to join another long march. This time, Graubart knew he would die, so he sneaked onto a pile of corpses and played dead. Two Dutch workers wheeled him off with several other real corpses to the crematorium; as they were about to slide him in, Graubart jumped up and said, "I'm alive!" In the end, it was humor that saved him: the Dutch workers were so amused they smuggled him into another camp of survivors. As the Allies approached, the German camp commander was ordered by his superiors to liquidate all the prisoners. To save his own skin, he disobeyed the order; and thus was Graubart liberated, on April 11, 1945.

For all the firsthand accounts Shaw wove into his fiction, he never did use Graubart's tale. He did use a story of Nazi cruelty that Paris agent and friend Alain Bernheim told him, of how Bernheim, as a teenager before the war, had broken his leg while skiing and been betrayed by a German ski instructor. That account became "Inhabitants of Venus," one of Shaw's best later stories. It worked because the cruelty depicted was refined, almost abstract—a color Shaw could absorb on his short story palette of fundamentally gentle hues. Graubart's story, on the other hand, was too graphic, too horrifying.

Some stories were better left alone.

CHAPTER SEVENTEEN

Still restlessly filling his time, Shaw agreed to write another, more felicitous piece for *Holiday:* a firsthand account of a Mediterranean cruise. Ever since his childhood days in Sheepshead Bay, Shaw had dreamed of having his own yacht, and the short trip he'd taken the previous year with Marian had only reinforced that desire. Now, with *Holiday* picking up half the tab of an expensive charter, he, Marian and eleven-year-old Adam set off from St.-Raphaël, on the Riviera, on June 13, 1961, with no greater goal than that of having the most fun they could while chugging eastward to Italy, south around the boot, across the Adriatic Sea to Yugoslavia, up the Yugoslavian coast and around to Venice in some six weeks' time.

The trip proved more of a floating cocktail party than anything else. In St.-Tropez, Françoise Sagan paid a visit. In Port'Ercole, Alan Moorehead, Shaw's old friend from wartime London and the postwar summers in Antibes, served as genial dinner host. In Naples, the Shaws ate fried squid and grilled rouget with Romain Gary. In Dubrovnik, Jim and Gloria Jones arrived by steamer from Venice, and the two couples spent several days at the Argentine Hotel, taking day trips up the Dalmatian coast and one memorable evening attending a production of *Hamlet* in Serbo-Croatian. Arriving at last in Venice, the Shaws lunched with Nancy Mitford, then met up with Martin and Arlene Gabel, with whom they drove north to Klosters.

Shaw wrote up his travels in a lighthearted vein that made fine copy for *Holiday.* Unfortunately, he proved unwilling to let the account die in the magazine's pages. That fall he proposed to Bennett Cerf that Random House publish *In the Company of Dolphins,* as he now called his travelogue, in hardcover book form. Donald Klopfer responded on Cerf's behalf with cautious approval, but Cerf, in a letter soon after, was bluntly candid. While *Dolphins* would make a fine magazine feature, he counseled, as a book it would seem of interest only to readers who either had taken or were contemplating a similar trip—and even for them, there were guidebooks available that offered much more useful information than Shaw's breezy descriptions. If the travelogue were deeply personal, Cerf added, it might have interest for Shaw's loyal readership, but the personal references were few and unrevealing. Considering also the high cost of printing a travel book that would presumably carry pictures, and the reluctance of booksellers to stock a volume that had appeared unabridged in a magazine already, the market prospects for *Dolphins* as a book were virtually nil.

There was much between the lines of that exchange. For Shaw, the decision to push *Dolphins* as a book indicated a deterioration of critical self-judgment. Despite a cool professionalism in the writing, *Dolphins* was lightweight work. Cloistered on his yacht, alighting only for meals and the requisite glance at a church or town square, Shaw had learned little of the places and cultures he'd passed through. Instead, there was a presumption in his writing that he himself was the subject of his piece, and that readers would thus take an inherent interest in the details of his trip. All in all, the piece only emphasized Shaw's image as a frivolous high-roller, and suggested once again that living well had become his revenge on dyspeptic critics. Cerf's reaction, in turn, revealed a growing impatience with Shaw as a writer and a new boldness in voicing negative opinions about his work. With his letter, the twenty-five-year relationship between the two men took another turn for the worse.

There were other small slights in the months that followed. Shaw made an enthusiastic pitch to Cerf for Salka Viertel, who wanted to write her autobiography. Perhaps, Shaw wrote, Cerf might consider signing her up with newly acquired Knopf. Politely, Cerf demurred. (The book eventually did get published by another house.) Then, in January, Shaw sent off the final draft of a project close to his heart: his first play in well over a decade. And again, Cerf's reaction was cool.

The play was a black comedy entitled *Children from Their Games.* More than anything else Shaw wrote in this period, it reflected his mood in the "dark year" that had just passed. Melvin Peabody, the play's Shaw-like protagonist, hobbles around his cluttered New York brownstone apartment like a modern-day Scrooge, full of bile for the outside world. His pretty blonde daughter-in-law, Melissa, acts as a foil for his rantings and offers consoling words. Unappeased, Peabody declares his intention to die forthwith. He can't kill himself, he says, because for all his ungodly views he's a Catholic. In an odd twist of logic, he demands that an old friend shoot him—a man whose life he once saved, and who thus feels obliged to pay Peabody back any way he can. As the play's two acts unfold, comic characters parade through Peabody's brownstone: a doltish southern football player who wants to marry Melissa; a real estate man who wants to buy Peabody's brownstone for big money because it's the last parcel blocking a proposed shopping mall; a doctor who announces he mixed up Peabody's X rays with another patient's, so that Peabody doesn't have a bleeding ulcer after all; and a divorced heiress who desperately wants to take Peabody away to live with her in her lovely suburban home.

Collectively, these tidings seem to solve Peabody's problems in one fell swoop, but the old curmudgeon finds fault with all of them, and demands that his appointed assassin, gun in hand, proceed. As a last resort, Peabody's old friend hypnotizes him. Peabody succumbs, and in dreamlike stupor finds his salvation.

Both Cerf and Klopfer found positive things to say about the play but agreed the end was a letdown—"flabby," as Cerf put it. They didn't mention the larger problem, that a character as unremittingly cynical as Peabody might seem unappealing, even irksome, to an audience. Perhaps the several inspired stretches of fast banter might tip the play from pathos into farce, provided the right actor play Melvin Peabody.

Though finished with the play, Shaw dragged his dark year with him into 1962. If he needed more reasons, they could be found in his movie dealings. *The Big Gamble* had opened in fall 1961 to disastrous reviews— Bosley Crowther wrote that, after a brilliant beginning, the movie "ends in a state of sheer confusion." More important, at MGM, where the eminent John Houseman was producing *Two Weeks in Another Town*, the film had run into serious problems.

Houseman, legendary cofounder of the Mercury Theatre with Orson Welles, had had a number of Hollywood successes in the past. After a five-year hiatus, however, he was encountering a chillier reception from new studio heads who seemed more bureaucratic and narrow-minded than his old colleague Dore Schary. His first effort, *All Fall Down*, with Warren Beatty, was mishandled in distribution. Now, with *Two Weeks*, Houseman's problems were worsening.

From the first, Shaw had hoped to write the screenplay for *Two Weeks*, but Houseman had ignored his repeated requests and assigned Charles Schnee, with whom he had worked on the not dissimilar *The Bad and the Beautiful*. Houseman's aim, indeed, was to create a film that would refer directly to his successful 1952 drama about a movie director, writer and star betrayed by their producer; clips of *The Bad and the Beautiful* would be shown at one point as the earlier work of the director Delaney in *Two Weeks*. To that end, he also hired the director and leading man of *The Bad and the Beautiful*, Vincente Minnelli and Kirk Douglas. It was an interesting notion, and an interesting if offbeat cast. Along with Douglas, it included Edward G. Robinson as Delaney, Claire Trevor as Delaney's wife, George Hamilton as the fiery young screenwriter and, most strangely, Cyd Charisse as the predatory ex-wife of the Kirk Douglas hero—"gorgeous to look at," Houseman wrote dryly, "but never entirely convincing as the Queen of the Jet Set."

A problem, as Houseman later admitted, was that while he and Minnelli knew well the Hollywood of *The Bad and the Beautiful*, neither of them was as familiar with the Rome of *Two Weeks*. Despite the location shooting, something was lost. "Unconsciously," Houseman wrote, "we found ourselves drifting into a Hollywood version of *La Dolce Vita*—without the intimate observation, the social and human attitudes and brilliant imagination that had given Fellini's film such an irresistible quality."

Shaw spent part of the winter writing his screenplay for *In the French Style*, a more satisfying piece of work than *Two Weeks* would have been in any event, because this time no producer or director would tinker with it. In May another sort of consolation came to pass: invitation to the Kennedy White House for a state dinner honoring André Malraux, France's minister for cultural affairs. The Shaws flew over by way of Paris, so that Marian could select a new gown for the event. Her first choice brought a couturier's warning that Jackie Kennedy had the same dress and might wear it at the dinner. Marian quickly chose another. So anxious was Marian about her appearance the night of the dinner that the Shaws arrived notably late to the White House; Shaw would rail about the embarrassment for years. Still, the evening turned out well. President Kennedy professed to have read Shaw's work; the two men had mutual friends, among them Ben Bradlee and William Walton; and as different as their backgrounds were, they felt a genuine kinship of quick wit and masculine swagger.

While Shaw was on the East Coast, he and Bob Parrish took the opportunity to pitch *In the French Style* as an independent package to Columbia Pictures in New York. Shaw's first thought for the female lead had been Barbara Harris, until he learned she was unavailable. It was his brother, David, who began lobbying for Jean Seberg. When Shaw and Parrish made inquiries, they learned that Seberg was on contract to Columbia. Mike Frankovich, Columbia's European head of production, read the screenplay and gave his tentative approval for Seberg to appear in it, though she would have the right to veto the project, and on the appointed day Shaw and Parrish, abetted by Irving Lazar, met Frankovich and a phalanx of executives in Columbia's corporate offices on Fifth Avenue.

Much to Lazar's dismay, Shaw and Parrish insisted they receive no upfront money. Instead, they stuck to their original plan, deferring their salaries in return for complete control over production, and accepting a percentage of any film profits down the line. The two partners had worked out a careful budget of $557,000, so eccentrically modest that Lazar was too embarrassed to ask for it. After a few minutes of small talk around the conference table with the Columbia executives, Lazar made Shaw and Parrish leave the room, then demanded and received the more comfortably round figure of $750,000. When he emerged to give his friends the news, Parrish was perplexed. What, he asked, would they do with the leftover money? Lazar looked at him incredulously. "Don't worry about it," he said. "We'll find a use for it."

After a brief return to Paris, Shaw was back in New York by July to oversee casting for *In the French Style* and work with Columbia to meet a shooting schedule that would begin in August. He took his now customary suite at the Ritz Tower for this New York swing, and it was there that a *Time* reporter interviewed him for a proposed cover story about jet-set society. The subject may have accounted for Shaw's suspicious demeanor, and of course, there was Shaw's long history of annoyance with the magazine. Sipping some alcoholic drink from a water glass—it was early evening—and sitting at a table littered with scripts of *Children from Their Games* and *In the French Style,* Shaw eyed his female guest warily. "You're not leveling with me, my dear. Why would *Time* do this story unless they were going to be nasty? If it's going to be nasty, you can dig it up yourself."

Induced to keep talking, Shaw professed impatience with the very notion of society as *Time* would define it. "It's supremely unimportant," he said. "It initiates nothing, it creates nothing, and it's worth nothing." Was there, at least, an international set? "You're trying to describe something that isn't there. It's too loose to define. Everyone who buys an airplane ticket is in it." While the reporter was there, Art Buchwald stopped by and offered his analysis of society on the Riviera and Capri: twenty percent money, eighty percent homosexuals and hangers-on. "The thing about the international set," added Buchwald, "is that nobody thinks they belong. They always think the other person belongs." After years of hobnobbing in Europe with generally wealthy people, most of whom would have described each other, if not themselves, as social, both Buchwald and Shaw sounded a bit disingenuous. What mattered, though, was that now Shaw was being sought out as much for his lifestyle as his work.

On this trip Shaw had come alone, and like a mischievous lad escaped from his mother's watchful eye, he came in search of fun. For Shaw, that meant lots of friends, lots of drinking and a good-looking blonde. This time her name was Doris Lilly.

Lilly was a witty and sexy gossip columnist for the *New York Post* who had also written the saucy bestsellers *How to Marry a Millionaire* and *How to Make Love in Five Languages.* The way she'd met Shaw, the year before, was straight out of a thirties screwball comedy.

"It was a very hot night in New York," Lilly recalls, "and I was taking a cab to '21.' I had the cab stop at the corner of 52nd Street and Fifth. Suddenly, I realized that all the doors had jammed. So I decided to crawl out of the window. I saw this man coming by and I said, 'Will you please help me.' He said, 'All right.' I had to take off my shoes. I couldn't go out feet first, and I had my handbag and a beautiful dress on, so I handed him the bag and my shoes, and then he took my arms and pulled me out backward. By now, of course, a small crowd had gathered. When he got me out and handed me back my bag, I said, 'I know you.' And he said, 'Yes, and I know *you.*' And of course, that was Irwin Shaw."

It was an amusing beginning to a happy affair. And perhaps for the first time, Shaw undertook an extramarital relationship with the thought that he might actually leave Marian; since the dark year of 1961, the Shaws' marriage had begun a steeper, and perhaps irreversible, decline. He and Lilly soon grew close enough to profess they loved each other, and while their sexual connection tapered off after a few years of occasional rendezvous in New York, Paris and Rome, they remained friends until Shaw's death.

Despite her sex-symbol image, Lilly was a shrewd judge of character. Early on, she realized that Shaw had found the perfect way to rationalize his philandering. "Irwin was a rogue," says Lilly. "He lived a life of doing all the wrong things—to his wife, to his girlfriends. So he developed this marvelous way of fending everybody off by not taking anything seriously." Lilly soon learned the price of going out with a married man. "I was deprived of going to the places with him that I wanted to go. We'd go to '21,' and we went to dinner with Swifty Lazar a few times. But Marian was here with Irwin a lot of the time. We'd go separately to the same dinner parties, and then he'd meet me afterward."

One mutual acquaintance they shared was Hemingway, whom both detested. Another was Budd Schulberg, with whom Lilly had conducted an early romance. Her continuing friendship with Schulberg gave her an unusually close perspective on each man's divided feelings about the other. "Budd used to mock Irwin for keeping Marian in Klosters while he was always somewhere else with another woman," Lilly recalls. "Budd would say, 'Marian must be the best skier in the world by now.'" Shaw, in turn, would imitate Schulberg's famous stutter: "M-m-m-m-marian m-must b-b-be the b-b-best sk-kier in the w-world b-by now."

The Irwin Shaw whom Lilly came to know in the summer of 1962 was still a magnetically attractive figure. "He wasn't handsome in a conventional way. But he had the most beautiful head of hair I'd ever seen, curled just the right amount. And a good head, and a good face, ugly but a little heroic, like a Medici. His eyes were like dartboards, so many lines around them. And of course he had that hawk nose. And his teeth—they were always giving him trouble, he was always going to the dentist, but he never complained about it. He had those great shoulders, and very short arms and legs—almost like an orangutan—and that great barrel chest. Very short fingers. Narrow and short. Almost delicate." In New York, at least, Shaw was also still a very dapper dresser, though by the early 1970s that would change. "He had a tailor and a bootmaker in Paris, and he was very, very vain about his clothes. Always wore dark gray suits, with good-looking red- or blue-striped ties."

As with virtually every woman who had ever made his acquaintance, Lilly found Shaw's overt masculinity compelling, but she was surprised by the disparity between his appearance and his sexual performance. Even if one allows for the subjective nature of such judgments—and the difference between a heavy-drinking middle-aged man and a young athlete—her report remains disconcerting. "I try never to talk about sex," says Lilly, "but in this case I'll break a rule, because it's really so revealing of Irwin's character. The fact is that Irwin, at least by the time I met him, was not a good lover. On a scale of one to ten, Irwin was a one. He was very enthusiastic, and he did everything, he didn't leave anything undone. But he didn't do it well. And as far as his physical endowment went, well, there wasn't much there. And I think that's why he pursued women as much as he did—to keep trying to prove to himself that there *was* something there."

In late July, while Shaw was in New York, a particularly bruising critique appeared on the front page of *The New York Times Book Review*. John Aldridge, whose assessment of Shaw and other postwar writers in *After the Lost Generation* had proven such a watershed work in 1951, was asked for an update. Aldridge found that all the writers he'd knocked a decade before had slid further than even he might have predicted. "Today nearly all these writers give one the impression that their best work is behind them," Aldridge declared. Norman Mailer, Truman Capote, Calder Willingham, Gore Vidal, Paul Bowles, Vance Bourjaily and James Jones came in for critical strafing, but Aldridge's dismissal of Shaw was more all-encompassing than most. "Irwin Shaw seems to have lost touch in Europe with the way present-day Americans talk and act," Aldridge wrote, "and a large part of his recent fiction has been seriously flawed by his tendency to make them talk and act in patterns which have long been out of date. Yet in Shaw's case one feels that the stoppage of experience occurred even earlier than the war, that in fact he has not really been creatively engaged with American life since the thirties—and then less with its actualities than with the fashionable representations of it to be found in certain modern novels."

It seems likely that Shaw's confrontation with Random House in August had something to do with the Aldridge piece. At the least, the piece sharpened the debate. Shaw told Cerf and Klopfer that he was fed up with Random House's minuscule advances—still $15,000 per book. He felt he was no longer getting the respect he deserved. Other writers were almost certainly receiving higher advances and more attention, and Shaw stood ready to leave if the house's founders didn't act quickly. If Cerf and Klopfer thought of Shaw as some postwar washup, why, there were other publishers who felt otherwise.

Cerf and Klopfer conferred worriedly, then went to Lazar with a new and very different offer. They would pay Shaw $55,000 by the end of the calendar year as an advance against a full-length novel. The manuscript would be delivered September 1, 1963. Reprint money would be divided with sixty percent to Shaw, forty to Random House, and Shaw would be referred to in the contract as a Random House employee, thus allowing the house to pay him through foreign channels abroad and have him avoid

U.S. taxes. Shaw, back in Paris by late August to help oversee the filming of *In the French Style*, wrote Cerf to say he accepted the terms and would be staying with Random House after all. To which Cerf responded with a note of undisguised relief. "I hope," he wrote happily, "we will be your publisher for the rest of all of our natural lives!"

That was destined to be a short-lived sentiment.

Even as Shaw plunged into production for *In the French Style* in Paris, *Two Weeks in Another Town* opened to scornful reviews in New York. Wrote Bosley Crowther in *The New York Times*: "The whole thing is a lot of glib trade patter, ridiculous and unconvincing romantic snarls and a weird professional clash between the actor and the director that is like something out of a Hollywood cartoon." The problem, *Time* declared, was that Vincente Minnelli and Kirk Douglas had in a sense worked too hard. "They are dead serious—and therein lies their error: the subject is too trivial for serious treatment." The film did hardly better with the public and soon sank from view.

Shaw's personal film bore all the earmarks of a more successful venture.

For one thing, Seberg had agreed to take the starring role. Bob Parrish had made a personal visit to Spain to show her the screenplay and stir her enthusiasm. Seberg had greeted him from a chair, with a broken foot and a cast to prove it. As soon as she scanned the screenplay, she announced the cast was coming off the next week. Only later did Parrish learn that the cast had been a ruse worked up by Seberg and her husband, Romain Gary, in case Seberg didn't like the script. It also allowed her to disguise her quite genuine, advanced pregnancy. When the film was in the can, Seberg confessed she had given birth five days before arriving on the set.

The choice of a male lead was less easily resolved. Initially, an agent sent Shaw and Parrish a young, unknown actor named Robert Redford, but Columbia insisted they go with a "name." Then Shaw suggested an ABC correspondent he knew socially. "He's on the television screen every week," Shaw reasoned. "So I know he's a good actor." Gently, Parrish suggested they put the correspondent through a screen test with Seberg. The correspondent froze up completely, gripped the café table as he delivered his lines, and nearly broke Seberg's neck as he bestowed the Capa farewell pat on her head. In the midst of this, Shaw repaired to the bar that conveniently adjoined the Billancourt studios where the film was to be shot. "Well, he's not that bad," he told Parrish afterward. When Seberg refused to play against the correspondent, however, Shaw caved in. "Let me break it to him gently," he said when the correspondent called the next day to learn how he'd done. Then Shaw took the phone and blurted out, *"Okay, kid, listen, you just can't act."* Finally, the partners went with the little-known—but at least professional—Stanley Baker.

A rare spirit of happy optimism prevailed at sound stage A in the Studios Cinema in Billancourt when filming began on August 27. Instead of having some anxious Hollywood producer on the set meddling with the director and muttering about schedules, there was ever jovial Irwin Shaw, who not only insisted Parrish make all his own decisions but cheerfully made script revisions on a daily basis. The most worrisome moment came with a seaside scene filmed on location in Nice. The scene called for calm waters, but the weather seemed unlikely to cooperate. Gamely, Shaw joined the cast and crew on the pier at seven on the morning of shooting, ready to rewrite the scene according to the height of the waves. Fortunately, blue skies dawned over a glassy blue sea.

His dark mood dispelled, Shaw gave several confident interviews that fall. To his new friend Larry Collins of *Newsweek*, he declared: "In Hollywood you start out with an endless series of conferences. Conferences always mean compromise. Conferences lead you to banality. That's what's always happened to me before." This time, Shaw said happily, he'd end up with a movie that wasn't a patchwork quilt, but "all one piece." And if it failed? "At least," Shaw said, "I damn well will have the satisfaction of having tried." Cynthia Grenier of *The New York Times* found Shaw willing to talk about his recent depression. "This all came out of a dark, bitter, melancholy year," Shaw told her. "It's true. Last year at Klosters in Switzerland was a dark, dark, but highly productive year for me. I got a play out of it—which is pretty much in keeping with my black mood . . . and a scenario for this movie, which is a lot more optimistic." John Crosby of the *New York Herald Tribune* asked Shaw more broadly how he felt about Europe now, after more than ten years as an expatriate. "The worst thing," Shaw replied teasingly, "is that all the tennis players are going home. I had a lot of American tennis partners—George Plimpton, for example—they've all gone home." How long, then, would he stay? "If I ever go home, it's because I've run out of tennis players."

To the partners' delight, *In the French Style* came in on schedule and even under budget. Shaw returned to Klosters for an especially festive Christmas, made more so by Adam's return from his first semester away at Le Rosey, the Swiss boarding school generally regarded as the world's most exclusive, where sons of oil sheikhs teamed up on verdant playing fields with sons of American corporate chairmen. For all his obvious intelligence and athletic good looks, Adam, the son of a writer, did not immediately fit in at the school, and more than once he was subjected to nasty brushes with anti-Semitism that made his furious father consider transferring him to one of the traditional New England prep schools. Eventually, he would graduate from Choate.

As it happened, these were not Adam's only problems. By the time he was twelve, it was apparent to people who met him that he was as spoiled as he was charming. Both his parents looked on him as something of a miracle, the perfect son after Marian's several miscarriages. Shaw adored him and felt that Adam, so handsome and bright, so beautifully proportioned, could do no wrong. Not untypically for a father who lived through the Depression, Shaw prided himself on his ability to provide his son with anything he desired, and equated financial generosity with successful parenthood. Increasingly, as time eroded Shaw's marriage to Marian, the surest bulwark that remained was his gratitude to her for bearing Adam and his loyalty to her for being Adam's mother.

Adam, in turn, received mixed messages from his mother and father. The boundaries of proper behavior seemed fuzzily drawn, and he continued to be recruited with emotional or tangible bribes by either parent in arguments with the other. Nor did any real work ethic get passed down. It was a standing joke in the family that at eight years old, Adam was asked what he wanted to be when he grew up. "A writer, like my father," he replied. "Why?" asked his interlocutor. "I want to ski all winter," Adam said brightly, "and play tennis in the summer." At about the age of twelve, Adam won a leading role in a school play. His parents came to see him, brimming with pride, as if enacting a scene from *The Troubled Air*, but Adam hadn't memorized his lines. The evening was a fiasco, and it marked the end of Adam's theatrical career. The perfect child was proving imperfect after all, a deep frustration to all three Shaws.

With Adam back in school, Shaw flew to New York for the start of rehearsals of *Children from Their Games* in mid-February 1963. There had been talk of Orson Welles's directing it, but Welles was more and more unpredictable, and plans had fallen through. Martin Gabel had also volunteered to direct, but Shaw had steered the play to Sam Wanamaker, known mostly as an actor, to direct as well as produce. The $75,000 cost of the production was borne by a consortium of backers who were among Shaw's closest friends: Arlene Francis, Harry Kurnitz, Robert Parrish, Frank Stanton, Max Pincus and Roger L. Stevens, with Shaw himself contributing $13,500.

The big setback at this point was in the casting of the lead. Shaw had very much wanted Walter Matthau to play the dyspeptic Melvin Peabody. It was an inspired choice, and Matthau was now a friend, having married Carol Marcus Saroyan not long before. Matthau had read the play and had expressed interest in taking the role. Unexpectedly, he had then been offered the role of his life, to star in a new play called *The Odd Couple*. Matthau offered sincere apologies to Shaw and said he couldn't pass up the Neil Simon part. "Irwin was furious," remembers Carol Matthau. "He said, 'That's the kind of thing you do to a person once in a lifetime.' And he never forgot it." Instead, the part went to Martin Gabel, the close friend who had seemed to cast a hex over so many of Shaw's plays in the past. "By putting Marty in the lead you almost had to wonder," muses Peter Viertel, "if Irwin wanted the play to fail."

Matthau's departure cast a deep shadow over the production as it struggled through rehearsals for an early tryout in New Haven in April. "If Walter had played the role, the play likely would have been a success. Maybe not a hit, but a success," says Sam Wanamaker. "He had the acerbic humor needed to bring it to life. Martin Gabel, while a good actor in many respects, simply didn't have that humor, and the play suffered accordingly."

With his usual truculence about rewriting, Shaw hardly helped matters. "We'd talk about changes in rehearsal," recalls Wanamaker, "and Irwin would say, 'Oh yes, I'll do them,' but then he wouldn't produce anything of significance, just a changed word or two. And he was in such an alcoholic daze throughout that it was hard to get through to him. I mean, he was affable and we all liked him, and he'd come to rehearsals and certainly laugh a lot, but he was really very drunk most of the time." It could not have helped that Shaw, who seemed to find more and more omens in the events around him, had just turned fifty, on February 27: a man at the perceived peak of life, looking down the other side, a long way from home.

In his New Haven hotel room, Shaw was asked by an interviewer why he'd chosen to write *Children* as a play after a fifteen-year-absence from the form. Because, said Shaw, he wrote any damned way he pleased. He was a storyteller, and he told his stories in whatever medium seemed most appropriate. He had had the idea for *Children* in his notes for five years as a possible story, he admitted, but its dark comic humor had seemed finally given to drama, and so he'd made it a play. He still liked the play form, he declared, but not the strains of production. "I don't like the rehearsals, the nervousness, the neuroses; the gambling in success—if one actor happens to be down on opening night the critics might call it a flop—and I don't like the hysteria of rewriting at 4 A.M. in your hotel room while anxious people stand behind you." Already sensing that he might be in for a tough time with the critics, Shaw made a typical effort to explain his play, much as he had a quarter-century before with *The Gentle People.* "The style of this story is kind of crazy," he said. "It's sort of a grotesque farce and I'm surprised that people take it so realistically. It's a fantasy."

By the time *Children from Their Games* opened, on April 11 at New York's Morosco Theatre, Marian had flown over to join her husband. She was nursing a torn shoulder muscle from a skiing accident in Klosters, only one of several unfortunate accidents to befall her in this period. Like the playwright and his wife in the lovely 1936 story "Flash in the Pan," Shaw and Marian went to the opening with mixed emotions, Marian with determined optimism, Shaw with a gnawing sense of dread. Much of what he saw on the stage was heartening: a top-energy performance by Martin Gabel, who had managed to stay on the wagon from the first out-of-town rehearsal; a wonderful Broadway debut by Gene Hackman, who would win a Clarence Derwent Award for most promising new actor of the season, in the role of Charles Widgin Rochambeau, the lovestruck southern football player; and a compelling performance by Brenda Vaccaro as the old curmudgeon's daughter-in-law. But the play seemed stillborn, and its hypnosis-scene ending, which Shaw had retained over Cerf's and Klopfer's objections, was as unsatisfactory as they had feared it would be. Among the unimpressed critics was Howard Taubman, who found that for all its "scorching mockery," the play "lacks a dramatic core. . . . Peabody is all but uninflected, and there is hardly any light or shade or development in any character."

Shaw had not intended to stay long in New York after *Children*'s opening, but the poor reviews seemed to hasten his departure the next day back to Klosters. He left behind a play that closed after only four performances and, as so often seemed to happen with Shaw, a chorus of head-scratching critics ruing the failure they had helped bring about. Despite its fatal flaws, wrote Richard Watts, Jr., "*Children from Their Games* represented the finest writing for the theater the talented author has ever offered. . . . The New York reviewers, possibly self-conscious over their uncertainty in such a matter, rarely blame the director for a play's defects, and there could be significance in the way several of us agreed that Sam Wanamaker's heavy-handed and emphatic staging of *Children from Their Games* failed to bring out the best in it. . . . This cannot exonerate Mr. Shaw from responsibility. . . . Yet *Children from Their Games* was a play with so many notable qualities that its hasty demise . . . was a misfortune to the theater. It is a shame there is no longer an audience for a striking though seriously flawed work by a talented playwright."

There was a new contriteness in the letters Shaw sent to friends from Klosters that spring, soliciting opinions about why *Children from Their Games* had failed. Cerf replied with warm sympathy that that was the question provoking endless debates in New York drawing rooms. At Garson Kanin's house, Cerf noted, Lillian Hellman, Kitty Hart, Walter Wanger and the Goddard Liebersons had joined with the Cerfs in a full twenty-minute discussion of the play and its bewilderingly fast close. One conclusion was that the pace had gone awry when Gabel, after ranting through most of the first act, was reduced to a sideline observer as other characters appeared. Another was that the ending simply didn't work. However, added Cerf, all agreed that *Children* was a work of power and originality— *certainly* better than the recently opened and overpraised *Who's Afraid of Virginia Woolf?*

Such was the judgment of an unimpeachable arts circle in the spring of 1963.

More as a gesture of friendship than anything else, Cerf offered to publish *Children* at Random House. Shaw, reviewing the play in the quiet of Klosters, replied with some renewed excitement that he saw new ways of improving it and would put off publication until he'd had the opportunity to make his changes. The only version ever published, as it turned out, was a standard Samuel French edition of the production draft. In June, Shaw and Marian visited with Adam, becoming a family again for ten days, as Shaw put it wryly in a letter to Jim Jones, by staying in a hotel in Évian, across the lake from Le Rosey. By July 1, Shaw was in New York—the old fighter, back on his feet—to start promotion on the scheduled fall release of *In the French Style.* Soon *Children from Their Games* slipped into the past, and with it Shaw's last bid for Broadway success. "The theater has, frankly, defeated me," he told an interviewer some years later, "and there's a time when you have to put the white flag up and surrender."

August brought the sadder surrender of another American dramatist. Clifford Odets, whose short, brilliant career of social-protest plays in the thirties had inspired Shaw's own, succumbed to cancer in Los Angeles. The comparisons made in those fevered years between Odets and Shaw had proved premature. Odets's best works, though dated, had preserved for him a secure place in the pantheon of twentieth-century playwrights, while Shaw's had not. Odets's later years as a screenwriter had been darkly tragic, however, unredeemed by any real critical or commercial success. As a result, the international edition of *Time* consigned his obituary to its "Milestones" column, and let a nameless junior writer report that "the contrast between Odets' early proletarian dramas and his Hollywood work inspired the celebrated jab, 'Odets, where is thy sting?' "

Back in Klosters, Shaw was thrown into a black rage when he read the obituary. He felt furious at his old nemesis *Time,* furious at the cavalier treatment of his old friend and fellow playwright, and perhaps furious too to think that he might one day be accorded the same treatment. He dashed off a blistering letter to the magazine's editors in which he pointed out, first, that like so many glib statements in *Time,* this one was inaccurate: the jab had been made about one of Odets's plays, long before he went out to Hollywood. More important, the obit had doubtless been written by a *writer,* as Shaw dryly put it, and what writer did not start off with the usual dreams of righting wrongs and helping humanity? Who then had sold out more completely, the playwright who had struggled against an unfortunate flaw in his character and the vicissitudes of time, or a writer who had traded his dreams to write a few polished paragraphs for the blood money that Henry Luce paid?

Shaw's letter, though never published by the magazine, did have a resonant effect: in September, when *Time* panned *In the French Style,* Shaw would conclude bitterly that the review was revenge, and would be provoked to write the most splenetic broadside of his life, against *Time* and the Luces.

Shaw came alone to New York in September for the opening of *In the French Style,* which gave him the opportunity to renew his relationship with

Doris Lilly. Proud of his work on the screen, anxious to see it succeed, he gave interviews to the daily papers and seemed not to mind when questions focused on his early career. "I remember those days—the 1930s—with a great fondness," he told one interviewer. "They were years of ferment and political hopefulness. Everybody was insecure—so everybody felt secure. There wasn't so much money around, so nobody cared too much about it. They didn't worry about their old age as they do now. And they seemed more generous." On the night of the opening, September 18, however, Shaw's fears of another critical failure got the better of him.

"I'll never forget that night," remembers Doris Lilly. "He had a little preview for his friends, a theater around Bloomingdale's, on Third Avenue." Afterward there was a party for 200 hosted by Irving Lazar, and Shaw found himself getting drunker and more cantankerous as the evening wore on, until he felt, in some wrathful way he didn't entirely understand, that he hated his friends and hated Lazar for luring him into the sort of celebrity bash he'd sworn to avoid for his non-Hollywood movie. In a letter to Lilly upon his return to Klosters, he spoke ruefully of his state of nervous shock that night, but for Lilly the evening was an embarrassment that put a damper on their relationship.

Generally, reviewers found the film to possess, as Bosley Crowther put it, "a certain melancholy charm." However, as the film's winsome story unfolded—with Jean Seberg as the young American girl first falling in love with her Frenchman, then, some years later, being visited in Paris by her anxious father, and finally falling dutifully for a homeward-bound American doctor—the critics noted a woodenness of dialogue and pace that suggested the film's director and screenwriter might have benefited from some studio supervision after all. "Just a bit too much self-deliberation, too much pondering 'should I do this or should I not' and then sitting around and brooding about it over the inevitable goblet of booze, goes on in this slowly-paced drama," intoned Crowther. Judith Crist observed that Jean Seberg had played the American girl in Paris one too many times (in *Breathless,* for example, and *Playtime*) for *In the French Style* to seem original. The previous films, she wrote, "give an over-all triteness to Mr. Shaw's tale, a weariness to its details." Despite a more enthusiastic reception in London, where the film opened simultaneously, moviegoers seemed nonplussed by what they saw, and after turning a modest profit, *In the French Style* drifted out of the theaters and into memory.

Buoyed by the London reviews, Shaw held out hope, upon his return to Klosters, that his film might yet emerge a major success; but by the time he flew back to New York in November, those hopes had been brushed away. A late review in *Time* seemed written expressly to throw salt in his wounds. "Year after year," it said, "Irwin Shaw wept bitterly in his champagne. The cinemoguls gave him heaps of dough to write movie scripts . . . but a man cannot live by bread alone. As an artist, Irwin earnestly and frequently explained to the press, he was hurt by what happened to his scripts after he turned them in. Words were changed. Sometimes whole scenes were struck out by some thick-fingered fur salesman who had never read anything more difficult than a ledger. Sizzling from Hollywood's ig- nominies (and loaded with Hollywood's gold), Scriptwriter Shaw last year at last devised a stratagem to baffle the barbarians. He wrote a picture and then produced it himself—at a cost of about a million." Concluded the reviewer: "Well, he can have it. For one thing, his script urgently requires the attention of that fur salesman. For another, it tells a story that has been told, and told more excitingly, a hundred times before. . . . If this picture does as well as it deserves to, he may soon be weeping bitterly in his beer."

Shaw had always been inordinately sensitive to poor reviews, but then, the reviews had often been inordinately insensitive. This time, he vowed in black fury, Henry Luce had gone too far.

Shaw's principal reason for this trip was to have a top-ranked New York dentist perform major surgery; for the rest of his life, he would pay for his parents' inability to pay for routine dental work in his youth. While staying at Delmonico's, however, he also agreed to write a diatribe against *Time* and the Luces for *fact*, a new fringe publication produced by Ralph Ginzburg, the mischievous left-wing publisher. Ginzburg, an eccentric character with round black glasses and a bristle-brush mustache, was clever enough to think of approaching Shaw for the piece. When Shaw invited him over to talk about it, Ginzburg asked if he could bring some of his editors with him. He showed up in hiking boots and shorts, backed up by a troop of twenty young radical colleagues. At *fact*, he explained to the rather surprised Shaw, ultimate democracy prevailed.

Still, Shaw agreed to join a host of well-known names whose bitter sentiments about *Time* were being rounded up by Ginzburg for *fact*'s inaugural issue in January. The other contributors, who included Bertrand Russell, Tallulah Bankhead, John Osborne and P. G. Wodehouse, re- stricted their responses to a pithy sentence or two. Not Shaw. Resolutely, he sat down to write page after page, the many years of resentment spilling out at last. He started by restating his recent exchange with the magazine's editors about the Clifford Odets obituary. Then he hinted darkly that *Time*'s review of *In the French Style* was an unsigned act of revenge. As well-bred and polite as *Time*'s reporters invariably seemed, as seasoned as their war correspondents were, the Machine in New York somehow trans- muted their words into the polished vitriole known as Timese. After bearing the brunt of that vitriole ever since his first appearance in the magazine in 1936, Shaw could hold his counsel no longer.

Nor, he went on to say, could he any longer feel obliged to keep a promise made to Clare Luce, back in 1937, never to write about the weekend spent with the Luces at their country estate in the Carolinas. For his own mischievous behavior that weekend Shaw reckoned he had earned a place on some list of names at the *Time* building under the heading "To Be Provoked at Every Opportunity." Not only had all his creative works been panned with unconscionable venom, but passing references had invariably been incorrect. Only recently, he observed, *Time* had reported in a story about the notoriously difficult Sam Spiegel an anecdote that "Writer Irwin Shaw, while working on the screenplay of *On the Waterfront*, woke up at three o'clock one morning and started shaving. When his wife awoke to ask what he was doing, Shaw said grimly, 'I'm going out to kill Sam Spiegel.' " Shaw had dashed off a wry note to the magazine to point out that he had never worked for or with Sam Spiegel, and that he was surprised to learn his name had become a nom de plume for Budd Schulberg. Some weeks later he had received acknowledgment of the mistake from *Time*'s head of researchers—but no correction in print. His follow-up letters were ignored, and there, he had come to realize, the matter would lie. In fact, the anecdote *would* remain uncorrected throughout Shaw's life, and then, in an irony he surely would have appreciated, resurface after his death in Sam Spiegel's obituary in *The New York Times*.

Doris Lilly, at Shaw's side throughout his November visit, read the *fact* piece and strongly advised him not to print it. "You're just too big to be doing this sort of thing," she said in genuine puzzlement. "This is so . . . *small*." Bob Parrish too advised Shaw to keep his anger private, but Shaw would not be dissuaded. "I'll show that sonuvabitch Luce," he insisted. The piece appeared to no particular fanfare in January, but it did provide a disturbing indication of Shaw's increasingly fragile ego. Lilly was right: he *was* too big to respond to carping critics. More than he ever had, however, he took the jabs as personal insults and nursed a bitter sense of rejection. By no coincidence, Shaw learned at about this time that he had an ulcer—beneath the jovial exterior, his dark brooding had done its work, abetted by drinking—and was forced to endure periods of abstinence that were invariably much shorter than his doctor suggested. More than any skiing accident of this period, the ulcer would throw off Shaw's happy balance of skiing by day to offset his drinking of the night before. As he felt less like exercising, he would feel more like drinking—and thus would the vicious circle of deteriorating health take hold.

There had been other signs of a new and more volatile bitterness in Shaw. Not long before in Paris, Shaw had shocked his friends and deeply embarrassed his family by punching a literary critic at a cocktail party hosted by Alain and Margery Bernheim. The critic was a diminutive Frenchman who thoughtlessly declared that Shaw's only good book had been *The Young Lions*, and that afterward Shaw had sold out. Enraged, Shaw hauled off and slugged him. "I looked up, and Irwin seemed to be climbing over this guy," recalls Bob Parrish. "Bernheim's mother was on his back saying, 'No, no, no.' " Shaw would have hit the fellow again if other guests hadn't restrained him and pushed him, with much effort, into the bedroom to cool off. A moment later, Shaw's rage passed and he turned in genuine anguish to Michael Mindlin, an old acquaintance and theatrical publicity man. "I can't believe I did that," he said forlornly. "Do you think it'll get in the papers?"

"Don't worry, Irwin," Mindlin said, trying to soothe him. "I don't think *Variety* has a sports section."

Back in Klosters, Shaw tried to put behind him the year's disappointments in theater and film, and to focus on the novel he was now obligated to write under Random House's new and more generous terms. For the first time in his writing career, he felt unable to summon the strength or enthusiasm to plunge into some long and sweeping tale. He felt tired, played out. The stories he had once turned out in a morning now took six months of tinkering. Somberly, he began sketching out a barely disguised reminiscence that might allow him to sift for meaning in his past, to understand how, at age fifty, he had come to this crossroads of success and sorrow. Its tone would be wistful, its style almost poetic, with a narrative that shifted back and forth between a present-day summer baseball game and the scattered memories of its Shaw-like protagonist sitting in the stands, watching his son play ball. Shaw began it as a story, with the working title "Lineaments of a Summer Day." When, after a checkered history, it appeared as a short novel two years later, it would announce itself more simply as *Voices of a Summer Day*.

It is not hard to see why Shaw would come to feel a special fondness for *Voices of a Summer Day*, and would even pronounce it the favorite of his dozen novels. Benjamin Federov, whose name evokes Shaw's lost family name, Shamforoff, is a fatalist. He knows life is a series of accidents, unmanageable passions, occasional victories and more frequent defeats, yet like his creator he has come to feel at peace with that process. He has, in effect, survived a midlife crisis. Throughout, there are glimmerings from Shaw's own life, set off with chronological chapter headings (usually a year or so off from Shaw's actual experiences): going to summer camp with his brother; falling in love and losing his virginity; witnessing his father's bankruptcy and collapse of spirit; marrying a Marian-like figure and conducting extramarital affairs with handsome, rich women.

The parallels between *Voices* and Shaw's own life are occasionally deceptive. As he often does in his novels, Shaw deliberately jumbles details to help put the book at a literary distance from reality. More important is his return to a Jewish protagonist after several novels of WASPy leading men, and with it a willingness to confront the brief but stinging instances of anti-Semitism in his own life. As a teenager, Benjamin Federov makes love to the daughter of a Methodist minister who then calmly informs him she can have an orgasm only with a "bestial Jew." He hears his father rant about the family's radical uncle, who has gone up to Boston to protest the

Sacco-Vanzetti trial, thus, his father declares, feeding the prejudices that all Americans harbor toward Jews. As a grown man, he sees two boys out in a rough surf in danger of drowning and walks up to a pair of prim matriarchs having drinks on the patio of a WASPy beach club to have them alert the management. The ladies look out at the boys and declare there's nothing they can do, because the boys aren't members.

The novel also draws a telling portrait of Marian, rechristened Peggy. Bright and outspoken as she is, she "surrounds" Federov in a way that becomes unbearably stifling. Left alone to brood about their marriage while he's off at war, she plans everything in maddening detail: the apartment decor, the meals to be served upon his return, the friends to be seen and the vacations to be taken. Nerve-rackingly jealous, she demands to know where Federov is having lunch, then calls the restaurant at midday to see if he's there. Federov isn't, of course; he's sneaked off from the office for a sexual rendezvous. But rather than have it justify Peggy's jealousy, Shaw uses the call to underscore why Federov has been driven to extramarital affairs in the first place.

There were other projects in the winter of 1963–1964. Shaw had written ten new stories over the last year or two, and had the notion of linking them together with little prose "bridges." At this point, he was still half convinced that Voices would simply run as one of those stories. He was also juggling several movie scripts, among them a project with Clement Wood called Quadrangle, about a school very much like Le Rosey. In February he and Marian took a chalet in Gstaad until Easter, both to spend time with Adam and to enable Shaw to work on the script with Wood. By mid-April he had finished Voices and decided its length definitely merited separate publication as a novel. The fact that he'd dispatched it in so short a time seemed not to bother him. To an interviewer the next year he would proudly tick off the decreasing periods each novel had taken him—four years on The Young Lions, two and a half each for The Troubled Air and Lucy Crown, one for Two Weeks in Another Town (a figure, it seems, arrived at by adding up intermittent work stretches) and now eight months on Voices—as if the sooner a novel could be written, the more proficient its author.

He sent a first draft off to Random House before heading down for a sybaritic spring trip to Antibes, where he stayed at the Résidence du Cap. By mid-May Cerf wrote to say that everyone at Random House found Voices a warm and bittersweet "story" that seemed likely to have broad appeal, and that the book would be scheduled for publication in November. The draft was not without its problems, however. Cerf enumerated a few of them, and it was agreed that Shaw would come to New York with a revised draft in June.

Despite the addition of two long scenes, the manuscript that Shaw bore under his arm to Cerf's office was by far the shortest novel he had ever submitted for publication—at roughly 200 pages in final print, about a quarter the size of *The Young Lions*. The length might not have mattered if Random House had been obligated to pay only the $15,000 advance it had paid Shaw in the past, but under the new terms of $55,000 per book, Cerf felt cheated by what he saw. Gently he told Shaw that while he liked *Voices of a Summer Day*, he felt it wasn't a "full-length novel," as the new contract stipulated. Random House would still publish it, he said, but some compromise was in order on the advance.

By this time, Shaw had changed editors, from the too formal Albert Erskine, with whom relations had been so strained, to the more genial Joe Fox. It was down to Fox's office that Shaw stormed after the meeting with Cerf. "His face was black with rage," Fox recalls, "and he was prowling around in that bearlike way of his, knocking over things, and saying, 'He called it a little book. A *little book!*' "

Days later, Shaw attended a weekend-long anniversary party at the Styrons' rambling farmhouse in Connecticut. The plan was to drive with Joe Fox and his wife to the Foxes' home in Bedford Village on a Friday, stay the night, and proceed to Connecticut in the morning. Also invited was Peter Matthiessen, whose literary reputation had risen steadily since the early *Paris Review* days. Matthiessen had just written his novel *At Play in the Fields of the Lord*, and several publishing houses were eagerly bidding on it. "I was wooing Peter," admits Fox, "so on the way up in the car I spent most of my time talking to him. He and I were in front, I was driving. And Irwin was sitting sullenly in the back listening to me." It didn't occur to Fox that Shaw might be insulted; it didn't occur to him that Shaw would ever leave Random House, despite the dustup with Cerf. "Irwin said very little until we drove into the Styrons' driveway," recalls Fox. "Then he suddenly announced from the backseat, 'I want you both to know that I've had six sets of friends in my life, and I'm ready to start on my seventh.' We sort of laughed, and went in to the party and got drunk, and that seemed the end of it. But it was the next week that he left Random."

Unbeknownst to Fox and Matthiessen, Shaw had encouraged Irving Lazar to find him another publishing house that would pay him more—and respect him more. Lazar had called Don Fine, the young, ambitious co-founder of Delacorte, a new line at Dell. Fine, after excited conversations with his publisher, Helen Meyer, had come through with an astounding six-figure offer.

Motivated too by his strong emotions of the moment, Shaw authorized Lazar to confront Cerf with Delacorte's terms and offer him the choice of either meeting them or letting Shaw go.

"Lazar walked into our office one day, obviously uncomfortable," Cerf recalled in his memoir *At Random*. "Lazar explained the situation and added, 'Of course, if you'll match this offer, Irwin will be happy; but if you won't, he knows that you will be decent enough to release him from his contract.'

"I hit the roof. I told Irving, 'You know perfectly well that this book has been under contract a long time.' I was so angry, I said, 'Get him out of here. I don't want to see him any more. He has an advance from us on this book—a considerable one.' Lazar said, 'Oh, he'll give you back the advance immediately.' . . . I said, 'That's very big of him. We have a contract. We could publish the damn thing and tell him to go to hell, but no, we'll send the manuscript back this afternoon. You send us the check for the advance, and let's forget about Irwin Shaw.' "

So furious was Cerf that before sending the manuscript over to Delacorte, he ordered Nan Talese to erase every one of the editing marks she'd made in pencil on the pages.

That night Shaw joined Lazar for dinner at Le Pavillon along with Arthur and Leonora Hornblow and an old Hollywood acquaintance, Frank Sinatra. Afterward they all drifted to "21" for a nightcap. There, across the room, they saw Bennett and Phyllis Cerf. Momentarily stunned, Shaw turned to Lazar and said, "I must go over and say hello." As the others watched, he walked stalwartly across to Cerf and held out his hand. Cerf hesitated, then shook it stiffly. But when Shaw then tried to kiss Phyllis Cerf on the cheek, she turned away.

More than a business arrangement had changed. A warm professional relationship of nearly thirty years had ended, and with it an important influence on Shaw as a writer. If Random House had not discovered Shaw, it had certainly helped establish him as a writer of distinction, published side by side with James Joyce, William Faulkner, Robert Penn Warren, John O'Hara and more recently Truman Capote and William Styron, among others. When Shaw had turned from stories to novels, Saxe Commins had played an enormously important role in cutting back and reshaping his sprawling manuscripts; there was no wiser editorial counsel to be had. If Random House, in the end, had been guilty of taking Shaw for granted, it was also true that Shaw had grown more sensitive to criticism with each passing novel. He wanted more reassurance than Cerf and Klopfer were able to give, and to a writer whose critical reputation had suffered, the truest reassurance was cash.

In the years to come, Shaw would make more money, more than he could imagine even now, and with his dogged daily output, he would double his output of novels in the last two decades of his life. The price would be a decline in quality. Shaw would claim that he wrote his best for whatever company published him, but his departure from Random House would come to seem a downward turning point. In a subtle way it seemed irreversibly to change his own self-image as a writer.

CHAPTER EIGHTEEN

The Delacorte colophon was barely a season old in the summer of 1964, when Shaw signed on as the line's first well-known author. What it had was money, and the new wild card of hard-soft royalty deals.

Delacorte's parent company was the long-successful paperback house of Dell. In 1963 Dell had acquired a hardcover house, Dial Press. Suddenly it seemed entirely reasonable to publish both the hard- and softcover editions of a book under one roof. Instead of the traditional arrangement by which a hardcover house first published a writer's work, then sold paperback rights and kept half the royalties, Dell would be able to offer writers one-hundred-percent paperback royalties without losing a cent. For the first time too, a paperback house might hope to have writers of its own, though to preserve tradition, a writer's work would still be published by the company's hardcover line before it came out in paperback.

The two Dell editors who began playing with the idea were as different from each other as Abbott and Costello. Ross Claiborne was the tall, reserved editor in chief of Dell's Delta and Laurel lines. Donald I. Fine, editor in chief of the money-making Dell line, was short, stocky and explosive. Despite their competitiveness with each other, it was agreed the pair would serve as co–editors in chief of the new line. Fine would go after commercial titles, while Claiborne would concentrate on more solid back-list titles. Each was given separate office space and staff in Dell's new quarters at 750 Third Avenue; each reported to Helen Meyer, Dell's president and publisher.

"We were regarded by the rest of the publishing industry as upstarts," recalls Ross Claiborne. "The attitude was: Who are these lowly paperback publishers and what do they know about hardcover publishing? They thought we were going to fall on our faces. And for a while we didn't have great success. But then we got Irwin and Jim [Jones]. And they became the bait that brought other writers in."

The terms Delacorte offered Shaw would have seemed extravagant for any top-selling author of the early sixties. For a writer like Shaw, whose earnings, as Claiborne admits, were in a "downward spiral," they were nothing short of extraordinary. Shaw would sign on for a two-novel deal, with *Voices of a Summer Day* as the first book. The second would likely be

295

a long work in progress called *The Uncaged Man,* an awkward title that would later be changed, at Claiborne's insistence, to *Rich Man, Poor Man.* The hardcover advance would be $100,000 per book, with $25,000 more each in performance bonuses. Shaw's next story collection would be published by Delacorte too, though its advance would be a modest $15,000. With book club advances and European rights thrown in, Shaw estimated his take on all three books could come to more than $350,000.

It was a deal that shocked the publishing world. Delacorte was accused of raiding Random House, a patently unfair charge. More accurately, editors and publishers complained that such an exorbitant advance would destroy the unwritten standards by which, in the early sixties, even bestselling novelists felt satisfied with advances in the neighborhood of $25,000 per book. Soon enough the business would become little more than a high-stakes money game, forcing out small publishers and turning writers into mercenaries.

That, in fact, did largely come to pass. "Irwin's breakup with Random House almost marked the end of the gentlemen's relationship between writer and publisher," recalls Nan Talese. "It was the beginning of the end of independent publishers too. But in a sense, Bennett [Cerf] led the way in that, by buying Alfred A. Knopf, then selling Random House to RCA. Suddenly there was big money in publishing." Shaw's move legitimized the process. Soon several hardcover houses would fight back by starting their own paperback lines, or buying existing ones, and the hard-soft royalty deal would become a staple of the business.

As soon as he could, Shaw flew back to Europe, leaving the furor behind him. As a reward to himself for signing into the big money, he bought, for $55,000, a fifty-foot yacht—a floating bar, as friends would come to refer to it. (Its name, *Xantippe,* must have amused him: Xantippe was the shrewish wife of Socrates.) Anchored in St.-Tropez, he took the time to write a sorrowful letter to Donald Klopfer, with whom he'd had no contact during the breakup. Itemizing the financial arrangements that made the switch irresistible, Shaw asked for Klopfer's understanding, and acknowledged the "long, good, warmhearted run" they'd had together. Klopfer immediately sent a gracious reply. He wouldn't have dreamed of standing in the way of such a wonderful business deal, he wrote, and yes, the two were still friends. Shaw was deeply grateful, and though Cerf would remain standoffish for the rest of his life, the Random House chapter seemed more happily concluded.

Money had always struck jarring chords in Shaw, and his new financial status did much to sharpen the dissonance. At last he could truly stop worrying about monthly bills: maintaining two homes, supporting Marian's often high-flown whims in clothes and entertaining, paying a private-school tuition that would soon escalate to college level. Instead of providing the peace of mind needed to work, however, money simply offered more temptations to play. And instead of liberating him to be an artist, the money seemed to underscore a new self-image for Shaw as a "professional," a term uttered with gruff pride by a seasoned writer who, like a boxer, took his lumps, kept on swinging, and walked away with the purse.

But to judge his own success by money made it all the more painful to learn someone else was earning more. That fall, back in New York and staying at the Ritz Tower, Shaw went to a ball game at Yankee Stadium with Gay Talese. They took a taxi—Shaw was not about to ride a subway at this stage of his life, no matter how much easier it was to reach the stadium that way—and en route the two men fell to talking about magazine writing. Since his wedding, Talese had gone on to be one of the hottest writers of a newly hot *Esquire,* pulling down as much as $4,000 per article. Editor Harold Hayes had just tapped Shaw to write an appreciation of football quarterback Y. A. Tittle. "Irwin told me he was getting two thousand dollars for the piece, and was that enough. I said, 'You could get more, Irwin.' I was saying this as a friend, that's all. But it hit him that *I* was getting more. I mean, I was writing pieces regularly, but still, he was Irwin Shaw, a man I'd looked up to before and now. I felt he should be making more than I was. But it didn't come out right. A week later I got a letter from Harold Hayes saying, 'Gay, when will you learn that your private relationship with me is something that should remain private?' He enclosed a letter from Irwin to him saying, in effect, 'I don't know why I should make less money than Gay Talese.' He was making big money already, of course; he didn't need more. It was his pride."

Shaw was much more deeply hurt later that fall, when Don Fine persuaded Jim Jones to become a Delacorte writer by offering $1 million for a four-book hardcover-softcover deal, complete with an employee clause for Jones and future financial safeguards for his family. When Shaw heard about the deal, his natural generosity, and his great love for Jones, were sorely strained: Why *had* Jones gotten more?

In truth, neither author's recent novels had measured up to his big war books, critically or commercially, but while Jones's *Some Came Running* had been published to almost universal condemnation, *The Pistol* and *The Thin Red Line* had regained for him much of his reputation as a first-rate war writer. Shaw, on the other hand, seemed to have dissipated his promise as a novelist, if not as a short story writer, and while Delacorte's contentious coeditors could always hope he'd surprise them, privately they admitted to having signed Shaw as much for the luster that his name would lend the new line as for the prospect of earning any financial return on their investment.

Certainly nothing Shaw published in the months after his contract-signing changed that outlook. In September 1964, *In the Company of Dolphins* appeared as a slim volume from Bernard Geis Associates, a little-known line distributed by Random House. (The book was already in production when Shaw broke with Random House.) Critics yawned, and the book immediately sank out of sight. *Voices of a Summer Day* followed early the next year. This time the response was more attentively hostile.

More than one critic duly noted that Shaw's intent in *Voices* was to limn not just his own past but that of his generation. Touching as it did on the Depression, the war, postwar hopes and failures, *Voices* did succeed at least in stirring sympathetic memories, but as a novel it fell short. Gerald Walker in *The New York Times* complained the flashbacks were forced, and that the baseball game to which Federov's thoughts keep returning "just does not yield a rich Proustian lode. . . . Irwin Shaw does not have the literary equipment; his rhetorical flight amounts to no more than a pop-up." *Time*'s critic took the opportunity to ask: "What ever became of Irwin Shaw?" Most cutting, though, was Stanley Kauffmann's appraisal in the Sunday *Herald Tribune*, an appraisal clearly tinged with the same personal venom Leslie Fiedler had shown almost a decade before.

Kauffmann lumped Shaw together with Herman Wouk, but pronounced Wouk the more admirable—"an honest merchant." He found "Shaw, on the other hand . . . a novelistic short-changer. He has not researched his subjects adequately enough to convey a sense of knowledge, he has not devised a suspenseful plot, he has not written with fast pace or color, he provides a much less meaty package—yet he charges the same price." Continued Kauffmann: "Shaw . . . exemplifies a relatively recent phenomenon. It dates, at a guess, from the Depression years. About that time we began to welcome shoddy art if it was concerned with pertinent subjects. (Shaw himself came to the fore in those days, derivative even then; his first work of note—the play *Bury the Dead*—reminded many of a previous play, Hans Chlumberg's *Miracle at Verdun*)." Both Wouk and Shaw were "cut-rate highbrows," Kauffmann concluded, but "although neither of their novels is of any importance, there is a grave difference, I think, between triviality and prostitution."

At about this time, a puzzled Don Fine asked Norman Mailer why it was that the New York literary establishment seemed to reserve such animosity for Shaw. "Because," said Mailer, "he's very rich, he likes martinis—and he's Jewish."

Mailer might have so described himself, and therein lay an intriguing comparison. Soon after Shaw, he too had signed on for the new big money, netting $125,000, for hardcover rights alone, from Delacorte's own Dial Press for *An American Dream*, the novel that had appeared serially in *Esquire* over the last year. But in 1965, as in 1948, the differences between Mailer and Shaw were at least as revealing as the similarities. The largest was that Mailer had stayed on home turf. Only two novels had come out of the long period between *The Naked and the Dead* and *An American Dream*, and both to scathing reviews that left Mailer's status as a fiction writer unclear even to him. In new and radical ways, however, Mailer had continued the exploration of American political and social issues begun in those novels. He had experimented liberally with drugs, explored psycho-analysis and mysticism, and tapped into the beat generation, black culture and youth rebellion. His journey had produced one landmark essay—"The White Negro"—and considerable chaos. Mailer's stabbing of his second wife, Adele, and his increasingly manic behavior, some of it drug-induced, all stirred endless speculation among his friends of his imminent mental collapse. Still, beginning with his profile of John F. Kennedy for *Esquire* in the heat of the 1960 election race, Mailer had found a new voice in journalism, and in *An American Dream* he used that voice to forge what critic John Aldridge called a "major creative breakthrough" in his fiction.

Over that same period, Shaw had continued to tell stories with the graceful and musical voice that had been his gift from the start, but while he hated to hear it, his decision to become an expatriate had kept him from participating in the maelstrom of American political and social change that inspired his best early work. Gradually, as a result, his voice had lost the passion that helped distinguish it. It seemed all too apt that in *Voices* Shaw's narrator would be mired in the past, searching for sense in the years that lay behind. Mailer, in *An American Dream*, was struggling to define the present, to come to terms with the sensuality of the sixties and see where it might lead. For all his experiments and mistakes, that search infused his writing with the energy and freshness that Shaw's work now lacked.

Mailer still envied Shaw his elegant style. "It was a damn good style," he says. "Irwin had his cutting edge. Some of his stuff is awfully good." But time, he felt, had revealed Shaw to be a stylist and not much else. The problem with Shaw, says Mailer, was that "he had no belief in either God or the devil, which does tend to reduce you as a writer. He really thought people got by on their personal style in life. A writer like John Cheever—whom I feel is much more important—was essentially doing the same thing with one huge difference: Cheever was a religious man. And the difference in their work is illumined by that. I don't think Irwin had this idea that we were here on this earth for any tremendous purpose. Maybe it was just a rotten, shitty world, and if so, the best thing was just to go through it and don't make any mess. In a sense, he got the worst of Hemingway."

By the mid-sixties, Mailer muses, "Irwin may have just made some tough estimate deep within himself that he had more of a talent for life than for becoming a great writer. To try to become a major American writer is a sacrifice. It's equal to joining a Trappist monastery. And I think Irwin decided, 'I've got a gift for life and I'm going to use it.'"

Did Shaw make such an estimate? Certainly none of the friends and lovers who erred in criticizing one of Shaw's works to his face at *any* time in his life would have felt he had. As confident as Shaw appeared out-wardly, however, his true self-image as a writer had remained unclear from his earliest successes on into the doldrums of the sixties. Perhaps he *had* been as uncomplicatedly delighted in his early promise as friends swore he was. And perhaps his first triumphs had built a carapace of confidence and ego around that self-image, as friends suggested, that preserved it from the critical onslaught that followed. But under that? "Irwin just thought he was the greatest writer around," says Doris Lilly. "His ego was *huge.*" On the other hand, Shaw himself would say some years later that "every day, when I wake up and have to work, I open my eyes in fear and trembling, because I don't know whether I still have it, whether I'm going to have it again or whether I'm going to be afflicted by the doubt that I never had it at all." At bottom a writer's self-image, even that of so seemingly brash a writer as Shaw, was just too fungible—brimming with confidence one day, doubt-riddled the next—to be so neatly defined. Still, Mailer's perception had an uncomfortable ring of truth.

Easier to discern was Shaw's image of Mailer: he didn't like him. The two had exchanged hardly a word since their unfortunate meeting at the Styrons' New York apartment in 1951, but over the years Shaw had heard reports of negative remarks made about him by Mailer, and on at least one occasion had been actively snubbed by his Brooklyn rival as Mailer swept by his table in a restaurant. Then too, Shaw had shared the literary world's fury with Mailer for the snide putdown of several of his peers, particularly James Jones, that had appeared as the title piece of *Advertisements for Myself,* a collection of essays published in the fall of 1959. Jones was livid with Mailer, and went so far as to keep a copy of *Advertisements for Myself* on a sideboard in the dining room of his Île St.-Louis apartment. Whenever he was visited by a writer who happened to be mentioned in the book, Jones would have the writer pen comments in the margin by the relevant passage. As it happened, Shaw was *not* mentioned in Mailer's essay, which may well have seemed the greatest insult of all.

On the evening of March 15, 1965, Dial Press threw a publication party for Mailer's *An American Dream* at the Village Vanguard. Somehow, despite the bad blood, Don Fine persuaded his two new prize Delacorte authors to make an appearance. James Jones walked in, only to be engaged immediately in a sparring match by a drunk and manic Mailer. Shaw stood off to the side, nursing his scotch and feeling mixed emotions: a certain amount of sympathy for Mailer, who seemed out of control, but also resentment. *An American Dream,* despite many negative reviews, was a major publishing event, and the book was clearly headed to the bestseller lists. *Voices of a Summer Day,* celebrated with a more civilized party two weeks before in the pool room of The Four Seasons, was already branded a failure.

Ironically, Shaw's best writing of the mid-sixties fell squarely in Mailer's camp. His profile of Y. A. Tittle, published in *Esquire* in January

1965, was a first-class piece that took a step or two toward New Journalism with a first-person voice. Reminiscences of his own days on the Brooklyn College gridiron were neatly interwoven with scenes of Tittle in practice and in the locker room. Shaw even sat on the New York Giants' bench for a game, marveling at the brutality of the play up close. It seemed little different from war, he wrote soberly. Deftly, Shaw managed to capture a sense of the embattled, thirty-eight-year-old quarterback while keeping a respectful distance—a nice choice—and throughout, he conveyed his own love and knowledge of the game, a passion almost as important to him as writing itself.

With less success, Shaw tried one final time to write a play—in fact, a pair of plays. He had an interesting notion to tell a two-generational family story set against two different wars. *A War Several Years Ago* featured a central character named Sawyer in Tel Aviv in 1943; *By the Old Moulmein Pagoda,* set in the sixties, followed Sawyer's son to a war in a "nameless Asian country." Unexpectedly, Shaw employed the Brechtian device of having a character address the audience with such pronouncements as: "This is a play. A play observes certain conventions." He also made an effort to invent his own Asian vocabulary. Both were risks he may have felt emboldened to take because he thought so little was at stake. To one interviewer at the time, Shaw acknowledged he was working on the plays, but added sadly, "Plays are my hobby and my cross, failure after failure." When the two plays were produced as *A Choice of Wars* in the winter of 1967 by the University of Utah's Babcock Theatre, *Saturday Review* was alert enough to send a reviewer, who came away impressed. While the first play was "mainly nostalgic and descriptive," wrote Henry Hewes, "the second one might well be expanded into a provocative full-length play dealing with the most important issue of the present day." If Shaw read the advice, he didn't heed it; the dual play was produced once again in Los Angeles, then dropped.

Not surprisingly, Shaw had conflicted feelings about the most important issue of the day. He knew all too well how appalling war could be, but as a veteran of World War II, he felt strongly that America was the watchdog of the free world, and he revered the late President Kennedy, under whose leadership the policy of sending American military advisors to Vietnam, begun under President Eisenhower, had been continued. At about this time, Don Fine remembers, Shaw launched into a defense of the war at a dinner party in Klosters. "Marian was in Paris, and Irwin had invited over some great-looking ladies. But then the subject of Vietnam came up, and Irwin started lecturing on it. His guests didn't know what the hell he was talking about. And Irwin just got madder and madder." For an anthology titled *Authors Take Sides on Vietnam,* Shaw was asked to weigh in with his formal opinion. It was almost shockingly sour. He began by noting that the intended book was reminiscent of a similar survey in the 1930s of authors on the Spanish Civil War. All but a few of the writers polled had declared themselves Loyalists and condemned Franco. Only a few years later, Shaw wryly noted, Franco had swept to victory and World War II was looming. Writers, in other words, loved to congratulate themselves on holding noble sentiments, without acknowledging how meaningless their protests were. Now, Shaw speculated, nearly all writers polled would doubtless condemn America's intervention in Vietnam, but again with no effect. He himself had no theories to offer, he wrote, on how to win the war tomorrow. He did know how President Johnson could rally reluctant doves to his side. The president could simply lend North Vietnam a few aircraft carriers, let them cruise safely off the coast of Cape Cod, and allow them to stage a sustained bombing raid (complete with napalm and defoliating chemicals) on Boston, New York and Philadelphia, preferably with a high number of casualties among children. At the same time, flyers would be dropped on the beleaguered cities explaining that the bombing was all for the greater good of international Communism. Best, Shaw suggested, if the maimed and murdered children came from families who, out of some twisted admiration for Communism, had secretly aided the invaders. After a year or two of that, every last American would rally around the flag, convinced that the war must be won at any cost, even if it meant a century of intervention.

"I don't think Irwin liked the sixties," Don Fine muses. "It was alien territory for him." Such was the distance Shaw had now traveled from *Bury the Dead,* and how out of touch he was, living in Europe, with the pulse of American culture and thought. It was a failing that, to a large degree, would account for the curious sense of unreality that marked his next novel, the panoramic tale of two brothers coming of age in postwar America, *Rich Man, Poor Man.*

In the spring of 1965, Shaw and Jones decided to travel again together, this time with the intention of writing up dual versions of their adventures for *Playboy.* They met with their wives in tow in Juan-les-Pins and drove to Antibes, where they boarded the *Xantippe* and began to cruise west along the French Riviera. Their plan was to motor up the Rhone to Arles, where they would attend bullfights in the town's historic Roman arena, but when the weather turned bad, they were forced to dock the boat and complete the journey by taxi. A series of day trips followed, with the cheery foursome returning each nightfall to sleep on the boat. Shaw and Jones christened their project "The Bouillabaisse Adventures" in tribute to their ample consumption of same. Later, each dutifully wrote up his own version of the trip; but when they compared their efforts, they agreed the versions were too similar, and the double chronicle was never published.

Soon after, Shaw retrieved his boat and headed back east on his own. In Port'Ercole, as he had four years before, he stopped to visit his old friend Alan Moorehead. As it happened, art critic Robert Hughes was living nearby as a young aspiring fiction writer, and he well remembers Shaw's arrival. "Apparently Shaw had had a bet with Moorehead and Luigi Barzini—both war correspondents—as to who would have the biggest boat in twenty years' time. Irwin, clearly, had won the bet. Moorehead had a thirty-two-foot ketch; Barzini had a black schooner that he'd gotten on a fire sale from some fascist notable because his book *The Italians* had come out that year. But Irwin's was a Genoa-built gin palace. I remember we all went on some picnic on the boat, and there was Irwin on the poop of this thing flourishing a chicken wing and saying, 'What else does a writer need?' "

One evening Hughes had them all over to dinner at his own modest digs, and took the opportunity to invite another acquaintance, Alwyn Lee. "Lee was one of Henry Luce's book reviewers for *Time* before the age of bylines, and had negotiated this deal whereby he could live in Italy and send his stories across," Hughes recalls. "He was a tall, gaunt fellow with a tube coming out of his stomach, thanks to booze and the pressure of grinding out these book reviews overseas.

"Anyway, Irwin got flown with the booze and launched into this tirade against *Time*, how the word had gone down that he was too left-wing, and to get him. He hadn't bothered to ask Alwyn what Alwyn did for a living, this was all off the cuff, but he ended his tirade by announcing that one day he would meet the sonuvabitch who had written those reviews and punch him out.

"Alwyn rose creakily to his feet, to his credit, and said, 'Well, you'd better start here, because I'm the one who wrote them.'

"Irwin looked at him in utter stupefaction and finally said, 'Well, we better have a drink, because this room is too small to fight in.' "

Shaw stayed just a few days on that port call, then came back about a month later. When he did, Hughes was in for another surprise. "The lady I was living with at the time decided a fifty-foot boat was a lot more fun than spending time with an impoverished Australian would-be writer," Hughes recalls. "So she signed on as Irwin's cook, officially, and off they sailed."

Not all of Shaw's romantic campaigns these days were conducted with such élan. Slim Hayward, separated from Leland, passed through Paris one day and got a call from "Irwee" insisting he take her to what she presumed was a dinner between two old friends. "We laughed a lot, and afterward we went to some little boîte to dance, and I had a marvelous pair of Schlumberger earrings that someone had given me, they had points of gold on them, and Irwee was being very flirty, which he wouldn't have been if I had been Leland's wife. He said something that was very funny, and leaned forward, laughing, and I caught him right on the edge of the nose with one of those jagged gold points. And his nose started to bleed as if he'd had a bull sword stuck in him. And that was the end of that: he had to go home and lie down with his feet up." On a trip to New York, Shaw tried to revive his romance with Nina de Vogt Fuller, who now ran a little antiques store in Greenwich Village. When Shaw showed up at the store to make his intentions known, Fuller told him she was involved with someone else, someone Shaw knew. "Who?" asked Shaw angrily. "Joe Kaufman," came the reply. "Oh my God," Shaw declared, "you can't go out with him. He doesn't work—and he *drinks.*" Since Shaw himself had clearly just consumed a monstrous quantity of scotch, Fuller remained unpersuaded.

The affairs at last were taking their toll—on the marriage, and on the man himself. Shaw was increasingly indiscreet about them, and Marian, rising to the bait, reacted with a jealousy so keen that even her good friends remarked on it. Routinely now, she went through Shaw's drawers and pockets, searching for evidence. She bridled if her husband so much as waved hello to another woman on the snowy streets of Klosters. If Shaw stepped off the little train at Klosters, back from New York or Paris, and reached to hug Adam first, Marian grew furiously upset.

Enid Boulting, separated from her husband (and not yet married to the Earl of Hardwicke), had a startling experience with Marian and Irwin in St. Moritz. The three had chosen to go skiing together; the Shaws stayed in one bedroom, Boulting in another. "One morning I didn't turn up for skiing, I was tired. So Irwin knocked on my door and came in and said, 'I think it's a disgrace you come here and don't ski, so listen, I've got a ski instructor waiting for you.' Marian saw him coming out of my room, and she thought we'd been sleeping together." Marian pressed the issue and wouldn't believe Boulting's remonstrances. "It was ludicrous. They had just spent the night together. Up to that point I had adored Marian, but after that I never spoke to her again." Checking back with friends in Klosters, Boulting found that her experience had not been untypical. "I was told that happened between them a lot," she recalls. "In fact, I was told that every season they picked someone and that that person had to be the nemesis for them."

It was a reading that jibed with other women's experiences over the years. Now, as then, Shaw seemed to have provoked Marian with some calculation. In the wide circle of Shaw's friends, it came to be assumed that Shaw had had an affair with Enid Boulting. Yet she earnestly denies she ever did. She says she'd have no reason to deny it if she had; it simply never came to pass. It thus seems possible that Shaw himself fostered the rumor, or at least made clear insinuations. This happened too with Gabby Van Zuylen, the glamorous expatriate related by marriage to the Rothschilds of Paris. Even today most of Shaw's friends have the vague notion that Shaw either told them or implied that he'd been a lover of Van Zuylen, yet Van Zuylen amusedly denies it. Why would a man who had conducted so many bona fide affairs with attractive women perpetuate—or at least fail to dispel—rumors of affairs he hadn't had? Almost certainly because of Marian. By now, provoking her jealousy had become the greater part of the game, if not the entire point of it.

Not unexpectedly, Shaw and Marian were spending more time apart as a result of these bruising experiences. The opportunities to leave had always been Shaw's. In the fall of 1965, however, Marian took an important step of her own, as the coproducer of a successful play in Paris.

Ira Wallach's *The Absence of a Cello* had proved a winning comedy on Broadway, and Marian, together with Claude Sainval, felt the play's premise—about a Gallic scientist submitted to an embarrassing investigation by the American industrial company for which he hopes to work—might survive an Atlantic crossing. Translated and rechristened *Le Mal de Test*, the production bowed September 8 at the Comédie des Champs-Élysées. To Shaw's shock and delight, French critics cheered, and Marian had a modest hit on her hands. It was the first in the family, as Shaw observed in a letter to James Jones, since 1939.

Marian had more than that, however. She also had a lover: Jean Daninos, an industrial engineer who had made a small fortune by designing the Facel Vega sports car. Daninos was a social friend of the Shaws, a short, bald man who lavished on Marian the attention she'd never won from her husband. With the success of *Le Mal de Test*, Marian began spending more time in Paris on her own, while Shaw held forth in Klosters or New York. Soon enough, word of the affair began to circulate among the Shaws' many friends, abetted by Marian's relative lack of secrecy about it: Enid Hardwicke, for one, remembers constantly running into Marian and Daninos together at Orly Airport in those years. Shaw, of course, would be the last to know. Still, he must have sensed that something would come of the longer separations, and he seemed to hunger for that change though he didn't have the nerve to force it overtly. "He felt very hemmed in, he wanted her to be more independent," recalls Liz Weicker Fondaras. "And I think that was the beginning of the trouble."

Love on a Dark Street, Shaw's first collection of new stories in eight years, appeared in October 1965 to almost universal critical silence—a terrible blow. One of the few New York critics to take note at all was Robert Cromie in *Saturday Review*, who admiringly declared the collection could stand on its own without comparison to Shaw's others. "He has the gift of all great storytellers: when he's really swinging, he creates characters as genuine as that odd couple across the street, the curious patrons of the corner bar, the tragic figures from the headlines. They are individuals who walk into the living room of your mind, ensconce themselves, and refuse to be dislodged." Another admirer was Paul West, who in the *New York Herald Tribune* observed that three or four of the collection's ten stories were "truly brilliant: assured, mordant, delving and acrobatically lively." West was particularly taken with "Once in Aleppo," a story about three street entertainers on bicycles with a monkey who startle a polite young American from Vermont who's come to Aleppo to teach. Ironically, the story had been written twenty years before, while Shaw's Africa experience was still fresh and his writing edge sharper, but he had put it aside when *The New Yorker* decided it was too risqué for its sensitive readers.

It didn't help that most of the stories in *Love on a Dark Street* had first appeared not in *The New Yorker* but in *Playboy*, where editor in chief A. C. Spectorsky, a longtime acquaintance known universally as Spec, happily served as Shaw's surrogate Ross. Yet the stories stand with dignity beside Shaw's better-known *New Yorker* favorites, and if they seem less neatly cornered, animated by more free-floating, even random, events, most live on the page as gracefully and vividly as their predecessors.

They do tend to run longer than the early *New Yorker* stories. Freed of any space restriction, Shaw was letting his latest works unfurl, many of them into novellas. The greater length allowed more complex story lines that could be resolved more fully, without requiring the multidimensional characters and interior world that Shaw had such trouble creating in his novels. Skeptics muttered that these longer stories simply made for likelier screen prospects, that indeed everything Shaw wrote now began as a screenplay or treatment, to be whipped into fiction only if Hollywood failed to nibble. A story like "Goldilocks at Graveside," however, gives the lie to that charge.

One of Shaw's best, "Goldilocks" opens with the funeral of an ex–State Department employee who resigned in the fateful year of 1952. The unexpected appearance of a slim, blond-haired man named Borden at the service stirs Victoria, the widow, to recall the events that bound their fates together. Back in the worst of the Communist witch-hunt days, when Victoria's husband was stationed at a certain unnamed embassy in "the desert," homosexuals began to be expunged from the State Department with the same alacrity as suspected Reds. One day Victoria happened to notice the embassy's brightest young star, a handsome consul she and her husband privately referred to as Goldilocks for his thick blond hair, emerging at midday with wet-combed hair from a downtown doorway. She wouldn't have noted the moment at all, had it not been for the furtive, guilty glance Goldilocks threw her before hurrying off in the opposite direction. Curious, Victoria checked the names by the buzzers and noted that of a well-known young homosexual. That very afternoon, the consul ordered Victoria's husband to resign, citing a messy extramarital affair that had in fact occurred some time before. Victoria and her husband went off to virtual exile, and to a misery relieved only by the news, some years later, that Goldilocks's secret homosexuality had finally become known, despite his cover-up marriage to a beautiful socialite. In the end, the same awful process in which he had collaborated had caught up with him too, forcing him to resign in dishonor. "Goldilocks" couldn't be a less likely film prospect, animated as it is by actions entirely unseen, and set against a more-than-decade-old backdrop that Hollywood was trying very hard to forget. It is simply Shaw at his storytelling best, trying to illumine a tortuous era in his past, and taking pleasure in his still strong powers.

Unlike Shaw's previous collection, the stories in *Love on a Dark Street* are not all set in Europe, but they do share a distinctly bitter view of love and life. Not only will accidents happen, but the world is full of bad people bringing those accidents down on good people, and as often as not, what drives the bad people is love in some twisted form. In "Noises in the City," a Shaw-like protagonist stops at a Greenwich Village bar for a nightcap and becomes the reluctant audience for a tortured, solitary drinker whose wife, it turns out, was raped and murdered. The assailant, a carpenter who had no criminal record, is being electrocuted up the river on this night. Grimly, the drinker checks his watch, makes a phone call, and comes back to report that the electrocution has just taken place. Shaken, the protagonist finds his way home to his safely sleeping wife and lies in bed listening to the noises of the city, newly aware of the madness they invoke.

Certainly Shaw found no grounds for optimism in his own life. In the winter of 1966, as he slogged through the writing of a screenplay of F. Scott Fitzgerald's *The Last Tycoon* for director Lester Cowan at MGM, Marian chose to take her newly honed producing skills from Paris to Broadway. In April *The New York Times* reported that "Marian Edwards, a former actress, wife of Irwin Shaw, the novelist, will make her debut as a Broadway producer in October with the $200,000 production of *Welcome to the Club.*" The comedy was the work of Clem Wood, the Shaws' good friend from Paris, whose debut novel by the same title would also appear in the fall. Wood explained his novel as "an attempt to write a comedy on the American race problem" during the American occupation in Japan; Wood himself had served in Japan as an infantry lieutenant.

Neither project came to pass, however. By December 1966, Cowan had scrapped Shaw's screenplay, telling gossip columnist Sheilah Graham: "I'm not satisfied with it. [Shaw] has made Stahr at the end too hard, too commercial. In the book he was efficient but a romantic idealist. Irwin is good where he sticks to the Fitzgerald book." More and more now, Shaw was being treated as a hack, and not a terribly good one at that. As for *Welcome to the Club,* it languished as a play prospect for lack of financing until it quietly expired. It did emerge as a film some years later, but that was of little help to Marian, whose late-blooming career as a theater producer never really recovered.

Journalist John Bainbridge came to Klosters at about this time to interview Shaw for a book about American expatriates in Europe, *Another Way of Living,* and his report remains a vivid verbal snapshot of the writer in middle age, toting up his debits and credits, ruminating on choices taken and not taken.

"There is no doubt," Bainbridge reported, "that Shaw is the number-one American in Klosters. If the postmaster or anybody else wants to locate any American who is visiting Klosters, or is expected, or has been there, Shaw is the authority consulted. The menu at the Chesa Grischuna, the most fashionable hotel in town, features a dish called Trout à la Shaw."

Bainbridge found Shaw affable and candid but also a bit gruff, even defensive. "Why do I live abroad?" Shaw echoed. "Everybody who comes to interview me here . . . makes that the first question. It's a sign of the political and cultural immaturity of the United States that this question is even asked. People have lived in countries other than their own since the beginning of civilization." To the question of why he'd come to live in Europe in the first place, Shaw offered the reply that had come to color all of his fiction: "By accident. People pretend that they do everything by design. I don't believe that. I mean, everybody, *everybody*, does everything by accident."

Shaw reported he was working seven days a week, despite his mother's protests. "She says, 'You're killing yourself with overwork.' And I have to keep reassuring her, 'Writing is not work. It's play. You do it for fun.'"

Inevitably, the conversation turned to the issue of taxes, and whether Shaw had moved to Europe to evade them. Shaw responded with the righteous indignation that the question always aroused, and pointed out that whatever advantages he had enjoyed in the 1950s were now a distant memory, thanks to the all-but-complete closing of the foreign-income loop-hole in 1963. An American claiming foreign residency in Europe now could claim an exemption only on the first $25,000 of his European-earned service income. As the result of tax agreements between the U.S. and most Western European nations, he also had to pay residence taxes to the country in which he claimed to live, which just about evened the score. Moreover, he couldn't deduct those Swiss taxes from his American income; and he couldn't deduct such expenses as secretaries, because they were paid for with untaxed income. Shaw could accept all that, he told Bainbridge, but here was the real rub: as a foreign resident, he couldn't vote in American elections, which amounted, he observed, to taxation without representation. "People always take the most venal view of your living here," he groused. "They always say it's a tax-dodge sanctuary. They say I'm just dying to live in America, but it's only to make money that I stay here. They don't know the facts."

So why did Shaw continue living in Switzerland? The clean air, the Alps, the helpfulness of the people. In New York, he observed, riders on a subway might witness two hoods beating up an old lady and do nothing about it. That, he said, would never happen here. And if Switzerland was more expensive than other European countries, there was good reason for that. "Prices are only low in backward countries," Shaw said. "The more civilized a country is, the more livable it is for the mass of its people, the higher the prices. Every time you go to a place that's cheap, you know the people are suffering. I don't like living in countries like that."

Swaddled as he was in comfort, suspicious as he was of what the sixties were stirring back home, the old lion still harbored a stubborn streak of social justice.

It was that streak which, in late May 1967, led Shaw to propose to filmmaker Jules Dassin that the two go to Israel, where war seemed about to erupt, and make a documentary.

The project was reminiscent, of course, of Shaw's book collaboration with Capa nearly two decades before. Dassin was an old friend, the brilliant director of such classic films as *Rififi* and *Never on Sunday*. Both men felt strongly about Israel's political situation, and for both, the prospect of filming history in the making soon seemed irresistible. Charged up, the new partners dropped all other commitments. Dassin recruited a camera crew of five in Paris, and Shaw set about getting permission for the team to enter the country. He had several good contacts, including Moshe Perlman, spokesman for the army under Moshe Dayan, who had become a Klosters regular during ski season. To Shaw's and Dassin's chagrin, however, permission failed to materialize until June 11—the day after the end of the Six Day War.

Swallowing their disappointment, the partners traveled from the Sinai Desert through Israel to Syria and Jordan, recording the aftermath of the war and the volatile peace negotiations between Israelis and Arabs. By the time they arrived in Jerusalem, a festive air prevailed, with such Jewish-American celebrities as Danny Kaye, Leon Uris and Leonard Bernstein on hand. Leon Davidoff, an affluent American Jew living in Mexico who had become an advisor and friend to several high-ranking Israeli politicians, arrived with seven Mexican journalists and remembers Shaw and Dassin vividly. "Jules and Irwin were like fire and water," Davidoff says. "Jules was the aggressive one, trying to do everything at once. He wanted to rent helicopters, and wasted time going from general to general trying to procure them. He wanted to film 150,000 Jews going on a holy day to the Wailing Wall, but the authorities wouldn't let him." So Dassin persuaded Jacques Graubart, the Belgian diamond merchant who had also rushed to the scene, to accompany him with a hidden camera. One night in Jerusalem, Davidoff threw a huge party for all the celebrities. "My stars were Dassin and Irwin," recalls Davidoff. "Then I invited Leon Uris. His wife got very excited at the prospect of meeting Irwin, but Uris was furious. He felt *he* was the better writer, and that Irwin was a hack."

Out of such a chaotic and unhappy trip came a fairly abortive documentary. Back home, in an effort to imbue it with an arty appeal, Dassin christened it *Rehearsal?* and intercut its journalistic scenes with footage of a ballet rehearsal, "to illustrate the title as well as the theme that this so-called small war could be a rehearsal for a bigger war," he told a reporter. By June 1968, when the film opened briefly in New York, Dassin had come to his senses, removed the ballet scenes and slapped on the more sober title of *Survival 1967*. Renata Adler, then working as a film critic for *The New York Times*, was less than impressed. "*Survival 1967* got to Israel on the seventh day of the six-day war and looks it," she declared. "Like some veteran who arrived at the front when the guns were still and who feels compelled for life to boast about what a brave war he spent, the movie keeps climbing truculently onto your barstool and being obnoxious. Missing the action seems to have broken the spirit of the really distinguished writer, Irwin Shaw, and the director, Jules Dassin, entirely." Adler went on to brand the film poor propaganda and poor reporting, a mélange of fuzzy interviews and "contrived, unmoving defensive travelogue, tacked on to a war."

Mercifully, the film died a quick death.

In the fall of 1967 Shaw's life began to change dramatically—the result of accidents, he would have said, that no one could predict or control.

He came to New York alone on a routine trip, to discuss with Ross Claiborne and Don Fine the big novel he hoped would redeem him at Delacorte after the mediocre sales of *Voices of a Summer Day*; to see old friends and take in the pleasures of New York in October; to attend a few parties. One of those was a dinner on October 24, in the Hunt Room of "21," to celebrate the opening of the movie *Camelot*. The dinner was hosted by Alan Jay Lerner, who had written the show's legendary lyrics, and his fifth wife, the much younger and quite beautiful Karen Gundersen. Lerner didn't know until the day of the party that Shaw was in town, and then invited him on the spur of the moment. "Alan said, 'How would you like to meet my old friend, Irwin Shaw?' " recalls Karen Lerner. "I said, 'Fine, but this is a seated, boy-girl-boy-girl dinner, so we'll need an extra woman. Who can we get?' " Lerner had no suggestions. "So I thought, Well, I can get my old roommate Bodie Nielsen. I called her at about five-thirty that afternoon, and she showed up in a long white dress looking great."

Lerner gave Bodie the choice of sitting next to Irwin Shaw—whom neither woman had yet met—or Frank Sinatra. Bodie chose Shaw. By the time the appetizers were served, the two were deep in spirited conversation.

Surprising as the match would seem to many of Shaw's friends, there was much about Bodie that appealed strongly and immediately to Shaw. At twenty-nine, she seemed invitingly young to a man in his mid-fifties. Like many of the women Shaw had pursued extramaritally, she was blond—it was almost as if blond hair itself represented extramarital sex. Certainly it indicated WASPdom, which had always been a draw: of Shaw's long line of lovers, hardly any was Jewish. Bodie was also curvaceous and

statuesque, several inches taller than Shaw, and taller still than Marian—
an intriguing novelty. In these and other ways, in fact, Bodie represented
a mirror opposite of Marian, which was exactly what Shaw seemed to want.

Unlike Marian, Bodie had grown up in an East Coast world of privilege and private schools. Her family was Danish, with aristocratic roots.
Her father ran a transatlantic shipping company and had brought up his
three daughters in a large, comfortable house in New Canaan, Connecticut, with summers spent in Denmark. Bodie was sent to Chatham Hall in
Virginia, where she excelled in riding, then to Vassar. These credentials,
however, told only half the story. Bodie was the black sheep of her family,
both liberated and literary. Early on, she took a special interest in writers.
Assigned at Vassar to shepherd the massive A. J. Liebling around campus
during a speaking engagement, she ended up holding long, boozy discussions with him and then having to fend him off at the end of the evening.
She became editor in chief of *The Vassar Review,* and at twenty wrote an
article for *The New York Times Magazine* titled "Vassar '58 Looks at the
World '58."

Upon graduating, Bodie moved into a spacious Manhattan apartment
with three roommates and began working as an editor for *Interiors,* a
prominent trade magazine of the decorating business. By age twenty-six she
was the magazine's managing editor, sharing a smaller apartment with
Karen Gundersen and leading a fast-paced social life of East Side parties
and older boyfriends. She liked to drink; she had a caustic sense of humor.
Somehow she also found time to read voraciously and acquire command
of five languages. She was, in short, the perfect date for a hard-drinking
writer: striking, indefatigable, full of fun, and able to hold her own at any
literary round table.

Bodie, for her part, was fascinated by Shaw the first night she met him,
by his talent and celebrity, by his own quick wit, by the sexy incongruity
between his Brooklyn longshoreman's appearance and his agile mind. But
despite an intimate dinner with Shaw three nights later at Le Pavillon, she
entertained no thought of becoming his next New York girlfriend and felt
content to write off her time with him as a short—unconsummated—
adventure. And there, indeed, is where the relationship might have remained, if Shaw's marriage had not at that time been collapsing in the wake
of Marian's disclosure that she had been carrying on a longtime affair with
Jean Daninos.

The accumulated baggage of a twenty-eight-year marriage would not
be sorted out overnight. More than two years of anger and legal threats
would pass before a divorce settlement was reached, but the confrontations
and negotiations would accomplish in detail what Marian's admission had
established in broad stroke. Shaw's marriage was over—and in meeting
Bodie, a dramatically new life would soon begin.

PART IV

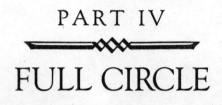

FULL CIRCLE

CHAPTER NINETEEN

As Shaw himself would put it in the introduction to his career-capping anthology of stories, *Five Decades,* he had always been a product of his times. Left-winger in the thirties, patriot in the forties, Red Scare–stung expatriate in the fifties, he had been tossed by the changing tides and then recorded them in his fiction. His stories and novels were soundings, taken from his own life or from the lives of those around him. If you were a fan you felt that writing had come to define a generation in all its evolving attitudes and expectations. If you weren't, you saw in his work a politics of convenience, and fiction that for all its craft must therefore be commercial literature. What the critics never properly considered was that the changes in Shaw's politics and literary perspective were not some calculated effort to keep in step with his times in order to sell books—they were his *life.* True as this had been in earlier decades, it would, in a subtler sense, be no less so in the late sixties and early seventies. The very fabric of American society seemed to be unraveling. Shaw's life was unraveling too, and as in the past, his personal crises and triumphs would end up, transmuted, at the heart of his fiction.

In America, the winter of 1967–1968 came to seem a dress rehearsal for the nightmarish spring and summer that would follow. Already, the so-called summer of love of 1967 had made national news of the Haight-Ashbury hippie movement; drugs, psychedelic music and the new sexual freedom, together with a burgeoning women's movement, were altering the cultural landscape. The escalating war in Vietnam was causing student marches on the Pentagon and campus riots around the country that would lead to the Columbia sit-ins and, later, Kent State. In Vietnam itself, the Tet offensive in late January 1968 made painfully clear how long the war would now stretch on and led President Johnson to abandon his hopes of reelection. In the South, civil rights protesters were gathering the momentum that would provoke a lone assassin to murder Martin Luther King, Jr., in April. Two months later, in the midst of a bitter three-way Democratic primary campaign, Robert Kennedy would be assassinated too. In August would come the riots of Chicago; in November this dark season would culminate with the election, by a .7-percent popular vote margin, of Richard Nixon as president.

From Klosters, where Shaw spent most of that winter, the headlines must have seemed unreal. Still, having always taken a passionate interest in the news of the day, he found himself galvanized by the prospect of trying to explain, in strictly allegorical terms, how the country had come to this terrible impasse. For years he had toyed with the idea of writing a novel as big and sweeping as *The Young Lions.* But only now did a story begin to emerge, of two brothers growing up in America's postwar period with lives, like those of the characters in *The Young Lions,* intertwined with the history of their era, from 1945 clear up to 1968. Not since *The Troubled Air* had Shaw even attempted to write a "big picture" book. The focus of the intervening novels had narrowed, from families against the backdrop of contemporary history to families isolated and divided, mourning small tragedies over large glasses of whiskey. Now, in *Rich Man, Poor Man,* he would broaden his scope again. That winter, dogged by the steadily diminishing success of his recent novels, Shaw settled down to work in earnest on the book that would, to his own astonishment, become a publishing phenomenon and introduce his name to the very generations engaged in such perplexing hysteria back in the States.

The winter of 1967–1968 was also the winter that Shaw's marriage fell apart.

The way Shaw would tell it to friends over the next rocky years, the breakup had begun abruptly over a lunch in which Marian dramatically announced the news of her affair with Jean Daninos. While she might consent to prolong the marriage until Adam got settled in college, she added, she was hereby calling an end to physical relations with her husband.

Shaw was shocked—and furious. The fact that he himself had engaged in dozens, if not scores, of extramarital affairs over the years seemed not to mitigate the severity of Marian's transgression in the least. In his frequent retelling of the story, Shaw would never waver in his righteous indignation, and when friends gently invoked the notion of a double standard, Shaw would hear none of it. Again and again, he would grow red-faced with fury. "I can understand that she might want to have an affair," he would say, not very convincingly. "But right here in Klosters? That's what I can't accept."

Unquestionably, Shaw's anguish was genuine and deep. But mixed in with it was wounded pride. On countless winter evenings in Klosters, Jean Daninos had been among the guests at Chalet Mia for dinner, an unremarkable man who had drunk Shaw's wine and laughed at his jokes. It was not only infuriating but also embarrassing to Shaw that this was the man with whom his wife had taken up. Far worse, Daninos had apparently grown accustomed to staying openly with Marian in Chalet Mia when Shaw was away. Shaw had been the classic cuckold.

How had he been so blind? And how could Marian have done this to him?

In *Evening in Byzantium,* the thinly disguised indictment of Marian that would be published a few years later, the Shaw-like protagonist learns of his wife's long-standing affair with a Daninos-like character not over a lunch but from a female friend. The friend confides that some time before, she invited Penelope and little Bertie Folsom to a fateful dinner. When the two became lovers as a result of it, Folsom took to sending her a dozen roses each year on the anniversary of the dinner. The female friend finds the custom both odious and smug, and is finally annoyed enough to report it to Jesse Craig. According to Bodie, the roses story was a true one; the recipient was a friend of the Shaws, Seusel de Dietrich.

However it became known to Shaw, the affair with Daninos was likely just one factor in a complex situation. Another was Shaw's drinking, and Marian's hardening attitude toward it.

Larry Collins, who had vowed upon first meeting Shaw to write his own big book and spend a writer's winter in Klosters, reached his goal just in time to be a reluctant ringside witness to the breakup of the Shaws' marriage. Having published *Is Paris Burning?* with Dominique Lapierre—for which he relied heavily on Shaw for descriptions of Liberation Day—he had now just finished a biography of a bullfighter, *Or I'll Dress You in Mourning.* In September 1967, he came to Klosters with his wife and their newborn first child. Almost as soon as they arrived, the Collinses were caught up in the daily battles between Irwin and Marian.

"Marian talked to my wife all the time," Collins recalls. "She was terribly concerned about Irwin's drinking. She was being a policeman. And there's no doubt that Irwin resented it. I think, quite frankly, that when Marian revealed she'd had an affair with Jean Daninos it became an excuse for Irwin." One night that winter, the Shaws attended a dinner party at the chalet the Collinses had rented a short distance from town. At the end of the evening, Shaw insisted on driving home, and was stopped by the local police, who made Marian drive the rest of the way. "Irwin was humiliated and furious," Collins recalls. "But then he went down to get something more to drink. And Marian was saying, 'Come on, Irwin, enough.' "

The Shaws were still together in the spring, when they moved into a new apartment in Paris at 185 rue de Grenelle, on the Left Bank near the Eiffel Tower. Together with the Joneses, they witnessed the student uprisings in May and tried to understand the anger that fueled them. Under the surface, though, the marriage had reached a stalemate.

It was against this backdrop that Shaw arrived at Bodie Nielsen's New York apartment on East 52nd Street on Halloween night, 1968. Fully a year had passed since their casual meeting. Shaw hadn't bothered to write or

call, and Bodie hadn't expected to see him again. She was still involved
with a man she had known the year before, and if Shaw had not seemed
so charming, standing in her doorway to whisk her off for a night on the
town, she might have turned him away. "But Irwin," as Bodie puts it, "was
just sort of an irresistible force."

That first evening, both Shaw and Bodie realized how excited they
were to see each other again. Cut loose from his marriage, Shaw found
himself appreciating Bodie not only as a prospective lover but also as a new
companion. As their affair began in earnest, they spent every evening of
the next month together, dining at the elegant restaurants Shaw loved.
Despite the seeming delicacy of his position, with divorce proceedings so
probable, Shaw proudly introduced Bodie to longtime friends; in matters
of the heart, and flesh, he had always done exactly what his brimming
emotions dictated. Shaw's friends, to be sure, were long accustomed to his
penchant for arriving at parties with women other than Marian, and the
only real snub came from Liz Weicker. "Oh, how nice," she told Bodie
when introduced. "We always like Irwin's girls."

Along with a quick wit and strong physical attraction, Shaw and Bodie
shared an excitement about politics and the arts that he had always found
lacking in his wife. Bodie would argue for Shakespeare's historical plays,
Shaw for the tragedies. Bodie would argue for Auden, Shaw for Yeats.
About his marriage, Shaw spoke dismissively. Marian had been a chorus
girl when he found her, he said. Within a year of marrying her, he had
realized he didn't love her, but loyalty had bound him to her. He certainly
didn't love her now, he said. She was pretentious; all she cared about was
going to the hairdresser, buying the next dress. By now, he said, they led
utterly separate lives, and it was only a matter of time before they divorced.

Acknowledging to herself that she was falling for a man twenty-five
years her senior, Bodie felt only one cause for concern as November
unfolded: Shaw's complex bond with Adam. That month Shaw got a
painful call from the University of Pennsylvania, where Adam was now in
his first year of an accelerated three-year program. Apparently Adam and
a girlfriend had been walking together when another student whistled at
the girlfriend. Adam had merely glowered for the moment, but he later
procured the student's name and dorm room number and went over to
beat the boy up. The student now lay seriously injured in the university
clinic, and Adam risked being expelled. By the time his father arrived for
consultations with the university psychologist, Adam had talked his way
out of expulsion, but the damage was done. So hurtful was the news, so
jarring to the picture Shaw clung to of Adam as the perfect son, that he
seemed to need to deny the whole experience. Instead of having a serious
father-son talk, he sat in strong silence over dinner, drinking without
surcease. Back in New York, Shaw recounted the episode as if Adam had
been maligned and the injured student had been the malefactor. For the

first time, Bodie sensed how unrealistic Shaw's view of his son was, and how destructive it might be to her own relationship. A more positive result was that a brooding concern with irrational violence would begin to color Shaw's work: not by chance would one of the two sons in *Rich Man, Poor Man* be characterized by outbreaks of violent temper.

During this time a conflict with her editor induced Bodie to leave her job at *Interiors*. But having a job suddenly didn't seem to matter anymore. In the last days before Shaw's return to Klosters, he and Bodie went to a boxing match at Madison Square Garden, courtesy of Mike Burke, Shaw's longtime friend who was now the Garden's manager. They went to Sardi's with actor James Mason. They went to Elaine's for dinner with Gay and Nan Talese, and sat in on the poker game that had become a minor legend at the venerable Upper East Side literary hangout. Gambling was illegal, of course, so the players traded IOUs, to be paid up later. To Shaw's great delight, Bodie turned out to be a ringer, by the end of the evening sweeping up chits for hundreds of dollars and adding to his attraction for her.

As he bid her farewell on December 3, Shaw felt strongly enough about Bodie to announce that he wanted to spend the rest of his life with her, no matter what happened when he got home. That he was in love with her seemed indisputable; whether or not he would have left Marian without the confluence of other factors is considerably less clear. He had been in love before and stayed married. Never before, though, had Marian insisted on maintaining a lover of her own: Daninos, no longer living at Chalet Mia with her, nevertheless remained close by in his own Klosters chalet, and the two saw each other in Paris.

It was a situation that both angered and depressed Shaw as he resumed his Alpine life. Through January of 1969, he dispatched several glum letters to Bodie. He had not written a chapter of his new novel since August, he reported, and couldn't seem to get back to work now. He went skiing every day and indulged in the endless round of parties that punctuated Klosters's winter season. He was bluff and hearty but not happy; it was not the same thing. He missed Bodie's mischievous smile, her sharp mind and biting wit, and the evenings of drinking and lovemaking in her deli-supplied apartment.

Heartsick and vulnerable, Shaw seized the opportunity when Marian left for Paris to arrange a rendezvous in St. Moritz with Bodie, who'd intended already to go skiing in nearby St. Anton. At the last minute, Shaw decided to leave a day earlier than planned and meet Bodie in St. Anton. He sent a telegram to alert her, but to the wrong hotel. Meanwhile, Bodie sent off a telegram to Chalet Mia to confirm that she would meet Shaw the next day at the Palace Hotel in St. Moritz. Halfway to St. Anton by car, Shaw turned back in new-falling snow to get his powder skis. When he walked into Chalet Mia, there was Marian, unexpectedly returned from

Paris, in receipt of Bodie's telegram. Despite her relationship with Daninos, she was furiously jealous—so much so that she had placed the telegram atop Shaw's rough manuscript for *Rich Man, Poor Man* and stabbed a knife as deeply as she could into the stacked pages.

The St. Moritz rendezvous, when it did come to pass, was brief because of Shaw's impending birthday: the date by now had become a cause for townwide celebrations in Klosters, and Shaw had to preside. With Marian due to leave town again, however, Shaw suggested Bodie come to Klosters the next week. Bodie returned to St. Anton for the interim—and blithely resumed the affair she'd already begun there with another man. When Shaw went down to the Klosters train station to welcome her, he immediately sensed the truth. "He took one look at me," Bodie recalls, "and shouted, 'You've been up all night with someone else!'"

Shaw was hurt, but fascinated. For the first time in his life, he was an old man with a younger woman who had the upper hand. It was oddly liberating; it was exciting. That winter, "small injuries" became the code phrase for infidelities, part joke, part reminder of the new order of things.

Over the next three days, Shaw introduced Bodie to all the charms of Klosters: meals at the Chesa; skiing (as in poker, Bodie proved the more adept of the two); and Chalet Mia (though Bodie stayed at the Silvretta). Then together they drove to Geneva, where Shaw sadly put Bodie on a plane home.

The plan now was for Shaw to fly to New York in early April. In daily letters and phone calls, he avowed his intent of making a final break with Marian at that point, of bringing in the lawyers. Meanwhile, he admitted to spending most nights at the Chesa's bar, getting drunk and holding earnest, rambling conversations with the waiters. Only half joking, he asked if anyone was criticizing him in New York for his actions. No matter, he declared when Bodie replied that no one was: he was condemning himself fervently enough these days to make up for that. He was working badly, skiing badly, drinking too much each night and starting every morning with a vow to go on the wagon, only to start in on Bloody Marys and white wine by noon. When he was young, he rued—and weighed only 182 pounds, all muscle, no fat—he had worked like a horse, drunk little, thought the world could be bettered, and confidently presumed he could best any rival at anything. Where had those days gone?

As if in some life-sized Shaw story, accident intervened days before Shaw's scheduled departure. Out on the slopes of Madrisa with Bob Parrish after a morning at the typewriter, Shaw skied into a snow-covered tree stump and tore his Achilles tendon. It was a painful injury that put him in bed for days, and Marian, back from Paris, rose to the occasion. Ignoring for the moment the gossip of Bodie's Klosters visit, she tended to Shaw's needs with nurselike devotion. Her husband, half impressed, half exasperated, wrote Bodie that Marian had always acquired a sort of beatific

The Chesa Grischuna, Klosters, Shaw's favorite haunt.

Chalet Mia, Klosters, named for Marian, Irwin and Adam and built in 1956.

Marlon Brando in *The Young Lions*, 1958. He and Shaw almost came to blows over Brando's portrayal of Christian Diestl. (20th Century–Fox)

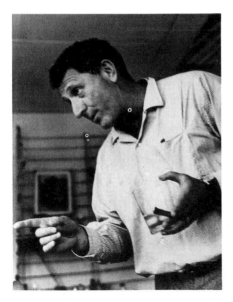

Shaw on the set of the film he coproduced, *In the French Style*, and with *French Style* director and coproducer Robert Parrish. (Robert Parrish Collection)

With Jigee Viertel. (Robert Parrish Collection)

Peter Viertel and Deborah Kerr. (Robert Parrish Collection)

"Famille Shaw" in Klosters, late 1950s. (Robert Parrish Collection)

Shaw with Marian on a trip to Yugoslavia, 1961. (Harry Ransom Humanities Research Center, University of Texas at Austin)

Shaw in the early sixties: in his
prime and about to shock the
publishing world once again.
(Pat York)

Paris, 1974, at the Brasserie Lipp.
(*Left to right*) Gloria Jones, Bodie
Nielsen, Jim Jones, Lauren Bacall,
Shaw, Ann and Art Buchwald.
(Gloria Jones Collection)

Literary eminences. *Above:* Jim Jones, Willie Morris and Shaw in East Hampton, 1976. (Nancy Crampton) *Below:* William Styron, Shaw and Jones in Paris, 1976. (Michel Ginfray, Gamma-Liaison)

Gloria Jones and Adam Shaw in Bridgehampton. (Gloria Jones Collection)

Shaw on his balcony in Klosters, 1983. (Francine Schoeller)

The aging lion in his garden, Southampton, 1981. "I seem to have sailed into an area of calm at last." (© Nancy Rica Schiff 1981)

grace when he was sick. His illness made her feel useful. As it did Clara Delaney, the old director's wife in *Two Weeks in Another Town*, it gave her a rare sense of power.

With neither Shaw nor Marian willing to abandon their extramarital ties, the truce soon collapsed and the marriage edged further toward formal separation. In early June, sporting an anvil-like shoe on his injured foot, Shaw left Klosters to meet Bodie in Cannes, where the two boarded the luxury liner *Raffaello* and settled in for the week-long crossing to New York—though in separate cabins to observe some decorum.

There was much talk en route of what terms Shaw would offer Marian. By Swiss law, he stood some chance of skewering Marian in court for the Daninos affair and thus having to pay her as little as $10,000. Shaw was certainly furious enough to consider that course of action, but for Adam's sake he hoped not to pursue it. He did intend to keep Chalet Mia. Marian, for her part, had announced she was compiling for the divorce proceedings a list of every woman Shaw had slept with throughout her marriage to him. Already the list had become a source of endless speculation and amusement in Klosters. Who was on it? How many dozens of names? And if so many beautiful women were named, was it more embarrassing to be *in*cluded—or *ex*cluded? "That list is a low blow," Shaw told Bodie, both flattered and alarmed. "After all, there're *married* women on it."

Almost as soon as they arrived in New York, Shaw received another deeply disturbing bulletin about Adam. Depressed by his parents' imminent divorce, and siding with his father as he always had, Adam had had a furious argument with his mother at the apartment in Paris. The argument ended with Adam's picking up a knife and Marian's locking herself in a bedroom to call friends for help. In a battery of long-distance calls, Shaw made plans to return to Europe, first to Paris to see Adam, then to Klosters. Resolutely, he decided to have Bodie join him in Klosters too.

Shaw flew back first, in late July. Two weeks later Bodie joined him; her decision brought the relationship squarely in the open and made clear that Shaw's marriage was indeed about to end.

From Paris the two drove south through the French countryside, staying overnight in Beaune, continuing to Zurich for a second night, and finally to Klosters. The trip, taken either south to Klosters or north to Paris, would become a signature of their time together, and of Shaw's life in these years: sybaritic, celebratory, the happy frolics of a writer in middle age who had decided that the gustatory pleasures of Europe, shared with a young, brainy blonde, were at least as important as anything he had to write.

With Marian in Paris, summer in Klosters seemed an idyll at first. Bodie stayed at the Chesa, but spent her days and evenings meeting the many friends who had begun to come in the off-season largely because Shaw did. The Parrishes were there, as were Shaw's good friends Geza and

Ann Korvin. Martha Gellhorn appeared, having set out to walk across the whole of Switzerland. Peter and Deborah Viertel were in the large wooden house they had built on an evergreen-studded hillside south of town. Salka Viertel was there too, having moved permanently to Klosters and established a court not so different from the one she'd had in Santa Monica. Regularly now, her longtime friend Greta Garbo took an apartment in town. Garbo would wear hats or sunglasses in the hope of not being recognized when she took to the streets, and she took long Alpine hikes on which Bodie began to accompany her. "We'd all go to Salka's place," recalls Parrish. "You'd look at the window, and there would be Greta, peeking in to be sure no one else was there. There were very few people she would see." Even to Peter Viertel, who had known her from his childhood, Garbo held an enduring fascination. "There was something about her; you couldn't keep your eyes off her, really. She was still strikingly beautiful—and very, very private. She cooked her own food, very rarely went out at all, except on her walks; liked to go to bed early."

Another Klosterite that summer was Gore Vidal, drawn in part by his own curiosity about Garbo. Vidal and Shaw had a surprising rapport, despite Vidal's tendency to look down his nose at a writer the likes of Shaw. Among other things, they shared a healthy liking for Dezaley wine: one night he and Shaw and Bodie together managed to polish off nine bottles of the stuff amid much laughter and political debate. Another night the three drove to dinner in Davos and emerged drunk enough to make the question of who would drive a real conundrum. Vidal finally insisted on taking the wheel, only to drive off the road on a hairpin curve. "Oh God," he said without missing a beat, "let's hope they don't print our obituaries in alphabetical order."

Vidal too had taken critical knocks not much less severe than Shaw's. "My reviews were just as bad as his," Vidal recalls, "but Irwin used to talk about his too much, he was very bitter about them. I'd tell him we just have to shrug them off, because there aren't any critics today, no one's keeping score; the last critic of any consequence was Edmund Wilson. But Irwin did take it seriously. He put a lot of it down to living abroad, he felt the critics resented that. I pointed out that Eliot and James had lived abroad and their reputations had only increased, but he couldn't be persuaded."

Late in August, Adam arrived, having spent the summer in London. It was the first time Bodie had met him, and the two were wary of each other. Bodie couldn't help but begrudge Adam's intrusion into her time with Shaw. Adam just as deeply resented this new woman in his father's life. Within days Shaw admitted to Bodie that Adam had reacted negatively toward her. It was a standoff that left him confused and torn.

Somehow despite the distractions and tensions, Shaw managed to stick to his early-morning writing routine, turning out as many as thirty pages a day to complete *Rich Man, Poor Man* by mid-October so that Delacorte could publish it the following summer.

In essence, the tale was as well worn as the Altsheller Civil War series of Shaw's childhood: the two Jordache brothers so opposite in nature, one a frustrated rebel who takes a low road of petty crime, the other a model student who becomes a perfect capitalist, scheming his way to great financial success. (Shaw later confessed he'd found the family name in a German phone book, only to learn after he'd written the book that the name was Romanian.) The novel's fast-paced events unfold against a thinly shaded postwar backdrop, with mentions of returning soldiers, the McCarthy years, the evolution of shopping malls, women's liberation and the Vietnam War.

The more intriguing aspect of *Rich Man, Poor Man*—and perhaps the underlying reason for its immense popularity with readers—is that one Jordache brother isn't simply virtuous while the other is evil. Each brother, in fact, tries to make the right moral choice at every turn. The choices are different only because the brothers' characters and circumstances are different. Morality, the novel argues, is shaped not by society but by the awesome influence of family. Here, as in his early novels, Shaw was making the careful choice to tell all sides, and to sympathize with each—thereby, to his mind, holding up an unblemished mirror to life.

Shaw's preoccupation with family had infused all of his novels. Now, as the complicated bonds of his own family appeared to be fraying— roughly fulfilling, as if by prophecy, the story line of *Lucy Crown*—he wanted to analyze, in an allegorical way, how one family would weather the years with two such different offspring. "All of literature comes out of the family—Oedipus, Hamlet—even Genesis is a family story," he would muse to an interviewer years later. "Storytellers always revert to the family—the people we're born from and the people born to us. It's impossible to exhaust."

The new note struck in *Rich Man, Poor Man* was one drawn from the calamitous events of the day, and from Shaw's own disturbing experiences with Adam. Violence, random and deadly, had come to exert an appallingly pervasive influence in the world. It was, Shaw sadly felt, the single most important societal change of the postwar period. In one sense, violence struck at you blindly from the outside world; thus the accidents of fate that Shaw's characters could expect might include muggings and senseless murder. In a deeper sense, random violence had to begin where everything else began: in the family.

Thus it is that Tom Jordache, rejected early on by his parents, nurtures a violent streak that shapes his morality and colors all his actions, while Rudy, the adored model son, grows up with no violence in his character at all, only the smooth ambition of the all-American boy. As the novel unfolds, each brother makes his choices accordingly. When Tom learns his sister has been sleeping with the local rich man on the hill, he vengefully places a burning cross on the man's front lawn, thus bringing on his own exile from the town. Rudy chooses to ignore his sister's indiscretion and let the rich man take a patronly interest in him. As a sparring partner in a boxing gym, Tom lays into the arrogant local contender, not caring that he'll lose his job when he does, because the contender has cruelly victimized the gym's aging manager in the ring. Rudy takes a dreary job after college in his town's department store, knowing he can manipulate the store's curmudgeonly owner to invest in his plans to build a lucrative shopping mall. Tom, of course, is the underdog one roots for, especially as his moral choices begin to seem more admirable than his brother's: when his father parts with $5,000 in precious savings to get Tom off the hook in a paternity suit, only to die soon after as a lonely suicide, Tom blackmails a blue-blooded member of the gym whom he's caught stealing wallets, then makes the already wealthy Rudy take the money as a payback on his father's behalf. Rudy, however, invests the money for his brother and eventually returns to him the much-increased sum. Cold and efficient, Rudy nonetheless is honest and well intentioned—he never does break the law in his climb to the top—and that, in the hands of a master storyteller, provides the balance that makes *Rich Man, Poor Man* so engrossing.

  Both brothers, sooner or later, get derailed by women. Tom marries a floozy who drags down his boxing career. Rudy carefully avoids getting involved with girls on his way up but finally marries a dipsomaniac who ruins his political career. The latter goes on to bring about Tom's death at the end of the novel. After a penultimate scene of seeming resolution—the two brothers reconciled on Tom's charter yacht on the French Riviera—Rudy's wife sneaks off board for a drink and gets in trouble with a violent type. Tom rescues her; a mechanical failure forces the happy group to stay dockside a few extra days; and the violent type thus has time to take his revenge.

  Throughout the novel, as its title suggests, both brothers grapple, in one way or another, with the all-pervasive issue of money. Rudy's moral choices are made in the pursuit of it; Tom's choices are forced by the lack of it. Each brother, in his way, seems to master money as the big book winds to its close, Rudy by abandoning his hubris, Tom by investing his onetime stake in the charter yacht that makes him truly happy. But then comes the accident to shatter dreams and rule the day. Life, as Shaw again makes clear, tends to end in such unforeseen tragedies. Still, he implies, we must make the best moral choices we can, based on the way we've been shaped. The only alternative is surrender.

  From first page to last, *Rich Man, Poor Man* is fluid storytelling. From a literary standpoint, it admittedly lacks the chiseled descriptions of Shaw's early stories, the carefully worked passages of *The Young Lions* and *The Troubled Air* or *Two Weeks in Another Town*. Nor does the novel seem to resonate with parallels to Shaw's own life. A few settings—an apartment in Greenwich Village, the boat scenes on the Riviera—offer a grainy stroke, here and there, against the gloss. Otherwise, the story unfolds with seamless detachment. The novel's careful moral balance between the Jordache brothers, however, and its unflagging narrative drive distinguish it at least as an extraordinary commercial novel.

So smoothly professional is *Rich Man, Poor Man* that one has to wonder if Shaw, embarrassed by the failure of his first book for Delacorte, deliberately set out to write a novel so all-American, so down the middle, that its financial success would be assured and thus fulfill his side of the bargain in his high-paying two-novel contract. Certainly *Rich Man, Poor Man* stands as an antithesis to *Voices of a Summer Day*, not only in its heft but also in its remoteness from the man who wrote it. By all accounts, however, Shaw was as cautiously proud of his new work as any he had written. He did encourage Bodie to read the manuscript and make copy-editing suggestions, and he accepted most of the many minor changes she proposed. Then, without further deliberation, he sent the book off.

The day after Shaw finished *Rich Man, Poor Man*, he met with a divorce lawyer and learned that Marian would be naming Bodie the corespondent in her divorce suit. She also wanted a considerable settlement.

Still sanguine, Shaw took Bodie to Paris for a post-book holiday. Again there were dozens of friends for her to meet. Chief among them were the Joneses, who had heard with some uneasiness the details of Shaw's collapsing relationship with Marian. Gloria in particular was nervous at meeting Bodie. Instinctively sympathetic to Marian as the edged-out wife, she felt insecure too about this younger blonde who had moved with such aplomb into a married man's life. To her own surprise, she and Bodie got along well, discovering they shared the same salty humor and joie de vivre. The two couples quickly formed a rare bond of true four-way affection and respect. Over the next half-dozen years, the times they spent together would be among their happiest.

By now the Joneses' Sunday-night poker games had become an institution at their rambling home on the Île St.-Louis, and both Bodie and Shaw enthusiastically joined in. Regulars included Bernie Frizell, the NBC correspondent Shaw had known since college, who had just walked away from his career to write a novel; and Jack Egle, a friend of Jones's who ran the International Student Exchange in Paris. Paul Jenkins, the abstract painter, would occasionally play, as would Françoise Sagan and Sydney Chaplin, while onlookers included artist Addie Herder, Clem and Jessie Wood, James Baldwin, publisher Eugene Braun-Munk, and Claude Dauphin and his wife, Ruda, who lived next door. The group would settle in to play after copious rounds of drinks and an inevitable spaghetti dinner—the custom had begun because Sunday was the cook's night off—and a certain boisterousness could always be counted on. "Gloria was a large part of why the games were special, she was so lively," recalls Frizell. "Irwin by this point in the evening would have consumed great quantities of booze and be rather quiet at the poker table. He was an earnest player, pretty good—not *that* good—but very good-natured and observant. By the end of the evening, he'd be utterly tanked but still stand up on his own two feet and still be observant."

By day Shaw and Jones would work—Shaw on correspondence during his Paris trips—while Gloria and Bodie went off to the races at Longchamp, St.-Cloud and Auteuil. With the rest of Paris, they would play the *tierce*, the three-way betting ticket purchased at any Pari-Mutuel Urbain on the day of a race. Shaw scoffed at the whole business until Bodie won—then began playing himself, though the sight of him trying to master the simple arithmetic involved was enough to send his friends into gales of laughter.

To maintain the pretense of separation required by the impending divorce case, Bodie stayed that fall at Addie Herder's apartment. But she was at Shaw's apartment every day, having drinks on the terrace as the shadow of the Eiffel Tower inched across it in the late afternoon. Bernie Frizell, for one, sensed that they had a strong and happy relationship but that Bodie, younger and brash-spirited, was in the dominant position. "Once we were at Irwin's talking about chess, which I'm very fond of and rather good at," Frizell recalls. "And Bodie said to me to amuse Irwin: 'Bernie, if you teach me how to play chess, I'll teach you how to fuck.'"

By mid-December Shaw was back in Klosters, sifting through revisions of *Rich Man, Poor Man* a final time before entrusting it to Bodie to take to New York. As further insurance, Shaw had Bodie take a Swissair flight piloted by Don Dixon, a relatively new drinking buddy who by now had made it a point to seek out Shaw in his down time between international flights. Dixon was a tall, genial bachelor, considerably younger than Shaw and not the least bit literary. Dixon had a masculine charm, however, and took great pleasure in serving as the Chesa's most visible Lothario, a role Shaw admired. Among these, Dixon was a favorite. As a tribute, Shaw later shaped his novel *Nightwork* around an ex-pilot forced to stop flying because of a loss of peripheral vision. Dixon had the same problem and eventually was forced to retire because of it.

The next act of Klosters's high domestic drama played before a local justice of the peace on December 23, 1969. Marian had arrived from Paris a few days before. She had tried to persuade Shaw to let her stay—alone—in Chalet Mia, but Shaw wouldn't be budged and she had had to resign herself to a hotel room. With holiday skiers streaming into town in droves, the Shaws aired their formal views in a modest municipal courtroom to gain a legal separation. The next day Shaw wrote to Bodie in New York that she had a poorer but happier friend. The terms were killing, but with any luck he would hang on to Chalet Mia, which was his greatest concern.

Within a week the provisional agreement collapsed amid bitter arguing. Feeling abandoned by both her husband and her son, Marian raised the stakes, demanding half her husband's estate. Also, she wanted the house—immediately. To help win her terms, she had her lawyer hire a detective. After a night on the job, the detective returned breathlessly to report that a woman had parked her car in front of Chalet Mia and gone in for the night. The woman, it turned out, was Fedora, the cook. Still, as a precaution, Shaw instructed Nielsen to send her letters sealed in envelopes addressed to Peter Viertel.

This was the start of the great Shaw standoff in Klosters, the wrathful, ongoing donnybrook that would transform the town's main street into what the regulars jokingly called High Noon, and the town itself into Peyton Platz. With Marian's latest round of demands, Shaw's wounded pride had turned into bearlike rage. It was one thing, he seethed to friends that winter, to make lawyerly demands for half the estate. It was quite another to insist on staying in Klosters—*his* town, after *her* betrayal—and to have the gall to demand Chalet Mia. Marian knew perfectly well how accustomed he'd become to writing in his cabin across the property's tiny stream, and how superstitious he, like any writer, felt about his work space. Clearly, he said, her only motive was revenge. True or not, Marian did succeed in convincing the local court authorities to grant her use of the house, pending final settlement of the case. In early January Shaw was forced to pack his bags and sublet Bob and Kathie Parrish's apartment, a pleasant walk-up in a chalet-style building in town that also housed Shaw's Swiss doctor, Jorge Egger.

Night after night Shaw poured out his rage and hurt to friends. Never, as Peter Viertel noted, had Shaw talked so openly about his emotions. Jacques Graubart stayed up all of one memorable night with him, trying to dissuade him from getting divorced at all. " 'You have to be more tolerant,' I'd say to him. But he wouldn't budge. It was a very sad time—for all of us. I remember people saying to Irwin, 'How can you do this to us?' "

That reproach was widely shared. The Shaws' separation meant the loss of a couple central to the social lives of all their many friends. Moreover, with Marian refusing to leave, and with both principals remaining in Klosters with their new lovers, friends were being thrown into the dilemma of choosing sides—a dilemma that both Shaw and Marian exacerbated by grimly lining up recruits. "That was one of the least attractive sides of Irwin, his vindictiveness toward Marian," recalls Larry Collins, who somehow managed to remain friendly with both Shaws through this period. Already the Chesa's owners, Hans and Doris Guler, were having to learn the fine art of seating Shaw and Marian at different ends of the hotel's small, wood-paneled dining room on these volatile winter evenings.

It was better to keep them from overlapping at all; on more than one occasion the two began shouting across the room at each other, to the astonishment of other guests.

As if these deliberations weren't ominous enough, that winter Shaw was indirectly involved in a fatal skiing accident. Larry Collins remembers it well: "Peter, Adam, Irwin and I, and a young Swiss female ski instructor all rode up together on the lift at the end of the day. It might have been snowing, or perhaps the weather had been warm, so there was definitely the possibility of avalanches. When we started down, Peter said, 'Let's take this cut which goes through some trees and across a couple gullies'—which were apt to come down. Irwin said, 'No, I don't think we should do that, I don't like the feel of it.' He said to me, 'Come on, Larry, let them go,' because Peter and Adam and the girl were better skiers. So we went our separate ways. And the mountain came down and the girl was killed." For Shaw, who had always tended to bomb down a slope without style or fear, the incident was a turning point; afterward he grew far more cautious, even timid, about the slopes he would take. Because of a worsening eye condition that kept him from distinguishing moguls in flat light, on certain days he wouldn't ski at all.

The Shaw wars took another turn for the worse with Bodie's arrival in late January 1970. Though she stayed at Kaiser's Hotel, Bodie's presence seemed calculated to give further offense to Marian, who retaliated by entertaining at Chalet Mia with Jean Daninos. "As Mrs. Shaw, Marian had had these wonderful dinners at Chalet Mia with Irwin presiding," recalls one frequent guest. "And everyone would adjourn to the living room and talk till midnight or one o'clock with cognac. With Daninos, Marian would just get him into the living room and he'd fall asleep in his corner, right in that same living room that Irwin had kept so animated. He was a very nice, decent man in the sense that he did everything to please Marian. But he wasn't Irwin Shaw." Not unexpectedly, in the deepening rivalry for recruits, Shaw tended to win more than Marian. "People were selfishly abandoning Marian," remembers a Paris friend, "because they didn't want to sacrifice Irwin's company."

Inevitably, the charged air clouded Shaw's relationship with Bodie too. Exasperated and defensive, she reacted by showing a cold shoulder to any of Shaw's friends perceived to sympathize with Marian. "She was appalling to us," recalls Liz Weicker Fondaras, "just appalling." Bodie resented the role she'd been asked to play, and began to long for the freewheeling life she and Shaw had found in Paris. For his part, Shaw was finding Bodie could be a prickly companion. She was also notably sloppy about her attire—the result, she liked to say, of a privileged childhood in which maids and nannies had picked up after her. Much to the bewilderment of Shaw's tony circle, she tended to wear blue jeans day after day, despite the ample wardrobe she'd brought along.

With some relief, Shaw left the whole fishbowl world of Klosters behind him in March, flying alone to New York to consult with his editors about *Rich Man, Poor Man,* and to tend to his aging mother, now in a posh Florida apartment complex for the elderly, with her bills paid by her two sons. The fractious Don Fine had left Delacorte to start his own imprint, Arbor House, so it was with Ross Claiborne, and an editor named Manon Tingue, that Shaw met to go over the novel that would salvage his career so dramatically.

Claiborne adored the book. "I was beside myself when I read the manuscript," he recalls. "I thought, Here we are, back to *The Young Lions,* to the early Irwin Shaw kind of success. I saw it as the book that was really going to make us a serious publisher." Despite the reluctance of some Delacorte executives who resented Shaw's commercial failure with *Voices of a Summer Day,* Claiborne pushed through a new two-book contract identical to the first: $100,000 for each of two novels (titles and plots to be determined later), the latter due in mid-1976.

Not long after he arrived in New York, Shaw drove up to spend a Sunday with the Styrons in Connecticut. There he met the courtly young Mississippian who at the age of thirty-two had rocked the literary world by becoming the editor of *Harper's* magazine, and immediately after had published his precocious, elegiac autobiography, *North Toward Home.* Willie Morris had not survived these triumphs unscathed. Just now he was going through a painful divorce, and he and Shaw were soon commiserating about their marital woes. The two men had much more than that in common, however. Despite their age difference, they shared passionate interests in both literature and sports. For Morris, a seminal experience had been reading "The Eighty-Yard Run" as a sixth grader in the Yazoo Public Library. "It was on pulp paper, in some sports anthology," he told Shaw, "but I realized even then that this was a story different from all the others I was reading. It was trying to tell me something more than just football, some quality of the emotions and time passing. There was a beauty to this story, something that caught me in the heart, about being alive on the Mississippi Methodist Lord's good earth, and about the difficulty of it all. That story was probably my first true introduction to great writing."

Not long after, over a boozy lunch at The Four Seasons—Morris, even then, could match Shaw drink for drink—the two agreed that Shaw would write a piece for *Harper's* on the Cannes Film Festival coming up in May. Shaw was due to attend anyway as a judge, so the magazine, with its chronically low budget, wouldn't have to pay his way. As for the fee, Morris could offer only $750. "He got a big kick out of that," Morris recalls. 'Seven-fifty?' he said, and shook his head. 'Sure, kid, sure.' " Shaw did go to the festival, and though the piece he submitted to *Harper's* would not be memorable, the experience would provide the genesis for his next novel, *Evening in Byzantium.*

With *Rich Man, Poor Man* due out in September, Shaw saw no reason to work in the meantime, and summer, traditionally, was a time to relax. With Bodie, he took a first-ever trip to Turkey, touring Istanbul's mosques and bazaars for five days in an old fin-backed purple Cadillac driven by an old Turk who, miraculously, had read all of Shaw's books in Turkish and insisted on escorting his famous rider for free. Then Bodie and Shaw flew down to join Sam Spiegel on his yacht, the SS *Malahne*, for a whirlwind Mediterranean cruise.

Rich Man, Poor Man appeared in September to decidedly mixed reviews—some of them rivaled the worst Shaw had so far received. "Irwin Shaw's big sixth novel, the one he was finally going to make a comeback with, is bad, bad," Christopher Lehmann-Haupt announced. "It's especially bad because it looks for a while as if he's going to pull it off—it's like a great old fighter who shows the great old moves in the early rounds and then begins to fall apart, swinging gracefully off target, staggering when he hasn't been hit, and finally collapsing from sheer exhaustion. *Rich Man, Poor Man* is finally so bad that one even begins to wonder if the great old fighter ever had it at all, whether we weren't taken in by the play *Bury the Dead*, the good short stories of the Thirties, and the novel *The Young Lions*." As a big-canvas social novel, Lehmann-Haupt went on to say, *Rich Man, Poor Man* lacked any vision of what society should be, mired as it was in senseless melodrama. The book did receive praise, but not of the most ringing sort. "Shaw still stakes his claim in the borderland where serious art and commercial sentimentalities blur comfortably," suggested R. V. Cassill in *The Washington Post*. "[But] it must be said that the milieus and situations he renders in his scenes are rendered masterfully. . . . Although Shaw has not really ripened as an observer of character or the times, his old superb skills have not failed him."

Late that fall, with the commercial fate of *Rich Man, Poor Man* uncertain at best, Shaw flew to Klosters to confront the prospect of an ugly divorce case in the local courts. He still refused to consider surrendering Chalet Mia, and he felt bitter about Marian's demand for half the estate, but as the court date neared, both Irving Lazar and Peter Viertel began working on him to compromise. Lazar, curiously enough, had insisted from the start that Marian was just in her demands. Viertel felt more sympathetic toward Shaw. "How can you set yourself up as a judge of this?" Viertel demanded of Lazar. "Shouldn't they work that out together?" But with Shaw and Marian at an impasse, Viertel and Lazar now became their unofficial surrogates.

After much negotiation Viertel persuaded Shaw to sacrifice half his estate—the only alternative, as Viertel observed, to a long and publicly reported court case. With that, he went back to Marian and Lazar. Marian was relieved but skeptical of how the estate would be divided. "So I went back and forth between Irwin and Marian for two days," recalls Viertel, "and I worked out an agreement, a property settlement. Whoever kept the house had to give the other one $100,000, and all stocks and other assets would be split. I said to Irwin, 'You love the house, and you're the earner— so keep it. Give Marian the $100,000, for Christ's sake.'"

Shaw, for all his protestations about never surrendering the house, balked at the prospect of selling long-held stocks. He had no idea yet of the money he stood to earn from *Rich Man, Poor Man,* and the idea of cashing in stocks went against his deepest conservative instincts. This way, though, he felt he was at least making the house choice himself. When Marian agreed to raise the $100,000 needed to fulfill her side of the bargain and keep the house herself, the warring couple at last came to terms.

"That night I was walking home after a late afternoon of skiing," Viertel recalls. "And Irwin and Marian drove up in the same car, off to see the lawyer or whatever it was. And they stopped and both jumped out and gave me a kiss and said, 'We'll never forget this.' I said something cynical like, 'Well, you'll probably both hate me two years from now.' But they made the agreement and the divorce went through as joint consent."

Shaw would indeed feel bitter toward Marian, as she would toward him—and in less than two years. Still, his life seemed wide open, perhaps for the first time since his ocean crossing to Europe nearly two decades before. Meanwhile, an odd turn of events was transpiring back in New York. *Rich Man, Poor Man,* for all its uncertain reviews, was stubbornly climbing the bestseller lists.

CHAPTER TWENTY

At a glance, Shaw's life after the settlement seemed not to change. He stayed rooted in Klosters and Paris, he saw all his old friends, and he remained remarkably disciplined in his writing habits: though capable of indulging in idle stretches, these were as carefully parceled out as any working man's corporate vacations. Freed of his shrewish wife, he told friends, he was simply happier than he had been in more than three decades. Without Marian's daily pressure to curb his drinking, however, Shaw's already excessive intake began to increase, and without the framework of family to put some limitation on his social life, he seemed to lose all discernment. More than ever before, his relentless socializing suggested that beneath the laughter Shaw harbored a tight knot of loneliness, and that he was more driven by it than his friends might have imagined.

One shrewd observer of Shaw at this time was Elinor Gruber, the Marcus sister who had first met him in New York when she was thirteen years old. In the early seventies, Gruber came to Klosters as a houseguest of Gore Vidal and found Shaw ringed by a court of well-intentioned but sycophantic admirers. True, there were the honest, close friends—the Parrishes, the Bernheims, the Viertels. But here too were dozens of new arrivals: ad agency executives, film distributors and Connecticut social climbers. "It was a clan, everyone gluing themselves to Irwin. And the sad thing was that he *wanted* to surround himself with these people. Yet I could see that the other Irwin, the Irwin I'd known so many years ago, was still there too. He never lost that. That was the conflict in his life, I felt: between his superficial self and the true man. He'd take small doses of the superficial side and then always revert to the more creative self." Gruber, for one, discounts loneliness as a motive. "It wasn't loneliness—it was *ego*. Vanity. One of the French philosophers said it best: 'If one has the choice of happiness or vanity, one will always choose vanity.' "

Not by chance, the apartment that would become Shaw's new home in Klosters lay directly in the middle of town. It was a walk-up above a jewelry store on Klosters's main boulevard, and its several rooms fronted the street, catercorner to the Chesa Grischuna, with a wide, long, chalet-style balcony from which Shaw, King of Klosters that he was, could wave cheerily down at his subjects passing by. Shaw greeted locals as affectionately as holiday skiers, and they adored him in return. Even the farmers, a stolid bunch who scowled at the spandex-clad foreigners in their midst, recognized and respected Irwin Shaw and felt included in his warmth.

Despite the divorce settlement, Bodie maintained an apartment of her own downhill, at the foot of town beside the Landquart River. She would see Shaw daily for lunch after his writing and participate in the dinners that gathered a dozen or more disparate guests every night of the skiing season. The very onslaught of Shaw's social life made a sanctuary essential, however. "I'd go to the butcher's and ask for chicken, and the butcher would say, 'No, you're having that at the Negropontes' tonight,' " Bodie recalls. "Except for the skiing, I was starting to hate Klosters. I hated the small-town gossips."

Not that the gossips could really be blamed: with Marian refusing to move out of town, colorful confrontations were as inevitable as scenes in an ongoing passion play. One day, typically, Shaw walked into the Chesa's dining room to see Marian at the head of a luncheon table of half a dozen well-coiffed ladies. Enraged, he bore down on them with fingers outstretched. "Do you know how this lunch is being paid for?" he shouted. "These fingers. These ten fingers are paying for your lunch today!" Another time Shaw found Marian giving a dinner party, again at the Chesa, and briskly pulled the tablecloth, laden with plates of food, off the table.

Privately Shaw liked to tell friends that he had been the big winner in the settlement. "I got Adam, and I got my cook Fedora," he often declared. But he also felt cheated and betrayed, and later, when Marian sold Chalet Mia for a reported $700,000 and bought an apartment near the railroad station, those feelings deepened. Not only had Marian made a windfall profit, she had callously divested herself of Shaw's favorite place in the world—deliberately, he believed, to hurt him.

Though he remained a generous host, in the wake of the settlement Shaw felt a new anxiety about money. Having managed to support his family handsomely all these years as a writer—still an extraordinary concept in American society—he suddenly found himself fearing he might end as his father had, destitute and defenseless, or at least forced to make considerable sacrifices. The fears were groundless: as of the previous mid-October *Rich Man, Poor Man* had hit the *New York Times* bestseller list and risen to the number-three position—*Love Story* was number one—where it would reside stubbornly until a slow decline in the spring. As of early 1971, however, Shaw had seen no royalties, and he worried that he might not be able to pay his taxes. The news in February was thus especially relieving: Swifty Lazar had sold the television rights to *Rich Man, Poor Man*.

The deal, which would later come to seem such a pittance to Shaw, had its origins in the changing nature of network television. Not long before, the "made-for-TV movie" had confounded skeptics to gain acceptance as a legitimate aspect of American television production. Hollywood executives felt considerably less excited by the simultaneous importation of English highbrow continuing dramas, but perhaps there *was* something in the notion of a more mainstream American . . . miniseries. Among the mavericks who began scanning the market for material was a young, ambitious vice-president of nighttime programming for ABC named Barry Diller.

From Diller's perspective, *Rich Man, Poor Man* was an obvious choice. The novel had sold well enough to have recognition value, yet no one would vie with him to make a feature of it. The studios tended to adapt only the biggest bestsellers of the year, and *Rich Man, Poor Man,* though doing well, fell short of that category. Moreover, the narrative spanned too long a time period: characters could not credibly age twenty-five years within a movie's two hours. That was exactly the sort of period, however, that lent itself to a six- or eight-episode miniseries. As if that were not enough, *Rich Man, Poor Man,* with its sure-bet premise of Good Brother versus Bad Brother, unrolled as pure, cinematic plot: twist upon twist, with virtually no interior monologue. The whole book, when he stopped to think about it, read like a treatment from first page to last.

Diller couldn't produce the miniseries himself. Like all network programs, *Rich Man, Poor Man* would be farmed out to an independent production company. It was a relationship of delicate interdependence that a network and production company shared, the networks exercising a near monopoly over television production companies, yet needing to fill airtime. Warily, the partners usually went through two deal-making stages. First they acquired a property, often splitting the cost. Then, after the production company had worked up a screenplay or in other ways advanced the project—usually at its own expense—the partners reconvened to decide what the network would pay for the right to air the program. The licensing fee, as it was called, was meant to provide a shooting budget and some profit to the production company; the network, of course, would make its money back by selling commercial time. (The production company would actually own the product and be free to sell future air rights as it pleased.) For *Rich Man, Poor Man,* Diller began by consulting with his boss at the time, ABC's president of entertainment, Marty Starger. Diller and Starger then called Sidney Sheinberg, president of MCA, which owned Universal Television. Sheinberg called Irving Lazar. The first stage of the deal, Diller told one interviewer later, took all of ten minutes.

The deal stipulated that ABC and Universal pay $110,000—$55,000 each—to Lazar on Shaw's behalf to acquire *Rich Man, Poor Man*'s television rights. To Lazar, it must have seemed like found money: personally, he thought the series would never come off. "A miniseries? Like those British things?" he told Ross Claiborne, among others. "It'll never work here." So there seemed no point in demanding further monies when the show was aired, or residuals for repeated showings. Nor did it seem to matter that Universal would retain all television rights to the novel's fictional characters. In the unlikely event that *Rich Man, Poor Man* should be a hit, the producers could go ahead and write a sequel any way they liked, without consulting Shaw and without paying him a cent. When Lazar told Shaw that he had sold the novel, he was not, for once, exaggerating. It was *gone.*

The sale, as Shaw wrote in a letter to Nan Talese, would help keep the wolf from his door for a few years. It did not keep him from growing ever more bitter toward Marian. All through 1971, Shaw poured his ire into the novel he had begun to consider at the Cannes Film Festival the year before.

In a disturbing number of ways, *Evening in Byzantium,* with its ironic title a tribute to the Yeats poem about an old man journeying to a land of immortal art, resembled *Two Weeks in Another Town.* As in *Two Weeks,* the Shaw-like protagonist, world-weary, embittered, is drawn to a glamorous European locale because of the film business. The setting has changed from Rome to Cannes, and this time the protagonist, Jesse Craig, is a has-been producer rather than a has-been actor. The thrust is the same, though: Craig wants to salvage his soul by persuading the hard-bitten deal-makers he meets to go with quality, in this case not by hiring a talented young director but in producing the script he's secretly written himself. As in *Two Weeks,* the protagonist stands all but immobile in his hotel room as a strange, attractive woman barges into his life (this time a journalist determined to interview Craig about his recent absence from the movie scene.) As in *Two Weeks,* he fields guilt-provoking long-distance calls from other women in his life, grimacing at their shrewish demands for his time and affection. The hotel scotch flows, the bitter memories unfold, and in the end Craig—never to blame for any of the tragedies that have befallen him—predictably fails to get his movie produced. As in *Two Weeks,* a medical emergency is the fateful determinant. This time the physical collapse is Craig's own.

Evening in Byzantium is far from the best of Shaw's novels. Quite startling, however, are the raw, open-nerved descriptions of Craig's wife, Penelope, so transparently a portrait of Marian that Marian reportedly gave serious thought to mounting a libel suit. Those passages are the best-written in the novel; plucked out and stitched together on their own, they would have made a first-rate short story.

The Penelope of *Evening in Byzantium* is a woman of hard-polished charm, somehow false for all her skills as a hostess, who leaves copious bills in her wake—clothes from Bergdorf's, hairstylings at Charles of the Ritz, a masseuse, medical treatments for her mother. (Marian's mother had died in October 1968.) While spending her husband's money, she has carried on an affair with bald little Bertie Folsom, an affair that everyone but Craig knows about, and has gone so far as to include Folsom in frequent social dinners at the Craigs' home. Yet she remains jealous enough of Craig to rifle through his papers in search of women's names, and when he is away, she continues to call him late at night, ostensibly to see if he's all right, in fact to be sure he's alone. She dissembles; she finds ways to push the blame his way whenever things go wrong. She invites mediocre people to dinner because she's cowed by intelligence and wit; she's pretentious. Worst of all, she's a bore.

In the past Craig let Penelope do as she pleased, wearily signing the checks for her expenditures and leaving all other financial dealings to his manager, a character with whom he has maintained a trusting relationship of handshake agreements, and who seems drawn from Irving Lazar. Now he's learned of the affair. Musing on how it could have come to pass, Craig realizes that for years he and Penelope have avoided candor, as he puts it, and thus gradually drifted apart. When Penelope visits his hospital room and suggests they call off the divorce, however, Craig is the one who takes the hard line. He's been cuckolded; he will not forgive her.

Shaw's first draft of *Evening in Byzantium* did not end with Jesse Craig's collapse and hospitalization. As if living his own novel, Shaw experienced the last scene in New York after submitting the book to Delacorte in early 1972.

Superstitious after *Rich Man, Poor Man*'s success, Shaw entrusted this new manuscript to Bodie and had her fly over in February on a Swissair plane piloted by Don Dixon. Peter Viertel, for one, read the book before Shaw sent it off and strongly advised his old friend to go over it again. The passages about Marian in particular seemed harsh, even libelous, an opinion in which Bodie concurred. But Shaw refused.

In Delacorte's executive offices, there was considerable anticipation about the next Shaw novel. *Rich Man, Poor Man* had remained on the *New York Times* bestseller list for thirty-three weeks, and hundreds of thousands of paperback copies were rolling off the presses—all bearing the Dell imprint, thanks to hard-soft publishing. Suddenly Shaw was hot again, having made a near-miraculous comeback for a writer whose sales had steadily declined over twenty-five years. To his chagrin, Ross Claiborne found the book dark and disappointing, as did editor Manon Tingue. "That first draft was unprintable," she recalls. "It was a purgative. What Irwin had created was a bizarre, grotesque portrait of Marian." According to Tingue, though, the corporate powers at Delacorte were reluctant to hold the book up for revisions. "Irwin was a name again, and Delacorte just wanted to publish it as it was." Eventually, she and Claiborne agreed to stand firm and insist that Shaw fly over for an editorial meeting.

During a stopover in London, Shaw apparently managed to contract hepatitis from eating bad shellfish. The illness was still incubating at the time he walked into Delacorte's offices in March to meet with Claiborne and Tingue, but he must have felt himself to be in ill health. Certainly to Claiborne and Tingue, his appearance was disconcerting. "Irwin was an unforgettable sight that day," Tingue recalls. "He was very uptight when he arrived; but then, he was always uptight until he got drunk. He was watching both of us like hawks that day. And he was trembling.

"Ross started out the meeting by saying, 'Irwin, the book is beautifully written—but of course you couldn't write badly.'

"Irwin sensed the mood, that that was of course just a prelude to criticism. And so at that point I took it apart as well as I could." Shaw, the young lion of the thirties and forties who had prided himself on never rewriting and on taking editorial suggestions only for cuts, seemed to take the criticisms with grace. "It's important to realize," Tingue says, "that Irwin was not a man unaccustomed to disappointment."

Two days after the Delacorte meeting and a whirl of New York social engagements with such friends as Pat Lawford, the Plimptons, the Matthiessens and the Lerners, Shaw collapsed in Bodie's apartment. To confirm the diagnosis of hepatitis, a doctor made Shaw urinate in a jar: the urine came out the color of Coca-Cola.

The sensible move was to enter a hospital, but Shaw was adamant about wanting to recuperate in Bodie's apartment. For the next three weeks, Bodie acted as nurse, caretaking for a patient too weak to stand, and keeping him to a fat-free—and alcohol-free—diet. It was a rare time of quiet, with no eager admirers barging in and Shaw for once under no compunction to play the all-embracing host. Ruminative and grateful for Bodie's ministrations, he talked seriously of marriage.

"When we had first gotten together," recalls Bodie, "Irwin would say, 'We're going to have the brightest football player at Harvard.' But his age had begun to get in the way. He couldn't ski much, for example. His arthritis was worsening—mostly in his hip—and he was adopting a sort of rolling walk from side to side. The drinking was obviously wearing him down considerably too, though he took great pride in how impervious he was to the effects of it—normal blood pressure and a strong constitution, that is. I used to kid him that his greatest search in life was not for his soul but for a doctor who'd tell him it was all right to drink. I adored him, but I was reluctant to think of getting married and having a child with a man so much older. I didn't want to be left a widow."

The hepatitis became a significant factor in Shaw's health, not so much for the time he was sick as for the way in which he chose to recover. Told he must not drink under any circumstances for six months after regaining his feet, Shaw complied in his own way: by stopping for six days. It was a gesture of nihilism that inspired the conclusion of the revised *Evening in Byzantium*. Jesse Craig, fresh out of the hospital after a life-threatening collapse, having been told he must not drink, walks blithely down the street into a bar and orders a scotch and soda. The liquor, as it goes down, tastes better than any drink he's ever had in his life. Ever the protagonist in the novel of his own life, Shaw knew exactly what he was risking by drinking again and had the perspicacity to portray himself with grim realism. But he was also now too weak, and too addicted to alcohol, to try to change the portrait.

In retrospect, Shaw's illness became a turning point for his relationship with Bodie. It brought them closer than they had ever been, but it also made clearer the impasse between them, of age and of intent.

Unquestionably, Bodie felt increasingly impatient with the life to which they returned in Klosters. "Irwin would make a joke of it," she recalls. " 'Well,' he'd say, 'it's time to put the lioness back in her cage.' " Bodie, in turn, castigated Shaw for allowing himself to be victimized by the endless admirers who came calling. She took a much tougher stand with invitations, and was roundly resented for it by those excluded. "They were all just social climbing," she says. "And I was a lot snottier about that than Irwin." At the first opportunity that spring of 1972, with Shaw struggling through his rewrite of *Evening in Byzantium*, Bodie went off to Paris alone for festive times with the Joneses.

Shaw, the more vulnerable of the two at this stage, lured Bodie back by agreeing to meet her for a holiday in Venice before returning to Klosters. A follow-up trip to Port'Ercole backfired, however, when Shaw invited Adam to join them. By now Bodie and Adam had a recognized standoff, bitter and entrenched, and could seem to agree only on the wisdom of not spending time together. Nor did Bodie hesitate to tell Shaw how much she felt he had indulged his son, and to what deleterious effect. Shaw, proud of Adam's success in landing a job after college as a UPI reporter in Abidjan in the Ivory Coast, refused to listen.

Shaw's rewrite of *Evening in Byzantium*, finished by early summer, provoked only more resentment. Bodie still thought the novel should not be published and made her opinions clear. On some level, she felt, Shaw seemed to agree, but he bridled at anyone else's negative opinion.

Despite periods now in which Shaw and Bodie literally refused to talk to each other, the relationship continued. One reason was that Bodie had sublet her apartment in New York and thus had no home to which she could easily return. By now, too, she and Shaw shared the same friends and the same lifestyle, all painful for her to consider giving up. Most important, beneath the murky tensions, and the hangovers when Shaw nursed black moods or felt, as he put it, "dreamy," there was still a strong emotional connection and more than a few good times.

One of the best was the first Calcutta Ski Race, orchestrated by Bodie as a celebration of Shaw's sixtieth birthday in February 1973. The idea was new to Klosters if not to the world of sport. Skiers of all levels were invited to join, with each team drawn up to consist of one excellent skier, one

average skier and one rank beginner. Team times would be combined, with
the overall time the only one that counted, and because experts would all
clock roughly the same downhill times, the bad skiers would, in a sense,
be the most important team members, making the whole race much fun-
nier and more festive.

The race succeeded beyond all expectations. It threw together the
town's different social factions, inspired a three-day spate of parties before
and after the event, and formalized the picture of Klosters as a happy court
paying homage to its ebullient king. With his usual good humor and grace,
Shaw officiated at the award ceremonies, in which the winning teams were
required to buy drinks for everybody else and the losing teams were presented statuettes of a donkey eyeing a snail, and gave a short, amusing
address that immediately became a regular part of the annual proceedings.

Somehow amid these frivolities, Shaw remained capable of returning
to his original self, as Elinor Gruber put it. Still waking early every morning, he settled in at the desk that looked out on Klosters's main street,
lighted up one of his many pipes, and banged away at his old Olivetti 44
manual typewriter. The novel he had in mind now was a light, escapist
adventure tale of a hotel clerk who accidentally finds $100,000 in a card-
board mailing tube and must decide what to do with it. *Nightwork*, as the
novel would be called, seemed again a deliberate reaction to the book that
had preceded it. For the first time in his career toor, Shaw seemed to be
making a conscious effort to tailor a story for the screen.

That was the winter two Shaw books appeared within a month of each
other. The year before, Shaw had tried to interest first Delacorte, then
Random House, in publishing a collection of five long stories that had run
in *Playboy* and *Esquire*. When neither had nibbled, Shaw had explained the
situation to Don Fine at a cocktail party, and Fine had jumped at the
chance to publish the collection under his new imprint, Arbor House.
Unfortunately, Fine couldn't afford to pay much. "So Irwin practically gave
them to me," Fine recalls. "I think I bought them for $1,000. Irwin and
I made the deal on our own, and then Lazar found out. He almost had a
heart attack. But Irwin had agreed." Eventually, the book did well enough
in hardcover for Fine to sell paperback rights to Dell—for $35,000. "Irwin
just loved that," says Fine.

God Was Here But He Left Early would prove to be Shaw's last collection of new short stories. Generally it earned grudging respect; in the
shifting cycles of critical opinion, Shaw's humbler station these days as a
commercial novelist seemed to have produced a swing back from envy and
anger to a rather generous-spirited appreciation of the long-distance writer
in the early autumn of his life. "Back in the days when the hallmark of
social concern in fiction was likely to be a polemicism, Irwin Shaw was
writing breezy, gutsy short stories that offered a punch in the mouth to the
unjust and a big hello to life," wrote Martin Levin in *The New York Times*

Book Review. "It's nice to see, from his newest batch, that custom has not staled his variety, nor has age withered his humanism."

In truth, none of the stories is among Shaw's best. Though the seasoned craftsman is everywhere apparent, still decorating character descriptions with unexpected flourishes, still building graceful and well-balanced narratives, the old Shaw passion, understated and taut, is nowhere to be found. At the same time, the three much longer stories of the collection strike a new note of engaging, winsome humor. They form a triptych, with each story framing the comic plight of some hapless fellow whose luck unexpectedly takes a turn for the better in a contemporary world of amorality and violence.

In "Whispers in Bedlam," a washed-up professional football player gains extrasensory hearing power. Able to discern the muttered commands of opposing quarterbacks in huddle, he suddenly becomes an outstanding player, always in on the tackle, and then goes on to hear people's thoughts. In "The Mannichon Solution," an unassuming lab chemist stumbles upon a solution that seems to kill anything yellow, and is soon swept up by a cabal of soulless colleagues who routinely channel the most profitable discoveries of their commercial lab work into secret private companies. The short and shy bookstore clerk of "Small Saturday" spends a morning bravely telephoning tall, beautiful women who regularly patronize his store, in search of a date for the evening. The women all report that they're busy but, hedging their bets, say they may be free later. All three protagonists are gentle people; their small victories in the harsh worlds of professional sports, science and sexuality, like those of the Brooklyn fishermen in *The Gentle People,* are cause for hope and delight.

The collection's two shorter stories share this vision, though they seem thrown in principally to lend heft to the three "novellas." More interesting is the preface, a short meditation on the particular pleasures of short story writing that also appeared at this time as an essay in *Esquire.* In it Shaw recalled how different the world was for a short story writer before World War II, when so many magazines eagerly bought fiction. Stories were more respected then; American writers, it was said, were arguably the masters of the form. Since then, Shaw observed, the quality of stories published had not declined, but the market had shriveled, the critical attention diminished. A pity, Shaw mused, because the pleasures of short story writing are unique. "In a novel or a play you must be a whole man. In a collection of stories you can be all the men or fragments of men, worthy and unworthy, who in different seasons abound within you," Shaw wrote. "It is a luxury not to be scorned."

The new critical respect for Shaw became more apparent with the appearance in March 1973 of *Evening in Byzantium.* Somehow Shaw's image had changed from that of a literary/political sellout to grizzled professional. "*Evening in Byzantium,*" reported Anatole Broyard in *The New York Times,* is "a real 'old pro' performance, full of smooth and knowing moves." At the same time, acknowledged Broyard, "it seems to me that the old pro syndrome has certain limitations or disadvantages. Given a choice of probable, consistent behavior or rupturing originality in a character, the old pro will usually settle for consistency. He's like a careful poker player who stays close to the vest and sticks to the odds. He never follows hunches or goes for long shots. The writer whose outstanding quality is his professionalism is also likely to give you craft—technical ingenuity—instead of inspiration." But, concluded Broyard, zagging back, "this is ungrateful. Mr. Shaw has worked hard at his craft—and mastered it, too. Sometimes he uses it to such good effect it sounds almost like art."

Shaw, so accustomed to snide dismissals, was rather pleased by Broyard's backhanded praise and that of the other critics who paid cavalier tribute to "the old pro." Soon after, Shaw found himself in New York on the *Today* show with fellow guests Budd Schulberg and Alvin Toffler, fielding earnest questions from hosts Barbara Walters and Hugh Downs about the corruptive effects of success. Though the show was taped early in the morning, Shaw took a few strong swallows of scotch before appearing in front of the cameras. Emboldened by the booze and irked by the line of questioning, he asked Hugh Downs during a commercial break how much *he* earned in annual salary. The answer: $500,000. All three writers were stunned.

While in the States, Shaw attended the wedding of Adam to Keren Ettlinger, a tall, striking blonde whose father, Don Ettlinger, was an old screenwriter friend of Shaw's. Though he admitted to mixed feelings about seeing his only son get married at the age of twenty-three—three years younger than Shaw himself had been at that turning point—there was also the traditional hope that marriage would provide the maturity and inner confidence Adam seemed to need. Not long before, Adam had also landed a reporter's job on *The Washington Post*—another encouraging sign. In fact, to many of the guests Adam may have seemed more mature than his parents: visibly uncomfortable, Irwin and Marian sat under the same roof civilly for the first time since the divorce settlement.

His literary and paternal duties done, Shaw flew back to Europe to embark on a late spring vacation. With Bodie, he drove his favorite Klosters-Paris route by way of Beaune's Hôtel de la Poste. The two went to the races at St.-Cloud with the Joneses and toasted *Evening*'s upward climb on the New York bestseller lists. They drove to St.-Tropez for another ritual: a weekend with Anatole and Sophie Litvak, just in time to catch a Monte Carlo auto race. For a week they holed up at the Résidence du Cap in Antibes with the Joneses and their Paris poker chum Jack Egle, taking over the hotel's common room for marathon poker games.

It was a vacation that didn't seem to end. Back to Paris, south again to Antibes, then on to Sardinia. Shaw went to social lunches, napped in the afternoons (while Bodie went with Gloria Jones to the track), went to more social dinners and nighttime pokerfests, until he walked slowly off, invariably drunk, to bed. Heavy as he was now, he managed, on more than one occasion, to break his hotel bed as he flopped down on it, and the incidents became a running joke.

Inevitably, the holiday excess took its toll. Shaw's increasing weight was symptomatic, as were the sharp stomach pains that beset him in Sardinia. The fact that he was in Sardinia at all seemed part of the excess. He agreed to write a fluffy piece about the place for *Travel & Leisure*—a respectable publication, but a far cry from those with which he'd been associated in the past. Happily accepting the free room and board that came with the assignment, he and Bodie spent much of their time mixing with an international yacht set, most of whom hadn't ever read Shaw, much less appreciated his work.

Hearing reports of Shaw's revelries, Marian told friends the blame lay with Bodie. Marian herself had always been a modest drinker and tried to curb her husband's excesses. Bodie, she felt, was a heavy drinker who encouraged Shaw's worst instincts and was steadily ruining his health. The truth was more complicated. Bodie did serve as a daily drinking buddy, and rarely did she try to restrain Shaw's intake—but Shaw was a hard man to restrain. A heavy drinker for years, he wasn't about to stop for anyone, nor would he even accept the idea that he might be an alcoholic. Throughout this period, as his body proved less and less able to absorb the abuse he inflicted upon it, he would stop drinking six or eight days at a time, be unremittingly tense and irritable, then start in again, satisfied he'd recovered his health. When he did, the charming, funny Shaw would return, a relief not only to Bodie but to everyone around him.

No matter how much he drank, Shaw never became a mean drunk, or a falling-down drunk, or anything else that might have alienated friends and provoked a reaction. Nor in Klosters, at least, did a drunken Shaw pose any traffic risk; he could always walk home. If Shaw's friends still felt guilty about not advising him to seek help, they also felt timid about raising the subject. Shaw was too famous a figure to take to task, and somehow, beneath the heartiness one sensed a temper that might easily be aroused. Tell Shaw not to drink? Says Bodie: "He just wasn't someone you talked to about that."

Ironically, as Shaw's personal life seemed to drift, his career continued its new upward climb. By September 1973, *Rich Man, Poor Man* had sold 100,000 copies in hardcover, as Shaw proudly noted in a letter to Jim Jones, with 1,500,000 paperback copies in print. Swept along by that success, *Evening in Byzantium* had racked up sales of 75,000 hardcover copies in six months. On the strength of those figures, Irving Lazar in November apparently managed to persuade Delacorte to "forgive" Shaw the second book still owed by his 1970 two-book contract, and to draw up a new two-book contract at $175,000 per book. The first of those would be the unfinished *Nightwork*; the second would be determined later. Significantly, the time period between novel deadlines was cut. Instead of three years per book, as his last contract had stipulated, Shaw agreed to write the first of his prospective novels in two years, the second in just one year. The lure of big money was proving more and more intoxicating. As the holiday season came on, Shaw repaired to Klosters to work on *Nightwork* in earnest—and through the prism of fiction bring to it musings on the very subject that had assured its creation.

First met, *Nightwork*'s Douglas Grimes seems a refreshingly untypical Shaw protagonist. He's younger than usual, puritanical, naive, a moderate drinker. He's also a lowly night clerk in a sleazy New York hotel, not some jaded American expatriate. But like his counterparts in *Two Weeks in Another Town* and *Evening in Byzantium*, Grimes once had more. A commercial pilot, he was grounded when a standard eye exam revealed a rare retinal condition affecting his peripheral vision. Having night-clerked for three years now, Grimes gets a lucky break as the novel opens. A disheveled whore rushes into the lobby at three in the morning, babbling about a corpse in the sixth-floor corridor. Grimes finds the corpse—a coronary case—clutching a cardboard mailing tube stuffed with $100,000 in small unmarked bills.

To his own surprise, Grimes finds himself coolly skipping town with the cash and leaving no forwarding address. First stop is Washington, D.C., to get a passport discreetly, with the help of an old friend now in the State Department. While there, Grimes agrees to give his dissipated brother $25,000 to invest in a long-shot business scheme and allows himself to be seduced by a tough lady lawyer in the Justice Department. (Mild-mannered as Grimes may be, the predatory women of the world can't restrain themselves from lunging for him any more than they can with beefier Shaw protagonists.) Then it's off to Europe, his cash in his suitcase, his options wide open.

A first hitch comes when Grimes realizes he's left Kloten airport in Switzerland with someone else's luggage. A second arises when, after much sleuthwork, Grimes discovers that the chap who mistakenly took his bag—and cash—is a rakish gambler named Miles Fabian. Until recently, Fabian's luck at cards tended to run out. Now he's turning far better profits investing his unquestioned windfall in everything from thoroughbred horses to porn movies. When Grimes demands his money back, Fabian talks him into becoming an equal partner—Fabian's business cunning, after all, seems a fair trade for Grimes's capital—and the two promptly embark on a champagne-and-caviar tour of Europe's finest hotels, dabbling with beautiful women and shrewd investments as they go.

The same winsome humor that Shaw tried out in the novellas of *God Was Here But He Left Early* is carried over here with considerable success.

Nightwork is *fun*, a lighthearted caper that weaves through its various European locales with obvious assurance and never tries to be more than the escapist entertainment it is. As an intrigue, it does lose steam early on: no one chases Grimes to Europe, so any lingering suspense is forgotten. Also, with no sense of purpose but to make their next investment and drink more champagne, Shaw's characters remain rather thin. As more than one reviewer would point out, however, there's something irresistibly delicious about a tale in which a lowly night clerk finds big money, decides to hang onto it—and basically gets away with it.

That he does said much about Shaw's changing view of the world. Writing *Nightwork* in the midst of the Watergate years, Shaw watched the collapse of the Nixon administration with fascination and horror, and brooded as always on the deeper ethical implications. If government was corrupt, what compelled the governed to abide by it? Legally, Doug Grimes was obligated to return his windfall to whoever claimed it, or at least to report it to the police. As Shaw pointed out in the novel, though, the stash almost certainly belonged either to the Mafia or to some Republican dirty-tricks team. Was Grimes wrong to use it to more honorable ends?

In late October Shaw put his book aside to make his autumn swing to Paris with Bodie. Besides seeing the usual crowd, they spent many evenings going no farther from Shaw's apartment on the rue de Grenelle than the local Italian restaurant, Chez Gildo, or Fontaine de Jade, a Chinese place around the corner. By Christmas the scene shifted back, as it always did, to Klosters. Many of the Paris revelers followed Shaw back, and the Hollywood crowd descended. Directors Norman Jewison, Robert Josephs and Robert Stigwood were prominent that year. So were Sam Spiegel and his son Adam, and Lauren Bacall and her son Sam. Shaw hosted a sprawling Christmas dinner for the Parrishes, the Viertels, Geza and Ann Korvin. Walter Haensli, a famous skier now involved with the Head ski company, gave the inevitable New Year's Eve party with his wife, Jane. On Shaw's birthday in February, the Second Annual Calcutta Ski Race convened.

Beneath the social routine, the bulwarks of Shaw's life were quietly shifting. In May he went again to the Cannes Film Festival, to serve as a judge and write a piece for *Travel & Leisure*. This time Bodie took the opportunity to arrange a rendezvous in Normandy with a new English lover. In the roughly five years she'd lived with Shaw, there had been other dalliances, but none so serious as this. Inevitably, it led to high domestic drama. Shaw grew suspicious upon his return to Klosters, and Bodie admitted the affair. When letters from the Englishman followed, Shaw put them unopened on Bodie's pillow. "Notice," he said, "I didn't put a knife through them." Soon after, the drama moved to Paris. The Englishman flew over from London to persuade Bodie to marry him, and after much soul-searching, Bodie turned him down. The Englishman, a former Cold-stream Guardsman and perfect gentleman, ended up calling Shaw on the phone to make a gracious surrender. "Well, old chap," he said, "she loves you much more than she loves me." Shaw declared the Englishman a wonderful fellow, and assured him Bodie would find him another woman to marry—which in fact she did. "That was the first time Irwin ever said thank you to me," Bodie recalls. "He never apologized or said thank you as a rule; he hated gushiness. But when I chose to stay with him in Paris, Irwin thanked me."

Another bulwark shifted in the summer of 1974. For several years now Europe had been growing more expensive as the dollar took a downward slide. Everywhere Shaw looked, he saw American expatriates packing to go home. He'd seen them leaving before and always vowed to remain; but when Jim and Gloria Jones decided to join the migration, it was time to reconsider.

Long as it had taken Shaw to move back for an extended stay, it took no time at all to decide where to go. The increasingly literary Hamptons, had they been represented on a Saul Steinberg map of America for expatri-ate writers in Europe, would have loomed large enough in the landscape to obscure every other destination but Manhattan and Hollywood, and perhaps Cape Cod. A sleepy and inexpensive haven in the 1950s for such painters as Jackson Pollock and Willem de Kooning, the Hamptons' lovely farming towns and rolling potato fields had long since been discovered by more affluent New Yorkers. Still, a sense of artistic community remained in the early 1970s, a precarious balance that would soon be lost amid rising real estate prices.

The artists now seemed outnumbered by writers. Peter Matthiessen, George Plimpton and others of the *Paris Review* crowd had come for the summer, if not year-round, as had Kurt Vonnegut, Jr., Truman Capote, E. L. Doctorow, Joseph Heller, Wilfrid Sheed, John Knowles and Dwight Macdonald. Willie Morris had moved out after a dramatic departure from *Harper's,* when the magazine's owners reacted negatively to his bold deci-sion to devote an entire issue to Norman Mailer's *The Prisoner of Sex.* The Joneses had spent the better part of two summers in the Hamptons already. Now they were headed back to stay with Adolph Green and Phyllis New-man before the start of Jones's year as a writer in residence at the University of Miami.

Shaw had spent time in the Hamptons himself. In addition to his 1950 summer in nearby Quogue, he had often visited his brother in Amagansett, where David Shaw and his family owned a house, and had become familiar enough with the area to use it as a backdrop for *Voices of a Summer Day.* Now he took the further step of renting a house sight unseen for the month of July. Situated in the Springs, a relatively unchic area, the house was the least expensive one available. Shaw had the money to afford a larger place, but he was surprisingly sensitive on the subject of rents—another lesson from the Depression. "Irwin would spend a fortune on a hotel room," Bodie observes, "but he hated it when his rents went up at all. He'd panic if our rent in Paris went up 150 francs, as it did once. 'They're robbing me blind!' he'd shout. At which point we'd go out for a consolation lunch that cost 1,500 francs. I'd point out the irony to him and he'd shout, 'You don't understand! Just forget it!' "

Still, there were more than enough distractions. Shaw's arrival was a major event, and soon the invitations piled on top of each other as thickly as in Klosters or Paris. Art and Joan Stanton, Mike Burke, Joe Heller and the Plimptons were only the first wave. The Joneses arrived July 11, just in time to settle in before Liz Weicker Fondaras's big Bastille Day party. For Shaw it was a time of family reunion as well: Adam came with his wife, Keren, and Shaw's mother made the trip from Florida to stay with David. Bodie had frankly hoped the month would persuade Shaw to start spending part of every year in the States, and in that sense the summer was a rousing success. By the time he left, Shaw sensed he had found a new home. As tribute, at the conclusion of *Nightwork*, he chose to have his hero settle happily in Sag Harbor, Long Island.

Back in Klosters, Shaw determined to finish *Nightwork*—still tentatively titled "Cold Pleasures"—in six weeks' time, and thus justify his summer of indolence. He was done two days before his self-imposed deadline, as he reported in a letter of September 12 to the Joneses in Florida. He had no real sense, he admitted, as to whether he'd produced "a work of art or a pile of junk," but added wryly that Christopher Lehmann-Haupt, the *New York Times* reviewer who had savaged *Rich Man, Poor Man*, would surely let him know in time.

With Bodie eager as always to get out of Klosters, Shaw accepted the invitation of his German publisher to come stay in Hamburg. Hopping quickly on to Copenhagen, Brussels and London, he and Bodie then flew to Miami to see the Joneses. It was a happy time in all but one respect: when Jones introduced Shaw as a surprise guest to his writing class, he spoke ardently of Shaw's brilliant short stories yet made no mention of his seven novels. Always terribly sensitive to real or imagined slights about his novels, Shaw was wounded enough to mention the incident years later to Bernie Frizell. To Jones and to the class, he betrayed no hint of his feelings.

Another bulwark of Shaw's life had shifted that summer. To Shaw's private dismay, after barely a year and a half, Adam quit *The Washington Post*, irked by the tedium of being a city beat reporter. By November he and Keren had moved into David Shaw's house in Amagansett, where Shaw went to visit him after seeing the Joneses. What he wanted to do now, Adam told his father, was write a book titled *Baby Journalist*, an account of his experiences as a UPI stringer. Suppressing any doubts, Shaw encouraged Adam to send an outline and a few sample chapters to Irving Lazar, who then sent them to Ross Claiborne at Delacorte.

"It was very promising," Claiborne recalls. "And since I knew how deeply Irwin cherished Adam, I thought this would be a good idea, we should sign this up. So we did. But it couldn't have been a worse idea. Adam finally sent in a manuscript that just didn't work. We went over it very carefully and wrote that in its present form it really was unpublishable. We tried not to be so severe as to freeze him, but it was still a very strong letter, we needed a total overhaul. Months, maybe years went by, and we never heard another word from Adam." Finally Shaw broached the subject with Claiborne and asked why he'd never responded to Adam's manuscript. "Because that was what Adam had told his father," says Claiborne. "So I felt compelled at that point to dig into the files and say, 'Irwin, this is how we responded.' Irwin just froze."

That was the year Anatole Litvak died of stomach cancer. Shaw and Bodie went to the December funeral service at Père-Lachaise in Paris, along with Peter and Deborah Viertel and other close friends through the years. Litvak had chosen to be cremated, a process that in Paris involves sliding the coffin into an open crematorium. The congregation hears the flames crackling, then sees the small box of ashes emerge from the other side. At Litvak's service, the effect was further heightened by the mournful Russian music Sophie Litvak had requested. It was an experience Shaw never forgot. Deeply shaken, he, Bodie and the Viertels adjourned to the Ritz to get seriously drunk.

Not for the first time, Shaw went on the wagon at New Year's in Klosters. Not for the last, he fell off within a week. More and more often he would wake long before dawn, nervously twitching from alcohol and the stress that writing, in a quiet, insistent way, bore upon him, and take Miltown tranquilizers—a precursor to Valium—to get back to sleep. More often, too, there were sharp stomach pains. Laid low for a week by the time his birthday came up in February, for the first time Shaw found all the attention infuriating: too many phone calls, too many presents, too many flowers.

Inevitably, his poor health affected his relationship with Bodie. Now that he no longer enjoyed skiing, she seemed impatient with him, and he resented that. In part because of the experience with Bodie's Englishman, he felt more suspicious of any men with whom she spent time, even if they were long-established friends, and sometimes accused her of having affairs with them. At a dinner party one night, Shaw watched Bodie talking at great length with Larry Collins over cocktails. When the guests proceeded into the dining room, he startled everyone around him by declaring: "All right: you two stop talking together!"

By March 1975, Bodie acknowledged wanting to leave. When Shaw went to Paris on a quick trip, she refused to join him. Shaw returned furious and retaliated by not contacting her at the riverfront apartment where she still lived. "He'd try to be indifferent to me," Bodie says. "He'd decided long ago that that was the best strategy. But he wanted me to be there. He was very aware of me at all times. Sometimes he really hated me. But he was never bored with me—nor I with him. Even when he'd say 'Fuck off,' he'd want to have lunch with me."

Guardedly, they went together to Paris that spring. Any hope of re-creating past springs was dashed, however, when Shaw learned he was to be evicted from his apartment.

Over the winter Shaw had invited the young daughter of a friend to stay in the apartment as a security measure—the place had been robbed twice during Shaw's tenancy. The young daughter had apparently transformed the place into a crash pad for an ever changing cast of drug-ingesting friends. After one too many nights of pounding music and raucous noise, Shaw's outraged landlady had resorted to the traditional means of evicting tenants from apartments in Paris, declaring to Shaw that her son was getting married and needed to move in. It didn't matter that Shaw's subtenant had moved out or that upon her return to pick up a few last possessions, Shaw and Bodie made clear just how they felt about her tenancy. The apartment was officially to pass out of Shaw's hands on December 1.

Shaw toyed briefly with the notion of renting another place, but rental apartments in Paris had always been difficult to find and now were only more so. Then too, the political situation in France seemed darker than it had in decades; the dollar was continuing its decline against the franc; and with the Joneses' recent decision to make their move back to the United States a permanent one, the American colony in Paris seemed terribly diminished. Suddenly Shaw realized, as he wrote in the preface to *Paris! Paris!,* a soon-to-be-published pastiche of his *New Yorker* and *Holiday* pieces about the city, that he "had no wish to be left stranded, a last, desolate, trans-Atlantic monument to a joyous invasion that had come and gone."

Ever since he'd met her, Shaw had never missed the chance to remind Bodie of her promise to take him across the Atlantic one day on one of her father's ships. The trip had become a standing joke. Now, as a sort of consolation prize for losing the apartment, Bodie called her father and made the arrangements. Not only would the ship bring them to New York for the start of a second summer in the Hamptons; for Shaw, it would also be a symbolic return passage from the trip he had made to Paris nearly twenty-five years before.

TWENTY-ONE

The *Pacific Skov*, a 25,000-ton dry-cargo boat, sailed from Antwerp for Montreal at noon on May 15, 1975, bearing captain, crew and two delighted passengers in the vessel's luxurious owner's quarters.

Shaw and Bodie had left Paris a few days before. Now they had this huge boat virtually to themselves for a ten-day passage that became one of their happiest times. They took enormous pleasure from their shipshape cabin suite, with its sliding mahogany doors and shelves, its two spacious rooms equipped with stereo, stocked refrigerator and wine cooler. Soon enough they struck up a hearty rapport with Captain Rasmus Lauritzen and spent hours trading talk about ships and the sea. To his great delight, Shaw was even put on "growler" watch, to look out for random iceberg bits. Meals were taken with the officers, and therein lay the only drawback: the food was terrible. By the second day, the passengers began to make do with cheese, crackers and wine.

After a rainy crossing, the *Pacific Skov* entered Montreal's St. Lawrence Seaway. Shaw and Bodie had reservations at a grand hotel but made their way back to the ship that evening for a boisterous farewell dinner with Captain Lauritzen and his first mate. The plan for the next day was to rent a car and drive to Sugarbush, Vermont, where Bodie's sister Hanne was expecting them. For whatever reason, no car was available. Not to be deterred, Shaw commandeered a huge, purple Cadillac taxi whose scruffy-looking black driver agreed to make the drive for $80. As soon as they set off, it became apparent that the driver was inebriated, presenting not only a threat to his passengers' lives but also a problem at the international border.

There was only one thing to be done. As the border station came into sight, Shaw convinced the driver to pull over, surrender the wheel, and hide in the trunk. Then, with Shaw impersonating a taxi driver and Bodie in the back, the Cadillac rolled up for inspection. The border guards were not taken in. One went so far as to ask Shaw to open the trunk. Out popped the black driver, crying, "It's just me! I just wanted to buy freedom!" Fortunately, the notion of a freedom train headed the wrong way across the border struck the border guards as vastly amusing, the motley crew was allowed to pass, and the trip continued without incident until the driver, behind the wheel again, lost his concentration on one of the last snowy curves and crashed gently into a tree.

Regrettably, the summer did not match that wonderful crossing.

It began happily enough, with the news that David Shaw would not be using his Amagansett house and that Shaw and Bodie were welcome to it. Like the dozens of houses that had since cropped up around it in the open dunes area known as Amagansett East, David's had the contemporary look of the new Hamptons: a gray-shingled beach house with cathedral-ceiling living room, wide plate-glass windows and a back deck. David had built a studio over the adjacent garage, and Shaw was excited at the prospect of working in it. On the summer's first hot day, however, its lack of air-conditioning transformed it into a sweat box. Soon enough too, the Hamptons social scene swept him up. Jim and Gloria Jones had rented Diana Vreeland's house in Sagaponack, a half-hour drive from Amagansett. Nearby lived Willie Morris, whose southern charm had captivated Jones as it did everyone who met him. Morris had been settled in Bridgehampton long enough now to help introduce Jones to the area's literary notables, and soon Shaw was knocking around on an almost daily basis with Morris or Jones, or both. Inevitably the group, including Gloria Jones and Bodie, would end up at Bobby Van's, the dark, unpretentious piano bar on Bridgehampton's Main Street that was already famous as the local writers' hangout.

Despite his own well-earned literary celebrity, Morris had never lost a certain sense of awe at the new company he kept. It was part of his charm: the Yazoo City, Mississippi, boy miraculously transplanted among such famous northerners. One of the first times he stood drinking with the two of them, Morris listened respectfully as they waded once again into wartime reminiscences. Finally, recalls Morris, "I said something like, 'I'm younger than you two, and I missed that war. I missed what you two experienced and I regret it.' And Irwin immediately said, 'No, you don't! You don't ever regret missing wars!' And Jim immediately agreed and said, 'I don't want to ever hear you say that again; I wouldn't wish a war on anybody.' "

At the same time, Morris never felt condescended to by his new drinking buddies. With Shaw he often talked sports; one of the things Shaw had missed most in Europe, he said, was the college football scores. "It was clear that wherever Irwin had lived, he'd never lost his quintessential Americanness," Morris observes. "He carried it with him wherever he went—as did Jim, which was certainly one of the reasons the two had formed such a strong bond in Paris." Morris found that particularly attractive about both men, and he loved listening to Shaw tell stories. "Actually, Irwin was much more comfortable than Jim at sitting around telling stories," says Morris. "He told them with more gusto and enjoyment." About their own writing, the drinking buddies talked hardly at all—as if observing some unstated literary code of the Hamptons. They did talk about reviews, and reviewers. "Irwin would talk about how he couldn't get a good review out of *The New York Times,*" recalls Morris. "But I didn't detect a bitterness so much as a wistfulness—the sort of wistfulness you often see in writers as they grow older."

One subject that did arouse Shaw's ire was the hasty deal on the *Rich Man, Poor Man* miniseries. From the start, Universal had given the project serious attention, assigning veteran screenwriter Dean Riesner and producer Harve Bennett to come up with a working script. Soon the planned series had ballooned from six to ten hour-long installments, consumed two and a half years, and run up expenses of $300,000. (Shaw had apparently expressed interest in writing the script himself and had come up with an outline which was passed on to Riesner, but it was hardly more than a day's work, with key pages of the novel simply pasted down on paper. Riesner's outline, by contrast, came to 118 pages.) For some time after that, Lazar's skepticism had seemed well-founded. Riesner's bulging script had been shelved in Barry Diller's office, seemingly unread, while Diller chose to work with another production company on another prospective miniseries, Leon Uris's *QB VII.* Then, in early 1974, Diller had handed the project to Brandon Stoddard, ABC's newly appointed vice-president of motion pictures for television. ABC still had no licensing agreement with Universal for *Rich Man, Poor Man,* and so the project was technically "frozen," but Stoddard began to take a strong, active interest in it, calling for revisions and increasing the number of installments to twelve. The airing of *QB VII* in April 1974 lent a certain momentum. While only modestly successful, it proved ABC was willing to risk the miniseries form. The greater factor may have been Diller's departure for Paramount soon after, which seemed to help bring ABC and Universal together to hammer out the licensing agreement. Typically, the deal was established, in January 1975 between ABC's Marty Starger and Universal's Frank Price, over a dinner at Chasen's restaurant. ABC would pay Universal $5 million to produce *Rich Man, Poor Man.* At that point Shaw, who received not a cent of the money, began nursing a long, slow burn about the subject of Irving Lazar. By summer, recalls Morris, he was livid. " '*That little bastid Lazar,*' Irwin would say, '*what's he doing to me?*' "

As in Klosters, friends from all stages of Shaw's life seemed to converge in the Hamptons that summer. Joseph Heller lived down the street. Over in the Springs was Robert Alan Aurthur, a jovial screenwriter who wrote a monthly column for *Esquire* called "Hanging Out." Budd Schulberg had settled in Quiogue; with some reluctance, Shaw and Bodie went to a Schulberg dinner party one night. Elia Kazan was in Montauk; Shaw and Bodie met him for lunch one day at Gosman's Dock restaurant. Charles Addams—friend from that fateful Quogue summer long before— came over in his marvelous Bugatti convertible. So did Ross Claiborne,

Don Fine and many others. Almost every day Shaw and Bodie would either host a luncheon party at the house or meet friends at a restaurant, often the Spring Close Inn in East Hampton, where the cocktails were even more generous than the portions of heavy Italian food. Every night there was more drinking with dinner. Almost every next morning Shaw would find himself too "dreamy" to work and would instead sit out back watching squirrels vie with sparrows around the house's large bird feeder.

Even Bodie admits that both she and Shaw began drinking too much that summer. Bodie would head off to the beach to take long, rejuvenating ocean swims; since her childhood summers in Denmark, she had prided herself on swimming in almost all weathers and still made a point of plunging into the Atlantic every New Year's Day, fully clothed to stave off hypothermia. But Shaw seemed to have lost all the desire to work off his hangovers that he had had when Bodie first met him. Overweight, increasingly arthritic, he spent hours in the house watching sports on television. One day Winston Groom, a *Washington Star* reporter who'd befriended Adam in Washington and whose *Better Times Than These* would soon establish him as a fine novelist, came by to meet the writer whose work he'd always admired. "There was Irwin in his underwear in the middle of this completely messy living room, shouting at the top of his lungs, '*Bodie, where are my pants?*' "

Shaw was hardly unaware of his deteriorating condition, but he preferred to blame his body's woes on athletics. Over a luncheon interview with Robert Alan Aurthur, he drank white wine on ice and ruefully declined an invitation to join Aurthur and Adam Shaw for waterskiing that afternoon. "Look at me," he said sadly to Aurthur. "The old football player, now a physical ruin. I've got hip arthritis that's killing me, and I can't raise my right arm higher than halfway, so my tennis game is a disaster. All from skiing. I've fallen off a cliff, ripped my Achilles tendon, torn all the ligaments in my right shoulder, and this scar under my eye is from five stitches after I hit a rock."

In part as a sign of advancing age, Shaw's view of the world was growing even darker. Politically he had swung back strongly to the liberal line in the later years of the Vietnam War, and the Watergate era had only confirmed his worst suspicions of the Republicans in general and Richard Nixon in particular (it didn't help his relationship with Lazar any that the agent had just signed on the ex-president as a client). Instead of reading hope into the resolution of those national tragedies, Shaw often talked to interviewers now in apocalyptic terms. To a *Women's Wear Daily* reporter, he spoke of "the destruction of the American way of life. If it continues, there will be a huge upheaval. . . . Within the next two years there may not be a disaster, but there will be a crisis. What I think will happen is that the state will become more powerful. Our lives will become more regulated. . . . Once that happens we'll have to be much more responsible for what the state does." For *Newsday*, Shaw penned a column that summer, only partly in jest, about a time within 400 years when the eastern end of Long Island, according to some scientists, would be swept under the waves of the Atlantic. Perhaps, Shaw speculated, the end would come sooner—as early as Labor Day, 1975. There might be "a high wind" to "announce the beginning of the end, followed by a cosmic rush of salt water and a sudden liquid silence." After that, no doubt, a nuclear explosion would rock the rest of the world. Archaeologists drifting over the area in glass-bottomed boats a few centuries later would be left to puzzle out the meaning of such high-density housing under the sea. Shaw's view of a world spinning out of control seemed not unrelated to the reality that he was losing control of his own life through drinking. In any event, it would come to color two of his last four novels.

Adam was around that summer as well. Having spent the winter and spring in David Shaw's house, he and Keren had moved into one of the two adjoining East Hampton houses owned by Muriel Murphy, a wealthy New Yorker and art patroness romantically involved with Willie Morris at the time. Adam was working on a new nonfiction book idea that had sprung out of a reporting assignment, about the emotional impact of a December 1974 jetliner crash on the families of its victims. Often that summer he would stop by to visit his father. It rankled Bodie that he came without calling and raided the refrigerator without asking. It bothered Adam that Bodie was there at all, a bristling watchdog between him and his father. One day, according to Bodie, Adam arrived in the early afternoon while his father was taking a nap. Bodie told him to come back later, and an argument flared up. In the midst of it, says Bodie, Adam broke a beer bottle on the counter and threatened Bodie with the jagged top end. The incident virtually ended their communication; but to Bodie's fury, Shaw even then took a soothing approach to his son.

The simultaneous arrivals of Jim Jones and Irwin Shaw that summer did much to raise the profile of the Hamptons as a literary colony. Sniffing a story, *New York* magazine's Anthony Haden-Guest came to raise a few glasses with the old lions at Bobby Van's and soak up the gossip. His report, published just in time for the Labor Day weekend, was droll and insightful. To more than a few of the writers mentioned, it also seemed needlessly snide. Shaw in particular was described as looking "roseate" and "sounding valedictory about the new, inflationary Europe." The real stab came from Dwight Macdonald, quoted as offering the rhetorical response: "Irwin Shaw? He's a *writer?*" Not long after the article appeared, Shaw spied Haden-Guest across the dining room of Elaine's. The way Willie Morris remembers hearing the story, Haden-Guest resorted to crawling under various tables and chairs in a circuitous course to the door to avoid confronting what he knew would be a furious Irwin Shaw. Haden-Guest remembers it somewhat differently. "Irwin became so irritated with me, it's true. Though I don't know why he was irritated with *me*; it was Macdonald who was so disparaging about Irwin in the story. Anyway, Irwin tried to pick a fight with me two or three times in Elaine's after that. It put me in quite an awkward position, when you think about it. On the one hand, here was this sixty-year-old man. On the other hand, he was reputed to be quite a good boxer. So if I beat him I'd look bad; if I lost I'd look worse. We did become reasonably friendly in the end, however."

To a few of Shaw's longtime friends, the real slight seemed self-inflicted. Gay Talese, fiercely loyal, felt sorry that, in a sense, Shaw had come down from his mountaintop in Europe to seek the company of the *Paris Review* crowd that once had come to him—a crowd that no longer paid him proper respect. "I think if a dancer gets older or a singer loses his voice, he's still worthy of respect," says Talese. "But I believe that when Irwin wrote books that weren't up to the standard of the early ones, they turned on him. In my rather primitive view of relationships, they owed him more respect. And so I was sorry he went into their turf at the end—Irwin, who'd been everywhere and done everything and knew better, going out there and trying to maintain a continuation of the good old days in Paris. Willie Morris was a good man, and James Jones was a good man, but I think a lot of the others—well, I think Irwin wanted them too much as colleagues and friends, and they were somewhat condescending to him now."

If he sensed such attitudes, Shaw was too proud to acknowledge them to himself. But by any count too, the ranks of those in the Hamptons who genuinely loved and admired him far outnumbered any snobbish detractors. And while he couldn't blind himself to the critical consensus that his best work lay behind him, Shaw still took real satisfaction from the ability, as Jim Jones put it, just to keep getting up, no matter how many times the envious critics knocked him down, and write another book. That, as Jones and Shaw assured each other, was what defined *real* writers.

In fact, the critics were quite respectful of *Nightwork* when it appeared in September. "Never mind if this isn't the Big Novel we've been expecting from Irwin Shaw ever since he wrote *The Young Lions*," reported *Newsweek* in a typically upbeat reaction. "[It] is great fun, enormously likable, a first-rate piece of entertainment." Christopher Lehmann-Haupt agreed: "If you're fond of money, you'll love *Nightwork*." Who cares, he added, that "no character or incident is convincing enough in itself to disguise its true purpose of manipulating the reader." And was Shaw, in providing such a happy ending for Douglas Grimes, "wheeling out a philosophy" to rationalize his own enjoyment of money over the years, Lehmann-Haupt mused? No matter. "It didn't occur to me to ask as I read it. I simply curled up with it one evening, let it agitate my sense of greed, and mindlessly enjoyed every minute of it."

To Shaw's delight, his tribute to money was soon climbing the bestseller lists. By late October director Frank Perry had agreed to buy film rights to *Nightwork* for $250,000—two and a half times what Douglas Grimes embezzled, as one reporter noted. Perry, whose earlier films had been serious dramas (*David and Lisa, Diary of a Mad Housewife*), was full of enthusiasm for what he called "the best Shaw story since *The Young Lions.*" Perry added: "It's funny and fast and posh as hell and I'm going to get all of this." It was, unfortunately, a prediction that would prove premature.

Despite Shaw's generous decision to dedicate *Nightwork* to Bodie's mother, Gerda, the summer had left deeply mixed feelings. Bodie felt suffocated by the relationship, and she stayed in New York when Shaw flew back to Paris to close up his apartment. By mid-September, Shaw wrote to say he missed her badly and called twice to persuade her to join him. Citing the need to live her own life for a while, Bodie refused. Furious, Shaw fired off a telegram telling her not to come after all. In mid-October a sad letter followed. Shaw was sure now, he wrote, that Bodie didn't love him anymore and that their relationship was over.

Feeling abandoned by the Joneses as well as by Bodie in Paris, Shaw spent a quiet fall packing, and putting the final touches on *Paris! Paris!*, the collection of essays about the city, accompanied by Ronald Searle illustrations, that would appear the next year. "He was flirting around with various women," recalls Enid Hardwicke, who saw him several times during that period. "But I knew that he was very sad and rather lonely. He told me there was nothing for him in Paris anymore. I sensed too that he must have been thinking of reconciling with Marian. He had never been a person who liked being alone." The person to whom he felt closest now, Hardwicke felt, was Adam. "His life was really centered around Adam emotionally. He'd start out a conversation by saying, 'I called Adam today.' You could see how important that relationship was to him." In late November, Shaw stored many of his belongings in Hardwicke's apartment. His furniture he gave to the international student exchange school run by his poker-playing friend Jack Egle. A sofa went to Addie Herder; the painting over his desk, a Postimpressionist still-life, went to Bodie, who flew over after all to be with him for his last few nights in Paris. To speed him on his way, his landlady cut off his heat, water and electricity. Shaw and Bodie, laughing helplessly at the heavy symbolism of it all, finished packing in the dark.

In the States for Thanksgiving, Shaw reluctantly embarked on a round of television talk-show appearances to help sustain the sales of *Nightwork*. One turned out to be memorable: Shaw and Irving Lazar appeared together December 3 on the Johnny Carson show, and Lazar took the opportunity to ask the urbane host to play the part of the con man in Frank Perry's prospective movie version of the novel. Casually, Lazar offered Carson a million dollars to do it. Assuming Lazar was jesting, Carson said he'd happily play Joan of Arc and get burned at the stake for a million dollars, upon which Lazar produced a legitimate check, already signed, for the amount. Carson quickly backpedaled.

For Bodie the hiatus had eased resentments. By mid-December she sublet her apartment again—a move that in effect signed her on for another season of life with Shaw—and flew back to Zurich with him. On the drive up to Klosters, she says, Shaw asked her again to marry him, but she refused, as she had in the past. Wary of the lifestyle that had driven her away before, she also insisted that she be the one to decide whom they would see; that they would see her friends at least as often as they saw his; that the dreaded blizzard of dinner invitations and social climbers would somehow be kept under control.

An unexpected, though not unpleasant, aspect of the Christmas holiday week was the arrival of a *People* magazine reporting team from New York to profile Shaw for the scheduled start of the *Rich Man, Poor Man* miniseries in February. Though he grumbled about Time Inc. and took issue with a recent *Time* review of *Nightwork*, Shaw was secretly delighted by this latest rise in visibility. When the reporter asked how he felt about his beleaguered literary status among the critics, Shaw declared, somewhat disingenuously, "I don't want to be remembered—I want to be read." Asked about his marital status, Shaw was no less adamant. "I'm never going to let another woman get a legal hold on me," he vowed, and added, "I'm not rich anymore. I lost most of it through divorce, extravagance, carelessness and taxes. An American divorce, financially speaking, is Armageddon."

Within weeks, the new arrangement began to collapse. Bodie flew to London on her own, ostensibly for doctors' appointments, but also to get away from the claustrophobia of Klosters. Then, in early February, she learned she had a deep skin cancer near her mouth.

The news coincided with a remarkable bulletin from New York: the first segment of *Rich Man, Poor Man,* aired on February 1, had attracted as many as 50 million viewers, an astonishing figure. Immediately, executives of ABC and Universal realized not only that they had a hit on their hands, but also that they still had enough time—just barely—to work up a *Rich Man, Poor Man: Book II* for the following season. (Television's other blockbuster miniseries, *Roots,* would also air within a year.) They had no story left, of course, but they owned the characters and could do anything they liked with them. Partly in deference to Lazar's phone calls, partly because even in Hollywood it made a certain sense to have the author of the original *Rich Man, Poor Man* bring his golden touch to the sequel, Universal agreed to fly Shaw out to California and pay him an exorbitant amount of money to help flesh out the new story lines. Shaw tried to persuade Bodie that she should fly over with him and seek medical help in New York; despite his love for all things Swiss, he had relied on New York doctors in every possible situation. But Bodie refused. She felt she could get fine care in nearby St. Gall, and went in for minor surgery. Within a day of the operation, she gathered her clothes and sneaked out of the hospital without permission.

The America that Shaw flew into on February 7, 1976, was a country mesmerized by the storytelling drama of Irwin Shaw. The number of viewers who had tuned in was unprecedented for a fictional drama, and to the delight of ABC and Universal executives, they *kept* watching. Clearly, the story's classic theme of sibling rivalry, woven with Shaw's narrative skills, accounted in part for *Rich Man, Poor Man*'s success. But there were other reasons too for the breakthrough of what television executives were already referring to simply as "The Series."

Those reasons—fortunate and unfortunate alike—could be traced to the show's unusually long gestation period. Fortunately, the scripts had been more carefully written, and rewritten, than those of standard dramas. Unfortunately, as far as Shaw was concerned, there had been time to doctor the plot by condensing three of the book's female characters into one. (Rudy's first love, Julie Prescott, assumed a prominent role, while the brothers' sister, Gretchen, and Rudy's alcoholic wife, Jean, were cut away completely.) The change made the story line easier to follow and perhaps more compelling for television audiences, but it also robbed key scenes of narrative punch. The drama was also hyped with various instances of sentimentality—a note deliberately absent from the novel—and distorted violence. Executive producer Harve Bennett was later quoted as saying he felt the changes made for a better story than the novel itself (a quotation Shaw saw and was infuriated by) and perhaps for television audiences he was right.

The twelve-hour script that emerged from those two and a half years seemed to require at least five months of filming. But no stars would allow their schedules to be tied up for so long. *Rich Man, Poor Man*'s producers thus had no choice but to cast unknowns in the leading roles, and compensate by casting stars in cameos. So was determined the series' most winning aspect, the inspired casting of Peter Strauss and Nick Nolte as Rudy and Tom Jordache. (Nolte, as *RMPM* producer Jon Epstein points out, was initially rejected for the part on the basis of mediocre film clips from his guest appearances on a few serial dramas. Only when casting director Geoffrey Fisher importuned director Boris Sagal to bring Nolte in for a film test did he win the role.) Once the series was cast, the projected budget of $6 million was cut back to $4.5 million by executives concerned they wouldn't make a profit. And yet this change too seemed to inject the production with a nervous energy, inspiring resourceful corner-cutting. (All shooting was done either in the studio, where sets were occasionally borrowed from other shows, or in the nearby countryside. An establishing

shot of New York City in 1954 was accomplished simply by panning the
skyline circa 1975, but no viewers seemed bothered by the twin towers of
the World Trade Center.) The epic scale, and the still extraordinary budget, in the end forced ABC to spend considerable money publicizing the
show to recoup its investment; and that same epic scale, as much as
anything else, lured curious viewers to the tube.

For the ABC and Universal executives who had taken such a huge
risk in producing the series, *RMPM*'s success was a tremendous vindication
(it would garner twenty-three Emmy nominations). For Shaw the experience must have seemed bittersweet. In one night more Americans had
become aware of his work than in the entire four decades of his writing
career—an astounding, quite incomprehensible fact—but what they had
seen, as far as Shaw was concerned, was a truncated version of his panoramic story. His one-time payment of $110,000, long gone, struck him now
as little more than highway robbery, and whatever fee he might receive for
contributing to *Rich Man, Poor Man: Book II* would hardly approach the
money he might have received if he had retained the rights to *RMPM*'s
characters. Meanwhile, Dell had been caught by surprise by the program's
popularity. Bookstores all over the country were being besieged by demands for *Rich Man, Poor Man,* but Dell had only 75,000 paperback copies
in print. Within the first week of the television airing, retailers logged ten
times that number of back orders for the book. In desperation, Delacorte
had its upstate printer work overtime and farm out to other printers. By
the end of March the novel had gone through six additional paperback
printings.

Shaw went to Los Angeles and met with *Book II*'s executive producer,
Michael Gleason, and soon set to work blocking out a series' worth of
stories. Unfortunately, Gleason wasn't excited by what Shaw produced.
"There was some really great stuff, some wonderful characters who come
in for a few scenes, really grab your attention—and then just disappear,"
Gleason told one interviewer later. "His outline would make a marvelous
novel. ... It would not make good TV." To Shaw's shock and outrage,
it turned out the ABC team had taken no chances on the old pro. In fine
Sam Spiegel style, two other television writers had been put on the job at
the same time. One day while he was in California, Shaw met Frank Perry
for lunch at the Beverly Hills Hotel and began fulminating about ABC.
"He told me when he sat down that he was on the wagon, but he was just
going to have a little glass of wine," Perry recalls. "He ordered half a bottle
of Soave and started to get angrier as he drank. By the end of the lunch,
he had gone through six half-bottles of Soave."

Shaw was back in Klosters in time to officiate at his birthday Calcutta
Ski Race, but his trip had left him debauched, as trips to the U.S. always
did. Bodie and Lillian Tucker made a point of trying to get him on the ski

slopes one day; it proved to be his last-ever trip up. "Irwin had hardly skied all winter, and his hip was bothering him," remembers Tucker. "But we thought it would boost his spirits. So we went to Madrisa, an easy run. But the morning sun vanished by the time we got up on the T-bar, and a fierce wind had blown up during the night, blowing many rocks bare. So here we were, and Irwin didn't like it a bit. He had no confidence at all. It was really rough getting him down; he was in a panic. We did get to the middle station, and then Irwin began to cheer up and think he could do it. 'We'll all go to the Rufini's Hotel and have trout,' he said. And that's just what we did. We had this marvelous French-style lunch at an outside table, and two great bottles of French wine. And that was the last time Irwin ever skied."

In late March Bodie learned she would have to undergo radiation treatments. When she insisted again on going to St. Gall rather than New York for treatment, Shaw grew furious. Whether his anger indicated deep concern or exasperation was hard to tell. At any rate, Bodie felt he could have been more sympathetic. "I resented that, and this time, I really felt I was getting ready to split." Daily, it seemed, Shaw's moods grew darker. "Even at the start of our relationship, when Irwin had been very happy with me, he'd had volatile moods. Often they were tied to his work." But now the moods were far more frequent. "It had everything to do with how he felt about work and reviews and Adam and Lazar and skiing and physical deterioration." In particular, Shaw would get angry at Bodie for skiing without him. "Irwin would often at this stage get into a drunken rage—irrationally drunk. There was no point in talking to him now when he was drunk."

When Shaw departed Klosters in early April, his relationship with Bodie effectively came to end. Bodie remained behind, refusing to commit to any future plans. Upon her arrival in New York a month later, she reclaimed her apartment and chose not to be in touch.

Within days of his return, Shaw made his way out to the Hamptons to visit Adam and Keren in East Hampton. As it turned out, the other of Muriel Murphy's two adjoining houses was unoccupied, and Shaw decided to move in for the season. His initial reaction to being on his own again was vast relief, and to more than one sympathetic listener he spoke of how fed up he was with Bodie. "I just can't take any more," he told Enid Hardwicke. "She's such a *slob*." When he met Addie Herder one day in Bridgehampton, he made her walk with him the length of Main Street, pulling her by the arm and saying, "Why can't Bodie pull herself together?"

With his newfound freedom, though, Shaw had trouble keeping himself together too. Daily he ended up at Bobby Van's, nursing a glass of wine by late morning, so that even among his heavier-drinking friends it began to be said that if you wanted to talk to Irwin and have him remember what you said, you had to find him before 11:00 A.M. As far as Shaw was concerned, matters definitely got out of hand the night of April 18, 1976. That was the night the East Hampton Village Police threw him into jail.

"Actually, it's a very funny story," recalls Willie Morris. "Irwin and Mike Burke were out that night having drinks at Bobby Van's, and they both got drunk as cooters. Adam came in and said, 'Dad, you've had enough, let's go home.' So they went home. Then Adam went off somewhere else. I showed up at Bobby Van's at a late hour—and there was Irwin. He'd snuck out of the house." Headed home the second time, Shaw, at the wheel of his latest Art Stanton Volkswagen, hit another car at the intersection of Main Street and Woods Lane in Wainscott. The officer who arrived at the scene quickly determined that Shaw was too drunk to drive and brought him to the village lockup. Utterly mortified, Shaw pleaded with the officer not to inform his mother of the arrest. At 2:00 A.M., Adam arrived to post the $100 bail, and a court date was set, eventually resulting in a modest fine.

It was a sad experience, made more so when *The East Hampton Star* included the news of Shaw's arrest in its regular police-blotter column, despite the earnest efforts of Adam to have the story spiked. It did have one beneficial result, though. From then on, Shaw made a dogged point of finding friends to drive him home at the end of an evening. Over the summers that followed, one of his most faithful escorts would be Winston Groom, who admits he often had the distinct impression Shaw was inviting him to a dinner party because he knew he'd need a sober hand at the wheel later on.

Shaw hadn't been back in East Hampton long before a new girlfriend, Ruth Batchelder, appeared on the scene. By all accounts—and there were many—Batchelder was a young woman with an agenda. An aspiring author and songwriter who had landed a job in New York assisting writer Jacqueline Susann, Batchelder impressed everyone she met that summer as a strong self-promoter, eager to meet Shaw's literary friends and land herself a book contract. The rumor that she had pursued a similar relationship with *Artie* Shaw, the bandleader, lent the situation a slightly madcap spin.

In fact, Batchelder did seem genuinely fond of Shaw, and solicitous of his very ragged health. "She did take good care of him," notes writer Alfred Allan Lewis, a longtime friend of Gloria Jones. "She ran his house, cooked his meals, tried to keep him off the sauce. She did all these nice things that were on the level. It's just that she also pushed hard on the level of her own selfish needs." For her part, Batchelder found the Hamptons literary crowd snobbish and unaccepting. As for the Shaw family scene, it was, she felt, right out of some dark O'Neill drama. Every night she would bring Shaw home roaringly drunk from some cocktail or dinner party, and then end up on the patio as he held forth, another drink in hand. By the end of her cameo role in Shaw's life, Batchelder says she was convinced of two things: that Shaw hated his mother, on whom his late-night invective often focused; and that with all the drinking, he had absolutely no interest in sex.

While the Hamptons literati were absorbing this sodden soap opera, a far more dramatic one exploded next door. For some time Adam's marriage to Keren Ettlinger had been less than harmonious. Whatever its problems, Keren felt dissatisfied enough to embark on a short romance with actor Kevin McCarthy—the same Kevin McCarthy who had appeared in the 1948 production of Irwin Shaw and Peter Viertel's play *The Survivors*. Keren described the romance in her diary and then, unwittingly or not, left the diary open. Adam read the fateful entry and reacted exactly as his father had to the news of Marian's relationship with Jean Daninos. With a few last shudders, the marriage came to an end.

Amid such *Sturm und Drang,* Shaw did little if any writing. Winston Groom remembers him as being in a sort of holding pattern: "not depressed, just floating." So substantial was his drinking that on at least one occasion, Shaw checked into Southampton Hospital with what he described as a flu but what friends believed to be delirium tremens. On July 16, however, Shaw delivered a long and lovely address at nearby Southampton College on writing and his own career. Filled with wise and gracious observations, the address belied his often reckless lifestyle these days and served as a reminder that no matter how dissipated he could appear on the outside, a brilliant mind kept ticking within.

To a large crowd that included his visiting mother, Adam and many friends, Shaw reminisced about his early days at Brooklyn College, his great love Elaine Cooper, radio serials, the overnight success of *Bury the Dead* and the writing life it had opened up for him. "People often ask me what drove me to being a writer," he reflected. "The question is more or less impossible to answer, since I started to be a writer, as far as I can remember, when I was eleven years old, and it's so far back in the mists of time that I have no notion of what really drove me into such a curious occupation." One likely reason, he admitted, "is that I had a rich Brooklyn accent, so that I couldn't talk very well. The second was that aside from a Brooklyn accent I mumbled, and people had great difficulty in understanding what I was saying when I spoke. My mother . . . kept saying all through my childhood, my adolescence, my youth and even up till today, 'Take the potatoes out of your mouth when you talk!' "

Shaw advised writers not to "disdain money. The chief gift is that it gives you time." A thick skin against critics was also useful, even imperative. The professor who had just introduced him, Shaw observed with amusement, "preferred to announce that I was very successful, etc. etc. and that made it sound as though my life has been one long happy procession of good reviews. My family, which is present tonight, knows this is hardly the case. Some of the reviews have been monstrous. And unfortunately,

writers never remember the thousand good reviews, but always remember
the one bad one. If you wish to survive, you have to remember it and still
get up off the floor, and keep on going."

With an eye toward his own posterity, Shaw suggested a writer not
only shake off the critics but ignore the fads. "We live in an age in which
almost every kind of writing, every kind of art, is acceptable or has an
audience or can be welcomed somewhere. That is, we don't have any
conventions like the heroic couplet or the iambic pentameter in drama or
the well-made story or the well-made novel. . . . [But] I think that if
somebody like myself feels that his style consists of being brief, concise,
lucid, clear, he should stick to it."

Above all, Shaw declared, a writer must remember that for all the
anguish and uncertainty it entailed, the practice of writing was play.

Within the Hamptons' wide literary/social circle, the relative eligibil-
ity of the Shaws *père et fils* did not go unremarked as the summer unfolded.
Interestingly enough, one of the first women to take an interest in Adam
ended up, after a short fling, with Adam's father instead.

Since Adam's teenaged years, there had existed between Shaw and his
son a not so subtle physical rivalry, whether on the slopes or in the
après-ski socializing at the bar of the Chesa Grischuna. Shaw took pride
in Adam's considerable athletic abilities and in his obvious attraction for
women, even to the extent of bragging to Bodie about how many girls
Adam was romantically involved with. At the same time, Shaw liked to feel
he could outcharm Adam when he set his mind to it. Now that his health
was declining more sharply, and his waistline expanding, he may have felt
the rivalry more keenly. But then, Diana Erwitt was just the sort of glamorous and gregarious blonde that Shaw had always admired.

As the wife of photographer Elliott Erwitt, Diana had often thrown
parties for a wide cross-section of the Hamptons crowd at her Colonial-
style home in Amagansett. Now, though, she and Erwitt were getting
divorced, so the party she threw for her own birthday on July 26 became
an opportunity, in part, to cast a few lines to attractive single men. When
photographer Jill Krementz told her that Adam Shaw was the newest
eligible bachelor in town, Diana, who had never met Adam, called to invite
him.

The two hit it off, and the next day, when Erwitt had to go by taxi
to Riverhead to appear before a judge about a ticket for speeding at ninety
miles per hour, she found herself paged at the courthouse: it was Adam,
holding a bouquet of zinnias. As he drove her back to the Hamptons,
Adam asked if she would cancel her lunch date to have lunch with him
and his father, and Erwitt agreed. "When we pulled up to the house Adam
said, 'Don't you want to comb your hair?' I could tell his father meant a
great deal to him and he wanted me to look my best. We got out, and it

was eleven in the morning, and his father said, 'You've just gotten back from court!' He was beaming with charm, there was such energy from his face, as if he was stranded in the Alps and I was his St. Bernard."

Shaw offered Erwitt a vodka, which she accepted, and the three ended up having lunch at the house rather than going out. "I sat opposite Irwin, who did most of the talking," recalls Erwitt. "I did most of the listening, and Adam did the glowering. There was obviously some rivalry here. As Adam and I left, he said, 'My father really liked you.' It was like out of some Edwardian novel; I felt I was one of the mill girls going up to the family that owned the mill. I had found Irwin so *simpatico,* so wonderful, so light and gay and charming, everything that seemed to be lacking in my life. But we were not going to see him again that summer." For the moment, Erwitt drifted into a short affair with Adam that was overshadowed by her mother's dying. When her mother died, on Labor Day, Erwitt and Adam parted company.

Meanwhile, it seemed only fitting that the summer's domestic dramas culminate in a hurricane. By August 9, when Hurricane Belle rose up from the south and appeared headed directly across eastern Long Island, Shaw had had just about all he could take of Ruth Batchelder. Hours before the hurricane hit, she made her last mistake.

It happened when Shaw got a call from Mike Burke's ex-wife, Timmy, who lived near the Murphy complex, to say she was alone and scared, and would Shaw stay the night at her house. The request was utterly innocent, but Batchelder took umbrage. That seemed to do the trick. Livid, Shaw banished her on the spot.

With the skies darkening, Batchelder sought refuge at Jim and Gloria Jonesos' newly purchased farmhouse in Sagaponack, where several people had gathered because the house was situated on some of the highest ground in the area, a bluff overlooking a patchwork of potato fields. Willie Morris and Muriel Murphy were there, as was Allan Lewis. Adam Shaw was there too, his typewriter at the ready; *The Washington Post* had given him an assignment to write a story on the effects of the storm on the Hamptons. Half afraid that these friends of Shaw would evict her too, Batchelder made herself useful by cooking up great pots of food. Shaw resolutely refused to leave his house for higher ground. "The hell with it," he told the Jones group by phone. "I don't care if there's a hurricane or not, I'm going to bed."

Despite predictions of a devastating storm, Shaw did exactly that. Soon after, the electricity went down. Adam began typing by candlelight, Ruth Batchelder kept stirring her pots as her prospective diners grew drunker and drunker, and the storm, such as it was, passed over. By the next morning, the brave band learned that Hurricane Belle had been a bust, leaving virtually none of the destruction wreaked by its legendary predecessor in 1938. As the skies cleared, Batchelder headed into Manhattan. There, by several reports, she checked into an expensive hotel on Shaw's account for the next day or two, and then flew out to California, where she managed to plant a prominent item in a newspaper gossip column about her intention to write a kiss-and-tell book that would expose the "real" Irwin Shaw.

Doris Lilly, still in touch with Shaw as a friend, clipped the gossip item and sent it on to Klosters, where Shaw was recovering after Labor Day from his summer indulgences. "In the letter I wrote him I said, 'Irwin, it's not so much fun now that you're not married, is it?' Cheating had been half the fun." Shaw wrote back to say he was hardly concerned about the tasteless rantings of an undereducated Jewess who wrote so badly that there was virtually no chance she would ever get a book published. Getting rid of her for the cost of a couple of days at an expensive hotel, he added, seemed a wonderful deal. After all the women with whom he had been involved, Batchelder was the only one who had left him feeling embittered, and one in an entire career of romances had to be expected. More cheerfully, he wrote, he was almost completely on the wagon, drinking only a glass or two of wine a day and slowly regaining a respectable figure.

The summer had done little for Shaw's writing career, but the continuing aftershocks of the *Rich Man, Poor Man* miniseries had made him a rich man after all. Each month since the miniseries, Dell had reissued another old Shaw novel in paperback, the covers identically designed, with each title in the same sweeping script used for *Rich Man, Poor Man*. As for the novel that had brought all this about, Dell now had 5.3 million paperback copies in print.

Shaw made his next career move as much out of pride as for profit. Furious at the tawdry production of *Rich Man, Poor Man: Book II* that would air that winter, he decided to write his own sequel, drawing on the story lines he'd worked up in Hollywood earlier in the year. With Irving Lazar's help, he persuaded Delacorte to draw up a separate contract for the book. He would still owe the novel he had agreed to write in 1973, but in the meantime he would be paid $200,000 to write *Beggarman, Thief,* as he titled his sequel—*within six months.* By a rider in the contract, Adam would be paid twenty percent of that advance in installments as "consultant and advisor to the author."

By late summer Shaw was hard at work, writing faster, and with less enjoyment, than he ever had in his life.

TWENTY-TWO

It was not unexpected, yet it came as a shock, profoundly affecting Shaw's work, his relationships—every aspect of the remaining years of his life. For an extraordinary number of people, Jim Jones's death in the spring of 1977 seemed to darken the sky as last summer's storm had only promised to do.

Shaw and other close friends already knew that Jones was afflicted with cardiomyopathy, a heart condition exacerbated by alcoholism. Unlike cirrhosis of the liver, with which it is often compared, cardiomyopathy cannot be reversed, only arrested. Jones's initial collapse had been at the Styrons' house in Martha's Vineyard in 1970. Since that time, he had managed to abstain from hard liquor, but not white wine.

The illness had influenced his decision to move back from Paris in 1974, and that move had helped persuade Shaw to follow him. During the last three summers Jones had clearly exhibited the telltale signs that his condition was worsening, particularly a shortness of breath that indicated his swollen heart was growing more impaired and allowing toxic fluids to collect. Still, his family and his many friends tried not to talk or think about the implications; and no one, certainly not Shaw, with his defiant Jesse Craig in *Evening in Byzantium* sauntering out of the hospital to order a scotch against doctor's orders, was about to dictate to Jones that he stop drinking altogether. The last slide, as Shaw would one day describe his own deteriorating condition, began in January.

All that winter, Shaw shuttled from Klosters to New York and back, carrying his Olivetti 44 portable typewriter with him and working, at either end, on *Beggarman, Thief*. In New York, he stayed in a suite at the Sherry-Netherland, that bastion of fusty elegance with sweeping views of Central Park and the Plaza Hotel. The Sherry had become Shaw's New York base now. He loved the hotel's understated charm, its small, dark lobby, the French-style decorative wood paneling of its elevators, the big, wide guest rooms furnished with overstuffed sofas and chairs. The Sherry wasn't for those who wanted brand-new appliances and telephones in the bathroom—the kitchenettes in its suites had a decidedly plain look about them, and the claw-footed bathtubs and old porcelain sinks struck some as unwelcome antiques—but to its regular guests, the hotel felt like home.

The novel that would emerge from Shaw's labors at the Sherry-Netherland would be dedicated to Jim and Gloria Jones. It would also carry an unusual prefatory note, explaining to readers that the novel bore no resemblance to television's *Rich Man, Poor Man: Book II*. In a sense, the entire plot of *Beggarman, Thief* would be a rebuke to the miniseries sequel—admittedly a less than ideal motivation for a novel.

Whereas the television sequel kills off many of its characters, *Beggarman, Thief* kills off no one, not even Tom Jordache's murderer Danovic, whom sixteen-year-old Wesley Jordache spends most of the novel trying to track down. (The miniseries did have to be constructed around Wesley, however, not just because Tom Jordache had been killed off at the end of *RMPM I*, but because Nick Nolte refused to participate in the project.) Indeed, the reflective tone of its characters, who indulge in considerable reminiscing with each other to remind the reader of the events of *Rich Man, Poor Man*, seems calculatedly antithetical to television's needs, an exercise in proving that a compelling story can be woven from yearnings and regrets as well as or better than by unremittingly violent episodes. Violence had become too prevalent a force in the civilized world to be ignored, but Shaw's aim was to sound an alarm by having characters react to offstage violence, not to contribute to the problem by adding more of it.

As in *Rich Man, Poor Man*, Shaw set his story against a backdrop of current events—talk of the Vietnam War, international terrorism, urban violence, women's liberation. There is no denying the story's weaknesses; even as commercial fiction, *Beggarman, Thief* is embarrassingly dreary. It does, however, underscore its author's continuing concern with the brooding issues of *Rich Man, Poor Man*—family, violence and the impact of money on each. Much of the novel is told through the eyes of Rudy, now the reluctant head of the Jordache clan, who comes increasingly to resemble his creator. Rudy has been battered by life, even to the extent of having, in fine Shaw fashion, a smashed nose. The battering, though, has ennobled him, making him newly aware of the importance of family above all else.

Beggarman, Thief shows a more philosophical attitude toward the vagaries of family—particularly of women in families—than anything Shaw had written to date. For the first time Shaw allowed a woman—Gretchen Jordache—to be sexual without becoming a virago, to be ambitious without being a female schemer, even to succeed in directing an excellent film. It seemed to reflect his own more tolerant views of the women in his life, a loosening of the infamous Shaw double standard, an awareness that women could embody as complicated a mix of desires and virtues as he.

One day in November 1976, early into the writing of *Beggarman, Thief*, Diana Erwitt happened into the Sherry-Netherland for dinner with a date. The dinner had gone badly, and Erwitt went storming out, only to run into Shaw, just off the plane from Europe. When Erwitt confessed why she was feeling so blue, Shaw swept her up to his suite for a few consolation drinks.

Finally she said she had to go. "As I got up to leave," recalls Erwitt, "Irwin said, 'You've got a new beau.' I said, 'Who?' He said, 'Me.'"

The two saw each other the rest of that fall, starting each day with a lunch that usually took up the whole afternoon. "When I came in the door," recalls Erwitt, "he would just stare at me and say, 'You look like a Charles Dana Gibson girl, right off the calendar.' He had a way of making you feel like the most beautiful, marvelous, clever, intelligent woman in the world." Once, as they were dining in the Sherry-Netherland's restaurant, a stunningly beautiful woman walked in. As she made her way down the bar every man in the restaurant turned to gawk at her—every man except Shaw. "Irwin didn't look over at her once," Erwitt marvels. "Finally, when she'd passed, I said, 'Irwin, I'm astonished, why didn't you look at her? Everyone else did.' And he said that no, a long time ago he'd learned not to do that when he was with another woman, that it was the height of rudeness, so he'd trained himself." If so, the author of "The Girls in Their Summer Dresses" had perhaps merely mastered a more effective strategy.

As a result of his latest, unexpected glow of celebrity, Shaw was constantly recognized and approached by admirers as he and Erwitt strolled off to lunch at Le Cirque or La Côte Basque. "He adored that," says Erwitt. "He loved being nice to people. He wouldn't suffer fools but he would suffer neophytes, kids who were doing stories on him for their college newspaper. People would come up to him in a bookstore, and the next thing I knew, we'd be up in the Sherry-Netherland with twenty perfect strangers from Omaha." Doormen and waiters recognized him too, and brightened when they did, for Shaw's generosity as a tipper had become legendary.

At the lunches, and at the equally long dinners, to which they ventured after a late-afternoon nap, Shaw would often speak of classic writers he loved and marvel that Erwitt hadn't read them. Erwitt was no fool, but as she explained, her Catholic education had left large gaps. "Irwin used to love teaching me things," she says. "He gave me lists of books to read—Euripides, Plutarch, Thackeray and Ben Jonson. Then he'd go out and buy me the books. He bought me a complete set of Thackeray. He bought me the Oxford English Dictionary. And in doing that he managed to be expansive without being pompous. Just tremendously young and energetic, a sort of combination Errol Flynn and intellectual figure."

Often talk turned to Marian. Erwitt was confused by the rumors she'd begun to hear—that Marian wanted to reunite with Shaw, that Shaw was considering it strongly. "Irwin would say, 'That old bitch, that geriatric case, what is she talking about?' He'd be choking with laughter." It was true, Shaw conceded, that now Adam was making a concerted effort to get his parents back together. While he would always be grateful to Marian as the mother of his son, however, Shaw said he was adamant about not getting remarried.

Unconvinced, Erwitt kidded Shaw about the revenges Marian would devise when he grew infirm in her care. " 'Those little accidents in the wheelchair when she forgets to turn on the brakes and you go down the hill and hit the dumpster? When she pins the bib through your collarbone and you can't say anything because you're drooling?' And Irwin would be screaming with laughter—just the image of him being in Marian's clutches like that, her getting back at him for all those years of infidelity."

Almost from the start, Shaw told Erwitt that he wanted to marry her. "I hemmed and hawed all through fall and winter on that one," she recalls. On the one hand, she felt she could be very happy married to Shaw. "I felt that the age difference was enough that he wouldn't be two-timing me. And I'm not sure I would have minded if he had. Irwin reminded me of that famous story about Bob Capa—the women loved him so much that one of them had tried to get into The '21' Club by saying, 'I'm one of Bob Capa's girls.' You just wouldn't mind. You might feel shortchanged, but when Irwin was with you he gave you his undivided attention." As if that were not enough, Shaw began sending occasional checks to Erwitt that fall—she was living at the Beekman Towers, a short walk from the Sherry-Netherland, and having trouble making ends meet after her divorce—and even bought her a Volkswagen (at the Art Stanton discount rate). The age difference was inhibiting, however, and the drinking bothered her—not only Shaw's, but her own while she was with him. A heavy drinker when she'd met Shaw, Erwitt was almost always hung over in the mornings at his suite in the Sherry-Netherland, waking groggily to the sound of Shaw's inevitable quicksilver typing. "Irwin said to me once, 'How the hell did we know drinking was so destructive?' I said, 'God, if you want to stop, why don't you?' And what he said, simply, was, 'I can't.' "

With Erwitt unbudgeable on the subject of marriage, Shaw still offered to support her. "He said come on, quit your job. But this was the funny part of it. Irwin never paid for anything, he used plastic and had some accountant pay his bills for him. He had no idea what the going rate for the yen was, for example. So he said, 'If you quit your job, I'll pay for your apartment—*and give you fifty dollars a week.*' He really thought that was a lot of money. It was like your grandfather giving you a quarter and saying, 'Go to a movie.' "

Amid such happy times, even an ultimate pro couldn't knock off a hefty novel in just six months. Shaw was forced to ask that his deadline be postponed to April 30, and to juggle the finishing of it with his inevitable holiday stay in Klosters. That winter, he and Marian startled the ski crowd by appearing in public together. Within hours, the news had flown around town that the Shaws had been seen lunching at the Alpina, a restaurant-hotel across from the railroad station. In fact, Adam and Keren had arranged the truce talk, but a mood of rapprochement was already in the air. By all accounts, Marian had tired of the wars sometime before Shaw and sent out peacemaking feelers through friends. She may not have pined for him with youthful passion, but she did feel solicitous for his drink-embattled health. Also, she missed being Mrs. Irwin Shaw, entertaining elegant friends with the immeasurably greater clout of her husband at her side. For his part, Shaw may have felt some vestigial bitterness toward the woman he had castigated in public for so long, but his latest turns around the track as an aging bachelor had begun to depress him, and the companionship of a lifetime mate was seeming unexpectedly attractive. Before the winter was out, the two ex-marrieds went a step further, taking a quiet side trip in the French countryside to sample the strange experience of being together again.

Bodie, meanwhile, remained a peripheral presence, having maintained her Klosters apartment on the Landquart River and made the decision to return to it for part of the winter. Years later, she bridles at the question of whether she and Shaw had actually ended their affair the previous spring, or if it continued in some fashion despite Shaw's summer dalliances and his new rapport with Marian. "There had been no real breakup," she says. "Neither Irwin nor I looked at life in such a parochial way. We remained close that winter; we were still an important part of each other's lives." Bodie had mixed feelings about Shaw's revived interest in Marian after serving for so long as an audience to his rage about her: bafflement, amusement, annoyance. But she says she understood Marian perfectly. "Marian had been extraordinarily tenacious about Irwin and always hoped she'd get him back. She was a voracious wife, and he'd become her property. It was an old-fashioned, almost nineteenth-century attitude, by which the wife had become all but subsumed by the marriage."

No less old-fashioned, however, was the attitude that prevailed when Bodie's separation from Shaw became an undeniable fact by the late spring of 1977. There was no talk of money changing hands, no financial compensation from a now wealthy man to his disenfranchised companion for a period that amounted to at least the seven years defined by common-law marriage. In part Bodie was to blame, for nursing an aristocrat's sense of pride about such things, despite the fact that she had abandoned her career to be with Shaw and now, without any private income, had no clear idea of how she would support herself. In part Shaw was to blame. Despite his characteristic generosity, he felt hostile, especially after the divorce years, about the prospect of doling out money to an ex-mate. Almost certainly, Marian was also to blame. As her role in Shaw's life continued to grow, her sheer presence, if nothing else, served to deter Shaw from sending Bodie money. "As far as Marian was concerned," Bodie observes, "I'd been a terrible influence. And I suppose it was hard to blame her. After all, I *had* borrowed her husband for eight years." Later, to help Bodie reestablish herself in New York, Shaw did send her a one-time compensation of $10,000.

Despite these distractions, by April 15, Shaw could stride into the Harvard Club in New York to meet E. J. Kahn, Jr., for lunch and announce, beaming, that he was writing the last sentences of *Beggarman, Thief* that very day. The manuscript, Shaw added, was 175,000 words long; within the last three months he had written 150 pages of it. "One great thing about Irwin Shaw," Kahn later wrote of the friend he hadn't seen in ten or fifteen years, "has always been that even when he isn't finishing a book he seems so exuberant. He is an unapologetic hedonist, and I suspect that his affability and jollity have had as much as anything to do with the fact that solemn critics are forever putting him down as a mere storyteller not to be alluded to in any profound discussion of serious literature. Irwin's attitude has always seemed to me to be: Let them wear hair shirts; cashmere's more comfortable."

Just days later came the sad news that Jim Jones had checked into Southampton Hospital and was fading fast. What Shaw found, in the waiting room of the hospital's coronary care unit, was a scene of desperate grief. Gloria Jones was being comforted by a succession of tearful friends; Kaylie and Jamie were hugging each other; and milling among them were nurses, doctors and lawyers. Despite hospital regulations, liquor was flowing freely; by the time Shaw arrived, Gloria had come to terms with the reality that Jim was literally dying and had made the decision to give him a cupful of bourbon, his first in five years. Meanwhile, Jones was talking, with effort, into a tape recorder, outlining the conclusion of his last novel, *Whistle*, as Willie Morris sat beside him taking backup notes. When Shaw came in, ashen-faced, to greet his old friend, Jones managed to say to him, "Irwin, you look worse than I do." To which Shaw shakily responded, "That's because you're sober and I'm not."

During Jones's last days, the vigil-keeping group would adjourn for lunch and dinner breaks to a restaurant called Herb McCarthy's, where with enough alcohol its members could begin to convince themselves that Jones was improving after all. Bodie was among the regulars, having come to stay with Gloria and offer full-time help. Adam was there too, and it was during the vigil that he first learned his father had been having an affair with Diana Erwitt—by hearing Shaw speak with her on a public telephone at the hospital. The evening Jones died—May 9, 1977—Shaw was having dinner with the Gabels and the Lazars in New York, where Bodie reached him by phone with the news. For Shaw, as for all of Jones's family and friends, it was a devastating experience that forced a somber reappraisal of life. Before the night was out, Shaw responded by placing a call to his companion of thirty years. In the harsh glare of mortality, Marian was the only woman in his life who seemed to count.

Not long before he died, Jones declared to his son, Jamie, and to Willie Morris that he wanted to be cremated, and for the two of them to take the urn filled with his ashes out on a boat. Then, instructed Jones, they were simply to throw the urn overboard. To Morris it was a dismaying notion. What if some fisherman brought it up in his net one day? Jones was adamant, though, and had the request included in his will. It was Shaw who prevailed on Jamie to help him persuade Gloria Jones to break the will. Recalls Morris: "Irwin told Jamie, 'Your father was a very great writer, and there are going to be scholars and admirers all through the years who will want to know where he's buried.' "

With Peter Matthiessen, Shaw then took charge of organizing a memorial service at the Bridgehampton Community House. A reception was to follow at the Joneses' house in Sagaponack, with a funeral the next day at a local cemetery. Only longtime residents of the town were allowed to be buried in the pretty, white-picket-fenced green, but Matthiessen persuaded the local authorities to grant an exception. First, though, the organizers had to deal with the cremation itself.

Morris was the one to make the arrangements with Southampton's Brockett Funeral Home, but he balked at the prospect of going to pick up the ashes alone. "I called Irwin," he remembers, "and we had Peter Matthiessen drive us over in his station wagon, the three of us. We had to sign out the ashes. Then Irwin picked up the urn in his big arms and we all headed back outside. I was walking behind Irwin, and he was kind of bouncing along on the balls of his feet, he was an aging athlete. At that point we didn't know what to do with the ashes, because Jamie had not decided at that point whether to bury them. So we decided to take the urn back to Peter Matthiessen's, because Peter had a Zen prayer room where he'd actually stored the urn that held his mother's ashes.

"We got there, and walked upstairs, and took off our shoes, and Irwin put his old buddy's ashes next to Peter Matthiessen's mother's ashes, and Maria, Peter's wife, made a little ceremonial tea. Then we went back downstairs to mix drinks. In the living room of Peter's house there's a wonderful piano, and almost out of instinct, I went over and picked out my favorite Protestant hymn, 'Abide with Me.' I was really playing to myself. All of a sudden, Irwin, who was sitting in a chair close to the piano, stood up and walked to a corner of the room, put his face in his hands and began sobbing like a child. It was like a thunderstorm, his whole big old body was racked with sobs, and it lasted about thirty seconds, forty seconds, and then all of a sudden he stopped. He sat back down and picked up his drink. And that was it."

William Styron, Willie Morris and Shaw were each to speak at the memorial service, and the three, still shaken, made a solemn vow not to drink until after the ceremony. When they arrived at the Bridgehampton Community House, a churchlike structure fronting Montauk Highway, Shaw went over to confer with the local firemen who were helping officiate as some 400 guests gathered. "You look like a man who needs a drink," said one of the firemen kindly to Shaw, and he pulled out a flask of whiskey. Feeling guilty but grateful, Shaw took a long, hard swig.

After words from Morris and Styron, Shaw stood to offer a somewhat simpler tribute, evoking in clear, bright images the life he and Jim and so many in the audience had shared in Paris. At the funeral service the next day, as Peter Matthiessen shoveled dirt on Jones's urn, Shaw said quietly, "Good-bye, Jim, the adventure is over."

Unresolved was the issue of how to deal with Jones's uncompleted manuscript of *Whistle*. Delacorte's editors wanted Styron and Morris to continue the narrative in Jones's voice, and with Jones's advance as leverage, their opinion held considerable weight. The two writers balked at that, however, and Shaw strongly supported their view. "I talked to Irwin about it," recalls Morris, "and he said we shouldn't do it that way. 'Absolutely not,' he said. 'It's unethical.' I remember how staunch Irwin was in his defense of Jim's posthumous book, loyal right to the end. Being very eloquent and damn professional about it too." Over a midtown lunch, Delacorte's editors, Gloria Jones, Willie Morris and Shaw decided that *Whistle* would be finished in outline form as the Jones team wished.

Shaw was at the Jones house in Sagaponack nearly every day for the next weeks, helping in any way he could. Loyal companion to Gloria, surrogate uncle to the children, he was a pillar of stability in this turbulent time, and the Joneses, who loved him already, never forgot it.

His own grief he expiated in an eloquent, heartfelt tribute that appeared in *The New York Times Book Review* in early June. Jones's war trilogy—or really, as Shaw suggested, his quartet, including *The Pistol*—constituted a unique "offer to posterity," the literature of a writer who truly understood the effects of World War II on the men who fought in it. Jones, he declared, had written "clearly, unsentimentally, bluntly, knowingly, with a craftsman's hard-earned skill." Those were words that might as easily have been used to sum up Irwin Shaw—as were Shaw's about Jones's persistent critics. "Not for the first time in the world of letters," Shaw wrote, "the success of his first book was used to damn his later work and his life style, whatever that means, which was commented upon by some critics to indicate that he had succumbed to greed at the expense of his art. Nothing could be further from the truth. He liked the freedom and the gewgaws of wealth and the immense generosity he could now afford, but the hard-bitten, dedicated soldier-artist never for a moment faltered in his task or changed his moral conception of the basic principles of his life."

In losing Jones, Shaw had lost more than a best friend. He had lost, in a very real sense, his soulmate, his counterpart, his other self.

The tribute seemed to have a cathartic effect. Soon after sending it off, Shaw, his effervescent spirits restored, sat for an interview at the

Sherry-Netherland with *Women's Wear Daily*'s Hillary Johnson and spoke of his "beeyu-dee-ful life." He explained that he usually worked better in Switzerland, in part because he couldn't understand the language. "In New York, unfortunately, I understand every word that is said—an overheard conversation can throw me for an entire day. But this time, I worked very well here just by locking myself in this gaudy, spacious room, which I hope my publishers are going to pay for." He expected, he said, that the critics would knock *Beggarman, Thief* hard because of the commercial success of *Rich Man, Poor Man.* "They'll say, 'Shaw's just in it for the money.'" Shaw denied that money was his motivation, but added, "There's a whole feeling that real writers ought to starve. Well, I did my amount of starving. And I don't want to starve now." Asked what he would change in his past if he could, Shaw cited only two regrets. "I wouldn't have written for the theater," he said frankly. "I wasted too much of my life there. I loved the theater, but I was a failure at it." The other regret was his divorce. "I made a mistake, not in getting married, but in getting divorced," Shaw said. "My wife feels the same. I don't know why we did it."

With Adam acting as mediator, a next stage in the cautious reconciliation between Shaw and Marian began, this one a planned two-week Caribbean cruise in the fall, with Adam along. If Shaw's heart was in it, though, his libido remained open to suggestion. That summer, ensconced in one of Muriel Murphy's two adjoining houses in East Hampton, he spent considerable time with Diana Erwitt. Now that Adam knew about the relationship, the situation, as Erwitt admits, was "very dodgy." At least Adam was not still renting Murphy's other house. Instead, he and Winston Groom had taken a cottage on a nearby property. But Adam rightly saw Erwitt as a threat to his plans of parental rapprochement and, backed by Groom, put whatever pressure he could on his father.

Shaw's own feelings were very mixed. From day to day he seemed to alternate between wanting to effect a reunion with Marian and wanting to marry Erwitt. A common denominator may have been his growing concern about his health, that he might soon be incapacitated and need a loyal wife's help. "I didn't realize he was in such a hurry," Erwitt recalls. "I think he was feeling very sick, very worried and depressed about his hip."

One proposal came on a day when Shaw and Erwitt drove out to Montauk for lunch at Gosman's Dock restaurant. After a boisterous, laughter-filled time with Rita Gosman, they drove slowly back and Shaw asked, more seriously than he had the previous winter, if Erwitt would marry him. "I said, 'Irwin, we're having so much fun the way it is, why get married?'" Erwitt recalls. "His mother was coming out to visit that day, and he said, 'Well, I'm not going to have you meet my mother and brother, then.' I said, 'Come on, don't be like that, don't punish me, but he really did.'"

As he and Erwitt were leaving Sardi's one night for Elaine's, Shaw tried one more time. "I said no and kind of looked him over," Erwitt recalls. "And he looked at me like, 'Look, I haven't got time for this.' It wasn't a young man's ardor. It was: 'Listen, I put my cards on the table, do you want to play or not?' It was the moment I should have said yes," Erwitt admits. "And I came to regret it."

Shaw spent time with other women that summer. One was a good-hearted Californian named Joan Bennett, who worked as a script girl for Robert Altman, a director Shaw had admired and come to know during Cannes film festivals. Another was actress Sylvia Miles, a choice that appalled the Hamptons literary set. Now, however, even Shaw recognized that his roguishness had played itself out. The rich and beautiful women he had courted in years past had somehow grown too young; the likelier prospects he pursued were either uninterested or unworthy. Instead of impressing two continents of friends with his sexual prowess, Shaw was starting to look ridiculous.

In a ruminative essay titled "What I've Learned About Being a Man" that would appear in *Playboy* just months before his death, Shaw wrote of having had to learn the "dismaying difference between being a roving bachelor at twenty and a sexagenarian lecher." Poignantly summing up his decision to return to Marian, he wrote, "The twilight hour comes when the thought of embarking on a sportive escapade with a beautiful young woman is outweighed by the claims of continuity, mutual and unexpressed understanding, private jokes, comfort in adversity, automatic support in times of trouble and hours spent in cordial silence in the long and tranquil evenings. In short—love. It is not the love of popular songs. It is not a blinding stroke of passion; it is not love at first sight but love at 1000th sight."

More than Shaw's sense of love was changing. Perhaps in part because of Jim Jones's death, in part because of his own decreasing physical vigor, Shaw was starting a new novel with a deeper satisfaction in writing than he had had in many years. In the sixties and early seventies he had often agonized over his prose, taking as long as two years to turn out a story or novella he liked—a draft put aside, picked up months later, rewritten, put aside again. Over the years he had come to write faster but with less pleasure, until with *Beggarman, Thief* he had reached an extreme of professionalism that no longer had anything to do with art. Now his own sense of mortality seemed to open him up. What mattered was the sheer joy of storytelling. That summer, Shaw turned out 60,000 words of a novel unlike any he had written. It was based on a dream he had had years before in Klosters, a dream so vivid that when he awakened with it still in his mind at three in the morning, he wrote it down in three pages, read it over the next day, and realized he had the kernel of a novel about an ordinary family in Manhattan whose lives are transformed by a wealthy man who wants to help them. For now, he was calling it simply "Number Ten"—as it was, in fact, his tenth novel. In addition, at Ross Claiborne's suggestion Delacorte had decided to publish a fat omnibus of Shaw stories. Tentatively, it was to include every one of the eighty-four Shaw had written and would appear in the fall of 1978.

By early August Shaw was back in Klosters, still based in his apartment over the jewelry store but spending considerable time with Marian. In a letter to Gloria Jones, Marian wrote of drifting along in a sort of haze, trying to define her own emotions and feeling somewhat foolish about that at her age. Shaw was still writing obsessively, playing tennis though not without pain. For both there was time for reading and reflecting. Marian confessed she did much more of the former than the latter.

In mid-September the Shaws as a family reconciled in earnest. Adam flew over from New York, and the three embarked from Antibes on a two-week Mediterranean cruise. In Sardinia they met up with Irving and Mary Lazar, and by all outward signs the trip was a great success. "Marian and I are back together again," Shaw announced to Ross Claiborne upon his return to New York. "But," he added more than once with a winning earnestness, "we don't have sex."

As Shaw set off with great reluctance on a short publicity tour for *Beggarman, Thief,* the reviews began to come in. Despite his own dire predictions, they weren't all bad. Christopher Lehmann-Haupt admitted that "having written off *Rich Man, Poor Man* as an embarrassing failure by a once promising writer, I found myself reading *Beggarman, Thief* with considerable enjoyment. How can this be explained?" One reason, Lehmann-Haupt suggested, was that it might be a better tale. "Where the plot of the first book was centrifugal—scattering the Jordache family, as it did, from its center in Port Philip, N.Y., to all parts of the world—the movement of the sequel is centripetal, bringing the family back together again." That the novel hinged on the effort of Tom Jordache's young son, Wesley, to find his father's murderer "gives the sequel more shape and concentration than the original had, and of course a good deal more suspense." At the same time, the *Times* critic added, he might have enjoyed the book more because his own expectations of Shaw as a writer had dropped. Now that all he looked for in a Shaw novel was an engaging yarn, by and large he got it.

Not all critics were so cavalierly amused. From Anita Brookner, writing for the London *Times Literary Supplement,* came the sort of withering pan to which Shaw was more accustomed. "Desperately bad writing," Brookner declared. "The man who once wrote *The Troubled Air* . . . has no business to put his name to this sadly computerized production. . . . Shaw's characters never know anything deeper than a sudden urge or itch—for drink, sex, money or trouble." Despite such ill-wishers, the novel, buoyed by the now established international Shaw market, gamely climbed the bestseller lists that fall, reaching *The New York Times* number-four spot and remaining in the top ten for several months.

Cheered by *Beggarman*'s commercial success, Shaw plunged ahead with "Number Ten," soon to be given its proper title of *Bread Upon the Waters*. More than its "dream" plot now distinguished it from Shaw's darkly autobiographical novels, and from the smoothly detached tales of late. A newly contemplative tone, unmistakably that of a writer wise with age, was evident. While in one way or another all of Shaw's works had been concerned with moral choices, here the entire story was an exercise in ethics that, when it appeared almost four years later, would elevate it to a place among the best of Shaw's novels—an unexpected triumph in the autumn of his career.

Shaw broke away from his writing to fly to New York for the publication party given for Jim Jones's *Whistle* on February 22, 1978. Appropriate to such a military-minded novel, the party was held in the fourth-floor mess and lounge of the Seventh Regiment Armory on Park Avenue, and as intended, it became a celebrity-studded tribute. As photographers clicked away, the literary lions gathered: William Styron, Norman Mailer, Willie Morris, Joseph Heller, Kurt Vonnegut, Jr., and many more. It was Shaw, though, who served as toastmaster. "We are not here tonight to mourn," he declared to the black-tie crowd when it fell silent. "We are here to celebrate. What we're celebrating is the completion of a massive monument, created by one indomitable man, out of his talent, his persistence and courage."

While he was in New York, Shaw accepted an invitation to return to Brooklyn College for the first time in the nearly half-century since he'd graduated. Soon after his years there, the college had moved from its ad hoc setting in the office towers of downtown Brooklyn to an official campus, deep in Flatbush, with a steepled church and red-brick classroom buildings. Shaw agreed to make an appearance if allowed to speak only, as he put it, "to the jocks and poets." Accordingly, members of the football team, the women's swimming and basketball teams, and staffers of the student newspaper and literary magazine gathered to meet the most famous alumnus in the college's history. Shaw was presented with a football and an old photograph that showed a leather-helmeted end running downfield, a pass in his hands, while a blurred figure raced after him; the blurred figure, upon close inspection, was Shaw.

"I stand before you now," Shaw said impishly, "a man who never worked a day in his life since he graduated." More seriously, he added, "I've had enormous ups and downs. Now, of course, I have a lot of scorn heaped on me because of the popularity. That's inevitable." When a student asked if Shaw had ever thought he'd become so famous and successful, Shaw replied immediately, with a beaming smile, "Sure! But this big, this much success . . . who could have imagined this?"

The irony, as Shaw knew, but was too gracious and too proud to mention, was that as famous as he had indeed become, these honors—the football, the photograph—were virtually the only official ones he had ever received. A couple of O. Henry citations, a $1,000 grant decades before from the American Academy of Arts and Letters—that was all. And now, as other writers of his generation were being heaped with honorary degrees and literary awards, Shaw was receiving none. Even inclusion in the American Academy of Arts and Letters, a seeming inevitability for a writer of Shaw's accomplishments, no matter how strictly one defined them, had somehow been denied him. "The Academy?" Shaw said once with great bitterness to George Weidenfeld. "They don't even know I exist." The literary establishment could not deprive Shaw of his great and enduring popularity. It could not rob him of the gathering fortune that now made him one of the richest writers in the world. But the establishment's inner circle had locked Shaw out—and would continue to do so for the rest of his life.

Not long after he returned to Klosters, Shaw showed up for dinner at Charlie and Lillian Tucker's chalet apartment with his Brooklyn College football in hand. "It had the names of all his erstwhile teammates on it," Lillian Tucker recalls. "He got very sentimental about it. He was also drinking rather heavily. And so he didn't remember, some months later, that he'd showed it to us, and he showed it to us again. Of course, we pretended we hadn't seen it before. But by now, sadly, the football had pretty much deflated."

TWENTY-THREE

If Jim Jones's death had exerted a profound influence on Shaw's life and work, the other, more pervasive influence was Shaw's own deteriorating health. Already, speeded along by drink, he had slid from the proud end of his prime into a premature old age: from the early 1970s, still the barrel-chested athlete with the strongly defined, Roman face, he looked now almost cherubic, his curly hair thinning and turning white, his face red and round, his belly distended. Even in February 1978, at age sixty-five, he might have presented the picture of a still vigorous younger man, if he had been off the sauce. Over the next few years, however, physical ailments would age him further, indeed would nearly cripple him. Ironically, they would also rekindle his love for Marian; and as always, the traumas in his life would work their way into his fiction.

The once married couple who came out together to the Hamptons for the summer of 1978 did not evince the signs of rediscovered passion. Rather, as Winston Groom put it, they seemed to be on best behavior. Shaw had again rented one of Muriel Murphy's two adjoining houses in East Hampton, and it was here that he brought a somewhat wary Marian. This summer too, Winston Groom rented the other house, and Adam, who had moved to Vail, Colorado—a Klosters of his own—came to visit. But a different, more formal mood prevailed. Instead of the boys'-club atmosphere that had characterized the last two summers, with a revolving door of attractive women and late nights at Bobby Van's, there were quiet dinners with an older crowd: the Stantons, the Gabels, the Lazars and sportscaster Jack Whitaker.

Behind the polite exterior, each of the Shaws found the family re-union at least as difficult as it was rewarding. For Marian, it was disconcerting to be on new social turf—the same turf on which Shaw had spent time with a succession of other women, particularly Bodie, during the last few summers. It embarrassed and depressed her to be the returning wife, and she couldn't help but feel hostile toward the Hamptons literati who had cheerfully condoned Shaw's short-lived affairs. Above all, she was bothered by Shaw's drinking, far worse even than when their marriage had collapsed a decade before. She felt strongly that Bodie had been largely responsible, and spoke vehemently about her to friends; but she knew that the Hamptons literary crowd exacerbated the problem too, and she resented the many well-intentioned hosts who made no effort to curb Shaw's intake. Joe Kaufman remembers being startled by the bitterness that still coursed beneath the Shaws' new peace. "Marian was very wary of anyone who'd seen Shaw with Bodie and was unsure, for example, how friendly I'd been with her, which was not at all. Anyway, they came to dinner one night and had a very bitter fight, a very unnerving fight right at the dinner table. It was unpleasant, and intimate, and everyone was very embarrassed."

As for Adam, he reportedly remained ambivalent about the reunion he had helped bring about. He felt strongly that Marian was the only woman who could curb his father's drinking and preserve his health. But suddenly he had a mother again, living virtually under the same roof and occasionally telling her grown-up son what to do. It didn't help that Adam's career as a writer was floundering. *Sound of Impact,* his journalistic book about the effects of an airline crash, published the previous year, had met a modest reception; of more concern, it hadn't seemed to point the way to a next nonfiction book. Instead Adam had tried his hand at a novel, but so far without success. Winston Groom, whose Vietnam novel *Better Times Than These* would appear later that summer, sympathized with his friend's dilemma—the son of the famous writer, both encouraged and burdened by that legacy—and discussed the matter with Adam's father. "Adam would write and rewrite, and Irwin would always pronounce it great," recalls Groom. "But he didn't sit down with the manuscript and really go over it. He told me once, 'If I help him, it will be confusing to him because his style is different from mine.' " Indeed, Adam had deliberately written in an elaborate European style to avoid his father's American style, but Irwin was also realizing that Adam might be too dependent on him. Recalls Groom: "Irwin said to me once, 'The trouble is, I'm condemning Adam for the very things I steered him toward—Le Rosey and the rest.' Now as a writer, Adam was trapped: that was his material."

Shaw himself was not exempt from the turbulent currents of family life. When the Shaws acquired a house in Southampton at 223 South Main Street at about this time—Marian's new aim with Arlene Francis was to redecorate old houses and sell them at a profit—Shaw worked in a separate wing closed off by two doors and without a phone. "When I'm writing I can't stand voices or music," he told one interviewer. "I especially can't stand the voices of my loved ones, because a loved one is someone who's always disagreeing with you all the time."

Still, Shaw felt relatively content that summer. A four-part television miniseries of *Evening in Byzantium* was to air in August, and if it seemed destined for Hollywood vulgarization (as indeed it was), the money was hardly unwelcome, nor was the effect of television on Shaw's paperback sales. In August *Time* reported on the generally increasing sales of paperbacks in America and placed *Rich Man, Poor Man* among the top ten sellers of the seventies, with 6.5 million copies in print. (The winner by far: *The Godfather*, with 13 million copies in print.) *Bread Upon the Waters* was continuing almost to write itself, and now appeared likely to rank among the longest of Shaw's novels. For now the imminent publication of Shaw's collected short stories seemed a no less satisfying prospect. But that was about to change.

In an elegiac preface to the collection's winnowed-down roster of sixty-three stories—the complete crop had proven too unwieldy for a single volume—Shaw stepped back to examine his long career as a writer within the context of his times. Ticking off the world events he'd lived through, and the places in which he'd written stories about those events, he suggested that in the aggregate his stories represented a kind of historical record—imperfect, with many omissions, but a record nonetheless. Reading them all again, he added, was not unlike the experience a drowning man is supposed to have, of seeing his life pass in front of him. "If the drowning man is devout," Shaw wrote, "it can be imagined that in those final moments he examines the scenes to determine that balance between his sins and his virtues with a view toward eventual salvation. Since I am not particularly devout, my chances for salvation lie in a place sometime in the future on a library shelf." Given the stories' ties to specific events, it was unfortunate, as one reviewer later noted, that the contents of the collection were presented in almost random chronological order, without dates to identify when each had been written.

A first disconcerting surprise came with the news that at almost the same time *Short Stories: Five Decades* was to appear in the fall, Random House would be publishing John Cheever's own omnibus collection of stories. Though the best of Shaw's stories could stand proudly with Cheever's, Shaw's old *New Yorker* colleague had garnered all the critical acclaim that continued to elude Shaw in recent years, and it was a safe bet that his collection would receive the larger coverage. Even discounting the brilliant packaging job that Random House would provide the Cheever book, with its distinctive, rich red cover, Delacorte's decision seemed ill-fated at best. "By the time we realized the Cheever collection was coming out, it was too late," rues Ross Claiborne. "We took all the ads we possibly could, but I'm afraid we were—well, I won't say beaten before we started, but it was very disappointing."

Delacorte's sales division hardly helped matters by deciding on a conservative print run of 15,000 copies. Clay Winters, then the director of marketing, was technically the executive to make the decision, but he says he made it with Claiborne's approval. "I was allowed to be the bad guy," he recalls, "so Ross could be the good guy."

To Winters, the choice was logical and inevitable. "Delacorte never wanted to be a literary house," he says. "It never wanted to have a Russian translation or a Pulitzer Prize–winning book." From the start, he points out, the house's sales force had sold Shaw as a commercial writer of bestselling novels. How could the salesmen work up a fervent pitch about a collection of stories—most of them, as the book's title implied, already decades old?

Apparently Shaw found out about the print order over a lunch with Ross Claiborne. Afterward he came storming into Winters's office, his face red, his hands shaking with rage. "How can you do this to me?" he railed at Winters. "Don't you know who I am?" Winters knew who Shaw was, but he knew his business too. The print order remained at 15,000.

As the Cheever book rose majestically into view, its sales outstripping all the expectations of traditional publishing wisdom, the appearance of *Five Decades*, with its somber black cover, seemed all the quieter, even funereal. Fortunately a few sympathetic critics, observing this, did their best to stir attention and respect for a collection that deserved to be accorded a significant place in the pantheon of twentieth-century American literature.

Stefan Kanfer in *Time* praised Shaw as a short story master whose supple prose was "dominated by sexual themes and by the attempt to lend common experience and ordinary people a secular grace." Kanfer declared that a critical revision on Shaw was overdue, and predicted that with the stories, "Shaw's claims for redemption can be written in the future definite." Jonathan Yardley in *The Washington Post* declared the stories "thoroughly professional, expertly crafted and more moving than one might expect. They are the work of a writer who knows what he is doing and, when he is at his best, does it very well indeed."

The most impassioned defense appeared in *The New York Times Book Review*. Screenwriter and novelist William Goldman, who well understood the rewards and sacrifices of commercial success, declared that under Shaw's own great popularity lay a consummate tale-teller, blessed with a gift for narrative and "the ability to write with an ease and a clarity that only Fitzgerald had. There is never a wrong word, a phrase that makes you stop, reread, make sure you've gotten the sense right." Goldman acknowledged that a few of the stories seemed manipulative. However, he added in a burst of perhaps excess enthusiasm, Shaw's best stories stood up better even than Hemingway's, whose "glorification of lunatic courage" simply didn't work anymore. "Do not look for symbolism in Irwin Shaw or Biblical puns," Goldman declared. "He is not interested in that. He wants only to get us safely through the terrors of the night."

Supportive as these reviews were, they failed to lift *Five Decades* to the prominence it deserved. By late October Cheever's collection had become the publishing story of the season, with the proud and somewhat surprised author heralded in the pages of national magazines. Shaw's collection sold modestly well—some 23,000 hardcover copies eventually. Clearly, though, it had failed to become, as had Cheever's, the critical capstone to a distinguished literary career. Under the circumstances, Shaw's tribute to Cheever in the pages of the short-lived magazine *Bookviews* was especially gracious.

"I will not pretend that this is a review in the ordinary meaning of the word," Shaw wrote. "Cheever and I have been friends since World War II, and I have always admired his work enormously. But in reading these stories at one stretch I have come to a greater appreciation of the world he has explored and for which he has drawn the boundaries." Shaw marveled at Cheever's "elegant, sonorous, guileful prose, filled with surprising and poetic felicities, of phrasing, little jokes, seemingly straightforward and conversational, full of arbitrary and delicious and sharply disciplined digressions, echoing with the autumnal sound of distant church bells coming to us over a harvest countryside, lit by a clear cool afternoon sunlight." Surely there could be no better exemplar than Shaw of Cheever's own oft-stated dictum, that writing was a noncompetitive game.

If Shaw harbored no resentment for his old colleague's success that fall, he did seem to feel bitter toward Delacorte for failing to promote his own collection aggressively enough, and it seems likely that that bitterness motivated a surprisingly ungracious demand in the early months of 1979.

Sometime that winter Shaw was asked by Paramount if he had any ideas for another television miniseries. He rummaged through his notes, fished out a plot sketch for a story about a daredevil skier, and promptly sold it. Shaw was to write the teleplay as well, but a falling-out with the producers involved would curtail his role. Meanwhile, he realized, there might be a novel in it; and considering the extraordinary boost that a television miniseries lent to book sales, why not try to write the novel so quickly it could be released concurrent with, or even before, the television production?

Even Shaw must have known that a novel spun out in three or four months could not possibly match the quality of his best work, but there were other considerations, principal among them his deteriorating health. Shaw's old hip injury was giving him increasing pain, and an operation to replace the damaged joint seemed all but inevitable. Though he maintained private medical insurance, he seems not to have qualified for Writers Guild pension benefits. Liam O'Brien, Shaw's old baseball teammate from the war days at Astoria, was on the Guild's board when Shaw's complaint came in, and handled it himself. "Irwin was angry because he'd been denied pension benefits for several scripts he'd done when he was living in Europe," recalls O'Brien. "When I looked into it, I learned it wasn't the Guild's fault, it was his agent's fault for not reading the contracts carefully enough to spot a loophole the studios had built in. What the studios did, to avoid paying the pension money to a writer in Europe, was send a new contract to their overseas office and have the writer sign it there. Unfortunately, the Writers Guild had a clause that said any writer who signed outside the continental U.S. wasn't eligible for benefits. We'd fought it like hell, but without success. At the same time, all Swifty had to do was read the contract carefully; the clause was right there in fine print. Instead, he'd had Irwin sign the goddamn contracts in London."

Feeling that much more vulnerable to the costs and possible consequences of a hip operation, Shaw now seemed determined to make whatever money he could, while he could, as a buffer against his old age and bedrock for his family. The cost of purchasing and redecorating the new Southampton house could have weighted these financial figurings only further. Even so, this hardly excused the strong-arm means by which Lazar presented the book deal to Delacorte.

Shaw still owed Delacorte a novel from his 1973 two-book deal, and as far as Claiborne knew, that novel was to be *Bread Upon the Waters*, not yet finished but already a sizable manuscript. Now, Lazar declared to Ross Claiborne, Delacorte had a choice. If Claiborne wanted to publish *Bread Upon the Waters* in a year or two, he would have to accept the skiing novel, soon to be titled *The Top of the Hill*, as an interim Shaw novel—at the same rate accorded the other two books. If Claiborne refused to publish the ski novel, why, that would free Shaw to shop it elsewhere. Shaw would still owe Delacorte a novel, but there were no guarantees it would be *Bread Upon the Waters*. Meantime, the rejection would poison Delacorte's relationship with Shaw and be embarrassing to both parties. Recalls Claiborne: "I did everything I could to avoid having *The Top of the Hill* injected into the contract. But Swifty said, 'Well, there are other publishers who want to publish it.' He had a gun to my head. When he wouldn't bend, I went to Irwin, but he wouldn't bend either."

As a result, Shaw was paid $175,000 for what amounted to a novelized screenplay treatment. "That was stiff," says Claiborne. "And it was very unfair of them, because there had been no previous discussion, while Irwin was writing it, that this would be part of the hardcover contract. It was dirty pool. Irwin justified it by saying he'd spent a lot of time turning this screenplay into a novel. But it never should have been published."

The higher price may have been that extracted from Shaw's reputation. *The Top of the Hill*, based loosely on a younger Shaw-like character who takes reckless risks in solo sports, is unquestionably the weakest of Shaw's twelve novels. Like *Beggarman, Thief*, its close second, *The Top of the Hill* carries an air of deliberate hackwork. Not even Shaw's usual pleasure in storytelling is evident in the dreary plot, about a young man who feels compelled to keep testing the limits of his physical courage in athletic endeavors, thanks to the enduring resentment he feels toward his overprotective mother. Is Michael Storrs in fact Adam Shaw, whose own subsuming interest in sports had led him from skiing to polo, and whose own mother often worried over the safety of her only son? As always, Shaw's characters seem amalgams of several real-life figures—a character trait drawn from one, an early past drawn from another—rather than clear-cut models. As Michael Storrs leaves his lucrative management-consulting job and breaks with his beautiful rich wife (who refuses to live like a prospective widow) to retreat to the Klosters-like ski town in Vermont where he once taught skiing, he comes to resemble Shaw *père* as much as Shaw *fils*; and his prowess as a lover as well as an athlete comes to seem suspiciously like the sexual fantasizing of an aging author whose conquests are behind him. If there's value in *The Top of the Hill*, it lies in the curious fact that in retrospect Michael Storrs seems a cannily drawn portrait of a yuppie—completed just before the word, and the concept, came into vogue. Shaw's own motivation in writing the novel thus acquires a wry, and perhaps not unintended, overlay of irony. With one foot now securely planted back in American culture, Shaw was offering at least a hint of his once formidable skills as an American social reporter.

To Claiborne, the *Top of the Hill* contract incident came to epitomize the tragedy of Shaw's late career. "Irwin valued his literary reputation to the death," says Claiborne. "And yet he could be swayed by money, over and over again. He didn't *guard* his reputation." As Claiborne observes, Delacorte might have published *The Top of the Hill* as a paperback to tie in with the television miniseries. That way, as he puts it, the book "wouldn't have really counted in the overall reckoning," but the money would have been less impressive. "In a way," says Claiborne, "we—Delacorte—really caused it to happen. Because we gave him that money, we started it with Jim [Jones] and with Irwin. It was corrupting; how could one help but be drawn by it? And the question is, Did Irwin ever write as well again?"

That spring, buttressed by the money from *The Top of the Hill*, the Shaws finished redecorating the large house at 223 South Main Street in Southampton. Its central structure was a nineteenth-century farmhouse, to which wings had been added. Out back were a lovely patio, a crescent-shaped pool and a sweeping lawn. Eventually Marian would convert a small outlying stable into a guest room.

Among Shaw's friends of previous summers, it was accepted fact that Marian had chosen a house in Southampton to keep her husband away from the hard-drinking crowd at Bobby Van's in Bridgehampton. If so, it was a campaign that largely failed. Like a schoolboy playing hooky, Shaw would drive over in the late mornings to Gloria Jones's, where a bottle of cold white wine could always be counted on, and where none of the friends who happened by would think to chastise Shaw for taking a pop or two before noon. "That was really the best time to see him," remembers Irma Wolstein, who with her husband, Ben, had been longtime friends of the Joneses. "In the mornings, he would tell marvelous stories, about his childhood, about Brooklyn College, about the war."

Ever proud of his Brooklyn College days, Shaw made a second happy return to his alma mater in May, this time to be inducted with nine other alumni into the college's athletic hall of fame. Among the many former classmates who gathered was novelist and poet Norman Rosten, whose own career had earned him critical respect but small readerships and almost no money. Generously, Shaw insisted that Rosten and his wife make use of either his Klosters or his Southampton house during the appropriate off-season. Rosten took him at his word and eventually stayed in both, using his host's typewriter to write him letters of gratitude while gazing wonderingly over Shaw's extensive collection of pipes.

Famous as Shaw was after *Rich Man, Poor Man*, Brooklyn College was making a serious effort to court him. Almost certainly, its officers were also hoping for a hefty bequest. Pressing its case, the college made Shaw its alumnus of the year in 1980, and again, dutifully, he returned. This time, at the end of the evening he came back alone to Elaine's, where a party was in progress for a book editor who had received some more distinguished literary award. "Irwin couldn't help but see the difference in awards and be hurt by it," recalls Elaine Kaufman.

Despite the lack of generosity in the literary world that deprived him of any sort of encomium, Shaw was still remarkably generous with other writers who sought him out. At Shaw's suggestion Bernie Frizell had cut 100 pages from the manuscript of his novel *The Grand Defiance*; it had gone on to be published to considerable praise. Winston Groom had sought and received Shaw's advice on *Better Times Than These*. In the early eighties, Kaylie Jones would be encouraged by Shaw's warm words about the manuscript of her own first novel, *As Soon As It Rains*. Really all a young writer needed to do to elicit Shaw's warm support was declare himself a writer; Shaw would do the rest. One night not long before his hip operation, Shaw was walking slowly on East 57th Street near the Ritz Tower—again his New York base since his reconciliation with Marian—when a young newspaperman and his girlfriend spotted him. The newspaperman, Vincent Cosgrove, screwed up the courage to introduce himself. "Fine," Shaw replied. "Let's go have a drink." Several memorable hours later, the young couple found themselves in Shaw's suite sharing a nightcap. The phone rang; it was Irving Lazar, furious that Shaw was hours late for a meeting. "What do you mean, 'Where have I been?'" Shaw barked into the phone. "I've been with Chris Killer and Vince Cosgrove." Downstairs, before bidding his new friends farewell and getting into a waiting limousine, Shaw advised them to get married and offered his Southampton home for the reception. The couple, who did go on to get married, were sensible enough to resist the invitation.

The limousine, in fact, had become a necessity. Shaw's hip was causing him such pain that he now walked with a pronounced limp. The only exercise he could manage was awkward swimming in his pool. Finally the operation was set for October 8. The night before, Shaw was treated to a Pipe Night at The Players club on Gramercy Park.

The Players club, a social bastion for actors and artists since its founding in the nineteenth century by Edwin Booth among others, was well-known for its Pipe Night "roasts" of venerable members or their guests. Shaw's old friend Martin Gabel was an important member of the club, and it was in the club's genteel townhouse quarters that an illustrious array of black-tie roasters gathered to pay Shaw tribute. "We have received, as you might imagine, many messages addressed to our guest of honor, Mr. Irwin Shaw," Gabel began in his famously deep, stentorian voice. "I shall read only one. 'Mr. Shaw, we congratulate you on being honored at the famed Players club and we want to thank you for the many years you have helped promote our cause. We, too, honor you. Signed, The Brothers Haig and Haig, Lord Dewar, Edgar Bronfman and all the boys of Seagram's.'"

In truth, a certain pathos underlay the soft gibes. Betty Comden and Adolph Green mugged their way through a piano routine in which they poked fun at the "true love/hate relationship" between Irwin Shaw and Irving Lazar—"two crazy kids who couldn't get along and couldn't get along without each other"—and imitated Marian as saying, 'Oh, listen, Irwin, I didn't mean that. I've just been testing you, I really love you." Others chose to pay earnest tributes to Shaw's achievements as a writer, tributes that emphasized the early stories and *The Young Lions* and delicately avoided mention of the later novels. Willie Morris declared "The Eighty-Yard Run" to have been a seminal influence on his decision to become a writer. Joseph Heller said the same of "Sailor off the Bremen." George Plimpton recalled Shaw as the first real writer he ever met, back in the early fifties, and joked, somewhat awkwardly, about the famous lost writers that Shaw must be keeping in his cellar to turn out his extraordinary volume of work. Kurt Vonnegut, Jr., praised *The Young Lions* as the best novel to emerge from World War II and added, "I know it's cruel on a man's ninety-second birthday to talk about nothing but his early work. But if I celebrate the early works of Irwin it is because I can celebrate my own youth too, long gone. I was crazy about everything Irwin wrote when I was young."

Oddly enough, the most refreshing tribute came not from a fellow writer but from an old Hollywood friend—Frank Sinatra. His very presence that night was a tribute to the remarkable range of twentieth-century figures who had made cameo appearances in Shaw's life these last five decades: from Laurence Olivier to André Malraux to Jack Kennedy. Though not close friends—often acquaintances of a few scattered evenings—they had been dazzled and drawn by Shaw, forming an often instant bond that somehow endured. It was an array one might find surrounding a person of tangible power—a politician, a corporate chairman, a rich New York hostess—but how often did one find it around a writer who, famous as he was, had only the power of his own personal charm to dispense?

"I'm happy to raise my voice in the chorus of love that has been spoken for Irwin Shaw," Sinatra began. "And I'm glad to be here tonight in honor of a guy who is an insult to a tuxedo."

Sinatra recounted having met Shaw in 1948—"when I begged him to use his influence to have me cast in the film version of his book *The Young Lions*. That shows you all the influence he had. Dean Martin got the part." On a more serious note, Sinatra added, "I love Irwin Shaw. . . . I love his talent, and it's a great gift he has, he strings words together like Cartier strings pearls." To Sinatra, Shaw "was one of the finest people who ever rolled a sheet of paper into an Olivetti and honored it with [his] words."

In its own joking way, the Players' Pipe Night was the most formal tribute from his peers that Shaw would receive.

Technically, the hip operation was a success. Shaw received a new hip joint, some of his pain was eased, and that fall he spoke optimistically of going skiing again when he returned to Klosters. If he did take a few test runs, however, they failed to lead to a newly active life; and drinking as much as ever, he continued to put on weight.

In late October Shaw could hardly have been cheered by the reviews that greeted *The Top of the Hill*, even from those critics who had grown to like the new commercial Shaw. "In his hands," wrote Christopher Lehmann-Haupt of Shaw, "Michael [Storrs's] case is lacking any historical or symbolic resonance. He seems to be one lone rat that Shaw has stumbled across in the laboratory of his imagination. And that is why, I suppose, Mr. Shaw remains a minor novelist, despite his manifest skills as an entertaining storyteller." The miniseries that had inspired the book aired the next February, and was promptly dismissed by John J. O'Connor as "pop trash."

With Marian serving as caretaker and watchdog, Shaw worked hard that winter and came close to finishing *Bread Upon the Waters*. A ruminative story from the start, it grows increasingly concerned with illness and mortality—at a pace roughly congruent with its author's own physical concerns. The first great surprise would be the prose of its opening pages: the novel marks a clear and courageous return to the careful, musical writing of Shaw's earlier career. The second would be its subject: instead of rich Americans gallivanting around Europe, *Bread* centers on a middle-class, tightly knit Manhattan family that seems drawn in part from Shaw's own early years in Brooklyn. More clearly than in any Shaw novel since *The Troubled Air*, this one was shaped as a tale of moral choices, and the impact of money upon them.

Allen Strand is a fifty-year-old teacher in the New York public school system—one of Shaw's gentle people, a loving, monogamous husband and devoted father to his three children. As is typical in Shaw, an accident upends the Strands' placid family life: one of the daughters returns home with a dazed older man who's just been mugged in Central Park. The man, who introduces himself as Russell Hazen, is deeply grateful for Caroline Strand's Good Samaritanism and wants to know how he can repay the entire family. The Strands assure him they want nothing, but Hazen, it turns out, is both determined and very rich. First come concert tickets, then social introductions for the children and weekend invitations to Hazen's rambling house in the Hamptons. As Hazen stirs the Strands' individual ambitions, the family's harmony begins to evaporate. The turning point comes when Strand has a heart attack while swimming in the ocean off Hazen's beach house. Helpless, he lets Hazen fly in specialists and pay for all his medical care. In the weeks that he remains bedridden, he can only watch as his all-providing host seems to replace him as the family's father figure.

To be sure, there were echoes of Shaw's own recent life, in the novel's Hamptons setting and in the bout of ill health that befalls Allen Strand, but as in *The Young Lions* and even *Rich Man, Poor Man,* Shaw seemed to be investing each of the two principal characters with a different side of his own conflicted spirit. In Strand, at first, resides the moral purity of the young Irwin Shaw—an honest member of a loving family, much like Noah Ackerman in *The Young Lions.* In Hazen, as in Michael Whitacre, lies a harsh, distorted version of the present-day, mature Shaw, well intentioned but jaded by his wealth and social power. Inexorably, Hazen corrupts Strand with his money, even as he tries to help him. Happily, Allen Strand in *Bread Upon the Waters* regains some moral equilibrium, but not without cost. His children scatter, his wife moves to Europe to be a painter (Strand spends a summer with her in an attempted reconciliation, but like Christian Darling in "The Eighty-Yard Run," he cannot accustom himself to his wife's new, artistic friends), and his career path is unclear.

In an early draft, apparently, Shaw accorded Strand a trouble-free return to his old teaching job in a New York public school. Jeanne Bernkopf, the Delacorte editor who worked on the manuscript, pointed out to him that no public school job would remain open for more than the year Strand and his family are caught up in Hazen's web. Shaw accordingly made his ending more uncertain, with Strand vowing to apply for his old job in the morning but not knowing if he would regain it. The revised ending is more in keeping with the harsh vision in Shaw's earlier novels: the odyssey in *The Young Lions* that brings Noah Ackerman through the war, only to see him killed by one last sniper's bullet; the abortive movie production in *Two Weeks in Another Town* that Jack Andrus manages to save, only to have it snatched in the end from his grasp; the happy life that Tom Jordache finds in *Rich Man, Poor Man,* shattered by a freak incident of random violence. Shaw's protagonists struggle to get through the moral thickets without losing their souls. Even if they emerge bloody and un-bowed, though, some pitfall awaits them around the next bend. That, as Shaw implies again and again, is always life's last joke.

If Shaw's ill health cast an amber light over his latest novel, in June 1980 it also led to a sudden and bitter break with the house that intended to publish it. Delacorte had been purchased by Doubleday, and under the larger company's aegis, new levels of bureaucracy had been added, which did not always facilitate the delicate diplomacy of contract negotiations with authors. That, at any rate, appeared to be the root cause of the conflict over Shaw.

With *Bread Upon the Waters,* Shaw would at last fulfill his 1973 two-book contract with Delacorte. Noting that, Don Fine at Arbor House had begun to make the same sort of overtures to coax Shaw from Delacorte that he had made on Delacorte's behalf some fifteen years before. Arbor House, the company Fine had formed in the late sixties, had recently been bought by Hearst. The acquisition had left Fine as editor in chief—for now—and imbued him with considerably more clout than he had had on his own. Warming to the battle, Fine offered Shaw a $3.75 million contract for the hard- and softcover rights to three novels.

Delacorte's response was to offer Shaw a two-book contract for roughly $2 million. As a younger man, Shaw might have gone with Fine's bigger money as he had once before, but after hearing various bids and counterbids, he decided to stay on with Delacorte, where his novels, at least, had been launched with such commercial success. "I have all the money I need," he reportedly told Don Fine. "And my wife and son have all the money they need. So I'm going to stay on at Delacorte."

The Delacorte contract was duly drawn up; Shaw was sent his copies to sign; and that was when the agreement fell apart. Jeanne Bernkopf vividly remembers getting the angry call from Shaw early one Saturday night in June. "It's all over," he said, terribly upset. "It's finished, I'm going to Arbor House." Shocked, Bernkopf asked why. "Because," shouted Shaw, "Doubleday has put a death clause into the contract."

The death clause was linked to an insurance rider that required Shaw to undergo a physical examination, and for an insurance policy to be determined accordingly—one that Delacorte would presumably pay. The rub was that if Shaw died before finishing a manuscript, his advance would have to be repaid by his estate out of what the lawyers called first monies. The advance would have to be paid back immediately, in other words, and no other debt or bill could take precedence over it. "It was appalling," says Ross Claiborne, who tried in vain to persuade Delacorte's bureaucratic powers to exclude the clause. "If Irwin *had* died before completing a book, they would have gotten their advance back without the first-monies busi-ness. We had nine or ten of Irwin's books in print, we could have gradually taken profits from their ongoing sales. The clause was totally unnecessary."

Within a week Shaw and Lazar had made the switch to Arbor House. "Naturally we don't encourage important authors to leave," Delacorte's president, Carl Tobey, stiffly told the press. It was just that "there were certain circumstances that came up."

Not long after, Claiborne himself left Delacorte in disgust.

Shaw managed to finish *Bread Upon the Waters*, which he dedicated to Swifty Lazar, after a calm summer in Southampton, but ill health continued to dog him. Now, in addition to his still ailing hip, he learned sometime over the winter of 1980–1981 that he would have to undergo a prostate operation. Once again, the issue of his health would affect his relationships—and his writing.

In the first week of July 1981, Shaw checked into New York's Columbia-Presbyterian hospital for what he and Marian told friends was a routine prostate operation. During the operation, complications developed. As Shaw began hemorrhaging, cancerous cells were discovered. Multiple transfusions were needed; the operation stretched on hour after hour. Very likely a weaker man would have succumbed. Shaw survived to be wheeled into the hospital's intensive care unit, only to contract viral pneumonia. For the next several days he wavered between drug-induced hallucinations and excruciating pain. Fluid would collect in his lungs because of the pneumonia, and an orderly would be required to pound his chest to dislodge the material; Shaw, in his delusionary state, grew convinced that the man was trying to kill him. Fed intravenously, hooked up to lifesaving machines and subjected to endless hypodermic injections, he became panicky and paranoid, a victim of what hospital authorities call intensive care unit syndrome.

That was when Marian took the measures that in Shaw's mind saved his life.

Before the operation, Shaw had felt toward Marian renewed affection, contentment, a strong conviction that reconciliation made the best sense for his family and his own old age. He had not lost interest in other women, however; even in the last two years, he had been known to head to Elaine's on a night when Marian was not in New York, and leave with some "young piece of fluff," as Elaine herself put it. Nor had he quite expunged his residue of bitterness toward Marian for her stern demands during the divorce.

The dire episode at Columbia-Presbyterian changed all that. Having kept a tense waiting-room vigil throughout the operation, Marian returned for long hours every day: easing Shaw's anguished thirst by swabbing his lips with lemons before he was able to drink, riding herd over doctors and nurses, and providing moral support that may have made the difference for Shaw between life and death. One evening Marian broke away to have dinner downtown with Marion Javits. "It was quite late after dinner," Javits recalls, "but Marian wanted to take one more look at Irwin. So I went up with her to Presbyterian, and when she walked into Irwin's room, I saw a look in his eyes, a look that could happen only after years of intimacy and love. You could tell he adored her. It was beautiful, and very touching."

Then, as the awful days in the intensive care unit stretched on, Marian apparently came to believe that the doctors were keeping Shaw in the ICU longer than necessary. Angrily, she demanded he be removed from the unit to a private room. Not long after that, she demanded he be allowed to leave the hospital to convalesce in Southampton. The doctors protested but finally acquiesced. In the months to come, Shaw would declare flatly to close friends like Bob Parrish and Larry Collins that Marian had saved his life. Within a year, for both emotional and financial reasons, he would demonstrate his gratitude by remarrying her.

Shaw's hospital stay had a no less important—but negative—effect on his relationship with Irving Lazar. Ever since the *Rich Man, Poor Man* television contract, Shaw's insults about Lazar had taken on a decidedly harder edge, but it was Lazar's action during the hospital stay that virtually severed relations between the two old friends.

By several accounts, Lazar paid Shaw a postoperative visit and brought with him documents pertaining to the as yet unproduced film version of *Nightwork*. In the nearly five years since Frank Perry had proudly announced his intention to direct a first-class production of the novel, several writers had turned out scripts at the behest of Perry's producer, Mike Frankovich. Perry had liked none of the scripts and finally written his own; when Frankovich's interest waned, that was the script he had taken to producer Elliott Kastner, who paid $250,000 to acquire the property.

For Perry, the decision to approach Kastner had become a nightmare. "Elliott kept saying he wanted to do it," recalls Perry, but a year after his initial show of interest, Kastner was still "dragging his heels—with no money paid to me." When Perry seized the chance to direct *Mommie Dearest* in the meantime, he recalls, "Kastner began serving me legal papers saying he was unable to move ahead. Eventually we made a settlement: I gave him the property in exchange for some money."

Kastner, a hard-boiled veteran whose films include *Farewell, My Lovely* and *The Missouri Breaks,* has a somewhat different version of the story that led to anguish for Shaw. "I had put up the money—Perry never put in a dime—and I had paid for Perry's 'reccies' to the south of France, to Venice, to Connecticut. I was on my way to putting some Band-Aids on the financing when I found out by accident that Perry had taken another job behind my back. Then he tells me, 'We'll do *Nightwork* after *Mommie Dearest.*' That, says Kastner dryly, is when "I really lost my erection for the project." Still, at about the time Shaw went in for his operation, Lazar talked Kastner into steering the project to CBS Theatrical Films, with Kastner to produce—and Lazar himself to serve as executive producer. "I told [Lazar] he would have to make full disclosure to Shaw," recalls Kastner, "which he assured me he would do, and subsequently assured me he did do. Nor did I have any reason not to believe that. Shaw was delighted to have Lazar get what he could off of any of his efforts, as long as it didn't come out of his own pocket. Lazar's always been meticulously clean and honest with me, so I know that he did discuss this with Shaw. It was just convenient for Shaw in the period when he knew he was dying to say anything that came to his mind."

Shaw's version, expressed later to several close friends, was that Lazar had gotten him to sign the papers approving the CBS deal while he was still groggily recovering in the hospital. Later, not only was Shaw impatient with Kastner; he was reportedly outraged at Lazar. Lazar himself emphatically denies this story, pointing out that he couldn't have gotten Shaw to sign any papers, because at that point there *were* no papers, and that Shaw was in intensive care, unable to sign anything anyway.

Whatever the true story, the hospital stay had one other important influence on Shaw. For weeks afterward, he stewed about his near-death experience, until at last he followed the most obvious path open to him. He resolved to exact revenge—by recounting it all in thinly disguised fiction.

TWENTY-FOUR

Worn out by his hospital ordeal, Shaw had never needed more the emotional boost of a well-received new novel. That August, as if fulfilling the prophecy of its own title, *Bread Upon the Waters* appeared to the most respectful acclaim of any Shaw novel since *The Young Lions.* The Book-of-the-Month Club proclaimed it a Main Selection—the first time Shaw had been granted that particular seal of approval. Delacorte called for an advance printing of 125,000 copies, then added a second printing before publication. It was ironic, Shaw pointed out to interviewers, that such excitement should be stirred by this of all his novels. What, after all, was commercially appealing about a middle-class Manhattan family beset with moral quandaries?

Not every critic admired the book. Novelist William Boyd in the London *Times Literary Supplement* declared acidly that "Shaw has been afflicted with ideas. He has a moral point of view, a modestly stoical theory of how to cope with the contemporary world—in itself quite commendable—that he wants to put across through the medium of fiction, and if necessary at its expense. Only this can explain the lifeless characters, such turgid dialogue. And Strand, the central consciousness through whose eyes we see all the action, must be one of the most boring narrators ever to make demands on a reader's time." But Evan Hunter in *The New York Times* commended the novel's "clean and spare" prose, "perfectly suited to the deceivingly plain tale [Shaw] appears to be telling. The first chapter alone could be taught in creative writing courses across the land as a model of concise exposition." In the *Chicago Tribune,* Merle Miller compared Shaw to Dickens. "Like Dickens, he has a social point to make. The point is that our civilization is threatened; there seem no longer to be any rules of conduct, and it is frightening." The novel, concluded Miller, "fulfills two much neglected duties of a novelist. It informs and it entertains."

The most insightful consideration of the novel—the most thoughtful look at Shaw the novelist from any journalist to date—appeared in *Saturday Review.* One spring day before the operation, Ross Wetzsteon, a senior editor at *The Village Voice,* had journeyed to Southampton to interview Shaw; he had studiously read not just the galleys of *Bread* but every previous Shaw novel as well. He was familiar, of course, with the critical consensus that Shaw was a commercial writer who had betrayed his early promise, that the quality of his prose had declined in inverse proportion to the escalating advances he was paid. "And yet," suggested Wetzsteon, "*Bread Upon the Waters*, with its unadorned moral severity, casts an arc of light back over [Shaw's] entire career. . . . Perhaps we have been misreading Shaw all along."

Wetzsteon found patches of poor prose in the more highly praised early novels; he felt the later works were not as weak as critics had claimed. In all the novels, however, was the common thread of moral choice. "Put another way," wrote Wetzsteon, "his strengths and weaknesses have been there all along, in each and every novel." Throughout, too, the novels offered an intriguingly ambivalent attitude toward money: "While on the one hand they're contemptuous of money, on the other they're enamored of glamour, and the hero's struggle is often an attempt to resolve this dilemma." Concluded Wetzsteon: "It seems possible, then, that what drives Irwin Shaw—and this would certainly help account for his enormous popularity with the reading public—is the desire to escape the economic constrictions of the lower-middle-class while at the same time retaining its moral values."

Cheered by *Bread*'s reception, Shaw began seeing old friends soon after his return to Southampton. Among the first invited was Don Fine, who tried without much success to hide his shock at Shaw's appearance. Shaw was disconcertingly thin, his skin sallow, his energy depleted, and he still suffered from the painful bedsores he had incurred during his hospital stay. A nurse was living at the house, offering round-the-clock care. "But I never found him dispirited," Fine recalls. One evening while Fine was there, Shaw insisted they go out to Cato's restaurant in Bridgehampton. Clem and Jessie Wood joined them, as did Gloria Jones and her friend Kennett Love, and of course Marian. "This was a major thing for him, and while he was there he was the host—booze on him, wine on him, everything was on Irwin. But then about eight-thirty, he stood up weakly and said he was going home, we were to carry on without him."

Many details of the operation were recounted that evening. None of Shaw's friends, however, was told that cancer had been discovered in Shaw's prostate, and that while the tumor had been excised, only time would tell if the cancer had been contained. Nor would they be told. Even when he suffered the relapse that would kill him, the secret, by and large, would hold. Like many cancer victims, Shaw worried that the news would brand him a dying man in friends' eyes and dampen the pleasures of whatever time remained. A psychological factor was involved too: if he avoided dwelling on it, worked hard at his writing, and kept his spirits up, perhaps the cancer might not return. Just possibly, too, there may have been the fear that Fine would hesitate to make an offer for the book Shaw now intended to write. Though Arbor House had not imposed an offending death clause, it had taken out an insurance policy on Shaw for double the advance.

Over a Sunday lunch at Ross Claiborne's house soon after Shaw's return from the hospital, Budd Schulberg remarked on the phrase that General Westmoreland so often used about troop casualties in Vietnam—"acceptable losses." Schulberg mused that the phrase might make a good title for his autobiography, and he remembers Shaw agreeing that it was a very good title indeed. The next year Schulberg was startled to see it gracing the cover of Shaw's latest and, as it happened, his last novel. Schulberg, who well remembered sharing his childhood reminiscences of Hollywood with F. Scott Fitzgerald, only to see them repeated virtually verbatim on the opening pages of The Last Tycoon, was annoyed but philosophical. "I guess," he reflects, "that that was an acceptable loss."

The novel that would acquire the title began tumbling out of Shaw's imagination at a dizzying speed when he returned to Klosters in late fall. Before the operation, he had intended his first work under the new Arbor House contract to be a multigenerational novel in the spirit of Rich Man, Poor Man; but he remained haunted by his hospital experience, and the only way to come to terms with it was to get it down on paper. Galvanized too by the success of Bread Upon the Waters and by the sheer joy of being alive, Shaw turned out five or ten pages a day and, to his own astonishment, completed a first draft in little more than three months. This was the pace at which he'd written Beggarman, Thief and The Top of the Hill, but there was a difference. Those were calculatedly commercial novels, by a still youthful man enjoying his newfound commercial success and the material pleasures it could bring. Acceptable Losses, even more than Bread Upon the Waters, is an old man's novel: dark, reflective, stippled with memories and soaked in stoic wisdom. Considering the speed with which it was written, it's also a surprisingly strong work.

Acceptable Losses is really two separate stories cobbled together. The first introduces Roger Damon, an aging, curmudgeonly literary agent whose quiet life is shattered by a late-night call from a man who identifies himself as Zalovsky and vows to kill him. Resistant until then to the outside world's increasing violence—and decreasing cultural standards—Damon is unnerved enough to start leaving lights on at night and putting new locks on his doors. His hard-drinking, caustic ex-wife Elaine—who suggests Bodie—advises him to start drawing up lists of any possible enemies he might have. His current wife, Sheila, who bears striking similarities to Marian, shares his fears as the list grows, with each name stirring memories of some professional or romantic rift.

In a typical story line of Shaw's later career, the threatening phone caller might turn out to have the wrong number or simply vanish; but in a return to the cause-and-effect narratives of Shaw's earlier work, the caller does materialize, and in a nocturnal confrontation is badly wounded as he

makes his escape. Once again the outside world's encroaching violence has
been fought off; the gentle people have won; a small parcel of civilization
has been saved.

Ended there, *Acceptable Losses* would stand as a good Shaw novella,
not written with the verve of his early work, but fast-paced and gripping
nonetheless. Instead the novel takes an odd, sharp turn. Recovering from
his midnight confrontation, Roger Damon begins to feel sharp stomach
pains, is reluctantly persuaded to submit for tests at a large New York
hospital referred to as Boylston General, and is then subjected to a harrow-
ing, badly botched operation. "It was an expression of my outrage at the
way the doctors had handled me," Shaw later claimed of the novel to
Richard Z. Chesnoff, a *Wall Street Journal* reporter who had become a
Klosters regular. "And," added Shaw, "at my own mortality."

Written with the horrors of his illness still fresh in his mind, those last
fifty pages of *Acceptable Losses* make a vivid and riveting testament that has
clear literary antecedents in Tolstoy's "The Death of Ivan Ilyich" and
Thomas Mann's *Death in Venice.* If in the end the testament seems more
personal than universal, the hospital section remains a strong and honorable last piece of work from a weak and tired man at the end of a remarkable career. As the novel closes, Damon, back home and slowly recovering,
looks gratefully at his wife as she brings two glasses of whiskey and soda.
" 'Healer,' " he calls her. " 'Giver of life.' " Sheila admonishes him not to
be sentimental, and adds, " 'I'm just the lady who brings you your whiskey
before dinner.' " To which Damon murmurs, in raising his glass, " 'What
a nice place to be.' "

Beginning in early December, Shaw worked daily writing and revising
Acceptable Losses with a new secretary, a sweet young local girl named
Francine Schoeller. Visibly weakened from his ordeal, Shaw stirred a
deeper, more solicitous affection now among his many admirers in Klosters:
less that accorded a king than a kindly grandfather to be cared for, protected, forgiven any small transgressions. Josh Mason, one of the many
second-generation holiday Klosterites who had come to look on Shaw as
part surrogate uncle and part close friend, vividly remembers what happened when he asked Shaw to serve as best man for his wedding on
December 29, 1981. The wedding was scheduled for early afternoon, so
Mason went over to collect Shaw late in the morning. "Of course, Irwin
was already over at the Chesa drinking wine," Mason recalls. "I said, 'Jesus,
Irwin, come on.' Irwin fixed me with this earnest look and told me how
important it was to be my best man—he had been a big admirer of my
mother, who had died not long before—and so of course I was moved
enough to sit down and start drinking with him." The two arrived at the
church fairly drunk, and Mason then gave Shaw the rings for bride and
groom. When the service began, the officiating minister asked the assembled guests to rise and then opened his Bible to begin. Shaw promptly put

his hand on the Bible. "He thought," says Mason, "that he was supposed to take an oath." Worse, it turned out that Shaw had lost the rings somehow in the lining of his baggy pants pockets. As the assembled group looked on in amusement, Shaw reached into another pocket, fished out the metal pull-tab from a Coca-Cola can, and gave it to Mason as a surrogate ring until the others could be found.

For the first time in its short history, in 1982 the town's Calcutta Ski Race had to do without the master of ceremonies whose birthday the race celebrated. In his annual letter to the scores of participants, Shaw made no mention of his weakened state, merely announcing that one of the town's socially active holiday skiers, Bob Beckwith, would now be orchestrating the festivities. As usual, Fred Chandon of Moët & Chandon would supply the free-flowing champagne; another regular named Hans Hartmann would supply the silver donkey-and-snail statuettes. Shaw attended the late February event, and managed to deliver his keynote speech, but anyone could see how quickly he tired, and how sadly diminished he was from the year before.

That spring the Shaws sneaked away from Klosters's social hubbub to rent a quiet, waterfront house on boulevard Maréchal in Antibes, the Villa l'Escale. Gazing out at much the same Mediterranean view that had epitomized their first happy summers in Europe in the late forties, they made calm, sober plans to be remarried. Renewed love was one motive, but fiscal prudence was another. Unswerving in his conviction that he owed his life to Marian, uncertain if or when his cancer might recur, Shaw wanted to remarry to assure that Marian could inherit the bulk of his now considerable estate as his widow and thus avoid onerous inheritance taxes. "It was really a deal," observed one close friend, "in which Irwin got an orderly home and manager and old pal, and Marian got the money and respectable behavior from Irwin."

The wedding, such as it was, took place in secret in the late afternoon of May 3, 1982, at the Klosters town hall. There were only four participants: Irwin and Marian and, as witnesses, Francine Schoeller and Alice Maissen, owner of the small apartment building in which Shaw lived. The ceremony simply involved applying for, and receiving, the wedding license, with the participants seated at a little table. Afterward there was a happy dinner at the nearby Walserhof restaurant. Adam was not present. The ceremony may have seemed too pro forma for him to make the journey from Spain, where he was now living as a still aspiring novelist and serious polo player. Possibly, too, Adam was undergoing a backlash of sentiment toward his parents' remarriage; sometime between the planning of the wedding and the establishing of a will in July 1983, Shaw and Marian would agree that Adam had been indulged enough as it was and should not inherit liquid assets.

Shaw's last novel was published in September, to the sort of mixed reviews that had dogged his entire writing career. John Jay Osborne, Jr., in *The New York Times Book Review* admired Shaw's goal in *Acceptable Losses* of trying "to combine the suspense of a thriller with the intimacy of a character study and serve it up in a fast-paced narrative of broad appeal." He admitted impatience with the novel's too-perfect protagonist: "Ultimately he bores us the way perfect Galahad bores us." Osborne found the hospital section gripping, though—so strong that it almost made him forgive the novel its faults. As for Christopher Lehmann-Haupt, he was this time gentler than usual. He admired Damon's search through memory for his possible killer, and pronounced the novel as a whole to be "a cleverly plotted and absorbing work of realism." However, added the *Times* critic, "With all its talk about writing and great works of literature, it seems to be hinting shyly that it might be judged by higher standards than those of good storytelling."

And that, of course, no modern-day critic would concede to Irwin Shaw.

Though he was plagued by more hip pain and new urological problems, Shaw did his best to struggle back to his typewriter—the indefatigable literary boxer—with yet another novel. This one was to be the multigenerational tale he had planned before the operation. As with the short-lived *A Choice of Wars,* it would be divided into two time frames, 1939 and 1984, and center on an Italian boy in America whose father owns a restaurant. But the novel would never be finished.

Under the terms of his new Arbor House contract, Shaw was due a sizable payment upon commencement of this next novel. Interestingly, he never asked for the money. Eden Collinsworth, an editor at Arbor House under Don Fine at the time, remembers being surprised by that. "I had the sense that Irwin knew he was ill and might not be capable of finishing the book, and that that was why he never asked for the money. But I must say, many other writers would have asked for that money, knowing it would be difficult for us to retrieve it after a death."

On his seventieth birthday—February 27, 1983—Shaw was honored by a townwide celebration that made even the Calcutta races of years past look modest by comparison. The local band serenaded both Shaws as they stood on their balcony over the jewelry store, a horse-drawn sleigh escorted him through the snowy streets as onlookers waved, the mayor presented him with a key to the town, and as a further gesture, the street signs on the town's main boulevard were changed officially, if temporarily, to read "Irwin Shaw Avenue." The festivities culminated, inevitably, at the Chesa Grischuna, where Shaw was presented with a huge cake, on top of which the titles of all twelve of his novels had been carefully written in icing. Visibly moved, Shaw thanked the assemblage for this celebration of his thirtieth consecutive birthday in Klosters and berated his well-wishers for reminding him of this official opening of his dotage. There are some, he added, who greet their old age by inviting all their friends to grow old with them. He was not one of those, Shaw declared. He wished them all to remain gloriously young, for the girls to be "as pretty as when I first saw them and the men to be as lively and witty." As the crowd stood in tear-glistening silence, Shaw gently concluded, "I hope that the night before my eightieth birthday, you will pass my window in the evening and see the light on my desk on and hear the sound of typing." On the actual date, he said, he hoped to be right where he was now, raising a glass among friends at the Chesa.

The New York Times' Herbert Mitgang, a Shaw admirer since their wartime meeting in Algiers on *Stars & Stripes,* seized on Shaw's seventieth birthday as an opportunity for an affectionate profile. "I cringe when critics say I'm a master of the popular novel," Shaw acknowledged to his old friend. "What's an *unpopular* novel? Can you beat the ending of the *Odyssey* or the Gospels? They're enormously entertaining. Now I'm sometimes regarded as just a popular writer, but so were Tolstoy, Dickens and Balzac and the ghost looking over all our shoulders, Shakespeare." Surely, Mitgang persisted, Shaw as a writer had changed since the early short stories. "I think I've grown more generous in my views," Shaw reflected. "When you're young, you look at things directly. Now I have peripheral vision. [But] I'm still trying to write clearly, and amusingly, without pretension."

That year, a longer tribute appeared in the form of a first book-length critical study of Shaw's oeuvre. James R. Giles, an earnest English professor at Northern Illinois University, had spent long days with Shaw in Southampton in the summer of 1980 and produced a respectful overview that noted the consistency of Shaw's concern with "gentle people." In his novels as well as his plays and stories, Shaw always returned to "the necessity of struggling to maintain individual integrity in the face of past mistakes and accidents, as well as awesome external forces." Over time, suggested Giles, Shaw's work revealed the "vision of a steadily increasing difficulty" in that struggle, "but of the absolute moral necessity" in making it. Shaw himself wryly summed up his aesthetic in one sentence for the professor: *"Believe in man, and take the accidents as they come."* Unfortunately, Giles's book, distributed by a small academic publisher in Boston, received modest attention and to date remains the only full-length critique of Shaw's work.

Not all the interviewers who came calling on Shaw in this sunset time were so respectful. Jeffrey Meyers, whose tough-minded Hemingway biography would appear two years later, journeyed to Southampton in early June 1983 to ask Shaw about his old literary nemesis and found the experience amusing. "When I mentioned his affair with Mary Welsh, thinking it was common knowledge, he 'shushed' me in a whisper so his wife, who evidently didn't know, wouldn't hear about it," Meyers recalls. "Also, though he lived in considerable splendor, he had to scream for the surly Negro woman to bring the excellent wine and allowed her to plunk it down on the table in a rude fashion. When he asked his wife if we could stay to lunch, she refused since he hadn't given her advance notice—this, despite two live-in servants. He was a bit gruff and hostile when we were discussing Hemingway, but warmed up, after two bottles of wine, when the talk centered on himself."

Surely the most glittering tribute to Shaw on American soil came on June 9 at Gay and Nan Talese's New York townhouse. The Taleses, who had never forgotten Shaw's generosity in arranging their wedding in Rome—a photograph of themselves with Shaw at the ceremony was displayed among many silver-framed photographs in their living room—had long planned to throw a large dinner in Shaw's honor on the occasion of their twenty-fifth wedding anniversary. "In fact, it would have been our twenty-fifth the following summer," Nan Talese recalls. "But we knew Irwin had been very sick, and we thought, wouldn't it be fun to give him a party. He had recovered, he seemed fine, but I just had a feeling he wouldn't last another year."

The dinner was for sixty, at round, blue linen–covered tables set out under the greenhouse roof that encased the Taleses' spacious back patio. The invited guests were Shaw's closest friends: Martin Gabel and Arlene Francis, Adolph Green and Phyllis Newman, Betty Comden, Rose Styron, George Plimpton and Slim Hayward—the great literary and social web of Shaw's life across two continents and seven decades. Above the hubbub of happy conversation, the reflections of candles in silver bowls at each table flickered on the greenhouse roof. Gay Talese stood up to offer a first toast. In the very competitive and insecure world of writers that most of these guests inhabited, Talese declared, there had never been a man of such unbounded generosity as Irwin Shaw. "And then," recalls Nan Talese, "people at table after table got up to give their toasts, one after another. It was an incredible tribute; it was a lavish outpouring of love."

Shaw spent the rest of June and much of July in Southampton, basking in the glow of tributes and invitations. Many of the friends the Shaws saw now were Marian's choices—Ahmet and Mica Ertegun, Geraldine Stutz—and there was no doubt that the set she had cultivated was less literary than social. "It was that Southampton decorator world," as one observer put it, and the Shaws' latest house, on Captain's Neck Lane, reflected that taste in its coolly modern and clean furnishings. (Though they intended to sell off the first house, enhanced as it was by Marian's redecorating work, they retained ownership of it for the moment.) Shaw didn't seem to bridle at Marian's social choices as he once might have. Nor did he seem to mind when Marian flew over to purchase a house in Mougins, a chic Riviera resort town set back in the hills a few miles in from the beach. The house Marian chose was situated on a steep hillside, and there were those who felt appalled on Shaw's behalf when they saw it, for Shaw, in his weakened state, and with his ailing hip, would be utterly unable to negotiate the area without a car. At least one close observer felt the writer knew perfectly well the house would be Marian's future home with Jean Daninos, whom she had continued to see, and went along with the purchase to make her happy. "It was the most elegant thing you could imagine a man doing." As it turned out, Shaw would not live long enough even to see the house.

What did continue to bother Shaw was Irving Lazar. Not long before, Lazar had suggested that Shaw sell the film rights for *Bread Upon the Waters* to his wife, Mary, who would serve as producer. Shaw had angrily refused. In addition, Lazar's putative production of *Nightwork* had turned into a fiasco. In fine Hollywood tradition, CBS had discarded Frank Perry's script—an impressive enough work that Dustin Hoffman had shown serious interest in starring in it and ordered up a new one that departed strongly from the novel. "I pleaded with Bill Self, the president of CBS films, not to send it to Shaw, particularly in his belligerent mood," says Kastner. "But he did. And Shaw exploded." Apparently Shaw then tried to reacquire the property, invoking a clause that remained in effect from his original deal with Frank Perry—namely, that if shooting didn't begin by a certain date, all rights reverted to him. By one account, Kastner then slapped Shaw with a $10 million lawsuit, claiming *Nightwork* had been unfairly yanked from him after he had invested significant money and time in its production. Kastner denies actually launching the suit. "I may have threatened to knock his socks off—that does sound like me. But I don't remember filing any lawsuit." In any event, the imbroglio had become a terrible emotional strain for Shaw, one that would consume much of his mental energy in the last months of his life. "He went berserk," says Kastner, without much pity. "It became the most important thing in his already fragile life." Eventually, a compromise was struck whereby CBS paid Shaw a consolation fee on the order of $100,000 ($10,000 of which he sent to Lazar) and granted him the right to approve the next screenwriter for the project. But the damage was done—to Shaw's spirit, and perhaps to his physical condition. "It was," admits the taciturn Kastner, "a very unpleasant period."

At least once since the operation, Lazar had gone to Klosters in an effort to cool his old friend's ire, but that was the trip that had ended in such acrimony, with Shaw erupting at Lazar in a black rage at the Chesa Grischuna and walking out in the middle of a meal. Now Lazar proposed visiting Shaw in Southampton in another reconciliation effort.

Bob Parrish, who with his wife, Kathie, had followed Shaw back from Klosters in 1980 to settle in Sag Harbor, remembers getting a call from Shaw one day that summer, canceling a lunch at Bobby Van's. "Look, kid,

Lazar's coming out," Shaw said in his usual way to Parrish. "We're going to have lunch at my house, and this will be the final confrontation. I'm tired of the lying and cheating, and this is it."

Shaw had certainly railed at Lazar in the past, but this time, Parrish thought, he sounded more deeply bitter and upset than ever before. In the early evening Shaw called again: Would the Parrishes join him for dinner? Parrish waited until they were seated to ask how the confrontation had gone. "And then Irwin looked at me with those hooded eyes," recalls Parrish, "and he said, 'How can you confront an amoeba?'"

"Well, what happened?" Parrish asked.

Shaw shrugged. "I accused him of cheating, and he denied it."

"So when did he leave?"

"A few minutes ago," Shaw said.

"But—what did you do with him the rest of the afternoon?"

"I helped him on his autobiography," Shaw replied.

Much of Shaw's last summer and fall were taken up with shuttling from one home to another with Marian: from the two houses in Southampton to Klosters to a rented house in Antibes, then back to Southampton. The travel disrupted Shaw's work on his new novel, but he did manage to turn out an essay titled "The Common Man" for *Esquire*'s golden fiftieth-anniversary issue, a rumination on the positive and negative aspects of the common man who had been the subject of so many of Shaw's early short stories. For Shaw, the assignment revived his tie with *Esquire* and brought an earnest invitation from the magazine's editors to help plan a first fiction supplement. It was Shaw who encouraged *Esquire*'s young co-owner Phillip Moffitt to take the gamble of devoting the entire "well," or middle, of the next year's August issue to a celebration of contemporary short fiction; the fiction issue has since become a much-touted annual event for the magazine.

Not to be outdone, *Playboy* persuaded Shaw to write an essay for its own thirtieth-anniversary issue of January 1984. Shaw was given a theme— "What I've Learned About Being a Man"—and told to do anything he wanted with it. Perhaps aware by now of a relapse of his prostate cancer, Shaw took the opportunity to write a memoir of sorts, a wistful reminiscence that covered far more ground than *Playboy*'s editors must have anticipated. How to weigh the triumphs and disasters of the last thirty years, Shaw mused, the ethical choices, the compromises, the small betrayals? In a seeming nod to those who might one day sift through the decisions of his life and try to judge them, Shaw suggested that a life defied such easy categorization. History, he observed, was filled with contradictions and countercurrents, and the only thing one could do was list them, in all their incongruity.

For himself, Shaw wrote, he found to his surprise that, at his ripe age of seventy, he felt "absurdly happy." The obvious reason was that he had survived an operation in which he had all but given himself up for dead, and now reveled in the simple pleasures of a springtime afternoon. In a darkening world, he also felt the "irrepressible joy" that any human being, no matter how dispirited, eventually regains.

At the same time, Shaw was forced to admit that the years had taken their toll. Three decades before, he had gone from tennis court to ski slope to late-night drinkfest, slept a few hours, and done it all again. Now, he admitted, he looked forward to quiet, early evenings, and he had to hide his dismay when pretty girls offered him their seats on a bus. If he had drunk less, Shaw asked himself, would he be so infirm? Like so many other questions, this one seemed unanswerable.

All around him, Shaw wrote, he saw the talented actors and writers and directors of his early days dying off. Yet he still considered himself, even in his old age, a lucky man. Lucky to have enjoyed a good first marriage, a good interim and a good second marriage (during which, he allowed, he had been a better husband than his first time out). Lucky to have a grown-up son who was becoming more and more a father figure himself while his own father became, as tradition dictated, more and more the son. "He may not be the man I might have wanted him to be," Shaw wrote of Adam, "but I hope he is the man *he* wants to be." It was a sentiment torn from the heart, admitting disappointment but also deep love about the person who had been perhaps more important to Shaw than any other.

Were there, Shaw said in closing, any regrets? In a sense, the list was endless. He regretted that he hadn't been born taller or swifter. He regretted that he'd never managed to seduce certain girls, and that he'd managed to seduce others. He regretted that wonderful friends had passed out of touch and that less wonderful ones had remained too much in touch. Also, he declared, he regretted "having met Hemingway and never having met T. S. Eliot, Stephen Crane, Delmore Schwartz, Alexandre Dumas or Willie Mays."

But given the chance, Shaw asked himself, would he live his life differently? He couldn't say; he didn't know. That, he declared, was just another of those unanswerable questions.

Shaw greeted 1984 as he had each of the last thirty or more years, drinking with family and friends at the Chesa, inviting scores of revelers to the traditional New Year's Day party at his apartment which always spilled out onto his balcony in the snow-glistening afternoon, and then hunkering down for a winter of work. This season's holiday skiers, however, could sense that Shaw, in a deep, irreversible way, was tiring. He was using a cane now even to walk across the street to the Chesa from his apartment. At the Calcutta Ski Race festivities that year, he came to sit quietly while Bob Beckwith did his businessman's best to give a humorous Shaw speech. Finally, Shaw indicated the microphone should be passed over, and he delivered a speech while sitting down. "Suddenly he was the old Irwin again," recalls John McCormack, a London advertising executive who had come to Klosters for years. "He was as funny as ever—ridiculed us and himself. The next day there was a dinner at his house, and again he was witty and warm and insulting."

The public charm now required enormous effort. Having lived for two years in the shadow, as he put it, of his first bout with cancer, Shaw was undeniably suffering a relapse. His whole system seemed to be surrendering. In trips to the nearby hospital in the larger town of Davos, down the valley, he learned of worsening problems with his heart, lungs and kidneys. On May 1, in response to a letter of affection and concern from Art Buchwald, Shaw wrote that for weeks now he had been unable to focus his vision. Typing had become impossible, and even penning a letter posed an arduous challenge. Finally the doctors had determined that in addition to all his other woes, Shaw had double vision. He hoped to return for medical treatment to Southampton Hospital, whose doctors he knew and trusted; but in any event, he wrote sadly, "my triumphs have probably just come to an end."

Another well-wisher who wrote Shaw in the last days was Ben Bradlee. "I had gotten into this kick, instead of writing [friends'] widows after they died, writing them before they died to tell them how much they'd meant to me," Bradlee recalls. "I got a wonderful letter back from Irwin, hand-written, about the elephants in the graveyard propping each other up. He was very aware that he was dying."

Peter Viertel, who had taken to spending more of the year in the south of Spain than in Klosters, came back to visit his old friend in early May. He found Shaw suffering and unable to speak with him for more than a few minutes at a time. "I'm tired, kid," Shaw confided to him. "I think this is the last slide." Viertel, who had watched Shaw's deterioration the last few years with dismay, left as soon as he could. "It's very, very sad to see someone that you liked all your life fall into that state, and I have a tendency if I can to shy away from that," Viertel admits. Not many years before, he had gone through the same process with his mother: Salka had died in Klosters after a long illness and was buried in the small graveyard beside the town's Protestant church.

The beginning of the end came at four in the morning on May 10. Andreas Maissen, whose mother owned the jewelry-store building and who lived with his wife, Susie, in the apartment above Shaw's, was awakened by the full-time nurse whom Marian had recruited to stay with Shaw.

The nurse was frantic: Shaw had collapsed. His lungs were filled with fluid, he was having trouble breathing, and he couldn't get up, though he was conscious. The Maissens hurried down to Shaw's apartment with the nurse and called an ambulance, and then all three worked together to lift Shaw from the floor and carry him down to the street. Shaw, who was in his pajamas, was confused and in pain, but managed to tell Maissen he wanted to bring three things to the hospital: his address book, his keys and some change to make phone calls. He kept telling Maissen to call Marian first, and Maissen kept assuring him he would. What Shaw didn't know was that Marian was in the south of France with Jean Daninos, who had continued to play a role in her life even after the Shaws' remarriage.

The hospital in Davos to which Shaw was speeded by ambulance rises several stories at the far edge of town, its nineteenth-century central building topped by gray metal cupolas. Shaw was put in Room 101 of the hospital's new wing, with a wide picture window looking east onto the snow-capped Silvretta mountains which separate Switzerland from Austria. Dr. J. Dannecker, a tall, young, heavy-smoking internist, attended him, together with a surgeon, Professor Matter. There was little they could do, however, and Shaw was conscious enough to realize that he had come to the hospital to die.

By the end of that first day, Marian had arrived at the hospital and begun the long vigil that seemed such a heartbreaking repeat of three years before. Eventually Shaw was placed in the hospital's intensive care unit. By May 15, it became clear that he had only hours or days to live. Adam flew in immediately. So did David Shaw, and Bob and Kathie Parrish; the three met up with each other in the Zurich airport and made the two-and-a-half-hour drive together. Recalls Kathie Parrish: "When David and Bob and I walked into Irwin's room in Davos, he was lying gaunt and ancient-looking, his breathing already raspy. He didn't seem aware, but when he saw David his eyes lit up with genuine, pure gold joy. Bob and I stood back as David went to the bedside and talked quietly with him." Parrish approached next. "Hello, Bobby," Shaw managed. "How're you doing?" Parrish asked. "Not very good," Shaw said, and turned away. "After Bob finished a few words with him he was tiring visibly," says Kathie Parrish. "I went to the bed, put my hand on his arm, looked into that dear, familiar face, and said, 'Thank you, darling, for all the good times.' I think his eyes flickered; I hope they did."

Startlingly, a beautiful Italian woman whom none of the friends recognized appeared just hours before Shaw died. She arrived at a time when Marian was not nearby, and insisted on being allowed to see Shaw alone. "I'm a friend of his," she said desperately to the floor nurse. "And I've driven all the way from Torremolinos. He helped me with my writing, he'll want to see me." Firmly, Adam went up to her. "I'm Irwin's son," he said. "My father is very sick, and he can't see anyone." The woman looked at him disbelievingly. "I'll go to Klosters and wait," she said—and vanished, never to be heard from again. Somehow the mysterious visit seemed in keeping with Shaw's fictional world, not to mention his real-life past.

At 6:10 P.M. on May 16, 1984, Shaw died, his wife on one side, his son, holding his hand, on the other. On the bedside table were two books he had been rereading, Thomas Mann's *Buddenbrooks* and a collection of Byron's poems.

The next day was full of confusion and sorrow. James Salter, the novelist who had come to revere Shaw in recent years, had paid money he could ill afford to fly from New York to bid Shaw good-bye; he arrived just hours too late. Peter and Deborah Viertel also arrived without having seen Shaw in the final days. To Viertel's dismay, a hastily arranged memorial service at the Klosters Protestant church featured not the distinguished speakers who would have come gladly if given more notice, but perorations from the local citizens, among them the Chesa's portly Hans Guler. The pews were also filled largely with local residents, the international ski crowd having long since left by mid-May.

Back in New York, news of Shaw's death was reported on the front page of the *Times* in a long, respectful obituary by Herbert Mitgang. "The author of a dozen novels," Mitgang wrote, "he was most admired for his short stories of the 1930s and 40s, which served as a model for an entire generation of writers." All across the country, the news was given prominent play—though, apparently by Marian's decision, the cause of death was reported as heart failure. To those older readers who had lived through Shaw's times with him, the old lion's death seemed to signal the death of a generation. To the younger generations of readers who had discovered Shaw with *Rich Man, Poor Man*, the details of Shaw's early successes were a cause of wonderment, a moment's curious reflection on the way to work.

Among Shaw's friends in New York, California and Europe, grief was mixed with concern about the seeming lack of funeral arrangements. Surely something appropriate would be done? In fact, no formal service would be held; Shaw had decreed in his will that there be no funeral of any kind.

The will, which Shaw had signed the previous year, included conditions that could not have been pleasing to Adam. Shaw stipulated that his library in Southampton, together with all possessions pertaining to the house, be given to Marian; Adam was to receive his father's library in Klosters. More important, Marian was to receive the houses—two in Southampton, one in Mougins. The rest of Shaw's estate, valued at some $3 million, was to go to a trust established in 1982, which would be administered by Marian. Adam was to become the literary executor and trustee, charged with making all business decisions about Shaw's published and unpublished work. Essentially, Marian held the purse strings.

The most pressing concern of the will was to fulfill Shaw's request to be cremated and, because he had died in Switzerland, to have his ashes scattered on the mountains above Klosters. In conversation, Shaw had refined the request slightly: he wanted the ashes to be scattered over the Gotschnagrat, a favorite ski run.

Marian and Adam duly had Shaw's body cremated. Scattering the ashes proved a more complicated task. The Swiss, it turned out, had strict rules about the dispersal of bodily remains, and casting ashes over ski runs was actually illegal. One bright May morning, Marian and Adam arranged with the ski patrol to ride up the snowless mountain on the Gotschnagrat ski lift. Along with the urn, Adam took a bottle of red wine to drink at the top, and in ship-christening fashion broke it open over a rock. Half of the ashes he scattered around him; the other half he kept, with the thought that they might one day be scattered in America, his father's other home. Five years later Adam would at last surrender the hope of rivaling his father as a writer and decide at age thirty-eight to become a commercial air pilot in the U.S., eventually establishing a new life in North Dakota, far removed from his family's watering holes. By several accounts, the decision would be a liberating one, allowing him to step out from his father's shadow and find a peace he'd never known.

For the scores of friends whose lives had been deeply and permanently touched by Irwin Shaw's charm and laughter, the lack of a proper ceremony seemed baffling. In Los Angeles there was a small memorial service orchestrated by Irving Lazar. Marian attended; Adam did not. If the service was intended in part as a peacemaking gesture, it failed: within a week or two of Shaw's death, Lazar and Adam, as literary executor, formally severed all business ties, each claiming to be the initiator. In Sag Harbor, Bob and Kathie Parrish decided to hold an informal service of their own. Neither Marian nor Adam was able to attend, but Lazar made a point of showing up.

"Kathie and I had just decided to have some of Irwin's friends over for a little wine and conversation," Parrish recalls with amusement. "I had some bottles of Dezaley, and also a Spanish wine that Irwin had unaccountably liked, Marqués de Riscal. We invited about twenty people—Gloria Jones, Betty Friedan, Clem and Jessie Wood, Peter and Maria Matthiessen, Bill Sheed, a few others—and among them was Slim Keith.

"When I called Slim to invite her, she said, 'Well, I can't come because I have a houseguest.' I said, 'Who's the houseguest?' Of course it was Irving. So I said, 'Oh, bring him along.' "

Lazar arrived at the Parrishes' house looking terribly despondent, and he pulled Parrish aside to say, "Look, please don't ask me to say a few words, I just wanted to pay my respects."

"So we all gathered and began to drink and talk," remembers Parrish. "And then suddenly Lazar stood up, took the floor, and made a formal, earnest speech."

There was just one other detail to be sorted out. Sometime after the Parrish ceremony, Marian returned to Long Island bearing her husband's still unscattered ashes. There was talk of trying to have them buried in the small Sagaponack cemetery near Jim Jones's, and Adam even asked Peter Matthiessen to intercede again with the local authorities. This time the authorities refused the request. For a while Marian stored them in a house that she and Arlene Francis bought for investment in Sagaponack, but when the house was sold, she gave the urn to Bob and Kathie Parrish for safekeeping. "I'll get them back from you at some point," she told Parrish.

Somewhat bewildered himself about where to store a burial urn, Parrish brought Shaw's ashes out to his garage. And there, five years later, they remain.

"Every time I have to go into the garage to get something," says Parrish, "I just look up on the shelf and think, 'Well, *there's Irwin.*'"

AFTERWORD

Five years after Irwin Shaw's death, more than a decade after the miniseries that revitalized his career, the books are still in print. As paperbacks they keep selling, still pulling in readers with their smooth, strong narratives, still surprising with their graceful prose. Inevitably, sales have tapered somewhat without the boost of a new book to bring fresh readers to the old ones. It is unclear whether that downward curve will steepen or steady, whether in five more years Shaw will be crowded off the shelves and consigned to the stewardship of literary historians—or continue to sell, helping to force a reassessment of his work.

Among his contemporaries, a critical reevaluation seems a doubtful prospect. William Styron, for one, admires the "wonderful lyrical feeling" of Shaw's early period and feels the stories have a resonance that has already proved more enduring than the work of a "surface" writer like John O'Hara. At the same time, Styron rues the quality of much of Shaw's later work.

"I always felt—and I don't mean this glibly," he says, "that there's not enough true pain in his work. True actual personified incarnated pain. And I'm not speaking of some mawkish, Dostoevskian sense, but it's as if he had the capacity for suffering and either shrugged it off or didn't allow it to enter his work. There was nothing superficial about Irwin's emotions as a person; he had a heart and feelings that were real. But somehow there was a filter that diverted it."

Norman Mailer has his own opinion on that matter. "There are so many of us, particularly writers, who get elevated when we're young, and we're like sailplanes," he says. "Unless we have our own motor, and most of us don't, it's just a question of how high they raise us before they cut us loose. And then the long-term tendency is to come down.

"I'm not sure Irwin had his own motor. He was very, very well received when he was young, and he was lifted up very high indeed. And that gave him a long ride, and he covered a lot of ground over thirty or forty years of writing. But he didn't have that crazy determination that's the next thing to insanity that writers like Faulkner and Hemingway had." And so eventually, suggests Mailer, Shaw simply floated down.

Perceptive as these judgments may be—and rendered by both men with genuine respect—the good early work still stands, and it merits Shaw the stature he strove to maintain for the rest of his life. Defined even as a play, a few dozen first-rate stories and a postwar novel, it is work that deserves the reconsideration that may yet resurrect it. Perhaps William Shawn puts it best. "If Irwin Shaw wrote, as he did, twenty or thirty fine stories, one should just be grateful for that," he says. "What gets into the books or becomes history is another question."

What stands too is the sweep of a glorious life, filled with color and drama and success, romance and friendship, fine wine and pure white ski runs, exuberance and laughter. A hearty life, a happy life, a life well lived.

A man could do worse.

SOURCES

Abbreviations

AMPAS   Academy of Motion Picture Arts and Sciences Library, Los Angeles
BL   Butler Library, Columbia University, New York
DN   New York *Daily News*
HRC   Harry Ransom Humanities Research Center, University of Texas, Austin
JA   New York *Journal-American*
MML   Mugar Memorial Library, Boston University
NY   *New York* magazine
NYHT   *New York Herald Tribune*
NYP   *New York Post*
NYT   *The New York Times*
NYTBR   *The New York Times Book Review*
SR   *Saturday Review*
SRL   *Saturday Review of Literature*
TN   *The Nation*
TNR   *The New Republic*
TNY   *The New Yorker*
WP   *The Washington Post*
WSJ   *The Wall Street Journal*
WT   New York *World-Telegram*

PROLOGUE   13–18

"This evening, the circle was . . ." Peter Viertel interview with the author.
"including, as Shaw had enjoyed pointing out . . ." Shaw profile by Herbert Mitgang, *NYT*, February 17, 1983.
" 'Irwin was like a cat' . . ." Leonora Hornblow interview with the author.
" 'Irwin courted fame' . . ." Gay Talese interview with the author.

PART I

ONE   21–33

"In the fall of 1920 . . ." Irwin Shaw, 'One Man's Brooklyn," *Holiday*, June 1950.
"And what brought it all suddenly . . ." This and other details of Sheepshead Bay history from Joseph Milgram, *An Informal History of Sheepshead Bay* (1970), Brooklyn Historical Society.
"For William Shamforoff, thirty-six . . ." Irwin Shaw birth certificate, State of New York; also William Shaw obituary, *NYT*, August 24, 1957.
"Nezhin was a cultural oasis . . ." Details about Nezhin from *Ukraine in Foreign Comments and Descriptions* (New York: Ukrainian Congress Committee of America, 1953).
"Israel's wife, Bessie . . ." 1900 New York City census.
"In 1892 . . . Israel Shamforoff made the decision . . ." 1900 New York City census.

"he traveled overland to the North German coast . . ." Israel Shamforoff 1909 naturalization petition, National Archives, New York branch, Bayonne, NJ.

"Two years later, Bessie Shamforoff . . ." 1900 New York City census.

"within a few years he would work . . ." Israel Shamforoff 1909 naturalization petition, National Archives, New York branch, Bayonne, NJ; also 1910 New York City census.

"In December 1904 . . ." Israel Shamforoff citizenship declaration, December 10, 1904, County Court of Kings County, State of New York.

"thus it seemed fitting . . ." William Shamforoff marriage certificate, September 18, 1911, Office of the City Clerk, New York.

"the couple moved to . . . 811 Ritter Place . . ." Irwin Shaw birth certificate, City Registrar's Office, State of New York.

"for the family eventually to play . . ." Benjamin Cheever, ed., *The Letters of John Cheever* (New York: Simon & Schuster, 1988), p. 125.

"Mixed feelings also attended . . ." Matthew Paris, "An Interview with Irwin Shaw," *The Brooklyn Literary Review*, no. 6, 1985.

"Young Irwin . . . resented the decision . . ." Clement Biddle Wood interview with the author.

"Within two years of Irwin's birth . . ." 1915 New York State naturalization records, National Archives, New York branch, Bayonne, NJ.

"while Irwin went to first grade . . ." Shaw, "One Man's."

" 'The beach was stained . . .' " Shaw, "One Man's."

" 'Stranded by one of the first waves . . .' " Shaw, "One Man's."

"Brighton Beach . . . was filling up . . ." Paris, "Interview."

"One family would buy . . ." Shaw, "One Man's."

"The Coney Island public school . . ." Shaw, "One Man's."

"One unpublished sketch called 'Champagne' . . ." Irwin Shaw collection, MML.

"Another, 'Important' . . ." Irwin Shaw collection, MML.

" 'A brooding, desert silence . . .' " Shaw, "One Man's."

"One of Irwin's first discoveries . . ." Shaw, "One Man's Brooklyn," original draft, Irwin Shaw collection, MML.

"From Altsheller, he went on . . ." Irwin Shaw, "In These Books Lived Great Friends . . . ," *NYTBR*, May 8, 1960.

"Irwin was skipped a grade . . ." Shaw, "One Man's."

"Closer to home . . ." Shaw, "One Man's."

"It was at the Montauk . . ." Jimmy Farber interview with the author.

"His hands grew hard . . ." Paris, "Interview."

"In Brooklyn he'd often gone . . ." Shaw, "One Man's."

"They'd go to Gray's Drugstore . . ." Jimmy Farber and Fred Malina interviews with the author.

"Not infrequently he would arrive . . ." Shaw, "One Man's."

"For the school paper . . ." Shaw, "One Man's."

"A few years later, Fred Malina . . ." Fred Malina interview with the author.

"Accordingly, the Shamforoff brothers had gone into business . . ." 1926 Brooklyn phone directory, Brooklyn Public Library.

"By 1926, all over the country . . ." Frederick Lewis Allen, *Only Yesterday* (New York: Harper & Row, 1986), chap. 11.

"At the mouth of the inlet . . ." Mersand, *Informal History*.

"The partners shifted their base . . ." Shaw, "One Man's."

"For Irwin at fourteen . . ." Shaw, "One Man's."

"One undeniable benefit . . ." Shaw interview by Bina Bernard, *People*, February 10, 1976.

"Plunking down his fifty-five cents . . ." Shaw, "One Man's."

"At one point Irwin took up . . ." Fred Malina interview with the author.

"He served summonses . . ." Irwin Shaw, "The Education of a Brooklyn Son," *Brooklyn College Alumni Association Bulletin*, Winter 1972.

"Not by coincidence had he dreamed . . ." Shaw, "One Man's."

TWO   34–49

"A stranger asking directions . . ." College history from *Broeklundian* (Brooklyn College yearbook), 1934, p. 37; Shaw's arrival date from Irwin Shaw, "My Days at Brooklyn College, or How I Came to Be a Writer," *Brooklyn College Alumni Association Bulletin*, Winter 1981.

" 'The diploma we sought . . .' " Shaw, "Education."

"Even so, Shaw was not thrilled . . ." Shaw, "Education."

"He had no luck . . ." Shaw, "One Man's"; also "My Days."

" 'It was at this period . . .' " Shaw, "One Man's."

"Shaw heard enough to write . . ." Irwin Shaw collection, MML.

"In earnest now, he began studying . . ." Paris, "Interview."

" 'How many times . . . have I reread . . .' " Paris, "Interview."

" 'His was a fake elegance . . .' " Paris, "Interview."

"Shaw began attending evening classes . . ." Shaw, "Education."

"On his few free evenings . . ." Shaw, "My Chancy Life as a Moviemaker," *Vogue,* September 1963; also "One Man's."

"He might still have been turned down . . ." Shaw, "My Days."

"he'd kept up with regular Sunday scrimmages . . ." Jimmy Farber interview with the author.

"For one thing, it had no field" This and other details of the Brooklyn College football team from interviews with the following former team members: Lawrence Beckerman, Louis Cohen, Albert Ehrlich, Mike Gelfat, Saul Goldberg, Mickey Green, Artie Holstein, Bernie Kristall and Irving (Stan) Stanislaw; also *Broeklundian,* 1934, p. 207.

" 'BROOKLYN COLLEGE LOSES IRWIN SHAW' " *The Brooklyn College Pioneer,* October 4, 1932.

"In fact, Shaw had merely found . . ." Shaw profile by Vincent Cosgrove, *DN,* May 18, 1984.

"The use of his father's gray Nash . . ." Jimmy Farber interview with the author.

"As many as four couples . . ." Shaw, "One Man's."

"among the several boys she'd already dated . . ." Sam Aaron interview with the author.

"When Shaw met her . . ." Information about Elaine Cooper from Mickey Green, Artie Holstein and Leon Labes interviews with the author; also Irwin Shaw, "Some Aspects of Writing in America," *Confrontation* (Long Island University), Summer 1977.

"Some 380 letters later . . ." Shaw, "Some Aspects."

"One was a wry fairy tale . . ." *The Odyssey* (Brooklyn College), January 1932.

" 'This obviously was designed . . .' " Shaw, "Education."

" 'The school has neither . . .' " *The Brooklyn College Pioneer,* February 15, 1933.

" 'Irwin was considered a great athlete . . .' " Bernard Frizell interview with the author.

"In . . . 'Romance Comes to Miss Brewster' . . ." Irwin Shaw collection, MML.

"Years later, Shaw would confide . . ." Paris, "Interview."

" 'Irwin was a very definite guy . . .' " Artie Holstein interview with the author.

" 'Except for a girl or two . . .' " Shaw, "Education."

"On a Wednesday afternoon . . ." David Driscoll interview with the author.

" 'The wine always makes . . .' " "A Brawl in a Tavern," Irwin Shaw collection, MML.

"speech teacher Arnold Moss . . ." Arnold Moss interview with the author.

"One other professor made . . ." Unpublished address by Shaw on the subject of Communism and the public school system, Irwin Shaw collection, MML.

"In addition to tutoring slow readers . . ." Shaw, "Education."

"One word that really stumped them . . ." Jimmy Farber interview with the author.

"Once again, President Boylan . . ." Shaw, "Some Aspects."

"Though the sketch seemed . . ." Tina Cohen interview with the author.

"La Guardia arrived with a police escort . . ." *Broeklundian,* 1934, p. 145.

" 'This generation turns over . . .' " *Brooklyn Citizen,* February 15, 1934.

"At about this time, the new *Fortune* . . ." As quoted in Frederick Lewis Allen, *Since Yesterday* (New York: Harper & Row, 1986), p. 160.

"At his father's insistence . . ." Shaw profile by Edna Manley, *NYHT,* May 3, 1936.

"With only slightly more interest . . ." Shaw, "Some Aspects."

"At this point, Shaw decided . . ." Shaw, "Some Aspects."

"All the search produced . . ." *The Brooklyn College Pioneer,* February 28, 1934.

"then turned into an unpublished short story . . ." Irwin Shaw collection, MML.

"One night he called David Driscoll . . ." David Driscoll interview with the author.

THREE 50–66

"radio had come a long way" Details about the history of radio from J. Fred MacDonald, *Don't Touch That Dial* (Chicago: Nelson-Hall, 1979).

"Brown . . . was about Shaw's age" Himan Brown interview with the author.

" 'I managed to write the equivalent . . .' " Shaw, "Some Aspects."

"At about the time Shaw had graduated . . ." Paris, "Interview."

"For a year or so in 1935–1936 . . ." Edith Messitte interview with the author.

"To a girl named Ruthie Strong . . ." Ruth Strong Conte interview with the author.

"In fact, the original manuscript . . ." Irwin Shaw collection, MML.

" 'The training was invaluable . . .' " Shaw, "Some Aspects."

"For now, radio's only unfortunate legacy . . ." Shaw, "Some Aspects."

"Shaw spent his Saturdays . . ." Robert Alan Aurthur, "Hanging Out," *Esquire*, October 1975.

"An unpublished play from this time . . ." Irwin Shaw collection, MML.

"in the summer of 1935 . . ." David Driscoll, Arnold Moss and Maurice Valency interviews with the author.

"A turning point had come . . ." Margaret Brenman-Gibson, *Clifford Odets, American Playwright: The Years from 1906 to 1940* (New York: Atheneum, 1982), p. 313.

" 'How I admired Odets! . . .' " Alfred Kazin, *Starting Out in the Thirties* (Boston: Atlantic/Little, Brown, 1962), pp. 81–82.

"In fact, it was Shaw's sixth . . ." George Plimpton, ed., *Writers at Work: The Paris Review Interviews, Fifth Series* (New York: Penguin, 1981), p. 155.

"He came up with a first draft . . ." Robert Garland, *WT*, March 20, 1936.

"In 1931 the Theatre Guild had staged . . ." Hans Chlumberg, *Miracle at Verdun* (New York: Brentano's, 1931).

"Just that month, Harry Hopkins . . ." John O'Connor and Lorraine Brown, eds., *Free, Adult, Uncensored—The Living History of the Federal Theatre Project* (Washington, DC: New Republic Books, 1978), pp. ix, 3.

"theater that must be . . . 'hot and spiteful . . .' " Clifford Odets, "The Awakening of the American Theatre," *New Theatre*, January 1936.

"Indeed, without the urging . . ." Jimmy Farber interview with the author.

"First prize was $50 . . ." Odets, "Awakening."

" 'Like spies for an invading army . . .' " Shaw, "One Man's."

"Shaw rented a two-room furnished apartment . . ." Irwin Shaw, "Another Time, Another Village," *NY*, July 6–13, 1981.

" 'At midnight it had the festive air . . .' " Harold Clurman, *The Fervent Years* (New York: Da Capo, 1983), p. 116.

"Five weeks before the scheduled performances . . ." Shaw, "Some Aspects."

" 'There are one or two extra-large . . .' " Shaw, "Notes on *Bury the Dead*," *NYT*, May 3, 1936.

"Shaw wrote a curtain-raiser . . ." Irwin Shaw collection, MML.

"to benefit the New Theatre League . . ." Robert Garland, *WT*, April 3, 1936.

"an impressive play' . . ." Herbert Drake, *NYHT*, March 16, 1936.

" 'not since Clifford Odets' . . .' " Robert Garland, *WT*, March 20, 1936.

" 'The Group offered to produce . . .' " Clurman, *Fervent Years*, p. 171.

"Producer Alex Yokel announced . . ." *NYT*, April 10, 1936.

"One was a call . . ." Shaw profile by Edna Manley, *NYHT*, May 3, 1936; also New York *Telegram*, April 7, 1936.

"The other call was from . . ." Bennett Cerf, *At Random* (New York: Random House, 1977) p. 120.

" 'We were surprised to find . . .' " Cerf, *At Random*, p. 121.

"By early April, Shaw was . . ." Shaw profile by Manley, *NYHT*.

"At the RKO lot . . ." Julian Blaustein interview with the author.

"he kept sending his shirts . . ." Shaw profile by Manley, *NYHT*.

"he stockpiled enough money . . ." Shaw interview by Ralph Tyler, *Bookviews*, December 1977.

"For the April 18 opening . . ." Shaw profile by Manley, *NYHT*; also *Variety*, April 22, 1936.

"The play had a new curtain-raiser . . ." Brooks Atkinson, *NYT*, April 20, 1936.

"an Armistice Day production . . ." From a short biography of Tennessee Williams in Leonard Unger, ed. in chief, *American Writers*, (New York: Charles Scribner's Sons, 1979), p. 381.

"*Bury* had been refined . . ." *Contemporary Dramatists* (New York: St. Martin's Press, 1982).

"The Saturday-night audience . . . broke into loud cheers . . ." Shaw profile by Herbert Mitgang, *NYT*, February 17, 1983.

" 'Mr. Shaw's grimly imaginative rebellion . . .' " Atkinson, *NYT*, April 20, 1936.

" 'Seen even at a dress rehearsal . . .' " John Mason Brown, *NYT*, April 18, 1936.

" 'Mr. Shaw stands in imminent danger . . .' " Gilbert Gabriel, New York *American*, as quoted on the first-edition dustcover of Irwin Shaw, *Bury the Dead* (New York: Random House, 1936).

" 'A symbol as complete and adequate . . .' " Joseph Wood Krutch, *TN*, May 6, 1936.

" 'Mr. Shaw says that the young men . . .' " Wolcott Gibbs, *TNY*, April 25, 1936.

" 'This play should not only harrow . . .' " Herbert Kline, *New Theatre*, April 1936.

"Out in California, Donald Ogden Stewart . . ." As reprinted in *New Theatre*, May 1936.
" 'I want to welcome him . . .' " Arthur Kober, as quoted in the colloquium reprinted in *New Theatre*, May 1936.
"Dudley Nichols . . . Clifford Odets . . . spoke too . . ." *New Theatre*, May 1936.

FOUR 67–87

"Fierce feelings had been building . . ." Details of Screen Writers Guild history from Nancy Lynn Schwartz, *The Hollywood Writers' Wars* (New York: Knopf, 1982).
" 'I am not a pacifist . . .' " Shaw, "Notes on *Bury the Dead.*"
"the apartment his relatives . . ." Shaw to Bennett Cerf, July 19, 1936.
"Her father . . . had started in vaudeville . . ." Snitz Edwards's professional credits as listed with the Screen Actors Guild.
"Eleanor Edwards . . . had also worked . . ." Eleanor Edwards's professional credits as listed with the Screen Actors Guild.
"the Edwardses lived comfortably . . ." Arnauld d'Usseau interview with the author.
"She took ballet lessons . . ." Richard Collins interview with the author.
" 'Jigee had very long dark hair . . .' " Maurice Rapf interview with the author.
" 'He envied people who spoke well . . .' " Ruth Strong Conte interview with the author.
"It was said that the town's . . ." Maurice Rapf interview with the author.
" 'I feel that life is too fragile . . .' " Shaw, "Notes on *Bury the Dead.*"
"In early July, Bennett Cerf . . ." Bennett Cerf to Shaw, July 9, 1936.
"Flushed with his new image . . ." Shaw to Bennett Cerf, July 19, 1936.
" 'Some sour commentators jeered . . .' " Clurman, *Fervent Years*, p. 202.
"That Shaw's limited role . . ." Details of Shaw's social activism from the FBI file on Shaw, provided to the author under the Freedom of Information Act; see also Herbert Mitgang, *Dangerous Dossiers* (New York: Donald I. Fine, 1988), pp. 124–128.
"By the end of summer 1936, Shaw was happy . . ." *NYT*, September 9, 1936.
"he had sublet . . ." Jimmy Farber interview with the author.
"Marian went back east . . ." Ruth Strong Conte interview with the author.
"She failed to get the Broadway role . . ." New York *Daily Mirror*, August 21, 1938; *NYP*, August 30, 1938.
"In September and early October . . ." *NYT*, September 9, 1936; October 24, 1936.
" 'Perhaps the most puzzling . . .' " Bosley Crowther, *NYT*, October 23, 1936.
"Pandro Berman . . . had told . . ." Shaw profile by Herbert Mitgang, *NYT*, February 17, 1983.
"That fall, he wrote . . ." *Variety*, November 4, 1936.
"Set on New Year's Day, 1937 . . ." Original drafts of *Siege*, Irwin Shaw collection, MML, and Library of Congress, Washington, D.C.
"For Shaw, who finished the play . . ." As noted on the copy of *Siege* in the Irwin Shaw collection, MML.
"Shaw took time to earn . . ." *NYT*, March 17, 1937
"Shaw also wrote . . ." CBS press release, Sunday, May 9, 1937; also on file at the Museum of Broadcasting, New York.
" 'The Columbia Workshop really became . . .' " Norman Corwin interview with the author.
"a pattern that continued . . ." *NYT*, July 21, 1937.
"For a story titled 'No Jury Would Convict' . . ." Shaw interview by Jerry Tallmer, *NYP*, May 8, 1973.
" 'not merely a publication but a cause . . .' " Kazin, *Starting Out*, pp. 10–11.
"he would make the doubtless honest mistake . . ." Irwin Shaw, "In Praise of the Short Story," *Esquire*, February 1973.
" 'So speedily are production plans advancing . . .' " *NYT*, September 8, 1937.
"Clurman found it 'weak and unclear' . . ." Clurman, *Fervent Years*, p. 218.
"Anguished, he prowled the neighboring streets . . ." Shaw profile by Mike Kaufman, *The Brooklyn College Ken*, March 10, 1953.
"Brooks Atkinson ridiculed Bel Geddes's . . ." Brooks Atkinson, *NYT*, December 9, 1937.
" 'The young writer . . . comes out . . .' " As quoted in Clurman, *Fervent Years*, p. 168.
"The most brazen and beguiling . . ." Details of Norden's background from Helen Lawrenson, *Stranger at the Party* (New York: Random House, 1972).
" 'Nice woman,' Shaw confided . . ." Joseph Heller interview with the author.
" 'Clare asked me to bring him . . .' " Lawrensen, *Stranger*, p. 105.
"*Time*'s unsigned notice . . ." *Time*, April 27, 1936.

"The first thing Shaw noticed . . ." Details of the weekend visit from Shaw's untitled essay on *Time for fact,* January–February 1964; also from Wilfrid Sheed, *Clare Boothe Luce,* (New York: E. P. Dutton, 1982), p. 108.

"In March 1938, Clurman took Shaw . . ." *NYHT,* March 13, 1938; also Brenman-Gibson, *Clifford Odets,* p. 495.

"Shaw was shocked . . ." Irwin Shaw, "Happy in Cannes," *Harper's,* September 1970.

"he hit upon another play idea . . ." Clurman, *Fervent Years,* p. 224.

"Galvanized, Shaw vowed to finish . . ." Shaw to Bennett Cerf, June 22, 1938.

"He took a house . . ." Shaw to Bennett Cerf, June 22, 1938.

"As Harold Clurman sailed back . . ." Clurman, *Fervent Years,* p. 228.

"The play . . . was subtitled . . ." Clurman, *Fervent Years,* p. 240.

" 'it was both delicate and melodramatic . . .' " Clurman, *Fervent Years,* p. 229.

"The Group actors disliked . . ." Clurman, *Fervent Years,* p. 237.

"as columnist Dorothy Bromley had already observed . . ." Dorothy Dunbar Bromley, *NYHT,* May 12, 1936.

"more tension arose with Clurman's choice . . ." Clurman, *Fervent Years,* pp. 238–239.

" 'The audience liked everything . . .' " Burns Mantle, *DN,* January 6, 1939.

" 'a peculiarly evocative and hintful parable . . .' " George Jean Nathan, *Newsweek,* January 16, 1939.

" 'an amiable yarn . . .' " Brooks Atkinson, *NYT,* January 6, 1939.

" 'fails to be convincing . . .' " Sydney Whipple, *WT,* January 6, 1939.

" 'absurd play . . .' " *Time,* January 16, 1939.

" 'the appearance of realism . . .' " Clurman, *Fervent Years,* p. 240.

" 'The gentle people of the title . . .' " John Anderson, *JA,* February 1, 1939.

FIVE   88–100

"Irwin Shaw . . . sat restlessly . . ." Plimpton, *Writers at Work,* p. 168.

" 'I knew I had something . . .' " Plimpton, *Writers at Work,* p. 168.

" 'The original manuscript . . .' " William Maxwell letter to the author, August 8, 1986.

" 'Sailor off the Bremen,' a very different sort . . ." Shaw interview by Hal Boyle, *NYP,* September 18, 1963.

"*Story* published the gently humorous . . ." *Story,* January–February 1939.

"As for 'Sailor,' Shaw submitted it . . ." Plimpton, *Writers at Work,* p. 167.

" 'he blew in and out . . .' " William Maxwell letter to the author, August 8, 1986.

"Maxwell . . . went down to Greenwich Village . . ." Plimpton, *Writers at Work,* p. 165.

" 'Irwin was one of the first . . .' " Brendan Gill interview with the author.

" 'We had a piano . . .' " Bruce Bliven, Jr., interview with the author.

" 'that butcher from the Grand Concourse' " Leila Hadley interview with the author.

" 'Irwin wouldn't have done . . .' " Edward Newhouse interview with the author.

" 'Irwin was tremendously charismatic . . .' " Andrea Simon interview with the author.

"Shaw went to El Morocco and to '21' . . ." Shaw, "Another Time."

" 'The one moment of absolute gravity . . .' " Shaw, "Another Time."

" 'Concurrently with this event . . .' " Clurman, *Fervent Years,* p. 248.

" 'I recognized him immediately . . .' " Irwin Shaw profile of Robert Capa, *Vogue,* April 1982. (Reprinted from *Paris/Magnum: Photographs 1935–1981* [New York: Aperture, 1982].)

"A fantasy about a rich young corporate chieftain . . ." From a rough draft of "Quiet City," Irwin Shaw collection, MML.

"In an effort to build enthusiasm . . ." Clurman, *Fervent Years,* pp. 242, 247.

"The play previewed . . ." Clurman, *Fervent Years,* p. 257. Elia Kazan states in his own autobiography that the play ran six Sundays as originally planned (*Elia Kazan: A Life,* New York: Alfred A. Knopf, 1988, p. 182).

"The winner was an unknown named Tennessee Williams . . ." Profile of Tennessee Williams in Unger, *American Writers,* p. 381.

"That spring Clurman also asked . . ." Lawrence Lee and Barry Gifford, *Saroyan: A Biography* (New York: Paragon House, 1988), p. 227.

"Shaw went to the opening . . ." Lee and Gifford, *Saroyan,* p. 227.

"tentatively titled 'Borough over the Bridge' . . ." As indicated by the author's note on Shaw in *Esquire,* June 1939.

" 'They think it comes so easy . . .' " Irwin Shaw obituary, Herbert Mitgang, *NYT,* May 17, 1984.

" 'He was very tall, and very thin' . . ." E. J. Kahn, Jr., interview with the author.

"One change he did sometimes suggest . . ." Plimpton, *Writers at Work*, p. 164.

" 'I never went there myself . . .' " Mary Cheever interview with the author.

" 'Irwin and Lobrano and I played together . . .' " Edward Newhouse interview with the author.

"That summer *The Gentle People* moved on . . ." *NYT*, July 6, 1939.

"Harold Clurman had hoped . . ." Clurman, *Fervent Years*, p. 256.

" 'I like Mr. Shaw's stories . . .' " Alfred Kazin, "Books and Things," *NYHT*, August 28, 1939.

"For a short story collection with a print run . . ." Random House print order, July 10, 1939, Random House collection, BL.

" 'storing up fat against the long winter' " Shaw to Bennett Cerf, October 8, 1939.

"on October 13, in a simple civil ceremony . . ." Irwin Shaw and Marian Edwards marriage certificate, California State Board of Health.

PART II

SIX   103–117

" 'I'll write fifty more plays' . . ." JA, May 9, 1936.

"It was a life the German-born Viertel . . ." Peter Viertel interview with the author; details about the Viertel family's background also from Salka Viertel, *The Kindness of Strangers* (New York: Holt, Rinehart & Winston, 1969).

"E. J. Kahn, Jr., a friend of both men . . ." E. J. Kahn, Jr., interview with the author.

"Shaw's principal project at this time . . ." Peter Viertel interview with the author.

"As it opens . . ." Original draft of "Retreat to Pleasure," Irwin Shaw collection, MML.

"Shaw sold the play . . ." Clurman, *Fervent Years*, p. 271; also Liam O'Brien interview with the author.

"The Shaws took a house . . ." Shaw to Bennett Cerf, June 26, 1940.

" 'Shaw had attempted to write . . .' " Clurman, *Years*, p. 271.

" 'I don't like Irwin Shaw's new play' . . ." Saxe Commins to Bennett Cerf, June 7, 1940, Random House collection, BL.

"Shaw wrote back a conciliatory letter . . ." Shaw to Bennett Cerf, June 26, 1940.

" 'We were all there, that summer of 1940 . . .' " Kazin, *Starting Out*, pp. 149–157.

"Marian landed a part . . ." New York *Sun*, October 2, 1940.

"The first problem with the *Retreat* production . . ." Clurman, *Fervent Years*, pp. 271–278.

"It was during a preview benefit performance . . ." Hume Cronyn interview with the author.

" 'the drollest writing of the season' . . ." Brooks Atkinson, *NYT*, December 18, 1940.

"Richard Watts found the core of the play . . ." Richard Watts, *NYHT*, December 18, 1940.

" 'discouraging . . . Mr. Shaw's main characters . . .' " Wolcott Gibbs, *TNY*, December 28, 1940.

" 'Here we have again . . .' " John O'Hara, *Newsweek*, December 30, 1940.

"despite a last-ditch rewrite . . ." *NYT*, December 27, 1940.

" 'That's sort of a touchy period . . .' " Budd Schulberg interview with the author.

"The magazine also published an anthology . . ." *Short Stories from* The New Yorker (New York: Simon & Schuster, 1943).

"As Shaw liked to point out . . ." Plimpton, *Writers at Work*, p. 167.

"When they turned it down . . ." Plimpton, *Writers at Work*, p. 167.

" 'I've noticed as an old athlete . . .' " Shaw interview by CBS News, for *Vital History* series, November 9, 1978 (Encyclopedia Americana/CBS Audio Resource Library, distributed by Grolier Educational, Danbury, CT).

" 'Irwin was always sending Marian . . .' " Mary Cheever interview with the author.

"By spring Shaw was back . . ." Script of *Mr. Twilight* dated May 13, 1941, Irwin Shaw collection, MML; also George Stevens collection, AMPAS.

"On his first Hollywood trip . . ." Shaw interview by Susan Winslow for George Stevens Jr.'s documentary film about his father, *Journey of a Filmmaker*, George Stevens collection, AMPAS.

"Stevens, who had gotten his start . . ." Details on George Stevens's life from *Journey of a Filmmaker*, by George Stevens, Jr.

" 'That's how I met Irwin . . .' " Carol Saroyan Matthau interview with the author.

" 'There was a circle' . . ." Elinor Gruber interview with the author.

"That January there was talk . . ." *NYT*, July 21, 1941; January 17, 1942; also Kazan, *Elia Kazan*, p. 302.

" 'The warmth of feeling . . .' " H. N. Doughty, *NYHT*, January 23, 1942.

" 'Irwin's Shaw's material is fresh . . .' " *Time*, February 16, 1942.

"with a script for RKO, *A Yankee Fable* . . ." *NYHT*, March 17, 1942.

SEVEN   118–128

"it was a colorful bunch . . ." Details from Kaufman-Astoria Studios archives; also Lee and Gifford, *Saroyan*, pp. 100–109.

" 'I lived at the barracks . . .' " Charles Addams interview with the author.

"The turning point may have come . . ." Kathie Parrish interview with the author.

"A multigenerational family story . . ." Irwin Shaw, *Sons and Soldiers*, (New York: Random House, 1944).

"In October Shaw sent the play . . ." Play analysis of *Labor for the Wind*, by Kathleen Millay for Katharine Cornell, October 5, 1942, Berg Collection, New York Public Library, main branch.

"Meanwhile, a long-awaited call . . ." Shaw interview for *Journey of a Filmmaker*, George Stevens collection, AMPAS.

" 'Marian was at every rehearsal . . .' " Gregory Peck letter to the author, January 5, 1988.

"Karl Malden . . . shared Peck's regrets" Karl Malden interview with the author.

"In a letter to his daughter . . . Joel Sayre . . ." Nora Sayre interview with the author.

"The night *Sons and Soldiers* opened . . ." *Stars & Stripes*, Middle East edition, May 14, 1943.

"Lewis Nichols . . . acknowledged . . ." Lewis Nichols, *NYT*, May 5, 1943.

" 'Irwin Shaw is such an accomplished writer . . .' " Wolcott Gibbs, *TNY*, May 15, 1943.

" 'a muddle and a mess' " Stark Young, *TNR*, May 17, 1943.

"*Time*, as usual, added its own special note . . ." *Time*, May 17, 1943.

"Shaw stayed on in Cairo . . ." *Stars & Stripes*, Middle East edition, May 14, 1943.

"he took a hot, slow train to Palestine . . ." Irwin Shaw, "Palestine Express," in *The Best from Yank* (Cleveland: World Publishing Company, 1945), p. 115.

" 'We were both really fucking off . . .' " Walter Bernstein interview with the author.

"and succeeded in prying loose . . ." Shaw interview for *Journey of a Filmmaker*, George Stevens collection, AMPAS; also original draft of "Africa Without Germans," Irwin Shaw collection, MML (final draft published in the *The Yale Review*, Summer 1944).

"His younger brother, David, had been assigned . . ." Original draft of "Africa Without Germans," Irwin Shaw collection, MML.

"In fact, David had tried . . ." Background details about David Shaw and his play from *Brooklyn Eagle*, February 5, 1942.

" 'Here was Irwin Shaw . . .' " Herbert Mitgang interview with the author.

"he wrote about a company of American bomber pilots . . ." *Stars & Stripes*, Algiers, June 25, 1943.

"Managing editor David Golding remembers . . ." David Golding interview with the author.

"What is certain is that on March 22, 1944 . . ." From the FBI file on Shaw, provided to the author under the Freedom of Information Act.

"Stevens made his way to Algiers . . ." Shaw interview for *Journey of a Filmmaker*, George Stevens collection, AMPAS.

"In early July . . . he and David spent . . ." Original draft of "Africa Without Germans," Irwin Shaw collection, MML.

"that very speech, reprinted in *Stars & Stripes* . . ." As reported in *NYHT*, August 26, 1945.

" 'Irwin got me a room . . .' " Walter Bernstein interview with the author.

"One memorable day, Shaw played football . . ." Shaw interview with Robert Alan Aurthur for his column, "Hanging Out," *Esquire*, October 1975.

"Shaw took the one recourse . . ." *Stars & Stripes*, Middle East edition, July 16, 1943; also Irwin Shaw, "The Common Man," *Esquire*, December 1983.

"August brought a reprieve . . ." Lee and Gifford, *Saroyan*, p. 106; also Budd Schulberg interview with the author.

" 'I was their project officer . . .' " Julian Blaustein interview with the author.

"Shaw played on a team called the Ten Old Men" Liam O'Brien interview with the author.

"Shaw wrote acidly of officers . . ." Irwin Shaw, "What I Think of the Army," *Salute*, April 1946.

"In an unsigned editorial . . ." *Stars & Stripes*, Middle East edition, September 10, 1943.

EIGHT   129–147

"with George Stevens's permission he attached himself . . ." Shaw interview for *Journey of a Filmmaker*, George Stevens collection, AMPAS.

" 'Since it was all taking place . . .' " Shaw interview in Lee and Gifford, *Saroyan*, p. 114.

" 'They were the two worst-dressed . . .' " Martha Gellhorn interview with the author.

"Already ensconced in the supposedly bombproof . . ." Details of Capa in London from Richard Whelan, *Robert Capa: A Biography* (New York: Alfred A. Knopf, 1985), pp. 207ff.

" 'They are both G.I.s, you know . . .' " Letter from Barry Bingham to Mrs. Barry Bingham, March 7, 1944.

"As a precaution, he began to make carbons . . ." Account by Shaw of writing *The Assassin, NYHT,* October 14, 1945.

" 'There were different social sets . . .' " William Walton interview with the author.

" 'If you were in a tough spot . . .' " Lael Wertenbaker interview with the author.

"a few years later, a blithely promiscuous woman . . ." Aram Saroyan, *Trio* (New York: Penguin, 1986), p. 79.

"Neither he nor his colleagues ever saw . . ." Shaw interview for *Journey of a Filmmaker,* George Stevens collection, AMPAS.

"Shaw was one of the unit's four writers . . ." Ivan Moffat interview with the author.

"That spring Shaw took a tour . . ." Irwin Shaw, "Oh, to Be in England Now," Irwin Shaw collection, MML.

"On another occasion, Shaw and Stevens . . ." Shaw interview for *Journey of a Filmmaker,* George Stevens collection, AMPAS.

"Welsh and her roommate, Connie Ernst . . ." Mary Hemingway, *How It Was,* (New York: Alfred A. Knopf, 1951), p. 106.

"That changed within the week . . ." Bernice Kert, *The Hemingway Women* (New York: W. W. Norton, 1983), p. 393.

"For Hemingway, it was a car accident . . ." Carlos Baker, *Ernest Hemingway: A Life Story* (New York: Charles Scribner's Sons, 1969), p. 390.

"For Shaw, it was a heartbreaking mixup . . ." Shaw interview for *Journey of a Filmmaker,* George Stevens collection, AMPAS; also Ivan Moffat interview with the author.

"Nor did another small Signal Corps group . . ." Ken Marthey interview with the author.

"In the unreal days that followed . . ." Ivan Moffat interview with the author.

"Shaw, for one, busied himself . . ." Richard Hoar Kent interview with the author.

"On or about June 21 . . ." Shaw interview for *Journey of a Filmmaker,* George Stevens collection, AMPAS.

"The first clue that the voyage . . ." Ivan Moffat interview with the author.

"The 1,200 men thus had to use the beds . . ." Shaw interview for *Journey of a Filmmaker,* George Stevens collection, AMPAS; also Ivan Moffat interview with the author.

"The men had barely reached . . ." Shaw interview for *Journey of a Filmmaker,* George Stevens collection, AMPAS; also Ivan Moffat interview with the author.

"Shaw was in a jeep team . . ." Richard Hoar Kent and Ken Marthey interviews with the author.

" 'The whole city was a shambles . . .' " William Walton interview with the author.

"A week later, Shaw's team recorded . . ." Shaw interview for *Journey of a Filmmaker,* George Stevens collection, AMPAS.

" 'A bullet went . . .' " Shaw, as quoted in James R. Giles, *Irwin Shaw* (Boston: Twayne, 1983).

"Along the way they ran into Capa . . ." Shaw profile of Capa, *Vogue,* April 1982.

"he looked up at a balcony . . ." Ruda Dauphin interview with the author.

"At a hilltop castle, artillery shells . . ." Shaw interview for *Journey of a Filmmaker,* George Stevens collection, AMPAS.

"Most memorable, though, was the afternoon . . ." Details about Mont-St.-Michel from Shaw's nonfiction account, "Stuff of Dreams," *The New Yorker,* January 5, 1946.

"this time nearly getting shot . . ." Shaw interview for *Journey of a Filmmaker,* George Stevens collection, AMPAS.

"When Hemingway ran into Shaw . . ." Jeffrey Meyers, *Hemingway: A Biography* (New York: Harper & Row, 1985), p. 406.

"That night he and his team . . ." Pinckney Ridgell interview with the author.

"he shared his comrades' amazement . . ." This and other details of Shaw's arrival in Paris from Shaw's nonfiction account, "Morts pour la Patrie," *The New Yorker,* August 25, 1945; also Philip Drell, Ken Marthey, Ivan Moffat and Pinckney Ridgell interviews with the author.

"In a fine display of hot-water one-upmanship . . ." Irwin Shaw, *Paris! Paris!* (New York: Harcourt Brace Jovanovich, 1976), p. 195.

" 'Mike Bessie was waiting . . .' " by David Schoenbrun, *America Inside Out* (New York: McGraw-Hill, 1984), pp. 134–135.

"the Special Coverage Unit established a headquarters . . ." Pinckney Ridgell interview with the author.

"Shaw's longest trip that fall . . ." Shaw interview for *Journey of a Filmmaker,* George Stevens collection, AMPAS.

"Hemingway referred to him snidely . . ." Drew Middleton interview with the author.

"On at least one occasion she even taunted Hemingway . . ." Meyers, *Hemingway,* p. 396; also Peter Viertel interview with the author.

"she flatly asked Shaw to marry her" Peter Viertel interview with the author.

"That November Shaw went home" Shaw interview for *Journey of a Filmmaker,* George Stevens collection, AMPAS.

"In December he wrote to Philip Drell . . ." Shaw to Philip Drell, December 15, 1944.

"In London, before the invasion . . ." Irwin Shaw, preface to *The Assassin* (New York: Random House, 1946).

" 'where the provinces had been . . .' " Sydney Gruson, NYT, March 23, 1945.

"this piece of 'stage journalism' . . ." W. A. Darlington, NYT, April 1, 1945.

"Shaw . . . headed back to Europe . . ." Shaw interview for *Journey of a Filmmaker,* George Stevens collection, AMPAS; also Philip Drell and Pinckney Ridgell interviews with the author.

" 'Part in a Play' . . . appeared that July . . ." July 7, 1945.

"On June 6, Capa and Shaw learned that Ingrid Bergman . . ." This story, and the accompanying note, from Ingrid Bergman, *Ingrid Bergman: My Story* (New York: Dell, 1981), p. 186.

"Sometime in that first whirlwind week . . ." Bill Graffis interview with Cornell Capa, Cornell Capa's personal records, New York.

NINE 148–164

" 'One week after I put on the gray suit . . .' " Shaw, "What I Think of the Army."

"Herbert Mitgang . . . remembers a huge party . . ." Herbert Mitgang interview with the author.

" 'Not having Martin Gabel's voice . . .' " Karl Malden interview with the author.

"*The Assassin* is not a good play . . .' " Lewis Nichols, NYT, October 18, 1945.

" 'more trite than trenchant . . .' " Howard Barnes, NYHT, October 18, 1945.

" 'there seems to be no line . . .' " Stark Young, TNR, October 29, 1945.

" 'It is not hard to suspect . . .' " Wolcott Gibbs, TNY, October 27, 1945.

"With grim humor, Shaw noted . . ." Shaw, preface to *The Assassin.*

"a much-discussed broadside was launched . . ." NYHT, March 8, 1946; also NYP, March 9, 1946.

"A. J. Liebling . . . titled his January *Esquire* column . . ." *Esquire,* January 1946.

" 'one of the theatrical documents . . ." Russell Maloney, NYT, March 24, 1946.

"Hayward was an unlikely Hollywood figure . . ." Details about Hayward's life from Slim Keith interview with the author.

"It was a colorful world . . ." Peter Viertel and Robert Parrish interviews with the author; also Michael Burke, *Outrageous Good Fortune* (Boston: Little, Brown, 1984), p. 125.

" 'I walked in the back door . . .' " Robert Parrish interview with the author.

" 'Marian's mafia' " Bernard Frizell interview with the author.

"In his foxhole in Normandy . . ." Ivan Moffat interview with the author.

"Capa had moved into the Garden of Allah . . ." Whelan, *Capa,* p. 242.

"A conservative Michigan congressman . . ." The Honorable George A. Dondero, as quoted in the FBI file on Shaw, provided to the author under the Freedom of Information Act.

" 'Once more Saroyan is full of love . . .' " Irwin Shaw, "Mr. Saroyan's Wartime Comedy," NYTBR, June 2, 1946.

"Shaw broke another bond . . ." NYT, July 11, 1946.

"A welcome reaffirmation . . ." NYT, May 6, 1946.

"the grant seemed to inspire . . . 'Prize for Promise' . . ." Irwin Shaw, *Short Stories* (New York: Random House, 1966).

"The title story . . . would be included . . ." *The* New Yorker *Book of War Pieces,* (New York: Reynal & Hitchcock, 1947).

" 'Irwin Shaw is a moral writer . . .' " Robert Gorham Davis, NYT, August 25, 1946.

"A particularly touching tribute came . . ." Budd Schulberg, PM, August 25, 1946.

" 'It was incredible' . . ." Peter Viertel interview with the author.

" 'I was going along . . .' " Shaw interview with Pete Hamill, *The Village Voice,* December 23, 1974.

"In a July letter to Bennett Cerf . . ." Shaw to Bennett Cerf, July 20, 1947.

"*The Survivors* had started as a movie idea . . .' " Peter Viertel interview with the author.

"Lazar . . . had come a considerable distance . . ." Background details on Irving Lazar from Jennifer Allen, "Swifty Lazar Is a Big Deal," NY, July 18, 1983.

"Bob Parrish remembers Lazar cornering him . . ." Robert Parrish interview with the author.

"among them John Chapman . . ." DN, as reported in *Time,* August 25, 1947.

"and Richard Watts, Jr., who . . . pointed out . . ." NYP, September 23, 1947.

"In his own first column . . ." TNR, September 29, 1947.

"a month of appraising . . ." *TNR*, October 20, 1947.

"The hearings were chaired by J. Parnell Thomas . . ." *NYHT*, October 21, 1947.

"Through his lawyer, Lloyd Paul Stryker . . ." *NYT*, October 25, 1947.

"He also joined a hastily formed Committee . . ." *NYHT*, October 25, 1947.

"Being a writer these days . . ." *NYT*, November 2, 1947.

"Years later, Shaw would see Jack Warner . . ." Irwin Shaw, "What I've Learned About Being a Man," *Playboy*, January 1984.

"As far as Shaw was concerned . . ." Irwin Shaw, "Win Some, Lose Some," *TV Guide*, February 25, 1978.

" 'Ah, well, it didn't bother him . . .' " Peter Viertel interview with the author.

"Paramount came fishing . . ." *NYHT*, November 6, 1947.

"Brooks Atkinson, for one, found the whole production . . ." *NYT*, January 20, 1948.

"The authors . . . sat up drinking . . ." Peter Viertel interview with the author.

"Howard Barnes, while noting the play's blend . . ." *NYHT*, January 20, 1948.

"Wolcott Gibbs simply damned the production . . ." *TNY*, January 31, 1948.

"This time Shaw had the odd opportunity . . ." *TNR*, February 2, 1948.

TEN   165–180

"No one at Random House seemed to like . . ." Saxe Commins to Shaw, April 14, 1948.

"Bennett Cerf had read it and declared   " Shaw interview by Ralph Tyler, *Bookviews*, December 1977.

"he had, with Commins's help, cut . . ." Plimpton, *Writers at Work*, p. 164.

" 'No work I have done . . .' " Saxe Commins to Shaw, June 2, 1948.

"From another Malibu beach house . . ." Shaw to Saxe Commins, June 2, 1948.

"a decision that assumed a special poignance . . ." Saxe Commins sympathy letter to Shaw, June 17, 1948.

"With screenwriter Charles Schnee . . ." Irwin Shaw collection, MML.

"With his brother, David, he wrote . . ." Shaw interview by Sidney Fields in the New York *Mirror*, January 30, 1949; also *NYHT*, June 19, 1949.

" 'Similarities? Well, there were and . . .' " Norman Mailer interview with the author.

" 'This is the moment Irwin Shaw's friends . . .' " Richard Match, *NYHT*, October 3, 1948.

" 'The reviewer is too close to it . . .' " William McFee, New York *Sun*, October 1, 1948.

"Marc Brandel agreed . . . more calmly . . ." *NYT*, October 3, 1948.

" 'When liberalism took its boldest stand . . .' " Diana Trilling, *TN*, October 9, 1948.

" 'Before the war, Irwin Shaw . . .' " *Time*, October 11, 1948.

"Shaw returned to New York in November . . ." Saxe Commins to Shaw, November 17, 1948; also Bennett Cerf to Shaw, January 5, 1949.

"In February Shaw let Peter Viertel . . ." Peter Viertel interview with the author.

"There were amusing distractions . . ." Robert Parrish interview with the author.

"The Shaws had spent the previous New Year's Eve . . ." Simon Michael Bessie interview with the author.

"Capa . . . talked a somewhat dubious Shaw into . . ." Shaw interview by Richard Whelan, for Whelan, *Capa*.

"Accordingly, in early May . . ." *NYT*, March 25, 1949; also dateline of May 12 on Irwin Shaw, "Letter from Tel Aviv," *TNY*, May 28, 1949.

"They started in Tel Aviv . . ." Shaw, "Letter from Tel Aviv"; also Whelan, *Capa*, p. 266.

"he traveled back to Rome . . ." Shaw to Donald Klopfer, May 23, 1949.

"By July the Shaws had settled . . ." Shaw to Donald Klopfer, July 5, 1949.

"The house's coastal side . . ." This and other details of Shaw's 1949 summer from Irwin Shaw, "How to Live Abroad," *Holiday*, July 1951.

"as Shaw wrote sheepishly to Donald Klopfer . . ." Shaw to Donald Klopfer, July 5, 1949.

"As soon as he and Mili arrived . . ." Details of the visit from Whelan, *Capa*, p. 277.

"*New Yorker* writer Bruce Bliven, Jr., . . . remembers . . ." Bruce Bliven, Jr., interview with the author.

"Sidney Simon . . . remembers Shaw . . ." Sidney Simon interview with the author.

" 'Cheever operated in a fantasy world . . .' " Edward Newhouse interview with the author.

" 'Then came the day . . .' " Leila Hadley interview with the author.

"Now he lit into Shaw . . ." Hemingway, *How It Was*, p. 300; also Meyers, *Hemingway*, p. 393.

"In November Hemingway had made good . . ." Peter Viertel interview with the author.

"at least one printed account . . ." Schwartz, *Hollywood Writers'*, p. 297.

ELEVEN 181–195

"There was an omen . . ." *NYHT,* April 23, 1950.
"In June the U.S. Supreme Court . . ." Stefan Kanfer, *A Journal of the Plague Years* (New York: Atheneum, 1973), pp. 100ff.
"The incident began . . ." Kanfer, *Journal;* also *NYT,* September 8, 1950.
" 'Several weeks ago . . .' " *NYT,* August 20, 1950.
"Theodore Kirkpatrick's announcement . . ." *NYT,* September 8, 1950.
"the predictable howl of outrage . . ." *The Daily Worker,* August 31, 1950.
"That New Year's Eve . . ." Joe Kaufman interview with the author.
" 'None of us knew Ted . . .' " Frank Zachary interview with the author.
" 'There was a little circle . . .' " Charles Addams interview with the author.
"William Walton . . . asked Shaw . . ." William Walton interview with the author.
" 'In those days . . .' " Marion Javits interview with the author.
"One evening Irwin ran into my wife . . ." Bruce Bliven, Jr., interview with the author.
" 'She was in a world . . .' " Carol Saroyan Matthau interview with the author.
"In September, Shaw became writer in residence . . ." *NYT,* March 9, 1950; also *Cue,* March 25, 1950.
" 'Mr. Shaw is probably the most artistic and articulate . . .' " William Peden, *SRL,* November 18, 1950.
" 'I know of no American writer . . .' " John J. Maloney, *NYHT,* October 22, 1950."
" '[Shaw] has his peers . . .' " John K. Hutchens, *NYHT,* December 23, 1950.
"Cerf was reluctant to let . . ." Bennett Cerf to Shaw, October 14, 1949.
" 'Lobrano was the managing editor . . .' " Edward Newhouse interview with the author.
"In October the archpatriotic Cecil B. DeMille . . ." Robert Parrish, *Growing Up in Hollywood* (New York: Harcourt Brace Jovanovich, 1976), pp. 201ff.
"Shaw moved into the Beverly-Carlton . . ." Various letters from Shaw at this time; also Arnold Moss interview with the author.
"Shaw managed to maintain a happy rapport . . ." Shaw to Leland Hayward, March 1, 1951.
"The hearings had opened in March . . ." Kanfer, *Journal,* p. 125.
" 'Irwin Shaw at his characteristic best . . ." Milton Rugoff, *NYHT,* June 10, 1951.
" 'It seems incredible' . . ." Stephen Stepanchev, *TN,* June 23, 1951.
" 'To those people as his audience . . .' " Lionel Trilling, *SRL,* June 9, 1951.
" 'Those wonderful people who in the 1930s . . .' " George E. Sokolsky, *JA,* July 8, 1951.
" 'Their leaving seemed rather sudden' . . ." Marion Javits interview with the author.

PART III

TWELVE 199–213

"I was en route to being assistant . . ." Ben Bradlee interview with the author.
"My first wife, Patsy . . ." Peter Matthiessen interview with the author.
" 'They were leading an F. Scott Fitzgerald life . . .' " Enid Hardwicke interview with the author.
"You just gravitated to him . . ." Slim Keith interview with the author.
"an exasperated Saxe Commins wrote . . ." Saxe Commins to Shaw, August 3, 1951.
"The tragedy of post–World War II writers . . ." John W. Aldridge, *After the Lost Generation* (New York: McGraw-Hill, 1951; New York: Arbor House, 1985, pp. 97ff).
" 'Writing about yourself . . .' " Irwin Shaw, *NYHT,* October 7, 1951.
"En route to Cherbourg . . ." Shaw, *Paris! Paris!,* pp. 4–5.
"Among the Shaws' new neighbors was Theodore White . . ." Theodore H. White, *In Search of History* (New York: Harper & Row, 1978), p. 352.
"Correspondent David Schoenbrun lived . . ." David Schoenbrun interview with the author.
" 'You'd say, "See you tonight . . ." ' " Art Buchwald interview with the author.
"The American Legion, of all groups . . ." Shaw, "What I've Learned."
"By October 17, Shaw was able . . ." Shaw to Leland Hayward, October 17, 1951.
"With Capa in particular . . ." Whelan, *Capa,* pp. 280–281.
" 'There was a group of men . . .' " Enid Hardwicke interview with the author.
"One of the first 'tall young men' . . ." Peter Matthiessen interview with the author.
" 'It was an extremely bohemian apartment . . .' " Patsy Matthiessen Southgate interview with the author.
"The big European tax loophole . . ." Peter Viertel interview with the author; also author interviews with Louis Mezzo and Scott Layne of Grant Thornton Accountants and Management Consultants, New York.

"Wertenbaker had retired from *Time* . . ." Lael Wertenbaker, *The Death of a Man* (New York: Random House, 1957).

" 'Wert was a little hostile . . .' " Joe Kaufman interview with the author.

" 'For something like twenty years . . .' " Kenneth Tynan, *The Observer* (London), March 31, 1968.

"In the late-summer light . . ." This and other details about Shaw's St.-Jean-de-Luz house from Plimpton, *Writers at Work*, pp. 139ff.

" 'The first story I got for him . . .' " Peter Matthiessen interview with the author.

" 'I had had this tremendous fixation . . .' " William Styron interview with the author.

" 'Seeing Irwin with them . . .' " Simon Michael Bessie interview with the author.

"It came out on the tennis court . . ." Joe Kaufman interview with the author.

"Not long afterward . . ." Peter Matthiessen interview with the author.

"Sitting one day . . ." Joe Kaufman interview with the author.

THIRTEEN 214–232

" 'Only Irwin could have foreseen . . .' " Ann Buchwald, *"Seems Like Yesterday* (New York: G. P. Putnam's Sons, 1980), pp. 112ff.

"As the party wound down . . ." David Schoenbrun interview with the author.

" 'God, it's great' . . ." Gabby Van Zuylen interview with the author.

"The story was based directly . . ." Robert Parrish interview with the author.

"In late March 1953 . . ." Shaw to Donald Klopfer, March 21, 1953.

"Soon after Shaw's arrival . . ." Tom Guinzburg interview with the author.

" 'Rose and I had met in Rome . . .' " William Styron interview with the author.

" 'I remember thinking how beautiful . . .' " Rose Styron interview with the author.

"One of the new arrivals . . ." George Plimpton interview with the author.

" 'I remember Marian as being . . .' " John Phillips Marquand, Jr., interview with the author.

"The two interviewers found Shaw . . .' " Plimpton, *Writers at Work*, pp. 139ff.

"Bob Capa came in August . . ." Whelan, *Capa*, p. 290.

"Hemingway . . . passed through St.-Jean . . ." Baker, *Hemingway*, p. 511.

" 'We stayed quite a ways outside Pamplona . . .' " Joe Kaufman interview with the author.

" 'Tip on a Dead Jockey' . . . based on his friend . . ." Ben Bradlee interview with the author.

"In a letter to Donald Klopfer . . ." Shaw to Donald Klopfer, September 6, 1953.

"By November 20, Shaw was able . . ." Shaw to Bennett Cerf, November 20, 1953.

"There was vague talk of returning . . ." Shaw to Simon Michael Bessie, November 20, 1953.

"This year too, they rented a chalet . . ." Shaw to Bennett Cerf, November 20, 1953.

"Even Salka Viertel came . . ." Viertel, *Kindness*, p. 335.

"Shaw extracted a solemn promise . . ." Shaw profile of Capa, *Vogue*, April 1982.

"There was good news from Hollywood . . ." *NYT*, January 23, 1954.

"with Shaw praised by Bosley Crowther . . ." *NYT*, February 12, 1954.

"With the news in March . . ." *NYT*, March 23, 1954.

"Shaw wrote Saxe Commins an uncharacteristic plea . . ." Shaw to Saxe Commins, March 27, 1954.

"On the plane he had time . . ." Donald Klopfer to Shaw, February 8, 1954.

" 'He is, I believe, a victim . . .' " As quoted in Dorothy Berliner Commins, *What Is an Editor? Saxe Commins at Work* (Chicago: University of Chicago Press, 1978), p. 151.

"a project, he confessed . . ." Shaw to Saxe Commins, March 27, 1954.

"By April 27, Shaw was . . ." Shaw to Bennett Cerf, April 27, 1954.

"It was a sweet, somewhat sad episode . . ." Betsy Gehman interview with the author.

"Shaw was in Antibes . . ." Shaw to Donald Klopfer, May 8, 1954.

"While in Japan, Capa had accepted . . ." Whelan, *Capa*, p. 291.

"In a letter that week to Saxe Commins . . ." Shaw to Saxe Commins, May 30, 1954.

"Shaw would get a call from Cornell Capa . . ." Shaw profile of Capa, *Vogue*.

"Ben Bradlee . . . came down on weekends . . ." Ben Bradlee interview with the author.

"One of our big things was . . ." Drew Middleton interview with the author.

FOURTEEN 233–246

"By early November . . ." Shaw to Donald Klopfer, November 7, 1954.

"In mid-December . . ." Wertenbaker, *Death*, pp. 126–127.

" 'The New Yorker* had this . . .' " Brendan Gill interview with the author.

" 'She was a real *femme formidable*' " E. J. Kahn, Jr., interview with the author.

" 'I know Shaw felt that way . . .' " Bruce Bliven, Jr., interview with the author.

" 'Irwin was very much respected. . .' " William Shawn interview with the author.

" 'Marian came in . . .' " Mary Jane Bacon interview with the author.
"The most frustrating of these . . ." Robert Parrish interview with the author; also Henry Fonda oral history, special collections, BL.
"All he knew for sure . . ." Shaw to Bennett Cerf, April 6, 1956.
" 'Irwin Shaw's forthcoming novel . . .' " NYT, January 16, 1956.
"Shaw accepted a lucrative offer . . ." Shaw to Bennett Cerf, February 9, 1956.
"Shaw was back in Klosters . . ." Shaw to Bennett Cerf, March 13, 1956.
" 'venture into fresh territory . . .' " Charles Rolo, NYT, April 1, 1956.
"Milton Rugoff . . . declared . . ." NYHT, April 1, 1956.
"James Kelly . . . found . . ." SR, March 31, 1956.
" 'Mr. Shaw came to the novel . . .' " Lewis Gannett, NYHT, March 30, 1956.
" 'The major stages of the plot . . .' " J. R. Willingham, TN, June 19, 1956.
" 'Though Lucy makes no visible mark . . .' " Time, April 2, 1956.
" 'Even though the reviews weren't signed . . .' " Bernard Frizell interview with the author.
"In July another review appeared . . ." Leslie A. Fiedler, "Irwin Shaw: Adultery, the Last Politics," Commentary, July 1956.
"At a dinner in Paris, Leonora Hornblow . . ." Leonora Hornblow interview with the author.
"David Schoenbrun also ran into Shaw . . ." David Schoenbrun interview with the author.
" 'a boy called Plympton [sic] . . .' " Shaw to Donald Klopfer, June 3, 1956.
" 'It was as close . . .' " Peter Matthiessen interview with the author.

FIFTEEN 247–262

"Marian supervised the construction . . ." Shaw to Bennett Cerf, December 29, 1956.
"One early example . . ." Lillian Tucker interview with the author.
"In 1954 he had submitted . . ." Susan Cheever, Home Before Dark (Boston: Houghton Mifflin, 1985), pp. 101–102.
"At some point on this trip . . ." Mary Cheever interview with the author.
"Shaw had thought to call it . . ." Shaw to Bennett Cerf, August 31, 1956.
"but then Cerf and Klopfer realized . . ." Bennett Cerf to Shaw, February 14, 1957.
"William Peden, writing in The New York Times . . ." NYT, July 7, 1957.
" 'The person who squirts this cold water . . .' " Bosley Crowther, NYT, August 9, 1957.
"Actually, Shaw wasn't to blame . . ." Robert Parrish interview with the author.
"producer Al Lichtman had bought . . ." Bob Thomas, Marlon: Portrait of the Rebel as an Artist (New York: Random House, 1973), p. 129.
"It was Dmytryk too who made the decision . . ." Edward Dmytryk oral history, special collections, BL.
"Brando, fiercely confident . . ." Thomas, Marlon, p. 131.
" 'The cameras were rolling . . .' " David Schoenbrun interview with the author.
"On Thursday, August 22 . . ." NYT, August 24, 1957; also WT, August 23, 1957.
"By December Shaw was able . . ." Shaw to Bennett Cerf, December 7, 1957.
" 'Irwin, you see, had always been . . .' " Clement Biddle Wood interview with the author.
" 'We were this young, aristocratic Harvard/Radcliffe couple . . .' " Gabby Van Zuylen interview with the author.
"Before heading down . . ." Shaw to Bennett Cerf, December 7, 1957.
"Also, as he confessed to Art Buchwald . . ." Art Buchwald, NYHT, August 18, 1957.
"For more than two years . . ." Irwin Shaw, "World of Achard is Airy, Sunny," NYHT, October 26, 1958.
"With Irving Lazar handling the negotiations . . ." NYT, February 26, 1958.
" 'Something is curiously missing . . .' " Bosley Crowther, NYT, March 13, 1958.
" 'It is not so much anti-Nazi . . .' " Bosley Crowther, NYT, April 3, 1958.
"It had much to commend it . . ." Shaw to Bennett Cerf, April 2, 1958.
"it had had a marvelous effect . . ." Bennett Cerf to Shaw, April 11, 1958.
"Kerr's husband . . . publicly accused . . ." DN, June 8, 1958.
"In mid-July Shaw opened a newspaper . . ." Shaw to Bennett Cerf, July 20, 1958.
"In a letter to Cerf . . ." Shaw to Bennett Cerf, July 20, 1958.
"In Paris producer Jean-Pierre Aumont . . ." John McClain, JA, October 21, 1958.
"as did his wife, Juliette . . ." Peter Viertel interview with the author.
" 'In Paris . . . Marcel Achard's Patate . . .' " Brooks Atkinson, NYT, October 29, 1958.
"Patate closed quietly . . ." NYT, October 31, 1958.

SIXTEEN   263–274

" 'What they had . . . was the war' " Gloria Jones interview with the author.
"It was in the early fall of 1958 . . ." Frank MacShane, *Into Eternity: The Life of James Jones, American Writer* (Boston: Houghton Mifflin, 1985), pp. 177ff.
"In the spring of 1959 . . ." Gay and Nan Talese interviews with the author.
" 'Albert is an absolutely brilliant editor . . .' " Joe Fox interview with the author.
"It was in Paris that fall . . ." Shaw, "What I've Learned," p. 226; also Irwin Shaw, *Voices of a Summer Day* (New York: Delacorte, 1965), pp. 169–170.
" 'The investing was very much against . . .' " Peter Viertel interview with the author.
" 'We were a group then . . .' " Elinor Gruber interview with the author.
" 'to investigate a scandal . . .' " Leonard Lyons, *NYP*, December 2, 1959.
"In Paris earlier that month . . ." Gabby Van Zuylen interview with the author.
" 'We shed our sicknesses . . .' " Richard Gilman, *Commonweal*, March 18, 1960.
" 'a penetrating story of modern life' . . ." Herbert Kupferberg, *NYHT*, January 31, 1960.
"Then too, there was the movie sale . . ." Shaw to Albert Erskine, December 23, 1959; also *Newsweek*, February 1, 1960.
"a new, lovely studio apartment . . ." Shaw to Bennett Cerf, April 20, 1960.
"Shaw took a quick trip to New York . . ." Shaw to Albert Erskine, June 30, 1960.
"For ten days he and Marian . . ." Shaw to Bennett Cerf, July 13, 1960.
"Kerr had gone on to procure a divorce . . ." *NYHT*, July 24, 1960.
"As for the rest of the summer . . ." Shaw to Albert Erskine, September 19, 1960.
"Jigee, the sparkling and flirtatious beauty . . ." Schwartz, *Hollywood Writers'*, pp. 297ff.
"Shaw wrote Erskine . . ." Shaw to Albert Erskine, June 12, 1961.
"Furious, Shaw dashed off a note . . ." Shaw to Bennett Cerf, October 9, 1961.
"On the ski slopes one day . . ." Robert Parrish interview with the author.
"Collins passed through Klosters . . ." Larry Collins interview with the author.
"James Salter . . . met Shaw in Paris . . ." James Salter interview with the author.
"Joseph Heller's first encounter . . ." Joseph Heller interview with the author.
"In late March, Shaw took on . . ." *JA*, April 6, 1961.
"Sitting in the courtroom . . ." Bill Pepper interview with the author.
"At the start of the trial Shaw . . ." *JA*, April 11, 1961.
"Eichmann's voice, Shaw reported . . ." *JA*, April 20, 1961.
"While Shaw was in Jerusalem, he met . . ." Jacques Graubart interview with the author.

SEVENTEEN   275–294

"Now, with *Holiday* picking up . . ." Shaw to Albert Erskine, June 12, 1961.
"In St.-Tropez, Françoise Sagan . . ." Irwin Shaw, *In the Company of Dolphins* (New York: Bernard Geis Associates, 1964), pp. 18ff.
"In Dubrovnik, Jim and Gloria Jones . . ." Gloria Jones interview with the author.
"That fall he proposed to Bennett Cerf . . ." Shaw to Bennett Cerf, October 26, 1961.
"Donald Klopfer responded on Cerf's behalf . . ." Donald Klopfer to Shaw, November 13, 1961.
"Cerf, in a letter soon after . . ." Bennett Cerf to Shaw, December 12, 1961.
"Shaw made an enthusiastic pitch . . ." Shaw to Bennett Cerf, January 23, 1962.
"And again, Cerf's reaction was cool" Bennett Cerf to Shaw, January 26, 1962.
"Bosley Crowther wrote . . ." *NYT*, September 2, 1961.
"After a five-year hiatus . . ." John Houseman, *Final Dress* (New York: Touchstone/Simon & Schuster, 1983), pp. 199, 209–214.
" 'Unconsciously . . . we found ourselves . . .' " Houseman, *Final Dress*, p. 210.
"The Shaws flew over . . ." Leonard Lyons, *NYP*, May 14, 1962.
"While Shaw was on the East Coast . . ." Robert Parrish, *Hollywood Doesn't Live Here Anymore* (Boston: Little, Brown, 1988), pp. 122ff; also Robert Parrish interview with the author.
"it was there that a *Time* reporter . . ." Shaw interview by Joyce Haber, July 3, 1962, Time Inc. library.
"This time her name was Doris Lilly" Doris Lilly interview with the author.
"In late July . . . a particularly bruising critique . . ." John Aldridge, "What Became of Our Postwar Hopes?" *NYTBR*, July 28, 1962.
"Shaw told Cerf and Klopfer . . ." Bennett Cerf to Shaw, August 21, 1962; also Donald Klopfer in-house memo to Cerf, August 30, 1962; also Cerf to Shaw, September 21, 1962.
"Shaw, back in Paris by late August . . ." Shaw to Bennett Cerf, September 17, 1962.

" 'I hope,' he wrote happily . . ." Bennett Cerf to Shaw, September 21, 1962.

" 'The whole thing is a lot . . .' " Bosley Crowther, *NYT*, August 18, 1962.

" 'They are dead serious . . .' " *Time*, August 31, 1962.

"Bob Parrish had made a personal visit . . ." Parrish, *Hollywood Doesn't*.

"Initially, an agent sent . . ." Robert Parrish interview with the author.

"filming began on August 27 . . ." Cynthia Grenier, "In Gallic Style," *NYT*, November 4, 1962.

" 'In Hollywood you start out . . .' " *Newsweek*, November 5, 1962.

" 'This all came out . . .' " Grenier, "In Gallic Style."

" 'The worst thing' . . ." John Crosby, *Signs of Living Abroad*, *NYHT*, September 24, 1962.

"more than once he was subjected . . ." Bodie Nielsen interview with the author.

" 'A writer, like my father' " Shaw, "Some Aspects."

"Adam won a leading role . . ." Peter Viertel interview with the author.

"Shaw flew to New York . . ." Shaw to Bennett Cerf, February 5, 1963.

"There had been talk of Orson Welles's . . ." Shaw to Bennett Cerf, January 23, 1962.

"The $75,000 cost of the production . . ." Shaw to James Jones, April 17, 1963, enclosing legal document from Paul, Weiss, Rifkind.

"Matthau had read the play . . ." Sam Wanamaker interview with the author.

" 'Irwin was furious' . . ." Carol Saroyan Matthau interview with the author.

" 'If Walter had played the role . . .' " Sam Wanamaker interview with the author.

"In his New Haven hotel room . . ." Shaw interview by Don Ross, *NYT*, April 7, 1963.

"for all its 'scorching mockery' . . ." Howard Taubman, *NYT*, April 12, 1963.

" '*Children from Their Games* represented . . .' " Richard Watts, Jr., *NYP*, April 21, 1963.

"Cerf replied with warm sympathy . . ." Bennett Cerf to Shaw, May 7, 1963.

"becoming a family again . . ." Shaw to James Jones, June 19, 1963.

"By July 1, Shaw was in New York . . ." Shaw interview by Jerry Tallmer, *NYP*, July 5, 1963.

" 'The theater has frankly defeated me . . .' " Shaw interview by Liz Drivan, CBS News, for *Vital History* series.

" 'the contrast between Odets' . . .' " *Time*, August 23, 1963.

"He dashed off a blistering letter . . ." Shaw to *Time* and to Howard Taubman of *NYT*, September 1, 1963, Rose Collection, New York Public Library at Lincoln Center.

"Shaw came alone to New York . . ." Doris Lilly interview with the author.

" 'I remember those days . . ." Shaw interview by Hal Boyle, *NYP*, September 18, 1963.

"until he felt, in some wrathful way . . ." Shaw to Doris Lilly, October 9, 1963.

" 'a certain melancholy charm' " Bosley Crowther, *NYT*, September 19, 1963.

"Judith Crist observed . . ." *NYHT*, September 19, 1963.

" 'Year after year' . . ." *Time*, October 11, 1963.

"He showed up in hiking boots and shorts . . ." Ralph Ginzburg interview with the author.

"He started by restating his recent exchange . . ." *fact*, January–February 1964.

"Shaw had shocked his friends . . ." Robert Parrish interview with the author; also Bill Wilson interview with the author, and Shaw, "What I've Learned."

"Shaw . . . had the notion . . ." Shaw to Bennett Cerf, January 28, 1964.

"In February he and Marian took a house . . ." Shaw to Bennett Cerf, February 9, 1964.

"By mid-April he had finished *Voices* . . ." Bennett Cerf to Shaw, April 27, 1964.

"To an interviewer the next year . . ." Lewis Nichols, "In and Out of Books," *NYTBR*, March 7, 1965.

"He sent a first draft off . . ." Shaw to Bennett Cerf, May 5, 1964.

"By mid-May Cerf wrote . . ." Bennett Cerf to Shaw, May 13, 1964.

"Despite the addition of two long scenes . . ." Shaw to Bennett Cerf, May 5, 1964.

"Random House would still publish it . . ." Joe Fox interview with the author.

"Lazar had called Don Fine . . ." Donald I. Fine interview with the author.

"Lazar walked into our office . . ." Cerf, *At Random*, pp. 121–122.

"So furious was Cerf . . ." Bennett Cerf oral history, special collections, BL.

EIGHTEEN 295–311

"In 1963 Dell had acquired . . ." This and other details of Delacorte's history from Carolyn Anthony, "Delacorte Now and Then," *Publishers Weekly*, May 27, 1988.

" 'We were regarded by the rest . . .' " Ross Claiborne interview with the author.

" 'Irwin's breakup with Random House . . .' " Nan Talese interview with the author.

"As a reward to himself for signing . . ." Lewis Nichols, "In and Out of Books," *NYTBR*, August 9, 1964.

"Anchored in St.-Tropez, he took . . ." Shaw to Donald Klopfer, July 17, 1964.

"Shaw went to a ball game . . ." Gay Talese interview with the author.

"Gerald Walker . . . complained . . ." Gerald Walker, NYTBR, February 28, 1965.

"Time's critic took the opportunity . . ." Time, March 5, 1965.

"Kauffmann lumped Shaw together . . ." Stanley Kauffmann, "Herzog, Schmerzog," NYHT, March 7, 1965.

" 'It was a damn good style . . .' " Norman Mailer interview with the author.

"On the other hand, Shaw himself would say . . ." Shaw, "Some Aspects."

"On the evening of March 15, 1965 . . ." Hilary Mills, Mailer: A Biography (New York: McGraw-Hill, 1984), pp. 284–285.

"Voices of a Summer Day, celebrated with a more civilized party . . ." Formal invitation to the party on file in the James Jones collection, HRC.

"To one interviewer at the time . . ." Lewis Nichols, "In and Out of Books," NYTBR, March 7, 1965.

"While the first play was 'mainly . . .' " Henry Hewes, SR, April 15, 1967.

"For an anthology titled Authors Take Sides . . ." Cecil Woolf and John Bagguley, eds., Authors Take Sides on Vietnam (New York: Simon & Schuster, 1967). Shaw's original reply is on file in the Berg Collection, New York Public Library, main branch.

"Shaw and Jones decided to travel . . ." James Jones to Shaw, February 25, 1965.

"They met with their wives in tow . . ." MacShane, Into Eternity, p. 210.

"As it happened, art critic Robert Hughes . . ." Robert Hughes interview with the author.

"Slim Keith, separated from Leland Hayward . . ." Slim Keith interview with the author.

"On a trip to New York . . ." Joe Kaufman interview with the author.

"Enid Boulting . . . had a startling experience . . ." Enid Hardwicke interview with the author.

"Marian had a modest hit . . ." Shaw to James Jones, September 13, 1965.

" 'He has the gift of all great storytellers . . .' " Robert Cromie, SR, October 2, 1965.

"Ironically, the story had been written . . ." Shaw interview by Mickey Friedman, San Francisco Examiner & Chronicle, November 19, 1978.

"as he slogged through the writing of a screenplay . . ." Leonard Lyons, NYP, September 16, 1965; also James Jones to Shaw, April 4, 1966.

" 'Marian Edwards, a former actress . . .' " NYT, April 13, 1966.

"Cowan had scrapped Shaw's screenplay . . ." Sheilah Graham, NYP, December 6, 1966.

" 'There is no doubt' . . ." John Bainbridge, Another Way of Living, excerpted in McCall's, April 1969.

"It was that streak . . ." NYT, October 15, 1967; also DN, June 9, 1968.

" 'to illustrate the title . . .' " NYT, October 15, 1967.

" 'Jules and Irwin were like . . .' " Leon Davidoff interview with the author.

"Survival 1967 got to Israel . . .' " Renata Adler, NYT, June 12, 1968.

" 'Alan said, "How would you like . . ." ' " Karen Lerner interview with the author.

PART IV

NINETEEN   315–331

"The way Shaw would tell it . . ." The account of Shaw's marital break drawn from Larry Collins, Bodie Nielsen, Robert Parrish and Peter Viertel interviews with the author.

"It was against this backdrop . . ." Details of Shaw's relationship with Bodie Nielsen from Nielsen's journals, letters and interview with the author unless otherwise noted.

" 'We'd all go to Salka's . . .' " Robert Parrish interview with the author.

" 'There was something about her . . .' " Peter Viertel interview with the author.

" 'My reviews were just as bad . . .' " Gore Vidal interview with the author.

"Shaw later confessed he'd found . . ." Shaw interview by Ralph Tyler, Bookviews, December 1977.

" 'All of literature comes . . .' " Shaw interview by Ross Wetzsteon, SR, June 1981.

"By now the Joneses' Sunday-night poker games . . ." Willie Morris, James Jones: A Friendship (New York: Doubleday, 1978), p. 119; also MacShane, Into Eternity, p. 233.

" 'Gloria was a large part . . .' " Bernard Frizell interview with the author.

"Claiborne pushed through a new two-book contract . . ." Delacorte contract with Shaw, April 6, 1970.

"It was on pulp paper . . .' " Willie Morris interview with the author.

" 'Irwin Shaw's big sixth novel . . .' " Christopher Lehmann-Haupt, NYT, September 28, 1970.

" 'Shaw still stakes his claim . . ." R. V. Cassill, WP, September 27, 1970.

" 'How can you set yourself up . . .' " Divorce settlement details from Peter Viertel interview with the author.

TWENTY 332–348

" 'It was a clan . . .' " Elinor Gruber interview with the author.

"The deal . . . had its origins . . ." Details of the *Rich Man, Poor Man* deal from Richard Anobile, *The Making of* Rich Man, Poor Man (New York: Berkley Medallion, 1976).

" 'A miniseries? Like those British things?' " Ross Claiborne interview with the author.

"The sale, as Shaw wrote in a letter . . ." Shaw to Nan Talese, February 18, 1971, Random House collection, BL.

" 'That first draft was unprintable' . . ." Manon Tingue interview with the author.

"Fine had jumped at the chance . . ." Donald I. Fine interview with the author.

" 'Back in the days when the hallmark of social concern . . .' " Martin Levin, *NYTBR*, February 4, 1973.

"a short meditation . . . that also appeared . . ." Irwin Shaw, "In Praise of the Short Story," *Esquire*, February 1973.

" '*Evening in Byzantium* is a real' . . ." Anatole Broyard, *NYT*, March 28, 1973.

"Shaw found himself in New York on the *Today* show . . ." Shaw, "Some Aspects."

"While in the States, Shaw attended . . ." Shaw interview by Jerry Tallmer, *NYP*, May 8, 1973.

"Irving Lazar . . . apparently managed to persuade Delacorte . . ." Delacorte contracts with Shaw, November 26, 1973; also Ross Claiborne interview with the author.

"In May he went again . . ." Irwin Shaw, "The Greatest Film Festival of Them All," *Travel & Leisure*, December 1974.

"He was done two days before . . ." Shaw to James Jones, September 12, 1973, James Jones collection, HRC.

" 'It was very promising . . .' " Ross Claiborne interview with the author.

"he 'had no wish to be left stranded . . .' " Shaw, *Paris! Paris!*, p. 6.

TWENTY-ONE 349–364

" 'I said something like . . .' " Willie Morris interview with the author.

"One subject that did arouse Shaw's ire . . ." Details of the *Rich Man, Poor Man* production from Anobile, *Making*.

" 'There was Irwin in his underwear . . .' " Winston Groom interview with the author.

"Over a luncheon interview with Robert Alan Aurthur . . ." *Esquire*, October 1975.

" 'the destruction of the American way . . .' " *Women's Wear Daily*, July 25, 1975.

"For *Newsday*, Shaw penned a column . . ." *Newsday*, July 27, 1975.

"Shaw in particular was described . . ." Anthony Haden-Guest, "Out Here in the Hamptons," *NY*, September 1, 1975.

" 'Irwin became so irritated . . .' " Anthony Haden-Guest interview with the author.

" 'Never mind if this isn't . . .' " *Newsweek*, November 3, 1975.

" 'If you're fond of money . . .' " Christopher Lehmann-Haupt, *NYT*, September 18, 1975.

"director Frank Perry had agreed . . ." *Variety*, October 29, 1975.

" 'He was flirting around . . .' " Enid Hardwicke interview with the author.

" 'I don't want to be remembered . . .' " Shaw interview by Bina Bernard, *People*, February 10, 1976.

"the first segment of *Rich Man, Poor Man* . . . had attracted . . ." Gerry Nadel, "50 Million Viewers Can't Be Wrong," *TV Guide*, December 18, 1976.

"Executive producer Harve Bennett was later quoted . . ." *DN*, January 25, 1976.

"a quotation Shaw saw and was infuriated by . . ." This and other details of the *Rich Man, Poor Man* production from Anobile, *Making*.

"Nolte, as *RMPM* producer Jon Epstein points out . . ." Jon Epstein interview with Cynthia Stuart.

"Dell had only 75,000 paperback copies in print . . ." Anobile, *Making*.

" 'There was some really great stuff . . .' " Nadel, "50 Million."

" 'He told me when he sat down . . .' " Frank Perry interview with the author.

" 'Irwin had hardly skied . . .' " Lillian Tucker interview with the author.

" 'Actually, it's a very funny story' . . ." Willie Morris interview with the author.

"Shaw . . . hit another car . . ." *The East Hampton Star*, April 22, 1976.

"despite the earnest efforts of Adam . . ." Winston Groom interview with the author.

" 'She did take good care . . .' " Alfred Allan Lewis interview with the author.

"For her part, Batchelder found the Hamptons . . ." Ruth Batchelder interview with the author.

"Keren felt dissatisfied enough . . ." Kevin McCarthy interview with the author.

"On July 16, however, Shaw delivered . . ." Reprinted as Shaw, "Some Aspects."

" 'When we pulled up to the house . . .' " Diana Erwitt interview with the author.

"It happened when Shaw got a call . . ." Alfred Allan Lewis interview with the author.

"In the letter I wrote . . ." Doris Lilly interview with the author.

"Each month since the miniseries . . ." Ross Claiborne interview with the author.

"As for the novel that had brought all this about . . ." *NY*, August 9, 1976.

"he persuaded Delacorte . . ." Delacorte contract with Shaw, June 6, 1976.

TWENTY-TWO   365–377

"Jones was afflicted with cardiomyopathy . . ." Details of Jones's illness from MacShane, *Into Eternity*, pp. 288, 292, 295–299.

"One day in November . . . Diana Erwitt . . ." Diana Erwitt interview with the author.

" 'One great thing about Irwin Shaw . . .' " E. J. Kahn, Jr., *About* The New Yorker *and Me* (New York: G. P. Putnam's Sons, 1979), pp. 198–199.

"What Shaw found, in the waiting room . . ." MacShane, *Into Eternity*, pp. 295–299.

"It was Shaw who prevailed . . ." Willie Morris interview with the author.

"His own grief he expiated . . ." Irwin Shaw, "James Jones, 1921–1977," *NYTBR*, June 12, 1977.

"Soon after sending it off . . ." Shaw interview by Hillary Johnson, *Women's Wear Daily*, June 10, 1977.

"a next stage in the cautious reconciliation . . ." Shaw interview by Ralph Tyler for *Bookviews*, December, 1977; also Ross Claiborne interview with the author.

"In a ruminative essay . . ." Shaw, "What I've Learned."

"That summer, Shaw turned out 60,000 words . . ." Shaw interview by Herbert Mitgang, *NYTBR*, November 13, 1977.

"It was based on a dream . . ." Edwin McDowell, "Reporter's Notebook," *NYT*, May 27, 1981.

"accepting a relatively modest advance of $40,000" Delacorte contract with Shaw, January 10, 1978.

"Marian wrote of drifting along . . ." Marian Shaw to Gloria Jones, August 9, 1977, James Jones collection, HRC.

" 'Marian and I are back together . . .' " Ross Claiborne interview with the author.

" 'having written off *Rich Man, Poor Man* . . .' " Christopher Lehmann-Haupt, *NYT*, October 17, 1977.

" 'Desperately bad writing' . . ." Anita Brookner, *Times Literary Supplement* (London), November 25, 1977.

" 'We are not here tonight to mourn' . . ." Judy Klemesrud, *NYT*, February 23, 1978.

"While he was in New York . . ." *NYT*, February 22, 1978.

" 'The Academy?' Shaw said once . . ." George Weidenfeld interview with the author.

" 'It had the names . . .' " Lillian Tucker interview with the author.

TWENTY-THREE   378–392

" 'Marian was very wary . . .' " Joe Kaufman interview with the author.

" 'Adam would write and rewrite . . .' " Winston Groom interview with the author.

" 'When I'm writing, I can't stand . . .' " Shaw interview by Mickey Friedman, *San Francisco Examiner & Chronicle*, November 19, 1978.

"In August *Time* reported . . ." *Time*, August 28, 1978.

" 'By the time we realized . . .' " Ross Claiborne interview with the author.

" 'I was allowed to be . . .' " Clay Winters interview with the author.

"Stefan Kanfer . . . praised Shaw . . ." Stefan Kanfer, *Time*, November 6, 1978.

"Jonathan Yardley . . . declared the stories . . ." *WP*, November 5, 1978.

"Screenwriter and novelist William Goldman . . . declared . . ." *NYTBR*, November 12, 1978.

" 'I will not pretend . . .' " Irwin Shaw, "Cheever Country," *Bookviews*, October 1978.

"Sometime that winter Shaw was asked . . ." Shaw interview by Judy Klemesrud, *NYT*, February 10, 1980.

" 'Irwin was angry because . . .' " Liam O'Brien interview with the author.

"If Claiborne wanted to publish . . ." Ross Claiborne interview with the author.

"Its central structure was . . ." Shaw profile by Esther Blaustein, *NYT*, August 12, 1979; also Paris, "Interview."

"Shaw made a second happy return . . ." *NYT*, May 16, 1979.

"Among the many former classmates . . ." Norman Rosten interview with the author.

" 'Irwin couldn't help but see . . .' " Elaine Kaufman interview with the author.

"One night not long before his hip operation . . ." Shaw profile by Vincent Cosgrove, *DN*, May 18, 1976.

" 'We have received, as you might imagine . . .' " Shaw Pipe Night tape, The Players club, New York.

" 'In his hands . . . Michael [Storrs's] case . . .' " Christopher Lehmann-Haupt, *NYT*, October 30, 1979.

"The miniseries . . . was promptly dismissed . . ." John J. O'Connor, *NYT*, February 6, 1980.

"In an early draft, apparently . . ." Jeanne Bernkopf interview with the author.

" 'Naturally we don't encourage . . .' " Claudia Cohen, *NYP*, June 23, 1980.

"During the operation, complications developed" James Brady, *NYP*, July 17, 1981.

" 'It was quite late after dinner' . . ." Marion Javits interview with the author.

" 'Elliott kept saying . . .' " Frank Perry interview with the author.

" 'I had put up the money . . .' " Elliott Kastner interview with the author.

"and Lazar himself to serve . . ." James Brady, *NYP*, October 27, 1981.

"He resolved to exact . . ." Shaw profile by Richard Z. Chesnoff, *WSJ*, March 21, 1984.

TWENTY-FOUR   393–408

"The Book-of-the-Month Club proclaimed it . . ." Ross Wetzsteon, "The Conflict Between Big Bucks and Good Books," *SR*, August 1981.

"Delacorte called for an advance printing . . ." James Brady, *NYP*, July 17, 1981.

" 'Shaw has been afflicted with ideas . . .' " William Boyd, *Times Literary Supplement* (London), July 31, 1981.

"Evan Hunter . . . commended the novel's . . ." *NYTBR*, August 28, 1981.

" 'Like Dickens, he has a social point . . .' " Merle Miller, *Chicago Tribune*, as quoted in blurb in 1981 Dell paperback edition of *Bread Upon the Waters*.

" 'And yet . . . *Bread Upon the Waters* . . .' " Wetzsteon, "Conflict."

" 'But I never found him dispirited . . .' " Donald I. Fine interview with the author.

"None of Shaw's friends, however, was told . . ." Clement Biddle Wood interview with the author.

"Arbor House . . . had taken out an insurance policy . . ." Wetzsteon, "Conflict."

"Budd Schulberg remarked on the phrase . . ." Budd Schulberg interview with the author.

"Shaw . . . completed a first draft in little more . . ." Shaw profile by Chesnoff, *WSJ*.

" 'It was an expression of my outrage . . .' " Shaw profile by Chesnoff, *WSJ*.

"Josh Mason . . . remembers what happened . . ." Josh Mason interview with the author.

"That spring, the Shaws sneaked away . . ." Shaw to Francine Schoeller, April 8, 1982.

"The wedding . . . took place in secret . . ." Shaw to Francine Schoeller, April 8, 1982; also Francine Schoeller interview with the author.

"Shaw and Marian would agree that Adam . . ." Shaw will, July 29, 1983, Surrogate's Court, Riverhead, New York.

"John Jay Osborne, Jr. . . . admired Shaw's goal . . ." *NYTBR*, October 3, 1982.

"As for Christopher Lehmann-Haupt . . ." *NYT*, September 28, 1982.

"This one was to be the multigenerational tale . . ." Francine Schoeller interview with the author; also Paris, "Interview."

" 'I had the sense that Irwin knew . . .' " Eden Collinsworth interview with the author.

"On his seventieth birthday . . . Shaw was honored . . ." Shaw profile by Chesnoff, *WSJ*.

"Shaw thanked the assemblage . . ." Shaw's speech provided to the author by Francine Schoeller.

" 'I cringe when critics say . . .' " Shaw profile by Herbert Mitgang, *NYT*, February 17, 1983.

"James R. Giles . . . produced a respectful overview . . ." Giles, *Shaw*.

"Shaw always returned to 'the necessity of struggling' . . ." Giles, *Shaw*, p. 10.

" 'When I mentioned his affair with Mary Welsh . . .' " Jeffrey Meyers letter to the author.

"The Taleses . . . had long planned . . ." Gay and Nan Talese interviews with the author.

"Lazar had suggested that Shaw sell . . ." As recounted by Shaw to Ross Claiborne.

" 'I pleaded with Bill Self . . .' " Elliott Kastner interview with the author.

"Bob Parrish . . . remembers getting a call . . ." Robert Parrish interview with the author.

"Much of Shaw's last summer and fall . . ." Correspondence between Shaw and Francine Schoeller.

"he did manage to turn out . . . 'The Common Man' . . ." *Esquire*, December 1983.

"It was Shaw who encouraged . . ." Rust Hills interview with the author.

" 'Suddenly he was the old Irwin again' . . ." John McCormack interview with the author.

"Finally the doctors had determined . . ." Shaw to Art Buchwald, May 1, 1984.

" 'I had gotten into this kick . . .' " Ben Bradlee interview with the author.

" 'It's very, very sad to see someone . . .' " Peter Viertel interview with the author.

"The nurse was frantic" Andreas Maissen interview with the author.

" 'When David and Bob and I . . .' " Kathie Parrish interview with the author.

" 'Hello, Bobby,' Shaw managed" Robert Parrish interview with the author.

"At 6:10 P.M. on May 16, 1984, Shaw died . . ." Dr. J. Dannecker interview with the author.

"On the bedside table were two books . . ." Shaw obituary by Herbert Mitgang, *NYT*, May 17, 1984.

" 'The author of a dozen novels . . ." Shaw obituary by Mitgang, *NYT*.

"The will . . . included conditions . . ." Shaw's will, July 29, 1983, Surrogate's Court, Riverhead, New York.

"Scattering the ashes proved . . ." Robert Parrish interview with the author.

WORKS BY IRWIN SHAW

PLAYS

Bury the Dead, New York: Random House, 1936.

Siege, produced in New York, 1937; original drafts on file in the Irwin Shaw collection, Mugar Memorial Library, Boston University, and at the Library of Congress, Washington, D.C.

Second Mortgage, in *One-Act Play Magazine* (New York), May 1938.

The Gentle People: A Brooklyn Fable, New York: Random House, 1939.

Quiet City, produced in New York, 1939; original draft on file in the Irwin Shaw collection, Mugar Memorial Library, Boston University.

Retreat to Pleasure, produced in New York, 1949; original draft on file in the Irwin Shaw collection, Mugar Memorial Library, Boston University.

The Shy and the Lonely, in William Kozlenko, ed., *American Scenes,* New York: Day, 1941.

Sons and Soldiers, New York: Random House, 1944.

The Assassin, New York: Random House, 1946.

The Survivors, with Peter Viertel, New York: Dramatists Play Service, 1948.

Patate, adaptation of a play by Marcel Achard, produced in New York, 1958.

Children from Their Games, New York: Samuel French, 1962.

In the French Style, screenplay and stories, New York: Macfadden, 1963.

A Choice of Wars, produced in Salt Lake City, Utah, and Glasgow, Scotland, 1967; original draft on file in the Irwin Shaw collection, Mugar Memorial Library.

SCREENPLAYS

The Big Game, 1936.

The Hard Way, with Daniel Fuchs and Jerry Wald, 1942.

The Talk of the Town, with others, 1942.

Commandos Strike at Dawn, 1942.

Take One False Step, with Chester Erskine and David Shaw, 1949.

Easy Living, with Charles Schnee, 1949.

I Want You, 1951.

Act of Love, 1954.

Ulysses, with others, 1955.

Fire Down Below, 1957.

This Angry Age, with René Clement, 1958.

Desire Under the Elms, 1958.

The Big Gamble, 1961.

In the French Style, 1963.

Survival 1967 (documentary), 1968.

NOVELS

The Young Lions, New York: Random House, 1948; London: Cape, 1949.

The Troubled Air, New York: Random House, and London: Cape, 1951.

Lucy Crown, New York: Random House, and London: Cape, 1956.

Two Weeks in Another Town, New York: Random House, and London: Cape, 1960.

Voices of a Summer Day, New York: Delacorte, and London: Weidenfeld & Nicolson, 1965.

Rich Man, Poor Man, New York: Delacorte, and London: Weidenfeld & Nicolson, 1970.

Evening in Byzantium, New York: Delacorte, and London: Weidenfeld & Nicolson, 1973.

Nightwork, New York: Delacorte, and London: Weidenfeld & Nicolson, 1975.
Beggarman, Thief, New York: Delacorte, and London: Weidenfeld & Nicolson, 1977.
The Top of the Hill, New York: Delacorte, and London: Weidenfeld & Nicolson, 1979.
Bread Upon the Waters, New York: Delacorte, and London: Weidenfeld & Nicolson, 1981.
Acceptable Losses, New York: Arbor House, and London: New English Library, 1982.

SHORT STORIES

Sailor off the Bremen and Other Stories, New York: Random House, 1939; London: Cape, 1940.
Welcome to the City and Other Stories, New York: Random House, 1942.
Act of Faith and Other Stories, New York: Random House, 1946.
Mixed Company: Collected Short Stories, New York: Random House, 1950; London: Cape, 1952.
Tip on a Dead Jockey and Other Stories, New York: Random House, and London: Cape, 1957.
Selected Short Stories, New York: Modern Library, 1961.
Love on a Dark Street and Other Stories, New York: Delacorte, and London: Cape, 1965.
Short Stories, New York: Random House, 1966.
Retreat and Other Stories, London: New English Library, 1970.
Whispers in Bedlam: Three Novellas, London: Weidenfeld & Nicolson, 1972.
God Was Here But He Left Early, New York: Arbor House, 1973; London: Pan, 1977.
Short Stories: Five Decades, New York: Delacorte, and London: Cape, 1978.

OTHER

Report on Israel, New York: Simon & Schuster, 1950.
In the Company of Dolphins, New York: Bernard Geis Associates, 1964.
Paris! Paris! (illustrated by Ronald Searle), New York: Harcourt Brace Jovanovich, and London, Weidenfeld & Nicolson, 1977.

MANUSCRIPT COLLECTIONS

Brooklyn College Library, New York
The Pierpont Morgan Library, New York
Mugar Memorial Library, Boston University

OTHER SOURCE MATERIAL COLLECTIONS

Random House Collection, Butler Library, Columbia University, New York
George Stevens collection, Academy of Motion Picture Arts and Sciences Library, Los Angeles

SELECTED BIBLIOGRAPHY

Aldridge, John W. *After the Lost Generation.* New York: Arbor House, 1985.

Allen, Frederick Lewis. *Only Yesterday.* New York: Harper & Row, 1986.

———. *Since Yesterday.* New York: Harper & Row, 1986.

Buchwald, Ann. *Seems Like Yesterday.* New York: G. P. Putnam's Sons, 1980.

Clurman, Harold. *The Fervent Years: The Story of Group Theatre and the Thirties.* New York: Da Capo, 1983.

Foley, Martha. *The Story of* Story *Magazine.* New York: W. W. Norton, 1980.

Giles, James R. *Irwin Shaw.* Boston: Twayne, 1983.

Gill, Brendan. *Here at The New Yorker.* New York: Random House, 1975.

Houseman, John. *Final Dress.* New York: Touchstone/Simon & Schuster, 1983.

Kanfer, Stefan. *A Journal of the Plague Years.* New York: Atheneum, 1973.

Kazin, Alfred. *Starting Out in the Thirties.* Boston: Atlantic/Little, Brown, 1962.

Kramer, Dale. *Ross and The New Yorker.* Garden City, NY: Doubleday, 1951.

Lawrenson, Helen. *Stranger at the Party: A Memoir.* New York: Random House, 1975.

Lee, Lawrence, and Barry Gifford. *Saroyan: A Biography.* New York: Paragon House, 1988.

MacDonald, J. Fred. *Don't Touch That Dial.* Chicago: Nelson-Hall, 1979.

MacShane, Frank. *Into Eternity: The Life of James Jones, American Writer.* Boston: Houghton Mifflin, 1985.

Manchester, William. *The Glory and the Dream.* Boston: Bantam/Little, Brown, 1980.

Meyers, Jeffrey. *Hemingway: A Biography.* New York: Harper & Row, 1985.

Mills, Hilary. *Mailer: A Biography.* New York: McGraw-Hill, 1984.

Mitgang, Herbert. *Dangerous Dossiers.* New York: Donald I. Fine, 1988.

Morris, Willie. *James Jones: A Friendship.* New York: Doubleday, 1978.

Parrish, Robert. *Growing Up in Hollywood.* New York: Harcourt Brace Jovanovich, 1976.

———. *Hollywood Doesn't Live Here Anymore.* Boston: Little, Brown, 1988.

Plimpton, George, ed. *Writers at Work: The* Paris Review *Interviews, Fifth Series.* New York: Penguin, 1981.

Saroyan, Aram. *Trio.* New York: Penguin, 1986.

Schoenbrun, David. *America Inside Out.* New York: McGraw-Hill, 1984.

Schwartz, Nancy Lynn. *The Hollywood Writers' Wars.* New York: Alfred A. Knopf, 1982.

Sheed, Wilfrid. *Clare Boothe Luce.* New York: E. P. Dutton, 1982.

Talese, Gay. *Fame and Obscurity.* New York: Dell, 1981.

Viertel, Salka. *The Kindness of Strangers.* New York: Holt, Rinehart & Winston, 1969.

Wertenbaker, Lael. *The Death of a Man.* New York: Random House, 1957.

Whelan, Richard. *Robert Capa: A Biography.* New York: Alfred A. Knopf, 1985.

White, Theodore. *In Search of History.* New York: Warner/Harper & Row, 1978.

Young, Peter. *The World Almanac of World War II.* New York: Bison, 1986.

INDEX

437